Financial Technology and Strategic AI Integration in FinTech: Transforming Banking, Payments, and Building a Sustainable Economy—Challenges and Opportunities

Financial Technology and Strategic AI Integration in FinTech: Transforming Banking, Payments, and Building a Sustainable Economy—Challenges and Opportunities

Guest Editors

Otilia Manta
Valentina Vasile
Shigeyuki Hamori

MDPI

Basel • Beijing • Wuhan • Barcelona • Belgrade • Novi Sad • Cluj • Manchester

Guest Editors
Otilia Manta
Center for Financial and Monetary Research "Victor Slăvescu", and CE-MONT
Romanian Academy
Bucharest
Romania

Valentina Vasile
Institute of National Economy
Romanian Academy
Bucharest
Romania

Shigeyuki Hamori
Graduate School of Economics
Kobe University
Kobe
Japan

Editorial Office
MDPI AG
Grosspeteranlage 5
4052 Basel, Switzerland

This is a reprint of the Special Issue, published open access by the journal *FinTech* (ISSN 2674-1032), freely accessible at: https://www.mdpi.com/journal/fintech/special_issues/63MD69HRU1.

For citation purposes, cite each article independently as indicated on the article page online and as indicated below:

Lastname, A.A.; Lastname, B.B. Article Title. *Journal Name* **Year**, *Volume Number*, Page Range.

ISBN 978-3-7258-8139-0 (Hbk)
ISBN 978-3-7258-8140-6 (PDF)
https://doi.org/10.3390/books978-3-7258-8140-6

Contents

Preface

The accelerated digitalization of financial systems, reinforced by the strategic integration of artificial intelligence, represents a profound transformation of global financial architecture. FinTech has moved beyond its initial role, related to improving operational efficiency, and has become a structural driver reshaping economic systems, institutional frameworks, and social interactions. In this context, this Special Issue brings together original and rigorous academic contributions that investigate how innovative financial instruments and artificial intelligence technologies are redefining banking systems, payment infrastructures, financial governance, and the pathways toward sustainable development.

The purpose of this Reprint is to provide a coherent and interdisciplinary overview of current research at the intersection of finance, technology, and sustainability. It is addressed to researchers, academics, practitioners, and policy makers interested in understanding the evolving dynamics of digital finance and its broader economic and societal implications. The selected works reflect the diversity of approaches and methods used to study FinTech innovation, including perspectives from finance, economics, data science, public policy, and ethics.

The motivation for this Reprint lies in the need to critically assess both the opportunities and challenges generated by rapid technological change. While FinTech and artificial intelligence offer significant potential for improving efficiency, inclusiveness, and sustainability in financial systems, they also raise complex issues related to regulation, ethics, and institutional adaptation. By bringing together these contributions, the Special Issue aims to support a deeper understanding of how digital transformation can be aligned with long term sustainable development objectives.

Overall, this Reprint seeks to provide an integrated academic resource that reflects the current state of knowledge and encourages further research into the evolving relationship between financial innovation, artificial intelligence, and sustainable economic progress.

Otilia Manta, Valentina Vasile, and Shigeyuki Hamori
Guest Editors

FinTech

MDPI

ditorial

Financial Technology and Strategic AI Integration in FinTech: Transforming Banking, Payments, and Building a Sustainable Economy—Challenges and Opportunities

Otilia Manta [1,2,*], Valentina Vasile [3] and Shigeyuki Hamori [4,5]

1 Romanian Academy, Centre for Financial and Monetary Research "Victor Slăvescu", 050711 Bucharest, Romania
2 Department of Finance and Banking, Faculty of Economic Sciences, Romanian-American University, 012101 Bucharest, Romania
3 Institute of National Economy, Romanian Academy, 050711 Bucharest, Romania; valentinavasile2009@gmail.com
4 Graduate School of Economics, Kobe University, Rokkodai, Nada-Ku, Kobe 657-8504, Japan; hamori@econ.kobe-u.ac.jp
5 Faculty of Political Science and Economics, Yamato University, Katayamacho, Suita 564-0082, Japan
* Correspondence: otilia.manta@rgic.ro or otilia.manta@icfm.ro

The accelerated digitalization of financial systems, intensified by the strategic integration of artificial intelligence (AI), marks a profound paradigm shift in the global financial architecture. FinTech has evolved beyond its initial role as a driver of operational efficiency, emerging instead as a structural force to reshape economic systems, institutional arrangements, and social interactions. In this context, the present Special Issue brings together original and rigorous academic contributions that examine how innovative financial instruments and AI technologies are transforming banking, payment infrastructures, financial governance, and pathways toward sustainable development.

The articles included in this Special Issue adopt interdisciplinary perspectives that intersect finance, economics, data science, public policy, and ethics. Collectively, they highlight both the transformative potential of FinTech and AI and the systemic challenges associated with rapid digital transformation, including regulatory uncertainty, ethical risks, and institutional adaptation.

1. Thematic Directions and Scholarly Contributions

The thematic directions outlined in this Special Issue reflect the multidimensional nature of contemporary FinTech ecosystems and the growing interdependence between technological innovation, institutional transformation, and sustainable development. Rather than addressing isolated technological applications, the contributions collectively illustrate how artificial intelligence, digital financial infrastructures, and decentralized technologies interact across markets, institutions, and societies. From predictive analytics and risk management to banking transformation, financial inclusion, blockchain governance, and sustainability-oriented finance, the selected studies form an integrated analytical framework that captures both micro-level mechanisms and macro-level systemic effects. This structure enables a comprehensive understanding of how FinTech and strategic AI integration simultaneously reshape financial performance, regulatory paradigms, ethical considerations, and long-term development trajectories in diverse economic contexts.

1.1. Artificial Intelligence, Predictive Analytics, and Financial Market Dynamics

A central thematic strand of this Special Issue focuses on the application of AI and advanced machine-learning techniques to financial forecasting, risk management, and

 https://doi.org/10.3390/fintech5020039

market behaviour analysis. These contributions illustrate the transition from traditional econometric models to adaptive, data-driven architectures capable of capturing non-linear dynamics and behavioural signals.

Within this direction, Ding Q., Guan C., Yu Y. introduce an innovative framework for forecasting IPO activity by integrating Long Short-Term Memory (LSTM) networks with aggregated music sentiment indicators in contribution 4. Their findings demonstrate that cultural and behavioural data can provide economically meaningful signals when processed through advanced neural architectures.

Complementarily, Ben Mekhlouf H., Moussaid A., Ghanimi F. investigate adaptive credit card fraud detection by comparing anomaly detection techniques with Deep Q-Network reinforcement learning agents, highlighting the advantages of continuous learning in highly dynamic fraud environments in contribution 3.

In the context of digital assets, Dutta A., Lakshmi M.G., Ramamoorthy A., Kumar P.K. explore the use of large language models for real-time "nowcasting" of cryptocurrency market conditions, revealing both their predictive potential and their limitations in highly volatile markets in contribution 5.

1.2. *Banking Sector Transformation and Institutional Performance*

A second major research project examines how FinTech and AI are reshaping the structure, performance, and resilience of the banking sector.

In contribution 9, Gaviyau W., Godi J. provides a comprehensive conceptual analysis of the evolution of banking systems from Banking 1.0 to Banking 5.0, emphasizing the growing importance of collaboration, digital ecosystems, and regulatory alignment.

From an empirical perspective, Fayad N.M., Awdeh A., Abou Mrad J., El Mokdad G., Nassar M. demonstrate that investments in digital human capital and intangible assets significantly enhance bank productivity in the United Kingdom, particularly in the post-pandemic context in contribution 8.

Similarly, Farag K., Ali L., Mutai N.C., Luqman R., Mahmoud A., Krasniqi N. show that income diversification, supported by machine-learning techniques, plays a critical role in improving bank stability across European banking systems in contribution 6.

Focusing on emerging markets, Robin I.A., Islam M.M., Alharthi M. highlight the positive impact of agent banking and FinTech-enabled distribution channels on the financial performance of commercial banks in Bangladesh in contribution 14.

1.3. *Financial Inclusion and Development in Emerging Economies*

Financial inclusion emerges as a cross-cutting theme throughout this Special Issue, reflecting the growing recognition of FinTech as a tool for inclusive growth.

In contribution 7, Farukh M.U., Taqi M., Vemavarapu K.R., Fadel S.M., Khan N.A. analyse how FinTech innovations are transforming rural financial ecosystems in India, demonstrating that digital payments, mobile banking, and micro-lending can significantly reduce financial exclusion when supported by appropriate regulatory and infrastructural frameworks.

In a complementary sustainability-oriented perspective, Magalhães R., Narracci F., Lowitzsch J. examine crowdfunding mechanisms for energy efficiency contracting, showing how digital financial platforms can democratize investment and support the green transition in contribution 13.

1.4. *Blockchain, Decentralized Finance, and the Reconfiguration of Trust*

Several contributions focus on blockchain and decentralized finance (DeFi) as foundational technologies for enhancing transparency, security, and efficiency in financial systems.

https://doi.org/10.3390/fintech5020039

In contribution 12, Kukman T., Gričar S. investigate the role of blockchain technology in improving transaction quality and operational efficiency, emphasizing its implications for financial quality management.

Extending blockchain applications beyond financial transactions, Agnola T., Ambrosini L., Beretta E., Gremlich G. present a blockchain-based platform for global supply chains, supported by empirical evidence from the coffee industry in contribution 2.

In the healthcare domain, Gonçalves Â.F.O., Norali S.F., Bechter C. analyse institutional resistance to AI-powered Buy-Now-Pay-Later smart contracts, highlighting behavioural, regulatory, and organizational barriers to adoption in contribution 10.

1.5. Governance, Ethics, and Public Policy in FinTech Ecosystems

The normative and institutional dimensions of FinTech development are addressed through contributions that emphasize governance, foresight, and ethical responsibility.

In contribution 11, Kayed S., Alhawwatma Z., Morshed A., Khrais L.T. apply a scenario-based multi-criteria decision analysis framework to FinTech governance in Kuwait, demonstrating how strategic foresight can enhance policy resilience under uncertainty.

Addressing ethical challenges, Alibašić H. proposes a multi-paradigm ethical framework for hybrid intelligence in blockchain and cryptocurrency governance, addressing tensions between algorithmic autonomy, decentralization, and institutional accountability in contribution 1.

1.6. FinTech, Artificial Intelligence, and Sustainable Development

In contribution 16, an integrative sustainability perspective is provided by Vasile V., Manta O. who examined the bidirectional relationship between FinTech, AI, and sustainable development. Their analysis highlights how digital financial technologies can support ESG objectives, green finance, and social inclusion, provided that technological innovation is aligned with coherent public policies and institutional support.

In contribution 15, this perspective is further reinforced by Zakia Siddiqui and Claudio Andres Rivera who developed a triangulated analytical framework for assessing sustainable FinTech models in Latvia, integrating Rogers' Innovation Diffusion Theory (IDT), De Meyer's Innovation Ecosystem framework, and Value Chain Theory. Their empirical findings show that the main competitive advantages of FinTech lie in flexibility, speed, customer-centricity, and trialability, while the main barriers remain regulatory complexity, uneven digital infrastructure, and institutional unreadiness. The study also emphasizes that strong collaboration among ecosystem actors supports innovation diffusion, but proactive regulatory engagement remains limited. Importantly, the authors argue that sustainable FinTech development depends not only on technological innovation itself, but also on institutional readiness, infrastructure capacity, agile public policy, and ESG integration. Their framework offers a replicable model for evaluating FinTech sustainability in small and highly regulated markets, demonstrating that long-term digital financial transformation requires a balance between innovation, compliance, and responsible governance.

2. Conclusions and Outlook Toward the Next Special Issue

The contributions assembled in this Special Issue provide compelling evidence that the strategic integration of FinTech and artificial intelligence represents a structural transformation of contemporary financial systems rather than a transient technological trend. Across diverse methodological approaches and geographical contexts, the studies demonstrate that AI-driven financial technologies are reshaping decision-making processes, risk assessment frameworks, institutional performance, and the architecture of financial intermediation. Collectively, the findings underscore the growing centrality of data-driven intelligence,

https://doi.org/10.3390/fintech5020039

digital infrastructures, and platform-based models in redefining how financial value is created, distributed, and governed.

Importantly, the insights generated in this Special Issue reveal that the impact of FinTech and AI extends well beyond efficiency gains and cost reduction. Several contributions highlight the emergence of new systemic interdependencies between financial institutions, markets, regulators, and users, raising fundamental questions related to transparency, algorithmic governance, ethical responsibility, and financial stability. At the same time, the evidence presented suggests that, when supported by adaptive regulatory frameworks and inclusive digital infrastructures, FinTech innovations can act as powerful enablers of financial inclusion, institutional resilience, and sustainable economic development.

These findings naturally open the path toward a broader and more integrative research agenda, addressed in the forthcoming *Special Issue AI × DeFi × Sustainability: Redesigning the Operating System of Global Finance*. While the current volume has primarily examined the strategic role of AI within evolving FinTech ecosystems, the next Special Issue advances the discussion by explicitly focusing on the convergence of artificial intelligence, decentralized finance (DeFi), and sustainability principles as a foundational redesign of the global financial "operating system." This shift reflects a transition from digitally enhanced financial systems toward intelligent, decentralized, and sustainability-oriented financial architecture.

The upcoming Special Issue aims to examine how this convergence is fundamentally transforming financial institutions, markets, and payment systems, while simultaneously supporting long-term economic, social, and environmental sustainability. In this context, AI-driven analytics, decentralized financial infrastructures, and sustainable finance frameworks are no longer treated as parallel developments but as mutually reinforcing components of next-generation financial ecosystems. Such architectures challenge traditional models of intermediation, governance, and trust, introducing new paradigms based on algorithmic coordination, distributed consensus, and embedded sustainability metrics.

By encouraging interdisciplinary research that spans finance, economics, data science, blockchain studies, and public policy, the next Special Issue seeks to advance scholarly understanding of both the opportunities and challenges associated with this convergence. Contributions are expected to explore how FinTech innovations contribute to resilient, inclusive, and responsible financial ecosystems, while also addressing critical issues related to systemic risk, regulatory design, ethical AI, and the environmental footprint of digital finance.

In this sense, the present Special Issue establishes the conceptual and empirical foundation for the next stage of inquiry. Together, the two Special Issues form a coherent scholarly trajectory that moves from the strategic integration of AI in FinTech toward a deeper exploration of how AI, DeFi, and sustainability jointly redefine the future of global finance. This continuity not only strengthens academic discourse but also provides valuable insights for policymakers, financial institutions, and technology developers seeking to navigate—and shape—the rapidly evolving financial landscape.:

Acknowledgments: The Guest Editors would like to express their sincere gratitude to the editorial team of FinTech for their professional support, guidance, and continuous assistance throughout the development of this Special Issue. Their dedication and editorial expertise were essential in ensuring a rigorous, transparent, and timely review process. The editors also warmly acknowledge all contributing authors for the quality, originality, and scholarly rigor of their research, as well as for their commitment to advancing knowledge at the intersection of financial technology, artificial intelligence, and sustainable development. Their contributions from the intellectual core of this Special Issue. Finally, the Guest Editors extend their appreciation to all partners, reviewers, and collaborators who supported this Special Issue through their expertise, constructive feedback, and

https://doi.org/10.3390/fintech502003

engagement. Their collective efforts significantly contributed to the successful completion and academic value of this Special Issue.

Conflicts of Interest: The authors declare no conflicts of interest.

List of Contributions:

1. Alibašić, H. A Multi-Paradigm Ethical Framework for Hybrid Intelligence in Blockchain Technology and Cryptocurrency Systems Governance. *FinTech* **2025**, *4*, 34. https://doi.org/10.3390/fintech4030034.
2. Agnola, T.; Ambrosini, L.; Beretta, E.; Gremlich, G. Empowering Global Supply Chains Through Blockchain-Based Platforms: New Evidence from the Coffee Industry. *FinTech* **2025**, *4*, 3. https://doi.org/10.3390/fintech4010003.
3. Ben Mekhlouf, H.; Moussaid, A.; Ghanimi, F. Adaptive Credit Card Fraud Detection: Reinforcement Learning Agents vs. Anomaly Detection Techniques. *FinTech* **2026**, *5*, 9. https://doi.org/10.3390/fintech5010009.
4. Ding, Q.; Guan, C.; Yu, Y. Mood in the Market: Forecasting IPO Activity with Music Sentiment and LSTM. *FinTech* **2026**, *5*, 12. https://doi.org/10.3390/fintech5010012.
5. Dutta, A.; Lakshmi, M.G.; Ramamoorthy, A.; Kumar, P.K. Large Language Models for Nowcasting Cryptocurrency Market Conditions. *FinTech* **2025**, *4*, 53. https://doi.org/10.3390/fintech4040053.
6. Farag, K.; Ali, L.; Mutai, N.C.; Luqman, R.; Mahmoud, A.; Krasniqi, N. Machine Learning for Predicting Bank Stability: The Role of Income Diversification in European Banking. *FinTech* **2025**, *4*, 21. https://doi.org/10.3390/fintech4020021.
7. Farukh, M.U.; Taqi, M.; Vemavarapu, K.R.; Fadel, S.M.; Khan, N.A. Fintech Innovations and the Transformation of Rural Financial Ecosystems in India. *FinTech* **2026**, *5*, 3. https://doi.org/10.3390/fintech5010003.
8. Fayad, N.M.; Awdeh, A.; Abou Mrad, J.; El Mokdad, G.; Nassar, M. The Impact of Technological Development on the Productivity of UK Banks. *FinTech* **2025**, *4*, 45. https://doi.org/10.3390/fintech4030045.
9. Gaviyau, W.; Godi, J. Banking Sector Transformation: Disruptions, Challenges and Opportunities. *FinTech* **2025**, *4*, 48. https://doi.org/10.3390/fintech4030048.
10. Gonçalves, Â.F.O.; Norali, S.F.; Bechter, C. AI-Powered Buy-Now-Pay-Later Smart Contracts in Healthcare. *FinTech* **2025**, *4*, 24. https://doi.org/10.3390/fintech4020024.
11. Kayed, S.; Alhawwatma, Z.; Morshed, A.; Khrais, L.T. Strategic Foresight for FinTech Governance: A Scenario-Based MCDA Approach for Kuwait. *FinTech* **2026**, *5*, 8. https://doi.org/10.3390/fintech5010008.
12. Kukman, T.; Gričar, S. Blockchain for Quality: Advancing Security, Efficiency, and Transparency in Financial Systems. *FinTech* **2025**, *4*, 7. https://doi.org/10.3390/fintech4010007.
13. Magalhães, R.; Narracci, F.; Lowitzsch, J. Crowdfunding and Energy Efficiency Contracting: Exploring New Pathways for Private Investment in Building Renovations. *FinTech* **2025**, *4*, 6. https://doi.org/10.3390/fintech4010006.
14. Robin, I.A.; Islam, M.M.; Alharthi, M. The Impact of FinTech on the Financial Performance of Commercial Banks in Bangladesh: A Random-Effect Model Analysis. *FinTech* **2025**, *4*, 40. https://doi.org/10.3390/fintech4030040.
15. Siddiqui, Z.; Rivera, C.A. Triangulated Analytical Framework for A Sustainable FinTech Model: The Case of Latvia. *FinTech* **2026**, *5*, 32. https://doi.org/10.3390/fintech5020032.
16. Vasile, V.; Manta, O. FinTech and AI as Opportunities for a Sustainable Economy. *FinTech* **2025**, *4*, 10. https://doi.org/10.3390/fintech4020010.

https://doi.org/10.3390/fintech5020039

FinTech

MDPI

Article

Triangulated Analytical Framework for a Sustainable FinTech Model: The Case of Latvia

Zakia Siddiqui * and Claudio Andres Rivera

Riga Business School, Riga Technical University, Ķīpsalas iela 6a, LV-1048 Riga, Latvia; claudio.rivera@rtu.lv
* Correspondence: zakia.siddiqui@rtu.lv

Abstract

This empirical study examines how FinTech innovation is adopted, scaled, and sustained in a small and highly regulated market, such as Latvia. The triangulated analytical framework is applied in this study, integrating Rogers' Innovation Diffusion Theory (IDT), De Meyer's Innovation Ecosystem framework, and Value Chain Theory. This framework analyses the relationship between innovation characteristics, ecosystem relationships, and restructuring in the value chain. The data was collected from FinTech leaders, conventional financial institutions (banks), regulators, and associations, and was analysed thematically. Based on interviews with stakeholders, the relative advantage of Latvian FinTech lies in its flexibility, speed, and trialability; however, barriers to adoption result in complex regulation, an uneven distribution of technology in infrastructure, and differences in institutional readiness. The authors found strong collaboration among the ecosystem's players but limited proactive regulatory engagement. This research provides a replicable model for cross-border or cross-sector analysis to assess the progress of innovation in regulatory and Environmental, Social and Governance (ESG) integration.

Keywords: FinTech; innovation ecosystem; value proposition; innovation diffusion; sustainable business model

JEL Classification: G23; O31; O33; M13; L26; L89

1. Introduction

The distribution of FinTech in the financial industry is driven by several factors, including its customer-centric approach, speed, and efficiency. Global corporate studies have shown that FinTech remains significant and is evolving in the financial sector despite fluctuations in investment cycles. FinTech remains relevant in the market, and this context reinforces the need for policies [1].

Such traits of FinTech solutions are due to Application Programming Interfaces APIs, FinTechs' work, and partnerships with traditional financial institutions [2]. The smaller the economy, the greater the impact of FinTech on a country's financial stability [3]. The ecosystem emerges more as a system of innovators, which has a transformative impact on society [4]. Such is the case in Latvia, which has over 100 FinTechs in operation [5]. A Europe-wide benchmarking study conducted by McKinsey & Company revealed that the performance of FinTech across Europe varies significantly. It demonstrated that the United Kingdom and Sweden are the leaders, while Slovakia and Romania are in the lower group for Fintech incorporation, and Latvia is listed in the middle of the third group [6].

The primary research question for this study is as follows: What roles do stakeholders in the FinTech ecosystem play in the diffusion, integration, alignment, and scaling of FinTech innovation in Latvia?

To answer this question, this study aims to achieve three objectives:

1. Identify the roles played by different FinTech stakeholders and their impact on the diffusion of innovation introduced by FinTech and their scaling.
2. Study the relationships that exist in the FinTech ecosystem in terms of trust, coordination, barriers, and collaboration between stakeholders.
3. Examine the value chain and operations made by FinTech stakeholders and how these link to FinTech growth/scalability and compliance.

This study contributes to the literature by applying a novel triangulated analytical approach (Innovation Diffusion Theory, the De Meyer Innovation Ecosystem model, and value chain analysis) to the empirical material and evidence from multiple stakeholders in a FinTech ecosystem for a mid-level economy in terms of maturity in the FinTech sector. Previous contributions address gaps by applying these theories separately, but not in a fully developed or integrated system applied to more mature FinTech ecosystems.

Roger's Innovation Diffusion Theory is a foundational lens through which to analyse the growth and innovation of the FinTech sector. Prior studies have utilised this theory to determine the adoption of digital banking [2] and investigate how the innovation of FinTech businesses affects the value chain activities of micro and small enterprises (MSEs) [7].

The second analytical lens of this study is the De Meyer Innovation Ecosystem model, which conceptualises the roles of stakeholders and their evolution from niche innovators to keystone players to orchestrators within the ecosystem's development, co-creating value through critical enablers such as human capital, infrastructure, and regulatory coordination [8].

Value chain analysis is another lens through which to analyse FinTech's contribution to the financial industry, particularly through its disruptive role and structural impact. One example is that FinTech enhances risk assessment, reduces costs, and streamlines various operations, ultimately leading to increased financial inclusion [9]. Also, in FinTech-driven ecosystems, supply chains tend to improve models' financial efficiency, which aligns with platform-based models [10].

Despite the global expansion of research on FinTech, the collective theoretical application of these three theories remains underexplored in small-market ecosystems, such as Latvia. Smaller countries offer a unique innovation environment compared to large economies due to their compact regulatory systems, limited talent pools, and export-oriented business models. Although these theories have been analysed separately in the past [2,8,9,11], they have not been examined using a single analytical approach.

The remainder of the paper follows the following structure: Section 2 presents the literature framework, Section 3 describes the methodology, Section 4 presents the findings and analysis, Section 5 discusses the results, and Section 6 presents the conclusions and contributions.

2. Literature Framework

Literature Framework. An iterative approach was used in this study, utilising keyword searches to identify the relevant academic literature. These searches were conducted on Google Scholar, Scopus, and Web of Science, using keywords related to FinTech, ecosystem, innovation diffusion, and value chain. The selected literature was screened to determine its relevance to the research question and the analytical lenses/theories. Articles from peer-reviewed journals and conference proceedings were prioritised.

Additionally, we included some seminal theoretical sources and high-quality corporate and industry reports as references by both industry and academia. Any duplicates, non-scholarly sources, or off-topic, unrelated sources were excluded. Moreover, the screening

https://doi.org/10.3390/fintech5020032

and selection of the literature were limited to English-language data only. Empirical work on FinTech was mostly performed from 2018 onwards, and older data was mainly used as the foundation of theoretical work. The most influential prior studies were identified by their citation counts, which complemented the present work analysing current development. To identify practical and relevant references, the authors applied citation chaining.

The three theoretical business models, IDT, De Meyer's ecosystem framework, and value chain analysis, have not been studied together before, but have been studied separately and independently in the FinTech literature [2,8,9]. Therefore, this study addresses this gap and utilises the Latvian FinTech Ecosystem as the anchor for the empirical analysis.

Innovation diffusion refers to the acceptance and eventual spread or diffusion of new products or services, ideas, or technologies [12]. Rogers' 1962 Innovation Diffusion Theory (IDT) suggests that five key attributes are involved in innovation diffusion: relative advantage, compatibility, complexity, trialability, and observability [13]. These are used to evaluate the acceptance and adoption of new technologies [14].

IDT has been used in prior studies to evaluate FinTech Innovation, for instance, for m-wallets [15,16], near-field communication (NFC) payments [17,18], mobile ticketing services [19], Open Data [20], commerce and payments [21], and digital banking [2].

In a volatile business environment, stakeholder collaboration is more important than competition [22], in terms of shared resources, knowledge spillovers, government support, local endowment, and network externalities [23]. Therefore, this ecosystem is used as the framework for elaborating, promoting, and persuading stakeholders to collaborate [24], resulting in the creation of innovative capabilities [25] and attaining a complex value proposition [26] due to their diversity [27] that eventually benefits the public [28] and attracts new entrants [29].

Tansley [30] coined the term Innovation Ecosystem. This was extended by Moore [31], who explored the competing players' framework, and by Basole & Karla [32], who identified its connectedness to co-development, solving complex problems, and knowledge sharing for sustainable development [33] from a global perspective [25].

De Meyer's Innovation Ecosystem has been utilised several times to explore the maturity of the FinTech Ecosystem and stakeholders, as well as the roles of different players [1,3,34]. Through this lens, the De Meyer Innovation Ecosystem framework is valid and relevant for understanding the growth and evolution of FinTech, as well as its interactions with other stakeholders within an ecosystem.

Finally, the third lens is the value chain framework. Value chain refers to how businesses create, deliver, and capture value [35]. The value delivered by FinTech is a modular and network-based rather than a firm-centric model, unlike traditional businesses [36,37]. For instance, by emphasising and creating value for partial processes, traditional methods are improved or replaced; FinTech creates value in onboarding (sign-up), compliance, payments, and scoring (credit) [38,39].

The value chain framework consists of three concepts: value proposition, value creation, and value capture [40,41]. Value proposition refers to the innovative products and services offered by companies that align with customers' needs [41]. Value creation refers to how a company delivers its value propositions, for example, through the use of technology, people, and partnerships [40,42]. Value Capture refers to how businesses earn revenues and profit. For example, financial capture could be profit margins or data monetisation [43].

Therefore, Value Chain Theory, as the third lens, studies how and where Fintech contributes functionally to the financial services sector in a small market like Latvia, adding operational value.

https://doi.org/10.3390/fintech502003

3. Methodology

An empirical, qualitative, multiple-case study approach was employed in this study, as Fintech is an emerging topic that requires in-depth data for inductive exploratory research. This study explores the innovations of the FinTech sector in a small country like Latvia, its collaboration within the ecosystem with its stakeholders, and its role in the value chain of financial services. This study employs semi-structured interviews with open-ended questions, grounded in a triangulated framework comprising IDT, De Meyer's Innovation Ecosystem framework, and Value Chain Theory. In this study, empirical findings are the result of qualitative interview coding; information is derived and structured according to the three analytical lenses mentioned.

The interviewees were FinTech leaders from the most successful Latvian FinTech subsectors, including lending, payment, and Information Technology–Data–Know Your Customer IT-Data-KYC [5], regulators, traditional financial institutions, and associations for multi-case design [44]. Table A1 in Appendix C provides a summary of the interviewees' profiles, including the category of stakeholders they belong to, their role, range of experience, mode of interview, and the duration of the interviews.

The authors employed a flexible and multimodal approach to collect data through interviews conducted from May to August 2025. The FinTech Latvian Association FLA facilitated the recruitment of participants/interviewees. The Managing Director of FLA introduced the researchers/authors to potential interviewees identified by the authors among the stakeholders. The reason for using this channel was to ensure timely responses and serious commitments from the participants, as the researcher knew some of these potential interviewees, while others were new contacts. Of the selected 15 FinTech stakeholders, 11 responded, yielding a 73% response rate. Additionally, all 8 of the other stakeholders responded, achieving a 100% response rate. Survey participants were given the choice to select three possible formats for the interviews, ensuring comfort, flexibility, and preference: face-to-face interviews, Zoom interviews, or completing a written questionnaire or survey.

All responses were anonymised for Qualitative Content Analysis (QCA). The questionnaires were designed to facilitate semi-structured interviews, incorporating all three theories within the triangulated theoretical framework: IDT [13], De Meyer's Innovation Ecosystem [45], and Value Chain Theory [35,40]. There were 15 questions related to these theoretical frameworks, with 5 questions for each theory to explore key components (see Appendix A). IDT questions were based on the following five attributes: relative advantage, complexity, compatibility, trialability, and observability. Innovation Ecosystem questions related to stakeholders' roles as orchestrators, enablers, or integrators. Value chain questions emphasised the FinTech companies' value proposition, value creation, and value capture. Also, there were two opening and three closing questions. The main questionnaire was created for FinTech firms, and a slightly modified version was administered to non-FinTech stakeholders, ensuring a theoretical context and allowing for cross-case analysis within the framework. In addition to the survey questions in Appendix A, Appendix D contains a detailed explanation of the interview process, including the recruitment process, the procedure for contact, the interview script, and whether it was one-to-one, specifying the mode (Zoom, in-person interviews, or written responses with the questionnaire).

A combined inductive and deductive coding approach was used to analyse the qualitative data gathered throughout the interviews. Based on the aforementioned academic theories, deductive codes were utilised. To capture recurring patterns in interview responses and stakeholders' insights, inductive codes were derived from the collected interview data.

With transparent and systematic coding, the QCA was conducted, resulting in the integration of evolving insights based on the theories [46,47]. As mentioned, initial codes were the result of recurring ideas; for example, one of the IDT attributes was relative advantage.

https://doi.org/10.3390/fintech5020032

Excerpts from the interview transcripts were labelled with initial codes, which were further grouped into sub-themes to avoid conceptual overlap. Furthermore, these sub-themes were grouped into grand themes, ensuring that all themes aligned with the theoretical lenses. The representation of the coding derived from raw excerpts during the interview to the initial codes, sub-themes, and grand themes is shown in Appendix B (Figure A3).

In total, 177 codes were identified or generated inductively from the responses of FinTech leaders, and 183 codes were obtained from non-FinTech stakeholders. These initial codes were recurring themes, concepts, or ideas, grouped into 78 and 81 sub-themes, respectively, and then into 41 and 42 grand themes, as shown in Table 1. The details of the coding procedure and how themes were developed are described in the next section, Findings and Analysis.

Table 1. QCA Coding summary—by authors.

	Non-Fintech Stakeholders' Initial Codes	FinTech Initial Codes	Non-Fintech Stakeholders Sub-Theme	FinTech Sub-Theme	Non-Fintech Stakeholder Grand Theme	FinTech Grand Theme
Total codes	183	177	81	78	42	41
Max	21	25	12	9	4	4
Min	4	4	2	4	2	2
Average	12	12	5	5	3	3

Basic rules concerning the participants involved were adhered to for this research. Interviewees were informed about the purpose and context of the study. Their participation was voluntary, and they could withdraw their participation at any time. Everyone provided their informed decision, either verbally or in writing via email to the primary author of this research. The details of all interviewees, including their names, titles, and the names of their companies or institutions, were kept confidential to protect their privacy. All interviews were recorded and stored safely; only the researchers have access to them. All interviews were recorded (those on Zoom and face-to-face were recorded only after permission was granted by the participants). The identities of the participants were kept anonymous throughout to ensure confidentiality. Direct quotations are anonymised; any quotations containing identifiable information would require approval for inclusion in the study.

4. Findings and Analysis

In this section, the authors present the findings that were reached through the Qualitative Content Analysis QCA performed on the data retrieved from the interviews. The analysis is based on the staged coding process as described in the Methodology, where excerpts from the interview transcripts were coded systematically and then grouped into sub-themes, which were further grouped and consolidated into grand themes. These themes were identified under the three analytical lenses: Innovation Diffusion Theory (IDT), De Meyer's Innovation Ecosystem framework, and Value Chain Theory. There are three tables in this section, which contain analytically interpreted results of the qualitative coding, followed by the synthesised coded themes. These were further compared across the stakeholder groups and further interpreted in light of the three lenses. Visual representations of the underlying coding structure and the development of the themes are shown as figures in Appendix B.

Coding method and development of themes: Qualitative Content Analysis was conducted using a stage-based coding flow for all questions across the three lenses employed in the framework, ensuring themes were generated transparently. Firstly, all interviews and writ-

https://doi.org/10.3390/fintech5020032

ten responses were carefully analysed and reviewed to determine their meaning and relevance to the theoretical framework, specifically regarding the IDT attribute (relative advantage). Secondly, these excerpts are then labelled with the initial code that was derived from recurring ideas and keywords (for instance, Instant Settlement, Time-to-Service: Faster Solution, Automation, AI-Generated Product Description, Faster Cross-Border Opportunities, Digital Money/Crypto, Compliance-Integrated Design, Easy Access, No Pre-Conditions, Serve Underserved, End-User Empowerment, Flexible and Lower Commission). Thirdly, these initial codes were clustered into sub-themes if they were conceptually related (for instance, Speed and Automation, Innovation in Design and Product, Innovation Inclusion + Access, User-Centric Utility and Cost, and Operational Disruption). Fourthly, consolidated grand themes were generated from the sub-themes (Technology-Centric Innovation, Human-Centric Value, and Market/Ecosystem-Centric Advantage).

Figure A3 shows the coding flow illustration for IDT (relative advantage). The same strategy or procedure was followed for all the questions in the questionnaire related to the triangulated framework. Further details on how the excerpts are converted into initial codes for the sub-themes and grand themes are provided in Appendix E, with coding details presented in Tables A2 and A3 for excerpts from FinTech and non-FinTech stakeholders, respectively.

In total, 177 initial codes were identified from the responses of FinTech leaders in the interviews, and 183 responses were derived from non-FinTech leaders. These initial codes were then grouped into 78 and 81 sub-themes, respectively, and 41 and 42 grand themes. This distribution of codes, sub-themes, and grand themes is summarised in Table 1, along with their distribution across stakeholder groups. The abovementioned codes formed the analytical basis for the findings, which are presented in the following subsections.

4.1. *Innovation Diffusion Theory (IDT)*

Table 2 and Figures A1–A3, A5 and A6 in Appendix B illustrate the findings on how FinTech Innovation is diffusing according to Roger's five attributes of IDT within the Latvian FinTech Ecosystem, as perceived by FinTech Stakeholders. The Latvian FinTech sector exhibits a relative advantage through speed, customer-centricity, and automation, supported by technology, including white-label and new B2B business models. FinTech must align with users' digital expectations, market scalability, and continuous KYC improvement. However, complexity increases due to limited collaboration, lack of trust, and regulatory ambiguity. Trialability can be achieved through both top-down processes, such as regulations implemented via innovation hubs and sandboxes, and bottom-up processes, including internal testing and freemium models. Observability is established through visibility from the regulator and associations, as well as users' testimonials and published success stories. Therefore, these approaches ensure that FinTech innovation diffusion aligns with Roger's five attributes; however, they are limited by the complexity of compliance and uneven infrastructure.

The key findings from the coded interviews are presented in Table 2, which compares how IDT attributes are perceived by FinTech and non-FinTech stakeholders in the FinTech sector. The results showed that relative advantage and compatibility are crucial factors supporting FinTech's diffusion, whereas complexity remains the most significant barrier, primarily due to uncertainty regarding regulatory and compliance requirements. Trialability and observability also play a vital role in the adoption of FinTech by reducing uncertainty and building confidence.

https://doi.org/10.3390/fintech5020032

Table 2. Findings based on interviews on IDT—by authors.

IDT Attribute + Coding Source Appendix B	FinTech Key Responses	Non-FinTech Key Responses
Relative Advantage Figure A3	Technology-centric reasons: speed, automation, and product innovativeness. Human-centric reasons: FinTech solutions serve underserved customers, increase end-user empowerment, provide digital platforms for accessibility, reduce costs through intermediary reduction, and supplement bank services. Market-centric reasons: operational disruption occurs for white-label strategies and new B2B models such as Platform as a Service (PaaS).	Ecosystem-centric advantage: transformation within collaboration. Market-centric advantage: speed and innovation. Consumer-centric advantage: access and inclusion. Compliance with regulations is identified as a major concern, causing tension between regulators and FinTechs.
Compatibility Figure A2	Technology-centric reasons: FinTech services complement the digital readiness of its audience, requiring automated solutions and digital onboarding. Human-centric reasons: FinTech services are customised to meet customers' needs (individual and business; banked or unbanked). Market-centric reasons: FinTech services fulfil the need for scalability for businesses.	Human-centric reasons: the Latvian market is prepared for digitalised financial services, but digital disparity persists across regions. Technology-centric reasons: banks develop iterative and agile digital products to improve competitiveness. Regulatory reasons: FinTechs must educate the public and businesses on innovation and digital security.
Complexity Figure A1	Technology-centric reasons: users prefer hybrid solutions combining new and familiar methods. Human-centric reasons: tech-knowledge gaps among demographic groups create demand for simpler solutions. Market-centric reasons: limited trust and regulatory uncertainty hinder collaboration.	Technology-centric reasons: strict regulations and licencing are justified for consumer protection. Human-centric reasons: lack of transparency leads to deficit trust and risk aversion. Market-centric reasons: negative social responsibility perceptions reinforce risk aversion.
Trialability Figure A6	Technology-centric reasons: FinTech develops services in agile form based on user feedback to meet market needs. Human-centric reasons: users test services internally and externally via freemium and pre-adoption models. Market-centric reasons: bottom-up trialability reduces risk and increases adaptability.	Technology-centric reasons: sandboxes and innovation hubs enable pilot testing. Human-centric reasons: regulators use experiments to educate and increase readiness. Market-centric reasons: trialability is seen as a top-down mechanism, contrasting the FinTech approach.
Observability Figure A5	Technology-centric reasons: sandbox initiatives enhance visibility and trust. Human-centric reasons: FinTech users are often unaware of the term "FinTech" despite using innovative services. Market-centric reasons: FinTechs publish reports and share success stories to build relationships with businesses and regulators.	Technology-centric reasons: licenced public registries and documentation provide visibility. Human-centric reasons: associations and events give FinTechs exposure. Market-centric reasons: cross-stakeholder collaboration increases observability and credibility.

https://doi.org/10.3390/fintech502003

4.2. De Meyer's Implications for Innovation Ecosystems in the FinTech Sector

Table 3 and Figures A4, A7–A9 and A12 in Appendix B present the findings on how the Latvian FinTech Ecosystem's stakeholders collaborate, interact, and co-create, as outlined in De Meyer's innovation orchestration model. The results show that the Latvian FinTech Ecosystem is still developing an organised stakeholder orchestration. Regulators remain the primary players, and collaboration among associations, banks, and investors remains mainly transactional. The primary barriers are ambiguous regulations and low trust, which hinder scaling and drive up integration costs. Regulator incentives remain slow and rigid; therefore, Latvian FinTechs rely on their own capabilities. According to the ecosystem's leaders, clear communication, trained human capital, and shared Anti-Money Laundering (AML)/KYC measures may help reduce transactional costs. In Latvia, informal knowledge sharing occurs; it is mostly partner-driven and occurs within a limited loop of institutional feedback. Hence, overall, the Latvian FinTech Ecosystem tends to be more reactive than proactive, thereby underscoring the need for agile, structured co-creation policy instruments.

The findings related to the ecosystem are shown in Table 3, based on the codes derived from the interviews. The results showed that, while regulators play a dominant role in shaping the ecosystem, collaborators, among other stakeholders, such as FinTechs, banks, and associations, are largely transactional and limited. As such, the FinTech ecosystem tends to be more reactive than proactive due to its regulatory ambiguity, high integration cost, and low trust, which limits innovation, scaling, and co-creation.

Table 3. Findings based on interviews on De Meyer's Ecosystem—by authors.

Ecosystem Component Coding Source Appendix B	FinTech Key Responses	Non-FinTech Key Responses
Stakeholder Integration Figure A4	Regulators are the most fundamental stakeholders for the guideline structures and compliance testing. In infrastructure development, traditional banks are perceived as both competitors and partners. Friction exists for interpretation and compliance. Investors, boards, and associations facilitate ecosystem growth. Sustained FinTechs act as orchestrators via partnerships and co-creation.	Regulators are crucial in both working groups and coordination at the EU level. Although the banks and associations support FinTech integration, they remain transactional. Slow collaboration is due to stricter bank rules. Integration among stakeholders is limited to shallow operational links. Focus on compliance is greater than co-creation.
Innovation Barrier Figure A9	Unclear relationships between FinTech and traditional businesses limit scaling. Ambiguous regulations and high integration costs result in slow innovation. Regulatory ambiguity limits cross-border growth. A lack of trust influences FinTech partnerships and reputation. Burden of compliance hinders new FinTech market entrants.	Uncertain and varying rules and their communication are highlighted by regulators. The risk-averse approach of regulators creates friction. Compliance is perceived as expensive, time-consuming, and overwhelming. The need for specialised compliance staff in FinTech increases costs. Regulatory ambiguity is the prime barrier.

https://doi.org/10.3390/fintech5020032

Table 3. *Cont.*

Ecosystem Component Coding Source Appendix B	FinTech Key Responses	Non-FinTech Key Responses
Incentivizing Innovation Figure A8	Most functions are maintained in-house to maintain speed and compliance. External partnerships are restricted due to low trust in regulation. Regulatory support exists; nevertheless, it is slow and inflexible. Industry recognition encourages continuity. Mature FinTechs switch from niche innovators to the leaders of the ecosystem.	Collaborations are not enough to incentivise innovation. Sandboxes tend to be more reactive than collaborative. Supervisory focus confines co-creation. Regulatory instruments are also reactive, not proactive. There is a need for deeper industry partnerships.
Reducing Transaction Cost Figure A7	Shared systems are essential with banks and regulators to improve and synchronise AML/KYC functions. Repetition and blurred rules waste resources. FinTechs create joint templates and checklists to shorten onboarding processes. Cross-institution co-operation helps reduce duplication. Efficiency leads to cost reduction.	To reduce errors, clear rules, improved infrastructure, and staff training are essential. There should be emphasis on clarity over cutting costs. For smooth implementation, hiring expert staff is fundamental. Tax breaks support low-cost models. Policy simplification is reviewed often at the institutional level.
Knowledge-Sharing Environment Figure A12	Knowledge exchange is largely informal and partner-driven; therefore, it has limited impact. Systematic learning and institutional follow-up are limited. Though events increase visibility, they do not increase infrastructure capacity. Gaps exist in consistent learning platforms for FinTech. Co-learning is essential with regulators.	Forums and working groups provide feedback and updates. Institutions conduct training in-house. Sector-specific education programmes are unavailable despite public education programmes. The sharing of policy-driven knowledge is mostly top-down. Iterative feedback loops are limited.

4.3. *Value Chain Theory Implications/Mapping in the FinTech Sector*

The summary in Table 4 and Figures A10, A11 and A13–A15 in Appendix B illustrates how Latvian FinTechs and traditional financial institutions restructure and adapt their value chains to achieve innovation while remaining compliant and scalable. FinTechs continue to maintain their customer-centric approach by diversifying their platforms, upholding ethical operations, and pursuing both profitability and inclusion. A selective outsourcing strategy, combined with in-house control, enables FinTech to achieve scalability. Automation, adaptive governance, and internal audits are used to integrate compliance and achieve transparency. FinTechs use Key Performance Indicators (KPIs), Service-Level Agreements (SLAs), and the volume of client acquisition to track performance, which together signal their maturity level and generate trust. Lastly, Latvian FinTechs embed ESG goals, implement digital strategies, and collaborate with policymakers to align with their value propositions. This way, Latvian FinTechs remain resilient and align with the European Union's (EU's) financial innovation goals.

https://doi.org/10.3390/fintech5020032

Table 4. Findings based on interviews on Value Chain Theory—by authors.

Value Chain Component Coding Source Appendix B	FinTech Key Responses	Non-FinTech Key Responses
Operational Structure Figure A10	Expand and diversify platforms for both global and local operations. Trust and visibility are built using awards and recognition. The main aim is to increase profits and scalability, along with reducing costs. Respect community-centric and ethical stewardship. Emphasis on agility, which is customer-centric.	Adopting agile methods and AI tools to align with FinTech models. Outsource non-core functions to FinTechs to remain efficient and reliant. Cultural change in regard to customer focus. Faster adoption is possible with reduced bureaucracy. Encourage collaborative agility.
Scalability vs. Compliance Figure A11	Core operations in-house to maintain control and efficiency. Outsource specific tasks (like legal documentation) whilst preserving integrity. Restrict over-dependence on third parties to restrict regulatory exposure. Selective outsourcing maintains responsiveness. Compliance rooted in growth strategies.	Unease regarding third-party risk and negative reputational exposure. Regulators tightly supervise FinTech growth to ensure user protection. FinTech maturity enhances trust and alignment. Outsourcing is overseen for systemic risk. Balance is needed to ensure innovation and security.
Transparency and Compliance Figure A15	Compliance is a fundamental characteristic of FinTech products. FinTechs use automation and architecture to internalise regulatory demands. Adaptive governance supported by internal audits and ecosystem co-operation. Automation and AI enrich the efficiency of oversight. Transparency enhances the trust of regulators in FinTech.	AI is designed for risk assessment and oversight of the broader governance framework. Associations have inconsistent levels of compliance. Emphasis on consumer protection and risk evaluation. Mutual responsibility across institutions. Culture of "doing things right", i.e., risk-averse environment.
Performance Metrics Figure A13	Track volume and revenue regularly to evaluate health. Non-financial metrics (for instance, testing, client acquisition) are linked to infrastructure needs and behaviour. Strategic goals are data-driven and adaptable. KPIs apprise partnership feasibility and trust. Metrics indicate sustainability and maturity.	For partnership and governance, KPIs and SLAs are used. Performance transparency builds trust. Metrics demonstrate sustainability to partners and associations. Indicators help evaluate the health of the ecosystem. It is encouraged to have shared benchmarking.
Value Proposition Alignment Figure A14	For modularity and quick market response, digital strategies are embedded in core models. Cloud-based structures, which are scalable, align with ESG goals. Co-operation with policymakers guarantees recognition along with compliance. Alignment supports scalability and resilience. Flexibility persists as a core differentiator.	For Digital Euro development and Open Finance, operational infrastructure is prioritised. Stability aligns with policy and ESG frameworks. Social fit and regulatory trust are vital for scaling. FinTechs are presumed to be partners in the implementation of the policy. Market access barriers lead to misalignment.

The main findings obtained from the coded interview data on the FinTech value chain are summarised in Table 4. The results showed that FinTech stakeholders tend to keep core operations in-house to maintain control and ensure compliance is not compromised. However, FinTech stakeholders also outsource non-core activities to help them scale and focus on their core business. Lastly, FinTech tends to emphasise trust, transparency, and different performance metrics to ensure sustainable growth, trust, and alignment with regulators and their ecosystem partners.

5. Discussion

In this section, the research questions are answered based on the findings.

The research question was as follows: What roles do stakeholders in the FinTech Ecosystem play in the diffusion, integration, alignment, and scaling of FinTech innovation in Latvia?

From De Meyer's Lens of Innovation Ecosystem:

https://doi.org/10.3390/fintech5020032

According to the findings, the role of each stakeholder differs based on their institutional position. FinTech stakeholders are the primary drivers of innovation diffusion and scalability, achieved through speed, digital capabilities, and synchronised, embedded modularity. On the other hand, non-FinTech stakeholders employ different tools for innovation diffusion, including requirements for compliance, trust expectations, and institutional coordination. In general, it was observed that innovation diffusion and scaling are enabled by (selective) collaboration and partnering in the private sector. However, diffusion and scaling are constrained by uneven infrastructure, regulatory complexity, and institutional unreadiness.

Therefore, the outcomes of this study indicate that ecosystem orchestration in the FinTech ecosystem is more institutionally constrained than market-driven, particularly in small, highly regulated markets.

From the Lens of Value Chain Theory:

The Latvian FinTech Ecosystem's stakeholders focus on the diffusion of innovation from the perspectives of flexibility, speed, and digital-first capabilities. However, this is restricted due to a complex regulatory framework, uneven infrastructure, and institutional unreadiness. FinTech emphasised agile, modular product designs and embedded compliance, whereas non-FinTech stakeholders focused on consumer trust and compliance integration. Collaboration is strong except with regulators. The FinTech value chain maintains its core operations in-house and selectively outsources specific tasks. Innovative strength and strategic partnerships contribute to the scaling of FinTech.

Thus, the findings of this study suggest that FinTech achieves scaling through partner integration and selective outsourcing, rather than completely externalising core functions.

From Rogers' Lens of Innovation Diffusion Theory IDT:

Both FinTech and non-FinTech leaders agree that flexibility, speed, and customer-centric service are the relative advantages of FinTech services over traditional financial solutions, modular designs, and API infrastructures. However, not all FinTech solutions are replacements; rather, they are supplements to conventional financial services. This viewpoint aligns with Roger's concept of relative advantage [13], Sharma et al.'s study [48] on the adoption of FinTech solutions, and Lee & Shin's opinion on efficient solutions to remain competitive [39]. Overall, the results show that the perceived relative advantage, an attribute of IDT, is the primary driver of innovation adoption, prioritising competitiveness and efficiency. Moreover, the Latvian FinTech sector plays a supplementary role in the traditional financial industry rather than substituting it completely.

FinTechs meet the digital expectations of tech-savvy and younger users, as well as niche B2B markets, with strong compatibility; however, such systems are weak in Latvia due to the gap that exists between local consumer demand and innovative design, aligning with the findings of Sun et al. [49]. Success stories, events, and testimonials enhance trust in FinTech, as stated by Zolkepli et al. [50]. As such, customers adopt user-friendly FinTech solutions. Complexity results from regulatory and compliance ambiguity, as well as associated costs. Demo or risk-free accounts, in addition to sandbox demos, increase FinTech adoption, lower perceived risk, and enhance trust and reputation, as stated by Sharma [48] and Thakur et al. [51]. The evidence from the Latvian FinTech sector suggests that perceived complexity is driven by institutional conditions rather than technology, despite high levels of observability and trialability. Institutional conditions depend on the cost and ambiguity of compliance.

Henceforth, the findings suggest that institutional readiness plays an important role alongside FinTech innovation attributes in the regulated market.

Private FinTech stakeholders synchronise their processes, collaborate with BaaS providers, payment processors, and card issuers, and engage in joint development Sprints and APIs. However, regulators tend to be reactive, extending guidance rather than providing structured

https://doi.org/10.3390/fintech502003

facilitation with policy tools, contrary to the conclusions of Williamson et al. [45] and Fenwick et al. [52]. Fintech partners with global networks to reduce operational costs and the burden of scaling. High compliance costs, the lack of a sandbox, and ambiguity in regulations are key barriers to aligning with Adner's [53] interdependence barrier.

This finding is contrary to the academic literature on the orchestration expectations of the ecosystem, which assumes that regulators usually act as proactive facilitators.

There is a partial knowledge-sharing ecosystem in Latvia, which is unstructured and misaligned with the framework presented by Sangwa et al. [54]. However, the regional policies could enable FinTech to earn trust and integration.

FinTechs customise functions by reorganising compliance, partner integration, and product development, and have transitioned from single-service models to a full-stack ecosystem. Banks also integrate APIs for alternative credit scoring. Most FinTechs consider that internal capabilities are vital, but external capabilities can also be leveraged through partnerships, which help scale and mitigate risks, aligning with the findings of Williamson & De Meyer [45] and Jangid et al. [55]. This is consistent with arguments in the value chain leadership that scaling is the result of partner integration and selective outsourcing. However, Latvian FinTech ensures that it does not lose control in-house and preserves core compliance, allowing it to manage regulatory exposure wisely. FinTech carefully scales, observing core functions in-house, to ensure it stays aligned with regulations. Regulators have stressed the importance of transparency and consumer protection for lasting viability. Financial innovation helps fulfil ESG goals [56], while AI solutions enable businesses to innovate more efficiently if they follow the rules [57].

Throughout the analysis, FinTech leaders displayed a strong relative advantage provided by FinTechs. Nonetheless, FinTech adoption barriers remain due to regulatory complexity and uneven readiness across businesses. FinTech has well-developed observability and trialability, with strong collaboration in the private sector. Based on these results, the authors conclude that advanced innovation diffusion and ecosystem growth rely heavily on institutional readiness, infrastructure capacity, and agile policy measures.

6. Conclusions and Contribution

The key goal was to understand how FinTechs and non-FinTech stakeholders perceive, develop, and scale their innovations. To explore this question, the authors developed a triangulated analytical framework using Rogers' IDT, Williamson's, and De Meyer's Innovation Ecosystem and Value Chain Theory.

6.1. Conclusions

a. FinTech innovation in the Latvian market is driven by automation, speed, and modularity; however, uneven institutional readiness and complexity of compliance are the biggest barriers.
b. As compared to regulatory facilitation, collaboration in the private sector is stronger. As a result, regulations create friction for integration and interpretation.
c. Partner integration with selective outsourcing can help FinTech scale innovations. However, FinTech often keeps governance and core compliance matters in-house to manage regulatory exposure.
d. A knowledge-sharing mechanism, combined with the infrastructure of AML/KYC, helps FinTech improve trust and reduce transaction costs, resulting in a progressively developing ecosystem.

https://doi.org/10.3390/fintech5020032

6.2. Contribution of This Study

a. This is the first study, to the best of the authors' knowledge, that combines IDT, De Meyer's Ecosystem Framework, and Value Chain and Business Models theory into a single triangulated analytical framework.
b. This framework can be replicated in small, highly regulated markets to analyse innovation in FinTech and other sectors undergoing technology convergence, such as health tech.
c. The questionnaire used to interview FinTech Ecosystem leaders can be adapted and reused for further studies, such as cross-sector or cross-country studies.

6.3. Limitation

This research has limitations: it is confined to one country (Latvia). Furthermore, a comparative study of the EU FinTech Ecosystem should be conducted to gain more insights. A longitudinal study should also be conducted to understand how the roles of regulators evolve. Moreover, further study is needed on how ESG elements are integrated into FinTech business models.

Author Contributions: Conceptualisation, Z.S., C.A.R.; methodology, Z.S.; software, Z.S.; validation, Z.S.; formal analysis, Z.S.; investigation, Z.S.; resources Z.S.; data curation, Z.S.; writing—original draft preparation, Z.S.; writing—review and editing, Z.S.; visualisation, Z.S.; supervision, C.A.R.; funding acquisition, Z.S. and C.A.R. All authors have read and agreed to the published version of the manuscript.

Funding: This research was funded by project No. 5.2.1.1.i.0/1/23/I/CFLA/001 "Knowledge and Research Capacity Strengthening of Anti-Money Laundering, Financial Sector Technology and Analysis".

Institutional Review Board Statement: Ethical review and approval were waived for this study due to the Latvian Law on Scientific Activity (Zinātniskās darbības likums, Law No. 107337) which defines the principles of scientific research and the responsibilities of researchers, including scientific integrity, objectivity, and responsible conduct of research, and does not establish a mandatory requirement for ethics committee approval for low-risk, non-biomedical research of this nature.

Informed Consent Statement: Informed consent was obtained from all subjects involved in the study.

Data Availability Statement: The datasets are available upon request.

Acknowledgments: The authors would like to thank RTU Riga Business School for its support in the writing of this paper.

Conflicts of Interest: The authors declare no conflicts of interest. The funders had no role in the design of the study; in the collection, analyses, or interpretation of data; in the writing of the manuscript; or in the decision to publish the results.

Abbreviations

The following abbreviations are used in this manuscript:

IDT	Innovation Diffusion Theory
ESG	Environmental, Social, and Governance
API	Application Programming Interface
MSE	Micro and Small Enterprises
NFC	Near-field Communication
IT-Data-KYC	Information Technology–Data–Know Your Customer
QCA	Qualitative Content Analysis
B2B	Business-to-Business
AML	Anti-Money Laundering
KPI	Key Performance Indicator

https://doi.org/10.3390/fintech5020032

SLA	Service Level Agreement
EU	European Union

Appendix A. Stakeholder Questionnaire—FinTechs BOD

I appreciate your willingness to participate in this research. This questionnaire is part of a study exploring stakeholder perspectives on Latvia's FinTech ecosystem. Please answer as thoroughly as you feel comfortable.

1. What is your professional background, and how did you become a board member of this FinTech?
2. How do you relate to the mission and vision of your FinTech company?
3. What innovations does your firm offer that improve on traditional financial services?
4. How do your products or platforms align with customer values and market needs? (Fit between the innovation and the target users' lifestyles or expectations)
5. What are the paramount usability or adoption challenges you've (or your users have) encountered?
6. How do you allow customers to test or pilot your products before full use?
7. What mechanisms help demonstrate the impact of your offerings (e.g., case studies, testimonials)?
8. Who are the most critical partners in your business ecosystem (e.g., enablers, regulators, adopters)?
9. What barriers have you encountered in navigating ecosystem relationships (e.g., with regulators or banks)?
10. How do you foster trust, co-creation, or collaborative development with other ecosystem players? (Mutual development of innovation with partners)
11. How does your firm contribute to or benefit from knowledge-sharing environments (events, consortia)?
12. How has your role evolved—from a niche innovator to a keystone or Orchestrator (if applicable)? (Lifecycle progression within the ecosystem)
13. How has your value proposition evolved since the company's inception?
14. What operational functions are handled in-house vs. outsourced, and why? (Internal capability vs. third-party reliance)
15. How do you structure your company to ensure scalability while staying compliant?
16. Do you track specific KPIs to evaluate business model performance?
17. How does your business model align with national or EU-level goals for FinTech?
18. What advice would you give to future FinTech board members or founders entering this space?
19. Can you share an anecdote or memorable board discussion about innovation or transformation?
20. How do you see your firm's role evolving within the Latvian FinTech landscape in the next 5 years?

Appendix B. Emerging Concepts from the QCA of the Interviews

Figures in Appendix B are organised by analytical lens and thematic grouping; figure numbering follows the order of first citation in the main text.

https://doi.org/10.3390/fintech5020032

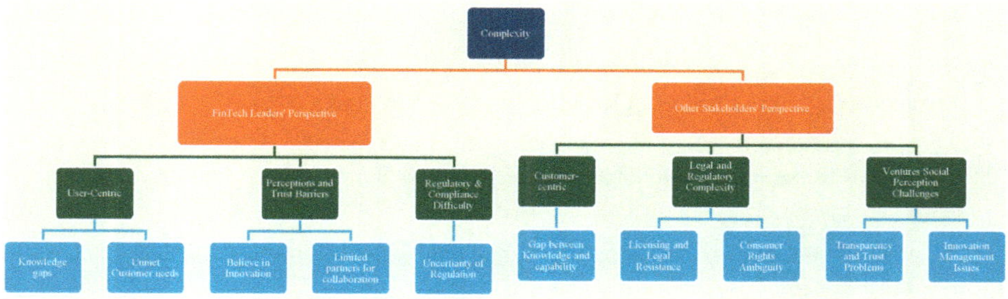

Figure A1. Rogers' Innovation Diffusion Theory for Complexity—developed by the author based on interviews, 2025.

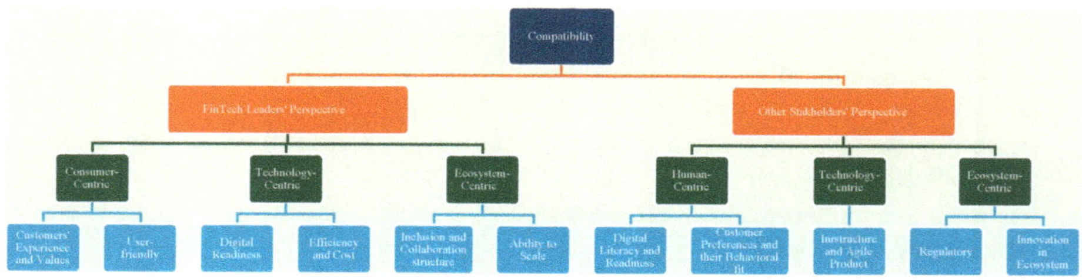

Figure A2. Rogers' Innovation Diffusion Theory for Compatibility—developed by the author based on interviews, 2025.

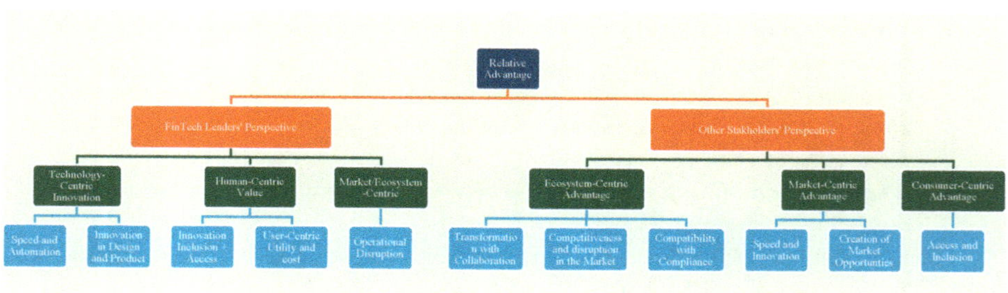

Figure A3. Rogers' Innovation Diffusion Theory for Relative Advantage—developed by the author based on interviews, 2025.

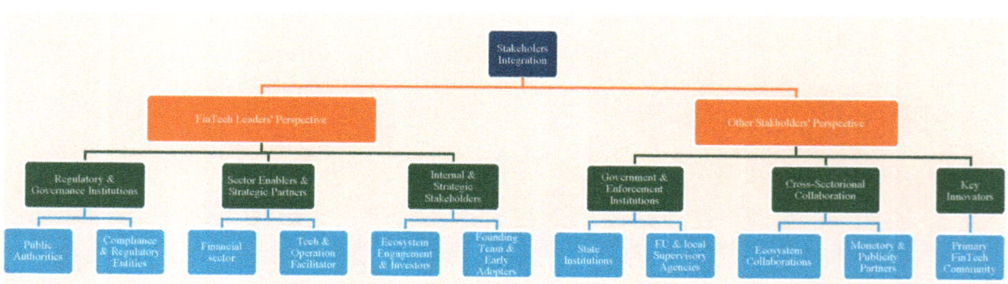

Figure A4. De Meyer's Innovation Ecosystem for Stakeholder Integration—developed by the author based on interviews, 2025.

https://doi.org/10.3390/fintech502003

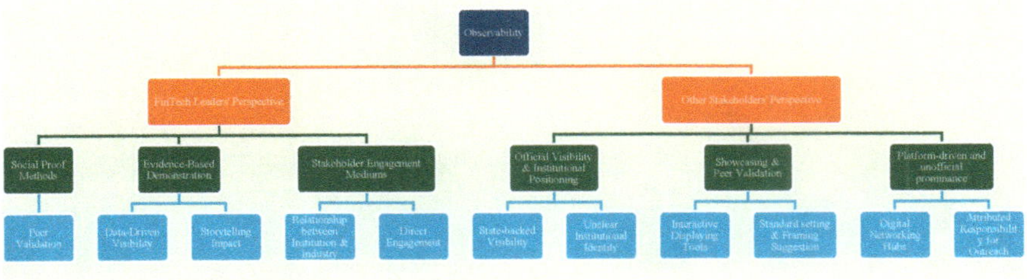

Figure A5. Rogers' Innovation Diffusion Theory for Observability—developed by the author based on interviews, 2025.

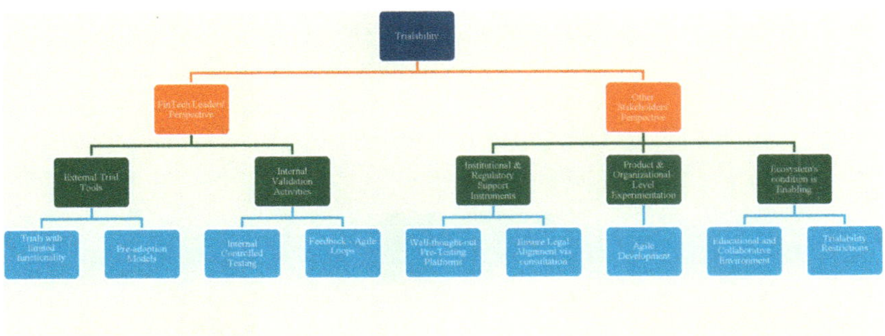

Figure A6. Roger's Innovation Diffusion Theory for Trialability—developed by the author based on interviews, 2025.

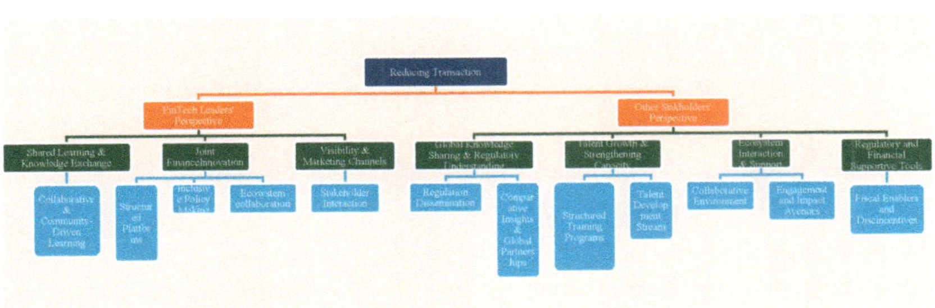

Figure A7. De Meyer's Innovation Ecosystem for Reducing Transactions—developed by the author based on interviews, 2025.

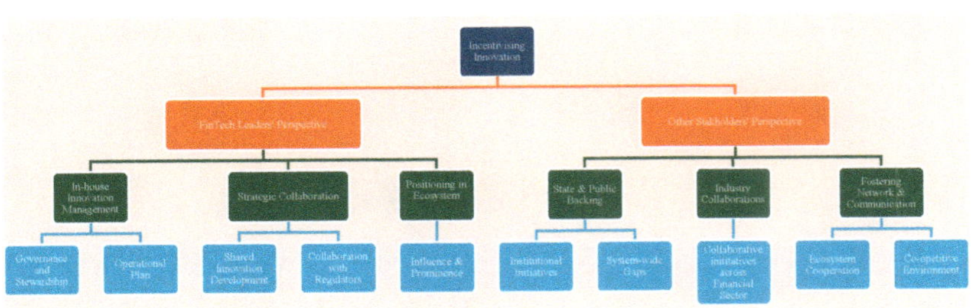

Figure A8. De Meyer's Innovation Ecosystem for Incentivising Innovation—developed by the author based on interviews, 2025.

https://doi.org/10.3390/fintech5020032

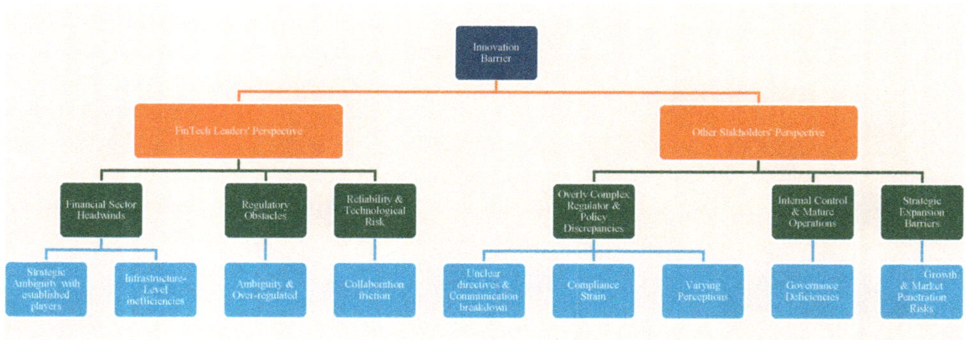

Figure A9. De Meyer's Innovation Ecosystem for Barriers to Innovation—developed by the author based on interviews, 2025.

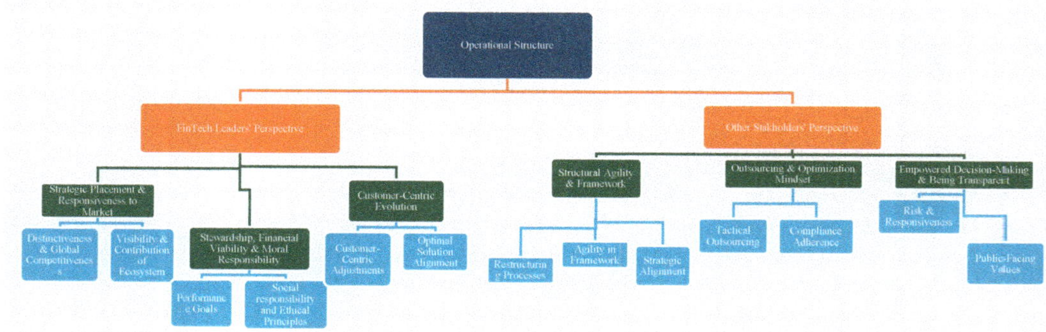

Figure A10. Value Chain Contribution to Operational Structure—developed by the author based on interviews, 2025.

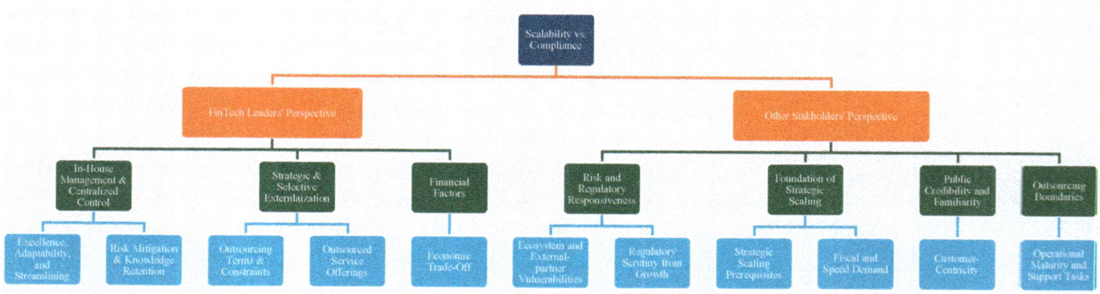

Figure A11. Value Chain Contribution to Scalability vs. Compliance—developed by the author based on interviews, 2025.

https://doi.org/10.3390/fintech5020032

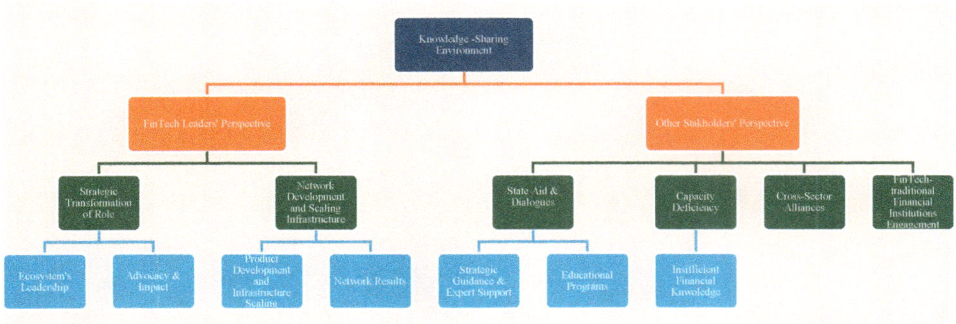

Figure A12. De Meyer's Innovation Ecosystem for a Knowledge-Sharing Environment—developed by the author based on interviews, 2025.

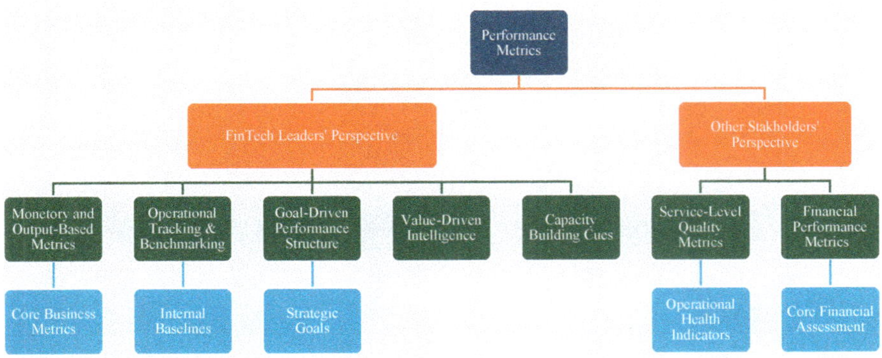

Figure A13. Value Chain Contribution to Performance Metrics—developed by the author based on interviews, 2025.

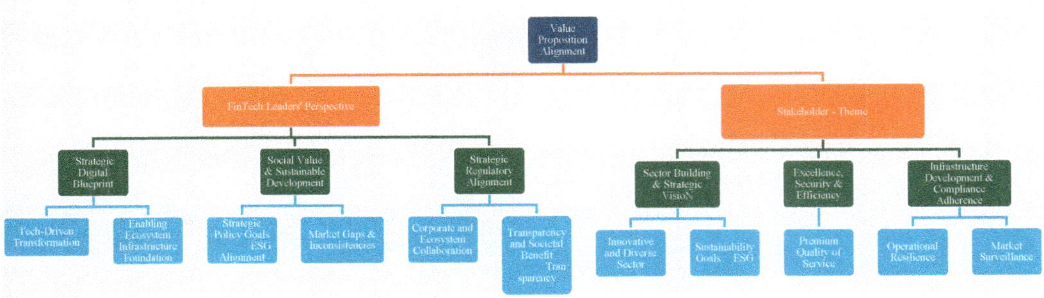

Figure A14. Value Chain Contribution to Value Proposition Alignment—developed by the author based on interviews, 2025.

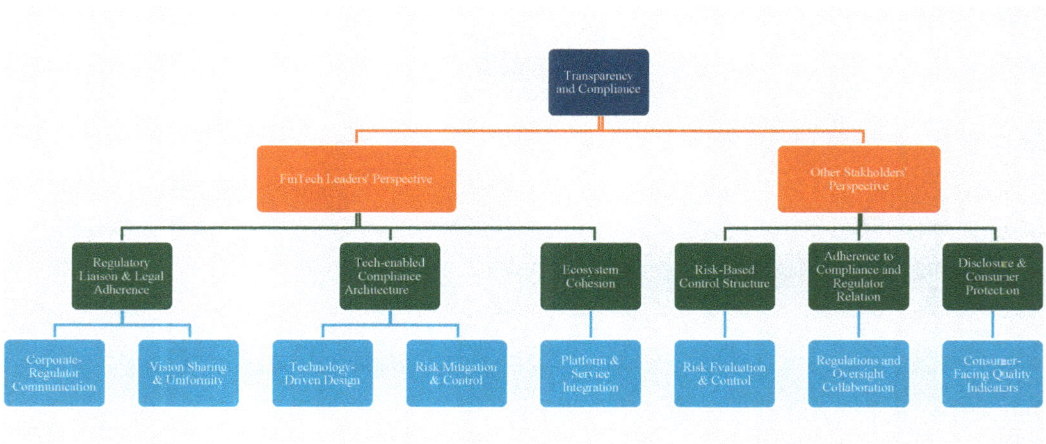

Figure A15. Value Chain Contribution to Transparency and Compliance—developed by the author based on interviews, 2025.

Appendix C. Profile of the Interviewees

Table A1. Profile of the interviewees, including stakeholder category, role, experience, interview mode, duration, and timing—developed by the authors based on interviews, 2025.

Interview ID	Role Type	Years of Experience	Mode	Duration	Month/Year
FinTech 1	Functional lead	29 years	Zoom	around 40 min	June 2025
FinTech 2	Executive leadership	14 years	Written	N/A	June 2025
FinTech 3	Executive leadership	16 years	Written	N/A	June 2025
FinTech 4	Executive leadership	22 years	Zoom	around 1 h	May 2025
FinTech 5	Senior Management	19 years	Zoom	around 50 h	June 2025
FinTech 6	Executive leadership	15 years	Written	N/A	May 2025
FinTech 7	Executive leadership	26 years	Written	N/A	May 2025
FinTech 8	Executive leadership	26 years	Written	N/A	May 2025
FinTech 9	Executive leadership	19 years	Written	N/A	June 2025
FinTech 10	Functional lead	16 years	Face-to-Face	around 1 h	May 2025
FinTech 11	Executive leadership	14 years	Written	N/A	May 2025
Regulator 1	Senior management	19 years	Zoom	around 1 h	June 2025
Regulator 2	Senior management	21 years	Written	N/A	May 2025
Regulator 3	Senior management	28 years	Zoom	around 1 h	May 2025
Regulator 4	Senior management	11 years	Written	N/A	August 2025
Commercial Bank 1	Senior management	26 years	Zoom	around 80 min	May 2025
Commercial Bank 2	Board-level governance	18 years	Zoom	around 75 min	May 2025
Association 1	Executive leadership	36 years	Face-to-Face	around 1 h	May 2025
Association 2	Executive leadership	24 years	Zoom	around 1 h	May 2025

Note: All roles of stakeholders and experiences are generalised to ensure anonymity. Moreover, the time taken for written responses cannot be determined.

https://doi.org/10.3390/fintech5020032

Appendix D. Interview Script

Contact and Recruitment Procedure: Purposive sampling was employed to recruit participants across various stakeholder groups. The stakeholder group included FinTechs from the three most successful subsectors of the FinTech sector, based on their financial performance from 2016 to 2022, traditional financial institutions (Commercial Banks), regulators, and associations. The Managing Director of the FinTech Latvian Association put the researcher or authors in contact with potential participants, some of whom were known to the authors, while others were new contacts. The introduction and initial communication were made via official emails by both authors and the Managing Director. The authors provided the initial guidelines and the questionnaire in advance. Additionally, participants could choose from three modes of response to prioritise their availability and flexibility: one-to-one interviews (either via Zoom or face-to-face) or written responses, which could be submitted as an attachment to the email.

Consent, Anonymity, and the Data: Once the initial contact was made, the authors then introduced themselves to and informed the participants of the purpose and context of the research. The information was provided to stakeholders to ensure they understood that the process was voluntary and that they reserved the right to skip questions or withdraw from the study at any point. All participants provided consent for both participating in the study and for a one-to-one interview, either verbally or in writing via email. Therefore, video recordings or audio recordings were used only when permission was granted. All responses were handled carefully to maintain confidentiality, and all the collected data were anonymised to maintain the confidentiality of the participants.

Additionally, no information, such as names, titles, or organisations, was used, and this was kept confidential throughout the research. If any direct quotation was necessary, it could not be shared without the prior approval of the participant. However, all recordings, their transcripts, and the written material are maintained and stored securely and are accessible only to the authors.

Interview Structure and modification in questions: Data were collected using a semi-structured questionnaire. The questionnaire was based on the triangulated theoretical frameworks of Rogers' Innovation Diffusion Theory (IDT), De Meyer's Innovation Ecosystems Framework, and the Value Chain Theory. The survey began with two introductory questions that asked participants about their role in their organisation and about the key developments in the Latvian FinTech Ecosystem. The introductory questions were followed by questions related to the three lenses. Five attributes of IDT were addressed in the IDT section (relative advantage, complexity, compatibility, observability, and trialability). De Meyer's Innovation Ecosystem examined how stakeholders interact and collaborate, the level of trust among them, and information such as who serves as the orchestrator, integrator, and enabler, as well as the key enablers and factors that act as barriers to diffusion and innovation scaling. Lastly, the value chain addressed value proposition, value creation, and how FinTech captures value by reshaping financial services, as well as the resulting constraints when scaling. Finally, the questionnaire concluded with three closing questions regarding their recommendations for new startups, recommendations on strengthening the FinTech Ecosystem, potential regulatory improvements, and any advice they wished to offer. The version of the questionnaire was slightly modified for non-FinTech stakeholders to ensure consistency, while simultaneously enabling comparison across cases.

Further information: In parallel to face-to-face or Zoom interviews, authors took notes as a backup. The written responses were also treated as qualitative data, equivalent to the one-to-one interviews, which were analysed using a Qualitative Content Analysis approach, similar to the analysis of the interview transcripts.

https://doi.org/10.3390/fintech5020032

Appendix E.

Coding Flow from Raw Responses to Themes: The first step was to identify responses to the questions from both the interview transcripts and the written responses. This was performed manually as the interviews were semi-structured and did not necessarily follow the same sequence. Excerpts answering specific questions were then identified and condensed into several keywords or labels, and they were named as the initial codes. The initial codes were then further grouped into sub-themes and aggregated into grand themes under the relevant theoretical lens. This process followed a structured flow: Identifying relevant excerpts from interviews (raw data), condensing meaning, generating initial keywords, grouping into sub-themes, aggregating into grand themes, and mapping to the theoretical lens.

For instance, one excerpt is taken from IDT on relative advantage below:

"Basically, we're taking the payment product and building the innovations on top of it, Mhmm. On top of it. One of our flagship products is our tipping solution. This way, you can pay the bill and leave the tip. And we do this tip, so the tip goes to the staff member's bank account, right, directly from the card machine. Mhmm. That's basically the innovation of it, it's built up on the IT on a back end that we are delivering directly from the machine to the staff, not through the business account, but, like, directly to the staff."

The initial codes identified were as follows: Innovative Product, Reduce Intermediaries/Disintermediation, Enhance Transparency, Lower Commission, Digital Solution, Cashless, Online Platforms/Apps, and Time-to-Service: Faster Solution. Similarly, all excerpts answering these questions were analysed to identify the initial codes. Then, these codes were grouped into sub-themes and subsequently into grand themes. Below, Table A2. is an example of the complete code derived from the initial code and the grand code for IDT relative advantage.

This table is illustrated in Figure A1. It is worth noting that the excerpts from the FinTech interviews were analysed separately from those of the non-FinTech interviews to compare viewpoints and triangulate frameworks from FinTech and non-FinTech stakeholders. The grand themes for the initial codes derived from non-FinTech stakeholders from the Latvian FinTech sector for IDT—relative advantage are given as follows in Table A3.

Table A2. Coding structure from initial codes to sub-themes and grand themes for IDT relative advantage from FinTech leaders perspective—developed by the authors based on interview data, 2025.

Grand Theme	Sub-Theme	Initial Codes
Technology-Centric Innovation	Speed and Automation	Instant Settlement
		Time-to-Service: Faster Solution
		Automation
		AI-Generated Product Description
		Faster Cross-Border Opportunities
	Innovation in Design and Product	Innovative Product
		Digital Solution
		Digital Money/Crypto
		Compliance-Integrated Design
		Easy Access
		No Pre-Conditions

https://doi.org/10.3390/fintech5020032

Table A2. *Cont.*

Grand Theme	Sub-Theme	Initial Codes
Human-Centric Value	Innovation Inclusion + Access	Serve Underserved
		End-User Empowerment
		Flexible
		Lower Commission
		Cashless
	User-Centric Utility and Cost	Online Platforms/Apps
		Customised Solution
		Enhances Transparency
		Transparency + Disintermediation
		Reduce Intermediaries/Disintermediation
		Supplement to Banking Solutions
Market/Ecosystem-Centric Advantage	Operational Disruption	White-label Strategy
		B2B Growth Model
		PaaS

Table A3. Coding structure of initial codes, sub-themes, and grand themes for IDT relative advantage from non-FinTech stakeholders perspective—developed by the authors based on interview data, 2025.

Grand Theme	Sub-Theme	Codess
Ecosystem-Centric Advantage	Transformation with Collaboration	Complements Banking Solutions
		Collaborators
	Competitiveness and disruption in the Market	Push Traditional Service Providers to Perform Better + Disruptors
		Competitors
	Compatibility with Compliance	Compliance
		Balance the Legal Needs
Market-Centric Advantage	Speed and Innovation	Faster Innovation
		Faster Response + Adaptable to Market Needs
	Creation of Market Opportunities	More Opportunities in the Market
		Reduce Cost
		Customised Products/Flexible Offerings
Consumer-Centric Advantage	Access and Inclusion	Underserved/Financial Inclusion
		Easy/Convenient Solutions

References

1. Kálmán, J. The Role of Regulatory Sandboxes in FinTech Innovation: A Comparative Case Study of the UK, Singapore, and Hungary. *FinTech* **2025**, *4*, 26. [CrossRef]
2. Shaikh, I.M.; Amin, H. Influence of Innovation Diffusion Factors on Non-Users' Adoption of Digital Banking Services in the Banking 4.0 Era. *Inf. Discov. Deliv.* **2025**, *53*, 12–21. [CrossRef]

https://doi.org/10.3390/fintech5020032

3. Koranteng, B.; You, K. Fintech and Financial Stability: Evidence from Spatial Analysis for 25 Countries. *J. Int. Financ. Mark. Ins Money* **2024**, *93*, 102002. [CrossRef]
4. Yáñez-Valdés, C.; Guerrero, M. Assessing the Organizational and Ecosystem Factors Driving the Impact of Transformativ FinTech Platforms in Emerging Economies. *Int. J. Inf. Manag.* **2023**, *73*, 102689. [CrossRef]
5. Siddiqui, Z.; Rivera, C.A. Mapping Fintech landscape in Latvia: Taxonomy-based classification and economic impact analysi *Pol. J. Manag. Stud.* **2024**, *30*, 304–319. [CrossRef]
6. McKinsey & Company. *Europe's Fintech Opportunity (Full Report)*; McKinsey & Company: New York, NY, USA, 2022; p. 27.
7. Chen, S.; Guo, Q. Fintech and MSEs Innovation: An Empirical Analysis. *arXiv* **2024**, arXiv:2407.17293. [CrossRef]
8. Takahashi, C.K.; Figueiredo, J.C.B.D.; Scornavacca, E. Investigating the Diffusion of Innovation: A Comprehensive Study c Successive Diffusion Processes through Analysis of Search Trends, Patent Records, and Academic Publications. *Technol. Forecas Soc. Change* **2024**, *198*, 122991. [CrossRef]
9. Cornelli, G.; Frost, J.; Gambacorta, L.; Jagtiani, J. The Impact of Fintech Lending on Credit Access for U.S. Small Businesses. *Financ. Stab.* **2024**, *73*, 101290. [CrossRef]
10. Guan, Y.; Sun, N.; Wu, S.J.; Sun, Y. Supply Chain Finance, Fintech Development, and Financing Efficiency of SMEs in China. *Adn Sci.* **2025**, *15*, 86. [CrossRef]
11. Rupeika-Apoga, R.; Wendt, S. FinTech in Latvia: Status Quo, Current Developments, and Challenges Ahead. *Risks* **2021**, *9*, 18 [CrossRef]
12. Kapoor, K.K.; Dwivedi, Y.K.; Williams, M.D. Rogers' Innovation Adoption Attributes: A Systematic Review and Synthesis o Existing Research. *Inf. Syst. Manag.* **2014**, *31*, 74–91. [CrossRef]
13. Rogers, E.M. *Diffusion of Innovations*, 5th ed.; Free Press: London, UK, 2003.
14. Tarhini, A.; Arachchilage, N.A.G.; Masa'deh, R.; Abbasi, M.S. A Critical Review of Theories and Models of Technology Adoptio and Acceptance in Information System Research. *Int. J. Technol. Diffus.* **2015**, *6*, 58–77. [CrossRef]
15. Kaur, P.; Dhir, A.; Bodhi, R.; Singh, T.; Almotairi, M. Why Do People Use and Recommend M-Wallets? *J. Retail. Consum. Ser* **2020**, *56*, 102091. [CrossRef]
16. Kapoor, K.K.; Dwivedi, Y.K.; Williams, M.D. Examining the Role of Three Sets of Innovation Attributes for Determining Adoptio of the Interbank Mobile Payment Service. *Inf. Syst. Front.* **2015**, *17*, 1039–1056. [CrossRef]
17. Tsai, J.-P.; Ho, C.-F. Does Design Matter? Affordance Perspective on Smartphone Usage. *Ind. Manag. Data Syst.* **201** *113*, 1248–1269. [CrossRef]
18. Zhang, X. Frugal Innovation and the Digital Divide: Developing an Extended Model of the Diffusion of Innovations. *Int. J. Inno Stud.* **2018**, *2*, 53–64. [CrossRef]
19. Kapoor, K.K.; Dwivedi, Y.K.; Williams, M.D. Empirical Examination of the Role of Three Sets of Innovation Attributes fo Determining Adoption of IRCTC Mobile Ticketing Service. *Inf. Syst. Manag.* **2015**, *32*, 153–173. [CrossRef]
20. Weerakkody, V.; Irani, Z.; Kapoor, K.; Sivarajah, U.; Dwivedi, Y.K. Open Data and Its Usability: An Empirical View from th Citizen's Perspective. *Inf. Syst. Front.* **2017**, *19*, 285–300. [CrossRef]
21. Sikandar, H.; Vaicondam, Y.; Khan, N.; Qureshi, M.I.; Ullah, A. Scientific Mapping of Industry 4.0 Research: A Bibliometri Analysis. *Int. J. Interact. Mob. Technol.* **2021**, *15*, 129–147. [CrossRef]
22. MINÀ, A.; Dagnino, G.B. Competition and Cooperation in Entrepreneurial Ecosystems: A Lifecycle Analysis of a Canadian IC Ecosystem. In *Innovation, Alliances, and Networks in High-Tech Environments*; Routledge: London, UK, 2015; pp. 65–81
23. Audretsch, D.B.; Cunningham, J.A.; Kuratko, D.F.; Lehmann, E.E.; Menter, M. Entrepreneurial Ecosystems: Economic, Technolog ical, and Societal Impacts. *J. Technol. Transf.* **2019**, *44*, 313–325. [CrossRef] [PubMed]
24. Colombo, M.G.; Dagnino, G.B.; Lehmann, E.E.; Salmador, M. The Governance of Entrepreneurial Ecosystems. *Small Bus. Econ* **2019**, *52*, 419–428. [CrossRef]
25. Reynolds, E.B.; Uygun, Y. Strengthening Advanced Manufacturing Innovation Ecosystems: The Case of Massachusetts. *Technol Forecast. Soc. Change* **2018**, *136*, 178–191. [CrossRef]
26. Talmar, M.; Walrave, B.; Podoynitsyna, K.S.; Holmström, J.; Romme, A.G.L. Mapping, Analyzing and Designing Innovatio Ecosystems: The Ecosystem Pie Model. *Long Range Plan.* **2020**, *53*, 101850. [CrossRef]
27. Etzkowitz, H.; Leydesdorff, L. The Dynamics of Innovation: From National Systems and "Mode 2" to a Triple Helix of University Industry–Government Relations. *Res. Policy* **2000**, *29*, 109–123. [CrossRef]
28. Cunningham, J.A.; Menter, M.; O'Kane, C. Value Creation in the Quadruple Helix: A Micro Level Conceptual Model of Principa Investigators as Value Creators. *R D Manag.* **2018**, *48*, 136–147. [CrossRef]
29. Ritala, P.; Agouridas, V.; Assimakopoulos, D.; Gies, O. Value Creation and Capture Mechanisms in Innovation Ecosystems: A Comparative Case Study. *Int. J. Technol. Manag.* **2013**, *63*, 244–267. [CrossRef]
30. Tansley, A.G. The Use and Abuse of Vegetational Concepts and Terms. *Ecology* **1935**, *16*, 284–307. [CrossRef]
31. Moore, J. Predators and Prey: A New Ecology of Competition. *Harv. Bus. Rev.* **1999**, *71*, 75–86.

https://doi.org/10.3390/fintech5020032

32. Basole, R.C.; Karla, J. On the Evolution of Mobile Platform Ecosystem Structure and Strategy. *Bus. Inf. Syst. Eng.* **2011**, *3*, 313–322. [CrossRef]
33. Granstrand, O.; Holgersson, M. Innovation Ecosystems: A Conceptual Review and a New Definition. *Technovation* **2020**, *90–91*, 102098. [CrossRef]
34. Stefanelli, V.; Manta, F. Digital Financial Services and Open Banking Innovation: Are Banks Becoming 'Invisible'? *Glob. Bus. Rev.* **2023**, 09721509231151491. [CrossRef]
35. Teece, D.J. Business Models, Business Strategy and Innovation. *Long Range Plan.* **2010**, *43*, 172–194. [CrossRef]
36. Zott, C.; Amit, R. Business Model Design: An Activity System Perspective. *Long Range Plan.* **2010**, *43*, 216–226. [CrossRef]
37. Adner, R. Ecosystem as Structure: An Actionable Construct for Strategy. *J. Manag.* **2017**, *43*, 39–58. [CrossRef]
38. Gomber, P.; Kauffman, R.J.; Parker, C.; Weber, B.W. On the Fintech Revolution: Interpreting the Forces of Innovation, Disruption, and Transformation in Financial Services. *J. Manag. Inf. Syst.* **2018**, *35*, 220–265. [CrossRef]
39. Lee, I.; Shin, Y.J. Fintech: Ecosystem, Business Models, Investment Decisions, and Challenges. *Bus. Horiz.* **2018**, *61*, 35–46. [CrossRef]
40. Clauss, T. Measuring Business Model Innovation: Conceptualization, Scale Development, and Proof of Performance. *R D Manag.* **2017**, *47*, 385–403. [CrossRef]
41. Morris, M.; Schindehutte, M.; Allen, J. The Entrepreneur's Business Model: Toward a Unified Perspective. *J. Bus. Res.* **2005**, *58*, 726–735. [CrossRef]
42. Johnson, M.W.; Christensen, C.M.; Kagermann, H. Reinventing Your Business Model. *Harv. Bus. Rev.* **2008**, *87*, 52–60.
43. Osterwalder, A.; Pigneur, Y. *Business Model Generation: A Handbook for Visionaries, Game Changers, and Challengers*; Wiley & Sons: New York, NY, USA, 2013.
44. Yin, R.K. *Case Study Research and Applications: Design and Methods*, 6th ed.; Sage Publication: Thousand Oaks, CA, USA, 2018.
45. Williamson, P.J.; De Meyer, A. Ecosystem Advantage: How to Successfully Harness the Power of Partners. *Calif. Manag. Rev.* **2012**, *55*, 24–46. [CrossRef]
46. Mayring, P. Qualitative Content Analysis. In *The Routledge Handbook of Research Methods in Applied Linguistics*; Routledge: Oxfordshire, UK, 2000.
47. Schreier, M. *Qualitative Content Analysis in Practice*; SAGE Publications Ltd.: London, UK, 2012; Volume 1.
48. Sharma, V.; Rupeika-Apoga, R.; Singh, T.; Gupta, M. Sustainable Investments in the Blue Economy: Leveraging Fintech and Adoption Theories. *J. Risk Financ. Manag.* **2025**, *18*, 368. [CrossRef]
49. Sun, H.; Fang, Y.; Zou, H. Choosing a Fit Technology: Understanding Mindfulness in Technology Adoption and Continuance. *J. Assoc. Inf. Syst.* **2016**, *17*, 377–412. [CrossRef]
50. Zolkepli, I.A.; Kamarulzaman, Y. Social Media Adoption: The Role of Media Needs and Innovation Characteristics. *Comput. Hum. Behav.* **2015**, *43*, 189–209. [CrossRef]
51. Thakur, R.; Srivastava, M. Adoption Readiness, Personal Innovativeness, Perceived Risk and Usage Intention across Customer Groups for Mobile Payment Services in India. *Internet Res.* **2014**, *24*, 369–392. [CrossRef]
52. Fenwick, M.; Vermeulen, E.P.M.; Corrales, M. Business and Regulatory Responses to Artificial Intelligence: Dynamic Regulation, Innovation Ecosystems and the Strategic Management of Disruptive Technology. In *Robotics, AI and the Future of Law*; Corrales, M., Fenwick, M., Forgó, N., Eds.; Perspectives in Law, Business and Innovation; Springer: Singapore, 2018; pp. 81–103.
53. Adner, R. Match Your Innovation Strategy to Your Innovation Ecosystem. *HBR Spotlight* **2006**, *84*, 98–107.
54. Sangwa, S.; Ndahimana, S.; Dusengumuremyi, F. Diffusion of Innovation vs. Dependence Theory: FinTech Inclusion in the AfCFTA Era. *SSRN J.* **2025**, *1*, 45–107. [CrossRef]
55. Jangid, H.; Bal, D.P.; Rao, N.V.M. Role of FinTech and Technological Innovation towards Energy, Growth, and Environment Nexus in G20 Economies. *Sci. Rep.* **2025**, *15*, 20057. [CrossRef]
56. Yong, J.Y.; Yusliza, M.; Ramayah, T.; Chiappetta Jabbour, C.J.; Sehnem, S.; Mani, V. Pathways towards Sustainability in Manufacturing Organizations: Empirical Evidence on the Role of Green Human Resource Management. *Bus. Strategy Environ.* **2020**, *29*, 212–228. [CrossRef]
57. Kouam, A.W.F. The Impact of Artificial Intelligence on Fintech Innovation and Financial Inclusion: A Global Perspective. *Res. Sq.* **2024**, *preprint*. [CrossRef]

https://doi.org/10.3390/fintech5020032

FinTech

MDPI

Article

Mood in the Market: Forecasting IPO Activity with Music Sentiment and LSTM

Qinxu Ding [1,*], Chong Guan [2,*] and Yinghui Yu [1]

1 School of Business, Singapore University of Social Sciences, Singapore 599494, Singapore
2 SUSS Academy, Singapore University of Social Sciences, 11 Eunos Road 8, #07-03, Singapore 408601, Singapore
* Correspondence: qinxuding@suss.edu.sg (Q.D.); guanchong@suss.edu.sg (C.G.)

Abstract

We examine whether aggregate "music mood" derived from globally popular songs can help forecast primary equity issuance. We build a Friday-anchored weekly panel that merges SEC EDGAR counts of priced Initial Public Offerings (IPOs) with features from the Spotify Daily Top 200 (audio descriptors such as valence, energy, danceability, tempo, loudness, etc.) and Genius-scraped lyrics. We extract lyric sentiment by tokenizing Genius-scraped lyrics and aggregating lexicon-based affect scores (valence and arousal) into popularity-weighted weekly indices. To address sparsity and regime shifts in issuance, we train a leakage-safe Long Short-Term Memory (LSTM) network on a smoothed target—the forward 4-week sum of IPOs—and obtain next-week forecasts by dividing the predicted sum by 4. On a chronological holdout, a single LSTM with look-back $K = 8$ outperforms strong baselines—reducing MAE by 13.9%, RMSE by 15.9%, and mean Poisson deviance by 27.6% relative to the best baseline in each metric. Furthermore, we adopt SHapley Additive exPlanations (SHAP) to explain our LSTM model, showing that IPO persistence remains the dominant driver, but music and lyrics covariates contribute incremental and robust signal. These results suggest that aggregate music sentiment contains economically meaningful information about near-term IPO activity.

Keywords: time series forecasting; neural networks; fintech; IPO activity

JEL Classification: C45; G17; G24; G41

1. Introduction

The timing and intensity of initial public offerings (IPOs) are famously cyclical, clustering into "hot" and "cold" markets that are only partially explained by fundamentals [1–3]. For practitioners and regulators, anticipating near-term IPO activity is operationally important: underwriters and exchanges allocate resources, issuers plan deal timing, and policymakers monitor market functioning during hot and cold markets. Many studies link IPO waves to capital market conditions, investor sentiment, and information friction [4]. In parallel, advances in computational social science show that high-frequency, crowd-scale proxies of sentiment—ranging from textual news to search queries and social media—contain predictive information about financial activity [5,6]. A behavioral finance perspective suggests that financing activity may also respond to broad investor mood and sentiment, which can shift risk tolerance and demand for risky assets. Classic evidence shows that mood fluctuations, such as seasonal depression, are associated with predictable market patterns [7], while more recent work documents that emotionally salient, widely shared experiences (e.g., national pride) can influence stock market outcomes [8]. These findings complement sentiment–valuation evidence [9] and motivate investigating high-frequency, scalable mood indicators.

This paper asks a simple question: do aggregate mood signals derived from popular music help forecast near-term IPO activity? The intuition is that the music people stream each day reflects contemporaneous affect, attention, and energy at scale; such changes in mood may co-move with risk appetite and issuance windows, much like weather, sports, or social media shocks have been shown to correlate with market outcomes [10,11]. Unlike sporadic textual events, music consumption yields dense, globally consistent time series with rich acoustic (e.g., valence, energy) and lyrical content that can be aggregated into leak-free weekly indices.

In order to examine whether music signals, such as audio and lyrical sentiments, provide incremental information to predict weekly IPO counts. We construct weekly predictors from daily popularity and sentiment measures, align them with a leakage-safe forecasting design, and evaluate their usefulness alongside standard time-series baselines and statistical count models.

Our main contributions are as follows:

- A reproducible, Friday-anchored weekly panel merging EDGAR IPO count with popularity-weighted music mood indices from audio features and lyrics, with leak-free aggregation.
- Feature primitives tailored to issuance timing (within-week dispersion, end-of-week shocks, lyrics–audio dissonance) that complement standard persistence and seasonality.
- Evidence that a lightweight LSTM trained on a smoothed count target outperforms naïve, MA, and Poisson GLM baselines on a common evaluation window.
- SHAP analyses confirm that music/lyrics covariates provide incremental predictive content alongside IPO persistence and make our model transparent.

The structure of the paper is as follows: Section 2 provides a comprehensive overview of the literature related to our work; Section 3 describes the data collection and preprocessing; Section 4 presents the methodology; Section 5 reports the experimental results and SHAP-based explanations; Section 6 concludes and discusses the limitations and future work.

2. Related Literature

Our study connects five strands of research: (i) IPO waves and issuance timing [2–4]; (ii) sentiment and markets using textual and alternative data [5,6,11]; (iii) deep learning for financial time-series forecasting [12,13]; (iv) explainable AI for deep models and financial decision-making, where we employ SHAP to attribute predictions [14]; and (vi) affect modeling, where we build on lexicon-based approaches to valence/arousal estimation [15,16]. To our knowledge, this is among the first studies to combine large-scale music mood (audio and lyrics) with issuance forecasting and to provide model-consistent, SHAP-based evidence that these covariates add incremental predictive content beyond persistence and seasonality.

IPO timing and issuance cycles. IPO activity is well known to cluster into "hot" and "cold" markets that are only partially explained by fundamentals. Classic and modern accounts attribute waves to time–varying adverse selection, information frictions, and learning [2,3,17]. Surveys synthesize evidence on market conditions, risk appetite, and institutional frictions shaping issuance [4]. Microstructure and cross-sectional studies document that issuers time offerings to exploit windows of investor demand and valuation [1,18]. Our forecasting target—near-term IPO counts—directly connects to this literature by quantifying short-horizon variation in issuance intensity.

Investor sentiment and alternative data. A large body of work links sentiment to market outcomes. Media tone, dictionaries tailored to financial text, and search/attention proxies predict returns, flows, and corporate actions [5,6,19]. Crowd-scale social data also carry predictive content [20,21]. Beyond text, mood proxies such as weather and national sports outcomes affect risk-taking and prices [10,11]. Baker and Wurgler's sentiment index links broad risk appetite to issuance dynamics [22]. The vast behavioral literature argues that transient mood states can affect risk-taking and pricing, especially when they shift investors' willingness to hold risky assets. For example, Kamstra et al. [7] document a seasonal pattern consistent with seasonal affective disorder (SAD), suggesting that changes in mood and risk tolerance can translate into systematic market outcomes. Related evidence shows that emotionally positive collective experiences, such as national pride, can affect market behavior [8]. Using a different setting, ref. [23] exploit the Eurovision Song Contest as a sentiment shock, further illustrating how music-related cultural experiences can generate measurable investor sentiment effects. Importantly, these mood channels need not be driven by fundamentals; they operate through investor psychology and attention, consistent with broader links between sentiment and aggregate valuation [9]. We extend this strand by proposing aggregate music mood—constructed from globally popular tracks' audio and lyrics—as a dense, internationally consistent sentiment proxy that complements event-driven textual measures.

Deep learning for financial time series. Recurrent and attention-based architectures capture nonlinear dynamics, regime changes, and mixed short/long memory in financial series. LSTMs improve equity prediction relative to linear benchmarks and tree ensembles [12]; systematic reviews summarize deep architectures for financial forecasting [13]. Hybrid pipelines combining denoising and feature learning with recurrent models further stabilize training on noisy data [24]. Recent sequence models (e.g., Temporal Convolutional Networks and Transformers) offer competitive performance and built-in mechanisms for handling seasonality and covariates [25,26]. Additionally, generative AI methods, such as Large Language Models (LLMs), demonstrate the ability to answer questions about financial time series [27,28]. Our design adopts a leakage-safe LSTM trained on a smoothed count target tailored to sparse, bursty issuance.

Explainable AI (XAI) for deep models and financial decisions. The adoption of complex models in finance raises transparency and accountability concerns. Model-agnostic tools such as LIME and SHAP attribute predictions to features via local surrogates and game-theoretic values [14,29], while surveys and critical perspectives discuss their promise and limitations [30–32]. On the other hand, differential equations provide an explicit framework for modeling neural network dynamics, which can enhance explainability and improve resistance to adversarial attacks [33–35]. In financial contexts, XAI has been applied to credit risk, market risk, and asset allocation to support validation and governance [36–38]. We use SHAP to document where our LSTM's gains arise: global attributions show IPO persistence dominates, whereas contemporaneous music and lyrics covariates provide incremental signal concentrated in recent lags—evidence that music-based sentiment adds economically meaningful information beyond persistence and seasonality.

Affect modeling foundations. Our construction of mood indices builds on lexicon-based emotion resources (valence and arousal) that have been widely used for large-scale affect measurement [15,16], alongside domain-specific financial dictionaries [6]. The audio side connects to music-information-retrieval studies focusing on mood from acoustic features [39,40]. Relative to prior sentiment proxies, music consumption yields dense, globally consistent time series that can be aggregated into leak-free weekly indices for issuance forecasting.

Guided by the IPO-cycle literature, which models issuance as a count time series, the sentiment literature linking mood to financing outcomes, and evidence that music-based indicators provide real-time sentiment signals, we examine whether music listening and lyric-derived sentiment add incremental predictive value for weekly IPO counts. Compared with prior work, our study shifts the prediction target from returns/pricing to issuance volume, combines audio and lyrics signals, uses a leakage-safe weekly forecasting design, and benchmarks against established time-series baselines.

We fuse (i) priced IPO count from SEC EDGAR with robust index retrieval, and (ii) daily Top 200 Spotify features and Genius-derived lyrics, processed into popularity-weighted mood measures (e.g., means, dispersion, end-of-week shocks, and lyrics–audio dissonance). We then train a leakage-safe sequence model (LSTM) on a smoothed forward 4-week target to forecast next-week IPO counts, comparing against strong persistence and Poisson Generalized Linear Model (GLM) baselines. LSTMs and related recurrent architectures are a natural fit for nonlinear, regime-switching time series in finance [12,13], and our design emphasizes reproducibility and strict temporal alignment.

On a chronological holdout, we evaluate metrics on the common test weeks to ensure fair cross-model comparability. A single LSTM with look-back $K = 8$ delivers consistent gains over strong baselines (naïve persistence, MA(4), MA(13), Poisson GLM): relative to the best baseline in each metric, the $K = 8$ model reduces MAE by approximately 13.9%, RMSE by 15.9%, and mean Poisson deviance by 27.6%. These improvements indicate that a compact sequence model exploiting recent history plus music sentiment captures temporal structure beyond simple smoothing and parametric count processes.

Deep learning models like LSTMs are usually considered a black box and lack transparency. To interpret the model and understand the importance of the features, we use SHAP [14] analysis. Global attributions from SHAP show that IPO persistence features (recent lags and moving averages) dominate in terms of importance, while contemporaneous music and lyrics covariates contribute incremental signal that improves short-horizon calibration. The explainability results suggest that aggregate music sentiment carries economically meaningful information about near-term IPO windows, even after accounting for persistence and seasonality.

3. Data

3.1. U.S. IPO Activity from EDGAR (2017–2023)

We construct weekly counts of U.S. initial public offerings (IPOs) from the SEC EDGAR system for 2017–2023. Consistent with market practice, we identify priced IPOs via 424B4 (final prospectus), explicitly excluding 424B2 structured notes:

$$\mathcal{I} = \{(\text{CIK}, t) : \text{form\_type} = 424B4\}. \tag{1}$$

Events are timestamped by EDGAR date_filed. We aggregate to Friday-anchored weeks using a Saturday 00:00 boundary. Let week(t) map a calendar date to the corresponding week start point (Saturday). For issuer i (identified by CIK), define the IPO event sets in week w:

$$\mathcal{I}_w = \{i : \exists\, t \text{ with } (i,t) \in \mathcal{I} \wedge \text{week}(t) = w\}. \tag{2}$$

We then construct distinct-issuer counts per week

$$\text{IPOCount}_w = |\mathcal{I}_w|, \tag{3}$$

https://doi.org/10.3390/fintech5010012

which prevents multiple same-week filings by the same issuer from inflating the totals.

The time series in Figure 1 displays a pronounced clustering of issuance into windows separated by droughts. From 2017 through 2019, weekly IPO activity is relatively moderate. Activity accelerates through 2020 and peaks in 2021, with several exceptionally high weeks, indicating a pronounced "hot market" episode. Thereafter, counts contract sharply in 2022–2023, with lower average levels and reduced volatility, and occasional near-zero weeks. This figure motivates a forecasting model that handles zero inflation and strong serial dependence.

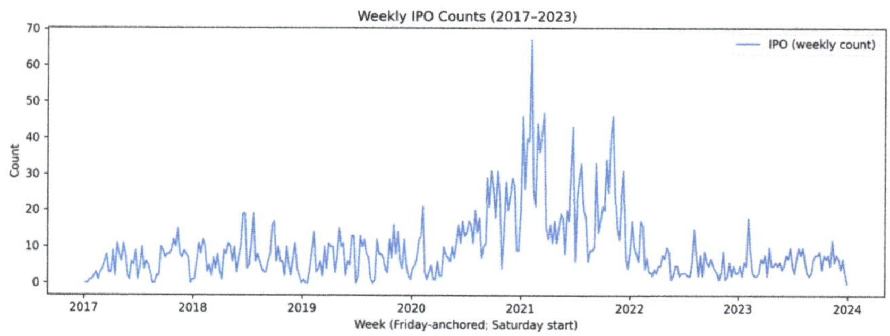

Figure 1. Weekly U.S. IPO counts, 2017–2023 (Friday-anchored weeks). The series exhibits zero inflation and clustered issuance windows.

Figure 2 reports the year-level average of weekly IPO counts from 2017–2023. Activity is relatively muted and stable in 2017–2019 (about 5.3, 7.3, and 6.8 IPOs per week, respectively), followed by a sharp boom in 2020 (13.1) that culminates in an exceptional peak in 2021 (23.8 average IPOs per week). Issuance then cools markedly in 2022 (5.6), with a modest rebound in 2023 (6.1). The pattern highlights a pronounced 2020–2021 IPO wave and a reversion toward pre-boom levels thereafter.

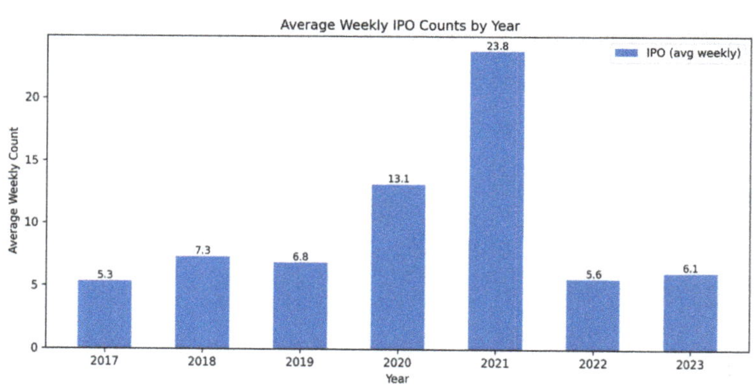

Figure 2. Average weekly U.S. IPO counts by year (2017–2023). Numbers above bars indicate the annual mean of weekly distinct-issuer IPO counts aggregated from EDGAR.

3.2. *Music Features (Spotify Top 200)*

We used the Spotify Daily Top 200 (Global) dataset as explanatory variables. Our sample spanned 25 January 2018 to 06 January 2022. The Top 200 data were obtained from a public, research-oriented distribution on Kaggle (https://www.kaggle.com/datasets/c0lydxmas/spotify-top-200-daily-global-2017-2021, accessed on 1 January 2025). and included track metadata (title, artist, rank, streams) and per-track audio descriptors.

https://doi.org/10.3390/fintech5010012

For each charted track, we collected the standard Spotify audio descriptors: danceability, energy, key, loudness, mode, speechiness, acousticness, instrumentalness, liveness, valence, and tempo. These features served as daily covariates summarizing the prevailing musical mood and acoustic profile of globally popular songs.

We fetched lyrics via the Genius API (https://docs.genius.com/, accessed on 1 January 2025) by querying with the song title and first listed artist. Extracted text was lightly normalized by removing prefaces (e.g., content before "Lyrics"), stripping bracketed section headers (e.g., [Chorus]), collapsing whitespace, and trimming ads/embeds, yielding a single cleaned lyric string per track aligned to the Spotify Top 200 entries. We computed continuous valence and arousal via a word-level lexicon with VAD scores [15].

3.3. Feature Engineering and Weekly Aggregation

Popularity weights. Let i index tracks and d index calendar days. When a popularity score $p_{i,d}$ is available, we map it to a bounded weight with a small floor to avoid zero–weight entries:

$$w_{i,d} = 0.1 + \frac{p_{i,d} - \underline{p}}{\overline{p} - \underline{p} + \varepsilon}, \qquad \varepsilon = 10^{-9}. \tag{4}$$

Here, $\underline{p} \equiv \min_{(i,d)\in\mathcal{I}} p_{i,d}$ and $\overline{p} \equiv \max_{(i,d)\in\mathcal{I}} p_{i,d}$ are the global minimum and maximum popularity values, computed over the entire sample index $\mathcal{I}$ (all observed track–day pairs). If popularity is unavailable, we set $w_{i,d} = 1$. All subsequent aggregates use $w_{i,d}$ as weights.

Daily standardization and dissonance. To place lyric and audio measures on a comparable within-day scale, we compute day-wise z-scores for each feature $x_{i,d}$ (e.g., lyric valence $v^L_{i,d}$, lyric arousal $a^L_{i,d}$, audio valence $v^A_{i,d}$):

$$\tilde{x}_{i,d} = \frac{x_{i,d} - \mu_d(x)}{\sigma_d(x) + \varepsilon}, \qquad x \in \{v^L, a^L, v^A\}. \tag{5}$$

Here, $\mu_d(x) \equiv \frac{1}{N_d}\sum_i x_{i,d}$ and $\sigma_d(x) \equiv \left(\frac{1}{N_d}\sum_i (x_{i,d} - \mu_d(x))^2\right)^{1/2}$ are, respectively, the cross-sectional mean and standard deviation across the N_d Top 200 tracks present on day d; $\varepsilon = 10^{-9}$ prevents division by zero on degenerate days. We define valence dissonance at the track–day level as

$$\delta_{i,d} = |\tilde{v}^L_{i,d} - \tilde{v}^A_{i,d}|, \tag{6}$$

which measures the absolute discrepancy between lyric- and audio-implied valence in standardized units.

Endweek of shocks. Let $\overline{\tilde{v}^L}_w$ and $\overline{\tilde{v}^A}_w$ be the (popularity-weighted) weekly means, and let $\tilde{v}^L_{\text{last},w}$ and $\tilde{v}^A_{\text{last},w}$ denote the last day's (Friday) standardized values. We define Friday shocks as

$$\text{shock}_w(\tilde{v}^L) = \tilde{v}^L_{\text{last},w} - \overline{\tilde{v}^L}_w, \qquad \text{shock}_w(\tilde{v}^A) = \tilde{v}^A_{\text{last},w} - \overline{\tilde{v}^A}_w. \tag{7}$$

Novelty of the chart. Let $\mathcal{S}_w$ be the set of unique track identifiers appearing in week w. The new-entry share is

$$\text{novelty}_w = \frac{|\mathcal{S}_w \setminus \mathcal{S}_{w-1}|}{\max\{1, |\mathcal{S}_w|\}}, \tag{8}$$

i.e., the fraction of titles in week w that did not appear in week $w-1$, which captures turnover and the influx of fresh content.

https://doi.org/10.3390/fintech5010012

Persistence (lags and moving averages). We include autoregressive signals of IPO activity:

$$\underbrace{y_{t-k}}_{\text{lags } k\in\{1,2,4,8,12\}}, \qquad \underbrace{\frac{1}{w}\sum_{j=0}^{w-1} y_{t-j}}_{\text{moving averages } w\in\{4,8,12\}}. \tag{9}$$

Seasonality. Let $w(t) \in \{1,\ldots,52\}$ denote the ISO week index of t. We encode annual seasonality with

$$week\_sin_t = \sin\left(\frac{2\pi\, w(t)}{52}\right), \qquad week\_cos_t = \cos\left(\frac{2\pi\, w(t)}{52}\right). \tag{10}$$

Weekly Aggregation and Leakage-Safe Alignment

Friday-Anchored Weeks: We map each calendar date d to a week key $w = \text{week}(d)$ using a Saturday 00:00 boundary, so each week spans Saturday–Friday and is anchored on the Friday date.

Daily Inputs: For each day d, we observe the Top 200 set of tracks $\mathcal{I}_d$. Each track $i \in \mathcal{I}_d$ has Spotify audio features (e.g., valence, energy, danceability, tempo) and lyric-based affect scores (valence/arousal) computed from the cleaned lyric text. We attach a nonnegative popularity weight $w_{i,d}$ as in Equation (4) and, for selected affect variables, compute within-day standardized values (day-wise z-scores) to make lyric- and audio-derived measures comparable.

Weekly (Popularity-Weighted) Means: For any track-day feature $x_{i,d}$ (audio or lyric), we define the weekly aggregate as a weighted mean over all track-day observations within week w:

$$\bar{x}_w = \frac{\sum_{d\in w}\sum_{i\in\mathcal{I}_d} w_{i,d}\, x_{i,d}}{\sum_{d\in w}\sum_{i\in\mathcal{I}_d} w_{i,d}}. \tag{11}$$

We use this operator to construct weekly audio averages (e.g., tempo_mean, energy_mean) and weekly lyric averages (e.g., lyrics_valence_mean, lyrics_arousal_mean).

Friday (Last-Day) Values and Shocks: Let $d = \text{Fri}(w)$ denote the Friday of week w. The Friday value is as follows:

$$\bar{x}_{\text{last},w} = \frac{\sum_{i\in\mathcal{I}_{\text{Fri}(w)}} w_{i,\text{Fri}(w)}\, x_{i,\text{Fri}(w)}}{\sum_{i\in\mathcal{I}_{\text{Fri}(w)}} w_{i,\text{Fri}(w)}}. \tag{12}$$

We define the Friday-anchored shock as $\text{shock}_w(x) = \bar{x}_{\text{last},w} - \bar{x}_w$.

Weekly Dispersion (e.g., Audio Valence): To capture heterogeneity in mood, we compute a weighted dispersion within week w, e.g., for standardized audio valence $\tilde{v}^A_{i,d}$:

$$valence\_audio\_z\_vol_w = \sqrt{\frac{\sum_{d\in w}\sum_{i\in\mathcal{I}_d} w_{i,d}\,(\tilde{v}^A_{i,d} - \bar{\tilde{v}}^A_w)^2}{\sum_{d\in w}\sum_{i\in\mathcal{I}_d} w_{i,d}}}. \tag{13}$$

Leakage Safety: All predictors for week w are computed using only information available up to (and including) the Friday of week w. The forecasting target is shifted one step ahead: we use week-w features to predict IPOCount_{w+1}, ensuring no future information enters the predictors by construction.

https://doi.org/10.3390/fintech501001[illegible]

4. Methodology

4.1. Problem Setup and Notation

Let $t \in \{1, \ldots, T\}$ index weeks (Friday–anchored). Let $y_t \in \mathbb{N}_0$ denote the number of IPOs observed in week t. Our one-step-ahead target is y_{t+1} ("IPO_next"). We collect a weekly feature vector $\mathbf{x}_t \in \mathbb{R}^F$ comprising music-derived indices, issuance persistence terms, and seasonal controls. To stabilize learning on sparse counts, we train on a smoothed target:

$$s_{t+1} = \sum_{j=1}^{4} y_{t+j}, \tag{14}$$

i.e., the 4-week moving sum that is forward-looking from $t+1$ to $t+4$. The model predicts $\log(1+s_{t+1})$; at inference, we invert the transform and divide by 4 to obtain a weekly prediction $\widehat{y}_{t+1} = \frac{\exp(\widehat{\log(1+s_{t+1})})-1}{4}$, then clip to $\widehat{y}_{t+1} \geq 0$. This preserves leakage safety because s_{t+1} is constructed by first shifting y_t to y_{t+1} and then applying a forward rolling sum; the last week (with unknown future) is dropped.

4.2. Sequence Construction and Train/Test Split

We adopt a chronological split: the last 20% of weeks form the test set, and the remainder form the training set. Given a sequence length K, we build overlapping windows

$$\begin{gathered}\mathbf{X}_t^{(K)} = \left[\mathbf{x}_{t-K+1}, \mathbf{x}_{t-K+2}, \ldots, \mathbf{x}_t\right] \in \mathbb{R}^{K \times F}, \\ \text{paired with label } z_t \equiv \log(1+s_t).\end{gathered} \tag{15}$$

On the train (test) set, windows start at the first index where K prior observations exist in the respective split.

4.3. LSTM Architecture and Optimization

We use a plain LSTM with a single recurrent layer and a linear head:

$$\mathbf{h}_t = \mathrm{LSTM}(\mathbf{X}_t^{(K)}; \text{units} = 16, \text{dropout} = 0.3), \qquad \widehat{z}_t = \mathbf{w}^\top \mathbf{h}_t + b, \tag{16}$$

trained with mean squared error on the smoothed log target:

$$\mathcal{L} = \frac{1}{N} \sum_{t \in \mathcal{T}_{\text{train}}} \left(\widehat{z}_t - \log(1+s_t)\right)^2. \tag{17}$$

We optimize with Adam (learning rate 10^{-3}), early stopping on training loss (patience = 25, best weights restored), and learning rate reduction on plateau (factor 0.5, patience = 10, floor 5×10^{-5}). Batch size is set adaptively (up to 32, roughly half the number of training sequences).

For reproducibility, Table 1 provides a compact specification of the LSTM model and training protocol. The table documents the input representation (a K-week feature sequence), the network architecture (LSTM layer and output head), optimization settings (loss, optimizer, learning rate), and regularization choices (dropout, early stopping, learning-rate scheduling). Together with the strictly chronological split and one-step-ahead target alignment, these details ensure the learning procedure is fully transparent and free of look-ahead leakage.

https://doi.org/10.3390/fintech5010012

Table 1. LSTM architecture and training protocol.

Component	Setting
Input	Sequence $X_t^{(K)} \in \mathbb{R}^{K \times F}$ (weekly features)
Recurrent layer	1-layer LSTM, units = 16, dropout = 0.3
Head	Linear Dense(1)
Training target	$\log(1+s_{t+1})$ where $s_{t+1} = \sum_{j=1}^{4} y_{t+j}$
Loss	Mean Squared Error (MSE)
Optimizer	Adam, learning rate 10^{-3}
Early stopping	Patience = 25, restore best weights
LR schedule	ReduceLROnPlateau, factor 0.5, patience 10, min lr 5×10^{-5}
Batch size	Up to 32 (approximately half the number of training sequences)
Split	Chronological; last 20% weeks as test

5. Experimental Results

5.1. Evaluation Metrics

Primary evaluation is on the weekly scale using the one–step–ahead target y_{t+1}:

$$\text{MAE} = \frac{1}{N_{\text{test}}} \sum_{t \in \mathcal{T}_{\text{test}}} \left| y_{t+1} - \widehat{y}_{t+1} \right|, \qquad \text{RMSE} = \left(\frac{1}{N_{\text{test}}} \sum_{t \in \mathcal{T}_{\text{test}}} (y_{t+1} - \widehat{y}_{t+1})^2 \right)^{\frac{1}{2}}. \tag{18}$$

We also report Poisson deviance on weekly predictions,

$$\text{Dev} = \frac{1}{N_{\text{test}}} \sum_{t \in \mathcal{T}_{\text{test}}} \left(\widehat{y}_{t+1} - y_{t+1} \log\left(\widehat{y}_{t+1} + \epsilon\right) \right), \quad \epsilon = 10^{-9}, \tag{19}$$

with $\widehat{y}_{t+1}$ clipped to be nonnegative.

5.2. Ablation on Sequence Length K

We vary the LSTM look-back window $K \in \{2, 4, 6, 8, 10\}$ (weeks of history) while keeping the architecture (1-layer LSTM, 16 units, dropout 0.3) and training setup fixed. The model is trained to predict $\log(1 + \sum_{j=1}^{4} \text{IPO}_{t+j})$ and mapped back to a weekly forecast by dividing the predicted 4-week sum by 4 (clipped at 0). For a fair comparison across K, all metrics (MAE, RMSE, mean Poisson deviance) are computed on the same 43-week test window. The results in Table 2 show that $K = 8$ achieves the lowest MAE, while $K = 6$ attains nearly identical RMSE and Dev, so we adopt $K = 8$ for the main LSTM results.

Table 2. Ablation over sequence length K for next-week IPO prediction. Metrics are computed on the common 43 test weeks (lower is better).

K	n	MAE	RMSE	Poisson Dev.
2	43	9.456	11.295	6.130
4	43	8.106	10.488	5.255
6	43	8.208	10.380	5.148
8	43	8.091	10.393	5.154
10	43	8.115	10.409	5.212

5.3. Baselines

Let t index Friday-anchored weeks and $y_t \in \mathbb{N}_0$ denote the IPO count in week t. The one-step-ahead prediction target is y_{t+1} ("IPO_next"). We evaluate all baselines on the same chronological split as the LSTM: the last 20% of weeks form the test set; earlier weeks form the train set. Seasonality controls use the ISO week number $w(t)$ encoded via $\sin(2\pi w(t)/52)$ and $\cos(2\pi w(t)/52)$.

https://doi.org/10.3390/fintech5010012

Naïve Last-Value: A persistence benchmark that predicts the next week by the current week's count:

$$\widehat{y}_{t+1}^{\text{naive}} = y_t. \tag{20}$$

This captures the short-run clustering of issuance and is leakage-safe.

Moving-Average (MA) Baselines: We include two smoothers that average recent weeks to reduce noise:

$$\widehat{y}_{t+1}^{\text{MA}(h)} = \frac{1}{h}\sum_{j=0}^{h-1} y_{t-j}, \qquad h \in \{4, 13\}. \tag{21}$$

MA(4) targets monthly seasonality; MA(13) approximates a quarter. Both are computed recursively on the full timeline so that the test segment can use trailing train observations without look-ahead.

Poisson GLM: To provide a strong classical count model, we fit a generalized linear model with Poisson mean and log link using only lagged IPO dynamics and seasonal terms:

$$\mathbb{E}[y_{t+1} \mid \mathbf{z}_t] = \mu_{t+1}, \tag{22}$$

$$\begin{aligned}\log \mu_{t+1} = \beta_0 + \beta_1 y_t + \beta_2 y_{t-1} + \beta_3 y_{t-3} + \beta_4 \text{MA}_t^{(4)} \\ + \beta_5 \sin(2\pi w(t)/52) + \beta_6 \cos(2\pi w(t)/52).\end{aligned} \tag{23}$$

Here, $\mathbf{z}_t$ collects $\{y_t, y_{t-1}, y_{t-3}, \text{MA(4)}, \text{seasonality}\}$; parameters β are estimated on the training window by maximum likelihood. Predictions $\widehat{\mu}_{t+1}$ are nonnegative by construction.

For each baseline, we report mean absolute error (MAE), root mean squared error (RMSE), and Poisson deviance on y_{t+1} over the test weeks in Table 3. All models are evaluated on the same set of $N = 43$ common prediction weeks. MAE is mean absolute error; RMSE is root mean squared error; Poisson Dev. is mean Poisson deviance, computed on nonnegative predictions. The LSTM trained on the smoothed 4-week sum achieves the best scores across all metrics: (i) MAE improves by ≈13.9% over the best baseline (Naive) (ii) RMSE improves by ≈15.9% over the best baseline (MA(4)), and (iii) Poisson deviance improves by ≈27.6% over the best baseline (MA(4)). These gains indicate that the sequence model captures temporal struc, ture beyond simple persistence/smoothing and a parametric Poisson GLM with seasonal controls.

Table 3. Performance on the common test weeks (intersection across all models; N = 43). Lower is better.

Model	N	MAE	RMSE	Poisson Dev.
LSTM (K = 8)	43	8.091	10.393	5.154
Naive (last value)	43	9.395	12.497	7.167
MA(4)	43	9.634	12.361	7.116
MA(13)	43	11.549	13.690	8.520
Poisson GLM	43	12.277	18.638	10.421

The realized series in Figure 3 is shown against Naive, MA(4), MA(13), Poisson GLM, and the LSTM (K = 8). The LSTM captures level shifts with less delay and avoids the GLM's extreme spikes during volatile periods; MA(13) is overly smoothed and lags peaks/troughs, while Naive and MA(4) respond faster but fail to anticipate reversals.

https://doi.org/10.3390/fintech5010012

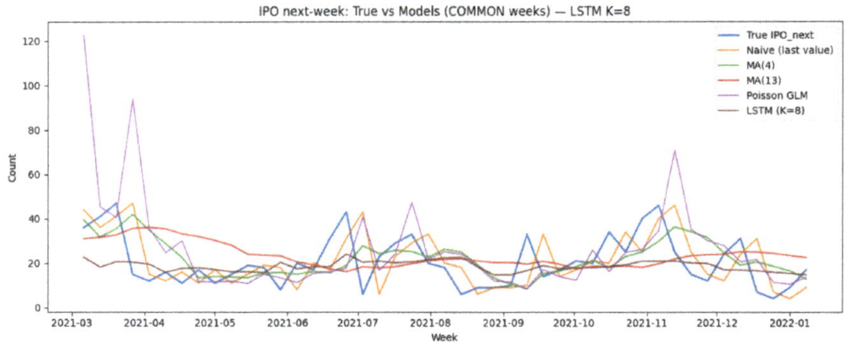

Figure 3. Next-week IPO forecasts on the common test weeks.

5.4. Sensitivity Test: Direct Next-Week Target vs. 4-Week Forward-Sum Target

The baseline LSTM is trained to predict the log-transformed 4-week forward sum $s_{t+1} = \sum_{j=1}^{4} y_{t+j}$ and is mapped back to the weekly scale by dividing the implied level prediction by 4, which can be interpreted as the average weekly issuance intensity over the next month. To test whether this target-smoothing choice is essential, we rerun an otherwise identical LSTM that is trained directly on the one-step-ahead target $\log(1 + y_{t+1})$ ("direct").

Following the evaluation protocol used for comparing models across different look-back lengths, we report results on the common 43-week test window induced by the largest look-back length (K = 10). The resulting common evaluation period spans 20 March 2021 to 08 January 2022 (43 weeks). Table 4 reports out-of-sample performance for both specifications (lower is better).

Overall, training on the 4-week forward-sum target yields equal or improved accuracy relative to direct training for most look-back lengths, particularly in MAE. For example, at K = 4 the MAE decreases from 9.096 (direct) to 8.106 (sum4), while Poisson deviance decreases from 5.742 to 5.255. At K = 6 and K = 8, the sum4 specification also attains lower MAE and lower Poisson deviance than the direct specification. At K = 2, the two approaches perform very similarly in MAE, while the direct specification yields a slightly lower Poisson deviance. These results support the motivation that target smoothing can improve learning stability under sparse and volatile weekly counts, while preserving the weekly one-step-ahead evaluation objective.

Table 4. Sensitivity to target definition on the common 43-week test window (20 March 2021 to 08 January 2022): direct next-week LSTM vs. 4-week forward-sum training (lower is better).

	Direct Next-Week Target			4-Week Sum Target		
K	MAE	RMSE	Dev.	MAE	RMSE	Dev.
2	9.465	11.048	5.918	9.456	11.295	6.130
4	9.096	10.922	5.742	8.106	10.488	5.255
6	8.639	10.557	5.357	8.208	10.380	5.148
8	8.759	10.773	5.599	8.091	10.393	5.154
10	8.718	10.432	5.250	8.115	10.409	5.212

A potential drawback of the 4-week target is that adjacent sums overlap, increasing serial dependence in training labels. However, this does not introduce look-ahead leakage because all predictors are computed using only week-t information and evaluation is conducted strictly out-of-sample under a chronological split.

Some notes on generalization of the smoothed-target advantage are as follows: the performance gains from forecasting the four-week forward sum (and scaling back to a

https://doi.org/10.3390/fintech501001

weekly rate) are consistent with the idea that IPO counts are noisy and often zero-inflated at weekly frequency, while issuance decisions reflect multi-week planning and execution. Therefore, smoothing the target can improve the signal-to-noise ratio and reduce sensitivity to week-to-week fluctuations. Although our empirical comparison is based on the available sample window, the underlying rationale is not specific to a particular sub-period and could plausibly extend to other time frames in which IPO activity remains lumpy and clustered.

5.5. Benchmark with Conventional Market Controls: Direct LSTM with vs. Without Market Variables

A potential concern is that the predictive content of music-based variables may proxy for broader market conditions that are known to shape IPO issuance windows (e.g., equity returns, volatility, and interest rates). To examine this issue in a minimal and leakage-safe manner, we augment the direct next-week LSTM with three standard market-condition controls observed up to week t (Friday-anchored): the S&P 500 weekly return, the log VIX, and the 10-year Treasury yield. We keep the LSTM architecture, training protocol, feature engineering for IPO persistence (lags and moving averages), seasonality, and the chronological split unchanged. We report performance on the common 43-week test window.

Table 5 compares the direct LSTM without market controls (direct_no_mkt) against the direct LSTM including market controls (direct_with_mkt). Overall, adding market controls does not uniformly improve out-of-sample performance in this setting. For $K = 6$, the market-augmented specification attains a slightly lower Poisson deviance (5.392 vs. 5.457), while MAE and RMSE remain comparable. For other look-back lengths (e.g., $K = 4$ and $K = 8$), the market-augmented specification yields higher MAE and Poisson deviance. These results suggest that, conditional on the model already incorporating strong issuance persistence and seasonal components, the incremental benefit of adding a small set of conventional market controls is limited in our weekly forecasting design. We interpret this benchmark cautiously: the goal is not to claim that market conditions are unimportant for IPO activity, but rather to show that the forecasting gains observed in our main specification are not trivially driven by the omission of a few standard market variables.

Table 5. Direct next-week LSTM with vs. without market controls on the common 43-week test window (lower is better).

	Direct LSTM (no Market Controls)			Direct LSTM (with Market Controls)		
K	MAE	RMSE	Dev.	MAE	RMSE	Dev.
2	9.579	11.176	6.008	9.695	11.455	6.272
4	8.966	10.749	5.567	9.500	11.613	6.338
6	8.587	10.643	5.457	8.681	10.563	5.392
8	8.428	10.574	5.395	8.580	10.683	5.512
10	8.769	10.644	5.473	8.808	10.474	5.296

5.6. Statistical Significance of Forecast-Accuracy Gains: Diebold–Mariano Test

To assess whether the LSTM's out-of-sample improvements over our baseline are statistically distinguishable from sampling variation, we apply the Diebold–Mariano (DM) test of equal predictive accuracy [41]. We compare the LSTM (sum/4 ensemble) against the Poisson GLM baseline on the set of common evaluation weeks, where both models produce non-missing forecasts. Let y_t denote the realized next-week IPO count, and $\hat{y}_t^{(A)}$ and $\hat{y}_t^{(B)}$ denote forecasts from the Poisson GLM (baseline) and the LSTM, respectively. Define forecast errors $e_t^{(A)} = y_t - \hat{y}_t^{(A)}$ and $e_t^{(B)} = y_t - \hat{y}_t^{(B)}$, and let the loss differential be as follows:

$$d_t = \left|e_t^{(A)}\right| - \left|e_t^{(B)}\right|, \tag{24}$$

so that $d_t > 0$ indicates lower absolute error for the LSTM. The DM test evaluates the null hypothesis $\mathbb{E}[d_t] = 0$. Because loss differentials in weekly time series can exhibit a short-horizon serial correlation, we report both the standard DM inference and a heteroskedasticity-and-autocorrelation-consistent (HAC) variant using Newey–West standard errors [42]. Given the finite evaluation sample, we interpret the results with standard small-sample caution [43].

Table 6 summarizes the absolute-error DM results. Without HAC adjustment (NW lag 0), the evidence is marginal (DM = 1.962, p = 0.056). Allowing for short-horizon serial correlation, the HAC-adjusted DM test becomes statistically significant at the 5% level (NW lag 4: DM = 2.205, p = 0.033; NW lag 8: DM = 2.151, p = 0.037). Overall, these results provide supportive evidence that the LSTM achieves lower out-of-sample absolute forecast error than the Poisson GLM on the common evaluation sample.

Table 6. Diebold–Mariano tests of equal predictive accuracy under absolute-error loss: Poisson GLM (baseline) vs. LSTM (sum/4 ensemble) on common evaluation weeks. Positive DM statistics indicate lower absolute error for the LSTM.

Newey–West Lag	DM Statistic	p-Value
0	1.962	0.056
4	2.205	0.033
8	2.151	0.037

5.7. SHAP Explanation Experiment (LSTM, K = 8)

Our objective in this subsection is to explain the next-week IPO forecaster (LSTM with look-back $K = 8$) that is trained on the target $y_t = \log\left(1 + \sum_{j=1}^{4} \mathrm{IPO}_{t+j}\right)$. At inference, we map back via $\widehat{S}_t = \exp(\hat{y}_t) - 1$ and report weekly $\widehat{\mathrm{IPO}}_{t+1} = \max(0, \widehat{S}_t/4)$. We use the same chronological split as the modeling. Features comprise IPO count, IPO persistence (lags $1, 2, 4, 8, 12$, moving averages $4, 8, 12$), seasonality (week_sin, week_cos), and music sentiment features (audio and lyric sentiment). Our LSTM to explain is a single-layer LSTM (16 units, dropout 0.3) $\rightarrow$ Dense(1), Adam (lr $= 10^{-3}$), MSE loss on y_t. We adopt KernelExplainer to obtain model-agnostic SHAP values and aggregate them over time by reporting mean |SHAP| per feature.

Figure 4 shows that IPO persistence dominates the explanation: ipo_count_ma4, ipo_count_ma12, ipo_count, ipo_count_lag1, and ipo_count_lag2 have the largest contributions. Music/lyrics covariates (e.g., valence_audio_z_vol, lyrics_valence_shock) provide secondary signal, while seasonality is modest.

The dispersion of audio valence (valence_audio_z_vol) summarizes the cross-track spread of perceived positivity in the globally popular songs during week t. Higher dispersion (i.e., a wider distribution of audio valence) indicates a less concentrated mood state in the listening population—consistent with elevated uncertainty, polarization, or mixed risk appetite. The LSTM assigns sizable importance to this dispersion measure, suggesting that how variable collective mood is can be as informative as where the mean mood sits when anticipating near-term issuance intensity.

End-of-week shocks in lyric-based valence (lyrics_valence_shock) captures within-week changes in the semantic polarity of lyrics (popularity-weighted), with an end-of-week focus designed to align with our Friday anchor. Large positive (negative) shocks reflect sudden improvements (deteriorations) in the textual affect of widely streamed songs, plausibly tracking rapid shifts in attention and sentiment. The model's high SHAP attributions on this shock variable indicate that recent, abrupt changes in crowd-level mood contain incremental information about next-week IPO timing beyond smoother persistence and seasonality patterns.

https://doi.org/10.3390/fintech5010012

Together, dispersion in audio valence and shocks in lyrical valence map onto two distinct behavioral channels: (i) uncertainty/heterogeneity in prevailing affect (captured by dispersion), and (ii) salient short-run updates in perceived mood (captured by shocks). These signals complement the persistence features: while lags/MAs encode slowly evolving issuance regimes, the music-derived measures provide high-frequency cues about shifts in risk appetite and attention that are not fully captured by historical IPO dynamics.

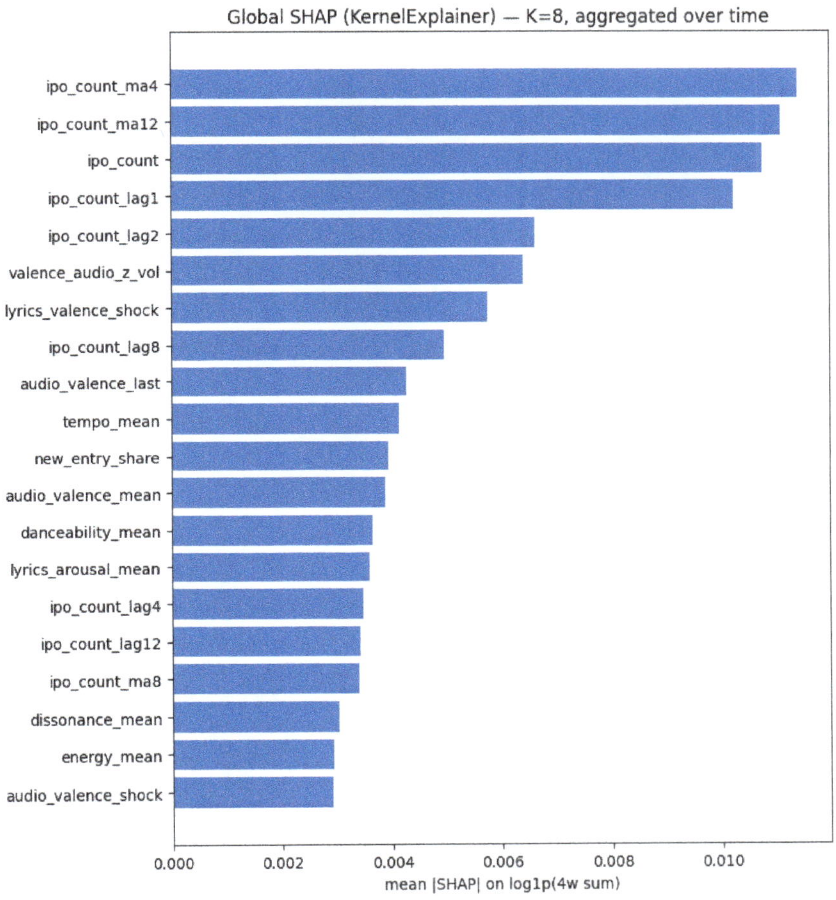

Figure 4. Global SHAP (KernelExplainer) for the LSTM with $K = 8$, aggregated over time.

The heatmap in Figure 5 visualizes time-by-feature attributions for the most recent explained case (columns $t-7$ to $t-0$; rows are features). Three patterns emerge:

(i) Short-Memory Concentration: Most attribution mass occurs at $t-1$ and $t-0$, consistent with short-horizon issuance dynamics. Specifically, ipo_count_lag2 and ipo_count_lag8 receive large positive contributions near $t-0$, while a smaller seasonal component appears far back, at $t-6$, for ipo_count. Older timesteps ($t-7$ to $t-3$) contribute little, indicating that the LSTM emphasizes very recent history.

(ii) Incremental Music/Lyrics Signal: Two non-persistence covariates stand out at the end of the window. lyrics_valence_shock loads heavily at $t-1$, implying that a sharp within-week change in lyrical polarity immediately precedes higher (or lower) predicted issuance. valence_audio_z_vol contributes moderately at $t-1$, consistent with contemporaneous affect in listening behavior complementing persistence cues.

https://doi.org/10.3390/fintech5010012

(iii) Transient Composition Effects: We observe a localized spike at $t-4$ in new_entry_share (share of tracks newly entering the Top 200). These mid-window attributions suggest occasional composition shocks in the popular-music basket—e.g., a burst of new releases or faster songs—that the model treats as informative but transient signals relative to last-week dynamics.

The heatmap supports the global-bar findings: persistence features dominate, but recent music/lyrics variables provide incremental information right before the forecasted week. The temporal localization of attributions to $t-1$ and $t-0$ aligns with a short effective memory for IPO intensity, while sparse mid-lag spikes reflect episodic, high-salience updates in the music-based covariates.

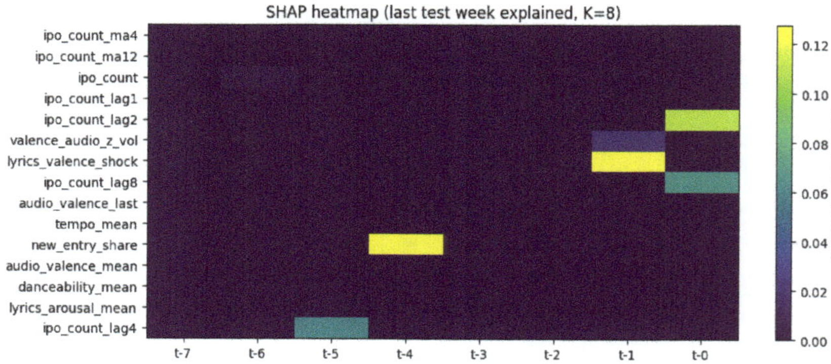

Figure 5. Per-example SHAP heatmap (last test week explained) for $K = 8$.

As expected, lagged issuance variables receive the largest global SHAP attributions, consistent with persistence in IPO cycles. More interestingly, several music-related variables exhibit non-trivial contributions. Among the music covariates, valence_audio_z_vol and lyrics_valence_shock consistently rank as the most influential, while new_entry_share appears as an episodic but meaningful signal (see Figures 4 and 5). Economically, these patterns support a mood–risk appetite channel: when broad sentiment and attention shift quickly, market receptiveness to risky equity issuance can change even after controlling for the slow-moving issuance regime captured by lagged IPO counts.

Dispersion of audio valence (valence_audio_z_vol) summarizes cross-track dispersion in perceived positivity within the popular music basket. Higher dispersion can indicate a less concentrated collective mood (mixed affect, polarization, or uncertainty), which may coincide with more fragile risk appetite. Its SHAP importance suggests that not only the level of mood, but also its heterogeneity, contains information relevant for near-term issuance intensity.

End-of-week lyric valence shock (lyrics_valence_shock) captures within-week changes in the semantic polarity of lyrics, measured as a Friday "shock" relative to the weekly average. A positive shock (lyrics becoming more positive late in the week) aligns with an improvement in sentiment close to the forecast origin and is consistent with higher subsequent IPO activity. This supports the interpretation that rapid mood updates can affect short-horizon issuance windows by shifting perceived market receptiveness.

Chart composition novelty (new_entry_share) measures turnover in the Top 200 basket. Spikes may reflect bursts of new releases or attention shifts that the model treats as transient signals. Its time-localized SHAP contributions are consistent with episodic attention or novelty shocks that complement persistence cues rather than replacing them.

Caution on interpretation: We emphasize that SHAP explains how the model uses features for prediction; it does not establish causality. A positive association between

https://doi.org/10.3390/fintech5010012

music mood and IPO activity may reflect underlying macroeconomic optimism, news, or broader demand conditions that jointly affect both cultural consumption patterns and capital-market activity. Accordingly, we interpret the music variables as predictive proxies for latent sentiment and attention rather than causal drivers of IPO waves.

Beyond the level of music mood (e.g., average valence or lyric sentiment), our feature set also captures dispersion—the cross-sectional variability of mood among popular songs within a week. A higher dispersion in valence indicates that listeners are consuming a more mixed or polarized set of songs (e.g., a combination of very upbeat and very downbeat tracks), rather than a uniformly positive or uniformly negative mood environment. From a behavioral finance perspective, such heterogeneity may reflect greater disagreement or uncertainty in underlying sentiment, which can be relevant for primary-market activity: IPO issuance tends to cluster when market conditions are more favorable and investor demand is easier to gauge, whereas more fragmented sentiment can coincide with cautious risk-taking and a weaker issuance window.

We also include a novelty proxy, measured as the share of new entries among popular songs (i.e., the new-entry share). A higher novelty value implies more frequent turnover in the set of trending songs, which can be interpreted as faster-moving attention and changing preferences in the broader market environment. Conceptually, novelty may track shifts in public attention and risk appetite: when novelty is elevated, the market may be in a more dynamic "search" state, potentially aligning with fluctuations in issuance timing. We emphasize that these interpretations provide economic intuition for the model explanations, while the empirical patterns remain predictive associations rather than causal claims.

5.8. Implications for Practitioners

Our findings show that cultural-mood indicators can enhance algorithmic issuance calendars, syndicate-desk dashboards, investor-sentiment monitors, and real-time risk assessments. By integrating music-derived sentiment signals, our study offers several operational pathways. Issuance desks and underwriters can utilize music-based mood indicators as early-warning signals for favorable or unfavorable issuance windows. In favorable windows, underwriters may accelerate feasible deals in the pipeline and plan less conservative execution assumptions; in unfavorable windows, they may increase marketing effort, widen pricing buffers, reduce deal size, strengthen the syndicate, or advise postponement. Positive mood shocks—such as sudden increases in lyrical valence—may signal elevated investor risk appetite and optimal timing for new filings [1,22]. This capability enables syndicate desks to refine their go-to-market timing strategies based on real-time cultural sentiment. FinTech market-intelligence providers can incorporate mood indices into analytics dashboards as complementary sentiment measures alongside traditional indicators such as news tone, search volume, and social-media sentiment [5,21]. The distinctive information content of music-based signals offers a unique value proposition within sentiment-monitoring markets.

While IPO underwriters and issuers are direct stakeholders, the ability to anticipate near-term IPO activity can also be useful for other financial institutions. For asset managers and wealth managers, expected issuance intensity can inform liquidity planning and tactical allocation decisions around primary-market supply. For broker-dealers and market makers, forecasts of IPO volume can support operational staffing, inventory/risk limits, and market-quality planning during anticipated "hot" weeks. For banks' treasury and risk functions, higher issuance periods may coincide with shifts in equity-market sentiment and financing conditions, so a high-frequency sentiment proxy can complement internal dashboards that monitor market risk. For exchanges, custodians, and post-trade service providers, expected IPO waves can help capacity planning and client onboarding preparation. Finally, for

https://doi.org/10.3390/fintech5010012

regulators and policy institutions, such indicators may serve as an additional, timely input for monitoring issuance conditions and potential overheating. We emphasize that these applications interpret the music-based indicators as predictive monitoring tools rather than causal drivers of issuance.

Our empirical and interpretability results suggest three recurring patterns linking music-based signals to short-horizon variation in IPO activity:

Pattern 1: Broad mood and risk appetite. Weeks characterized by a more positive and higher-energy "music mood" (as reflected in our listening- and lyrics-based indicators) are followed by higher IPO activity. This pattern is consistent with a behavioral channel in which improved mood increases risk tolerance and demand for risky assets, thereby strengthening market conditions for equity issuance and making IPO timing more favorable.

Pattern 2: Attention and hot-market amplification. The predictive content of music mood appears most informative around elevated issuance periods. This suggests that sentiment signals may matter more when market attention and coordination among issuers and intermediaries are higher. In such "hot" markets, shifts in mood and attention can translate more quickly into book-building conditions, investor demand, and issuance decisions.

Pattern 3: Complementarity with standard predictors. Music mood features do not merely replicate lagged IPO counts or seasonal effects. Instead, they provide incremental predictive information relative to standard time-series and count-model baselines. This complementarity supports the interpretation that music-based indicators capture a latent sentiment component that is not fully reflected in conventional financial predictors at a weekly frequency.

6. Conclusions

This paper introduces a reproducible pipeline that (i) builds issuance targets from SEC EDGAR with priced-offering screens and robust index fallbacks, (ii) derives daily, popularity-weighted music features from the Spotify Daily Top 200 and cleaned Genius lyrics, and (iii) aggregates them into leakage-safe, Friday-anchored weekly predictors (means, end-of-week shocks, dispersion, lyrics–audio dissonance, and related covariates). We train a leakage–safe LSTM on a smoothed forward 4-week target and obtain next-week forecasts by dividing the predicted sum by four.

On a chronological holdout, evaluating models on the common test window ($n = 43$ weeks), a single LSTM with look-back $K = 8$ outperforms strong baselines—naïve persistence, MA(4), MA(13), and a Poisson GLM with seasonality—reducing error by 13.9% in MAE, 15.9% in RMSE, and 27.6% in mean Poisson deviance relative to the best baseline for each metric. These gains indicate that a lightweight sequence model, trained on a stabilized count target, captures temporal structure beyond simple smoothing and parametric count processes.

To interpret the model, we apply SHAP to the $K = 8$ LSTM. Global attributions show that IPO persistence features (recent lags and moving averages) dominate importance, while contemporaneous music/lyrics covariates contribute incremental and robust signal; per-example heatmaps reveal that contributions concentrate on recent timesteps, consistent with short-horizon issuance dynamics. Taken together, these findings suggest that aggregate music sentiment carries economically meaningful information for near-term IPO activity, complementing persistence and calendar seasonality.

Our results motivate incorporating high-frequency cultural signals into issuance forecasting and monitoring (e.g., window-timing dashboards). Future work could (i) extend this work to SEOs and cross-market issuance, (ii) test alternative architectures (temporal CNNs/Transformers) and multitask targets (e.g., intensity and zero-inflation), (iii) refine

https://doi.org/10.3390/fintech5010012

affect modeling beyond lexicons (contextual embeddings for lyrics; non-linear audio sentiment), and (iv) study causality and stability under regime shifts via rolling/bootstrapped evaluations and policy-relevant stress tests.

6.1. Theoretical Contribution

We introduce a novel channel for market prediction by constructing large-scale music-based mood indices from audio features and lyrics. This extends the expanding literature on alternative sentiment sources—including news tone [5], financial text dictionaries [6], search-based attention [19,44], social-media mood [20,45] and lyrics-only metrics [46]—by demonstrating that cultural-mood signals from both sonic and lyrical features contain predictive information relevant for capital markets.

Our study contributes to the literature on IPO timing by providing new evidence on the role of investor sentiment. First, we construct a novel music-based sentiment index that captures broad investor mood while remaining plausibly orthogonal to IPO-specific institutional features, such as regulatory calendars, reporting cycles, and underwriting capacity. Second, exploiting within-wave variation in IPO issuance, we show robust evidence that sentiment helps explain fluctuations in IPO volume beyond fundamentals [3] and mechanical seasonality. Using explainable-AI methods, we further decompose predictive contributions and demonstrate that music-based sentiment provides economically meaningful incremental information relative to persistence and calendar-based predictors traditionally used to model IPO activity.

Our findings are consistent with a behavioral channel in which broad mood and sentiment shape risk-taking and demand for equity issuance, complementing prior evidence that mood proxies can influence market outcomes [7,8,23]. The music-based indicator contributes to this literature by offering a scalable, high-frequency sentiment proxy that is not restricted to a specific country-level holiday or discrete event. While we do not claim music causes IPO waves, the predictive content of music mood suggests that cultural-consumption signals can help track latent sentiment relevant for issuance timing and market participation.

6.2. Methodological Contribution

First, we develop a reproducible, leakage-safe forecasting pipeline anchored on a Friday-based weekly dataset with forward-looking smoothing targets, chronological splits, and temporal alignment. These design principles address the field's emphasis on rigorous, time-ordered AI modeling, where data leakage represents a challenge to the validity of sequential prediction systems [13]. Second, we demonstrate that a compact LSTM model [12,47] significantly outperforms naïve persistence, moving-average baselines, and Poisson-generalized linear models with seasonality in forecasting next-week IPO counts. This finding contributes to the growing evidence that deep architectures effectively capture the nonlinear, regime-switching dynamics characteristic of financial time series [13,26]. Third, we employ SHAP [14] to interpret our LSTM model, addressing the critical need for transparency in financial AI systems. This approach aligns with increasing regulatory and practitioner emphasis on explainability and auditability in financial machine learning [30,32,36].

Author Contributions: The conceptualization, methodology, validation, formal analysis, investigation, and writing of the paper were completed by Q.D., C.G. and Y.Y. equally. All authors have read and agreed to the published version of the manuscript.

Funding: This research received no external funding

Institutional Review Board Statement: Not applicable.

https://doi.org/10.3390/fintech5010012

Informed Consent Statement: Not applicable.

Data Availability Statement: The data presented in this study are available on request from the corresponding author due to their ongoing use in further analyses related to future research.

Conflicts of Interest: The authors declare no conflicts of interest.

References

1. Lowry, M. Why does IPO volume fluctuate so much? *J. Financ. Econ.* **2003**, *67*, 3–40. [CrossRef]
2. Lowry, M.; Schwert, G.W. IPO market cycles: Bubbles or sequential learning? *J. Financ.* **2002**, *57*, 1171–1200. [CrossRef]
3. Pástor, L.; Veronesi, P. Rational IPO waves. *J. Financ.* **2005**, *60*, 1713–1757.
4. Ritter, J.R.; Welch, I. A review of IPO activity, pricing, and allocations. *J. Financ.* **2002**, *57*, 1795–1828.
5. Tetlock, P.C. Giving content to investor sentiment: The role of media in the stock market. *J. Financ.* **2007**, *62*, 1139–1168.
6. Loughran, T.; McDonald, B. When is a liability not a liability? Textual analysis, dictionaries, and 10-Ks. *J. Financ.* **2011**, *66*, 35–6
7. Kamstra, M.J.; Kramer, L.A.; Levi, M.D. Winter blues: A SAD stock market cycle. *Am. Econ. Rev.* **2003**, *93*, 324–343. [CrossRef]
8. Abudy, M.M.; Mugerman, Y.; Shust, E. National pride, investor sentiment, and stock markets. *J. Int. Financ. Mark. Inst. Mone* **2023**, *89*, 101879.
9. Brown, G.W.; Cliff, M.T. Investor sentiment and asset valuation. *J. Bus.* **2005**, *78*, 405–440. [CrossRef]
10. Hirshleifer, D.; Shumway, T. Good day sunshine: Stock returns and the weather. *J. Financ.* **2003**, *58*, 1009–1032.
11. Edmans, A.; Garcia, D.; Norli, Ø. Sports sentiment and stock returns. *J. Financ.* **2007**, *62*, 1967–1998.
12. Fischer, T.; Krauss, C. Deep learning with long short-term memory networks for financial market predictions. *Eur. J. Oper. Re* **2018**, *270*, 654–669. [CrossRef]
13. Sezer, O.B.; Gudelek, M.U.; Ozbayoglu, A.M. Financial time series forecasting with deep learning: A systematic literature review 2005–2019. *Appl. Soft Comput.* **2020**, *90*, 106181. [CrossRef]
14. Lundberg, S.M.; Lee, S.I. A unified approach to interpreting model predictions. In Proceedings of the 31st Internationa Conference on Neural Information Processing Systems, Long Beach, CA, USA, 4–9 December 2017; pp. 4766–4777.
15. Mohammad, S. Obtaining reliable human ratings of valence, arousal, and dominance for 20,000 English words. In Proceedings o the 56th annual meeting of the association for computational linguistics (Volume 1: Long Papers), Melbourne, Australia, 15–2 July 2018; pp. 174–184.
16. Demszky, D.; Movshovitz-Attias, D.; Ko, J.; Cowen, A.; Nemade, G.; Ravi, S. GoEmotions: A dataset of fine-grained emotion *arXiv* **2020**, arXiv:2005.00547.
17. Ibbotson, R.G.; Jaffe, J.F. Hot Issue Markets. *J. Financ.* **1975**, *30*, 1027–1042.
18. Helwege, J.; Liang, N. Initial Public Offerings in Hot and Cold Markets. *J. Financ. Quant. Anal.* **2004**, *39*, 541–569. [CrossRef]
19. Da, Z.; Engelberg, J.; Gao, P. In Search of Attention. *J. Financ.* **2011**, *66*, 1461–1499. [CrossRef]
20. Bollen, J.; Mao, H.; Zeng, X. Twitter Mood Predicts the Stock Market. *J. Comput. Sci.* **2011**, *2*, 1–8. [CrossRef]
21. García, D. Sentiment During Recessions. *J. Financ.* **2013**, *68*, 1267–1300.
22. Baker, M.; Wurgler, J. Investor Sentiment and the Cross-Section of Stock Returns. *J. Financ.* **2006**, *61*, 1645–1680.
23. Abudy, M.M.; Mugerman, Y.; Shust, E. The winner Takes it all: Investor sentiment and the Eurovision Song Contest. *J. Bank Financ.* **2022**, *137*, 106432.
24. Bao, W.; Yue, J.; Rao, Y. A Deep Learning Framework for Financial Time Series Using Stacked Autoencoders and Long-Shor Term Memory. *PLoS ONE* **2017**, *12*, e0180944. [CrossRef]
25. Borovykh, A.; Bohte, S.; Oosterlee, C.W. Conditional Time Series Forecasting with Convolutional Neural Networks. *arXiv* **2017** arXiv:1703.04691.
26. Lim, B.; Arık, S.Ö.; Loeff, N.; Pfister, T. Temporal Fusion Transformers for Interpretable Multi-Horizon Time Series Forecasting *Int. J. Forecast.* **2021**, *37*, 1748–1764. [CrossRef]
27. Ding, Q.; Ding, D.; Wang, Y.; Guan, C.; Ding, B. Unraveling the landscape of large language models: A systematic review an future perspectives. *J. Electron. Bus. Digit. Econ.* **2023**, *3*, 3–19. [CrossRef]
28. Lee, D.K.C.; Guan, C.; Yu, Y.; Ding, Q. A comprehensive review of generative AI in finance. *FinTech* **2024**, *3*, 460–478. [CrossRef
29. Ribeiro, M.T.; Singh, S.; Guestrin, C. "Why Should I Trust You?": Explaining the Predictions of Any Classifier. In Proceedings o the 22nd ACM SIGKDD International Conference on Knowledge Discovery and Data Mining (KDD), San Francisco, CA, USA 13–17 August 2016; pp. 1135–1144.
30. Arrieta, A.B.; Díaz-Rodríguez, N.; Del Ser, J.; Bennetot, A.; Tabik, S.; Barbado, A.; García, S.; Gil-López, S.; Molina, D.; Benjamins R.; et al. Explainable Artificial Intelligence (XAI): Concepts, taxonomies, opportunities and challenges toward responsible AI. *Inf Fusion* **2020**, *58*, 82–115. [CrossRef]
31. Molnar, C. *Interpretable Machine Learning*; Lulu.com: Durham, NC, USA, 2020.

https://doi.org/10.3390/fintech5010012

32. Rudin, C. Stop Explaining Black Box Machine Learning Models for High Stakes Decisions and Use Interpretable Models Instead. *Nat. Mach. Intell.* **2019**, *1*, 206–215. [CrossRef]
33. Kang, Q.; Song, Y.; Ding, Q.; Tay, W.P. Stable neural ode with lyapunov-stable equilibrium points for defending against adversarial attacks. *Adv. Neural Inf. Process. Syst.* **2021**, *34*, 14925–14937.
34. Kang, Q.; Zhao, K.; Ding, Q.; Ji, F.; Li, X.; Liang, W.; Song, Y.; Tay, W.P. Unleashing the potential of fractional calculus in graph neural networks with FROND. *arXiv* **2024**, arXiv:2404.17099. [CrossRef]
35. Zhao, K.; Li, X.; Kang, Q.; Ji, F.; Ding, Q.; Zhao, Y.; Liang, W.; Tay, W.P. Distributed-order fractional graph operating network. *Adv. Neural Inf. Process. Syst.* **2024**, *37*, 103442–103475.
36. Bussmann, N.; Giudici, P.; Marinelli, D.; Papenbrock, J. Explainable Machine Learning in Credit Risk Management. *Comput. Econ.* **2021**, *57*, 203–216. [CrossRef]
37. Wang, Y.; Ding, Q.; Wang, K.; Liu, Y.; Wu, X.; Wang, J.; Liu, Y.; Miao, C. The skyline of counterfactual explanations for machine learning decision models. In *Proceedings of the 30th ACM International Conference on Information & Knowledge Management*; ACM Digital Library: New York, NY, USA, 2021; pp. 2030–2039.
38. Beckmann, L.; Broszeit, S.; Stieber, S. Understanding the Determinants of Bond Excess Returns Using Explainable Artificial Intelligence. *J. Bus. Econ.* **2023**, *93*, 1817–1849. [CrossRef]
39. Hu, X.; Downie, J.S. When Lyrics Outperform Audio for Music Mood Classification: A Feature Analysis. In Proceedings of the 11th International Society for Music Information Retrieval Conference (ISMIR), Utrecht, The Netherlands, 9–13 August 2010; pp. 619–624.
40. Laurier, C. Automatic Classification of Musical Mood by Content-Based Analysis. Ph.D Thesis, Universitat Pompeu Fabra, Barcelona, Spain, 2009.
41. Diebold, F.X.; Mariano, R.S. Comparing predictive accuracy. *J. Bus. Econ. Stat.* **2002**, *20*, 134–144. [CrossRef]
42. Newey, W.K.; West, K.D. A simple, positive semi-definite, heteroskedasticity and autocorrelationconsistent covariance matrix. *Econometrica* **1986**, *55*, 703–708. [CrossRef]
43. Harvey, D.; Leybourne, S.; Newbold, P. Testing the equality of prediction mean squared errors. *Int. J. Forecast.* **1997**, *13*, 281–291. [CrossRef]
44. Mou, J.; Liu, W.; Guan, C.; Westland, J.C.; Kim, J. Predicting the cryptocurrency market using social media metrics and search trends during COVID-19. *Electron. Commer. Res.* **2024**, *24*, 1307–1333. [CrossRef]
45. Guan, C.; Liu, W.; Cheng, J.Y.C. Using social media to predict the stock market crash and rebound amid the pandemic: The digital 'haves' and 'have-mores'. *Ann. Data Sci.* **2022**, *9*, 5–31. [CrossRef]
46. Guan, C.; Yu, Y.; Ren, J.; Ding, D. From Chart to Chart: Analyzing Lyric Content in Music Streaming Charts for Predicting Stock Prices Using LSTM. In *Machine Learning and Modeling Techniques in Financial Data Science*; IGI Global Scientific Publishing: Hershey, PA, USA, 2025; pp. 295–320.
47. Hochreiter, S.; Schmidhuber, J. Long short-term memory. *Neural Comput.* **1997**, *9*, 1735–1780. [CrossRef]

https://doi.org/10.3390/fintech5010012

FinTech

MDPI

Article

Adaptive Credit Card Fraud Detection: Reinforcement Learning Agents vs. Anomaly Detection Techniques

Houda Ben Mekhlouf [1], Abdellatif Moussaid [2,*] and Fadoua Ghanimi [1]

1 Laboratory of Electronic Systems, Information Processing, Mechanics and Energetics, Faculty of Sciences, University Ibn Tofail, Kenitra 14000, Morocco; houda.benmekhlouf@uit.ac.ma (H.B.M.); fadoua.ghanimi@uit.ac.ma (F.G.)
2 College of Agriculture and Environmental Sciences, Mohammed VI Polytechnic University (UM6P), Benguerir 43150, Morocco
* Correspondence: abdelatif.moussaid@gmail.com

Abstract

Credit card fraud detection remains a critical challenge for financial institutions, particularly due to extreme class imbalance and the continuously evolving nature of fraudulent behavior. This study investigates two complementary approaches: anomaly detection based on multivariate normal distribution and deep reinforcement learning using a Deep Q-Network. While anomaly detection effectively identifies deviations from normal transaction patterns, its static nature limits adaptability in real-time systems. In contrast, the DQN reinforcement learning model continuously learns from every transaction, autonomously adapting to emerging fraud strategies. Experimental results demonstrate that, although initial performance metrics of the DQN are modest compared to anomaly detection, its capacity for online learning and policy refinement enables long-term improvement and operational scalability. This work highlights reinforcement learning as a highly promising paradigm for dynamic, high-volume fraud detection, capable of evolving with the environment and achieving near-optimal detection rates over time.

Keywords: credit card fraud detection; reinforcement learning; Deep Q-Network; anomaly detection; imbalanced data; online learning; adaptive systems; transaction security

JEL Classification: G21; G28; C45; C38

1. Introduction

Financial fraud detection represents one of the most pressing challenges in the modern digital economy, with serious consequences for financial institutions, businesses, and consumers worldwide. Moreover, the rapid digitization of financial services has created new opportunities for fraud, making it essential to develop advanced detection systems capable of identifying malicious transactions in real time.

Financial fraud can manifest itself in various forms, including credit card fraud, identity theft, money laundering, insurance fraud, and payment system exploitation. Among these, credit card fraud has emerged as one of the most common and financially damaging types, with global losses projected to reach $49.32 billion by 2030 [1,2].

In addition, the field of credit card fraud detection has evolved considerably from traditional rule-based systems to sophisticated artificial intelligence (AI) techniques. Early detection methods relied on static rules and threshold-based alerts, which often proved insufficient against adaptive fraudsters constantly developing new evasion strategies [3].

 https://doi.org/10.3390/fintech5010009

In this way, the adoption of machine learning (ML) and deep learning (DL) methods has revolutionized fraud detection, allowing systems to learn complex patterns from historical transaction data and identify subtle anomalies indicative of fraudulent activity [4,5].

Furthermore, Hafez et al. [6] conducted a systematic review of AI-based techniques for credit card fraud detection, highlighting the effectiveness of ML, DL, and meta-heuristic optimization algorithms. Their analysis showed that integrated AI approaches substantially improve the detection of different types of fraud. However, limitations persist in the ML and DL models, necessitating continuous development to keep pace with evolving fraudulent behaviors.

Ensemble methods have also shown significant promise. Alkhozae et al. [7] proposed an explainable credit card fraud detection model that combines multiple classifiers, including XGBoost, LightGBM, Random Forest, and MLP. This framework achieved remarkable performance with 99.86% precision, 96.36% precision, and 80.59% recall, while incorporating SHAP-based explainability and reinforcement learning for dynamic threshold tuning. As a result, the system successfully blocked 91% of fraudulent transactions while maintaining a 7.8% false-positive rate.

Moreover, the issue of class imbalance has been extensively addressed through sampling techniques. Gutiérrez-Gallego et al. [8] introduced a Balanced Underbagging Ensemble approach for highly imbalanced datasets common in financial applications. Their method outperformed 100 combinations of oversampling and undersampling techniques, demonstrating superior recall for both majority and minority classes across different ML algorithms.

In addition, evolutionary algorithms have been applied to optimize imbalanced learning. Safder et al. [9] utilized Genetic Algorithms (GA) for synthetic data generation, surpassing methods such as SMOTE, ADASYN, GAN and VAE in multiple metrics, including accuracy, precision, recall, F1-score, ROC-AUC and AP curve.

Deep learning architectures have further advanced fraud detection capabilities. Salem et al. [10] proposed the local search-based binary Griffon vulture optimization algorithm (BGVOA-LS), integrating optimized feature selection with ML to improve accuracy. Their approach reduced the feature count by 67% while achieving up to 99.8% accuracy. Similarly, generative models have been applied to address data imbalance. Pavan et al. [11] employed adversarial ML based on chaotic variational autoencoders, while Ab Yajid et al. [12] developed a hybrid Big Bang-Big Crunch with cuckoo search (HB3C2S) for feature selection combined with DCNN, achieving accuracy up to 95.61%.

Unsupervised learning approaches are increasingly important for detecting new fraud patterns. Kennedy et al. [13] combined SHAP-based feature selection with autoencoder-generated labels, significantly improving label quality and model performance. Walauskis et al. [14] extended this work using ensemble unsupervised methods with percentile thresholding, effectively overcoming the challenge of severely unbalanced data labeling. Moreover, Darwish et al. [15] utilized Artificial Bee Colony (ABC)-based sampling to generate realistic synthetic fraud samples, improving model learning without biasing towards non-fraudulent transactions. Their method improved detection accuracy while reducing false alarms, improving the reliability of the system.

Explainable AI (XAI) has also gained attention due to the black-box nature of complex models. Vadlamudi et al. [16] explored the explanations of LIME and SHAP along with transformer-based models such as BERT, XLNet, and RoBERTa. Their CheMO multi-algorithm optimization approach achieved 97–98% accuracy while providing interpretable decisions. Similarly, Hirnschall [1] proposed semi-supervised Bayesian GANs with logarithmic signs, improving uncertainty-aware fraud detection and improving trustworthiness. In addition, Sundaravadivel et al. [17] demonstrated that the Adaboost and Decision Tree

https://doi.org/10.3390/fintech5010009

models outperformed ANN in predicting credit card defaults, achieving 82% accuracy versus 78%.

Hybrid and metaheuristic methods have further strengthened detection capabilities. Alsowail [18] combined the random light Gradient-based CatBoost Ensemble with the Enhanced Gold Rush Algorithm, attaining 99.1% accuracy. Priatna et al. [19] proposed a hybrid Autoencoder-Transformer framework for fraud in e-commerce, surpassing conventional DNN, LSTM, and RNN models in precision, precision, recall, F1-score, and AUC. Moreover, metaheuristic optimization has been applied for feature selection and hyperparameter tuning. Atban et al. [20] demonstrated that the PSO + VQC combinations achieved 94.54% precision, while Abadlia et al. [21] and Chakraborty [22] showed the effectiveness of particle swarm and sand cat swarm optimization techniques for stacked autoencoders and CNN-based detection, respectively.

Real-time and scalable architectures have also been explored. Madhavappa et al. [23] employed an optimized CNN-RNN framework for the detection of online transactions. Federated learning approaches have addressed privacy concerns while maintaining high accuracy. For example, Damanik et al. [24] proposed explainable and balanced federated learning with neural networks, while Xia et al. [25] introduced FinGraphFL, which combines graph-based learning and federated principles. In addition, El Hlouli et al. [26] proposed a fully connected deep network that combines Autoencoder and MLP architectures, achieving superior evaluation metrics in multiple unbalanced credit datasets.

Recent advances in advanced neural architectures have also improved detection performance. Shabiya et al. [27] proposed LSO-RVAE, achieving 99.80% accuracy, 100% recall, and an AUC of 0.998. Chugh et al. [28] integrated Firefly Optimization with logistic regression, improving MCC by 34.94%. Furthermore, Adejoh et al. [29] combined autoencoders, self-organizing maps, and RBMs with adaptive reconstruction thresholds, achieving high accuracy and F1-scores. In addition, Ahmad et al. [30] utilized Tomek Links undersampling to enhance the balance of the data set and improve ANN performance.

Comparative analyzes provide valuable information on algorithmic performance. Tayebi et al. [31] demonstrated that XGBoost with Bayesian optimization outperformed other ML models with high detection rates accuracy and high AUC. Similarly, Andrade-Arenas et al. [32] showed that Random Forest and XGBoost consistently outperformed alternatives using SMOTE to minimize imbalance. In addition, Theodorakopoulos et al. [33] implemented distributed big data-driven ML using PySpark, XGBoost, and CatBoost, achieving scalable real-time detection, while Akouhar et al. [34] proposed Kolmogorov-Arnold networks driven by dynamic sampling to improve adaptability across benchmark datasets.

Unsupervised and anomaly detection techniques are increasingly relevant. Karnavou et al. [35] employed Isolation Forest, one-class SVM, and deep autoencoders for unsupervised detection, while John Berkmans et al. [36] used heterogeneous multi-view graph neural networks, demonstrating substantial gains in accuracy. Additionally, Hancock et al. [37] combined SHAP with one-class classifiers for efficient feature selection in highly imbalanced data.

Despite these advances, significant limitations remain. Models often struggle with extreme class imbalance, the continuous evolution of fraud patterns, privacy restrictions, and limited interpretability. Hayat et al. [38] highlighted that evaluation flaws can exaggerate model performance, while Feng et al. [39] addressed imbalance and missing values with Gradient Boosted Decision Trees. Similarly, Chen et al. [40] integrated LSTM with logistic regression to capture spatiotemporal correlations, improving predictive performance.

This study addresses three key research questions: Can Deep Q-Networks effectively learn fraud detection policies from extremely imbalanced transaction data? How does the adaptive, sequential learning of DQN compare to static anomaly detection in fraud

https://doi.org/10.3390/fintech501000

detection performance? And is reinforcement learning a viable paradigm for real-time, adaptive fraud detection in dynamic financial environments?

To answer these, we propose a reinforcement learning agent-based framework for credit card fraud detection, which builds a predictive model, primarily using Deep Reinforcement Learning, to classify transactions as either fraudulent or non-fraudulent. The model relies on a small set of easily available transactional features, including the transaction ID, date and time, customer ID, terminal ID, transaction amount, and the fraud label indicating legitimate or fraudulent transactions. In this way, the RL agent can continuously learn from transaction streams, adapt to emerging fraud patterns, and optimize long-term detection strategies. Moreover, because it only requires basic transactional data that are automatically generated during normal operations, the framework is practical, scalable, and privacy-preserving, enabling financial institutions to deploy adaptive fraud detection without extensive data collection or additional infrastructure.

In summary, the main contributions of this paper are threefold: (1) We propose a reinforcement learning-based framework using Deep Q-Networks for adaptive fraud detection in highly imbalanced transaction data. (2) We provide a comparative analysis between anomaly detection and reinforcement learning, highlighting the long-term learning advantages of DQN in dynamic environments. (3) We demonstrate through structured experiments that DQN can achieve sustained performance improvement over time, making it suitable for real-time deployment in systems such as ATM networks.

2. Materials and Methods

2.1. Problem Statement

The main task of this study is to perform a binary classification to identify whether each transaction is legitimate (0) or fraudulent (1). The primary difficulty lies in the strong imbalance between the two classes, which tends to bias models toward predicting the majority class. As a result, the model may not detect rare fraudulent cases. In addition, fraud patterns can evolve, requiring models that are capable of continuous learning and adaptation.

To address these challenges, two modeling strategies are proposed. These approaches were selected based on their demonstrated effectiveness in the literature: anomaly detection for handling extreme class imbalance [8,13], and reinforcement learning for adapting to evolving fraud patterns [6,25].

The first strategy is anomaly detection, also known as outlier detection. This approach is particularly effective for unbalanced data. Instead of directly distinguishing between legitimate and fraudulent transactions, the model learns the pattern of normal transactions. Any transaction that deviates significantly from this learned behavior is flagged as a potential fraud. This makes the method suitable when fraudulent examples are rare and diverse.

The second strategy is reinforcement learning (RL). In this framework, fraud detection is treated as an interactive process between an agent (the detection model) and an environment (the stream of transactions). The agent makes decisions such as approving or flagging transactions, and receives rewards for correct decisions and penalties for incorrect ones. Over time, the agent learns an optimal decision policy that adapts to changing and new fraud behaviors. This continuous learning capability makes RL promising for dynamic financial systems.

https://doi.org/10.3390/fintech5010009

2.2. Data

2.2.1. Data Description

The data used in this study is the Kaggle "Credit Card Fraud Detection" data set, which includes transactions made by European cardholders [41]. This dataset has been extensively studied in the fraud detection literature, with numerous works documenting its characteristics and preprocessing requirements [17,33]. This benchmark dataset does not contain explicit temporal sequencing information.

It contains 284,807 transactions, among which only 492 are fraudulent, representing about 0.172% of the total. This highlights the severe imbalance in the class distribution.

The data set contains 31 features: transaction time, the transaction amount, class label, and 28 anonymized features (V1–V28) that were obtained using principal component analysis (PCA). The PCA transformation was applied to protect confidentiality and reduce dimensionality, resulting in numerical features that capture most of the variance in the original data. The distribution of these variables is shown in Figure 1.

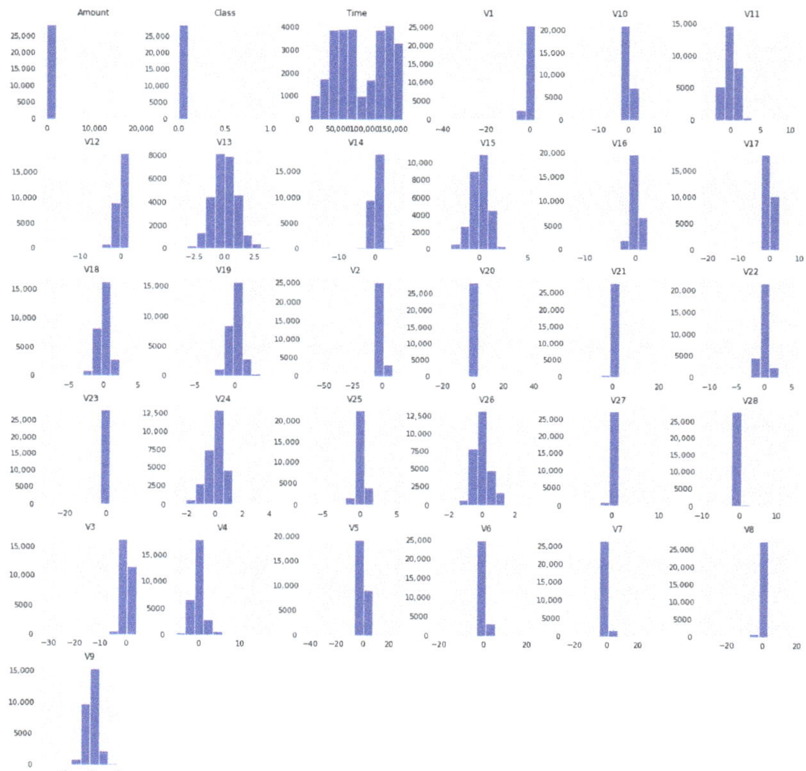

Figure 1. Distribution of the PCA-derived features in the Kaggle credit card fraud dataset.

2.2.2. Data Visualization

A preliminary investigation was conducted to ensure data quality and consistency. Duplicate transactions were identified and removed, reducing the data to 283,726 entries. No missing values were found, which simplifies preprocessing. After cleaning, the data contained 283,253 legitimate transactions and 473 fraudulent transactions.

The imbalance between classes is visually represented in Figure 2. Fraudulent transactions represent only a very small portion of the dataset.

https://doi.org/10.3390/fintech5010009

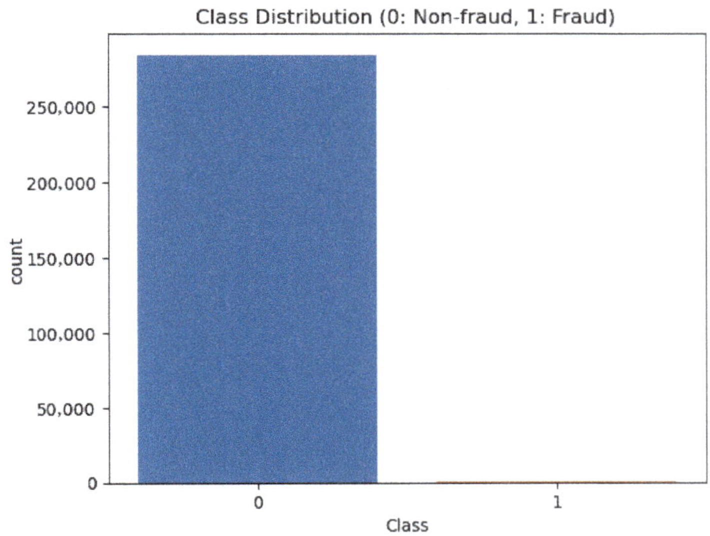

Figure 2. Class distribution showing legitimate (0) vs. fraudulent (1) transactions.

On the other hand, understanding the distribution of transaction amounts is important, as fraudulent transactions often exhibit distinctive patterns of monetary amounts. Figure 3 presents this distribution.

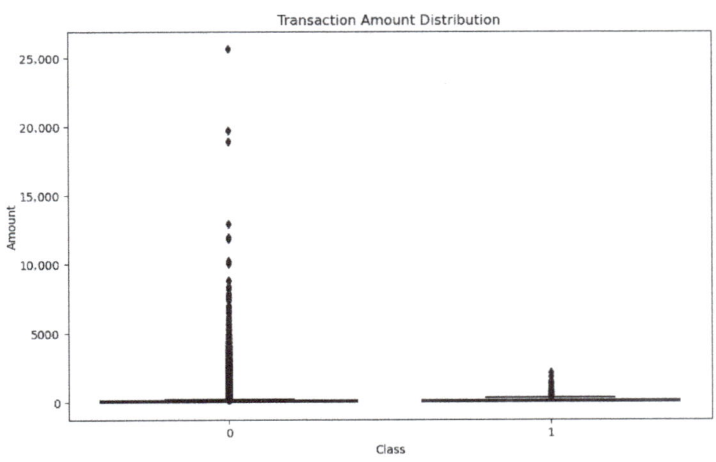

Figure 3. Transaction amount distributions for legitimate (0) and fraudulent (1) classes.

Fraudulent transactions may involve either small amounts—used to test the validity of the card—or larger amounts aimed at maximizing illegal profit before the card is blocked. Recognizing such differences is essential for designing features that can help models detect these patterns effectively.

In addition, a correlation analysis was performed to identify the features that are most closely related to the target variable.

The correlation matrix in Figure 4 illustrates the relationships between all features, including the target.

https://doi.org/10.3390/fintech5010009

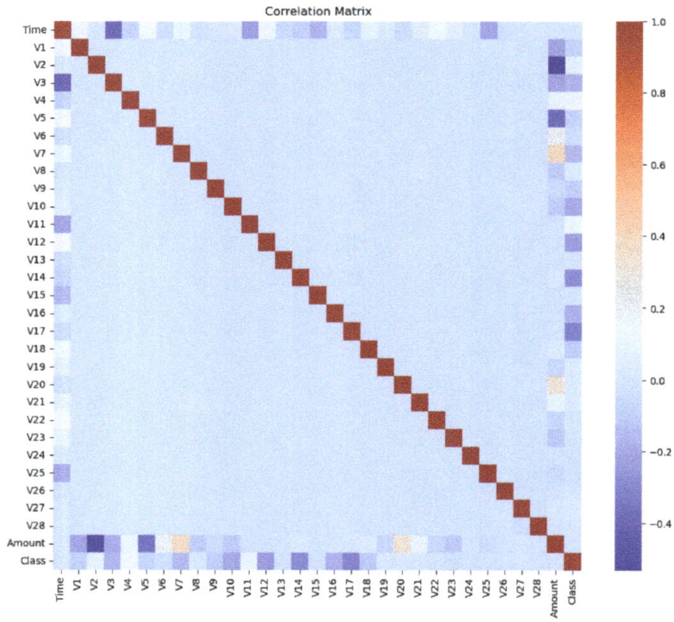

Figure 4. Correlation matrix of all 31 features, including the 28 PCA components.

The correlation heat map reveals that several PCA-derived features have notable relationships with fraud. Components such as V14, V17, V12, and V10 typically show strong negative correlations, indicating that smaller values in these components are associated with a higher probability of fraud. In contrast, components such as V11, V4, V2, and V7 show positive correlations with fraudulent activity.

The features Time and Amount have weak correlations with the target. Time shows minimal influence, while Amount may have a slight positive relationship, suggesting that fraudulent transactions might differ in their typical value distribution.

Because the V-features are uncorrelated due to the PCA transformation, they provide a suitable input space for machine learning algorithms. This property reduces redundancy and helps models learn effectively from independent features.

Technically speaking, correlation analysis is therefore a critical step in identifying which variables most contribute to distinguishing fraudulent transactions. These features will be prioritized in future modeling to enhance both accuracy and interpretability.

In this analysis, a feature was considered to have a "significant linear correlation" with the target if its absolute correlation coefficient $|r| > 0.2$. This threshold is commonly used in feature selection for fraud detection to identify meaningful relationships while avoiding noise [17]. Features such as V14, V17, and V11 met this criterion and were prioritized in subsequent modeling.

As a synthesis, this exploratory data analysis has quantitatively and visually confirmed the profound class imbalance that defines the fraud detection problem. More importantly, it has successfully identified a subset of principal components (notably V2, V4, V7, V11, V12, V14, and V17) that exhibit significant linear correlations with the target variable. These features are strong candidates for being the primary drivers in our subsequent classification models. The insights derived from the transaction amount distribution and these key correlations provide a critical, empirically grounded foundation for the next phase of this study: building and evaluating predictive models that are specifically designed to be

https://doi.org/10.3390/fintech501000

robust to imbalance and capable of leveraging these discriminative signals for accurate fraud identification.

2.3. Models and Methodology

In this study, we used two different machine learning approaches. Each method solves the problem differently.

The first model is the anomaly Detection Model. This model works well with unbalanced data. It learns what normal transactions look like and flags transactions that are very different as potential fraud. However, this model needs to be retrained when new data arrives, which can be impractical for credit card systems that process transactions continuously.

The second model is a Reinforcement Learning Model (DQN). This model can learn and adapt automatically over time. Although it is harder to train at first, it can improve itself with each new transaction without needing manual retraining. This makes it suitable for dynamic environments like fraud detection.

2.3.1. Anomaly Detection Using Multivariate Normal Distribution

The anomaly detection algorithm aims to identify transactions that deviate significantly from normal behavior. In our case, we model the normal transaction patterns using the Multivariate Normal Distribution, which captures both the mean behavior and the covariance structure of multiple features simultaneously.

The probability density function for a vector of characteristic d of dimensionality $\mathbf{x}$ is given by the following:

$$p(\mathbf{x};\boldsymbol{\mu},\boldsymbol{\Sigma}) = \frac{1}{(2\pi)^{d/2}|\boldsymbol{\Sigma}|^{1/2}} \exp\left(-\frac{1}{2}(\mathbf{x}-\boldsymbol{\mu})^T\boldsymbol{\Sigma}^{-1}(\mathbf{x}-\boldsymbol{\mu})\right) \tag{1}$$

where:

- $\mathbf{x} \in \mathbb{R}^d$ is the feature vector that represents a transaction,
- $\boldsymbol{\mu} \in \mathbb{R}^d$ is the mean vector of the normal transactions,
- $\boldsymbol{\Sigma} \in \mathbb{R}^{d\times d}$ is the covariance matrix that captures the correlations of features,
- d is the number of selected features.

For computational simplicity and interpretability, we assume that the features are statistically independent. Under this assumption, the joint probability density function is factorized into a product of univariate normal distributions:

$$p(\mathbf{x}) = \prod_{j=1}^{d} \frac{1}{\sigma_j\sqrt{2\pi}} \exp\left(-\frac{1}{2}\left(\frac{x_j-\mu_j}{\sigma_j}\right)^2\right) \tag{2}$$

where μ_j and σ_j denote the mean and standard deviation of the j-th feature, respectively.

Due to the extreme class imbalance in fraud detection, the model is trained exclusively on normal transactions. and the dataset partitioned as follows:

$$\begin{aligned} \mathcal{D} &= \mathcal{D}_0 \cup \mathcal{D}_1, \\ \mathcal{D}_0 &= \{\mathbf{x}_i \mid y_i = 0\} \quad \text{(Normal transactions)}, \\ \mathcal{D}_1 &= \{\mathbf{x}_i \mid y_i = 1\} \quad \text{(Fraudulent transactions)}, \\ \mathcal{D}_{train} &\subset \mathcal{D}_0 \quad \text{(Training set contains only normal transactions)}. \end{aligned} \tag{3}$$

Based on prior feature correlation and importance analysis, we selected the following features for the model: `['V4', 'V11', 'V12', 'V14', 'V16', 'V17', 'V18', 'V19', 'Time']`.

The developed anomaly detection algorithm operates in three main steps as mentioned in Algorithm 1.

https://doi.org/10.3390/fintech5010009

Algorithm 1 Anomaly Detection Process

1: **Step 1:** Compute the probability density for each feature individually:

$$p(x_j) = \frac{1}{\sigma_j\sqrt{2\pi}} \exp\left(-\frac{1}{2}\left(\frac{x_j - \mu_j}{\sigma_j}\right)^2\right)$$

2: **Step 2:** Combine the probabilities for all features assuming independence:

$$p(\mathbf{x}) = \prod_{j=1}^{d} p(x_j)$$

3: **Step 3:** Flag the transaction as anomalous if the joint probability is below a threshold ϵ:

$$\text{if } p(\mathbf{x}) < \epsilon \text{ then classify as FRAUD}$$

2.3.2. Deep Q-Network for Reinforcement Learning

In this approach, fraud detection is formulated as a sequential decision-making problem under the Reinforcement Learning paradigm.

The agent interacts with an environment that represents the transaction data set and learns to distinguish between normal and fraudulent transactions through trial-and-error.

The environment of the model is defined as follows:

- **States:** The feature vector of each transaction (after preprocessing and normalization).
- **Actions:** Discrete choices: 0 (normal) or 1 (fraudulent).
- **Rewards:** $+1$ for the correct classification, -1 for the incorrect classification.
- **Goal:** Learn an optimal policy π^* that maximizes the expected cumulative discounted reward:

$$\pi^* = \arg\max_{\pi} \mathbb{E}\left[\sum_{t=0}^{\infty} \gamma^t R(s_t, a_t)\right], \tag{4}$$

where $\gamma \in [0, 1]$ is the discount factor. This formulation treats fraud detection as a sequential decision process, a common abstraction for applying RL to classification-like tasks [22,25].

The Deep Q-Network approximates the Q-value function $Q(s, a; \theta)$ using a feedforward neural network as an algorithm. The network architecture is as follows:

$$\begin{aligned} \text{Layer 1:} \quad & \mathbf{h}_1 = \text{ReLU}(\mathbf{W}_1\mathbf{s} + \mathbf{b}_1) \\ \text{Layer 2:} \quad & \mathbf{h}_2 = \text{ReLU}(\mathbf{W}_2\mathbf{h}_1 + \mathbf{b}_2) \\ \text{Output:} \quad & \mathbf{q} = \mathbf{W}_3\mathbf{h}_2 + \mathbf{b}_3 \end{aligned} \tag{5}$$

Here, both hidden layers contain 24 neurons, the hidden activation function is ReLU, and the output layer is linear, representing the predicted Q-values for each action.

The neural network is trained by minimizing the mean squared error (MSE) loss derived from the Bellman equation:

$$\mathcal{L}(\theta) = \mathbb{E}\left[\left(r + \gamma \max_{a'} Q(\mathbf{s}', a'; \theta) - Q(\mathbf{s}, a; \theta)\right)^2\right] \tag{6}$$

Moreover, two key strategies improve training stability and convergence:

https://doi.org/10.3390/fintech5010009

- **Experience Replay:** Past transitions $(\mathbf{s}_t, a_t, r_t, \mathbf{s}_{t+1}, d_t)$ are stored in a memory buffer (deque). Random batches are sampled for training, breaking temporal correlations between consecutive samples:

$$\mathcal{D} = \{(\mathbf{s}_t, a_t, r_t, \mathbf{s}_{t+1}, d_t)\}. \tag{7}$$

- **Exploration vs. Exploitation: Otilia Manta, Valentina Vasile, Shigeyuki Hamori** The agent follows an ϵ-greedy policy to balance exploration and exploitation:

$$\pi(\mathbf{s}) = \begin{cases} \text{random action} & \text{with probability } \epsilon, \\ \arg\max_a Q(\mathbf{s}, a; \theta) & \text{with probability } 1 - \epsilon. \end{cases} \tag{8}$$

  The exploration rate ϵ decays over episodes from 1.0 to a minimum of 0.01.

  The DQN training procedure is summarized in Algorithm 2:

Algorithm 2 DQN Training for Fraud Detection

Initialize DQN agent with state dimension n_s and action space n_a
Initialize experience replay memory with capacity 2000
for each episode $e = 1, \ldots, E$ **do**
  Reset environment to initial state s_0
  for each step in episode **do**
    Select action a_t using ϵ-greedy policy
    Execute action, observe reward r_t and next state s_{t+1}
    Store $(s_t, a_t, r_t, s_{t+1}, d_t)$ in replay memory
    Sample random mini-batch from memory
    Update network weights via gradient descent on loss $\mathcal{L}(\theta)$
    Decay exploration rate ϵ
    if done **then**
      break
    end if
  end for
end for

The model was implemented using `TensorFlow` and `Keras` frameworks. and the key hyperparameters used are:

- Learning rate: 0.001
- Discount factor γ: 0.95
- Replay memory size: 2000 transitions
- Mini-batch size: 32
- Hidden layers: 2 layers, 24 neurons each, ReLU activation
- Exploration rate: ϵ decays from 1.0 to 0.01
- Episodes: 100 for training

2.4. Data Preprocessing

A comprehensive data preprocessing pipeline was implemented across all experimental setups, beginning with data quality, where duplicate transactions were identified and removed, eliminating 1081 records to reduce the dataset from 284,807 to 283,726 entries, resulting in a final class distribution of 283,253 legitimate (Class 0) and 473 fraudulent (Class 1) transactions. Feature engineering involved removing the Time feature to focus on transactional patterns rather than temporal sequence, while the Amount feature

https://doi.org/10.3390/fintech50[illegible]0009

was normalized using StandardScaler, which transforms features using the mathematical formulation:

$$z_i = \frac{x_i - \mu}{\sigma} \tag{9}$$

where

$$\mu = \frac{1}{n}\sum_{i=1}^{n} x_i \tag{10}$$

represents the feature mean and

$$\sigma = \sqrt{\frac{1}{n}\sum_{i=1}^{n}(x_i - \mu)^2} \tag{11}$$

represents the standard deviation, ensuring zero mean and unit variance across all features.

For the anomaly detection model, feature selection was performed based on prior correlation analysis, resulting in the selection of the most discriminative features: ['V4', 'V11', 'V12', 'V14', 'V16', 'V17', 'V18', 'V19', 'Time']. The data splitting strategy was tailored to each modeling approach, with standard 80%/20% stratified splits used for DQN models on both balanced and unbalanced samples, while for anomaly detection, a specialized split was implemented where training utilized only legitimate transactions and validation and test sets contained both classes for comprehensive evaluation. The different sample sizes reflect the operational paradigms of each model: anomaly detection as a static batch model versus DQN as an incremental online learner.

2.5. Model Evaluation

After training the models on the prepared datasets, we proceed to the evaluation phase, where we test each model on unseen test data and compare the predictions with actual values.

Given the critical nature of fraud detection and the imbalanced characteristics of our data, we employ a comprehensive set of evaluation metrics that provide meaningful insights beyond traditional accuracy measures.

In binary classification, accuracy is defined as:

$$\text{Accuracy} = \frac{TP + TN}{TP + TN + FP + FN} \tag{12}$$

However, in our highly imbalanced dataset, where fraudulent transactions represent only 0.172% of all transactions, accuracy becomes a misleading metric. A naive classifier that always predicts "non-fraud" would achieve the following:

$$\text{Accuracy} = \frac{283{,}253}{283{,}253 + 473} \approx 99.83\% \tag{13}$$

This apparently excellent score does not detect any fraudulent transactions, rendering it useless for practical fraud detection.

To ensure a robust evaluation, we employ four key metrics that provide a balanced assessment of the performance of the model.

$$\text{Precision} = \frac{TP}{TP + FP} \tag{14}$$

$$\text{Recall (Sensitivity)} = \frac{TP}{TP + FN} \tag{15}$$

https://doi.org/10.3390/fintech501000

$$\text{F1-Score} = 2 \times \frac{\text{Precision} \times \text{Recall}}{\text{Precision} + \text{Recall}} = \frac{2TP}{2TP + FP + FN} \quad (16)$$

$$\text{F2-Score} = 5 \times \frac{TP}{5 \times TP + 4 \times FN + FP} \quad (17)$$

where :

- **Precision**: Measures how many of the predicted frauds are actual frauds. High precision means when the model flags a transaction as fraudulent, it is likely correct. This minimizes false alarms and customer inconvenience.
- **Recall**: Measures how many of the actual frauds are correctly detected. High recall means the model catches most fraudulent transactions, minimizing financial losses for the bank.
- **F1-Score**: The harmonic mean of precision and recall, providing a balanced measure between the two. This is particularly useful for balanced datasets.
- **F2-Score**: Gives twice the weight to recall compared to precision ($\beta = 2$), making it our primary optimization metric for unbalanced fraud detection. This specific weighting reflects typical financial industry risk assessments where undetected fraud is estimated to be 2–4 times more costly than false positives. This aligns with our business objective, where missing fraudulent transactions (false negatives) is more costly than false alarms (false positives).

The anomaly detection model used a specialized evaluation with F2-score optimization during threshold tuning:

$$\alpha^* = \underset{\alpha \in [0.001, 0.05]}{\arg\max} \; F_2(\alpha) \quad (18)$$

where the anomaly threshold $\epsilon = \alpha^d$ and d is the feature dimension. This approach explicitly prioritizes fraud detection capability.

For reinforcement learning experiments, we created specialized dataset samples to address different aspects of the fraud detection problem:

- **Unbalanced Sample:** From the original cleaned dataset (283,726 transactions), we randomly selected 3000 legitimate transactions and all 473 fraudulent transactions to create a more manageable but still highly imbalanced dataset for DQN training.
- **Balanced Sample:** Using the 2023 credit card dataset that contains more than 550,000 records, we created a balanced subset with 1000 legitimate and 1000 fraudulent transactions to evaluate model performance under balanced class conditions.

This sampling strategy allows us to test our models under both realistic (imbalanced) and idealized (balanced) scenarios, providing comprehensive insights into their behavior across different data distributions.

3. Results and Discussion

3.1. Experimental Results

The experimental evaluation revealed distinct performance patterns across the three modeling approaches. Table 1 presents the comprehensive results obtained from rigorous testing on their respective datasets.

It is important to note that while the anomaly detection model demonstrates superior immediate performance, the DQN framework represents a different paradigm: one focused on incremental adaptability rather than static detection. The lower initial metrics for DQN reflect the challenge of learning from extreme imbalance. At the same time, its reinforcement learning architecture provides the foundation for continuous improvement as more transaction data becomes available.

https://doi.org/10.3390/fintech5010009

Table 1. Performance Comparison of Credit Card Fraud Detection Models.

Model	Dataset	Accuracy	Precision	Recall	F1-Score	F2-Score
Anomaly Detection	Full Dataset	0.996	0.749	0.831	0.788	0.813
DQN (Unbalanced)	3K/473 Sample	0.686	0.268	0.635	0.377	0.536
DQN (Balanced)	1K/1K Sample	0.690	0.689	0.675	0.682	0.678

The multivariate normal distribution approach performed exceptionally well, achieving an accuracy of 99.6% and the highest F2-score of 0.813 among all models. Its recall was 83.1%, showing a strong ability to identify most fraudulent transactions. The precision of 74.9% indicates that about one in four flagged transactions was false positive. Although this may cause some inconvenience for customers, it helps minimize financial losses from undetected fraud.

In comparison, the DQN model showed very different results depending on the data distribution. The unbalanced DQN struggled with precision, achieving only 26.8%, while maintaining a moderate recall of 63.5%, resulting in a low F1-score of 0.377. However, the balanced DQN performed much more evenly, with a precision of 68.9% and recall of 67.5%, which led to an F1-score of 0.682.

The strong performance of the anomaly detection model comes from its mathematical foundation in multivariate normal distribution. By modeling the full covariance structure of legitimate transactions, it captures normal behavior very accurately. Training exclusively on normal transactions (283,253 samples) allows the model to learn intricate patterns without being influenced by the rare fraud cases. In addition, the probabilistic framework provides natural confidence scores for its predictions.

The high recall of 83.1% is particularly valuable in Credit card fraud detection, as it ensures that most fraudulent transactions are caught, reducing financial losses. Although the precision of 74.9% means that some false positives occur, this trade-off is acceptable in financial security contexts where missing fraud is more costly than occasional false alarms.

The DQN results highlight several important insights into reinforcement learning for fraud detection. First, data distribution has a strong impact: the unbalanced precision of the DQN shows that extreme class imbalance can cause frequent misclassifications of legitimate transactions. Second, the learning process demonstrates steady improvement, with average rewards rising from initial random performance to 29.28 for the unbalanced model and 36.86 for the balanced model after 100 episodes. Finally, balanced DQN achieves more stable and consistent performance in both precision and recall, showing that with appropriate data balance, reinforcement learning can learn robust decision policies.

While the current experimental setup shows modest DQN performance compared to anomaly detection, the reinforcement learning architecture inherently supports ongoing policy refinement. In real-world deployment, where fraud patterns continuously evolve, this adaptive capability could enable DQN to progressively close the performance gap with static models over time. Future work with temporally segmented datasets is needed to fully quantify this long-term adaptation potential.

3.2. Practical Implementation Considerations

The choice between anomaly detection and reinforcement learning approaches involves several operational and performance considerations.

The anomaly detection model demonstrates high reliability, achieving 99.6% accuracy and 83.1% recall, ensuring minimal disruption to legitimate transactions while providing strong financial protection. Its computational efficiency allows for fast inference suitable for high-volume transaction processing. However, the model is static: it requires complete

https://doi.org/10.3390/fintech5010009

retraining to adapt to new fraud patterns, cannot learn continuously from new data, and requires regular updates to maintain performance.

In contrast, the DQN reinforcement learning approach offers continuous adaptation and autonomous learning. The agent improves with each new transaction, automatically adapting to evolving fraud patterns without manual intervention. This real-time optimization makes it particularly suitable for dynamic environments where local fraud patterns differ from global trends and new attack vectors constantly emerge.

From an ATM deployment perspective, the continuous learning capability of DQN models is highly advantageous. Modern ATMs embedded systems can host these models with inference times well within acceptable limits, allowing multiple ATMs to operate independently while developing specialized fraud detection policies tailored to local transaction patterns. Reinforcement learning provides scalable protection while reducing the dependency on network connectivity for updates.

When comparing operational outcomes, anomaly detection would miss approximately 17% of fraudulent transactions, whereas the balanced DQN would initially miss slightly more. However, due to its ability to learn continuously from every transaction, the DQN model can improve over time and approach progressive improvement in detection rates. In high-transaction environments like ATMs, where thousands of operations occur daily, this learning from the environment allows the model to quickly refine its policy, reducing both false negatives and false positives, and achieving superior long-term performance.

In general, reinforcement learning emerges as the most promising solution for fraud detection in dynamic, high-volume environments. Its continuous adaptation, autonomous operation, and capacity to leverage every transaction for incremental improvement make it highly effective for maintaining optimal detection rates and minimizing financial losses. This approach ensures that, unlike static anomaly detection models, the system naturally evolves with emerging fraud patterns, ultimately delivering a more robust and future-proof solution.

4. Conclusions

This study demonstrates three key findings: DQN can effectively learn fraud detection policies despite extreme class imbalance, achieving competitive F2-scores with balanced data; while anomaly detection provides superior immediate performance, DQN offers unique adaptive capabilities for evolving fraud patterns; and reinforcement learning represents a viable paradigm for real-time fraud detection, particularly in distributed systems like ATM networks.

This study demonstrates the powerful potential of reinforcement learning for dynamic fraud detection. The Deep Q-Network agent continuously learns from transaction streams, autonomously improving its decision policy as new fraud patterns emerge. Unlike static models, DQN can adapt in real time, making it ideally suited for high-volume and distributed environments, such as ATM networks, where thousands of transactions occur daily.

Balanced DQN models, trained with carefully prepared datasets, achieve robust performance across precision and recall metrics and steadily improve over time. Using every transaction as a learning opportunity, the reinforcement learning framework can approach progressive improvement in detection rates, reducing false negatives and false positives while maintaining operational efficiency.

The current study establishes the theoretical foundation and preliminary evidence for DQN's applicability to fraud detection. Future research should investigate DQN's learning trajectory through more extensive temporal analysis, including dataset segmentation to simulate the evolution of fraud patterns and longer training periods to validate sustained

https://doi.org/10.3390/fintech5010009

performance improvements. Such work would provide stronger empirical validation of DQN's potential to surpass static detection methods in dynamic environments.

Although anomaly detection provides strong initial performance and interpretable confidence scores, reinforcement learning offers compelling advantages in long-term adaptability, scalability, and resilience to evolving threats. Future work should focus on rigorous robustness testing across multiple random seeds, incorporating explainability frameworks such as SHAP to interpret the DQN's policy, and enriching the reinforcement learning formulation with more complex reward structures and sequential decision dynamics. These advancements would further solidify reinforcement learning as a leading paradigm for the next generation of autonomous, adaptive financial fraud detection systems.

Author Contributions: Conceptualization, H.B.M., A.M. and F.G.; methodology, H.B.M., A.M. and F.G.; software, H.B.M.; validation, H.B.M., A.M. and F.G.; formal analysis, H.B.M.; investigation, H.B.M.; resources, A.M. and F.G.; data curation, H.B.M.; writing—original draft preparation, H.B.M.; writing—review and editing, A.M. and F.G.; visualization, H.B.M.; supervision, A.M. and F.G.; project administration, A.M. and F.G.; funding acquisition, not applicable. All authors have read and agreed to the published version of the manuscript.

Funding: This research received no external funding.

Data Availability Statement: The data used in this study are publicly available from Kaggle. Specifically, we used the "Credit Card Fraud Detection" dataset, which is described and cited in Section 2.2 of the manuscript.

Conflicts of Interest: The authors declare no conflicts of interest.

References

1. Hirnschall, D. Semi-Supervised Bayesian GANs with Log-Signatures for Uncertainty-Aware Credit Card Fraud Detectio *Mathematics* **2025**, *13*, 3229. [CrossRef]
2. Mekhlouf, H.B.; Moussaid, A.; Ghanimi, F. Financial Fraud Detection Using Machine Learning: A Review of Literature. I Proceedings of the International Conference on Advanced Technologies for Humanity, Rabat, Morocco, 25–26 December 202 Springer: Cham, Switzerland, 2023; pp. 49–54.
3. Edge, M.E.; Sampaio, P.R.F. A survey of signature based methods for financial fraud detection. *Comput. Secur.* **2009**, *28*, 381–39 [CrossRef]
4. Awoyemi, J.O.; Adetunmbi, A.O.; Oluwadare, S.A. Credit card fraud detection using machine learning techniques: A comparativ analysis. In Proceedings of the 2017 International Conference on Computing Networking and Informatics (ICCNI), Lagos, Nigeria 29–31 October 2017; IEEE: New York, NY, USA, 2017; pp. 1–9.
5. Liu, D.; Zhao, Y.; Xu, H.; Sun, Y.; Pei, D.; Luo, J.; Jing, X.; Feng, M. Opprentice: Towards practical and automatic anomaly detectio through machine learning. In Proceedings of the 2015 Internet Measurement Conference, Tokyo, Japan, 28–30 October 201 pp. 211–224.
6. Hafez, I.Y.; Hafez, A.Y.; Saleh, A.; Abd, El-Mageed, A.A.; Abohany, A.A. A systematic review of AI-enhanced techniques in credi card fraud detection. *J. Big Data* **2025**, *12*, 6. [CrossRef]
7. Alkhozae, M.; Almasre, M.; Almakky, A.; Alhebshi, R.M.; Alamri, A.; Hakami, W.; Alshahrani, L. An Explainable Credit Car Fraud Detection Model using Machine Learning and Deep Learning Approaches. *J. Appl. Data Sci.* **2025**, *6*, 2838–2857. [CrossRef
8. Gutiérrez-Gallego, A.; Garnica, O.; Parra, D.; Velasco, J.; Hidalgo, J. Balanced Underbagged Ensemble Approach for Classifyin Highly Imbalanced Datasets in the Insurance and Financial Sectors. *Intell. Syst. Account. Financ. Manag.* **2025**, *32*, e7001 [CrossRef]
9. Safder, M.U.; Naveed, S.S.; Khurshid, K.; Salman, A.; Nizami, I.F. Optimizing imbalanced learning with genetic algorithm. *Sc Rep.* **2025**, *15*, 34857. [CrossRef]
10. Salem, A.H.; Azzam, S.M.; Emam, O.E.; Abohany, A.A. From chaos to clarity: Unraveling credit card fraud with BGVCA-LS. *J. Bi Data* **2025**, *12*, 215. [CrossRef]
11. Reddy, D.P.V.S.; Vivek, Y.; Pranay, G.; Ravi, V. Chaotic variational auto encoder-based adversarial machine learning. *Comput. Elect Eng.* **2025**, *128*, 110646. [CrossRef]
12. Yajid, M.S.A.; Bhosle, N.; Sudhamsu, G.; Khatibi, A.; Sharma, S.; Jeet, R.; Sivaranjani, R.; Bhowmik, A.; Santhosh, A.J. Hybrid Bi Bang-Big crunch with cuckoo search for feature selection in credit card fraud detection. *Sci. Rep.* **2025**, *15*, 23925. [CrossRef]

https://doi.org/10.3390/fintech501000

13. Kennedy, R.K.L.; Villanustre, F.; Khoshgoftaar, T.M. Unsupervised feature selection and class labeling for credit card fraud. *J. Big Data* **2025**, *12*, 111. [CrossRef]
14. Walauskis, M.A.; Khoshgoftaar, T.M. Unsupervised label generation for severely imbalanced fraud data. *J. Big Data* **2025**, *12*, 63. [CrossRef]
15. Darwish, S.M.; Salama, A.I.; El-Zoghabi, A.A. Intelligent approach to detecting online fraudulent trading with solution for imbalanced data in fintech forensics. *Sci. Rep.* **2025**, *15*, 17983. [CrossRef]
16. Vadlamudi, M.N.; Doma, S.; Sayeedunnisa, S.F.; Hijab, M.; Chinnem, R.M.; Sankara Babu, B. Towards Transparent Fraud Detection: Explainable AI and Multi-algorithm Optimization in Financial Security. *Int. J. Intell. Eng. Syst.* **2025**, *18*, 698–712. [CrossRef]
17. Sundaravadivel, P.; Isaac, R.A.; Elangovan, D.; KrishnaRaj, D.; Rahul, V.V.L.; Raja, R. Optimizing credit card fraud detection with random forests and SMOTE. *Sci. Rep.* **2025**, *15*, 17851. [CrossRef] [PubMed]
18. Alsowail, R.A. Optimizing Network and Systems Management for Fraud Detection: A High-Performance Approach Using Random Light Gradient-Based CatBoost Ensemble with Enhanced Gold Rush Algorithm. *J. Netw. Syst. Manag.* **2025**, *33*, 96. [CrossRef]
19. Priatna, W.; Warta, J.; Rasim; Mayadi; Mahbub, A.R.; Hidayat, A. Anomaly detection in e-commerce fraud using a hybrid autoencoder-transformer. *ICIC Express Lett.* **2025**, *19*, 1081–1089.
20. Atban, F.; Küçükkara, M.Y.; Bayilmis, C. Enhancing variational quantum classifier performance with meta-heuristic feature selection for credit card fraud detection. *Eur. Phys. J. Spec. Top.* **2025**, *234*, 3705–3718. [CrossRef]
21. Abadlia, H.; Smairi, N. Enhanced particle swarm optimization-based hyperparameter optimized stacked autoencoder for credit card fraud detection. *Int. J. Data Sci. Anal.* **2025**, *20*, 1239–1253. [CrossRef]
22. Chakraborty, D. Bill safe: Intelligent forgery detection with CNN and upgrade sand cat swarm optimization. *Discov. Comput.* **2025**, *28*, 84. [CrossRef]
23. Madhavappa, T.; Sathyanarayana, B. An efficient framework based on optimized CNN-RNN for online transaction fraud detection in financial transactions. *Int. J. Syst. Assur. Eng. Manag.* **2025**, *16*, 3354–3374. [CrossRef]
24. Damanik, N.; Liu, C.-M. Towards Explainable and Balanced Federated Learning: A Neural Network Approach for Multi-Client Fraud Detection. *Int. J. Adv. Comput. Sci. Appl.* **2025**, *16*, 373–382. [CrossRef]
25. Xia, Z.; Saha, S.C. FinGraphFL: Financial Graph-Based Federated Learning for Enhanced Credit Card Fraud Detection. *Mathematics* **2025**, *13*, 1396. [CrossRef]
26. El Hlouli, F.Z.; Riffi, J.; Mahraz, M.A.; Ali, A.; El Fazazy, K.; Tairi, H. Deep neural network for detection of fraudulent transaction. *Multimed. Tools Appl.* **2025**, *84*, 41991–42008. [CrossRef]
27. Shabiya, M.I.; Chandrika, R.R. LSO-RVAE: Latent space optimization with sparrow search and residual variational autoencoder for Credit card fraud detection. *Eng. Res. Express* **2025**, *7*, 035244. [CrossRef]
28. Chugh, B.; Malik, N.; Gupta, D. Firefly Optimization-Based Logistic Regression Classifier for Credit Card Fraud Detection. *J. Circuits Syst. Comput.* **2025**, *34*, 2550204. [CrossRef]
29. Adejoh, J.; Owoh, N.; Ashawa, M.; Hosseinzadeh, S.; Shahrabi, A.; Mohamed, S. An Adaptive Unsupervised Learning Approach for Credit Card Fraud Detection. *Big Data Cogn. Comput.* **2025**, *9*, 217. [CrossRef]
30. Ahmad, H.; Rawashdeh, E.; Al Tawil, A.; Al-Ramahi, N. EFC-Tomek: An effective undersampling technique for credit card fraud detection. *Int. J. Data Netw. Sci.* **2025**, *9*, 845–852. [CrossRef]
31. Tayebi, M.; El Kafhali, S. A novel approach based on XGBoost classifier and Bayesian optimization for credit card fraud detection. *Cyber Secur. Appl.* **2025**, *3*, 100093. [CrossRef]
32. Andrade-Arenas, L.; Yactayo-Arias, C. Comparative Analysis of Machine Learning Models for Credit Card Fraud Detection Using SMOTE for Class Imbalance. *Int. J. Saf. Secur. Eng.* **2025**, *15*, 893–901. [CrossRef]
33. Theodorakopoulos, L.; Theodoropoulou, A.; Tsimakis, A.; Halkiopoulos, C. Big Data-Driven Distributed Machine Learning for Scalable Credit Card Fraud Detection Using PySpark, XGBoost, and CatBoost. *Electronics* **2025**, *14*, 1754. [CrossRef]
34. Akouhar, M.; Ouhssini, M.; El-Fatini, M.; Abarda, A.; Agherrabi, E. Dynamic oversampling-driven Kolmogorov–Arnold networks for credit card fraud detection: An ensemble approach to robust financial security. *Egypt. Inform. J.* **2025**, *31*, 100712. [CrossRef]
35. Karnavou, E.; Cascavilla, G.; Marcelino, G.; Geradts, Z. I know you're a fraud: Uncovering illicit activity in a Greek bank transactions with unsupervised learning. *Expert Syst. Appl.* **2025**, *288*, 128148. [CrossRef]
36. John Berkmans, T.; Karthick, S. Anomaly detection in online credit card data using optimized multi-view heterogeneous graph neural networks. *Knowl.-Based Syst.* **2025**, *324*, 113767. [CrossRef]
37. Hancock, J.T.; Bauder, R.A.; Khoshgoftaar, T.M. SHAP as a Data Reduction Technique for Highly Imbalanced Big Data. *Int. J. Artif. Intell. Tools* **2025**, *34*, 2540001. [CrossRef]
38. Hayat, K.; Magnier, B. Data Leakage and Deceptive Performance: A Critical Examination of Credit Card Fraud Detection Methodologies. *Mathematics* **2025**, *13*, 2563. [CrossRef]
39. Feng, X.; Kim, S.-K. Statistical Data-Generative Machine Learning-Based Credit Card Fraud Detection Systems. *Mathematics* **2025**, *13*, 2446. [CrossRef]

https://doi.org/10.3390/fintech5010009

40. Chen, T.; Yang, X.; Ni, L. Credit Card Fraud Detection Algorithm Based on a Stacked Ensemble Model. *Int. J. Softw. Eng. Knowl. Eng.* **2025**, *35*, 1177–1200. [CrossRef]
41. Credit Card Fraud Detection. Retrieved from Kaggle. 2013. Available online: https://www.kaggle.com/datasets/mlg-ulb/creditcardfraud (accessed on 1 June 2025).

https://doi.org/10.3390/fintech5010009

FinTech

Article

Strategic Foresight for FinTech Governance: A Scenario-Based MCDA Approach for Kuwait

Salah Kayed [1], Zaid Alhawwatma [2], Amer Morshed [2,*] and Laith T. Khrais [3]

1 Department of Accounting, Business School, The Hashemite University, P.O. Box 330127, Zarqa 13133, Jordan
2 Department of Accounting, Faculty of Business, Al-Zaytoonah University of Jordan, P.O. Box 130, Amman 11733, Jordan
3 Department of Business Administration, Faculty of Business, Middle East University, P.O. Box 383, Amman 11831, Jordan
* Correspondence: a.morshed@zuj.edu.jo or amermurshed1@gmail.com

Abstract

This study investigates how strategic foresight can enhance FinTech governance and policy resilience in emerging economies, using Kuwait as an illustrative case. It aims to identify which foresight interventions should be prioritized across alternative futures to strengthen innovation, security, and institutional adaptability within the digital finance ecosystem. A scenario-based Multi-Criteria Decision Analysis (MCDA) framework is applied, combining the Analytic Hierarchy Process (AHP) and the Technique for Order Preference by Similarity to Ideal Solution (TOPSIS). Expert evaluations were conducted to assess five foresight interventions against eight policy and performance criteria across three plausible scenarios: Optimistic Growth, Status Quo, and Crisis and Contraction. Sensitivity analyses were performed to validate the stability of intervention rankings. The results reveal distinct priorities under each scenario: SME-oriented digital finance platforms and talent development dominate under growth and stability, while cybersecurity investment becomes paramount during crisis conditions. Regulatory fast-tracking maintains a consistent, moderate influence across all contexts. These outcomes underscore the need for adaptive, context-sensitive policy design that accommodates uncertainty. The framework provides policymakers with a structured approach to align FinTech strategies with long-term national visions such as Kuwait's Vision 2035, while offering transferable insights for other emerging economies. The study's originality lies in integrating strategic foresight and MCDA for FinTech governance—a methodological and practical contribution to foresight-informed policymaking.

Keywords: strategic foresight; FinTech governance; scenario planning; MCDA; Kuwait Vision 2035; digital transformation

JEL Classification: G28; O33; O16

1. Introduction

The rapid expansion of financial technology (FinTech) has redefined how financial services are delivered, regulated, and accessed, providing emerging economies with opportunities to foster innovation, strengthen financial inclusion, and diversify their growth models. In Kuwait, FinTech is increasingly recognized as a driver of national priorities under Kuwait Vision 2035, which emphasizes digital transformation as a strategic pillar.

https://doi.org/10.3390/fintech5010008

Yet, Kuwait's FinTech ecosystem remains at an early stage, marked by regulatory fragmentation, weak infrastructure coordination, and the absence of structured foresight tools in policy planning [1].

The international literature consistently stresses the role of strategic foresight in anticipating disruption, guiding innovation, and supporting adaptive policymaking. Tools such as scenario planning, horizon scanning, and Delphi methods have been applied in advanced economies to embed foresight within governance and regulatory frameworks. However, within the Gulf, much of the FinTech scholarship has focused on adoption readiness, regulatory reform, or ecosystem benchmarking, with limited attention to how foresight approaches can be operationalized to guide long-term FinTech strategies [2,3]. This leaves a significant gap in the integration of foresight with FinTech governance, particularly in contexts like Kuwait where vulnerabilities linked to cybersecurity, energy reliability, and human capital remain unresolved.

This gap motivates the study's central research question: Which strategic foresight interventions should be prioritized to strengthen Kuwait's FinTech ecosystem under alternative future scenarios?

To address this question, the research applies a scenario-based Multi-Criteria Decision Analysis (MCDA) framework, combining the Analytic Hierarchy Process (AHP) and the Technique for Order Preference by Similarity to Ideal Solution (TOPSIS). Drawing on expert input, the model evaluates five strategic foresight interventions against eight criteria under three plausible scenarios: optimistic growth, status quo continuation, and crisis and contraction. This approach ensures that interventions are prioritized not in isolation but with sensitivity to different possible futures, consistent with foresight theory and adaptive governance principles.

The contribution of the study is twofold. Theoretically, it advances the literature by linking foresight research with decision-support methods, showing how priorities shift depending on scenario assumptions. Practically, it provides structured evidence that can guide policymakers in aligning national FinTech strategies with long-term uncertainty. While the focus is on Kuwait, the framework offers transferable insights for other emerging economies where foresight integration into financial governance remains underdeveloped.

This study addresses key theoretical and methodological gaps by integrating strategic foresight with decision-support tools to operationalize adaptive governance in FinTech policy. It applies a scenario-based MCDA (AHP–TOPSIS) to evaluate the robustness of policy interventions across multiple futures, providing an evidence-based framework that aligns Kuwait Vision 2035 with long-term uncertainty and sustainable digital transformation.

The remainder of the paper is structured as follows: Section 2 reviews the literature and conceptual framework; Section 3 details the methodology; Section 4 presents the findings; Section 5 discusses the results; Section 6 outlines implications; and Section 7 concludes with limitations and future research directions.

2. Literature Review

2.1. Strategic Foresight in Digital Finance

Strategic foresight refers to a structured, long-term approach for anticipating future developments and informing present-day decision-making [4]. In sectors such as financial technology (FinTech), foresight enables policymakers to prepare for uncertainty, navigate disruption, and align innovation with national priorities. As digital finance expands through blockchain, open banking, and AI-driven credit scoring, foresight has become essential for sustaining competitiveness, regulatory coherence, and financial inclusion [5].

Recent scholarship emphasizes that foresight is not only about forecasting but also about building adaptive governance capacities. This distinction highlights an important

https://doi.org/10.3390/fintech501000

debate in the literature: predictive foresight, which seeks to identify the most likely future, versus adaptive foresight, which prepares institutions for multiple plausible futures. Adaptive approaches are increasingly viewed as more effective in volatile environments such as FinTech, where technological change is rapid and regulatory risks are systemic [6].

Operational tools include scenario planning, horizon scanning, Delphi surveys, and trend impact analysis. These methods help policymakers uncover systemic weaknesses, test resilience under uncertainty, and anticipate second-order effects of innovation. In developed markets, foresight is embedded within regulatory structures: Singapore uses regulatory sandboxes and policy labs to experiment with digital finance regulation, while the UK applies agile supervision and RegTech initiatives to adapt its frameworks to innovation cycles [7]. Such practices show how foresight supports both innovation and stability.

By contrast, many emerging economies, including those in the Gulf, rely on reactive rather than anticipatory policy responses. Although national visions such as Kuwait Vision 2035 and Saudi Vision 2030 outline digital ambitions, explicit foresight frameworks tailored to FinTech remain absent or fragmented. This limits the ability of regulators to anticipate vulnerabilities such as cyber risks, talent shortages, energy constraints, and geopolitical shocks, all of which can undermine digital transformation [2,3].

In this context, the integration of strategic foresight interventions into FinTech policymaking is not only a technical exercise but a governance necessity. It enables governments to move beyond compliance-driven responses and align regulation, infrastructure, and innovation ecosystems with the uncertainties of digital finance. This study adopts an adaptive foresight orientation, focusing on preparing for multiple plausible futures rather than predicting a single trajectory.

2.2. Economic and Sectoral Foundations of FinTech Governance

FinTech has transformed the economics of financial intermediation by lowering transaction costs, improving efficiency, and expanding access, yet it also introduces coordination and stability challenges. Ref. [8] argues that FinTech enhances efficiency by reducing overhead and information frictions but depends on regulatory systems that often evolve too slowly to match innovation. Ref. [9] similarly shows that FinTech reshapes risk-sharing, liquidity management, and competition in banking, requiring adaptive governance to balance innovation and systemic stability. Ref. [10] adds that while digital finance improves inclusion, it can also amplify instability if regulation and consumer protection lag behind technology. Empirical evidence from [11] further demonstrates that weak regulatory frameworks in emerging markets can expose investors to governance failures—underscoring the centrality of regulatory clarity, cybersecurity, and inclusion as foresight criteria in FinTech governance. Beyond these theoretical foundations, FinTech's influence spans multiple sectors of the economy. In business finance, digital platforms facilitate factoring, accounting, and debt collection, strengthening SME liquidity [12]. For individuals, digital lending and personal finance tools expand credit access and financial literacy, though they raise new concerns about data privacy and bias [13]. In capital markets, mobile trading and robo-advisory services democratize investment but may heighten volatility [14]. Meanwhile, cybersecurity-focused FinTech firms play a stabilizing role by safeguarding digital transactions, a public good essential for maintaining trust in financial ecosystems [15].

Overall, FinTech's economic and sectoral breadth highlights its dual character as both a catalyst for inclusion and a potential source of systemic vulnerability. Static regulation cannot fully manage these trade-offs. Therefore, foresight-based and adaptive governance—such as the scenario-based MCDA framework applied in this study—offers a structured means to anticipate how innovation, regulation, and resilience interact under uncertain futures. This integrative perspective bridges economic theory with practical foresight,

https://doi.org/10.3390/fintech5010008

positioning FinTech governance as both an economic coordination problem and a strategic policy challenge.

2.3. Futures Literacy and Anticipatory Governance in FinTech

Futures literacy, defined by UNESCO as the capability to "imagine, anticipate, and respond to change" [16], has become a critical dimension of strategic foresight. Rather than focusing solely on predicting probable futures, futures literacy emphasizes developing institutional capacity to recognize multiple possibilities and adapt accordingly. This perspective is particularly relevant for FinTech, where technological disruptions such as blockchain innovations, decentralized finance (DeFi), and AI-driven credit scoring reshape financial systems in nonlinear and uncertain ways.

Closely linked is the concept of anticipatory governance, which refers to the systematic integration of foresight practices into decision-making processes to manage emerging risks and opportunities [17]. Anticipatory governance frameworks stress proactive policy design, early stakeholder engagement, and iterative adaptation, helping governments to align regulation with evolving innovation cycles. For FinTech ecosystems, this implies embedding foresight not only in high-level visions but also in regulatory sandboxes, digital infrastructure planning, and consumer protection frameworks.

By linking futures literacy with anticipatory governance, policymakers can shift from reactive regulation toward building adaptive capacity in FinTech governance. This study reflects this perspective by evaluating how scenario-based foresight interventions can strengthen Kuwait's ability to anticipate risks and seize opportunities in its digital finance transformation.

2.4. FinTech Ecosystem Development: Kuwait in Comparative Perspective

The development of FinTech ecosystems varies significantly across national contexts, shaped by institutional capacity, regulatory flexibility, infrastructure maturity, and strategic vision. In Kuwait, FinTech remains at a formative stage. The Central Bank of Kuwait (CBK) has introduced a regulatory sandbox and issued a draft Open Banking Regulatory Framework in 2025, yet implementation delays, fragmented infrastructure, and weak cross-sectoral coordination continue to hinder progress compared to regional peers.

In contrast, the UAE and Bahrain have implemented governance models that combine regulatory foresight with institutional support. The UAE, through the Dubai International Financial Centre (DIFC) and Abu Dhabi Global Market (ADGM), has established internationally recognized sandboxes, digital banking licenses, and agile consultation mechanisms that integrate foresight into financial policymaking [18]. Bahrain's FinTech Bay serves as a dedicated innovation hub, coordinating regulatory flexibility, open banking adoption, and experimentation with Islamic FinTech applications [19]. Saudi Arabia has similarly advanced by embedding FinTech within its Vision 2030 framework, supporting development through SAMA's regulatory sandbox and the Fintech Saudi initiative, which align private-sector innovation with national objectives [20].

Global leaders reinforce how foresight-based governance can drive FinTech resilience. The United Kingdom's Financial Conduct Authority (FCA) integrates regulatory technology (RegTech), data-driven supervision, and consumer-protection safeguards into its FinTech oversight. Singapore's Monetary Authority (MAS) complements regulatory sandboxes with foresight grants, policy labs, and structured scenario planning, enabling policymakers to stress-test digital finance strategies under conditions of cyber risk and geopolitical uncertainty [21,22]. These cases illustrate that foresight, when embedded institutionally, enables innovation while mitigating systemic risk.

https://doi.org/10.3390/fintech5010008

By comparison, Kuwait faces persistent structural barriers that compromise foresight potential. These include underdeveloped cybersecurity systems, low levels of SME digital literacy, bottlenecks in energy infrastructure, unregulated cryptocurrency activity, and a shortage of FinTech-specific human capital [2]. The absence of integrated foresight frameworks exacerbates these vulnerabilities, leaving policy largely reactive and fragmented. Without anticipatory mechanisms, regulators struggle to prioritize interventions, sequence reforms, or coordinate ecosystem stakeholders.

Although Kuwait possesses considerable potential, it lacks the governance mechanisms that distinguish more advanced ecosystems. Addressing these gaps requires embedding strategic foresight interventions into FinTech policy design to accelerate ecosystem preparation, reduce systemic vulnerabilities, and align national strategy with long-term digital transformation goals.

2.5. Comparative Literature Survey on FinTech Governance and Foresight

Existing research on FinTech foresight and governance in emerging economies remains fragmented and largely descriptive. Studies conducted in Kuwait have evaluated Vision 2035 and the regulatory sandbox, emphasizing institutional readiness but without applying structured foresight or multi-criteria evaluation. Similar analyses in Saudi Arabia and the United Arab Emirates have relied on scenario narratives and expert consultations to identify cybersecurity and infrastructure priorities, but they did not incorporate quantitative weighting or sensitivity testing [18,23].

The present study advances this literature by combining strategic foresight with Multi-Criteria Decision Analysis (MCDA) to assess how FinTech priorities shift across alternative futures. Unlike prior qualitative approaches, the integrated AHP–TOPSIS model quantifies expert judgment and enables systematic comparison of trade-offs among regulation, inclusion, and resilience. This framework provides a replicable, data-driven approach that links foresight analysis with measurable policy implications, contributing to a more rigorous understanding of FinTech governance in Kuwait and offering methodological value for other emerging economies.

2.6. Scenario-Based Foresight in National Innovation Strategies

Scenario-based foresight has emerged as one of the most widely applied approaches in innovation strategy and public policy, particularly in complex and uncertain technological environments. By mapping multiple plausible futures, scenarios enable policymakers to uncover systemic weaknesses, test resilience, and develop strategies that remain effective under different conditions [24]. Unlike predictive models that assume a single trajectory, scenario-based foresight supports adaptive governance, where decisions are stress-tested against volatility and disruption.

Globally, several countries have institutionalized scenario planning within their innovation ecosystems. The Netherlands and Finland use long-term scenario workshops and policy labs to guide digital infrastructure and sustainability transitions. Singapore's Committee on the Future Economy employed scenario foresight to anticipate financial risks from geopolitical and cybersecurity shocks, leading to targeted reforms in data protection and infrastructure investment [25]. These examples demonstrate that scenario-based foresight functions as both a planning tool and a policy instrument, allowing governments to prepare proactively rather than reactively.

In the Gulf, scenario-based foresight is referenced in high-level national visions—such as Saudi Vision 2030 and Kuwait Vision 2035—but remains absent at the sectoral or regulatory level. Without structured foresight processes, financial governance is characterized by short-term responses, leaving states ill-prepared for shocks such as cyberattacks, capital

https://doi.org/10.3390/fintech5010008

flight, or technological obsolescence [26]. In Kuwait, this gap is particularly evident in FinTech governance, where the absence of futures analysis limits the ability to prioritize interventions and align regulatory design with long-term uncertainty.

Thus, scenario-based foresight interventions provide distinctive value for FinTech policy. They capture the sector's nonlinear risks—ranging from delayed open banking implementation to talent migration—and allow policymakers to pre-emptively identify strategies that are robust across different futures [27].

2.7. Multi-Criteria Decision Analysis (MCDA) in Technology and Policy Decision-Making

Multi-Criteria Decision Analysis (MCDA) provides a structured framework for evaluating alternatives against multiple, often conflicting criteria, making it especially relevant for policy and technology domains where trade-offs are unavoidable [28]. By incorporating both quantitative and qualitative judgments, MCDA facilitates transparent and systematic prioritization in uncertain environments, enabling stakeholders to balance efficiency, resilience, and innovation.

Among the most widely used methods, the Analytic Hierarchy Process (AHP) structures expert judgments into weighted priorities through pairwise comparisons, while the Technique for Order Preference by Similarity to Ideal Solution (TOPSIS) ranks alternatives based on their closeness to an "ideal" outcome. When applied together, AHP and TOPSIS allow researchers and policymakers to evaluate competing strategies in a participatory and reproducible manner [29].

In governance and policy research, MCDA has been used extensively to support decision-making in urban planning, environmental management, energy transitions, and digital transformation strategies. It has enabled governments to clarify stakeholder preferences and weigh competing objectives such as cost versus sustainability or innovation versus regulation. In digital policy specifically, MCDA has been employed to assess smart city strategies, e-government platforms, and ICT investment priorities [30].

However, its application to FinTech governance and foresight remains rare. Most existing FinTech studies focus on adoption models or short-term performance indicators, overlooking how structured decision-support tools can guide long-term strategic planning. The integration of MCDA with scenario-based foresight is especially limited, even though such combinations have proven effective in fields like energy security and environmental sustainability [31].

This gap is significant in the FinTech domain, where uncertainty around regulation, infrastructure, cybersecurity, and talent development demands structured prioritization across divergent futures. By combining AHP and TOPSIS with scenario analysis, this study extends decision-support methodologies into FinTech governance, offering a replicable framework for policymakers to evaluate the robustness of foresight interventions under uncertainty.

2.8. Research Gaps, Theoretical Contribution, and Hypotheses Development

Despite the rapid growth of FinTech scholarship, much of the literature remains focused on adoption models and institutional readiness, often framed through TAM, UTAUT, or TOE. While valuable for understanding user behavior and organizational uptake, these approaches offer limited insight into how policymakers and regulators can anticipate shocks, manage systemic risks, or prioritize interventions under uncertainty. This leaves a substantial gap in foresight-oriented approaches to FinTech governance, particularly in emerging economies.

Globally, advanced jurisdictions such as Singapore and the UK illustrate how foresight and anticipatory governance can be embedded in regulatory practice through policy

https://doi.org/10.3390/fintech501000

labs, scenario exercises, and regulatory sandboxes. Regionally, the UAE, Bahrain, and Saudi Arabia have begun integrating foresight into national FinTech strategies, aligning innovation with long-term visions. By contrast, Kuwait's ecosystem remains fragmented, constrained by delayed regulatory implementation, weak infrastructure, limited cybersecurity capacity, and shortages of skilled talent. Although Vision 2035 articulates digital ambitions, it does not provide operational foresight mechanisms for guiding FinTech policy under technological or geopolitical uncertainty.

At the methodological level, Multi-Criteria Decision Analysis (MCDA) has been successfully applied to policy domains such as energy, environment, and digital transformation. Yet, its integration with scenario-based foresight in FinTech governance is almost absent. Most existing studies emphasize short-term adoption metrics or performance outcomes, overlooking structured decision-support frameworks that can evaluate the robustness of policy interventions across multiple possible futures.

This study addresses these gaps in three key ways. First, it integrates strategic foresight theory with decision-support methods, bridging futures literacy [16] and anticipatory governance [32] with MCDA. Second, it introduces a scenario-based AHP–TOPSIS model that prioritizes foresight interventions under divergent conditions, testing the stability of strategies across optimistic, status quo, and crisis scenarios. Third, it situates Kuwait as an illustrative case, highlighting both the risks of fragmented governance and the potential of foresight-based planning. The framework provides theoretical value by extending foresight research into FinTech governance and practical value by offering policymakers in emerging economies a replicable tool for aligning innovation strategies with long-term uncertainty.

2.9. Hypotheses: Exploring Trade-Offs in Foresight-Based FinTech Governance

Drawing on strategic foresight theory and contingency-based scenario planning, this study reconceptualizes its hypotheses as exploratory propositions designed to reveal how the prioritization of FinTech policy interventions changes across alternative futures. Rather than confirming predetermined expectations, the analysis seeks to uncover empirical trade-offs—how long-term innovation and inclusion objectives interact with short-term resilience and regulatory stability under varying conditions [16,33].

H1. *Regulatory clarity will generally remain an enabling factor but may not dominate across all future scenarios.*

While transparent and predictable regulation is widely viewed as a "no-regret" condition for FinTech growth [14], its relative importance may decline in crisis settings where immediate resilience and cybersecurity take precedence. This hypothesis examines whether regulatory certainty functions as a stable baseline or whether it competes with more urgent interventions under stress.

H2. *Infrastructure-oriented strategies (e.g., cybersecurity and energy resilience) will gain priority in crisis or high-risk scenarios compared with stable or optimistic contexts.*

Foresight and risk governance literature emphasize that external shocks amplify latent vulnerabilities [3]. This hypothesis tests whether expert preferences systematically shift toward resilience investments when uncertainty and systemic risk intensify.

H3. *Human-capital and inclusion strategies (e.g., talent development and SME digital finance) will dominate under stable or growth-oriented scenarios but may lose priority during crises.*

https://doi.org/10.3390/fintech5010008

Futures literacy theory suggests that capability-building thrives when resources and institutional confidence are high [34]. The hypothesis explores whether long-term inclusion remains valued when macroeconomic conditions deteriorate or whether short-term stabilization displaces developmental goals.

H4. *The prioritization of foresight interventions will vary significantly across scenarios, reflecting adaptive—not fixed—governance preferences.*

In line with contingency theory, this hypothesis tests whether shifts in macro-financial and institutional assumptions generate measurable changes in the ranking of interventions [35]. It positions adaptability itself as an indicator of foresight maturity within governance systems.

Together, these four hypotheses frame the MCDA analysis as an exploratory test of contextual variation rather than confirmation of static expectations. Each hypothesis corresponds to one or more foresight domains—regulatory (H1), infrastructure (H2), innovation and inclusion (H3), and integrated adaptability (H4)—allowing the scenario-based framework to assess how FinTech governance priorities evolve under uncertainty.

Figure 1 illustrates the methodological flow of the study rather than causal relationships among variables. The three parallel scenarios—Optimistic Growth, Status Quo, and Crisis and Contraction—serve as distinct analytical settings feeding into the AHP–TOPSIS evaluation, which generates scenario-specific rankings of foresight interventions. The framework highlights how each scenario independently informs the prioritization process, reflecting the study's adaptive foresight orientation. Accordingly, the scenarios should be viewed as parallel and non-sequential, and the figure's layout has been adjusted to remove any implication of temporal or hierarchical dependence among them.

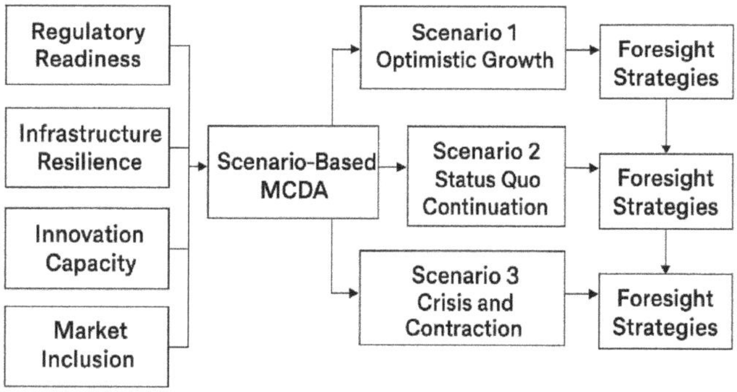

Figure 1. Conceptual framework.

3. Methodology

3.1. Research Design

This study applies a scenario-based Multi-Criteria Decision Analysis (MCDA) framework to evaluate foresight challenges and strategic priorities in Kuwait's FinTech sector. MCDA is suitable for contexts with multiple, conflicting criteria and high uncertainty, where linear forecasting provides limited guidance [28]. By integrating MCDA with scenario planning, the framework enables evaluation of interventions across divergent futures, strengthening strategic planning and policy resilience.

The design is grounded in strategic foresight theory, which emphasizes preparation for multiple plausible futures rather than single-point predictions. It also draws on anticipatory governance, which embeds foresight capacities into decision-making to manage

https://doi.org/10.3390/fintech5010008

risks and opportunities proactively [14,36]. From a decision theory perspective, MCDA operationalizes these ideas by structuring expert judgments into weighted priorities.

For consistency, the study defines strategic foresight interventions as governance measures to strengthen FinTech ecosystems (e.g., regulatory clarity, cybersecurity, SME financing, talent development, infrastructure resilience). The MCDA approach combines two methods: the Analytic Hierarchy Process (AHP), which derives weights through pairwise expert comparisons, and the Technique for Order Preference by Similarity to Ideal Solution (TOPSIS), which ranks alternatives by their closeness to an ideal outcome [29].

This framework links foresight and decision theory, enabling structured prioritization of FinTech strategies under uncertainty and offering a replicable model for emerging economies [37].

3.2. Intervention Identification

The five foresight strategies were identified through a structured three-stage process combining horizon scanning, Delphi consultation, and stakeholder validation. First, an extensive review of policy reports, regional foresight frameworks, and FinTech governance studies was conducted to map recurring themes within the four conceptual domains—regulation, infrastructure, innovation, and market. Second, two Delphi rounds with experts from academia, regulatory authorities, and the FinTech sector refined these themes into actionable policy measures that achieved consensus (median importance ≥ 4.0, IQR ≤ 1.0). Third, a validation workshop aligned the proposed measures with Kuwait's Vision 2035 priorities. This process yielded five interventions: Regulatory fast-tracking, Cybersecurity investment fund, Talent development, National coordination body, and SME digital financing platforms, each corresponding to a specific foresight domain and empirically tested in the MCDA framework.

3.3. Scenario Development

To examine foresight strategies under uncertainty, this study developed three plausible scenarios for Kuwait's FinTech environment to 2030. The process followed the structured foresight methodology proposed by [38], which builds scenario logics around key drivers of change and critical contextual uncertainties.

The scenario-building process unfolded in four steps. First, horizon scanning was conducted using Central Bank of Kuwait policy reports, international FinTech outlooks, and academic literature to identify drivers of change in regulation, technology, macroeconomics, energy, and human capital. Second, two critical uncertainties were selected through stakeholder discussions: (i) the adaptability of regulatory frameworks, and (ii) the stability of Kuwait's macro-financial environment. Third, these uncertainties were mapped into a scenario matrix, which generated contrasting pathways. Finally, draft scenario narratives were developed to illustrate implications for FinTech development and governance [39].

The resulting three scenarios reflect alternative macroeconomic, regulatory, and technological trajectories:

- Scenario 1—Optimistic Growth: Effective execution of Vision 2035, stronger regulation, cybersecurity investment, venture capital inflows, and global partnerships.
- Scenario 2—Status Quo Continuation: Slow regulatory progress and uneven infrastructure; adoption grows moderately, led by incumbent banks with limited SME engagement.
- Scenario 3—Crisis and Contraction: Reform stagnation caused by cyberattacks, energy grid strain, or macroeconomic shocks, resulting in weakened investor confidence and declining trust in digital finance.

https://doi.org/10.3390/fintech5010008

Twelve national stakeholders—representing startups, banks, regulators, academia, and investors—participated in scenario construction. A second consultation round validated plausibility, internal consistency, and policy relevance, ensuring scenarios provided a robust foundation for the MCDA evaluation.

3.4. Criteria Identification

Selecting evaluation criteria is a critical step in MCDA, as it determines how foresight strategies are assessed and compared. In line with foresight and decision-support literature, this study defines evaluation criteria as the dimensions that capture essential conditions for FinTech governance under uncertainty (Tables 1 and 2).

Table 1. Final foresight evaluation criteria by domain.

Domain	Code	Criterion
Regulatory Readiness	R1	Regulatory Clarity
	R2	Open Banking Implementation
Infrastructure	I1	Cybersecurity Framework Strength
	I2	Energy Infrastructure Resilience
Innovation Ecosystem	E1	Availability of Skilled FinTech Talent
	E2	National Digital Literacy
Market Readiness	M1	SME Access to FinTech Financing
	M2	Domestic and Foreign Investment Attractiveness

Table 2. Definitions of evaluation criteria.

Criterion	Definition
Regulatory Clarity	Transparency and predictability of financial regulations and compliance processes.
Open Banking Implementation	Extent of adoption and enforcement of open banking standards.
Cybersecurity Framework Strength	Maturity of digital security measures protecting financial infrastructure.
Energy Infrastructure Resilience	Stability and reliability of energy supply for digital financial services.
Skilled FinTech Talent	Availability of professionals with technical and financial expertise.
National Digital Literacy	Population-level awareness and ability to use digital financial services.
SME Access to FinTech Financing	Accessibility of alternative financing tools for small and medium enterprises.
Investment Attractiveness	Capacity to attract domestic and foreign capital into FinTech ventures.

A two-round Delphi method was applied to ensure both rigor and consensus. Delphi is widely recognized in foresight research for refining expert knowledge and building convergence around uncertain or contested issues. The panel included 20 experts from Kuwait's FinTech ecosystem—policymakers, bankers, startup founders, cybersecurity professionals, and academics. This sample size aligns with prior Delphi studies, where 15–25 experts are considered adequate for diverse representation while allowing iterative feedback [40].

In Round 1, participants proposed key factors influencing FinTech foresight success. These inputs were clustered into four domains: regulatory readiness, infrastructure resilience, innovation ecosystem, and market readiness. In Round 2, experts rated each item on a 5-point Likert scale (1 = not important; 5 = extremely important). Criteria with a median score $\geq$4.0 and interquartile range $\leq$1.0 were retained, resulting in eight final evaluation criteria [41,42]

These criteria, validated through the Delphi process, form the foundation for the AHP weighting and TOPSIS ranking, ensuring structured prioritization of foresight interventions across scenarios.

https://doi.org/10.3390/fintech501000

3.5. Expert Recruitment and Panel Composition

To enhance transparency and validity, the recruitment, composition, and participation of experts in the Delphi, AHP, and TOPSIS stages are described in greater detail below.

Experts were recruited through a purposive sampling strategy designed to capture diverse perspectives from across Kuwait's FinTech ecosystem. Invitations were extended through three channels:

1. professional and academic networks linked to the Central Bank of Kuwait, Kuwait University, and regional FinTech associations;
2. nominations by national regulators and incubator programs;
3. open calls circulated via LinkedIn and professional mailing lists.

To ensure independence and reduce group conformity, all data collection rounds were conducted individually and anonymously, with no group deliberations. Participation was voluntary, and informed consent was obtained under approved ethical protocols (ZUJ-REC-2025-014).

The final Delphi panel comprised 20 experts, of whom 18 participated in the AHP and TOPSIS evaluations. Panelists were selected for demonstrated expertise in financial regulation, technology, entrepreneurship, or academia. The group represents a balanced mix of institutional backgrounds (Table 3).

Table 3. Composition of expert panel.

Stakeholder Group	Number of Experts	% of Total	Typical Roles/Affiliations
Regulators & Policy Officials	7	35%	Central Bank of Kuwait, Capital Markets Authority
Financial Institutions (Banks & Investment Firms)	4	20%	Digital banking, payments, investment services
FinTech Entrepreneurs & Startups	4	20%	SME financing, cybersecurity, blockchain firms
Academics & Researchers	3	15%	Universities and think tanks specializing in finance and technology
Consultants & Independent Experts	2	10%	Legal, risk, and digital strategy consultants
Total	20	100%	—

Potential conflicts of interest were managed by excluding respondents directly affiliated with policy initiatives evaluated in the study (e.g., regulatory sandbox management). To minimize bias, responses were anonymized before aggregation.

3.6. Subgroup Comparison and Robustness

To evaluate representativeness and potential bias, subgroup analyses were conducted. Rankings generated by regulators, entrepreneurs, and academics were compared using Spearman rank correlation tests. While absolute scores differed slightly—for example, regulators emphasized cybersecurity and governance, while entrepreneurs prioritized SME financing—the top three strategies were consistent across groups, with correlations above 0.85. This convergence supports the robustness of the findings while acknowledging contextual variation in expert perspectives.

3.7. Weighting and Method

To determine the relative importance of the foresight criteria identified in Section 3.3, this study applied the Analytic Hierarchy Process (AHP). AHP is widely recognized for expert-based decision-making, as it accommodates both qualitative judgments and quantitative measures while ensuring logical consistency.

Using Saaty's 9-point scale, the 20 Delphi panel experts conducted pairwise comparisons of the eight criteria under conditions of uncertainty. Each expert response generated a comparison matrix, for which a Consistency Ratio (CR) was calculated. Matrices with CR

https://doi.org/10.3390/fintech5010008

values greater than 0.10 were excluded to maintain reliability. Normalized weights from consistent matrices were aggregated using the geometric mean to form the final criteria weight vector [43,44].

Table 4 presents the resulting weights, which reflect strong emphasis on regulatory clarity (0.160), cybersecurity (0.145), and investment attractiveness (0.145), with digital literacy and energy resilience receiving lower relative weights.

Table 4. Final weights of foresight criteria (AHP results).

Code	Criterion	Weight
R1	Regulatory Clarity	0.160
R2	Open Banking Implementation	0.125
I1	Cybersecurity Framework Strength	0.145
I2	Energy Infrastructure Resilience	0.090
E1	Skilled FinTech Talent	0.120
E2	National Digital Literacy	0.080
M1	SME Access to Financing	0.135
M2	Investment Attractiveness	0.145

These weights were then incorporated into the TOPSIS model, where each foresight intervention was evaluated under the three scenarios developed in Section 3.2. TOPSIS allowed ranking by proximity to an "ideal" intervention, while sensitivity analysis tested robustness to weight variation. This integration ensured a transparent, replicable process linking foresight theory with structured decision support.

3.8. Alternative Evaluation Using TOPSIS

Following the AHP weighting of foresight criteria, this study applied the Technique for Order Preference by Similarity to Ideal Solution (TOPSIS) to evaluate and prioritize foresight interventions under the three scenarios developed in Section 3.2. TOPSIS is widely used in MCDA as it identifies the best alternative by measuring each option's distance from an "ideal" and "anti-ideal" solution, based on weighted performance scores [45].

Through expert consensus and stakeholder validation, five strategic foresight interventions were identified as most relevant for Kuwait's FinTech ecosystem: (1) regulatory fast-tracking, (2) talent development programs, (3) cybersecurity investment fund, (4) national coordination body, and (5) SME-focused financing platforms. Each intervention was rated against the eight criteria (Table 1) across all three scenarios, using a scale from 1 (very low impact) to 9 (very high impact). Ratings were provided by 18 experts after scenario-specific briefings to ensure contextual relevance.

The TOPSIS procedure involved six steps: (i) constructing the decision matrix, (ii) normalizing values to remove unit differences, (iii) applying AHP-derived weights, (iv) identifying ideal and anti-ideal solutions, (v) calculating Euclidean distances from these reference points, and (vi) computing relative closeness coefficients for ranking.

Applying TOPSIS within each scenario generated differentiated rankings, highlighting which strategies remained robust and which shifted depending on external conditions. Sensitivity analysis, conducted by varying criteria weights within $\pm 10\%$, confirmed the stability of the main results. This scenario-based use of TOPSIS provided a transparent and adaptive prioritization framework, strengthening the methodological rigor of the study and ensuring practical relevance for policymakers.

3.9. Sensitivity and Robustness Checks

To guarantee the robustness and the reliability of the rankings of the foresight strategy derived by the TOPSIS method, various sensitivity analyses were applied. They assessed

https://doi.org/10.3390/fintech5010008

the result's stability in conditions of variable uncertainty, indicative of the uncertainty of the strategic foresight as well as of the experts' judgment [46].

3.9.1. Variation in Scenario Weighting

Although each scenario was treated with equal weight in the initial analysis, additional simulations were performed to evaluate how changes in scenario likelihood would affect strategy rankings. Three weight distributions were tested:

- Scenario-Dominant Model: 70% weight to one scenario, 15% to the others.
- Risk-Averse Model: Higher weight assigned to Scenario 3 (Crisis and Contraction).
- Growth-Optimistic Model: Higher weight assigned to Scenario 1 (Optimistic Growth).

In all cases, the top-ranked foresight intervention remained within the top two positions, confirming the resilience of the strategic priority set.

3.9.2. Criteria Weight Perturbation

To examine the influence of expert-derived criteria weights, the AHP weights were systematically perturbed ±10% and ±20%. The TOPSIS rankings were recalculated for each case. The Spearman rank correlation coefficients between the original and perturbed rankings ranged from 0.87 to 0.95, indicating high stability [47].

3.9.3. Stakeholder Subgroup Comparison

Subgroup analysis was conducted by comparing rankings generated from three stakeholder groups: regulators, entrepreneurs, and academics. While some variation in individual scores existed, the overall ranking of top interventions showed convergence across groups, further supporting the validity and consensus of the results.

These sensitivity checks demonstrate that the scenario-based MCDA model is not only methodologically sound but also resilient to uncertainties in assumptions and inputs, making it a credible tool for strategic foresight in Kuwait's evolving FinTech sector.

3.10. Ethical Considerations

This study received ethical approval from Al-Zaytoonah University of Jordan (Ref. No.: ZUJ-REC-2025-014). All participants were provided with an information sheet and signed informed consent prior to taking part in the Delphi, AHP, or TOPSIS stages. Participation was voluntary, with the right to withdraw at any point.

To ensure confidentiality, no identifying data were recorded or disclosed. All responses were securely stored and used solely for academic purposes. No incentives were offered. The study involved minimal risk and adhered to institutional and international ethical guidelines for expert-based research.

4. Findings

4.1. Overview of Evaluation Matrix and Data Quality

The evaluation matrix was constructed from expert judgments provided by 18 panelists, who assessed five foresight strategies against the eight AHP-weighted criteria under three scenarios: Optimistic Growth, Status Quo, and Crisis. Each strategy was rated on a 9-point scale, and the aggregated values were processed through the TOPSIS procedure to determine each strategy's relative closeness to the ideal solution [48].

To ensure methodological rigor, only AHP responses with a consistency ratio (CR) ≤ 0.10 were retained. Missing values (<2%) were corrected using within-group mean substitution. Experts received standardized scenario briefings and instructions to reduce interpretation bias. Robustness checks confirmed that rankings were stable across replications, enhancing confidence in the data's reliability.

https://doi.org/10.3390/fintech5010008

In addition to the mean closeness scores, dispersion statistics were calculated to capture the degree of consensus among experts. Across all scenarios, the standard deviation of expert ratings for each strategy ranged between 0.58 and 0.91 (on a 1–9 scale), indicating moderate variation in perceived impact. The average coefficient of variation was approximately 12%, suggesting that while general agreement existed on the ranking order, some heterogeneity remained regarding the intensity of each intervention's importance. Notably, the highest disagreement occurred for "Talent Development" in the Crisis scenario (SD = 0.91), reflecting differing views on its relevance under economic stress. Conversely, "Cybersecurity Investment Fund" in the same scenario showed the lowest dispersion (SD = 0.58), implying strong expert consensus that cybersecurity dominates under adverse conditions. Including these dispersion measures strengthens confidence in the reliability of the aggregated rankings while highlighting areas where policy preferences diverge.

Table 5 and Figure 2 present the scenario-based closeness scores. The results indicate clear scenario-dependent priorities: SME Digital Financing Platforms scored highest under Optimistic Growth and Status Quo, emphasizing inclusion and access, while the Cybersecurity Investment Fund dominated in Crisis, reflecting resilience needs. Regulatory Fast-Tracking maintained steady mid-level importance across all contexts, highlighting its consistent though secondary role in FinTech foresight.

Table 5. Scenario-based TOPSIS closeness scores for strategic interventions.

Strategy	Optimistic Growth	Status Quo	Crisis and Contraction
Regulatory Fast-Tracking	0.660	0.648	0.556
Talent Development Programs	0.710	0.632	0.481
Cybersecurity Investment Fund	0.674	0.594	0.712
FinTech Coordination Body	0.652	0.617	0.565
SME Digital Financing Platforms	0.723	0.654	0.603

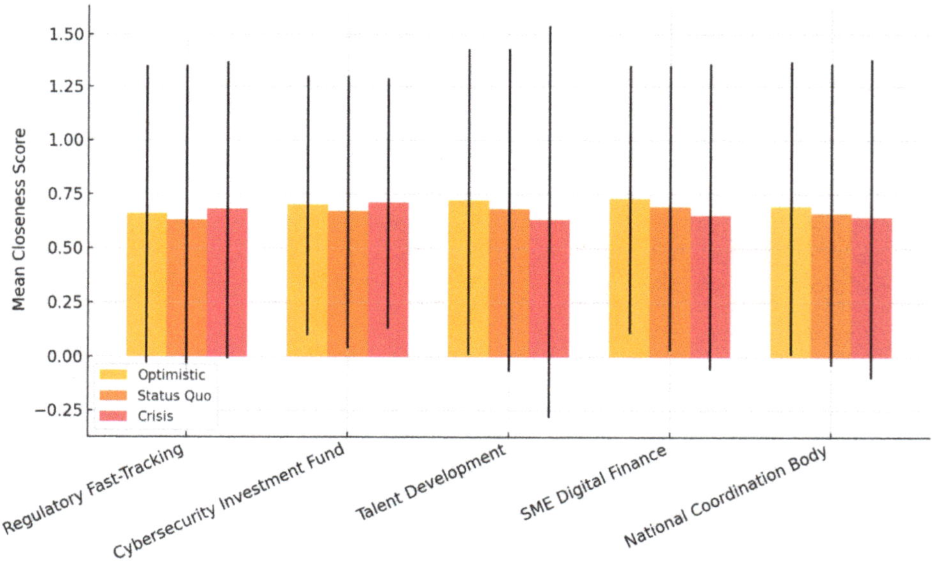

Figure 2. Cross-scenario comparison of foresight strategy rankings.

This radar graph shows the relative effectiveness of five foresight strategies against three future scenarios. Talent growth and SME financing platforms appear as highest priority in the Optimistic Growth scenario, indicative of concern for inclusion and capacity

https://doi.org/10.3390/fintech501000

building. Conversely, in the Crisis scenario, cybersecurity investment is the most important intervention, showing the requirement for resilience. Regulatory fast-tracking shows steady priority in all scenarios, showing its essential function in facilitating FinTech growth in the face of different conditions.

4.2. Scenario 1—Optimistic Growth

Under the Optimistic Growth scenario, Kuwait's FinTech sector benefits from sustained economic expansion, effective regulatory reforms, and infrastructure investments consistent with Vision 2035. In this favorable environment, foresight priorities shift toward capacity building and ecosystem expansion rather than short-term resilience.

The TOPSIS results (Table 6) show that SME Digital Financing Platforms ranked highest (0.723), followed closely by Talent Development Programs (0.710). Experts emphasized that SME platforms would expand credit access, increase adoption among underserved groups, and foster diversification beyond oil. Similarly, talent development was viewed as critical for meeting labor market needs and sustaining FinTech-driven innovation.

Table 6. TOPSIS scores for scenario 1—optimistic growth.

Strategy	Closeness Score
SME Digital Financing Platforms	0.723
Talent Development Programs	0.710
Cybersecurity Investment Fund	0.674
Regulatory Fast-Tracking	0.660
FinTech Coordination Body	0.652

The Cybersecurity Investment Fund (0.674) ranked third, indicating that even in stability, digital trust remains an enabling condition. Regulatory Fast-Tracking (0.660) and the FinTech Coordination Body (0.652) were moderately prioritized, reflecting their supportive role in creating a conducive environment, though not seen as immediate growth levers.

These findings partially support H1 (regulatory clarity as a consistent enabler), strongly support H3 (talent and inclusion strategies dominate in stable contexts), and provisionally support H4 (scenario-specific ranking shifts). They highlight the foresight principle that in optimistic futures, long-term enablers—financial inclusion and skills—carry the greatest strategic weight [49].

The dominance of SME Digital Financing Platforms and Talent Development Programs under optimistic conditions aligns with adaptive foresight theory, emphasizing capacity building and inclusion when environmental uncertainty is low. These findings reflect the absorptive-capacity principle in anticipatory governance, where institutions leverage stability to invest in long-term innovation and human capital rather than short-term resilience.

4.3. Scenario 2—Status Quo Continuation

The Status Quo scenario assumes moderate FinTech progress, marked by incremental regulatory reforms, uneven infrastructure, and limited cross-sector coordination. Without major shocks or breakthroughs, foresight priorities emphasize sustaining momentum while addressing inefficiencies.

The TOPSIS results (Table 7) place SME Digital Financing Platforms highest (0.654), reaffirming financial inclusion as a core driver of ecosystem stability. Experts emphasized that supporting SMEs in this context would expand usage of digital services while compensating for limited innovation from larger incumbents.

https://doi.org/10.3390/fintech5010008

Table 7. TOPSIS scores for scenario 2—status quo continuation.

Strategy	Closeness Score
SME Digital Financing Platforms	0.654
Regulatory Fast-Tracking	0.648
Talent Development Programs	0.632
FinTech Coordination Body	0.617
Cybersecurity Investment Fund	0.594

Regulatory Fast-Tracking (0.648) ranked second, reflecting concerns about bureaucratic delays and fragmented implementation of open banking and data governance. Its elevated position compared to the optimistic scenario underscores the perceived need to accelerate reforms when growth is modest.

Talent Development Programs (0.632) remained important but dropped slightly, suggesting that resource limitations under steady conditions constrain investment in long-term skills. The FinTech Coordination Body (0.617) and Cybersecurity Investment Fund (0.594) ranked lowest, indicating that structural resilience and institutional alignment are not viewed as urgent in stable environments.

These findings support H1 (regulatory clarity remains a consistent enabler), confirm H3 (talent and SME strategies are prioritized under stable conditions), and reinforce H4, as the ranking differs from Scenario 1, reflecting scenario-dependent shifts.

The high ranking of Regulatory Fast-Tracking and sustained importance of SME Digital Financing Platforms illustrate anticipatory governance in incremental environments. Here, foresight acts as a mechanism for maintaining adaptability within policy inertia. The shift in priority from capacity-building to procedural efficiency supports the adaptive foresight notion that moderate uncertainty requires institutional agility and regulatory coherence to sustain progress

4.4. Scenario 3—Crisis and Contraction

The Crisis and Contraction scenario envisions a future where Kuwait's FinTech sector faces structural disruptions, including cyberattacks, energy shortages, regulatory stagnation, or geopolitical shocks. In such conditions, foresight priorities shift from ecosystem expansion to resilience and systemic trust.

The TOPSIS results (Table 8) show the Cybersecurity Investment Fund as the highest-ranked strategy (0.712). Experts stressed that government-backed or hybrid investment in cybersecurity is indispensable for safeguarding digital platforms and sustaining confidence when financial and energy risks converge.

Table 8. TOPSIS scores for scenario 3—crisis and contraction.

Strategy	Closeness Score
Cybersecurity Investment Fund	0.712
SME Digital Financing Platforms	0.603
FinTech Coordination Body	0.565
Regulatory Fast-Tracking	0.556
Talent Development Programs	0.481

The second-ranked strategy, SME Digital Financing Platforms (0.603), indicates that inclusion remains important even under stress, with SMEs viewed as vulnerable actors requiring targeted support to maintain business continuity. The FinTech Coordination Body (0.565) ranked third, suggesting that institutional alignment gains some importance during instability, though not as urgently as direct resilience measures.

https://doi.org/10.3390/fintech5010008

By contrast, Regulatory Fast-Tracking (0.556) and Talent Development Programs (0.481) dropped to the bottom, reflecting that longer-term reforms and capacity-building are deprioritized when short-term stabilization takes precedence [50].

These findings partially support H1 (regulation less critical under crisis), strongly support H2 (infrastructure resilience, especially cybersecurity, becomes dominant), align with H3 (talent and inclusion lose priority in adverse futures), and confirm H4, as the ranking diverges sharply from Scenarios 1 and 2.

The prominence of the Cybersecurity Investment Fund during crisis scenarios embodies the resilience logic central to foresight and risk governance frameworks. When systemic shocks dominate, foresight transitions from growth-enabling functions to trust preservation and systemic stability. This supports theoretical propositions that adaptive foresight prioritizes immediate resilience over long-term expansion under adverse futures

4.5. Cross-Scenario Comparison of Strategy Rankings

A cross-scenario comparison reveals distinct shifts in strategic priorities depending on contextual assumptions, underscoring the value of a scenario-based MCDA approach.

Table 8 summarizes the rank order of strategies across the three scenarios. SME Digital Financing Platforms ranked first in both Optimistic Growth and Status Quo, and second in Crisis, indicating strong robustness as a consistently important intervention. Talent Development Programs, by contrast, fell from second under growth to last in crisis, illustrating high sensitivity to environmental stability. The Cybersecurity Investment Fund rose from third in growth to first in crisis, confirming that resilience-oriented measures become decisive under adverse conditions.

Regulatory Fast-Tracking maintained moderate but steady importance, ranking between second and fourth, suggesting it is widely valued as an enabling condition though not perceived as transformative. The FinTech Coordination Body consistently occupied middle-to-lower positions, implying limited independent impact but supporting roles in governance alignment.

These patterns provide strong evidence for H4, as rankings vary significantly across scenarios. They also support H1 (regulation remains important but not dominant), H2 (infrastructure resilience dominates in crisis), and H3 (talent and inclusion are prioritized in favorable conditions).

Overall, the analysis highlights that while some strategies demonstrate robustness across futures (e.g., SME financing), others are highly contingent on scenario dynamics (e.g., talent vs. cybersecurity), reinforcing foresight's role in adaptive policymaking (Table 9).

Table 9. Rank order of strategies across scenarios.

Strategy	Optimistic Growth	Status Quo	Crisis and Contraction
SME Digital Financing Platforms	1	1	2
Talent Development Programs	2	3	5
Cybersecurity Investment Fund	3	5	1
Regulatory Fast-Tracking	4	2	4
FinTech Coordination Body	5	4	3

4.6. Sensitivity Analysis Results

To confirm the robustness of the scenario-based MCDA findings, multiple sensitivity tests were conducted. These analyses examined whether strategy rankings would shift under different assumptions regarding scenario weights, criteria weights, and stakeholder perspectives.

https://doi.org/10.3390/fintech5010008

4.6.1. Scenario Weight Perturbation

Alternative weighting schemes were applied to reflect policy emphasis on growth or risk aversion. For example, a growth-biased model (60% Optimistic, 20% Status Quo, 20% Crisis) and a risk-averse model (20% Optimistic, 20% Status Quo, 60% Crisis) were tested. Across all schemes, the top-ranked strategies shifted by at most one position. This stability indicates that recommendations remain valid even when policymakers prioritize particular futures.

4.6.2. Criteria Weight Perturbation

Each AHP-derived criterion weight was perturbed by ±10% and ±20%, with recalculated rankings compared to the baseline. Spearman rank correlations ranged from 0.87 to 0.96, confirming a strong preservation of rank order. This suggests that no single criterion dominates outcomes, reducing the risk of bias from expert weighting.

4.6.3. Stakeholder Subgroup Analysis

When analyzed separately, regulators, entrepreneurs, and academics showed minor variations in absolute scores—for instance, entrepreneurs ranked SME financing slightly higher, while regulators emphasized cybersecurity. However, the top three strategies remained consistent across groups, reinforcing the generalizability of the results.

Overall, the sensitivity tests demonstrate that strategy rankings are not fragile to model assumptions or subgroup perspectives. This reliability enhances confidence in the MCDA framework, ensuring that the identified priorities—such as SME financing in stable conditions and cybersecurity in crises—can inform robust and adaptive foresight planning for Kuwait's FinTech ecosystem.

5. Discussion

5.1. Theoretical Contributions

This study applied a scenario-based MCDA model to evaluate foresight priorities in Kuwait's FinTech sector, extending foresight theory into an underexplored policy domain. The findings support prior calls for anticipatory governance in digital finance, especially in emerging economies where foresight is often reactive or absent [4,51]. Consistent with evidence from advanced ecosystems such as Singapore and the UK, the study demonstrates that structured foresight tools enable policymakers to anticipate shifts in strategic priorities under different conditions [26].

By combining AHP and TOPSIS with scenario analysis, the research also addresses a methodological gap in the application of MCDA to FinTech governance [28,52]. The robustness checks conducted confirm that the framework is reliable, offering a replicable approach for integrating foresight into digital financial policy planning.

5.2. Scenario-Specific Insights

The results reveal how foresight strategies vary with contextual assumptions, enriching debates in foresight literature that emphasize adaptive, rather than fixed, planning [3,38]. The mid-to-high ranking of regulatory fast-tracking across scenarios underscores its foundational importance for FinTech ecosystems, consistent with studies highlighting regulatory clarity as a precondition for innovation [27]. However, its reduced priority during crisis scenarios suggests that regulatory reform alone cannot safeguard systemic stability.

The consistent prioritization of SME digital financing platforms aligns with calls for inclusion-led FinTech growth [2,49]. Even in contraction scenarios, experts regarded SME financing as a resilience strategy, positioning inclusion as both a growth enabler and a stabilizer. Conversely, the decline of talent development in crises reflects a strategic shift

https://doi.org/10.3390/fintech501000

from long-term capacity-building to immediate stabilization, adding nuance to literature that often frames human capital development as a universal priority [18]. The sharp rise of cybersecurity investment in crisis scenarios highlights the context-dependent nature of resilience strategies, reinforcing foresight theory's focus on adaptive priorities.

5.3. Policy Relevance and Adaptive Governance

Regionally, the findings highlight the risks of Kuwait's reactive policymaking compared to foresight-driven approaches in the UAE and Bahrain, where national FinTech strategies embed structured foresight mechanisms. Unlike those peers, Kuwait's regulatory fragmentation and lack of anticipatory frameworks hinder long-term digital finance resilience. By showing that strategic priorities shift under growth, stability, and crisis scenarios, this study provides policymakers with a pathway to move beyond short-term compliance. The model aligns with Kuwait Vision 2035 by offering a structured, adaptive framework to harmonize foresight, regulation, and innovation in national FinTech governance.

5.4. Theoretical Extension and Adaptive Orientation

This study extends foresight theory by showing how scenario-based MCDA operationalizes adaptive foresight in FinTech governance. Unlike predictive models focused on single outcomes, the AHP–TOPSIS integration quantifies how policy priorities shift across alternative futures, demonstrating foresight as a continuous learning and adjustment process. This approach transforms foresight from qualitative anticipation to a structured analytical method, strengthening its explanatory and practical value in uncertain policy environments.

5.5. Adaptive vs. Predictive Foresight Models

The findings validate an adaptive foresight model. Variations in strategy rankings across growth, stability, and crisis contexts confirm that FinTech governance requires flexibility rather than prediction. Adaptive foresight views uncertainty as a resource for institutional learning—encouraging iterative evaluation and recalibration instead of fixed planning.

5.6. Economic Interpretation of Scenario-Based Rankings

The scenario-based MCDA results indicate economically meaningful trade-offs rather than minor preference shifts. The TOPSIS closeness coefficient (C_i) is a dimensionless, bounded (0–1) index that summarizes each strategy's relative proximity to the ideal alternative in the weighted criteria space, rather than a direct percentage change in any single outcome. To convey magnitude, we interpret score gaps on a proportional basis, $(\Delta C / C_{\text{ref}}) \times 100$, where C_{ref} is a representative benchmark level (Table 5: mean ≈ 0.632; range 0.481–0.723). Under this scaling, $\Delta C = 0.05$ corresponds to ~7.9% of the mean (0.05/0.632) and ~6.9–10.4% across the observed range, hence the description of a 0.05 difference as roughly a 5–10% variation in the composite performance index implied by the MCDA criteria [8,10]. Under optimistic scenarios, higher rankings for SME digital finance and talent development reflect greater potential for long-term growth and inclusion, consistent with [9] argument that innovation-driven intermediation enhances productivity. In contrast, during crisis scenarios, the prominence of cybersecurity and regulatory clarity suggests stronger short-term welfare effects through the preservation of trust and risk containment [11].

Overall, these results imply that FinTech governance priorities are context-dependent: inclusion and capability strategies yield higher marginal returns in stability, while resilience-oriented measures mitigate losses in volatility. This reinforces the foresight principle

https://doi.org/10.3390/fintech5010008

that effective policy design must balance capacity building and crisis resilience, aligning adaptive governance with established financial intermediation dynamics.

6. Implications

6.1. Practical Implications

The results offer targeted guidance for policymakers, regulators, and industry stakeholders in Kuwait's FinTech ecosystem. The repeated top ranking of SME digital financing platforms in optimistic and status quo scenarios indicates that inclusion-oriented strategies are both growth enablers and stabilizers in favorable conditions. This suggests that long-term policy planning should institutionalize SME-focused digital platforms to ensure wider access to credit and support diversification beyond large financial institutions.

Regulatory fast-tracking emerged as moderately important across all three scenarios. Its consistent presence in the middle-to-high range confirms its role as a structural enabler, but its decline in crisis conditions underscores that regulation alone cannot address systemic risks. This highlights the need to pair regulatory reforms with complementary resilience strategies, such as investments in infrastructure and security, to maintain ecosystem stability.

Cybersecurity investment, by contrast, shifted from a secondary concern in stable futures to the highest-ranked priority during crises. This demonstrates that digital trust becomes the defining factor when the ecosystem is under pressure. Practical implications include the establishment of cybersecurity investment funds, stronger technical standards, and incentives for startups to adopt robust security frameworks. Proactively embedding resilience into digital finance policy will ensure that shocks—whether technological, economic, or geopolitical—do not derail long-term FinTech ambitions.

Taken together, these findings show that adaptive policymaking is essential. Strategies that prioritize inclusion and capacity-building in growth phases must be balanced with resilience measures that dominate in crises. Policymakers in Kuwait can use this insight to align Vision 2035 goals with the dynamic realities of digital transformation.

6.2. Research Implications

For academic research, the study demonstrates the utility of integrating scenario-based foresight with multi-criteria evaluation techniques. By showing how strategic priorities shift under varying assumptions, it highlights that foresight interventions cannot be assessed in static contexts. This methodological approach provides a template for extending foresight studies beyond descriptive analysis into structured, evidence-based evaluation.

The framework also opens avenues for comparative studies. Applying the model to other Gulf states would reveal whether the patterns identified in Kuwait—such as the dominance of inclusion strategies in stable conditions and cybersecurity in crises—are regionally consistent or context-specific. Expanding the expert base and incorporating mixed methods could further validate the findings and provide richer insights into stakeholder perspectives. Finally, future research could examine how foresight-driven policy tools interact with adoption behavior, cross-border regulation, and emerging technologies, offering a broader theoretical contribution to digital governance studies.

7. Conclusions

This study applied a scenario-based Multi-Criteria Decision Analysis (MCDA) framework to evaluate strategic foresight interventions for Kuwait's FinTech ecosystem. By integrating AHP and TOPSIS with structured scenario planning, the research demonstrated how policy priorities shift depending on whether the future is characterized by optimistic

https://doi.org/10.3390/fintech5010008

growth, status quo continuation, or crisis and contraction. The results show that SME digital financing platforms and talent development dominate in favorable futures, while cybersecurity investment becomes the leading priority during crises. Regulatory fast-tracking remained moderately important across all scenarios, confirming its role as a foundational enabler rather than a transformative driver.

The findings underline that foresight strategies are highly context-dependent. Interventions cannot be assumed to hold equal relevance across all futures; instead, their importance changes with underlying assumptions about stability, growth, and disruption. This highlights the value of adaptive policymaking and provides a replicable model for aligning FinTech strategies with uncertain environments. While applied to Kuwait, the framework can be adapted to other emerging economies facing similar challenges in digital transformation.

At the same time, the study is not without limitations. The reliance on a relatively small expert panel, while sufficient for exploratory foresight, may restrict the diversity of perspectives included. Expanding stakeholder participation in future studies—particularly by incorporating consumers and international investors—could enhance robustness. The analysis also drew on qualitative expert judgments rather than quantitative performance data, and further research could combine mixed-method approaches to validate and extend the findings. Finally, the focus on Kuwait constrains generalizability, and applying the framework to other Gulf or emerging economies would provide valuable comparative insights.

Future research should also examine how foresight-driven strategies interact with emerging developments such as digital assets, cross-border regulation, and AI-enabled financial services. Exploring these dynamics would advance understanding of how adaptive governance models can support resilience and innovation in fast-evolving digital ecosystems.

While this study applies the foresight-based MCDA framework to Kuwait's FinTech ecosystem, its design is intentionally hybrid—combining context-specific insights with generalizable methodological elements. The framework reflects Kuwait's institutional priorities, such as Vision 2035, the regulatory sandbox, and the country's energy and human-capital conditions. These contextual anchors enhance policy relevance but also limit direct transferability to economies with different institutional capacities or regulatory maturity.

Nonetheless, the core structure of the framework—spanning regulation, infrastructure, innovation, and market readiness—is adaptable to other emerging economies seeking to align FinTech development with resilience and inclusion goals. Future research could extend the model through cross-country comparisons or larger expert panels to test its robustness under varying institutional settings. By treating Kuwait as a case study of anticipatory governance in FinTech, the paper contributes both a national illustration and a transferable analytical method for managing digital transformation under uncertainty.

Author Contributions: Conceptualization, S.K., Z.A., A.M. and L.T.K.; methodology, A.M. and L.T.K.; formal analysis, A.M. and L.T.K.; investigation, S.K. and Z.A.; data curation, A.M.; writing—original draft preparation, A.M. and L.T.K.; writing—review and editing, S.K., Z.A., A.M. and L.T.K.; visualization, A.M.; supervision, S.K.; project administration, S.K. All authors have read and agreed to the published version of the manuscript.

Funding: This research received no external funding.

Institutional Review Board Statement: The study was conducted in accordance with the Declaration of Helsinki and approved by the Research Ethics Committee (REC), Al-Zaytoonah University of Jordan (Protocol Code: ZUJ-REC-2025-031; Date of Approval: 15 March 2025).

Informed Consent Statement: Informed consent was obtained from all subjects involved in the study.

https://doi.org/10.3390/fintech5010008

Data Availability Statement: The data supporting the findings of this study are available from the corresponding author upon reasonable request.

Conflicts of Interest: The authors declare no conflicts of interest.

References

1. Morshed, A. Navigating Tradition and Modernity: Digital Accounting and Financial Integration in Family-Owned Enterprises i the Arab Gulf. *Sustain. Futur.* **2025**, *9*, 100680. [CrossRef]
2. Musleh Alsartawi, A. The Diffusion of Financial Technology-Enabled Innovation in GCC-Listed Banks and Its Relationship wit Profitability and Market Value. *J. Financ. Report. Account.* **2024**. [CrossRef]
3. Lytras, M.D.; Alkhaldi, A.; Malik, S.; Serban, A.C. Artificial Intelligence for Smart City Vision 2040 in Gulf Region. In *Th Emerald Handbook of Smart Cities in the Gulf Region: Innovation, Development, Transformation, and Prosperity for Vision 2040*; Emeral Publishing Limited: Leeds, UK, 2024; pp. 515–525.
4. Alsmadi, A.A.; Al-Okaily, M. Future Front of Finance: The Role of FinTech Strategies, Competitiveness Dynamics and Sustainab Solutions. *Compet. Rev. Int. Bus. J.* **2025**. [CrossRef]
5. Huang, Y. Fintech as a Catalyst for Sustainable Development: A Bibliographic Review of Drivers, Technologies, Econometric and Regional Insights. *J. Account. Lit.* **2025**. [CrossRef]
6. Naji, K.K.; Gunduz, M.; Alhenzab, F.; Al-Hababi, H.; Al-Qahtani, A. Assessing the Digital Transformation Readiness of th Construction Industry Utilizing the Delphi Method. *Buildings* **2024**, *14*, 601. [CrossRef]
7. Shamsuddin, J. Fintech Development: International Experiences and Lessons for Malaysia. *Public Adm. Law Rev.* **2025**, *2*, 4–1 [CrossRef]
8. Philippon, T. *The Fintech Opportunity*; National Bureau of Economic Research: Cambridge, MA, USA, 2016.
9. Thakor, A.V. Fintech and Banking: What Do We Know? *J. Financ. Intermediation* **2020**, *41*, 100833. [CrossRef]
10. Ozili, P.K. Impact of Digital Finance on Financial Inclusion and Stability. *Borsa Istanb. Rev.* **2018**, *18*, 329–340. [CrossRef]
11. Mugerman, Y.; Hecht, Y.; Wiener, Z. On the Failure of Mutual Fund Industry Regulation. *Emerg. Mark. Rev.* **2019**, *38*, 51–7 [CrossRef]
12. Rijal, P. Fintech Catalyst in the Evolution of Credit Markets. In *The Palgrave Handbook of Fintech in Africa and Middle East: Connectin the Dots of a Rapidly Emerging Ecosystem*; Palgrave Macmillan: Singapore, 2025; pp. 29–51.
13. Hesami, S. Navigating the AI-Driven Transformation of Personal Finance: Opportunities, Challenges, and Ethical Imperative *Strategy Leadersh.* **2025**. [CrossRef]
14. Hidayat-ur-Rehman, I.; Alam, M.N.; Alsolamy, M.; Alharbi, S.H.H.; AlAnazi, T.M.B.; Bhuiyan, A.B. Examining Investor Interactio with Digital Robo-Advisory Systems: Green Value and Interface Quality in a Socio-Technical Context. *Systems* **2025**, *13*, 78 [CrossRef]
15. Morshed, A.; Khrais, L.T. Cybersecurity in Digital Accounting Systems: Challenges and Solutions in the Arab Gulf Region. *J. Ris Financ. Manag.* **2025**, *18*, 41. [CrossRef]
16. Jennische, U.; Sörbom, A. Governing Anticipation: UNESCO Making Humankind Futures Literate. *J. Organ. Ethnog* **2023**, *12*, 105–119. [CrossRef]
17. Mustafa, J.A. Integrating Financial Literacy, Regulatory Technology, and Decentralized Finance: A New Paradigm in Fintec Evolution. *Investig. Manag. Financ. Innov.* **2024**, *21*, 213–226. [CrossRef]
18. Yaseen, H.; Al-Amarneh, A. Adoption of Artificial Intelligence-Driven Fraud Detection in Banking: The Role of Trust, Trans parency, and Fairness Perception in Financial Institutions in the United Arab Emirates and Qatar. *J. Risk Financ. Manag.* **2025**, *1* 217. [CrossRef]
19. AlBenJasim, S.; Takruri, H.; Al-Zaidi, R.; Dargahi, T. Development of Cybersecurity Framework for FinTech Innovations: Bahrai as a Case Study. *Int. Cybersecur. Law Rev.* **2024**, *5*, 501–532. [CrossRef]
20. Noreen, U. Mapping of FinTech Ecosystem to Sustainable Development Goals (SDGs): Saudi Arabia's Landscape. *Sustainabilit* **2024**, *16*, 9362. [CrossRef]
21. Dasilas, A.; Karanović, G. The Impact of FinTech Firms on Bank Performance: Evidence from the UK. *EuroMed J. Bu* **2025**, *20*, 244–258. [CrossRef]
22. Sreevas, V.T.K.; Hendra, H.; Kulkarni, P.; Pandiya, B.; Sharma, A.K. International Cooperation in Fintech Regulation. In *Examinin Global Regulations During the Rise of Fintech*; IGI Global: Hershey, PA, USA, 2025; pp. 163–186.
23. Al-Daoud, K.I.; Abu-AlSondos, I.A. Robust AI for Financial Fraud Detection in the GCC: A Hybrid Framework for Imbalanc Drift, and Adversarial Threats. *J. Theor. Appl. Electron. Commer. Res.* **2025**, *20*, 121. [CrossRef]
24. Sossa, J.W.Z.; Posada, N.G.; Montoya, L.H.B.; Monsalve, A.M.Z.; Piedrahíta, J.C.P.; Mendoza, G.L.O.; Grisales, L.V.; Cano, L.F.C Foresight Study Using Scenarios and the Delphi Method in the Leather Agroindustrial Chain to 2035-Alignment of Results wit Open Innovation. *J. Open Innov. Technol. Mark. Complex.* **2024**, *10*, 100374. [CrossRef]

https://doi.org/10.3390/fintech501000

25. Pauliukevičienė, G.; Stankevičienė, J.; Binh, D. Strategic Insights: Evaluating SDG 4, SDG 8, SDG 9 and SDG 16 in Driving Sustainable Growth in the Global FinTech Landscape. *Rev. Int. Bus. Strategy* **2025**, *35*, 27–46. [CrossRef]
26. Shaban, O.S.; Omoush, A. AI-Driven Financial Transparency and Corporate Governance: Enhancing Accounting Practices with Evidence from Jordan. *Sustainability* **2025**, *17*, 3818. [CrossRef]
27. Carayannis, E.G.; Papamichail, G.; Zotas, N.; Askounis, D. Corporate Foresight: Navigating Uncertainty in a VUCA World. *J. Knowl. Econ.* **2025**, *16*, 17494–17515. [CrossRef]
28. Digkoglou, P.; Papathanasiou, J. Application of Multiple Criteria Decision Aiding in Environmental Policy-Making Processes. *Int. J. Environ. Sci. Technol.* **2025**, *22*, 6967–6982. [CrossRef]
29. Venčkauskas, A.; Toldinas, J.; Morkevičius, N. Improving Multi-Class Classification for Recognition of the Prioritized Classes Using the Analytic Hierarchy Process. *Appl. Sci.* **2025**, *15*, 7071. [CrossRef]
30. Pahsa, A. Financial Technology Decision Support Systems. *J. Electr. Syst. Inf. Technol.* **2024**, *11*, 5. [CrossRef]
31. Škrabal, J.; Vybíral, M. Regional Potential for Brownfield Regeneration in the Czech Republic Using Multi-Criteria Decision Analysis. *Acta Acad. Karviniensia* **2025**, *25*, 72–88. [CrossRef]
32. Ferla, G.; Mura, B.; Falasco, S.; Caputo, P.; Matarazzo, A. Multi-Criteria Decision Analysis (MCDA) for Sustainability Assessment in Food Sector. A Systematic Literature Review on Methods, Indicators and Tools. *Sci. Total Environ.* **2024**, *946*, 174235. [CrossRef]
33. Morton, A.; Fasolo, B. Behavioural Decision Theory for Multi-Criteria Decision Analysis: A Guided Tour. *J. Oper. Res. Soc.* **2009**, *60*, 268–275. [CrossRef]
34. Campanella, F.; Ferri, L.; Serino, L.; Zampella, A. Driving Sustainability: How FinTech Transforms SDG Performance in SMEs. *J. Glob. Responsib.* **2025**. [CrossRef]
35. Demneh, M.T.; Zackery, A.; Nouraei, A. Using Corporate Foresight to Enhance Strategic Management Practices. *Eur. J. Futur. Res.* **2023**, *11*, 5. [CrossRef]
36. Taqa, S.B.A. The Mediating Role of Remote Communication on the Relationship between Electronic Human Resource Management Practices and Organizational Performance in Iraqi Commercial Banks. *Middle East J. Commun. Stud.* **2025**, *5*, 2.
37. Ram, C.; Montibeller, G. Exploring the Impact of Evaluating Strategic Options in a Scenario-Based Multi-Criteria Framework. *Technol. Forecast. Soc. Change* **2013**, *80*, 657–672. [CrossRef]
38. Wilkinson, A.; Kupers, R.; Mangalagiu, D. How Plausibility-Based Scenario Practices Are Grappling with Complexity to Appreciate and Address 21st Century Challenges. *Technol. Forecast. Soc. Change* **2013**, *80*, 699–710. [CrossRef]
39. Ahmed, A.K.; Nahar, H.M.; Manajrah, M.M.N. Effect of Social Media on Shaping the Agenda of the Communicator in the Jordanian TV Channels. *Middle East J. Commun. Stud.* **2023**, *3*, 3.
40. Talukder, B.; Hipel, K.W. Review and Selection of Multi-Criteria Decision Analysis (MCDA) Technique for Sustainability Assessment. In *Energy Systems Evaluation (Volume 1) Sustainability Assessment*; Springer: Berlin/Heidelberg, Germany, 2021; pp. 145–160.
41. Manzolli, J.A.; Yu, J.; Miranda-Moreno, L. Synthetic Multi-Criteria Decision Analysis (S-MCDA): A New Framework for Participatory Transportation Planning. *Transp. Res. Interdiscip. Perspect.* **2025**, *31*, 101463. [CrossRef]
42. Al-Muntasir, M. The Phenomenon of Information Flow from Traditional and New Media about the Corona Pandemic from the Perspective of Newly Graduated Media Professionals in Yemen. *Middle East J. Commun. Stud.* **2022**, *2*, 1.
43. Kriswardhana, W.; Toaza, B.; Esztergar-Kiss, D.; Duleba, S. Analytic Hierarchy Process in Transportation Decision-Making: A Two-Staged Review on the Themes and Trends of Two Decades. *Expert Syst. Appl.* **2025**, *261*, 125491. [CrossRef]
44. Oreqat, A. The Degree of Satisfaction of Facebook Users about Its Features, Usage Motives and Achieved Gratifications: An Applied Study on Students of the Faculty of Mass Communication at the Middle East University. *Middle East J. Commun. Stud.* **2021**, *1*, 1.
45. Thuannadee, S. Comparison of the Financial Performance of Thai Public Hospitality Firms: Using the Technique for Order of Preference by Similarity to Ideal Solution. *Int. J. Bus. Excell.* **2025**, *36*, 1–15. [CrossRef]
46. Shuwandy, M.L.; Alasad, Q.; Hammood, M.M.; Yass, A.A.; Abdulateef, S.K.; Alsharida, R.A.; Qaddoori, S.L.; Thalij, S.H.; Frman, M.; Kutaibani, A.H. A Robust Behavioral Biometrics Framework for Smartphone Authentication via Hybrid Machine Learning and TOPSIS. *J. Cybersecur. Priv.* **2025**, *5*, 20. [CrossRef]
47. Liu, J.; Bao, X.; Chen, L. Artificial Intelligence in Educational Technology and Transformative Approaches to English Language Using Fuzzy Framework with CRITIC-TOPSIS Method. *Sci. Rep.* **2025**, *15*, 25542. [CrossRef]
48. Kalura, P.; Pandey, A.; Chowdary, V.M.; Dayal, D. A TOPSIS-Based Multicriteria Assessment of Hydrologic Model Calibration Using Satellite-Derived Evapotranspiration and Streamflow Data. *Hydrol. Process.* **2025**, *39*, e70191. [CrossRef]
49. Badra, S.; Jain, S.; Vichore, S. Fintech and Financial Inclusion: Conceptual Foundations and Research Landscape. *Glob. Knowl. Mem. Commun.* **2025**. [CrossRef]
50. Alshari, H.A.; Lokhande, M.A. Analysis of Constraints and Their Impact on Adopting Digital FinTech Techniques in Banks. *Electron. Commer. Res.* **2023**, *25*, 3131–3164. [CrossRef]

https://doi.org/10.3390/fintech5010008

51. Alshehadeh, A.; Elrefae, G.; Belarbi, A.; Qasim, A.; Al-Khawaja, H. The Impact of Business Intelligence Tools on Sustaining Financial Report Quality in Jordanian Commercial Banks. *Uncertain Supply Chain Manag.* **2023**, *11*, 1667–1676. [CrossRef]
52. Alshehadeh, A.R.; Elrefae, G.; Injadat, E. Influence of Traditional Performance Indicators on Economic Added Value: Evidence from Insurance Companies. *Corp. Gov. Organ. Behav. Rev.* **2022**, *6*, 18–27. [CrossRef]

https://doi.org/10.3390/fintech5010008

FinTech

Article

Fintech Innovations and the Transformation of Rural Financial Ecosystems in India

Mohd Umar Farukh [1], Mohammad Taqi [2,*], Koteswara Rao Vemavarapu [2], Sayed M. Fadel [2] and Nawab Ali Khan [1]

1 Department of Commerce, Aligarh Muslim University, Aligarh 202001, India
2 School of Business, Bahrain Polytechnic, Isa Town 33349, Bahrain
* Correspondence: mohammad.taqi@polytechnic.bh

Abstract

Background: Fintech companies have revolutionized the financial services industry in India in recent years. This is especially true for the growth of digital payment methods. India's unbanked are being introduced to banking by fintech companies. Despite the country's strong banking system, many residents find it difficult to get government financial services. This is particularly true for rural or low-income people. This vacuum has been addressed by fintech solutions including digital banking, micro-lending applications, mobile wallets, and UPI platforms. Objectives: to study the impact of financial technology businesses on increasing financial inclusion for India's underbanked and unbanked population and Challenges encountered by financial technology enterprises in their endeavors to access unbanked populations, encompassing concerns of infrastructure with special reference to western Uttar Pradesh. Method: This mixed-methods study examines how FinTech is narrowing the financial gap for unbanked people using quantitative econometric analysis and qualitative case study assessments. Results: Digital financial innovation and regulatory support encourage inclusive growth in underdeveloped economies, whereas rich nations benefit from sophisticated banking institutions. This is indicated by the small influence of GDP per capita ($\beta = 0.22$–0.32, $p < 0.05$). Findings: The study found that inclusive finance is revolutionized when FinTech is used with the help of robust regulatory frameworks and digital infrastructure. Policymakers should prioritize cybersecurity, public-private partnerships to improve digital literacy, and rural connection if they want more people to take part in the digital financial ecosystem. Implications: FinTech can remove obstacles to accessing financing. The proper coordinated improvements in regulatory frameworks, digital infrastructure and financial literacy among the people are necessary to achieve full financial inclusion.

Keywords: Fintech; digital payments; financial inclusion; unbanked communities; India; mobile banking; UPI; digital literacy; financial access

JEL Classification: E42; G21; O16; O33; D14

1. Introduction

The term 'fintech' describes the new wave of financial technology that emerged in response to the 2007–2008 financial crisis and has subsequently brought about a sea change in the industry. The expansion of contemporary banking may be traced back to two mainstays: technological banking and technologically enabled banking [1]. One of the main

https://doi.org/10.3390/fintech5010003

factors driving this cause in India over the past decade has been the rapid expansion of mobile networks into underserved areas and communities [2,3]. With the rise of payment banks, customers in rural and semi-urban areas now have another option besides online and mobile banking. This has helped streamline operations and cut costs for service provision. Secondly, an expanding economy brings in more individuals to work in finance and the economy, funding growth factors, such as expanding opportunities for savings mobilization and entrepreneurship, decreasing risk susceptibility, and improving people's quality of living, inclusive financial breakthroughs can reduce poverty [4]. Over 330 million formerly unbanked individuals were able to access formal financial institutions in FY2023 as the financial inclusion index increased from 43.4 to 60.1, according to the Reserve Bank of India. India's Reserve Bank (2023) [5] Digital payment systems have sped up socioeconomic transition in addition to being convenient. By promoting competition among financial service providers, transparency in all financial operations, and the effectiveness of government subsidy programs, they decreased costs and enhanced service delivery. According to the Digital India project, these platforms integrate conventional banking services to contemporary financial needs and foster economic progress [6,7]. Fintech employs technology to improve the accessibility, efficiency, and delivery of financial services.

1.1. India's Unbanked Community

With barely 35 per cent of individuals holding an account with a financial institution, India has one of the lowest percentages of account penetration among developing nations, and it is also home to the biggest unbanked population [8,9]. In Andhra Pradesh and Delhi NCR, about half of the adults have a formal account, while in Gujarat, Kerala, and Maharashtra, it's around 40 per cent. However, in Bihar, Orissa, and Rajasthan, that number drops to less than 30 per cent. There are almost 1.22 billion people living in India, and according to 2011 census statistics, 65 per cent of individuals there do not have access to official financial services [10]. World Bank data shows that just 35.2 per cent of Indian people over the age of 15 hold an account with a bank or other formal financial institution. Formal financial institutions have deposit accounts with 55 per cent of the population and credit accounts with only 9 per cent. One bank branch for every fourteen thousand people is what the numbers reveal. Very few people use credit cards, and even fewer use debit cards (18 per cent vs. 2 per cent). In India, there may have been an increase in the number of bank branches after the reform period, but there are still only 48,000 commercial banks (including RRBs and SCBs) servicing 6 lakh villages. That means out of 12.5 communities, there is just one bank branch. People without bank accounts in India and the other BRICS countries have said that opening a formal account is difficult [9,11].

1.2. Role of FinTech Startups in Serving the Unbanked in India

Most rural Indians do not have access to traditional banking services; however, this can change with the help of financial technology. Small and medium-sized enterprises (MSME) have a significant challenge when it comes to money. However, there is hope in the form of fintech firms that may help alleviate this problem by providing simpler and faster access to loans [7]. To increase the penetration of financial services in India, FinTech startups are utilizing big data, machine learning, and alternative data to improve the customer experience in areas such as accessibility, convenience, personalization, transparency, and the development of credit scores and underwriting credit [1].

1.3. Mobile Banking and Digital Payment Frameworks

Indian National Payments Corporation (NPCI) and explored NPCI's function within the country's burgeoning digital payment sector. All of India's retail payment systems are unified under NPCI. By establishing a foundation based on massive volumes and

https://doi.org/10.3390/fintech501000

scale, it will be possible to provide payment services for a fraction of the current cost structure [12]. In May 2016, after only four years of operation, RuPay captured 38 per cent of the market with 267 million debit cards. Due to its cost-effectiveness, RuPay-based e-commerce transactions have experienced a 20 per cent increase in volume and a 22 per cent increase in value month-over-month. The Pradhan Mantri Jan-Dhan Yojana (Jan-Dhan Yojana) aims to provide banking services to everyone and is helping to spread RuPay [9]. The recipients will receive RuPay Debit cards that have an accident insurance policy with a maximum coverage of Rs 100,000. In the future, RuPay's market share would be increased thanks to the debut of their credit card in December 2016, brand awareness campaigns in metropolitan areas, and partnerships with 8 payment banks and 10 small financing institutions [13,14].

1.4. Integration of Biometric Systems with Electronic Know Your Customer (e-KYC)

Every citizen of India is assigned a distinct identity a random 12-digit number through the government's Aadhaar program. A customer's Aadhaar number, together with fingerprint and/or iris scan technology, allows a Digital Financial Service (DFS) provider to authenticate the customer's identity [12]. The customer due diligence process is made easier for DFS providers since they depend on Aadhaar authentication results without further identification verification. A portion of the Aadhaar Act pertaining to the commercial sector's utilization of e-KYC was declared unlawful by the Indian Supreme Court in September 2018. Because of this, the private sector was not provided with access to e-KYC services. There was no change to the availability of e-KYC for public services including social assistance payments [15,16]. In 2019, a policy was put in place to permit the private sector to utilize e-KYC. This legislation specifically permits DFS providers and telecommunication companies to do so.

1.5. Direct Benefit Transfers (DBTs) and Government Initiatives

In India, the Janani Suraksha Yojana utilized the conditional cash transfers program. Nevertheless, Unconditional Cash Transfers (UCT) were the cash transfer method that was perceived in the 2010–2011 economic survey. Reducing food insecurity among the ultra-poor is one of the goals of well-targeted UCT, which also increases household consumption and asset ownership. Therefore, to endorse and implement a solution for direct transfer of subsidies, the Indian government established a task force headed by Nandan Nilekani in the 2011–2012 budget speech. The report on this initiative is titled 'Report of the Task Force on Direct Transfer of Subsidies on Kerosene, LPG and Fertilizer, 2011. To replace kerosene, LPG, and fertilizer subsidies with cash transfers, the committee proposed several systems, one of which is the Core Subsidy Management System (CSMS). This system would integrate Aadhaar, ERP (Enterprise Resource Planning) systems, the Nodal Bank and Payment Gateway, and modules for logistics, training, education, and outreach [17,18]. Mobile technology and the AEPS system have made financial aid more transparent, speedier, and dependable. This has decreased middleman and corruption and increased rural trust and involvement. FinTech has successfully combined technical innovation and social welfare governance to drive economic growth and achieve social justice and inclusion [19].

1.6. Financial Literacy and Consumer Empowerment

The term 'financial literacy' refers to the ability to understand one's own financial situation and make educated decisions to improve one's own financial situation. Through the provision of information, instruction, and/or objective advice, financial education enables consumers and investors to gain a better understanding of financial products, concepts, and risks [5,20]. It also empowers them to become more self-aware of financial risks and opportunities, make educated choices, know where to get assistance, and take

https://doi.org/10.3390/fintech5010003

other effective actions to improve their financial well-being. From what has been said thus far, it is evident that education and financial literacy are closely connected ideas. Government and institutional initiatives like the Digital Literacy Campaign (DISHA) and the Reserve Bank Innovation Hub (RBIH) have helped promote financial literacy. The Digital Personal Data Protection Act (2023) protects consumer data and privacy by addressing these challenges [21].

1.7. Growth Factors of Indian FinTech Sector

Key elements that contribute to the success of fintech organizations include customer loyalty, the funding climate, technology and IT infrastructure, value proposition, innovative data utilization, and operational costs [22]. In the next three to five years, the following seven things will most certainly propel the Indian financial technology industry forward: Consistent expansion of the economy accompanied by rather low access to banking services. Public sector insurers and large public sector banks are falling behind the market [23,24].

1.8. Regulatory Forbearance Toward FinTech

Millennials in India are climbing the digital financial services adoption S-curve at a quick pace, which is making them feel more pressure from established players. India Infrastructure and connectivity for digital financial services may be enhanced by the spread of data on the internet and stacks [25]. Potentially enabling subsidization without constructing scale are technological advancements and cloud service adoptions that result in asset light models with nearly nil unit costs at transaction levels. A decline in India's real interest rates [26].

1.9. Supervisory Legal Framework and Government Initiatives for Fintech in India

India lacks a comprehensive regulatory framework for financial technology (fintech) due to the sector's overlapping and non-linear business patterns. Depending on the specifics of the firm, many laws and regulations may apply to a fintech company [4,16,19,20]. Standard regulatory bodies include the Reserve Bank of India (RBI), the Securities and Exchange Board of India (SEBI), the Insurance Regulatory and Development Authority of India (IRDAI), the Pension Fund Regulatory and Development Authority (PFRDA), and the Insurance and Financial Services Regulatory and Development Authority of India (IFSCA7) [27,28]. Payment aggregators and gateways, data and privacy, lending and deposit collecting, insurance product and service provision, trading of securities and derivatives, etc. are all areas that fall under the purview of the agencies. Many financial offers need previous permissions and licenses from the RBI, SEBI, or IRDAI before a firm may launch operations. With initiatives like the Unified Payment Interface (UPI), Aadhaar, and open application programming interfaces (APIs), the government has paved the way for the Fintech industry to offer creative and adaptable digital banking. Additionally, the government publishes policies that will either directly encourage investments in tech, fintech, and startup companies in India or would have a beneficial effect on these industries. In addition, the IFSCA has instituted an incentive program for both Indian and international FinTech's who are looking to expand their customer base outside of India's borders [4]. Among the several tax relief proposals put up by the government was a postponement of the transfer of cash to IFSC GIFT City from 31 March 2023 to 31 March 2025. Introducing the Tamil Nadu FinTech Policy 2021: A Path to Success for Selected FinTech Startups [23,24,27,29].

National Payments Corporation of India (NPCI) [4,7,30–32]: Multiple circulars about payments over the Unified Payments Interface (UPI).

SEBI [5,27,31–33]: Mutual Funds Circular for the Year 2021.

https://doi.org/10.3390/fintech5010003

IRDAI [5,7,28,30,33,34]: Insurance Policy Electronic Issuance and Repository Guidelines, 2015. A guide to online insurance shopping, 2017. Indian Rules for the Regulatory and Development Agency of Insurance (Issuance of e-Insurance Policies), 2016.

IFSCA [4,5,27,31,32]: The 2019 International Financial Services Centers Authority Act. Guidelines for Financial Technology Entities in International Financial Services Centers (IFSCs), 2022.

Over 450 million people have been able to open new bank accounts thanks to the Jan Dhan Yojana, making it possible for them to receive direct benefits transfers and use a variety of financial services like insurance, pensions, remittances, and credit. Fintech businesses may use this to their advantage when developing technological goods for the vast Indian consumer market. To tackle India's challenging issues with presence-less, paperless, and cashless service delivery, the country has developed a stack of application programming interfaces (APIs) that governments, corporations, startups, and developers may use on a one-of-a-kind digital infrastructure. In 2016, the National Payments Corporation of India created UPI, a sophisticated mobile app-based payment system that allows users to transfer payments across bank accounts. This technology has been a driving force behind India's Fintech boom. More than 6.28 billion transactions totaling 10.62 lakh crore were recorded in July 2022 by 338 banks registered under the platform. The E-Rupee, also known as the Central Bank Digital Currency (CBDC), was recently introduced by the Indian government [5,19,35]. A digital money alternative, it will spur expansion in India's financial technology sector. Mumbai, Bandra Kurla Complex, FinTech Valley in Vizag, O-hub in Bhubaneswar, and FinTech Hub in Kolkata are all parts of the fintech cluster. Governments often establish Fintech Hubs, which are essentially parks, to encourage investment in the state's economic infrastructure and to entice large financial institutions and investors to establish headquarters there [5,17,24,36].

1.10. Issues to Be Considered Seriously by Fin Techs for Future Development

International money transfers are still unexplored for Fin Techs: Fin Techs still lack experience with international payments, even though they have a lot of room to grow. Migrant workers find it challenging to utilize remittance services due to their high cost and many international money transfers use correspondent banks [37]. Further price increases and a resurgence of unofficial, unregulated payment networks are possible outcomes of a decline in the number of correspondent banks Even if there are a lot of personal remittances flowing in, cross-border transactions in India are sluggish compared to domestic payments and there aren't many possibilities. For various payment systems to communicate with one another, it is necessary to convert payment instructions into a common language [5,12,27,38].

High Concern regarding use, protection & privacy of Data: Concerns about data usage, protection, and privacy may become more prevalent as FinTech continues to gain traction, especially if the roles and duties of service providers are not clearly defined. There is a risk that machine learning algorithms may perpetuate prejudice by ignoring or downplaying the experiences of marginalized communities [39]. The Indian populace is generating an unprecedented amount of data due to the proliferation of mobile phone and Internet connections. Legal and legislative action must be taken to ensure that customers have control over the data they generate. The public need to be able to manage their personal information just like they would have any other possession. They need to follow strict rules, keep systems locked down, and react fast when something goes wrong. CERT-In keeps an eye on threats and helps coordinate responses, while the RBI expects companies to stick to tough global security standards like International Organization for Standardization/International Electrotechnical Commission 27001 (ISO/IEC 27001) [40].

https://doi.org/10.3390/fintech5010003

That means building strong information security systems to protect customers and keep things running smoothly. The RBI requires regulated enterprises to follow ISO/IEC 27001 security standards. This standard highlights the need for an ISMS to protect client data and maintain operations [5,20,40,41].

1.11. Enhancement of Consumer Protection and Digital Education

Online education and consumer safety should take precedence. Regulators should educate the public on digital and financial literacy at the same time to prevent fraud from happening in the first place. To entice low-income groups, safety standards and problem-solving processes need to be made clearer and easier to use. Good digital hygiene and financial awareness might not be sufficient, though. Using cash as a payment method is a habit that is difficult to overcome, according to evidence from throughout the globe. Even beggars, street merchants, and buskers in China accept electronic payments [42,43].

1.12. Regulators Must Maintain a Neutral Approach

The last point is that regulators should be impartial. The Working Group on FinTech and Digital Banking Report [5] cautions that regulators should not unfairly benefit new entrants by providing them with differing regulations compared to established enterprises. With the rise of large digital payment corporations comes the inevitable tension between data-fueled oligopoly and the necessity to re-align incentives to foster a competitive environment by rewarding smaller, more creative businesses [44,45].

2. Review of Literature

Zavolokina et al. (2016) [45] explain the consensus among journalists and the public on the FinTech framework of thought. Getting the word about FinTech in the hopes that it will be covered in academic journals is the main objective. Exploratory and descriptive research methodologies were employed. The results show that academics seldom broach the topic of financial technology (FinTech), which should encompass more than just technological concerns. Nicoletti et al. (2017) [39] delves into FinTech's predicted future by speculating that the business would soon take on a new shape, with many clients relying on it. The primary objective is to highlight the substantial advantages of FinTech endeavors. Key findings provide more evidence of prevailing economic tendencies. Sanmath, A. (2018) [46] deliberated on the function of financial technology (Fintech) in Indian banking, financial services, and financial gateways, and on the prospect of future banking partnerships with Fintech. The Reserve Bank is reportedly keeping up its initiatives to provide safe and reliable payment and settlement systems so that we may all live in a cashless world. India is now leading the pack in terms of digital infrastructure for financial universalization. One of its indigenous stacks, JanDhan, Aadhaar, and Mobile (JAM), is helping us go from a data-poor to a data-rich nation. Badruddin et al. (2017) [1] considered how to conceptualize FinTech's efficacy in expanding access to financial services. He delivered well-organized research work that drew on a variety of resources, including personal journals, books, online resources, and more. The development of FinTech, she said, has lowered prices and simplified the microfinance concept. The present scenario makes the viability of FinTech evident, she concluded her analysis by noting. This company continues to look at the problems even though they exist. Vijai (2019) et al. [28] focuses on the evolution of FinTech technology in India and the possibilities and threats it faces. Customers benefit from FinTech since it allows safer and quicker transactions. His study demonstrates how FinTech is influencing the Indian financial services sector. Priya et al. (2019) [4] find out what financial technology is, how it works, and what opportunities and challenges it poses to businesses in India. Financially and technically, fintech firms need to be nurtured.

https://doi.org/10.3390/fintech501000

As is to be expected in other areas of finance, the majority of successful start-ups are located in the payments industry, according to the report. There are several ways in which the government and regulatory bodies may bolster the financial technology sector. This research aims to identify different fintech innovations and modern transformational steps of rural financial ecosystem in India with special reference to western Uttar Pradesh, India. The information was gathered from the local people of rural and semi-urban areas of this region to know, how people are familiar with digital payment platforms and fintech services, how often they use them, any problems they encounter.

3. Objectives

- Evaluate the impact of financial technology businesses on increasing financial inclusion for India's underbanked and unbanked population.
- To study challenges encountered by financial technology enterprises in their endeavors to access unbanked populations, encompassing concerns of infrastructure, data security, and digital literacy.

4. Research Methodology

This research analyses quantitative data and human case studies to determine how Financial Tech (FinTech) has increased banking access. Secondary data, economic models to assess FinTech growth, and comparative case studies of digital financial services usage are employed in the study. This comprehensive and holistic approach may help you comprehend how digital technology might assist unbanked people with access money in many economic and legal circumstances [6,30,47].

Sample size: Total 350 respondents have been taken by this survey conducted.

Study area: People in Western Uttar Pradesh's (India) rural and semi-urban areas were the targets of structured surveys. The poll aims to gather data on how people are familiar with digital payment platforms and fintech services, how often they use them, any problems they encounter, and how they perceive these topics overall.

Data collection: To acquire first-hand information from respondents, this study will use primary data gathering methods, particularly structured questionnaires. Surveys and interviews with legislators, financial service companies, and FinTech users can be part of future study to gather primary data. In this geographical setting, the study intends to use direct survey methods to collect genuine preferences, trends, and difficulties pertaining to the research subject [41]. Secondary sources were Peer-reviewed journal articles and working papers from Elsevier's ScienceDirect, SpringerLink, and IEEE Xplore provide conceptual and theoretical frameworks to empirical data. An econometric model of FinTech acceptance and financial inclusion is created using panel data regression analysis [48,49]. Financial inclusion variables such as adult financial account access, mobile money transactions per capita, and digital lending volume are examined in the model, along with the effects of blockchain-based financial services and AI-driven credit assessment. This study's central equation is:

$$FI_{it} = \alpha + \beta_1\, FinTech_{it} + \beta_2\, GDP_{it} + \beta_3\, RegQuality_{it} + \beta_4\, DigitalInfra_{it} + \varepsilon_{it}$$

4.1. Case Study

This study compares how different FinTech solutions change financial access on the ground. Putting people's needs before your own is more important than focusing on financial gains. Consider digital loans in India. Platforms such as Google Wallet, Paytm, and PhonePe are utilizing AI-driven credit checks to expand access to micro-loans for low-income individuals, bringing them closer to the financial system. This study explores the

https://doi.org/10.3390/fintech5010003

reasons for the usage of various fintech solutions, the challenges presented by legislation, the social and economic impacts, and the variables that led to the success of each example. This study offers a simple framework that draws on findings from government publications, industry white papers, and financial inclusion surveys to highlight the successes, failures, and present situation of different financial ecosystems.

4.2. Ethical Considerations and Limitations

This study conforms to data privacy laws and ethical research standards as it relies on secondary sources and publicly accessible datasets. The data come from reliable sources and never use personally identifiable information (PII). However, there are a few limitations to the study that should be mentioned. These include data discrepancies across reporting agencies, the fact that official records might not include informal financial transactions, and the fact that legislation around FinTech is often changing, so they might not be included in the future. Researchers in the future may refine this method by speaking with politicians, financial service providers, and FinTech users to get primary data. By combining econometric modeling with comparative case study analysis, this study adopts a rigorous mixed-methods research technique to evaluate FinTech's influence on increasing financial inclusion. Integrating quantitative and qualitative data analysis is key to understanding the game-changing impact of digital financial services on those without bank accounts. Results from future research on the connection between FinTech, economic growth, and financial accessibility, as well as discussions on regulatory and legislative frameworks, will be informed by this technique. This study uses fixed effects (FE) and random effect (RE) models to control differences among countries. A key component of this equation is Gross Domestic Production (GDP) per capita. It has a strong relationship with the availability of financial services and economic progress. Greater access to banking and digital finance is a natural consequence of people's increased propensity to interact with formal financial institutions as their earnings rise. Digital financial services are in high demand in rising economies since a higher GDP per capita usually means more buying power, more employment prospects, and more economic activity [31,48,49]. These variables capture economic strength and the institutional environment, two things that really shape how fintech evolves and how many people get included financially. By bringing both into the analysis, we reduce big differences between countries in terms of their economies and governance, which gives us a clearer idea of fintech's real, independent impact.

4.3. Data Transformation and Normalization

The Fixed Effects (FE) model is a handy tool when you're working with panel data essentially, data that tracks various countries or regions over time. FE helps account for those hidden factors that remain constant, like cultural attitudes towards banking or long-standing policies. This way, it can really understand the impact of things like fintech adoption or digital infrastructure on financial inclusion, since the study is focusing on changes within each country over time rather than just making comparisons between different countries [34,47,49]. Variance Inflation Factor (VIF). VIF is used to check if any of your independent variables are too closely related, which can throw off your regression analysis. When two variables are too correlated, it becomes tricky to determine which one is actually influencing the outcome. A VIF score above 10 is a warning sign. In this case, VIF helped ensure that GDP per capita, mobile penetration, and digital infrastructure were independent enough to trust the regression results. Additionally, when necessary, all variables are log-transformed to ensure they can be compared fairly. Hausman tests are also conducted to determine whether fixed-effects or random-effects models are a better fit for the data, and variance inflation factors (VIF) are calculated to check for multicollinearity.

https://doi.org/10.3390/fintech5010003

4.4. Variables for Conducting Data Analysis

To summarize important variables, descriptive statistics are calculated prior to regression analysis. The following Table 1 is an example of the output:

Table 1. Descriptive statistics for Variables.

Variable	Mean	Std. Dev.	Min	Max
Financial Inclusion (FI)	64.3%	18.2	22.1%	98.5%
FinTech Adoption (%)	48.7%	22.5	5.2%	91.3%
GDP per Capita (USD)	12,345	8765	1200	78,900
Internet Penetration (%)	58.4%	24.3	10.1%	98.7%

4.5. Statistical Analysis

In Stata 17.0, a battery of diagnostic tests ran to check for heteroskedasticity and possible autocorrelation in the panel data, and robust standard errors were used to make sure the econometric results were solid. First, the Breusch-Pagan/Cook-Weisberg test was used to check for heteroskedasticity. It turned out that the residual variance was not constant, so White's robust standard errors were applied, which are estimators that are robust against heteroskedasticity. Furthermore, the incorporation of countries and period fixed effects reduced the weak serial correlation that was revealed by the Wooldridge test for autocorrelation. All variables showed VIF values below 5, indicating that multicollinearity was not an issue, when the Variance Inflation Factor (VIF) was used to evaluate it [7]. The absence of any impact of FinTech adoption on financial inclusion is suggested by the null hypothesis (H_0:$\beta_1 = 0$), in contrast to the positive effect proposed by the alternative hypothesis (H_1:$\beta_1 > 0$). Computed coefficients demonstrate that the adoption of FinTech has a positive and statistically significant effect on financial inclusion, since the *p*-value is less than 0.05 at the 1 per cent, 5 per cent, and 10 per cent significance levels [17,26,47,50].

4.6. Rationale for Variable Selection

When choosing variables for the panel regression model, the study leaned on both real-world data and theory about how fintech, financial inclusion, and economic development connect. Both Fixed Effects and Random Effects models help deal with differences between countries. The main regression equation includes:

Financial Inclusion Index (FI_{it}): The dependent variable, based on the World Bank Global Findex Database (2021) [32,35,47,51,52] tracks the share of people with formal bank accounts. It also covers how often people use digital payments and whether they have access to credit.

FinTech Adoption ($FinTech_{it}$): This is the key explanatory variable. It measures how much people use mobile money or digital payment systems per capita. Basically, it shows how digital platforms connect the unbanked to financial services.

Gross Domestic Product per Capita (GDP_{it}): This control variable measures a country's economic well-being. Higher incomes usually mean better financial products and cheaper access to technology.

Regulatory Quality ($RegQuality_{it}$): This WGI measure looks at how effective the government is, how well it protects consumers, and how transparent its policies are. The idea is to see if strong regulation really does drive fintech growth and build user trust.

Digital Infrastructure ($DigitalInfra_{it}$): This statistic quantifies the proportion of individuals using the internet and examines how connectivity facilitates online financial platforms. Robust digital infrastructure facilitates FinTech adoption [29].

https://doi.org/10.3390/fintech5010003

Mobile Penetration (MobilePen$_{it}$): This variable denotes mobile phone ownership rates and is essential for comprehending mobile banking and digital wallet utilization, particularly in rural areas [12,14].

4.7. Hypothesis

H1: *There is significant relationship between impact of financial technology businesses on increasing financial inclusion for India's underbanked and unbanked population.*

H2: *There is a significant relationship between challenges faced by financial technology businesses in their efforts to reach those without bank accounts, including issues related to infrastructure, data security, and digital literacy.*

5. Results and Analysis

In Table 2 a wide range of ages, genders, educational backgrounds, professions, income levels, and geographic locations are represented in the 350 respondents' socio-demographic distribution. The sample is mostly composed of young adults, with a majority falling between the 18–30 years (28.6 per cent) and 31–45 years (25.7 per cent) age categories. Only 5.7 per cent of the participants are below the age of 18 and 17.1 per cent are above the age of 60. A minor percentage (2.9 per cent) classified as other, whereas 54.3 per cent were male and 42.9 per cent were female. The gender distribution suggests a little male preponderance. Nearly 29 per cent of the samples had a bachelor's degree or above, 25.7 per cent had a master's degree, and 8.6 per cent had no formal education at all, indicating that the sample is well-educated [3,49,53]. Of the many occupations represented among the respondents, the largest groups were those working in the service industry (25.7 per cent of the total) or as students (20 per cent), followed by those in agriculture (17.1 per cent), small business/retail (14.3 per cent), and daily wage workers (11.4 per cent). About yearly income, most participants fell into the lower and middle-income brackets; specifically, 28.6 per cent earned between ₹1,00,001 and ₹3,00,000, 22.9 per cent earned below ₹1,00,000, and 8.6 per cent earned more than ₹10,000. In terms of geography, there is a reasonable distribution: 37.1 per cent live in metropolitan areas, 34.3 per cent are rural, and 28.6 per cent are semi-urban. The results are more broadly applicable since the sample is diverse in terms of demographics and socioeconomic status, which increases the likelihood that respondents' opinions will be accurately represented [6,38,54].

In terms of digital payment systems, 40 per cent of respondents utilize UPI-based applications like BHIM, Google Pay, and similar services, making them the most popular is shown in Table 3. There are a lot of people using Paytm (20 per cent) and PhonePe (17.1 per cent), which shows how popular they are for everyday transactions. With a 12.9 per cent use rate, debit and credit cards remain the most popular digital payment options. With lower acceptance rates, choices like mobile wallets (5.7 per cent) and other platforms (4.3 per cent) appear to be more specialized. In general, the results show that UPI is the most popular digital payment method, with other platforms being adopted selectively based on user desire, accessibility, and their level of convenience [33,52].

Among the 350 respondents, the most prevalent purpose for digital payment usage is grocery shopping (25.7 per cent). This suggests that digital modes are becoming a regular element of family purchasing as shown in Table 4. This reflects the increasing dependence on digital platforms for both personal and professional activities, as it is followed by the payment of utility bills (20 per cent) and business transactions (17.1 per cent). There is a high rate of use for mobile data recharge (14.3 per cent) and receiving payments (15.7 per cent), which might indicate that service-based transactions and peer-to-peer transactions are prevalent. Digital payments were used for entertainment, travel, and other miscellaneous

https://doi.org/10.3390/fintech501000

costs by a lesser percentage of respondents (7.1 per cent). Groceries and energy bills are the main drivers of digital payment use, while the statistics show that it is extensively used across necessary and commercial activities [43,55].

Table 2. Socio-demographic Distribution of Respondents.

Variables	Categories	Frequency (*n*)	Percentage (%)
Age	Below 18	20	5.7
	18–30	100	28.6
	31–45	90	25.7
	46–60	80	22.9
	Above 60	60	17.1
Gender	Male	190	54.3
	Female	150	42.9
	Other	10	2.9
Education Level	No formal education	30	8.6
	Primary	50	14.3
	Secondary	80	22.9
	Higher Secondary	90	25.7
	Graduate and above	100	28.6
Occupation Sector	Agriculture	60	17.1
	Small Business/Retail	50	14.3
	Daily Wage Worker	40	11.4
	Service Sector	90	25.7
	Student	70	20.0
	Other	40	11.4
Annual Income	Below ₹1,00,000	80	22.9
	₹1,00,001–₹3,00,000	100	28.6
	₹3,00,001–₹6,00,000	80	22.9
	₹6,00,001–₹10,00,000	60	17.1
	Above ₹10,00,000	30	8.6
Location	Urban	130	37.1
	Semi-urban	100	28.6
	Rural	120	34.3

Concerns about security and dependability in digital transactions were highlighted by the study of respondents' most prevalent worries regarding digital payment methods, which include the risk of fraud (22.9 per cent) and transaction failures (20 per cent). A rising number of people are becoming more comfortable and confident with digital payment methods, since a sizeable majority of respondents (18.6 per cent) stated that they had no problems. Problems with digital literacy and infrastructure are evident in instances like not knowing how to utilize apps (17.1%) and not having access to the internet (12.9 per cent). Just 8.6 per cent of people said that not having access to smartphones was a problem. Although digital payments are becoming more popular, there are still certain issues that users face when trying to utilize them. These include fears of fraud, unsuccessful transactions, and a lack of user education is shown in Table 5. The study's empirical results

https://doi.org/10.3390/fintech5010003

use econometric modelling, statistical analysis, and case-specific assessments to examine FinTech adoption and financial inclusion. Panel regression, variance inflation factor (VIF) analysis, and hypothesis testing provide the findings. To verify variable connections, structural equation modelling (SEM) is used [43,49].

Table 3. Distribution of Digital Payment Platforms ($n = 350$).

Digital Payment Platform	Frequency (n)	Percentage (%)
UPI (BHIM, GPay, etc.)	140	40.0
Paytm	70	20.0
PhonePe	60	17.1
Debit/Credit Card	45	12.9
Mobile Wallets	20	5.7
Other	15	4.3
Total	350	100

Table 4. Distribution of Digital Payment Usage ($n = 350$).

Usage Purpose	Frequency (n)	Percentage (%)
Utility bills	70	20.0
Mobile/Data recharge	50	14.3
Grocery shopping	90	25.7
Business transactions	60	17.1
Receiving payments	55	15.7
Other	25	7.1
Total	350	100

Table 5. Distribution of Challenges in Digital Payments ($n = 350$).

Challenges	Frequency (n)	Percentage (%)
Lack of internet access	45	12.9
Lack of smartphone	30	8.6
Fear of fraud	80	22.9
Not understanding how to use apps	60	17.1
Transaction failures	70	20.0
No challenge faced	65	18.6
Total	350	100

5.1. Descriptive Statistics and Correlation Matrix

Table 6 summarizes the descriptive statistics of the important variables before moving on to regression analysis.

The usage of FinTech is significantly associated with financial inclusion ($p < 0.01$), as shown in Chart 1. Based on the data in Table 6, it appears that more people can access financial services when they use mobile banking and digital payments more often [12,32].

https://doi.org/10.3390/fintech5010003

Table 6. Summary Statistics of Key Variables.

Variable	Mean	Std. Dev.	Min	Max
Financial Inclusion (%)	64.3	18.2	22.1	98.5
FinTech Adoption (%)	48.7	22.5	5.2	91.3
GDP per Capita (USD)	12,345	8765	1200	78,900
Internet Penetration (%)	58.4	24.3	10.1	98.7
Mobile Phone Penetration (%)	78.2	15.1	30.2	98.9

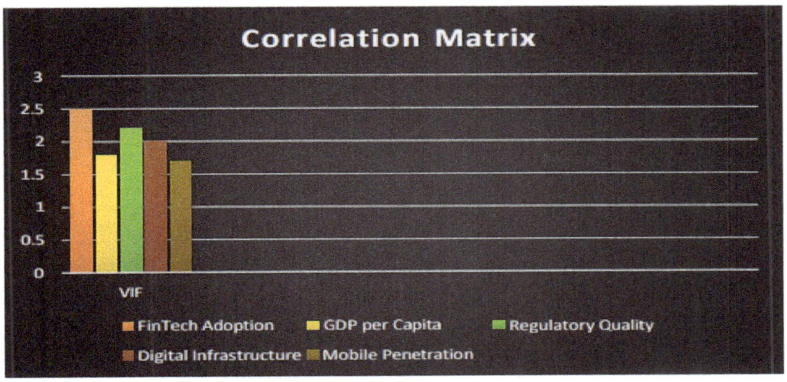

Chart 1. Substantial Positive Association between FinTech Use and Financial Inclusion.

5.2. Regression Results: Fixed and Random Effects Models

Panel data regression analysis quantifies FinTech's influence on financial inclusion. Fixed-effects (FE) and random-effects (RE) models are estimated, employing Hausman tests to find the best specification. Estimated regression equation:

$$FI_{it} = \alpha + \beta_1\ FinTech_{it} + \beta_2\ GDP_{it} + \beta_3\ RegQuality_{it} + \beta_4\ DigitalInfra_{it} + \beta_{5Mobile}\ Pen_{it} + \varepsilon_{it}$$

Based on Hausman test ($\chi^2 = 15.8$, $p < 0.05$), the Fixed-Effects Model is the recommended specification, indicating that country-specific factors substantially affect financial inclusion results [20] in Table 7 and Chart 2. A VIF analysis: to test multicollinearity, VIF scores are calculated:

$$VIF_k = \frac{1}{1 - R^2{}_k}$$

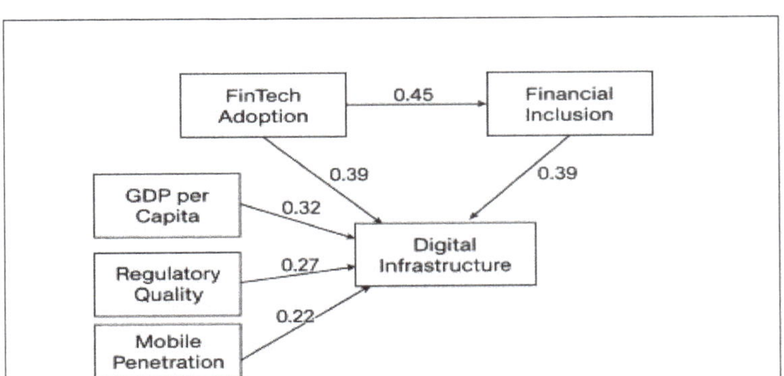

Chart 2. Model Path.

https://doi.org/10.3390/fintech5010003

Table 7. Regression Results.

Variable	Fixed Effects (FE)	Random Effects (RE)
FinTech Adoption	0.45 ** (0.08)	0.41 ** (0.09)
GDP per Capita	0.32 * (0.12)	0.30 * (0.13)
Regulatory Quality	0.27 * (0.10)	0.25 * (0.11)
Digital Infrastructure	0.39 ** (0.07)	0.36 ** (0.08)
Mobile Penetration	0.22 * (0.11)	0.19 * (0.12)
Constant	12.3 (4.8)	13.1 (5.1)
Observations	600	600
R^2	0.72	0.68
Hausman Test (χ^2)	15.8 ($p < 0.05$)	

* Statistical significance at the 5% level ($p < 0.05$), ** Statistical significance at the 1% level ($p < 0.01$).

5.3. Structural Equation Modeling (SEM) Validation

SEM was used to validate direct and indirect links between FinTech adoption, digital infrastructure, and financial inclusion. The SEM path analysis showed that FinTech adoption had a substantial direct impact on financial inclusion ($\beta = 0.45$, $p < 0.01$) and an indirect influence via digital infrastructure ($\lambda = 0.39$). FinTech penetration measured by the percentage of adults using mobile wallets or digital payment apps directly increases the chance of people utilizing formal financial services including savings, credit, and insurance. Strong digital infrastructure (e.g., internet availability, mobile network quality) enhances this relationship by facilitating financial engagement through technical accessibility, the model path illustrates in Chart 2 [41].

5.4. Hypothesis Testing and Interpretation

The null hypothesis (H_0: FinTech does not impact financial inclusion) was rejected at 1 per cent significance level, providing strong evidence that FinTech adoption improves financial inclusion outcomes. The correlation $\beta_1 = 0.45$ indicates that a 10 per cent increase in FinTech adoption, such as mobile money or digital banking usage among adults, leads to a 4.5 per cent increase in financial inclusion. More people, especially in underbanked rural and semi-urban areas, can access formal savings accounts, credit facilities, and digital payment systems elaborate in Chart 3. The mediation effect ($\lambda = 0.39$) indicates that digital infrastructure quality greatly enhances this association. FinTech adoption boosts financial inclusion by 40 per cent in nations with strong internet and mobile network infrastructure. Mobile penetration helps, but FinTech innovation needs solid digital ecosystems and user confidence to maximum inclusion [11,14,56].

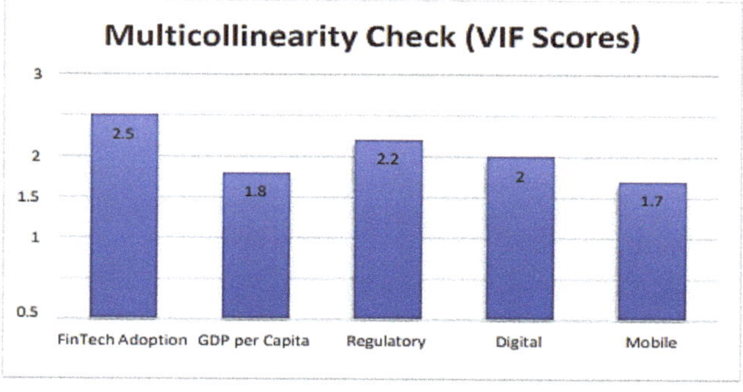

Chart 3. Multicollineraity Check (VIF scores).

https://doi.org/10.3390/fintech501000

6. Discussion and Policy Implications

6.1. The Role of Digital Infrastructure

The analysis shows that digital infrastructure, economic growth, and smart regulations all matter a lot. There is a strong link between financial inclusion and people using FinTech ($\beta_1 = 0.45$, $p < 0.01$). Basically, digital services open the door for people who have always been left out of the formal banking world Varga (2018) [36] backs this up, pointing out that when digital payment tools are easy, safe, and just work, even people with very little money can join in. Due to low levels of financial literacy and internet availability, the poll also reveals a FinTech gap in rural areas. To bridge this gap, digital literacy programs in rural India is needed, microfinance instruments powered by artificial intelligence, and subsidies for mobile banking [13,27,29,57]. The findings of the regression indicate that the success of FinTech is influenced by the quality of the regulations ($\beta_3 = 0.27$, $p < 0.01$), and that countries with strict laws protecting consumer data and privacy also have higher levels of digital financial inclusion. Locations that have consistent internet access and cell penetration tend to have faster increase in digital banking usage, as indicated by the substantial influence of digital infrastructure ($\beta_4 = 0.39$, $p < 0.01$). Compared to GDP growth, the adoption of fintech can have a greater impact on inclusion. The results are corroborated by Alipay in China and M-Pesa in Kenya [13,44]. The Unified Payments Interface (UPI), DigiLocker (run by the Reserve Bank of India), and the Open Network for Digital Commerce (ONDC) are a few examples of the government-backed digital ecosystems that have revolutionized financial services in India. Societal advantages have resulted from a 36% increase in financial access in low-income communities made possible by mobile banking. Digital financial innovation and regulatory support encourage inclusive growth in underdeveloped economies, whereas rich nations benefit from sophisticated banking institutions. This is indicated by the small influence of GDP per capita (β = 0.22–0.32, $p < 0.05$). The study found that inclusive finance is revolutionized when FinTech is used with the help of robust regulatory frameworks and digital infrastructure. Rural connection, public-private digital literacy partnerships, and cybersecurity should be prioritized by policymakers in order to promote equal participation in the digital financial ecosystem. Real-time FinTech transaction data and AI-based credit risk models should be used in future research to improve forecasting accuracy and knowledge of developing economic financial access dynamics [58–60].

6.2. Policy Implication

Invest in 5G and high-speed internet networks. A one-point boost in the digital infrastructure index is linked to a 0.39-point rise in financial inclusion. The following conclusions are drawn from the data obtained from surveys and regression analysis in the semi-urban and rural areas of Western Uttar Pradesh. The $\beta_3 = 0.27$ coefficient shows that trust and regulation are important for long-term FinTech adoption. To make regulations stronger, make cybersecurity and data protection legislation harsher. The government should subsidize mobile banking services and promote microfinance platforms powered by artificial intelligence to reduce the disparity in mobile banking usage between urban and rural areas. As a result, policy interventions are necessary to expand 5G and internet connectivity to unserved regions such as Amroha, Baghpat, and Muzaffarnagar. To compensate, the government might incentivize telecom firms to construct towers in underserved regions. More collaboration between the government, the RBI, and FinTech businesses is needed to maintain people's trust while promoting innovation; this should be replicated with initiatives like DigiLocker, UPI, and ONDC.

https://doi.org/10.3390/fintech5010003

7. Conclusions

Financial technology (FinTech) may aid non-bankers' access to the financial system, according to this study. An exhaustive investigation found a connection between digital financial services, great legislation, widespread mobile use, and economic progress. The usage of FinTech has a greater influence on access to money than GDP per capita, according to the research ($\beta 1 = 0.45$, $p < 0.01$). The growth of mobile networks, the internet, and blockchain technology have all contributed to the increased trust and acceptance of FinTech. The government must put money into 5G networks, cybersecurity, and financial systems powered by artificial intelligence if FinTech is to keep growing. Due to low levels of financial literacy and internet availability, the poll also reveals a FinTech gap in rural areas. The Unified Payments Interface (UPI), DigiLocker (run by the Reserve Bank of India), and the Open Network for Digital Commerce (ONDC) are a few examples of the government-backed digital ecosystems that have revolutionized financial services in India. Through these initiatives, millions of individuals and small businesses are brought into the formal digital economy through the interoperability of e-commerce platforms, banks, and FinTech. Societal advantages have resulted from a 36% increase in financial access in low-income communities made possible by mobile banking. Digital financial innovation and regulatory support encourage inclusive growth in underdeveloped economies, whereas rich nations benefit from sophisticated banking institutions. This is indicated by the small influence of GDP per capita ($\beta = 0.22$–0.32, $p < 0.05$). The study found that inclusive finance is revolutionized when FinTech is used with the help of robust regulatory frameworks and digital infrastructure. Rural connection, public-private digital literacy partnerships, and cybersecurity should be prioritized by policymakers in order to promote equal participation in the digital financial ecosystem. Real-time FinTech transaction data and AI-based credit risk models should be used in future research to improve forecasting accuracy and knowledge of developing economy financial access dynamics.

Author Contributions: Conceptualization, M.U.F.; Methodology, M.T.; Validation, S.M.F.; Formal analysis, M.U.F.; Investigation, M.T.; Resources, K.R.V.; Data curation, S.M.F.; Writing—original draft preparation, M.U.F.; Writing—review and editing, M.T.; Visualization, K.R.V.; Supervision, N.A.K.; Research Paper Administration, N.A.K. All authors have read and agreed to the published version of the manuscript.

Funding: This research received no external funding. The authors conducted the study independently without any financial support from institutions, agencies, or organizations.

Institutional Review Board Statement: Approval Waived. We would like to clarify that in India, there is currently no formal requirement for any local Institutional Review Board (IRB) or ethics committee for studies of this nature. Nevertheless, the authors have strictly adhered to ethical principles while conducting this research, in line with the standards outlined in the Declaration of Helsinki (1975, revised 2013).

Informed Consent Statement: All participants were informed about the purpose of the study, and their consent was obtained prior to participation.

Data Availability Statement: The data presented in this study are available on request from the corresponding author. No publicly archived datasets were generated or analyzed during the current study. The data supporting the findings are derived from secondary sources and publicly available reports and can be shared upon reasonable requests. The data supporting the findings of this study are available from the corresponding author upon reasonable request. No publicly archived datasets were generated or analyzed during the study.

Conflicts of Interest: The authors declare no conflict of interest. The authors conducted this research independently, and there was no influence from any external party in the study's design, execution, interpretation, or publication decision.

https://doi.org/10.3390/fintech5010003

References

1. Badruddin, A. Conceptualization of the effectiveness of FinTech in financial inclusion. *Int. J. Eng. Technol. Sci. Res.* **2017**, *4*, 960–965.
2. Chavan, P.; Birajdar, B. Micro finance and financial inclusion of women: An evaluation. *Reserve Bank India Occas. Pap.* **2009**, *30*, 109–129.
3. Singh, S.; Goyal, S.K.; Sharma, S.K. Technical efficiency and its determinants in microfinance institutions in India: A firm level analysis. *J. Innov. Econ. Manag.* **2013**, *1*, 15–31. [CrossRef]
4. Priya, P.K.; Anusha, K. FinTech issues and challenges in India. *Int. J. Recent Technol. Eng.* **2019**, *8*, 904–908. [CrossRef]
5. Reserve Bank of India. Financial Inclusion and Digital Payments Report FY. 2023. Available online: https://www.rbi.org.in (accessed on 21 May 2025).
6. Frost, J.; Gambacorta, L.; Huang, Y.; Shin, H.S.; Zbinden, P. BigTech and the changing structure of financial intermediation. *Econ. Policy* **2019**, *34*, 761–799. [CrossRef]
7. Iqbal, S.; Nawaz, A.; Ehsan, S. Financial performance and corporate governance in microfinance: Evidence from Asia. *J. Asian Econ.* **2019**, *60*, 1–13. [CrossRef]
8. Goswami, S.; Sharma, R.B.; Chouhan, V. Impact of financial technology (Fintech) on financial inclusion in rural India. *Univers. J. Account. Financ.* **2022**, *10*, 483–497. [CrossRef]
9. GSMA. Enabling Rural Coverage: Regulatory and Policy Recommendations to Foster Mobile Broadband Coverage in Developing Countries. 2018. Available online: https://www.gsma.com/solutions-and-impact/connectivity-for-good/mobile-for-development/gsma_resources/enabling-rural-coverage-report/ (accessed on 17 April 2025).
10. Rathod, S.; Arelli, S.K.P. Aadhaar and financial inclusion: A proposed framework to provide basic financial services in unbanked rural India. In *Driving the Economy Through Innovation and Entrepreneurship*; Springer: New Delhi, India, 2013; pp. 731–744.
11. Wieser, C.; Bruhn, M.; Kinzinger, J.P.; Ruckteschler, C.S.; Heitmann, S. *The Impact of Mobile Money on Poor Rural Households: Experimental Evidence from Uganda*; Policy Research Working Paper No. 8913; World Bank Group: Washington, DC, USA, 2019; Available online: https://openknowledge.worldbank.org/handle/10986/31978 (accessed on 4 June 2025).
12. Aron, J. Mobile money and the economy: A review of the evidence. *World Bank Res. Obs.* **2018**, *33*, 135–188. [CrossRef]
13. Jack, W.; Suri, T. Risk sharing and transaction costs: Evidence from Kenya's mobile money revolution. *Am. Econ. Rev.* **2014**, *104*, 183–223.
14. Kim, M.; Zoo, H.; Lee, H.; Kang, J. Mobile financial services, financial inclusion, and development: A systematic review. *Electron. J. Inf. Syst. Dev. Ctries.* **2018**, *84*, e12044. [CrossRef]
15. Mbiti, I.; Weil, D.N. The home economics of e-money: Velocity, cash management, and discount rates of M-Pesa users. *Am. Econ. Rev.* **2013**, *103*, 369–374. [CrossRef]
16. Noreen, M.; Mia, M.S.; Ghazali, Z.; Ahmed, F. Role of government policies to fintech adoption and financial inclusion: A study in Pakistan. *Univers. J. Account. Financ.* **2022**, *10*, 37–46. [CrossRef]
17. Bollinger, B.; Yao, S. Risk transfer versus cost reduction on two-sided microfinance platforms. *Quant. Mark. Econ.* **2018**, *16*, 251–287. [CrossRef]
18. Masino, S.; Niño-Zarazúa, M. Improving financial inclusion through the delivery of cash transfer programmes: The case of Mexico's Progresa–Oportunidades–Prospera programme. *J. Dev. Stud.* **2018**, *56*, 151–168. [CrossRef]
19. Sunita, R.; Siddik, M.M. A study on fintech and the future of financial services with reference to Chennai. *J. Surv. Fish. Sci.* **2023**, *10*, 6550–6557.
20. Pessanha, A.H.U.C. How FinTechs and Their Partnerships with Financial Institutions are Closing the Banking Gap: Challenges and Opportunities. Ph.D. Thesis, Catholic University of Lisbon, Lisbon, Portugal, 2019.
21. Umamaheswari, S. Role of artificial intelligence in the banking sector. *J. Surv. Fish. Sci.* **2023**, *10*, 2841–2849.
22. Donovan, K.P. Mobile money for financial inclusion. *Inf. Commun. Dev.* **2012**, *61*, 61–73.
23. Kamal, M.; Rahmani, S.; Alam, M.R. Beyond traditional banking: How fintech is reshaping financial access in India. *Int. Adv. Res. J. Sci. Eng. Technol.* **2025**, *12*, 234–247. [CrossRef]
24. Qamruzzaman, M. Does financial innovation foster financial inclusion in the Arab world? *PLoS ONE* **2023**, *18*, e0287475.
25. Singh, N.D.; Singh, H.R. Social impact of microfinance on SHG members: A case study of Manipur. *Prabandhan Indian J. Manag.* **2012**, *5*, 43–50. [CrossRef]
26. Mia, M.A.; Zhang, M.; Zhang, C.; Kim, Y. Are microfinance institutions in South-East Asia pursuing objectives of greening the environment? *J. Asia Pac. Econ.* **2018**, *23*, 229–245. [CrossRef]
27. Government of India. Digital India Initiative. 2019. Available online: https://www.digitalindia.gov.in (accessed on 11 May 2025).
28. Vijai, C. FinTech in India—Opportunities and Challenges. *J. Bank. Insur. Res.* **2019**, *8*, 42–54. [CrossRef]

https://doi.org/10.3390/fintech5010003

29. Kumar, P.; Sharma, B. Pilot study leading to gap identification on diversification and digital strategy deployed by payments ban in India. *Int. J. Bus. Res. Manag.* **2024**, *18*, 928–943.
30. Ghosh, S. Financial inclusion in India: Does distance matter? *South Asia Econ. J.* **2020**, *21*, 216–238. [CrossRef]
31. Neelam, K.; Bhattacharya, S. Financial technology solutions for financial inclusion: A review and future agenda. *Australa Account. Bus. Financ. J.* **2022**, *16*, 170–184. [CrossRef]
32. Abiona, O.; Koppensteiner, M.F. Financial inclusion, shocks, and poverty: Evidence from the expansion of mobile money i Tanzania. *J. Hum. Resour.* **2022**, *57*, 435–464. [CrossRef]
33. Anitha, G.; Ravichandiran, C.; Paramasivan, C. Role of Fintech in the Financial Sector in India. *Int. J. Innov. Technol. Explor. Eng* **2025**, *14*, 106–111.
34. Iqbal, B.A.; Shaista, S. Role of banks in financial inclusion in India. *Contad. Adm.* **2017**, *62*, 644–656. [CrossRef]
35. Tian, H.; Siddik, A.B.; Pertheban, T.R.; Rahman, M.N. Does fintech innovation and green transformational leadership improv green innovation and corporate environmental performance? *J. Innov. Knowl.* **2023**, *8*, 100396. [CrossRef]
36. Varga, D. Fintech: Supporting sustainable development by disrupting finance. *Bp. Manag. Rev.* **2018**, *8*, 231–249.
37. World Bank. *Migration and Development Brief No. 31*; World Bank Group: Washington, DC, USA, 2019. World Bank Migration an Remittances portal. Available online: https://documents1.worldbank.org/curated/en/099743108132442498/pdf/IDU14f9949a 1807f146a91917b16a5166334a79.pdf (accessed on 16 June 2025).
38. Bhagat, A.; Roderick, L. Banking on refugees: Racialized expropriation in the fintech era. *Environ. Plann. Econ. Space* **2020**, *5* 1498–1515. [CrossRef]
39. Nicoletti, B. *The Future of FinTech: Integrating Finance and Technology in Financial Services*; Springer International Publishing: Cham Switzerland, 2017. [CrossRef]
40. *ISO/IEC 27001*; Information Security, Cybersecurity and Privacy Protection—Information Security Management Systems– Requirements. ISO: Geneva, Switzerland, 2022.
41. Black, W.; Babin, B.J. Multivariate Data Analysis: Its Approach, Evolution, and Impact. In *The Great Facilitator*; Springe Berlin/Heidelberg, Germany, 2019; pp. 121–130.
42. Gomber, P.; Koch, J.A.; Siering, M. Digital finance and Fintech: Current research and future research directions. *J. Bus. Econ.* **201** *87*, 537–580. [CrossRef]
43. Roberts, J.A.; Lunsford, R. Reducing the financial inclusion gap through digital transformation. *Glob. Conf. Bus. Financ. Pro* **2023**, *18*, 127–133.
44. Suri, T.; Bharadwaj, P.; Jack, W. Fintech and household resilience to shocks: Evidence from digital loans in Kenya. *J. Dev. Econ* **2021**, *153*, 102697. [CrossRef]
45. Zavolokina, L.; Dolata, M.; Schwabe, G. The FinTech phenomenon: Antecedents of financial innovation perceived by the popula press. *Financ. Innov.* **2016**, *2*, 16. [CrossRef]
46. Sanmath, A. FinTech banking—The revolutionized digital banking. *Int. J. Trend Sci. Res. Dev.* **2018**, *9*, 172–180. [CrossRef]
47. Datta, D. The future of financial inclusion through fintech: A conceptual study in post-pandemic India. *Sachetas* **2023**, *2*, 11–1 [CrossRef]
48. Greenacre, J. What regulatory problems arise when fintech lending expands into fledgling credit markets? *Wash. Univ. J. La Policy* **2020**, *61*, 229–260.
49. Lakshman, K.; Raj, V. A study on the impact of fintech companies with reference to growth of the Indian economy. *J. Emerg Technol. Innov. Res.* **2023**, *10*, d581–d590.
50. UIDAI. Aadhaar: Enabling Financial Inclusion. 2021. Available online: https://uidai.gov.in (accessed on 3 July 2025).
51. Reena, A. Role of fintech companies in increasing financial inclusion. *J. Appl. Manag. Jidnyasa* **2022**, *14*, 24–36.
52. Adbi, A.; Natarajan, S. Fintech and banks as complements in micro entrepreneurship. *Strateg. Entrep. J.* **2023**, *17*, 585–61 [CrossRef]
53. Sarma, M.; Pais, J. Financial inclusion and development. *J. Int. Dev.* **2011**, *23*, 613–628. [CrossRef]
54. McKinsey. What Digital Finance Means for Emerging Economies. 2016. Available online: https://www.mckinsey.com (accesse on 29 May 2025).
55. Arner, D.W.; Barberis, J.N.; Buckley, R.P. The evolution of Fintech: A new post-crisis paradigm? *Georget. J. Int. Law* **2016**, *4* 1271–1319. [CrossRef]
56. Abbasi, K.; Alam, A.; Brohi, N.A.; Brohi, I.A.; Nasim, S. P2P lending fintech's and SMEs' access to finance. *Econ. Lett.* **202** *204*, 109890. [CrossRef]
57. Duncombe, R.; Boateng, R. Mobile phones and financial services in developing countries: A review of concepts, methods, issue and evidence. *Third World Q.* **2009**, *30*, 1237–1258. [CrossRef]
58. Kehinde-Peters, O. Fintech and financial inclusion: Closing the gender gap. In *Women and Finance in Africa: Inclusion an Transformation*; Springer Nature: Cham, Switzerland, 2024; pp. 75–89.

59. Adegbite, O.O.; Machethe, C.L. Bridging the financial inclusion gender gap in smallholder agriculture in Nigeria: An untapped potential for sustainable development. *World Dev.* **2020**, *127*, 104755. [CrossRef]
60. Arner, D.W.; Buckley, R.P.; Zetzsche, D.A.; Veidt, R. The identity challenge in finance: From analogue identity to digitized identification to digital KYC utilities. *Eur. Bus. Organ. Law Rev.* **2018**, *19*, 55–80. [CrossRef]

https://doi.org/10.3390/fintech5010003

FinTech

Article

Large Language Models for Nowcasting Cryptocurrency Market Conditions

Anurag Dutta [1,*], M. Gayathri Lakshmi [2], A. Ramamoorthy [3] and Pijush Kanti Kumar [4]

[1] Department of Computer Science and Engineering, Government College of Engineering and Textile Technology, Serampore 712201, West Bengal, India
[2] Department of Mathematics, Saveetha Engineering College, Chennai 602105, Tamil Nadu, India; gayathrilakshmi@saveetha.ac.in
[3] Department of Mathematics, Vel Tech Rangarajan Dr. Sagunthala R&D Institute of Science and Technology, Chennai 600062, Tamil Nadu, India; drramamoorthya@veltech.edu.in
[4] Department of Information Technology, Government College of Engineering and Textile Technology, Serampore 712201, West Bengal, India; pijush752000@gcetts.ac.in
* Correspondence: anuragdutta@ieee.org

Abstract

Large language models have expanded their application from traditional tasks in natural language processing to several domains of science, technology, engineering, and mathematics. This research studies the potential of these models for financial *"nowcasting"*–real-time forecasting (of the recent past) for cryptocurrency market conditions. Further, the research benchmarks capabilities of five state-of-the-art decoder-only models, `gpt-4.1` (OpenAI), `gemini-2.5-pro` (Google), `claude-3-opus-20240229` (Anthropic), `deepseek-reasoner` (DeepSeek), and `grok-4` (xAI) across 12 major crypto-assets around the world. Using minute-resolution history of a day in USD for the stocks, `gemini-2.5-pro` emerges as a consistent leader in forecasting (except for a few assets). The stablecoins exhibit minimal deviation across all models, justifying the *"nowcast strength"* in low-volatility environments, although they are not able to perform well for the highly erratic assets. Additionally, since large language models have been known to better their performance when executed for a higher number of passes, the experimentations were conducted for two passes (`Pass@1` and `Pass@2`), and the respective nowcast errors are found to be reduced by 1.2156% (on average).

Keywords: large language models; nowcasting; cryptocurrencies; market volatility

JEL Classification: G17; C53; C45

1. Introduction

Cryptocurrencies have emerged as a major class of decentralized digital assets that trade continuously, without the closure periods typical of traditional equities and commodities. Their constant operation, combined with extreme fluctuations, heterogeneous liquidity, and sentiment-driven price swings, creates markets that are structurally more volatile than most conventional financial assets [1–3]. These characteristics make cryptocurrencies ideal for short-horizon prediction, or *nowcasting*, where the objective is to infer the immediate future or most recent present state of the market from high-frequency data. Traditionally, high-frequency financial prediction and market volatility modeling have been studied extensively in the financial-technology literature using *classical parametric* techniques like ARCH, and GARCH models [4,5], capturing volatility clustering and conditional heteroskedasticity. Further, *realized-volatility* methods use intraday returns for intraday construction of (instantaneous) market variability [6,7]. Nowcasting, which was initially developed in macroeconomics for studying real-time estimates of economic variables, is now getting absorbed in *fintech* to capture the data streams from the recent past (observations) for immediate decision-making [8].

While existing methods [9,10] tend to work well for traditional assets and forecast over larger windows, they fail to *"nowcast"* well. Nowcasting [8], unlike forecasting [11], infers the most recent past or predicts the very near future market states from incoming data streams. In the context of cryptocurrencies, minute resolution data provide rich but very noisy signals due to irregular patterns and sudden shifts in market trends [12–14], which makes it difficult even for the state-of-the-art machine learning techniques to predict asset prices. A core methodological decision in short-horizon market prediction is whether to model price levels, log-prices, or returns. Financial time series data are generally non-stationary in levels but exhibit more stable properties in returns or log-returns; similarly, realized volatility aggregates intraday return variability and is often the target for high-frequency nowcasts. Traditional deep-learning models (e.g., long short-term memory, transformers, convolutional networks, etc.) are efficient at learning temporal and spatial patterns from structured data [9], but their predictive capabilities are insufficient for medium to high frequency, needing minute-scale predictions. **LLMs tend to overcome these challenges by processing online financial news, expert commentaries, and social media, allowing models to interpret market dynamics in more depth.** Recent studies have shown these large language models with more promise (or in some cases, competitiveness) than many state-of-the-art neural models for time series forecasting. Zhou et al. [15] suggest coupling with LLM-generated text analysis and analyzing indicators like RSI, moving averages, etc., adding context, and therefore refining them using FinBERT [16] through sentiment analysis. Similarly, the hybrid models proposed by Chen et al. [17,18] and Wang et al. [19] use LLM capabilities to extract and encode noisy market signals, which, when fused with neural architectures, deliver better accuracy, especially in turbulent or sentiment-driven conditions. Comparative analyses consistently show that LLM-based or LLM-augmented methods demonstrate improved robustness, better adaptability to new market information, and superior prediction metrics (e.g., lower RMSE and MAE) over deep learning models relying solely on numeric inputs. The strength of LLMs lies not only in their ability to process vast textual information but also in offering *"expert analyst"*-like interpretations [20] that complement quantitative signals. As a result, literature increasingly points to LLM-augmented or LLM-guided systems as better in terms of predictive performance and ability to generalize across volatile regimes than traditional deep learning alone. While these advances come with greater computational demands and require careful integration, the consensus in recent studies is that the multimodal fusion of LLMs with deep-learning architectures sets a new benchmark in financial forecasting, achieving an enhanced, context-aware understanding of market fluctuations and outperforming the traditional techniques.

This research aims to study the efficiency of leading LLMs (standalone) for nowcasting cryptocurrency market conditions. Cryptocurrencies have some unique characteristics—(a) extreme fluctuations [2,3], (b) market microstructure effects [21], and (c) heterogeneous data sources [22] that benefit from the deep contextual understanding and multi-level reasoning strategies of LLMs. Additionally, the state-of-the-art LLMs possess mechanisms like *speculative decoding*, *mixture-of-experts* layers, and *dynamic attention* spans that improve performance on irregular financial time series. In this research, nowcasting capabilities of five leading decoder-type LLMs, `gpt-4.1` (OpenAI), `gemini-2.5-pro` (Google), `claude-3-opus-20240229` (Anthropic), `deepseek-reasoner` (DeepSeek), and `grok-4` (xAI), have been evaluated on minute-resolution price data for twelve major cryptocurrencies, comprising both highly volatile assets and a few stablecoins. Besides, it also benchmarks the top-2 LLMs against established econometric and neural baselines from the ARCH, and GARCH families, HAR-volatility models, and Recurrent Neural Networks—for each of the cryptocurrencies. **LLMs outperform the classical econometric models by ≈9.47% and the neural models by ≈4.63%.** This benchmarking enables identification of (a) model rankings in nowcasting, (b) quantification of the benefits of multi-pass reasoning (two passes were made for this research) over classical models, and (c) exploration of the robustness of the models for low- and high-volatility assets.

The organization of this manuscript is as follows: Section 2 presents the background and preliminaries of this research. The methodology for "*nowcasting*" is described thoroughly in Section 3, and the experimentation is laid out in Section 4 with presentation of the comparative result. Finally, the work is concluded in Section 5 addressing both the merits and demerits of the work.

2. Preliminaries

This section discusses the necessary preliminaries for the establishment of the research: (a) cryptocurrency market volatility, for understanding the dynamics of price fluctuations, and (b) large-language models, for understanding the operation of decoder-only type models.

2.1. Cryptocurrency Market Volatility

In financial markets, volatility is the quantification of the degree of variation in the price of an asset over time. For cryptocurrency, this "*degree of variation*" is often extreme due to 24/7 trading, low liquidity in some tokens, and rapid shifts in market sentiment. Empirically, it can be observed that the returns of large-cap cryptocurrencies are "*fat-tailed*" [3], i.e., the probability of extreme returns decays much slower than under a Gaussian assumption, and clusters by volatility; thus, the large (or small) price moves tend to be followed by large (or small) moves, reflecting persistence in conditional variance. The volatilities are also impacted by the "*leverage effect*" [23] because of which negative returns often increase future volatility more than positive returns of the same magnitude, implying an asymmetric response of risk to shocks. Additionally, the financial market is expected to have a long memory, i.e., autocorrelations in absolute or squared returns decay hyperbolically over long temporal horizons. These occurrences are conditionally *heteroskedastic* by nature, which makes use of both direct and nonparametric insights from the market, making the forecast of these fluctuations challenging. As mentioned in the Introduction itself, classical techniques like ARCH [4] and GARCH [5] are precise in capturing volatility clustering and conditional heteroskedasticity. Similarly, high-frequency approaches [6,7] realized volatility by aggregating intraday returns. In fintech, this family of models has been applied with a mixed (balanced) set of observations [24,25], primarily because of extreme jumps in the stock prices at times, intra-day trading, and most importantly, sentiment-driven shifts. **This research aligns with this econometric tradition but evaluates whether modern LLMs (the leading technology behind the current AI revolution), when used as autoregressive generators, can match or complement these established baselines.**

2.2. Decoder-Only Large Language Models

Transformer architecture, which serves as the building blocks of large language models today, was introduced by Vaswani et al. in a groundbreaking inception ("*Attention Is All You Need*", 2018) [26], using the existent self-attention mechanisms to model sequence data over the standard recurrence or convolutional modules. In a standard Transformer (*encoder-decoder* type), an input sequence is first embedded and then processed through stacked layers of multi-head self-attention [27] and position-wise feed-forward networks [28], each followed by residual connections [29] and layer normalization [30]. Apart from the "*encoder-decoder*" type, there are two different architectures of transformer models—"*encoder-only*" and "*decoder-only*". Figure 1 presents a detailed architectural comparison between the three transformer-based model types. Decoder-only Transformers (GPT-type models) are the foundational blocks to every large language model; these are *autoregressive sequence generators* (in layman's terms), where each next-token prediction *conditions* on prior tokens [31–33]. In nowcasting stock prices, these decoder-only LLMs are used for minute-level market observations.

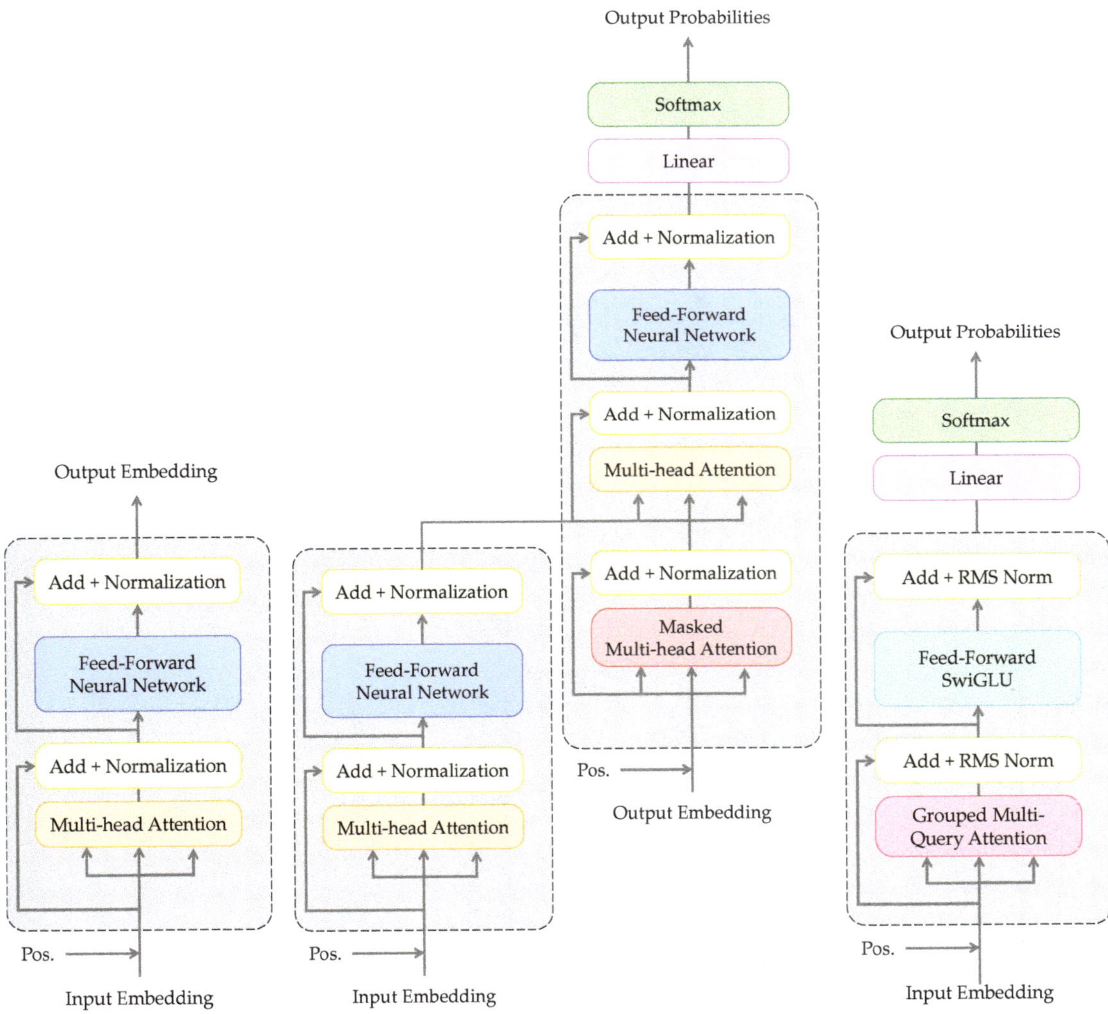

(**a**) Encoder only (BERT) (**b**) Encoder-Decoder (Original Transformer) (**c**) Decoder only (LLaMA)

Figure 1. Architectural comparison of common Transformer-based models: encoder-only (**a**), encoder-decoder (**b**), and decoder-only (**c**).

3. Methodology

This section presents the structured framework to evaluate the nowcasting capability of decoder-only large language models (LLMs) on high-frequency cryptocurrency time series. The pipeline consists of (a) data preparation, (b) input encoding using "prompt" engineering, (c) autoregressive inference with optional multi-pass sampling, and finally (d) quantitative performance evaluation. **The objective, therefore, in this pipeline is to determine the capabilities of LLMs to provide insights into financial markets under volatility and noise.**

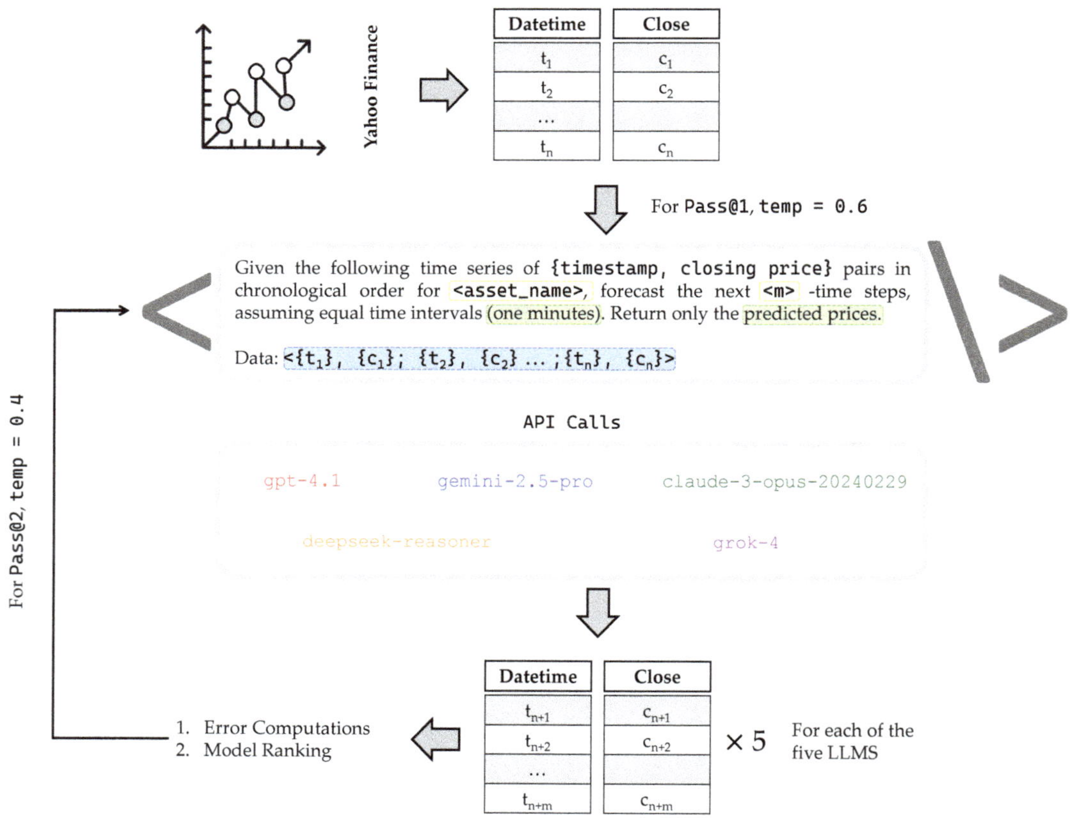

Figure 2. Methodology for nowcasting crypto-market trends using the large language models.

3.1. Data Acquisition and Preprocessing

Let $\mathcal{C} = \{C_1, C_2, \ldots, C_K\}$ denote a set of $K = 12$ cryptocurrency assets (e.g., bitcoin, ethereum, dogecoin, etc.) For each asset $C_k \in \mathcal{C}$, minute-level OHLC (Open-High-Low-Close) data for a fixed trading day. The timestamp–close pairs are extracted as,

$$[\boldsymbol{\mathcal{D}}_k]_{((n+m)\times 2)} = \{(t_1^{(k)}, c_1^{(k)}), (t_2^{(k)}, c_2^{(k)}), \ldots, (t_{n+m}^{(k)}, c_{n+m}^{(k)})\}, \tag{1}$$

where, $t_i^{(k)}$ is the ith minute timestamp (in UTC) and $c_i^{(k)}$ is the closing price of C_k at $t_i^{(k)}$ (in USD).

To control scale variance across assets, the first n points are normalized to have zero mean ($\mu = 0$) and unit variance ($\Sigma = 1$). Thus, the sequence in Equation (1) are bounded as,

$$c_i^{(k)} \leftarrow \frac{c_i^{(k)} - \mu_k}{\Sigma_k}, \quad \mu_k = \frac{1}{n}\sum_{i=1}^{n} c_i^{(k)}, \quad \Sigma_k = \sqrt{\frac{1}{n}\sum_{i=1}^{n}\left\| c_i^{(k)} - \mu_k \right\|^2}$$

The LLMs are then allowed to observe the entire set n tuples, partitioned into,

1. **Context window** $\mathcal{X}_k = \{(t_1^{(k)}, c_1^{(k)}), \ldots, (t_n^{(k)}, c_n^{(k)})\}$ (input to the model), and
2. **Forecast window** $\mathcal{Y}_k = \{(t_{n+1}^{(k)}, c_{n+1}^{(k)}), \ldots, (t_m, c_m)\}; \quad \exists\, m < 2 \cdot n$ (used for evaluation).

3.2. Prompt Encoding and Autoregressive Inference

Decoder-only LLMs process data via tokenized input prompts. To feed structured time series into this format, the context window $\mathcal{X}_k$ is flattened and fed as a text sequence,

> Given the following time series of timestamp, closing price pairs in chronological order for <asset_name>, forecast the next <m> -time steps, assuming equal time intervals (one minutes). Return only the predicted prices. Data: <t1, c1; t2, c2...;tn, cn>

The prompt is formatted as natural language while preserving syntactic structure for ease of parsing. Models are queried using their public APIs with default inference hyperparameters,

1. **Temperature** [34] (T) which controls the sampling entropy. For the first pass (`Pass@1`, encouraging diversity) of the model, $T_1 = 0.6$ was set and for the second pass (`Pass@2`, favoring refinement) $T_2 = 0.4$ was set.
2. **Max token length** [35] set to allow at least m scalar predictions.
3. **Decoding strategy** [36]: all models use top-p sampling with nucleus $p = 0.95$.

Given the prompt $\mathcal{P}_k$, each LLM $\mathcal{M}^{(j)}$ produces a response, $\hat{\mathcal{Y}}_k^{(j)} = \mathcal{M}^{(j)}(\mathcal{P}_k; T, m)$, where $\hat{\mathcal{Y}}_k^{(j)} = \{\hat{c}_{n+1}^{(j)}, \ldots, \hat{c}_{n+m}^{(j)}\}$ is the predicted price sequence from model j.

3.3. Multi-Pass Sampling and Refinement

Since auto-regressive LLMs gives different outputs for different stochastic decoding, **multi-pass sampling** was performed to investigate *stability* and *refinement*. For each model j, two passes were conducted,

1. `Pass@1`: *"one-shot"* prediction with $\mathcal{P}_k$ and temperature $T_1 = 0.6$,
2. `Pass@2`: re-query using the same $\mathcal{P}_k$ and a reduced temperature $T_2 = 0.4$ to reduce variance and encourage convergence.

These are denoted as,

$$\hat{\mathcal{Y}}_k^{(j,1)} = \mathcal{M}^{(j)}(\mathcal{P}_k; T_1), \quad \hat{\mathcal{Y}}_k^{(j,2)} = \mathcal{M}^{(j)}(\mathcal{P}_k; T_2).$$

The performance differential $\Delta\text{RMSE}_k^{(j)} = \text{RMSE}^{(j,1)} - \text{RMSE}^{(j,2)}$ is computed to assess refinement. In principle, increasing the number of passes (`Pass@k`, $k > 1$) should reduce variance in predictions and improve RMSE. However, practical limitations apply: proprietary LLMs monetize token usage, constraining feasible k. In our experiments, we evaluated up to $k = 5$. Beyond $k = 2$, most models did not exhibit substantial gains; instead, performance often deteriorated due to hallucinations or unstable numeric continuations, particularly in volatile series. Therefore, we report only the first two passes: the first reflects the *"one-shot"* baseline, while the second captures the benefit of sampling diversity without incurring instability. Figure 2 presents the methodology workflow as discussed above.

4. Experimentation

This section presents the experimental setup and results of evaluating the nowcasting performance of five decoder-only large language models (LLMs) across twelve major cryptocurrencies using minute-resolution price data.

4.1. Dataset

This research considers a diverse set of twelve cryptocurrencies, $\mathcal{C} = \{C_1, C_2, \ldots, C_{12}\}$, comprising high-volatility assets (e.g., BTC, ETH) and stablecoins (e.g., USDT, USDC). The assets, their abbreviations, and corresponding metadata are summarized in Table 1. Each asset C_k has a context length n (the number of minute-resolution points used as input) that varies between 230 and 1147, and a nowcast horizon m (the number of steps predicted) that varies between 58 and 287. Figure 3 shows one-day, minute-resolution closing prices for the selected cryptocurrencies. The reason behind the choice of the selected twelve cryptocurrencies is to keep the set of assets diverse (intentionally) and to balance observational explainability. At one-minute granularity, each asset produces $\approx$1.4 k points daily, which skypes up to $\approx$17 k across the portfolio, with sufficient statistical depth for model evaluation. The portfolio covers *"flagship high-volatility"* tokens (BTC, ETH), *"mid-cap coins"* (ADA, SOL, TRX, XRP), *"ecosystem-specific"* tokens (BNB, STETH, WTRX), and *"stablecoins"* (USDT, USDC) containing distinct market microstructure regimes, liquidity conditions, and volatility profiles. The existent literature affirms that predictive behavior is largely driven by volatility class and liquidity structure rather than by the idiosyncrasies of individual tokens; thus, once these representative regimes (mentioned above, in *italicized* text) are included, additional assets result in poor explanation of the observations, because of which we limited the choice to the 12 crypto-assets (refer to Table 1). This makes the chosen portfolio *tractable*, *representative*, and *feasible* with the potential to engage in robust conclusions about the relative forecasting capabilities of LLMs.

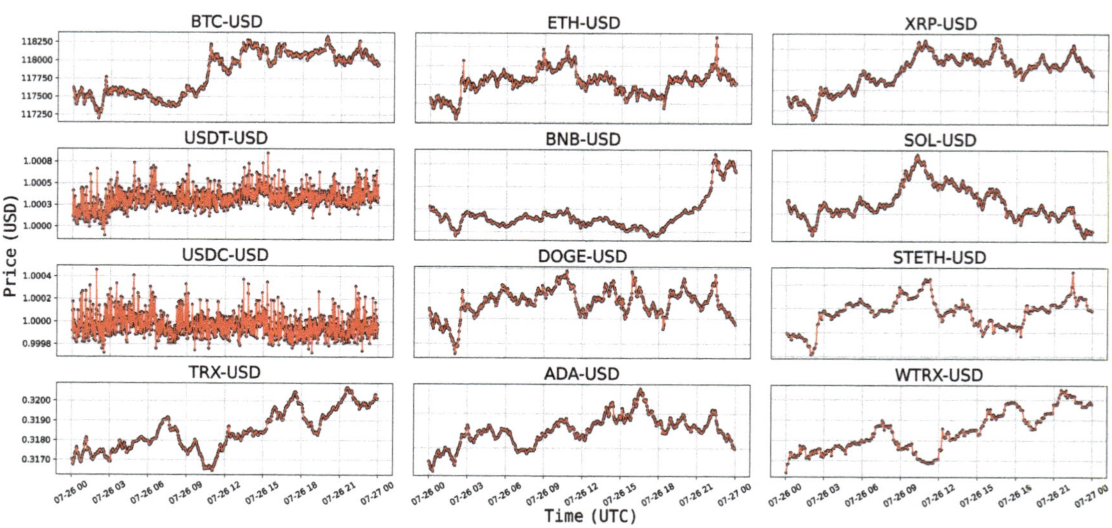

Figure 3. The variations in closing cap for different cryptocurrencies were sampled at a granularity of 1 min for a window of a whole day. It can be inferred from the plots that none of the assets (refer to Table 1) model seasonality or any repetition in patterns, making the nowcast challenging.

Table 1. Different cryptocurrencies, their abbreviations, their context and nowcast lengths, along with their descriptions. For the experiments, the context is fed as plain-text input, and the LLMs are asked to generated the forecast (here, nowcast).

Cryptocurrency	Abbreviation	Context	Nowcast	Crypto Description
Cardano	ADA-USD	996	250	Smart contract platform with research approach
Binance Coin	BNB-USD	1060	265	Utility token used within Binance ecosystem
Solana	SOL-USD	1126	282	Fast blockchain focused on scalability and speed
Bitcoin	BTC-USD	1084	271	First and most known decentralized cryptocurrency
Dogecoin	DOGE-USD	948	238	Meme-inspired coin for community support
Ethereum	ETH-USD	1128	282	Smart contract leader for decentralized apps
Lido Staked Ether	STETH-USD	230	58	Tokenized ETH staked using the Lido protocol
TRON	TRX-USD	1060	266	Network for digital content and media sharing
USD Coin	USDC-USD	1127	282	Regulated stablecoin backed by dollar reserves
Tether	USDT-USD	1147	287	Leading stablecoin pegged to the U.S. dollar
Wrapped TRON	WTRX-USD	230	58	Ethereum-compatible token version of TRON
Ripple	XRP-USD	1081	271	Crypto for fast global payments and settlements

4.2. Experimental Results

This subsection evaluates five large language models (refer to Table 2): `GPT-4.1` (OpenAI), `Gemini-2.5-Pro` (Google), `Claude-3-Opus` (Anthropic), `DeepSeek-Reasoner` (DeepSeek), and `Grok-4` (xAI). Each model is tested using two passes of inference: `Pass@1` with temperature $T_1 = 0.6$, and `Pass@2` with $T_2 = 0.4$. Tables 3 and 4 present the Root Mean Square Error (RMSE) and Mean Absolute Error (MAE) for each asset across the five models, accurate up to six decimal places. The best result for each asset (per metric and pass) is **highlighted**. Figure 4 displays the mean model ranking (lower is better) aggregated over all assets and both passes. `Gemini-2.5-Pro` exhibits the best average performance, followed closely by `GPT-4.1`, especially in high-volatility scenarios. Table 5 presents the comparison of the top-2 LLMs with established *econometric* models – GARCH (1, 1), GJR-GARCH (1, 1), and HAR-RV; and *neural* models – GRU, and LSTM.

Table 2. Layer-wise architecture summary of the large language models used for this research.

Model	**Architecture Type**	**Context Window**	**Per-Layer Highlights**	**Special Mechanisms**
`gpt-4.1`	Decoder-only	∼1 M	Masked multi-head self-attention Feed-forward network (GELU) Layer norm + residual Long-span (dynamic attention)	Instruction-tuned Multimodal embeddings Speculative decoding
`gemini-2.5-pro`	Decoder-only Mixture of Experts	∼1 M	Grouped-query attention (GQA) Mixture-of-Experts FFN Residual + layer norm	"Deep Think" reasoning Multimodal fusion layers
`claude-3-opus-20240229`	Decoder-only	∼200 K	Masked multi-head self-attention Feed-forward network (GELU) Layer norm + residual	Dual θ/λ generate + verify Hallucination mitigation

Table 2. *Cont.*

Model	Architecture Type	Context Window	Per-Layer Highlights	Special Mechanisms
`deepseek-reasoner`	Decoder-only RL model	∼128 K	Chain-of-Thought token paths Inference loop (self-verification) RoPE positional embeddings	RL-first reasoning pipeline Cold-start SFT + RL fine-tuning
`grok-4`	Hybrid design	∼256 K	Modular attention routing Specialized transformer subsystems Residual + layer norm	Multi-agent "Heavy" mode Native tool & real-time search Symbolic (math) co-processors

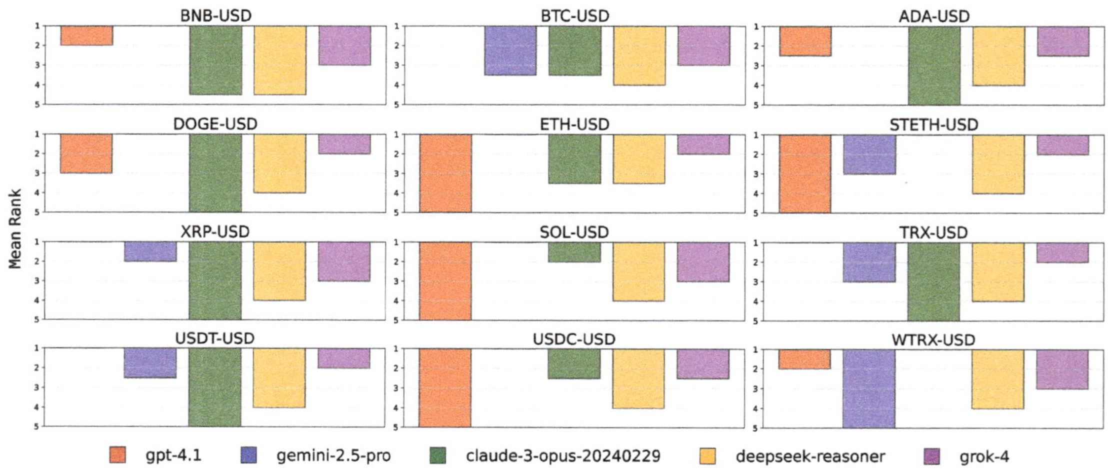

Figure 4. Mean Rank (averaged over both the passes, y-axis) for each of the five models (x-axis) evaluated on the 12 cryptocurrency assets. **Shorter bars depict better rank than the longer bars.**

Table 3. Nowcasting performance (RMSE, and MAE) in `Pass@1` of the five large-language models competing against each other. The best results are **highlighted**.

Cryptocurrency	Metrics	`gpt-4.1` (OpenAI)	`gemini-2.5-pro` (Google)	`claude-3-opus-20240229` (Anthropic)	`deepseek-reasoner` (DeepSeek)	`grok-4` (xAI)
Cardano	RMSE	0.0036	**0.0024**	0.0053	0.0040	0.0035
	MAE	0.0029	**0.0019**	0.0047	0.0034	0.0030
Binance Coin	RMSE	8.1722	**7.4841**	10.3506	8.9133	8.4246
	MAE	6.6000	**5.9315**	8.5815	7.2627	6.8126
Bitcoin	RMSE	**113.5952**	120.7385	121.9678	119.5055	118.0289
	MAE	92.1119	**85.6062**	96.8550	92.4466	90.6021
Dogecoin	RMSE	0.0027	**0.0011**	0.0047	0.0031	0.0025
	MAE	0.0022	**0.0009**	0.0040	0.0026	0.0021
Ethereum	RMSE	14.8038	**7.4333**	12.4757	12.1862	10.9557
	MAE	12.0619	**5.0465**	9.4482	9.4312	8.2732

Table 3. *Cont.*

Cryptocurrency	Metrics	gpt-4.1 (OpenAI)	gemini-2.5-pro (Google)	claude-3-opus-20240229 (Anthropic)	deepseek-reasoner (DeepSeek)	grok-4 (xAI)
Solana	RMSE	2.4482	**0.5466**	0.6789	1.3979	1.0512
	MAE	2.2033	**0.4801**	0.5099	1.2255	0.9034
Lido Staked Ether	RMSE	10.9444	9.1565	**6.4742**	9.2257	8.4909
	MAE	8.6561	6.8606	**4.3686**	6.9800	6.2768
TRON	RMSE	**0.0011**	0.0015	0.0020	0.0016	0.0014
	MAE	**0.0010**	0.0014	0.0018	0.0015	0.0013
USD Coin	RMSE	0.0002	**0.0001**	0.0001	0.0002	0.0001
	MAE	0.0002	**0.0001**	0.0001	0.0001	0.0001
Tether	RMSE	**0.0001**	0.0001	0.0001	0.0001	0.0001
	MAE	**0.0001**	0.0001	0.0001	0.0001	0.0001
Wrapped TRON	RMSE	0.0009	0.0011	**0.0008**	0.0009	0.0009
	MAE	0.0007	0.0010	**0.0007**	0.0008	0.0008
Ripple	RMSE	**0.0105**	0.0187	0.0400	0.0256	0.0206
	MAE	**0.0085**	0.0145	0.0340	0.0212	0.0168

Table 4. Nowcasting performance (RMSE, and MAE) in `Pass@2` of the five large-language models competing against each other. The best results are **highlighted**.

Cryptocurrency	Metrics	gpt-4.1 (OpenAI)	gemini-2.5-pro (Google)	claude-3-opus-20240229 (Anthropic)	deepseek-reasoner (DeepSeek)	grok-4 (xAI)
Cardano	RMSE	0.0033	**0.0024**	0.0049	0.0041	0.0034
	MAE	0.0028	**0.0018**	0.0043	0.0035	0.0028
Binance Coin	RMSE	7.6002	**6.7357**	9.1085	9.1807	7.9191
	MAE	6.2700	**5.4588**	7.7233	7.4079	6.4720
Bitcoin	RMSE	**106.7787**	111.0792	107.4139	120.7005	113.3071
	MAE	88.4688	**79.6137**	87.1695	94.2955	86.0710
Dogecoin	RMSE	0.0025	**0.0011**	0.0044	0.0032	0.0024
	MAE	0.0021	**0.0009**	0.0036	0.0027	0.0020
Ethereum	RMSE	13.6195	**7.1352**	11.7262	12.4301	10.4089
	MAE	11.4588	**4.8951**	8.6918	9.6190	7.7810
Solana	RMSE	2.2763	**0.5242**	0.6244	1.4390	0.9931
	MAE	2.0931	**0.4665**	0.4793	1.2500	0.8572
Lido Staked Ether	RMSE	10.2905	8.7902	**5.8260**	9.4103	8.0654
	MAE	8.3100	6.5176	**4.0191**	7.1896	5.9022
TRON	RMSE	**0.0010**	0.0014	0.0018	0.0016	0.0014
	MAE	**0.0010**	0.0013	0.0017	0.0015	0.0013
USD Coin	RMSE	0.0002	**0.0001**	0.0001	0.0002	0.0001
	MAE	0.0002	**0.0001**	0.0001	0.0001	0.0001

Table 4. *Cont.*

Cryptocurrency	Metrics	gpt-4.1 (OpenAI)	gemini-2.5-pro (Google)	claude-3-opus-20240229 (Anthropic)	deepseek-reasoner (DeepSeek)	grok-4 (xAI)
Tether	RMSE	**0.0001**	0.0001	0.0001	0.0001	0.0001
	MAE	**0.0001**	0.0001	0.0001	0.0001	0.0001
Wrapped TRON	RMSE	0.0008	0.0010	**0.0008**	0.0010	0.0008
	MAE	0.0007	0.0009	**0.0007**	0.0008	0.0008
Ripple	RMSE	**0.0098**	0.0176	0.0360	0.0261	0.0196
	MAE	**0.0080**	0.0139	0.0313	0.0218	0.0158

Additionally, Figure 5 visualizes minute-resolution of closing prices for various cryptocurrencies, segmented into (a) "*training context*" (in red), representing the historical price points observed by the large language models during inference, (b) "*true future*" prices (in blue), denoting the actual ground-truth values withheld for model evaluation, and (c) nowcasted predictions (in orange) for the forecasted price trajectory for `Gemini-2.5-Pro` (averaged over both passes).

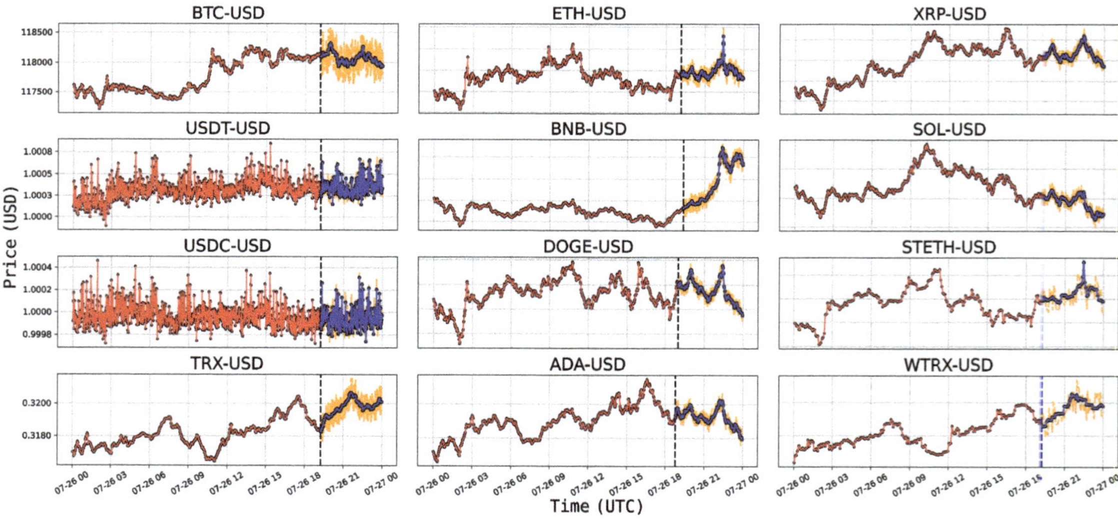

Figure 5. The variations in closing cap (train-red), true predictions (test-blue), and the nowcast (predictions-orange, averaged over both the passes) for the cryptocurrencies.

Table 5. Step-ahead nowcast accuracies (averaged over both the passes for the LLMs) for two representative cryptocurrencies from each asset class, compared to established *econometric*, *neural*, and *large language models*.

Cryptoasset Type	Token	Classical Models			Neural Models		Large Language Models	
		GARCH (1,1)	GJR-GARCH (1,1)	HAR-RV	GRU	LSTM	gemini-2.5-pro	gpt-4.1
High-volatility	BTC	0.5762	0.5904	0.6295	0.6316	0.6388	0.6880	0.6973
	ETH	0.5806	0.5982	0.6347	0.6323	0.6495	0.6719	0.6683

Table 5. *Cont.*

Cryptoasset Type	Token	Classical Models			Neural Models		Large Language Models	
		GARCH (1,1)	GJR-GARCH (1,1)	HAR-RV	GRU	LSTM	`gemini-2.5-pro`	`gpt-4.1`
Mid-cap coins	ADA	0.6275	0.6303	0.6376	0.6546	0.6709	0.6877	0.6753
	SOL	0.6128	0.6286	0.6319	0.6522	0.6597	0.6851	0.6790
Ecosystem-specific	BNB	0.6081	0.6252	0.6406	0.6389	0.6437	0.6790	0.6803
	STETH	0.6133	0.6349	0.6539	0.6542	0.6657	0.6947	0.6925
Stablecoins	USDT	0.6350	0.6614	0.6705	0.6789	0.6835	0.7018	0.7011
	USDC	0.6285	0.6524	0.6615	0.6760	0.6779	0.6959	0.6967

4.3. Observations

From the experimental results, as in Section 4.2 (Tables 3–5, and Figures 4 and 5), the following observations can be made:

1. `Gemini-2.5-Pro` consistently outperforms other models (refer to the mean rank in Figure 4 and per-asset accuracies in Table 5). It achieves the lowest average RMSE for eight out of twelve assets in `Pass@2` (Tables 3 and 4).
2. Model performance has a strong positive correlation with the particular class the assets belong to. Stablecoins (USDT, USDC) have very few errors (Tables 3 and 4) and the highest directional accuracy (Table 5), due to their low volatility and tight mean-reversion dynamics. In contrast, high-volatility assets such as BTC and ETH produce substantially larger errors and lower accuracy (Tables 3–5). Thus, it can be stated that extreme intraday variations remain difficult to capture for both econometric and LLM approaches, although the overall accuracy of LLM models for such assets is better by ≈5–6%.
3. `Pass@2` improves accuracy across all models by an average reduction of ≈1.2156% in RMSE from `Pass@1` to `Pass@2`.
4. Some LLMs (e.g., `claude-3-opus` in the experiments) produce unstable numeric outputs on assets like XRP, ETH, etc., which results in error outliers (Tables 3 and 4). This suggests that some models under certain settings hallucinate, requiring post-processing of the incorrect (or even sometimes, non-numeric tokens).
5. When benchmarked against classical econometric models (here, GARCH (1,1), GJR-GARCH, and HAR-RV) and neural baselines (GRU, LSTM), the top LLMs outperform (refer to Table 5): the mean accuracy of LLMs exceeds the classical-model mean by ≈9.47% and the neural-model mean by ≈4.63%. These improvements are uniform but are smallest for the most volatile assets and largest for mid-cap assets.

These observations suggest that even *off-the-shelf* (proprietary) decoder-only LLMs outperform existent classical models in terms of their forecast strengths, robustness, and adaptability across cryptoassets (of different types). But, even in the current strata, the LLMs can't overturn the need for these classical models because of their inherent architectural responsibilities and limitations (like hallucination, catastrophic forgetting, etc.). Therefore, the need of the hour is to develop hybrid strategies that can transfer LLM-informed volatility inputs to strong econometric models. Additionally, the LLMs experimented with in this research are all-purpose models; fintech domain-specific models can also be built by training them on a large corpus of historical economic data, and therefore these models are expected to perform well in practice when conjugated with classical models.

5. Conclusions

This research benchmarked the capabilities of state-of-the-art decoder-only large language models (LLMs) for *"nowcasting"* minute-resolution cryptocurrency price series. The evaluation is being performed on five leading models, `GPT-4.1`, `Gemini-2.5-Pro`, `Claude-3-Opus-20240229`, `DeepSeek-Reasoner`, and `Grok-4`, across twelve assets with varying volatility profiles, becoming the first research to benchmark on such a large variety of crypto-assets. **To the best of our knowledge, the paper is the first contribution to the community on medium-to-high frequency *"nowcast"* in cryptocurrency market conditions. The results confirm that off-the-shelf LLMs, when properly prompted, can capture short-term directional trends in both stable and moderately volatile cryptocurrencies, e.g.,** `Gemini-2.5-Pro` **being the consistent achiever, as observed in this research.** However, all models performed poorly on highly erratic, volatile assets like bitcoin (BTC) and ethereum (ETH), suggesting scopes of improvement for the existing models for purely auto-regressively modeling the intra-day spikes (extreme events). The poor performance of the (most) volatile assets reinforces well-established findings from the literature in financial econometrics, wherein traditionally for volatility clustering and leverage effects models like GARCH-type struggle, although LLMs perform at a higher cap than them, they still struggle to provide explicit structure to these assets with extreme returns. While the best LLMs outperform classical techniques by $\approx$7.48%, the room for improvement in modeling of such extreme events in fintech is large. This study highlights the necessity for hybrid approaches mapping both the traditional (classical as well as neural) techniques with state-of-the-art large language models.

Additionally, the multi-pass sampling protocol (`Pass@1` with temperature $T_1 = 0.6$, and `Pass@2` at $T_2 = 0.4$) observes a measurable reduction in forecast error with an average improvement of 1.2156% in RMSE (particularly) across models and assets, both. From a layman's point of understanding, it is better for LLMs with stochastic sampling to be run for $k > 1$ passes for achieving substantial improvement in accuracies. Although these multi-pass samplings improve statistical accuracy, these gains may not necessarily translate into economic value, especially when the improvement margin is tiny (as is the case for volatile crypto-assets).

Besides architectural constraints arising from numeric sequence extrapolation by these LLMs, some financial-specific limitations remain, such as assessment of long-memory effects, regime shifts, seasonality, etc. Another shortcoming of this proposed methodology for forecasting financial markets using large language models is the reliance on raw close-price series at one-minute resolution. We adopt raw prices here for interpretability and compatibility with autoregressive LLM prompting but acknowledge that return-based validation can be an important direction for future work. Future works can study these aforementioned issues as motivation for research alongside other rising concerns in the present time, like cross-asset spillovers, liquidity shocks, and news releases (macroeconomic), which are lately found to have positive correlation with econometric modeling.

Author Contributions: Methodology, P.K.K.; Software, A.D. and A.R.; Formal analysis, M.G.L.; Data curation, A.D. and A.R.; Writing—original draft, A.D. and M.G.L.; Supervision, P.K.K.; Project administration, A.R. All authors have read and agreed to the published version of the manuscript.

Funding: This research received no external funding.

Institutional Review Board Statement: Not applicable.

Informed Consent Statement: Not applicable.

Data Availability Statement: The original contributions presented in this study are included in the article. Further inquiries can be directed to the corresponding authors.

Conflicts of Interest: The authors declare no conflicts of interest.

References

1. Dutta, A.; Voumik, L.C.; Ramamoorthy, A.; Ray, S.; Raihan, A. Predicting cryptocurrency fraud using ChaosNet: The Ethereum manifestation. *J. Risk Financ. Manag.* **2023**, *16*, 216. [CrossRef]
2. Begušić, S.; Kostanjčar, Z.; Stanley, H.E.; Podobnik, B. Scaling properties of extreme price fluctuations in Bitcoin markets. *Phys. A Stat. Mech. Its Appl.* **2018**, *510*, 400–406. [CrossRef]
3. Bruzgė, R.; Černevičienė, J.; Šapkauskienė, A.; Mačerinskienė, A.; Masteika, S.; Driaunys, K. Stylized facts, volatility dynamics and risk measures of cryptocurrencies. *J. Bus. Econ. Manag. (JBEM)* **2023**, *24*, 527–550. [CrossRef]
4. Engle, R.F. Autoregressive conditional heteroscedasticity with estimates of the variance of United Kingdom inflation. *Econom. J. Econom. Soc.* **1982**, *50*, 987–1007. [CrossRef]
5. Bollerslev, T. Generalized autoregressive conditional heteroskedasticity. *J. Econom.* **1986**, *31*, 307–327. [CrossRef]
6. Andersen, T.G.; Bollerslev, T.; Diebold, F.X.; Labys, P. Modeling and forecasting realized volatility. *Econometrica* **2003**, *71*, 579–625. [CrossRef]
7. Hautsch, N. *Econometrics of Financial High-Frequency Data*; Springer Science & Business Media: Berlin/Heidelberg, Germany, 2011. [CrossRef]
8. Giannone, D.; Reichlin, L.; Small, D. Nowcasting: The real-time informational content of macroeconomic data. *J. Monet. Econ.* **2008**, *55*, 665–676. [CrossRef]
9. Fan, C.; Zhang, X. Stock price nowcasting and forecasting with deep learning. *J. Intell. Inf. Syst.* **2024**, *63*, 639–656. [CrossRef]
10. Richardson, P. Nowcasting and the use of big data in short term macroeconomic forecasting: A critical review. *Econ. Et Stat.* **2018**, *505*, 65–87. [CrossRef]
11. Bok, B.; Caratelli, D.; Giannone, D.; Sbordone, A.M.; Tambalotti, A. Macroeconomic nowcasting and forecasting with big data. *Annu. Rev. Econ.* **2018**, *10*, 615–643. [CrossRef]
12. Stosic, D.; Stosic, D.; Ludermir, T.B.; Stosic, T. Collective behavior of cryptocurrency price changes. *Phys. A: Stat. Mech. Its Appl.* **2018**, *507*, 499–509. [CrossRef]
13. Kyriazis, N.; Papadamou, S.; Corbet, S. A systematic review of the bubble dynamics of cryptocurrency prices. *Res. Int. Bus. Financ.* **2020**, *54*, 101254. [CrossRef]
14. Soloviev, V.N.; Yevtushenko, S.P.; Batareyev, V.V. Comparative analysis of the cryptocurrency and the stock markets using the random matrix theory. In *Computer Science & Software Engineering: Proceedings of the 2nd Student Workshop (CS&SE@SW 2019), Kryvyi Rih, Ukraine, 29 November 2019*; National Academy of Pedagogical Sciences of Ukraine: Kyiv, Ukraine, 2019; Volume 2546, pp. 87–100. Available online: https://lib.iitta.gov.ua/id/eprint/720100/ (accessed on 28 September 2025).
15. Zhou, L.; Zhang, Y.; Yu, J.; Wang, G.; Liu, Z.; Yongchareon, S.; Wang, N. Llm-augmented linear transformer–cnn for enhanced stock price prediction. *Mathematics* **2025**, *13*, 487. [CrossRef]
16. Kim, J.; Kim, H.-S.; Choi, S.-Y. Forecasting the S&P 500 index using mathematical-based sentiment analysis and deep learning models: A FinBERT transformer model and LSTM. *Axioms* **2023**, *12*, 835. [CrossRef]
17. Chen, Q.; Kawashima, H. Stock price prediction using llm-based sentiment analysis. In Proceedings of the 2024 IEEE International Conference on Big Data (BigData), Washington, DC, USA, 15–18 December 2024; pp. 4846–4853. [CrossRef]
18. Chen, Q. Stock price prediction with LLM-guided market movement signals and transformer model. *Fintech Sustain. Innov.* **2025**, 1–7. [CrossRef]
19. Wang, S.; Ji, T.; Wang, L.; Sun, Y.; Liu, S.-C.; Kumar, A.; Lu, C.-T. Stocktime: A time series specialized large language model architecture for stock price prediction. *arXiv* **2024**, arXiv:2409.08281. [CrossRef]
20. Törnberg, P. Large language models outperform expert coders and supervised classifiers at annotating political social media messages. *Soc. Sci. Comput. Rev.* **2024**, 08944393241286471. [CrossRef]
21. Almeida, J.; Gonçalves, T.C. Cryptocurrency market microstructure: A systematic literature review. *Ann. Oper. Res.* **2024**, *332*, 1035–1068. [CrossRef]
22. İçellioğlu, C.Ş.; Öner, S. An investigation on the volatility of cryptocurrencies by means of heterogeneous panel data analysis. *Procedia Comput. Sci.* **2019**, *158*, 913–920. [CrossRef]
23. Sözen, Ç. Volatility dynamics of cryptocurrencies: A comparative analysis using GARCH-family models. *Future Bus. J.* **2025**, *11*, 166. [CrossRef]
24. Katsiampa, P. Volatility estimation for Bitcoin: A comparison of GARCH models. *Econ. Lett.* **2017**, *158*, 3–6. [CrossRef]
25. Dyhrberg, A.H. Hedging capabilities of Bitcoin. Is it the virtual gold? *Financ. Res. Lett.* **2016**, *16*, 139–144. [CrossRef]
26. Vaswani, A.; Shazeer, N.; Parmar, N.; Uszkoreit, J.; Jones, L.; Gomez, A.N.; Kaiser, Ł.; Polosukhin, I. Attention is all you need. *Adv. Neural Inf. Process. Syst.* **2017**, *30*. [CrossRef]

27. Wu, C.; Wu, F.; Ge, S.; Qi, T.; Huang, Y.; Xie, X. Neural news recommendation with multi-head self-attention. In Proceedings of the 2019 Conference on Empirical Methods in Natural Language Processing and the 9th International Joint Conference on Natural Language Processing (EMNLP-IJCNLP), Hong Kong, China, 3–7 November 2019; pp. 6389–6394. [CrossRef]
28. Geva, M.; Schuster, R.; Berant, J.; Levy, O. Transformer feed-forward layers are key-value memories. *arXiv* **2020**, arXiv:2012.14913. [CrossRef]
29. He, K.; Zhang, X.; Ren, S.; Sun, J. Deep residual learning for image recognition. In Proceedings of the IEEE Conference on Computer Vision and Pattern Recognition (CVPR), Las Vegas, NV, USA, 27–30 June 2016; pp. 770–778. [CrossRef]
30. Ba, J.L.; Kiros, J.R.; Hinton, G.E. Layer normalization. *arXiv* **2016**, arXiv:1607.06450. [CrossRef]
31. Brown, T.; Mann, B.; Ryder, N.; Subbiah, M.; Kaplan, J.D.; Dhariwal, P.; Neelakantan, A.; Shyam, P.; Sastry, G.; Askell, A.; et al. Language models are few-shot learners. *Adv. Neural Inf. Process. Syst.* **2020**, *33*, 1877–1901. [CrossRef]
32. Kaplan, J.; McCandlish, S.; Henighan, T.; Brown, T.B.; Chess, B.; Child, R.; Gray, S.; Radford, A.; Wu, J.; Amodei, D. Scaling laws for neural language models. *arXiv* **2020**, arXiv:2001.08361. [CrossRef]
33. Ouyang, L.; Wu, J.; Jiang, X.; Almeida, D.; Wainwright, C.; Mishkin, P.; Zhang, C.; Agarwal, S.; Slama, K.; Ray, A.; et al. Training language models to follow instructions with human feedback. *Adv. Neural Inf. Process. Syst.* **2022**, *35*, 27730–27744. [CrossRef]
34. Renze, M. The effect of sampling temperature on problem solving in large language models. In *Findings of the Association for Computational Linguistics: EMNLP 2024*; Association for Computational Linguistics: Stroudsburg, PA, USA, 2024; pp. 7346–7356. [CrossRef]
35. Xue, F.; Fu, Y.; Zhou, W.; Zheng, Z.; You, Y. To repeat or not to repeat: Insights from scaling LLM under token-crisis. *Adv. Neural Inf. Process. Syst.* **2023**, *36*, 59304–59322. [CrossRef]
36. Shi, C.; Yang, H.; Cai, D.; Zhang, Z.; Wang, Y.; Yang, Y.; Lam, W. A thorough examination of decoding methods in the era of LLMs. *arXiv* **2024**, arXiv:2402.06925. [CrossRef]

FinTech

MDPI

Article

Banking Sector Transformation: Disruptions, Challenges and Opportunities

William Gaviyau * and Jethro Godi *

Department of Finance Risk Management and Banking, University of South Africa (UNISA), Pretoria 003, South Africa
* Correspondence: gaviyw@unisa.ac.za (W.G.); godinj@unisa.ac.za (J.G.); Tel.: +27-(0)-12-429-3757 (J.G.); Fax: +27-(0)-86-569-8848 (J.G.)

Abstract

Banking has evolved from ancient times of using grain banks and temple lending to modern banking practices. The transformation of the banking sector has ensured that banks play the crucial role of facilitating faster and efficient service delivery. This paper traced the evolution of banking and examined associated disruptions, opportunities, and challenges. With the specific objective of influencing policy-oriented discussions on the future of banking, this study adopted a literature review methodology of integrating various sources, such as scholarly journals, policy reports, and institutional publications. Public interest theory and disruptive innovation theory underpinned this study. Findings revealed that banking has evolved from Banking 1.0 to Banking 5.0 due to disruptive factors which have been pivotal to the significant structural sector changes: Banking 1.0 (pre-1960s); Banking 2.0 (1960s to 1980s); Banking 3.0 (1980s–2000s); Banking 4.0 (2000s–2020s); and Banking 5.0 (2020s to the future). Despite the existence of opportunities in the transformation, challenges include regulations, skills shortages, legacy systems, and cybersecurity that must be addressed. This calls for a coordinated response from stakeholders, with banking's future requiring collaborations as cashless economies, digital economies, and digital currencies take centre stage.

Keywords: banking evolution; fintech; digital banking; banking sector transformation; artificial intelligence; regulatory framework; cybersecurity; customer experience

JEL Classification: G21

1. Introduction

In a digitalized world, the financial intermediation role of banks is heightened and remains pivotal. To ensure the provision of safe and secure customer-centric financial services, digital technologies play a crucial role in facilitating faster and efficient delivery. Notably, banking is evolving from traditional to digital banking. Characteristically, traditional banking has been associated with conventional banking methods and banking services provided mainly in bricks-and-mortar structures. On the other hand, digital banking driven by technological innovations introduces digital access in the execution of banking services.

Ref. [1] concurs with [2] that digital banking has transformed and reshaped the traditional financial services landscape through operational efficiencies, improved service delivery, and customer experiences among others. For instance, instant bank transfer

 https://doi.org/10.3390/fintech4030048

options are now available, whereas they previously took longer. Also, there is now an easier online customer onboarding process, which previously required customers to physically visit the bank. Indeed, these developments have been influenced primarily by a tech-savvy generation, improved internet penetration rates, and increased availability of affordable mobile gadgets which have spurred the integration of fintech and banking [3,4]. All these have disrupted the approaches and services associated with traditional banking. Noticeably, the integration of financial technologies (fintech) and banking has seen an increase in the development of digital banking platforms, usage of banking cards in transactions, and a shift toward a cashless society.

Fintech players provide innovation and creative solutions, while financial institutions provide a regulatory compliance framework and a customer base. For the fintech to scale up and ensure long-term success, they require the regulatory expertise and customer base possessed by the banking sector. Meanwhile, the banking sector requires adaptive innovations to meet the demands of a dynamic operating environment. In fact, a mutually reinforcing relationship exists between fintech and financial institutions. Hence, the development of regulatory sandboxes in most countries, with the United Kingdom through the Financial Conduct Authority (FCA) being the first in its attempt to accommodate technological innovations [5]. For sustainable success, collaboration is key in the coexistence of fintech and financial institutions. Thus, through collaboration, synergistic benefits accrue to the economy and industry by capitalizing on the strengths of both parties [2]. The synergistic benefits drive innovation and growth in the financial services sector [6–8].

Originally, the emergence of fintech companies in the financial services sector was viewed as disruptive, with the potential to eliminate traditional bank dominance [9,10]. This view was dominant especially after the 2007/8 Global Financial Crisis (GFC). By contrast, ref. [11] observed inconsistences associated with disruptive innovation theory's suggested strategies for disruptors. Furthermore, they revealed strategies adopted by incumbents as collaborative. Progressively, the disruptive nature is evolving into collaborative partnerships.

Ref. [6] observed that fintech solutions bridged the infrastructure gap within the traditional banking system by capitalizing on digital innovations to provide crucial financial services such as savings, credit, and insurance. For example, digital microcredit facilities accessed on smartphones via app-based lenders have recorded growth in Kenya [12]. Not only have fintech solutions addressed financial inclusion, but they have also stimulated economic growth and transformed banking. According to the hypothesis of [13], banking will become more focused and connected to technology, customers, products, and life. The four pillars of [13] summarise the future of banking as "Bank = technology," "Bank = client," "Bank = product," and "Bank = life." It is further postulated that a human being is Homo financial in the digital age, which means they possess financial literacy and financial thinking.

In terms of prior studies, ref. [14] conducted an exploratory qualitative study to identify and analyse the challenges associated with digital transformation in the retail and commercial banking in Germany. The study revealed that the barriers were mainly in product market knowledge, participation of employees and customers, and public benefits. These barriers contributed varied magnitudes to the digital transformation process of banks. On the same subject of digital transformation, ref. [15] focused on India with [16], focusing on Indonesia. They both revealed that banks should address the challenges for them to remain competitive. Thus, a research gap exists, in that these three studies [14–16] were country-specific, meaning that the outcomes cannot be generalized to other countries. Additionally, they highlighted the opportunities and challenges without identifying the disruptive forces behind.

Another study by [17] focused on the way employee skill sets have to evolve to keep up with the banking sector's changing digital landscape. To remain competitive and innovative, ref. [17] concluded that financial institutions should invest in workforce upskilling. Alternatively, ref. [18] conducted a systematic literature review on the digital transformation in banking. The study highlighted that stakeholders should strike a balanced approach in encouraging innovation and promoting financial inclusion.

From the digital transformation journey of the banking sector, scant studies have traced the transformation and highlighting the existing challenges, opportunities, and disruptive forces. Hence, this study aims to fill that gap by tracing the evolution from Banking 1.0 to Banking 5.0.

Accordingly, this paper traces the transformation of the banking sector from the ancient times of barter trade to the modern banking practices. Also, this paper examines the associated disruptions, opportunities, and challenges. Significantly, the paper's findings aim to inform and influence policy-oriented discussions on the future of banking. This paper is organised into six sections. Firstly, Section 1 is the introduction on the subject under study. Secondly, Section 2 outlines the research approach adopted. Thirdly, Section 3 is the literature review in which the evolution of banking sector and theories are discussed. Fourthly, Section 4 discusses the disruptions, opportunities, and challenges in the banking transformation. Fifthly, Section 5 highlights this study's policy implications. Finally, Section 6 provides the conclusion and proffers future directions of study.

2. Research Approach

With the specific objective of influencing strategic policy discussions in the banking sector, this study adopted a literature review methodology as its primary research technique. This study traced both historical and current change drivers alongside assessing the strategic policy implications to the banking sector. The approach enabled the integration of various sources, such as scholarly journals, policy reports, and institutional publications. Additionally, this study allowed flexibility in interpreting emerging themes across multi-disciplinary domains [19,20].

This review fosters thematic exploration, historical contextualization, and policy-relevant synthesis, which are essential to comprehending multi-faceted disruptions like technological innovation, regulatory change, and organizational structure shifts, in contrast to systematic reviews that prioritize thorough coverage and stringent inclusion criteria [21]. This approach was relevant for generating insights that promote evidence-based decision-making and has been confirmed through effective application in similar research focused on digital finance and regulatory innovation among others [22–25]. This strategy was consistent with this study's objective of stimulating policy-oriented discussion on the opportunities and challenges influencing banking's future.

3. Literature Review

This paper's literature review is organised into two areas, the theoretical underpinnings and evolution of banking.

3.1. Theoretical Framework

Two theories underpinned this study, namely public interest theory and disruptive innovation theory. The first to be discussed is public interest theory.

3.1.1. Public Interest Theory

This theory was advanced in 1920 by Pigou. Pigou was of the view that regulations were designed with the regulatory aim of correcting market imperfections [26–28]. This was based on the implied assumption that businesses do not operate to serve public interests. Hence, regulations are usually induced by public crises or discontent. For example, The Dodd-Frank Act of 2010 in USA was enforced to address banks' risk-taking behaviour after the 2007/8 GFC. Additionally, the European Union (EU) enforced the General Data Protection Regulations (GDPR) in 2018 to address data security issues associated with the digital operating environment requirements.

Critique of this theory has centred on the capture of regulations by industry players as well as failure to adapt in an evolving environment [26,29]. Applying the theory to this study, regulations are designed and developed with the overall objective of aiding attainment of regulatory mandates such as financial stability and integrity. Failure to address these mandates results in a contagion effect in the economy [30], leading to the inclusion of consumer protection and financial inclusion mandates to the traditional regulatory mandates [31,32]. In the era of modern banking with evolving technologies, failure to have adaptative regulations results in regulatory arbitrage. Regulatory arbitrage can be viewed as market failure.

To overcome public interest theory criticisms and minimise risks of capture by industry players, regulators need a balanced approach to regulating banking in the evolving fintech era. The balanced approach should promote innovation and be sustainable without stifling competition. To broaden understanding on the subject, the disruptive innovation theory is discussed in the next section.

3.1.2. Disruptive Innovation Theory

The theory was developed by Christensen in 1997. The theory explains how new entities enter existing markets using innovative technologies as a competitive edge to disrupt or reshape existing markets. As a result, new services and products are on offer, new consumer segments are created, and new approaches to business are introduced into an existing market among others. By leveraging on innovative technologies, this ensures efficient and cheaper service delivery. However, these innovative approaches disrupt the traditional market players (incumbents). Hence, disruptive innovation.

Ref. [33] revealed that in Indonesia, branchless banking has transformed the financial services sector by leveraging on innovative technologies to provide service access to the unbanked population. Furthermore, with fintech innovations, customised financial products and services have been developed targeting the underbanked and unbanked population [6]. In [34], the smart mobile phone technology was identified as a disruptor to incumbent banks' models. For instance, mobile network service providers such as MTN, Airtel, and Glo have transformed by integrating the traditional banking system and mobile banking [35,36].

Applying the theory to this study, technologies continue to play a key factor in transforming the banking sector. This has resulted in new products, services, and players. However, some view technology as a disruptor while others view it as requiring collaborative partnerships.

Having discussed the two theories applicable to this study, the evolution of banking is reviewed in the next section. As part of the literature review, combining the two theories and evolution of banking provides an enriched foundation to understand the drivers which can influence policy-oriented discussions.

3.2. Evolution of Banking (Banking 1.0 to Banking 5.0)

The historical developments of banking assist in having better perspectives on the factors that have been pivotal to the significant structural sector changes. In this respect, previous studies on the evolution of banking, industry and Information Communication Technologies (ICTs) have served as the basis for the categorisations [37–40].

The categorisations to be discussed are Banking 1.0 (pre–1960s); Banking 2.0 (1960s to 1980s); Banking 3.0 (1980s–2000s); Banking 4.0 (2000s–2020s); and Banking 5.0 (2020s to the future):

3.2.1. Banking 1.0 (Pre–1960s)

Banking began thousands of years ago with its origins dating back to roughly 2000 BC in Assyria and India, when traders lent money to purchase grain [41]. During the same period, temples in ancient Greece and Rome started taking deposits, making loans, and even trading money. With time, these Italian banking practices spread throughout the rest of Europe. In 1926, Italy enacted regulatory supervision legislation for deposit-taking institutions [42,43]. Notably, advancements occurred in Amsterdam under the Dutch Republic during the 17th century while in London, these commenced in the 18th century. These advancements laid the foundation for Europe's modern banking systems.

Ref. [39] observed that Banking 1.0 referred to the conventional banking model that existed prior to 1960, when branches operated at scheduled times and banking services were customised. Characteristically, during this period, money was physically transferred, records were kept on paper, and bank managers then knew the clients facially, by name, and every aspect of a client's life [37]. The decision to lend was based on the reputation and character. Regulations were not stringent with banking transactions, mostly performed in good faith and followed by a handshake.

Historically, incorporation of technological innovations in the financial services sector began in 1945 when cheques were first accepted as a form of payment [37,40]. This was followed by the first credit card in 1957 in the United States of America (USA), the Diners credit card which was mass marketed [44,45]. However, with the manual system in operation, there was slow service, alteration in cheque payments, and the system was prone to human error [41].

In general, operations during this era created the backbone of today's financial system with core principles of trust and customer service. According to modern banking theory, commercial banks play a crucial role in the economy's wealth distribution when combined with other financial intermediaries [39,46,47].

3.2.2. Banking 2.0 (1960s–1980s)

In this era, showing progression from Banking 1.0 to Banking 2.0, banks' branch operations and networks expanded [37]. Due to the inefficiencies associated with manual systems under Banking 1.0, mainframe computers for data storage and accounting were introduced [40]. For instance, bank transactions were bulk processed at the end of the day.

In the 1960s, Barclays Bank was the first bank globally to introduce Automated Teller Machines (ATMs) which eased financial transactions [48,49]. Later, debit cards were released as a means of conducting transactions. This advancement unlocked the global network of automation in the banking sector, which benefited both banks and clients.

The 1970s saw the creation of the Society for Worldwide Interbank Financial Telecommunications (SWIFT), a global, automated financial messaging service which eventually harmonized worldwide cross-border foreign transactions [50,51]. To participate in the SWIFT platforms, banks have a unique ID known as SWIFT or Bank Identifier Code (BIC) universally accepted by the central banks [52].

Various technologies were introduced within the banking system during Banking 2.0. Consequently, there were advancements due to electricity being incorporated into the industrial functions in line with Industrial Revolution 2.0 [46]. Thus, [40] referred to this period as the data processing years.

3.2.3. Banking 3.0 (1980s–2000s)

The client server period stretched from the 1980s to 2000s, also known as Banking 3.0. Ref. [40] revealed that during this period, banks facilitated information technology-based infrastructures to enable bank clients to interact with the bank. Consequently, banks offered new services. Furthermore, ref. [48] concurred with [53] who opined that new service offerings such as internet banking were popularised in the 1990s with the advent of banks having world-wide websites. For instance, ref. [54] revealed that in 1997, Singapore had five banks with customized websites for internet banking namely [48] Post Office Savings Bank (Postbank), Overseas Union Bank (OUB), Development Bank of Singapore (DBS Bank), United Overseas Bank (UOB), and Overseas-Chinese Banking Corporation (OCBC).

Services which came along with internet banking included paying bills, transferring funds, printing statements, and account balance inquiries. The availability of these technologies enabled faster speed and data flow exchange within the banking sector. Thus, electronic business was performed at a faster rate than the previous analogue period, with millions of bank transactions taking place every day. Internet banking represented one of the evolutionary stages of banking [55]. This resonated with the industrial automation associated with Industrial Revolution 3.0 [56].

In response, banks began using data warehouses to store a record of all transactions [57]. This enabled data mining in the creation of customized marketing strategies based on historical consumer interactions data. Even though the warehouses represented the commencement of data analysis in the banking sector, the branches' one-day processing lag was still restricting the delivery of real-time data [40,56,58].

3.2.4. Banking 4.0 (2000s–2020s)

According to [40], the predictive period is the period when banks started processing real-time transactions. For instance, the bank responds promptly and maintains customer's satisfaction if a customer lodges a complaint with the call centre [40]. Accordingly, the Banking 4.0 era enabled banks to utilise forecasting or prediction models based on historical transactions. During this era, financial and non-financial firms retained data virtually and limitlessly due to the cheap cost of data storage [59]. Banking 4.0 embraced the innovative solutions offered through financial technology companies and specialized in providing customized customer-oriented experiences through digital channels [56].

Banking operations are crucial to banks performing and executing customer transactions seamlessly. In [60], it was discovered that over the last two decades of the 20th century and the first part of the 21st century, banking operations had changed. They changed from traditional ledgers to automated ledger posting machines (ALPMs) to current core banking systems (CBSs).

The predictive period known as Banking 4.0 encouraged collaboration and innovation in the financial services ecosystem. Ref. [39] emphasized that Banking 4.0 was premised on promoting collaboration between customers and financial institutions. Collaboration remains key as evidenced by the products and service offering being driven by customers in need of convenience. So, this resonates with Industrial 4.0 which is based on the development of smart products and services that rely on the integration of internet of things [37] and application of big data analysis [61].

3.2.5. Banking 5.0 (2020s to the Future)

Banking 5.0 is going to be characterised by exchange-traded funds (ETFs), cryptocurrencies, high-frequency trading, intelligent banking, robo-advisors and cobots, embedded banking, and responsible banking. The emphasis is going to be placed on sustainability issues. Thus, Banking 5.0 will require greater collaboration between human and intelligent systems [37,62].

To improve client experiences, Banking 5.0 emphasizes the seamless integration of technology with human interfaces, with a particular emphasis on sustainable banking. In Banking 5.0, banks would serve as platforms that collaborate with different partners in the ecosystem to offer a wide range of financial and non-financial services.

The emergence of technologies like voice recognition, virtual and augmented reality, and artificial intelligence, which together provide a powerful combination for improving banking services and addressing current banking issues, is more responsible for the transition towards Banking 5.0 rather than solely new inventions [63].

When comparing Banking 4.0 and Banking 5.0, collaboration in Banking 4.0 centred on financial institutions with fintechs while Banking 5.0 is centred on human and intelligent systems. This shows significant advances in the interactions which require traditional banks to move away from legacy systems.

Traditional banks are anticipated to undergo major transformation and create alliances with fintech start-up businesses [37,64]. Therefore, there is little chance that traditional banks would cease operating. However, it is anticipated that the spread of fifth-generation technology would facilitate easier innovative banking models to be adopted and shared. So, the model includes digital banks with a different approach to service offering.

In terms of the banking evolution, Banking 1.0 to 5.0's key features are summarized as follows. Firstly, Banking 1.0's key features were the reliance on manual banking systems with physical record keeping. Furthermore, the traditional banking concept of relationship banking was established. Also, during this era, cheques and credit cards were introduced. Secondly, Banking 2.0 had growth in branch networks and bulk transaction processing associated with analogue systems. Main frame computers, debit cards, and the SWIFT international platform were introduced into the banking system. Thirdly, Banking 3.0 had internet banking, accessing banking services 24/7, and batch transaction processing. In addition, relationship banking continued to drive banking. Fourthly, Banking 4.0's features included instant and real-time transaction processing, digital record keeping, reduced branch networks, mobile banking, banking apps, and digital wallets. Lastly, Banking 5.0's features include customer-driven banking, usage of robots, application of quick response (QR) codes to access banking services, licensing of digital banks, and mobile wallets.

The next section highlights the disruptions, challenges, and opportunities associated with the banking evolution.

4. Disruptions, Challenges, and Opportunities

Banking has evolved from the barter system used in ancient times, the industrial revolution propelling trade and commerce, and embracing digital solutions in the financial intermediary role [2,13,65]. The changes reflect technological advancements, evolving customer behaviour, and regulatory developments. Nevertheless, [13] pointed out that banking sector changes were revolutionary not evolutionary. This indicates radical and significant structural changes within the banking sector.

Ref. [2] argued that the future of bank success was hinged on overcoming regulatory, ethical, and technological challenges. Ref. [46] identified technology, together with political and economic factors, as the drivers of future banking. Meanwhile, ref. [13] highlighted innovation and competition as the drivers of banking transformation. Globalization, capital concentration, the creation of new banking models, and a new banking culture are some of the unique drivers of the banking sector's evolution. Notably, these factors have significantly changed the competitive and highly regulated banking sector.

The transformation has disrupted the banking sector and created opportunities and challenges for the stakeholders which are summarised in Table 1. The disruptions, challenges, and opportunities are discussed and analysed hereafter.

Table 1. Summary of each banking era's characteristics, disruptions, challenges, and opportunities.

Banking Era	Characteristics	Disruptions	Challenges	Opportunities
Banking 1.0 (pre-(1960s)	Traditional relationship banking Physical cash transportation Manual system and physical record keeping	Credit card Cheque Mass banking	Limited banking services Slow service delivery Cheque fraud Regulations	Foundational banking principles
Banking 2.0 (1960s–1980s)	Expanding branch networks Analogue system; bulk transaction processing; relationship banking	Debit and credit card SWIFT international payment platform Mainframe computers	Regulations Risk management Limited banking access	More customers and development of more products Development of risk management strategies and credit scoring models
Banking 3.0 (1980s–2000s)	Data warehouse; internet banking; Banking access 24/7; relationship banking; batch transaction processing; expanding branch networks	Electronic banking Financial liberalisation Globalisation ICT-based infrastructure	Regulations Financial instability	ATM cash access outside banking hours Increased automation
Banking 4.0 (2000s–2020s)	Instant and real-time transaction processing; digital record keeping; reducing branch networks; mobile banking; banking apps and digital wallets	Financial innovation Regulation arbitrage and competition between fintech and traditional financial institutions 2007/8 Global Financial Crisis Artificial Intelligence Blockchain Big data	Cybersecurity Compliance Data ethics and privacy Reduced traditional earnings Customer behaviour	Data Analytics Collaboration between banks and non-banks Digital banking Ancillary earnings
Banking 5.0 (2020s–future)	Customer-driven banking; electronic fund transferring; robots; application programming interface (APIs); and bots; instant and real-time transaction processing; mobile banking apps—digital payments, online deliveries, and mobile wallets; use of QR codes to access banking services; digital banks; digital currency	Cloud computing Artificial Intelligence Blockchain ESG and Sustainable Finance Lifestyle banking	Risk Management Data ethics Regulations	Collaboration between human and intelligent systems Ancillary earnings

Source: Researcher's synthesis.

4.1. Disruption Factors

These are the factors that resulted in structural sector change. Disruptions have been identified in four areas—regulations, technology, human capital, and customer behaviour.

4.1.1. Technology

The banking sector has and continues to witness an unparalleled wave of technological disruptions due to the emergence of fintech, blockchain, and artificial intelligence (AI). By providing quicker, easier, and more user-friendly services through digital-only platforms, these innovations have placed traditional banks' dominance to the test [53,66,67]. In offering real-time, customized financial services, fintech companies and non-banking startups have applied agile development models and client data, prompting traditional banks to reorganize their digital strategies and IT infrastructure. Modern banking operations nowadays heavily rely on technologies like chatbots driven by artificial intelligence, biometric authentication, and smartphone apps.

Traditional banking practices have been severely reshaped by technological developments, mostly because of the emergence of fintech businesses that provide modern financial services. Agility and customer-focused strategies serve as key characteristics, with platforms such as Revolut challenging traditional banks by offering a range of services through user-friendly mobile applications, currency exchange, international money transfers, and cryptocurrency support [68–70]. Revolut and Monzo are among the digital banks that have brought competition to the traditional banks in the UK [69]. In a similar vein, Stripe has revolutionized online payments by providing developers with simple application programming interfaces (APIs) to incorporate payment processing, which aids organizations in streamlining intricate financial processes [71,72].

In reaction to these technology disruptions, traditional banks are adopting open banking initiatives and forming strategic partnerships with fintech companies. For example, Goldman Sachs and Apple collaborated to produce the Apple Card, integrating technical innovation with financial knowledge to provide smooth user experience [73]. A more competitive and customer-focused financial environment is promoted by open banking, which is made possible via APIs and enables third-party developers to create new financial products. As an example, Deutsche Bank made the decision to capitalize on the prospects presented by open banking in 2015 by developing an API programme [74]. Through the Deutsche API programme, Deutsche Bank enabled its partners and customers to integrate banking data as well as financial products and services into their own applications and products. As a result, partners can provide their clients with financial services right when they need them. In the long run, these big tech and fintech players would be dominant players in the financial services sector and competitive edge. Technology as a competitive edge has been identified as a disruptor by the disruption innovation theory.

Cloud computing, blockchain, and artificial intelligence (AI) have all been incorporated into banking, further accelerating technological disruption. While blockchain technology guarantees safe and transparent transactions, AI-powered chatbots and robo-advisors improve customer service by offering immediate, individualised responses [75]. Because cloud computing provides scalable infrastructure, banks may quickly and effectively roll out services to satisfy the changing needs of tech-savvy customers.

Progressively, from Banking 1.0 to Banking 5.0, technology has been the greatest driver in the transformation of the banking sector and ultimately reconfiguration of banking models [76]. For instance, the adoption of the internet under Banking 3.0 prompted the development of electronic banking and accessing banking services 24/7 which was not possible under Banking 2.0 and Banking 1.0.

These developments challenge established revenue sources including fees from intermediary providers and reduce dependency on physical branches. While banks that embrace transformation are reinventing business models to include innovation as an essential competence, those that do not face the risk of losing market share. However, all these technological developments present new challenges in the areas of cybersecurity, data security, and system compatibility, putting pressure on banks to innovate while safeguarding consumer trust.

4.1.2. Regulations

The presence of fintech has forced countries to design guidelines which either foster innovation or enforce stringent control [77]. The main reason for regulatory restrictions includes cybersecurity concerns such as fraud, money laundering, and data breaches. In addition to promoting fintech innovation, financial regulators have an enormous duty of striking a balance on the regulatory mandates such as consumer protection, competition, and financial stability [31,78].

To oversee fintechs in the USA, a market-driven approach is applied. Regulators enforcing this are the Security Exchange Commission (SEC) and Office of Comptroller Currency (OCC). In the UK, through the Financial Conduct Authority (FCA) and Prudential Regulation Authority (PRA), the country has an approach that fosters innovation through the regulatory sandboxes, whereas China enforces stringent government-led oversight. The enforcements are carried out by the People's Bank of China (PBOC) and the China Banking and Regulatory Insurance Commission (CBRIC). In the EU, using the revised Payment Services Directive (PSD2), they have promoted open banking, giving fintechs access to banking information. This is carried out through European Central Banking (ECB) and European Banking Authority (EBA). This is similar to South Africa, where the South Africa Reserve Bank (SARB) advances the fintech innovation agenda in collaboration with banks.

Regulatory disruption has significantly improved banking operations. The emergence of data-driven compliance mechanisms and regulatory technology (RegTech) offers banks another chance to improve their governance and risk management frameworks. Banks are being forced to update compliance systems and reporting procedures because of the introduction of frameworks like open banking, data privacy regulations such as the General Data Protection Regulation (GDPR), and more stringent anti-money laundering (AML) regulations. Regulatory technology, or RegTech, is becoming an essential investment, according to [79], as it enables institutions to automate compliance and adjust to changing legal requirements. Also, it streamlines compliance tasks including fraud detection, anti-money laundering (AML) monitoring, and reporting obligations, which not only improves regulatory responsiveness but also lowers administrative burdens and human error.

Failure of the Silicon Valley Bank (SVB) in March 2023 shows that regulatory control has been a challenge despite regulatory technology developments. This was viewed as the third largest bank failure in USA [73]. Regulatory enforcement deficiencies were highlighted by the San Francisco Federal Reserve's reluctance to take meaningful action despite identifying problems in prior years with SVB's risk management methods [80]. In order to avert systemic risks, such occurrences highlight the necessity for more proactive and coordinated regulatory actions. For example, customer onboarding processes have now been automated by banks which allows ongoing client risk assessment. Incorporation of AI into the banking service provision provides personalised and predictive services. AI algorithms analyse service users to offer customised services [81].

To drive institutions toward accessibility and seamless integration, regulators now encourage banks to securely exchange consumer data with approved third parties using standardized APIs. In particular, in the EU, with the PSD2 which allows information sharing with prior consent, a credit scoring model has been developed which allows customer evaluation in the absence of established data sets [82]. Failure to address the regulatory approaches on data sharing in the digital operating environment can threaten the stability of the sector. In South Africa, Discovery Bank has made a significant investment in behavioural banking, drawing on its knowledge of the Vitality program and Discovery Health to leverage behavioural data to support improved financial health [83]. Regulations should not be used as a deterrent but to encourage and promote competition within the confines of consumer protection. On the other hand, these transformations place an enormous load on legacy infrastructure and make operations more difficult, even as they encourage innovation. To ensure that bank systems can adapt to changing requirements without negating performance or user experience, traditional banks must find a balance between innovation and regulatory compliance.

Within the transformation landscape, banks' operational expenses and capacity for innovation have also been hampered by the growing regulatory constraints. Adhering to conflicting legislation frequently results in high operating costs, while reducing innovation expenses and possibly impeding the creation of new financial services and products [77]. In line with the digital operating environment, banks are spending money on regulatory technology (RegTech) solutions that automate compliance procedures, thereby reducing operational expenses and increasing productivity. After all, the financial regulatory landscape has grown deeper, with new frameworks designed to improve consumer protection and transparency among others.

4.1.3. Human Capital

The banking sector is changing due to artificial intelligence (AI) technology such as chatbots, robotic process automation (RPA), and machine learning algorithms [84]. Employees with expertise in data analysis, cybersecurity, and digital product development are in greater demand as conventional operations are replaced by automation and artificial intelligence. To stay relevant in the changing banking landscape, banks fund reskilling initiatives to perform more sophisticated and strategic tasks. For instance, BankCo's FORWARD project [85]. As a result, banks are being forced to change from being product-focused entities to becoming experience-driven, adaptable ecosystems.

Organizational structures and employment approaches must be rethought considering the banking sector's digital transformation. The banking sector has two major obstacles, overcoming a shortage of digital skills in the workforce and adjusting to a demographic of digitally native consumers that anticipate multi-channel, seamless experiences [84,85]. On the other hand, [86] posits that though bank operational efficiencies are expected to improve, job security and skills extinction concerns arise. Thus, to manage tech-driven operations, HR must upskill staff in analytics and innovation and encourage agile mindsets.

The banking sector's digital transformation demands an adjustment to more flexible and agile work environments. Cross-functional teams are replacing traditional hierarchical organizations because they can react quickly to changes in the market and in technology. The shift necessitates a cultural shift that values cooperation, ongoing education, and flexibility [85,87]. Agile, digitally enabled approaches that prioritize employee empowerment, data analytics, and collaboration are displacing traditional HRM approaches. Banks are investing more effort into creating agile work cultures that allow teams to employ design thinking and provide customer-focused solutions.

Adjustment to more flexible and agile work environments in the digital world requires competent employees and the development of appropriate working culture. This concurs with digital innovation theory which implies that a competitive edge relates to competent and organisationally fit employees. In Ref. [88], it was argued that failure to adapt and remain rigid with resistance to change results in underutilisation of technology. However, the organisational culture transition process requires a customised approach that is not costly and leaves the organisation vulnerable. Employee errors can be devastating for the organisation which could result in regulatory sanction and penalties, which undermines corporate compliance culture. For example, in 2009, Lehman Brothers and Royal Bank of Scotland (RBS) were closed due to employee errors which eventually caused lapses in the systems [89].

From the employee's perspective, the digital transformation can be viewed as a threat or opportunity. Task automation, such as cash-depositing automated teller machines that reduced the job tasks for bank tellers, can be seen as a threat, although from an organisation and customer perspective, this is viewed as an opportunity for efficient financial service delivery. Clearly bank tellers would need to focus on other strategic and operational activities and might require upskilling. These developments show the transition from Banking 1.0 when the ATM was introduced by Barclays Bank to the Banking 5.0 era of cash-depositing ATMs.

In a study of Jordanian SMEs, the findings revealed that organisational culture played a dual role of being a moderator and driver in the digital transformation process [90]. Further innovation and learning remained critical. Therefore, positive attitudes, continuous learning, and innovation are prerequisites in managing the transition to digital environment. The author of [91] posited that to maximize the full benefits of digital transformation the culture should align with technology adoption and organisational goals.

The COVID-19 pandemic hastened the adoption of digital technologies for collaboration and remote work and also the shift to a hybrid work model that blends in-person and remote labour [92]. Establishing secure communication platforms and remote access systems was necessary as institutions swiftly adjusted to virtual work settings. Many banks are now considering long-term hybrid work models because of this change, which not only guaranteed company continuity during the crisis but also showed the viability and advantages of flexible work arrangements. Although, organisations ought to encourage hybrid models that incorporate mental health initiatives, flexible work schedules, and individualized well-being programs [93]. Maximizing the advantages of hybrid work arrangements and maintaining a resilient and balanced labour market require addressing the support mechanisms and updating labour regulations [94].

HR leaders must take a proactive and strategic approach to successfully integrate AI and automation in the workforce. Adopting AI-driven innovations requires a workforce that is both literate and flexible, which calls for the development of new career pathways and positions focused on AI, creative employment models, and extensive upskilling initiatives. In the era of AI, HR must serve as a mediator between people and machines [87]. In addition, it must ensure a smooth transition by addressing skill transitions, job insecurity, and changes in workplace culture [84]. To maintain a motivated workforce, organizations must assist employees through engagement, training, and having open communication channels.

4.1.4. Customers Behaviour

The banking sector is facing significant disruption because of shifting consumer expectations. Consumers of modern banking prefer fast, simple, and customized experiences on a variety of channels [95]. Ref. [71] concurred with [20] that banks have been forced to redesign their digital engagements and provide more value through personalization. This was as a result of competition with tech giants that provide quick satisfaction and user-friendly interfaces [71]. To sustain engagement and loyalty, customers now need real-time information, integrated digital wallets, and AI-driven recommendations.

Modern consumers demand seamless, customized digital banking experiences. They are seeking services that can be accessed on any device, at any time, and from any location. In response to customer demands for ease and personalization, banks such as JPMorgan Chase have created mobile applications that provide real-time transaction alerts and customized budgeting tools [65]. The rise in digital-only banks, like Ally Bank, which has no physical branches and provides affordable fees and competitive interest rates, is a result of consumers' preference for the convenience of online banking. These banks challenge established banks to improve their digital offerings by appealing to tech-savvy customers who value time and efficiency [65,68,69].

Banks are customizing their products using customer journey mapping and big data to match expectations. This change in design from a product-centric to a customer-centric approach represents a profound cultural shift in bank operations [73]. However, it takes a significant investment in infrastructure, data management, and cybersecurity to achieve these objectives. Banks must constantly reinvent their platforms while maintaining privacy and trust since customer loyalty is becoming more and more linked to digital experiences. Failure to do so faces the risk of losing clients to agile competitors.

Banks are using AI-driven virtual assistants in their customer service operations with the goal of fulfilling changing customer demands. For example, Bank of America's Erica enhances client engagement and satisfaction by offering swift responses to questions, proactive financial guidance, and tailored insights [65]. These developments highlight how crucial it is to leverage technology to fulfil the ever-changing demands of customers.

4.2. *Opportunities*

The ability of institutions leveraging on technological innovations in utilizing data analytics, designing flexible business models to boost customer interaction, and improving financial service delivery in promoting equitable and sustainable economic growth constitutes a few of the opportunities in the banking sector transformation.

4.2.1. Efficiency and Cost Reductions

Cloud computing, AI-driven analytics, and robotic process automation (RPA) are examples of digital solutions which provide opportunities to reduce administrative costs and streamline processes. Banks can increase efficiency and decrease human error by digitizing internal procedures and automating repetitive tasks [20]. For instance, robotic process automation (RPA) has proved to significantly reduce costs for compliance reporting and loan processing time at India's ICICI Bank. Thus, banks' total agility is increased by this resource reallocation, which allows them to concentrate on strategic innovation and client engagement.

Digital transformation has enhanced the development of banking agency models and integrating mobile technologies contributing to financial inclusion. In low- and middle-income nations, mobile financial services have been helpful in reducing the disparity in financial access [96]. Low-cost banking has been made possible in South Africa by mobile platforms such as ABSA's cashsend and Standard Bank's Instant Money, especially for those living in rural areas. By doing away with the requirement for physical infrastructure, these services enable banks to lower overhead expenses while reaching a wider audience.

Banks can provide individualized goods and services and gain a deeper understanding of consumer behaviour by utilizing big data analytics [97]. Utilizing customer retention tactics, cross-selling, and targeted marketing, this generates new revenue potential. AI-driven platforms that personalize financial suggestions and identify early indicators of financial stress were first introduced by banks such as DBS in Singapore. These programs raise lifetime value, promote digital engagement, and enhance consumer experience.

With technological innovation driving the transformation of the banking sector, stakeholders in the sector placed emphasis on efficiency as demanded by consumers. Notably, the COVID-19 pandemic decimated the presence of the physical bank branches. In the United Kingdom, HSBC Bank and Barclays Bank closed one hundred and fourteen (114) branches and one hundred and sixty-five (165) branches, respectively, in 2023, due to increased customer migration from physical banking to digital banking [98] Customer demand for convenience has forced traditional banks to introduce digital banking services. However, will this trend continue in Banking 5.0 as some customers prefer banks with physical branches for security reasons?

4.2.2. Digital Financial Solutions

Information technology-induced financial services are also promoting accessibility, efficiency, and innovation [99]. To promote financial inclusion and reduce barriers for marginalized people, banks are using digital technologies to offer secure transactions, effective payment systems, and individualized financial advice. Additionally, emerging opportunities for improved decision-making and fraud prevention are being made possible by technologies such as blockchain and artificial intelligence [100].

As mobile phones and the internet become more widely used, the use of digital payment methods has increased dramatically on a global scale [101]. By eliminating the presence of middlemen and reducing transaction costs, these technologies enable smooth cross-border transactions. Therefore, digital payments have become widely used due to their speed and convenience, which has substantial implications for both businesses and consumers. Global payment providers such as PayPal and Alipay have drastically reduced transaction costs and processing times while enabling real-time financial tracking and management for consumers [6,102].

Cybersecurity concerns continue to increase in the modern world, and these threaten customers' access to financial services [103]. For example, fraud, phishing, identity theft, and ransomware are some concerns that affect the utilization of digital banking platforms. With the increase in technological developments, some innovative solutions have been developed which strengthen financial security. These include multi-factor authentication (MFA), blockchain-based secure transactions, and artificial intelligence (AI)-driven fraud detection. Real-time transaction analysis and flagging by AI models enable prompt action, including transaction red flagging or suspending accounts [104]. This preventative strategy minimizes the adverse effects of fraud on consumers and financial institutions. Likewise, the decentralized and irreversible ledger of blockchain technology has raised security and transparency in financial transactions, lowering the possibility of fraud and boosting confidence in financial systems [6,105].

Ref. [106] observed that mobile money is transformative in nature by making use of mobile phones to conduct financial transactions. In Africa, the mobile money technology transfer platform gained prominence in Kenya through M-PESA which was launched by Safaricom in 2007. Safaricom, the licenced cellular network, initiated the mobile money transfer services with support from development-oriented stakeholders [107,108]. These included the Commercial Bank of Africa which provided traditional banking infrastructure. In [109], it was posited that M-PESA has evolved with registered users now able to send and receive money globally. Indeed, this has contributed significantly to increasing financial service access to marginalised members of society.

4.2.3. Innovative Collaborative Partnerships

The financial landscape is transforming primarily due to the convergence of fintech and traditional banking approaches [110]. As a result, traditional banks have been compelled to reconsider strategies and adjust to remain competitive. Through these partnerships, by embracing the fintech revolution, traditional banks can leverage the use of digital innovations and provide a seamless digital banking experience [111] (Sunitha & Madhav, 2020). Financial and non-financial players, including BigTech such as Facebook, PayPal, Google, and Apple, fintech firms, telecommunications companies, and retailers are making inroads into the mobile banking market [112,113]. Undoubtedly, the growing demand for mobile banking services has been brought about by the growing adoption of smartphones.

Mobile banking has evolved by integrating mobile technologies with the financial services system [114]. Nevertheless, integration has been more prevalent in developed countries such as the USA and European Union while in developing countries, the focus was on using mobile technologies to bridge the financial inclusion gap. The mobile money services were evident in Ghana with MTN Mobile Money, Kenya with M-PESA, and Zimbabwe with Ecocash. Admittedly, in the late 2000s, banks were the key users of SMS-based banking, which changed to app-based banking as smartphones became more widely used [115,116].

Innovative offerings like m-wallets, which enable users to maintain and utilize bank cards as well as merchant loyalty cards, and mobile payments utilizing near-field communication (NFC) technology have been made possible with the adoption of mobile banking [113,117]. NFC enables contactless payments such as Apple Pay, Google Pay, and Samsung Pay. Mobile banking utilizes portable devices that includes smartphones, tablets, or other mobile devices to conduct transactions and access banking services. Mobile banking apps allow users to pay bills, deposit, transfer money, and check account balances. Though mobile banking provides easier accessibility and convenience, which are essential, this underscores the drivers of a growing and interconnected global financial ecosystem.

Risks arise with the increasing adoption of mobile banking and expansion of payment systems [118,119]. The risks include but are not limited to cyber security, data breaches, and fraud and require concerted efforts to protect consumers and ensure financial system integrity. Thus, stakeholders should prioritize enhancing regulatory frameworks, incorporating advanced security technologies, and educating consumers.

Ref. [120] opined that as digital banking adoption continues to grow, digital banks face the threats of gaining customer acceptance and trust, which traditional banks have built over time. Despite the threats to the bank model, significant opportunities for collaboration exists both for traditional and digital banks. Crucially, collaboration remain key in shaping future of the banking sector.

Comparing Banking 4.0 and Banking 5.0, collaboration in Banking 4.0 centred on financial institutions with fintechs while Banking 5.0 is centred on human and intelligent systems. Banking 4.0 had regulatory sandboxes with Banking 5.0 having robots and cobots. This shows great advancement in the interaction, requiring traditional banks to move away from legacy systems.

4.2.4. Explore Additional Revenue

Ref. [2] observed that the disruptive nature has not only affected the traditional revenue streams but forced the institutions to focus on earning through offering value-added services and fee-based earning models. Revenue for banks is earned from a range of banking activities they offer. Traditionally, banks' earnings are in the form of commissions, fees, and net interest income. So, to operate profitably and sustainably in the future, banks should explore a new and innovative approach to reconnect with their traditional customers and connect with new customers. Notably, the new category of customers is tech savvy, young, and enterprising.

The changing customer demographic requires banks to be strategic in market positioning by aligning with the expected future environment. These include earning income from ancillary services being offered such as cross-selling, that is, offering additional products to existing customers [37,39]. For instance, offering legal and insurance services to an existing customer. This entails additional income and enhancing customer satisfaction. Similarly, in the fintech era, banks collaborating with fintech have additional sources of income.

4.2.5. Customer Engagement Channels

Delivery channels refer to the vehicles or ways in which bank customer interacts or engages with the bank. Significantly, interaction to access banking services such as cash withdrawals, payment processing, account opening, debit order activation, and funds transfer. Traditionally, customers have interacted with the bank using the single channel, either face to face or physical visits to the branch [37,39]. Another is multi-channels which are independent channels aimed at satisfying several market segments [121]. Various channels that have gained traction and transformed interactions are through electronic channels such as ATMs, mobile phones, and computers. These channels operate independently with no interface between these channels.

Ref. [122] identified cross channel as an attempt to partially integrate traditional and online channels. Omni channel refers to a channel integrating physical and digital channels which includes digital assistants, online, mobile, and in-person, to give clients an efficient banking experience [37]. In particular, through omni channel, customers can initiate a service request online via apps and complete by physically visiting a branch. So, customers can utilize a variety of methods in accessing bank accounts to perform transactions. Additionally, this channel facilitates communication and allows accessibility from any location at any time and across all devices. Under Banking 1.0, delivery channels were through physically visiting the bank during specified times and has evolved to 24/7 engagement through various apps in Banking 5.0.

In fact, the financial services sector has evolved from the Banking 1.0 era and continues to evolve. This has been precipitated by the technological innovations and customer preferences among others. Banks now operate in a customer-centric environment, where clients select financial service providers according to preferences for speed, flexibility, and personalized banking [123,124]. Generally, banking services and delivery channels have gone through an enormous shift from traditional processes supported by bank employees, to fully automated and self-service. In the process, this has limited usage of physical branches to more complicated transactions. Admittedly, [125] observed the significant digitalisation of banking services in the last two decades. This shift encourages efficiency and promotes financial accessibility.

4.3. Challenges

Even though there are many potential benefits to the banking sector's transformation, there are also numerous challenges to overcome. These call for a coordinated response.

4.3.1. Data Privacy and Cybersecurity Threats

The banking sector's digital transformation, which has been facilitated by the adoption of technologies such as cloud computing, big data analytics, and artificial intelligence, has greatly increased vulnerability to cybersecurity risks and data privacy issues [126]. According to [127], cyber risks cost global banks an estimated USD 2.5 billion a year, with over 20,000 cyberattack incidents recorded. This has resulted in financial liabilities valued at more than USD 12 billion during the past two decades. These figures highlight the importance of cybersecurity in ensuring institutional resilience and financial stability. As digital platforms manage ever-increasing amounts of private client data, protecting data against ransomware, fraud, and breaches becomes not only a technical issue but also an inherent business necessity [128].

Identity theft, phishing, malware, and ransomware are just some of the risks related to cybersecurity that have greatly impacted digital banking. According to [118], these threats were cited as the most significant barriers to the implementation of digital banking in South Africa. The gross losses increased by 45% to approximately ZAR 438 million in 2021, despite an overall 18% decrease in digital banking fraud incidences. This underscores the growing sophistication of cyberattacks [129]. Common strategies that undermine customer confidence and discourage wider utilization of digital services include social engineering, ATM card skimming, malware-injected platforms, and phony banking websites [126,130].

The willingness of individuals to utilize digital banking systems is significantly affected by how they perceive associated risks [131,132]. Risks are made worse by limited bank communication and the absence of customer awareness of online security procedures. Additional systemic risks are brought about through using untrustworthy third-party vendors and unencrypted data transmission [133]. Research conducted in developing nations reveals a significant gap in public cybersecurity education and technical infrastructure, thereby exposing consumers and institutions to frequent attacks [134]. Such constraints undermine banks' reputations and compromise the credibility of digital financial systems.

Ref. [135] posited that cybersecurity is becoming increasingly complex and complicated with the push for AI and data standards. In [118], some important ways of mitigating these threats were outlined. These consist of client education initiatives, antiviral software, intrusion detection systems, secure application development, and strong password standards. Enhancing regulatory compliance, encouraging information-sharing cultures, and upholding current security procedures are crucial to boosting user confidence and the robustness of digital banking.

Technology lowers the compliance costs while information privacy and security concerns remain a threat [136]. Personal information can be misused and stolen by third-party agents. There is a need to minimise this downside of technology with the economy deriving greater benefits. Reliance on third parties is now a threat to the transformation of the banking sector and is growing. Ref. [137] envisioned a convergence of regulation, technology, and ethical practices to address the security and trust issues.

4.3.2. Legacy Systems

Over the past 20 years, financial services have been the major users and purchasers of ICT services globally [20,138,139]. Legacy systems refer to information systems that have been in existence for some time and are used by traditional banks in service delivery. Crucially, these systems have been the core of traditional bank's profitability and hold substantial value [37].

Ref. [140] argued that traditional bank legacy systems contribute to failure to innovate and adopt new technologies. Furthermore, legacy systems result in compliance being expensive and it being very slow to obtain requested information or data [141,142]. For example, an online customer onboarding process using legacy systems costs at least USD 10 million and is implemented over a two-year period [143]. However, the same process carried out using modern technologies, costs USD 0.3 million and is implemented over a three-month period.

Likewise, fintechs can acquire modern systems without huge capital outlay and be the competitive edge. Essentially, with the current environment of big data, banks can have better insights by making data-driven decisions in real time. The decisions are derived from analysis of current and historical data. Compliance-based data requires data extraction from different sets within the banking system; integration, algorithm-based data aggregation and automation can only be achieved using modern technologies. Notably, modern customers prefer a better customer experience which can be offered by fintechs rather than traditional banks.

When integrating new digital technologies with legacy systems, banks encounter significant organizational and technological challenges. Security shortcomings and operational inefficiencies are frequently brought about by incompatibility between outdated and modern systems [98]. Furthermore, the ability to integrate operations and risk functions is based on access to high-quality data which is consistent across the organisation [144]. Challenges associated with legacy systems' modernisation include regulatory compliance, legacy data migration, disruption risk, and organisational resistance. As a result, this affects agility and scalability.

Legacy systems dominated the transition from Banking 1.0 to Banking 3.0. Post 2007/8 global financial crisis (GFC), banks invested in new technologies with compatible digital systems than analogue-based systems used before. So pre-2007/8 GFC, ICT systems were designed and developed when the banking system technologies were not integrated while post-2007/8 GFC which is current, future banking systems have integrated systems. Whilst the integrated systems are good, these advancements have introduced ethical challenges, algorithmic bias, and data privacy concerns [145].

4.3.3. Systemic Risk

Ref. [6] argued that the rise in unregulated or minimally regulated fintech companies, which might function beyond the authority of traditional financial regulators, further increases the possibility of market disruption. Because such entities might engage in unethical activities without being subject to the same level of surveillance as traditional financial institutions, this might result in systemic risk. Furthermore, the financial system may be affected if a key fintech company fails, especially if it is linked to other financial institutions [146].

Digital innovation can result in financial disruptions due to unidentified weaknesses during the trial stages of new innovations. Strategies to reduce the risks associated with fintech while promoting innovation include regulatory sandboxes, mentorship programs, and improved collaboration between regulators and fintech companies. In addition to having appropriate safeguards in place to protect customers and maintain financial stability, these strategies seek to create an atmosphere that is more conducive to fintech innovation [147,148].

4.3.4. Changing Customer Demographics

The financial services sector is undergoing transformation which has largely been attributed to technological innovations. Furthermore, [149] noted that the financial services sector continues to evolve due to technological innovations, changing regulatory mandates, growing customer preferences, and changes in demographics. These have compelled service providers to adjust the way they offer services in conformity to changing customer segments.

In line with the demographic transition theory, consumer decision-making is influenced by demographic factors [150,151]. The theory further argues that as people grow so do preferences. For example, in consumer purchasing decision-making, men, children, and women interpret information differently resulting in different decisions. Hence, the role of demographic factors in consumer decision-making cannot be ignored.

There are five categories of generation, namely baby boomers, gen X, gen Y, gen Z, and gen A [152–154]. Baby boomers were born between 1946 and 1964. Gen X was born between 1965 and 1980. Gen Y, also known as Millennials, was born between 1981 and 1996.

Gen Z was born between 1997 and 2012. Gen Alpha (A) was born in 2012 to date. The most important thing in identifying the generation categories is to customise marketing messages and strategies based on the group preferences. Notably, baby boomers prefer cash transactions and physically visiting the bank.

Generation Z is a significant consumer generation born between the mid-1990s and the early 2010s [152]. Ref. [153] referred to this group as post-millennials or centennials. In [154], this group was also identified as the iGeneration. In making purchase decisions, they place reliance on digital channels and social media influences. Also, they prefer a highly personalised tech experience. As the Gen Z population grows, notable shifts in customer preferences are expected. To remain competitive with this generation, customized marketing strategies should be adopted. For instance, millennials and Gen Z, as digital natives, are leading the shift towards digital banking, and their preferences and behaviours play a crucial role in shaping next generation-centric banking.

Some of the banking services are now being provided online with a few requiring physical branch visits. Services available online include bank transfers, statement requests, balance enquiries, and loan applications. Ref. [155] claimed that although internet banking and mobile bank apps were previously exclusive and optional, the banks of today cannot compete as long as they do not offer convenient online services.

In Tanzania, [4] revealed that geographic, demographic, and psychographic constructs of market segmentation had a positive influence on the bank's profitability. Based on the results, the authors recommended that markets should be segmented based on these three constructs. Therefore, banks should customize marketing strategies in line with the unique requirements of each market segment. This study by [4] highlighted how crucial customer demographics are in the development of marketing strategies as they affect profitability.

A study was conducted by [150] to determine the criteria used by Indian bank customers in selecting banks and how these affect demographic subgroups. The factors identified in bank selection were convenience and service delivery. However, these factors differed significantly based on demographic attributes such as gender, age, income level, education level, and occupation. These results indicate the practical implications in the development and design of customized demographic-driven marketing strategies.

Ref. [156] conducted an analysis study on psychographic segmentation in Canada's banking sector. The study identified three different customer groups namely conservatives, sceptics, and visionaries. These groups approached digital banking differently; hence, marketing approaches should be customized. The most important finding is not to focus solely on demographic constructs but incorporate psychographic constructs as well.

The studies by [4,156] concur with [150] as they all stressed the importance of customized demographic-driven marketing strategies especially in a digital-driven evolving landscape. However, [156] further identified the psychographic element in designing the marketing strategies.

4.3.5. Skills Shortages and Upskilling

Significant gaps in employee readiness have been revealed by the banking sector's rapid digital transformation, especially in the areas of data analytics, digital literacy, and flexible working arrangements. Ref. [135] highlighted that the cyber skills gap has widened in 2024 with 67% of the companies reporting a moderate to critical skills gap. Only 14% of the organisations were confident that they had the requisite people and skills.

Ref. [19] revealed that employee deficiencies in technological skills to effectively utilize the latest technology adds to the challenges of legacy systems and antiquated infrastructure. To remain relevant in a changing workplace, employees are constantly required to renew their skill sets. Thus, to maintain long-term competitiveness in digital banking environments, the importance was highlighted of moving from simply technical competence to broader digital skill sets [19,157].

Ref. [149] posited that HR transformation processes must rethink the HR department as a business partner and co-creator of digital strategy, going beyond simple upskilling. This includes building tech-enabled, human-centred solutions that require cross-departmental collaboration, especially with marketing and finance. Further, paradigm shifts in the way banks manage people and performance should move toward design thinking, human-centred design, and agile techniques. Upskilling initiatives run the risk of becoming dispersed and inadequate in the face of continuous digital disruption.

5. Policy Implications

From a policy perspective, the findings of this study revealed that digital technologies are transforming the financial services sector by placing reliance on third parties. For example, Bigtech, which is the data-driven firms that are driving the payment platforms with Apple and Google taking a share of the banking. Also, Regtech, which is the technology-based companies aiming to provide regulatory compliance solutions to banks. Interestingly, when relying on third parties, the delegated authority remains with the banks. However, these give rise to risks such as cybersecurity, ethical, and information risks.

A pragmatic approach is required to ensure that technological outcomes are met without compromising regulatory mandates outcomes. To minimise conflicting objectives, a balance should be struck among regulators, customers, financial institutions, and technology players. These conflicting objectives might result in financial instability, unfair competition, and consumer protection issues. But who will play that oversight role of ensuring a balance of stakeholders' objectives given that the unregulated technology companies continue to transform the banking sector?

In the Asian Pacific (APAC) region, financial regulators have been criticised for trying to regulate or control new areas which they do not know or appreciate [158]. Digital innovations have entailed different regulatory approaches in understanding and application. Accordingly, with the new world order of technology-driven solutions to problems there is need to guide future policy direction by accommodating technological innovations effectively.

6. Conclusions and Future Directions

This study has highlighted the evolution of banking from ancient times to modern times. Banking has evolved through five eras, Banking 1.0 to Banking 5.0. Banking 1.0 being the period pre-1960s while Banking 2.0 was the period from 1960s to 1980s, Banking 3.0 was from 1980s to 2000s, Banking 4.0 started from 2000s to 2020s, and Banking 5.0 represents the 2020s to the future. Admittedly, the exact timelines are difficult to establish, hence using indicative periods. Despite using indicative periods, these provide a representative timeframe to understand key transformations that occurred within the banking sector. The evolution followed the industrial evolution that occurred during the almost similar indicative periods. As a result, significant structural sector changes were observed. These changes were induced by factors such as regulations, technology, human resources, and customer behaviour.

Theories assisted in enhancing knowledge of banking. Public interest theory revealed regulation development considerations and evolving operating environments. Hence, requiring careful thoughts to minimize regulatory capture and regulatory arbitrages among others. On the other hand, disruptive innovation theory highlighted how new entities enter existing markets using innovative technologies as a competitive edge to disrupt or reshape existing markets. These two theories indicated that the modern banking sector requires greater collaboration to understand the operating environment dynamics and how regulation should be designed by balancing the interest of stakeholders.

In this study, the significant findings were that opportunities and challenges exist in the banking sector's transformation which are associated with a dynamic banking operating environment. Opportunities include development of new business models such as digital banks and integration with non-banking providers which improve service delivery and performance of data analytics among others. Despite the existence of opportunities, challenges include regulations, skills shortages, legacy, and cybersecurity that must be addressed.

The findings suggest a multi-disciplinary stakeholder-coordinated response on the future of banking both at a micro and macro level. Thus, at a micro level, the institutions should conduct an internal review assessment to identify strengths and weaknesses. This should inform the strategic positioning of the institution in the new operating environment. Also, at a national, regional, and global level, policy-oriented discussions and regulatory formulation should be given priority in the dynamic banking operating environment. Importantly, the future of banking requires collaborations as digital economies, digital currencies, cashless society, customer-centric banking institutions, and artificial intelligence take centre stage. These findings add to the growing body of research on the future of banking-related areas such as cybersecurity disclosures, integration of artificial intelligence, and data standards sharing, regulatory uncertainty, and collaborative models of banking.

Author Contributions: Conceptualization, W.G. and J.G.; methodology, W.G. and J.G.; software, W.G.; validation, W.G. and J.G.; formal analysis, W.G.; investigation, W.G.; resources, W.G.; data curation, W.G.; writing—original draft preparation, W.G.; writing—review and editing, J.G.; visualization, W.G.; supervision, J.G.; project administration, W.G.; funding acquisition, J.G. All authors have read and agreed to the published version of the manuscript.

Funding: The APC was funded by the University of South Africa.

Institutional Review Board Statement: Not applicable.

Informed Consent Statement: Not applicable.

Data Availability Statement: The original contributions presented in this study are included in the article. Further inquiries can be directed to the corresponding authors.

Conflicts of Interest: The authors declare no conflicts of interest.

References

1. Ahmad, N.R. Financial Inclusion: How Digital Banking is bridging the Gap for Emerging Markets. *J. Appl. Linguist. TESOL (JALT)* **2025**, *8*, 894–902.
2. Awaliyah, T.; Safitri, N.; Hartaty, S.; Felani, F.; Judijanto, L. The Impact of Financial Technology Innovation on Banking Service Transformation: A Case Study in the FinTech Industry. *Glob. Int. J. Innov. Res.* **2023**, *1*, 306–313. [CrossRef]
3. Acharya, S.; Joshi, S. Impact of cyber-attacks on banking institutions in India: A study of safety mechanisms and preventive measures. *PalArch's J. Archaeol. Egypt/Egyptol.* **2020**, *17*, 4656–4670.
4. Mbura, O.K.; Kagoya, S.M. Consumer Market Segmentation Adoption and Its Influence on the Performance of Tanzania's Banking Industry. *ORSEA J.* **2024**, *14*, 111–131. [CrossRef]
5. Kálmán, J. The Role of Regulatory Sandboxes in FinTech Innovation: A Comparative Case Study of the UK, Singapore, and Hungary. *FinTech* **2025**, *4*, 26. [CrossRef]
6. Sanyaolu, T.O.; Adeleke, A.G.; Azubuko, C.F.; Osundare, O.S. Exploring fintech innovations and their potential to transform the future of financial services and banking. *Int. J. Sch. Res. Sci. Technol.* **2024**, *5*, 54–72. [CrossRef]
7. Khuan, H. Fintech and the Future of Banking. Collaboration and Innovation for Better Financial Services. *Econ. Stud. Bank. J. (DEMAND)* **2024**, *1*, 75–79. [CrossRef]
8. Bhasin, N.K.; Rajesh, A. Impact of E-collaboration between Indian banks and fintech companies for digital banking and new emerging technologies. *Int. J. e-Collab. (IJeC)* **2021**, *17*, 15–35. [CrossRef]
9. Aysan, A.F.; Nanaeva, Z. Fintech as a financial disruptor. A bibliometric analysis. *FinTech* **2022**, *1*, 412–433. [CrossRef]

10. Chiu, I.H. Fintech and disruptive business models in financial products, intermediation and markets-policy implications for financial regulators. *J. Tech. L. & Pol'y* **2016**, *21*, 55.
11. Zalan, T.; Toufaily, E. The promise of fintech in emerging markets. Not as disruptive. *Contemp. Econ.* **2017**, *11*, 415.
12. Upadhyaya, R.; Weitzberg, K.; Bonyo, L. Digital Credit Providers, Regulatory Frameworks, and Structural Power. A Case Study of Digital Microcredit Regulation in Kenya. *Financ. Soc.* **2025**, *2025*, 1–23. [CrossRef]
13. Korobov, Y. Global banking: Transformation, innovation & competition. *SHS Web Conf.* **2017**, *39*, 01012. [CrossRef]
14. Diener, F.; Špaček, M. Digital Transformation in Banking: A Managerial Perspective on Barriers to Change. *Sustainability* **2021**, *13*, 2032. [CrossRef]
15. Sahoo, R.K. Digital Strategy and Transformation: Opportunities and Challenges in the Banking Industry in India. Ph.D. Thesis, SSBM Geneva, Geneva, Switzerland, 2024.
16. Jameaba, M.S. Digitalization, Emerging Technologies, and Financial Stability: Challenges and Opportunities for the Indonesian Banking Industry and Beyond. *Qeios* **2022**, 1–39. [CrossRef]
17. Ewim, C.P.M.; Omokhoa, H.E.; Ogundeji, I.A.; Ibeh, A.I. Future of work in banking: Adapting workforce skills to digital transformation challenges. *Future* **2021**, *2*, 45–56.
18. Munira, M.S.K. Digital transformation in banking: A systematic review of trends, technologies, and challenges. *Strateg. Data Manag. Innov.* **2025**, *2*, 78–95. [CrossRef]
19. Abdul Latif, K.; Nik Mahmood, N.H.; Mohd Ali, N.R. Exploring sustainable human resource management change in the context of digital banking. *J. Environ. Treat. Tech.* **2020**, *8*, 779–786. Available online: https://core.ac.uk/display/334606668 (accessed on 20 April 2025).
20. Arner, D.W.; Barberis, J.; Buckley, R.P. The Evolution of Fintech: A New Post-Crisis Paradigm? University of Hong Kong Faculty of Law Research Paper No. 2015/047. 2015. Available online: https://ssrn.com/abstract=2676553 (accessed on 20 April 2025).
21. Zetzsche, D.A.; Buckley, R.P.; Arner, D.W.; Barberis, J.N. From FinTech to TechFin: The regulatory challenges of data-driven finance. *NYU J. Law Bus.* **2020**, *16*, 379–460. [CrossRef]
22. Cele, N.N.; Kwenda, S. Do cybersecurity threats and risks have an impact on the adoption of digital banking? A systematic literature review. *J. Financ. Crime* **2025**, *32*, 31–48. [CrossRef]
23. Demirgüç-Kunt, A.; Klapper, L.; Singer, D.; Ansar, S.; Hess, J. *The Global Findex Database 2017: Measuring Financial Inclusion and the Fintech Revolution*; World Bank: Washington, DC, USA, 2018.
24. Puschmann, T. Fintech. *Bus. Inf. Syst. Eng.* **2017**, *59*, 69–76. [CrossRef]
25. Beck, T.; Demirgüç-Kunt, A.; Levine, R. Financial institutions and markets across countries and over time-data and analysis. *World Bank Policy Res. Work. Pap.* **2009**, 4943.
26. Colm, G. In defense of the public interest. In *Classics in Institutional Economics, Part II*; Routledge: London, UK, 2024; Volume 9, pp. 376–389.
27. Croley, S.P. *Regulation and Public Interests: The Possibility of Good Regulatory Government*; Princeton University Press: Princeton, NJ, USA, 2009.
28. Ugochukwu Uche, C. The theory of regulation: A review article. *J. Financ. Regul. Compliance* **2001**, *9*, 67–80. [CrossRef]
29. Stigler, G. The Theory of Economic Regulation. *Bell J. Econ. Manag. Sci.* **1971**, *2*, 3–21. [CrossRef]
30. Su, F.; Zhai, L.; Zhou, Y.; Zhuang, Z.; Wang, F. Risk contagion in financial markets: A systematic review using bibliometric methods. *Aust. Econ. Pap.* **2024**, *63*, 163–199. [CrossRef]
31. Allen, H.J. Regulating fintech: A harm focused approach. *Comput. Law Secur. Rev.* **2024**, *52*, 105910. [CrossRef]
32. Claessens, S.; Rojas-Suarez, L. *Financial Regulations for Improving Financial Inclusion*; Center for Global Development: Washington, DC, USA, 2016; Volume 2, pp. 44–53. Available online: https://www.cgdev.org/sites/default/files/CGD-financial-regulation-task-force-report-2016.pdf (accessed on 20 April 2025).
33. Sintha, L. Branchless banking as a disruptive innovation in Indonesia. In Proceedings of the 2nd Annual Conference on Blended Learning, Educational Technology and Innovation (ACBLETI 2020), Online, 23–24 October 2020; Atlantis Press: Dordrecht, The Netherlands, 2021; pp. 380–385.
34. Pai, V.S. Innovation and Market Disruption: Some Exploratory Thoughts. *KIM J. Bus. Res.* **2022**, *2*, 1–8.
35. Monye, M.; Osio, J. Adapting to Digital Disruption: Evaluating Implementation Challenges and Effective Strategies in Nigerian Banking Marketing. *J. Policy Dev. Stud.* **2024**, *17*, 129–151. [CrossRef]
36. Pang, Z.; Abdullah, M.Y. Disruptive Innovation and Its Impact on Traditional Business Models: A Multi-Industry Study. *Uniglobal J. Soc. Sci. Humanit.* **2024**, *3*, 294–300.
37. Chougule, P.S.; Dudekula, C.S. Banking in the Future: An Exploration of Underlying Challenges. In *The Adoption of Fintech Using Technology for Better Security, Speed, and Customer Experience in Finance*; Jafar, S.H., Hemachandran, K., Akhtar, S., Parvez, A., Khan, P., Hani El-Chaarani, H., Eds.; Routledge: New York, NY, USA, 2024; pp. 160–191.
38. Rathnayake, N.D.N.B. The Era of the transition–from traditional to digital banking. In *Transformation for Sustainable Business and Management Practices: Exploring the Spectrum of Industry 5.0*; Emerald Publishing Limited: Leeds, UK, 2023; pp. 41–55.

39. Mehdiabadi, A.; Shahabi, V.; Shamsinejad, S.; Amiri, M.; Spulbar, C.; Birau, R. Investigating Industry 5.0 and Its Impact on the Banking Industry: Requirements, Approaches and Communications. *Appl. Sci.* **2022**, *12*, 5126. [CrossRef]
40. Megargel, A.; Shankararaman, V.; Reddy, S.K. Real-time inbound marketing: A use case for digital banking. In *Handbook of Blockchain, Digital Finance, and Inclusion*; Academic Press: Cambridge, MA, USA, 2018; Volume 1, pp. 311–328.
41. Utami, B.S.A. The impact of the COVID-19 pandemic on the MSME sector in Indonesia. *Econ. J. Econ.* **2021**, *3*, 97–103.
42. Molteni, M.; Pellegrino, D. The establishment of banking supervision in Italy: An assessment (1926–1936). *Bus. Hist.* **2024**, *66*, 1442–1470. [CrossRef]
43. Dermine, J. Banking in Europe: Past, present and future. *Transform. Eur. Financ. Syst.* **2003**, *21*, 31–95.
44. Burugulla, J.K.R. Enhancing Credit and Charge Card Risk Assessment Through Generative AI and Big Data Analytics: A Novel Approach to Fraud Detection and Consumer Spending Patterns. *Cuest. Fisioter.* **2025**, *54*, 964–972.
45. Fry, T.H. For Everything Else, There's Taxes: Why Credit Card Rewards Should Stop Being Priceless. *Boston Coll. Law Rev.* **2025**, *66*, 121–172.
46. Mehdiabadi, A.; Tabatabeinasab, M.; Spulbar, C.; Karbassi Yazdi, A.; Birau, R. Are we ready for the challenge of banks 4.0? Designing a roadmap for banking systems in Industry 4.0. *Int. J. Financ. Stud.* **2020**, *8*, 32. [CrossRef]
47. Bhattacharya, S.; Thakor, A.V. Contemporary banking theory. *J. Financ. Intermediat.* **1993**, *3*, 2–50. [CrossRef]
48. Bansal, N. The Impact of Financial Security Enhancement Through One Time Password in ATM Cash Transactions: The Impact of Financial Security Enhancement. In *Organizational Sociology in the Digital Age*; IGI Global Scientific Publishing: Hershey, PA, USA, 2025; pp. 453–468.
49. Batiz-Lazo, B. Emergence and evolution of ATM networks in the UK, 1967–2000. *Bus. Hist.* **2009**, *51*, 1–27. [CrossRef]
50. Sharmin, S.; Kalam, F.A.; Islam, A.F.; Aubhi, R.U.H. Impact of emotional intelligence on employee performance: A bibliometric approach. *J. Hum. Resour. Sustain. Stud.* **2024**, *12*, 243–262. [CrossRef]
51. Kumar, R. The evolution of banking through digital payment systems. *IJEETE J. Res.* **2025**, *11*, 284–295.
52. Metzger, J.; Paulowitz, T. Seeking common legal entity standards to facilitate cross-border payments. *J. Paym. Strategy Syst.* **2018**, *12*, 365–370. [CrossRef]
53. Omarini, A.E. Banks and Fintechs: How to Develop a Digital Open Banking Approach for the Bank's Future. *Int. Bus. Res.* **2018**, *11*, 23–36. [CrossRef]
54. Tan, M.; Teo, T.S. Factors influencing the adoption of Internet banking. *J. Assoc. Inf. Syst.* **2000**, *1*, 5. [CrossRef]
55. Safari, K.; Bisimwa, A.; Buzera Armel, M. Attitudes and intentions toward internet banking in an underdeveloped financial sector. *PSU Res. Rev.* **2022**, *6*, 39–58. [CrossRef]
56. van Thiel, D. On The Human-Centred AI Transformation of Banking. Dissertation. 2025. Available online: https://repository.tilburguniversity.edu/server/api/core/bitstreams/51f89b64-ce94-4e59-8077-d2208d5037b9/content (accessed on 19 April 2025).
57. D'Andrea, A.; Limodio, N. High-speed internet, financial technology, and banking. *Manag. Sci.* **2024**, *70*, 773–798. [CrossRef]
58. Del Gaudio, B.L.; Porzio, C.; Sampagnaro, G.; Verdoliva, V. How do mobile, internet and ICT diffusion affect the banking industry? An empirical analysis. *Eur. Manag. J.* **2021**, *39*, 327–332. [CrossRef]
59. Arslanian, H.; Fischer, F. Fintech and the future of the financial ecosystem. In *The Future of Finance: The Impact of FinTech, AI, and Crypto on Financial Services*; Springer International Publishing: Cham, Switzerland, 2019; pp. 201–216.
60. Saxena, D. Regaining legitimacy after an information systems implementation failure: Case of a National Blood Bank Service. *J. Inf. Technol. Teach. Cases* **2022**, *12*, 50–54. [CrossRef]
61. Rajeshkumar, L. Financial Evolution: Tracing the Roots of Al in Finance. In *AI, Economic Perspectives, and Firm Business Management*; IGI Global Scientific Publishing: Hershey, PA, USA, 2025; p. 45.
62. Rathnayake, M.R.M.C.J.K. Impact of Cross Generational Knowledge Sharing on Innovative Behaviour: Role of Edge Organization Factors. 2023. Available online: http://www.dr.lib.sjp.ac.lk/bitstream/handle/123456789/12860/Abstract.pdf?sequence=1&isAllowed=y (accessed on 25 April 2025).
63. Shahabi, V.; Azar, A.; Faezy Razi, F.; Fallah Shams, M.F. Simulation of the effect of COVID-19 outbreak on the development of branchless banking in Iran: Case study of Resalat Qard–al-Hasan Bank. *Rev. Behav. Financ.* **2020**, *13*, 85–108. [CrossRef]
64. Elsaid, H.M. A review of literature directions regarding the impact of fintech firms on the banking industry. *Qual. Res. Financ. Mark.* **2023**, *15*, 693–711. [CrossRef]
65. Ranjan, R. Behavioural Finance in Banking and Management: A Study on the Trends and Challenges in the Banking Industry. *Asian J. Econ. Bus. Account.* **2025**, *25*, 374–386. [CrossRef]
66. Prayoga, R.G. Digital Banking and Traditional Banking: A Comparative Study on Advanced Financial Service. *SUKUK Int. J. Bank. Financ. Manag. Bus.* **2023**, *2*, 35–51.
67. Arner, D.W.; Barberis, J. Regulating FinTech Innovation: A Balancing Act. Asian Institute of International Financial Law. [Электронный ресурс]. 2015. Available online: http://www.law.hku.hk/aiifl/regulating-fintech-innovation-a-balancing-act-1-april-1230-130-pm (accessed on 25 March 2025).

68. Rybacki, P. Revolut's Revolution: The Rise of a Digital Bank. 2022. Available online: https://knowledge.uchicago.edu/record/4 59?v=pdf (accessed on 27 April 2025).
69. Polasik, M.; Widawski, P.; Lis, A. Challenger bank as a new digital form of providing financial services to retail customers in th EU internal market: The case of Revolut. In *The Digitalization of Financial Markets*; Marszk, A., Lechman, E., Eds.; Taylor & Franci Abingdon, UK, 2022.
70. Boda, V.V.R.; Immaneni, J. Streamlining FinTech operations: The power of SysOps and smart automation. *Innov. Comput. Sci.* **2019**, *5*, 36–50.
71. Sen, S. The Effect of Consumer Trust on the Growth of Online Payment Platforms: A Case Study of PayPal and Stripe. *Shod Sagar J. Commer. Econ.* **2024**, *1*, 17–21.
72. Gomber, P.; Kauffman, R.J.; Weber, B.W. Financial IS, Underlying Technologies, and The FinTech Revolution. In *A Call for Paper Special Issue of the Journal of Management Information Systems*; University of Delaware: Newark, DE, USA, 2016; Available onlin https://jmis-web.org/cfps/JMIS_SI_Fintech.pdf (accessed on 30 May 2025).
73. Casey, A. Silicon Valley Bank A case study in Post crisis Bank Failures. *Bank. Financ. Law Rev.* **2024**, *41*. Available onlin https://chicagounbound.uchicago.edu/law_and_economics/1057/ (accessed on 30 May 2025).
74. Hensen, J.; Kötting, B. From open banking to embedded finance: The essential factors for a successful digital transformatio *J. Digit. Bank.* **2022**, *6*, 308–318. [CrossRef]
75. Mohan, P. Technologies for Digital Disruption in Banking. *South Asian J. Soc. Stud. Econ.* **2025**, *22*, 22–34. [CrossRef]
76. Palmieri, A.; Nazeraj, B. Open banking and competition: An intricate relationship. *EU Comp. Law Issues Chall. Ser. (ECLIC)* **202** *5*, 217–237.
77. Sharma, P. Fintech Startups and Traditional Banking: Rivals or Collaborators. *Comput. Fraud. Secur.* **2024**, *2024*, 357–370.
78. Nayak, R. Banking regulations: Do they matter for performance? *J. Bank. Regul.* **2021**, *22*, 261–274. [CrossRef]
79. Zetzsche, D.A.; Arner, D.W.; Buckley, R.P. Decentralized finance. *J. Financ. Regul.* **2020**, *6*, 172–203. [CrossRef]
80. Conti-Brown, P.E. Lessons from History. *Finance & Development Magazine*, March 2023. Available online: https://www.imf.org en/Publications/fandd/issues/2023/03/book-review-lessons-from-history-conti-brown (accessed on 30 May 2025)
81. Wagner, G.; Eidenmuller, H. Down by algorithms: Siphoning rents, exploiting biases, and shaping preferences: Regulating th dark side of personalized transactions. *U. Chi. L. Rev.* **2019**, *86*, 581. [CrossRef]
82. Saia, R.; Giuliani, A.; Pompianu, L.; Carta, S. From payment services directive 2 (PSD2) to credit scoring: A case study on a Italian Banking Institution. *IC3K* **2021**, *1*, 164–171.
83. Hyland, L.; Sebastian, A.; Seetharam, Y. An application of behavioural finance in banking: The Discovery Bank case. *J. Eco Financ. Sci.* **2021**, *14*, 10. [CrossRef]
84. Zuhrofi, A. Human Capital Optimization Strategy in Bank BNI 46 to Improve Innovation and Services. *Akad. J. Econ. Bus. Stu* **2025**, *5*, 29–38.
85. Li, M.; Li, Z.; Pan, S.L. Spanning knowledge boundaries in offshore insourcing through organizational learning: A case study o bankco. In Proceedings of the 18th Pacific Asia Conference on Information Systems PACIS 2014, Chengdu, China, 24–28 June 201 p. 187. Available online: http://aisel.aisnet.org/pacis2014/187 (accessed on 25 April 2025).
86. Bessen, J. Automation and jobs: When technology boosts employment. *Econ. Policy* **2019**, *34*, 589–626. [CrossRef]
87. Tenakwah, E.S.; Watson, C. Embracing the AI/automation age: Preparing your workforce for humans and machines workin together. *Strategy Leadersh.* **2025**, *3*, 32–48. [CrossRef]
88. Oko-Odion, C.; Angela, O. Risk management frameworks for financial institutions in a rapidly changing economic landscape. *In J. Sci. Res. Arch.* **2025**, *14*, 1182–1204. [CrossRef]
89. Financial Conduct Authority. The Financial Services Practitioner Panel Annual Report 2011/12: FCA. 2011. Available onlin https://www.fca.org.uk/panels/practitioner-panel/publication/annualreport2012.pdf (accessed on 16 July 2025).
90. Hasan, E.F.; Alzuod, M.A.; Al Jasimee, K.H.; Alshdaifat, S.M.; Hijazin, A.F.; Khrais, L.T. The Role of Organizational Culture i Digital Transformation and Modern Accounting Practices Among Jordanian SMEs. *J. Risk Financ. Manag.* **2025**, *18*, 147. [CrossRef
91. Vial, G. Understanding digital transformation: A review and a research agenda. In *Managing Digital Transformation*, 1st ed Routledge: London, UK, 2021; pp. 13–66.
92. Cahyono, N.D. Adaptive Leadership Strategies for Hybrid Workforces: Navigating the Future of Human Resource Managemen *J. Acad. Sci.* **2025**, *2*, 12–20.
93. Telu, S.; Kumar, S. Towards a sustainable future: A comprehensive review of employee well-being in hybrid work settings. *Mana Sustain. Arab. Rev.* 2025; *ahead-of-print*. [CrossRef]
94. Singh, S.K.; Sharma, P. Role of Hybrid Entrepreneurship in the Gig Economy. In *Entrepreneurial Ecosystems Driving Econom Transformation and Job Creation*; IGI Global Scientific Publishing: Hershey, PA, USA, 2025; pp. 29–56.
95. Mohsen, S.E.; Hamdan, A.; Shoaib, H.M. Digital transformation and integration of artificial intelligence in financial institution *J. Financ. Report. Account.* **2025**, *23*, 680–699. [CrossRef]

96. Yang, F.; Tajul, A.M. Role of financial inclusion and digital transformation on bank credit risk. *J. Int. Financ. Mark. Inst. Money* **2024**, *91*, 101934. [CrossRef]
97. Wu, H.; Hung, J.-L.; Liu, L. Impact of big data analytics on banking: A case study. *J. Enterp. Inf. Manag.* **2023**, *36*, 459–479.
98. Shivaramakrishna, D.; Nagaratna, M. A novel hybrid cryptographic framework for secure data storage in cloud computing: Integrating AES-OTP and RSA with adaptive key management and time-limited access control. *Alex. Eng. J.* **2023**, *84*, 275–284. [CrossRef]
99. Amoo, O.O.; Osasona, F.; Atadoga, A.; Ayinla, B.S.; Farayola, O.A.; Abrahams, T.O. Cybersecurity threats in the age of IoT: A review of protective measures. *Int. J. Sci. Res. Arch.* **2024**, *11*, 1304–1310. [CrossRef]
100. Djibran, F. Enhancing SME Growth Through Online Banking Solutions: Opportunities And Challenges In The Digital Era. *J. Ris. Multidisiplinary Edukasi* **2025**, *2*, 413–426. [CrossRef]
101. Babu, S.K.; Hameed, A.; Nair, R.R.; Babu, T.; Sharma, R.; Chinnaiyan, R.; Sungheetha, A. Analyzing the Digital Transformation and Evolution of Financial Technology (Fintech) Across Various Industries. In Proceedings of the 2024 4th International Conference on Innovative Practices in Technology and Management (ICIPTM), Noida, India, 21–23 February 2024; IEEE: Piscataway, NJ, USA, 2024; pp. 1–8.
102. Vives, X. The impact of FinTech on banking. *Eur. Econ.* **2017**, *2*, 97–105.
103. Adejumo, A.; Ogburie, C. Strengthening finance with cybersecurity: Ensuring safer digital transactions. *World J. Adv. Res. Rev.* **2025**, *25*, 1527–1541. [CrossRef]
104. Lam, A.Y. Artificial Intelligence Applications in Financial Technology. *J. Theor. Appl. Electron. Commer. Res.* **2025**, *20*, 29. [CrossRef]
105. Zohar, A. Bitcoin: Under the hood. *Commun. ACM* **2015**, *58*, 104–113. [CrossRef]
106. Siano, A.; Raimi, L.; Palazzo, M.; Panait, M.C. Mobile banking: An innovative solution for increasing financial inclusion in Sub-Saharan African Countries: Evidence from Nigeria. *Sustainability* **2020**, *12*, 10130. [CrossRef]
107. Foster, C. Intellectual property rights and control in the digital economy: Examining the expansion of M-Pesa. *Inf. Soc.* **2024**, *40*, 1–17. [CrossRef]
108. Omwansa, T. M-PESA: Progress and prospects. *Innovations* **2009**, *107*, 476.
109. Musembi, P.M. Africa's Contributions to Digital Technology: A Case of M-Pesa Technology in Kenya. In *Contributions of Africa's Indigenous Knowledge to the Wave of Digital Technology: Decolonial Perspectives*; IGI Global: Hershey, PA, USA, 2024; pp. 260–289.
110. Karani, G.; Jadhav, B. How Traditional Banks Adapt to the Fintech Revolution in Banking and Finance Sector. In *Shaping Cutting-Edge Technologies and Applications for Digital Banking and Financial Services*; Routledge: London, UK, 2025; pp. 214–225.
111. Sekhar, S.C.; Kumar, M. An overview of cyber security in digital banking sector. *East Asian J. Multidiscip. Res.* **2023**, *2*, 43–52. [CrossRef]
112. Aliu, N.F.; Ikharo, A.B.; Jegede, A.J. Enhancing Regulatory Compliance in the National FinTech Ecosystem: A Centralized RegTech Approach. *Univ. Ib. J. Sci. Log. ICT Res.* **2024**, *12*, 1–11.
113. Arner, D.; Buckley, R.; Charamba, K.; Sergeev, A.; Zetzsche, D. Governing FinTech 4.0: BigTech, platform finance, and sustainable development. *Fordham J. Corp. Fin. L.* **2022**, *27*, 1. [CrossRef]
114. Iyelolu, T.V.; Agu, E.E.; Idemudia, C.; Ijomah, T.I. Legal innovations in FinTech: Advancing financial services through regulatory reform. *Financ. Account. Res. J.* **2024**, *6*, 1310–1319. [CrossRef]
115. Chaimaa, B.; Najib, E.; Rachid, H. E-banking overview: Concepts, challenges and solutions. *Wirel. Pers. Commun.* **2021**, *117*, 1059–1078. [CrossRef]
116. Gupta, P.K. Internet banking in India–Consumer concerns and bank strategies. *Glob. J. Bus. Res.* **2008**, *2*, 43–51.
117. Dhumal, K. Virtual business card using NFC technology. In *Recent Advances in Sciences, Engineering, Information Technology & Management*; CRC Press: Boca Raton, FL, USA, 2025.
118. Jumayev, B. Big data: Customer credit analysis using digital banking database. *Int. J. Artif. Intell.* **2025**, *1*, 1056–1059.
119. Hassan, A.O.; Ewuga, S.K.; Abdul, A.A.; Abrahams, T.O.; Oladeinde, M.; Dawodu, S.O. Cybersecurity in banking: A global perspective with a focus on Nigerian practices. *Comput. Sci. IT Res. J.* **2024**, *5*, 41–59. [CrossRef]
120. Zhang, Y.; Liu, Q.; Li, X. The strategic value of cybersecurity in digital banking transformation. *J. Financ. Technol. Innov.* **2023**, *5*, 221–240.
121. Xuan, Q.T.; Truong, H.T.H.; Quang, T.V. The impacts of omnichannel retailing properties on customer experience and brand loyalty: A study in the banking sector. *Cogent Bus. Manag.* **2023**, *10*, 2244765. [CrossRef]
122. Cao, L.; Li, L. The impact of cross-channel integration on retailers' sales growth. *J. Retail.* **2015**, *91*, 198–216. [CrossRef]
123. Al-Okaily, A.; Al-Okaily, M.; Teoh, A.P.; Al-Debei, M.M. An empirical study on data warehouse systems effectiveness: The case of Jordanian banks in the business intelligence era. *EuroMed J. Bus.* **2023**, *18*, 489–510. [CrossRef]
124. Tanda, A.; Schena, C. Digital Transformation and Digital Disruption. In *FinTech, BigTech and Banks*; Palgrave Pivot: Cham, Switzerland, 2019; Volume 4, p. 52. [CrossRef]
125. Shaikh, A.A.; Hanafizadeh, P.; Karjaluoto, H. Mobile banking and payment system: A conceptual standpoint. *Int. J. E-Bus. Res. (IJEBR)* **2017**, *13*, 14–27. [CrossRef]

126. Wang, S.; Asif, M.; Shahzad, M.F.; Ashfaq, M. Data privacy and cybersecurity challenges in the digital transformation of the banking sector. *Comput. Secur.* **2024**, *147*, 104051. [CrossRef]
127. International Monetary Fund (IMF). *Global Financial Stability Report 2024*; IMF: Washington, DC, USA, 2024; Available online https://www.imf.org (accessed on 20 April 2025).
128. Meduri, K. Cybersecurity threats in banking: Unsupervised fraud detection analysis. *Int. J. Sci. Res. Arch.* **2024**, *11*, 915–925 [CrossRef]
129. SABRIC (South African Banking Risk Information Centre). Annual Crime Statistics 2021. Available online: https://www.banking.org.za/news/sabric-annual-crime-stats-2021/ (accessed on 20 April 2025).
130. He, Z.; Zhang, T.; Lee, R.B. Attacking and protecting data privacy in edge–cloud collaborative inference systems. *IEEE Internet Things J.* **2020**, *8*, 9706–9716. [CrossRef]
131. Njeru, P.W.; Gaitho, V. Investigating extent to which cybercrime influences performance of commercial banks in Kenya. *Int. J Econ. Commer. Manag.* **2019**, *8*, 489–514.
132. Apau, R.; Koranteng, F.N. Impact of cybercrime and trust on the use of e-commerce technologies: An application of the theory of planned behavior. *Int. J. Cyber Criminol.* **2019**, *13*, 228–254.
133. Alzoubi, H.M.; Ghazal, T.M.; Hasan, M.K.; Alketbi, A.; Kamran, R.; Al-Dmour, N.A.; Islam, S. Cyber security threats on digital banking. In Proceedings of the 1st International Conference on AI in Cybersecurity (ICAIC), Houston, TX, USA, 15–17 March 2022 pp. 1–4.
134. Mphatheni, M.R.; Maluleke, W. Cybersecurity as a response to combating cybercrime: Demystifying the prevailing threats and offering recommendations to the African regions. *Int. J. Res. Bus. Soc. Sci.* **2022**, *11*, 384–396. [CrossRef]
135. WEF. Cybersecurity Disclosures Under the Spotlight, and Other Cybersecurity News to Know This Month: World Economic Forum. 2025. Available online: https://www.weforum.org/stories/2025/04/effective-cybersecurity-communications-other-cybersecurity-news-this-month/?utm_source=whatsapp&utm_medium=social (accessed on 20 April 2025).
136. Pillai, S.E.V.S.; Hu, W.C. Security and Privacy Challenges and Opportunities in FinTech. In Proceedings of the 2024 Cyber Awareness and Research Symposium (CARS), Grand Forks, ND, USA, 28–29 October 2024; IEEE: Piscataway, NJ, USA, 2024 pp. 1–6.
137. Odumuwagun, O. Future of Security in FinTech: Balancing User Privacy, Compliance, and Technological Advancements. *Int. J. Res. Publ. Rev.* **2025**, *6*, 1296–1310. [CrossRef]
138. Sharma, V.K.; Kumar, A. Determinants of online banking adoption in India: An empirical investigation. *Int. J. Bus. Innov. Res* **2025**, *36*, 229–247. [CrossRef]
139. Tsingou, E. Effective horizon management in transnational administration: Bespoke and box-ticking consultancies in anti-money laundering. *Public Adm.* **2021**, *100*, 522–537. [CrossRef]
140. Saksonova, S.; Kuzmina-Merlino, I. Fintech as financial innovation–The possibilities and problems of implementation. *Eur. Res Stud. J.* **2017**, *20*, 961–973. [CrossRef]
141. Chittoor, D.S. Implementing data lineage frameworks in financial institutions: A systematic analysis of compliance, efficiency and risk management. *Int. J. Sci. Res. Arch.* **2025**, *14*, 353–361. [CrossRef]
142. Stulz, R.M. Fintech, bigtech, and the future of banks. *J. Appl. Corp. Financ.* **2019**, *31*, 86–97. [CrossRef]
143. Sekhar Nanda, A. Technology Advantage in Finance: Revolutionizing the Rise of IT-Enabled Financial Services in the Digital Age *Int. J. Comput. Sci. Inf. Technol. Res. (IJCSITR)* **2025**, *5*, 62–71.
144. Chinamanagonda, S. Revitalizing Legacy Systems: Proven Strategies for Successful Application Modernization. *J. Comput. Inf. Technol.* **2024**, *4*, 1–8.
145. Vettriselvan, R.; Velmurugan, P.R.; Regins, J.C.; Maheswari, S.U.; Joyce, R. Best Practices, Ethical Challenges, and Regulatory Frameworks for AI Integration in Banking: Navigating the Future. In *Artificial Intelligence for Cloud-Native Software Engineering* IGI Global Scientific Publishing: Hershey, PA, USA, 2025; pp. 377–410.
146. Enriques, L.; Ringe, W.G. Bank–fintech partnerships, outsourcing arrangements and the case for a mentorship regime. *Cap. Mark. Law J.* **2020**, *15*, 374–397. [CrossRef]
147. Khan, H.H.; Kutan, A.M.; Qureshi, F. Fintech integration: Driving efficiency in banking institutions across the developing nations *Financ. Res. Lett.* **2024**, *67*, 105772. [CrossRef]
148. De Koker, L.; Morris, N.; Jaffer, S. Regulating financial services in an era of technological disruption. *Lawin Context* **2019**, *36*, 90–112. [CrossRef]
149. Kuchciak, I.; Warwas, I. Designing a Roadmap for Human Resource Management in the Banking 4.0. *J. Risk Financ. Manag.* **2021**, *14*, 615. [CrossRef]
150. Kaur, H.; Arora, S. Demographic influences on consumer decisions in the banking sector: Evidence from India. *J. Financ. Serv. Mark.* **2019**, *24*, 81–93. [CrossRef]
151. Warf, B. Demographic transition. In *Encyclopedia of Geography*; Warf, B., Ed.; SAGE: Thousand Oaks, CA, USA, 2010; pp. 708–711

52. Salam, K.N. Gen-Z Marketing Strategies: Understanding Consumer Preferences and Building Sustainable Relationships. *Gold. Ratio Mapp. Idea Lit. Format* **2024**, *4*, 53–77. [CrossRef]
53. Seyfi, S.; Hall, C.M.; Strzelecka, M. Introduction: Gen Z, tourism, and sustainable consumption. In *Gen Z, Tourism, and Sustainable Consumption*; Seyfi, S., Hall, C.M., Strzelecka, M., Eds.; Routledge: London, UK, 2024; pp. 3–17.
54. Goh, E.; Okumus, F. Avoiding the hospitality workforce bubble: Strategies to attract and retain generation Z talent in the hospitality workforce. *Tour. Manag. Perspect.* **2020**, *33*, 100603. [CrossRef]
55. Arkhipova, N. Impact of Demographic Trends on Retail Banking. *Procedia Comput. Sci.* **2022**, *214*, 831–836. [CrossRef]
56. Fares, O.H.; Aversa, J.; Lee, S.H. The digital divide: Psychographic segmentation in the Canadian banking context. *J. Mark. Anal.* **2024**, 1–16. [CrossRef]
57. Kornelakis, A.; Kirov, V.; Thill, P. The digitalisation of service work: A comparative study of restructuring of the banking sector in the United Kingdom and Luxembourg. *Eur. J. Ind. Relat.* **2022**, *28*, 253–272. [CrossRef]
58. van der Laan, L.; Yap, J. Strategy and Asia Pacific Futures. In *Foresight & Strategy in the Asia Pacific Region: Practice and Theory to Build Enterprises of the Future*; Springer: Singapore, 2016; pp. 59–89.

FinTech

MDPI

Article

The Impact of Technological Development on the Productivity of UK Banks

Nour Mohamad Fayad [1], Ali Awdeh [2,*], Jessica Abou Mrad [3], Ghaithaa El Mokdad [4] and Madonna Nassar [5]

1 Department of Economics, Faculty of Business Administration, Lebanese International University, Beirut P.O. Box 1464/04, Lebanon; nour.fayad@liu.edu.lb
2 Faculty of Economics and Business Administration, Lebanese University, Beirut P.O. Box 6573/14, Lebanon
3 Faculty of Business Administration, Modern University for Business and Science, Beirut P.O. Box 113/7501, Lebanon; jaboumrad@mubs.edu.lb
4 Faculty of Business Studies, Arab Open University, Beirut P.O. Box 20584518, Lebanon; gmokdad@aou.edu.lb
5 General Directorate of the Presidency of the Council of Ministers, Beirut P.O. Box 3170/11, Lebanon; madonnanassar@gmail.com
* Correspondence: ali.awdeh@ul.edu.lb

Abstract

This study investigates the impact of digitalisation and intangible investment—specifically digital skills and software adoption—on productivity in the United Kingdom's banking sector. Software adoption is captured through banks' investment in enterprise systems (CRM/ERP, cloud computing, and related applications), rather than a single software version. Drawing on detailed bank-level data from six major UK banks over the period 2007–2022, this research provides empirical evidence that higher intensities of digital human capital and intangible assets are positively associated with improvements in both employee productivity and overall bank performance. A standard deviation increase in software specialist employment is associated with productivity gains of 10.3% annually, though this upper-bound estimate likely combines direct effects with complementary factors such as concurrent IT investments (e.g., cloud infrastructure) and managerial innovations. The findings also highlight substantial heterogeneity across banks, with younger institutions experiencing more pronounced benefits from intangible investment due to their greater flexibility and innovation capacity. Furthermore, this study reveals that the adoption of high-speed internet and investment in IT hardware have a strong positive effect on bank productivity, particularly in the wake of the COVID-19 pandemic, which accelerated digital transformation across the sector. However, the observational nature of the study and the limited sample size necessitate caution in generalising the findings. While the results have implications for digital workforce development and technology infrastructure, policy recommendations should be interpreted as preliminary, pending further validation in broader samples and diverse institutional settings. This study concludes by advocating for targeted strategies to expand digital skills, promote software diffusion, and modernise infrastructure to facilitate productivity convergence, while emphasising the need for future research to address potential endogeneity and external validity limitations.

Keywords: digital transformation; technological development; bank productivity; FinTech adoption

JEL Classification: D24; E44; G21; L86; O33

1. Introduction

Over the past few years, the global economy has witnessed a rapid spread of disruptive technologies, leading to fundamental shifts in business models across all economic sectors. One of the most significantly affected sectors was the financial industry, which is currently undergoing a major transformation driven by digital innovation. Since the 1950s, the financial sector has seen continuous technological evolution, beginning with the introduction of Automated Teller Machines (ATMs), which enabled self-service banking and reduced reliance on human factors. This was followed by the invention of payment cards, which reduced the need to carry cash.

According to Breidbach et al. [1], the adoption of new technologies in the financial sector has been gradual yet consistent. The rise in internet access in the 1990s enabled customers to perform online banking transactions 24/7. In the 21st century, technologies such as cryptocurrencies and block chain have made it possible to conduct financial transactions without relying on traditional centralised intermediaries.

Interestingly, despite substantial technological advancements over the past six decades, the financial industry has not been destabilised; on the contrary, it has thrived [2]. Established financial institutions, particularly large banks, have been compelled to adopt new strategies to meet evolving customer expectations. Meanwhile, new entrants—commonly referred to as "FinTech" companies—have seized opportunities to deliver services that traditional banks were either unable or too slow to provide. These new players have introduced innovative solutions such as mobile wallets, payment applications, crowdfunding platforms, and automated investment advisory tools, fundamentally reshaping the financial landscape.

From a theoretical perspective, the relationship between technological development and productivity is anchored in classical and modern production theory, which posits that productivity increases when firms enhance their ability to generate more output from a given set of inputs. In the banking sector, this is achieved primarily through reductions in transaction costs, improved information processing, enhanced intermediation efficiency, and service innovation. The digital transformation introduces three core mechanisms that drive productivity gains in banking: (1) Automation and Process Efficiency, (2) Scalability and Cost Reduction, and (3) Complementarity with Intangible Capital. Moreover, drawing from the endogenous growth literature (e.g., [3]), innovation in financial services not only enhances firm-level productivity but also contributes to broader sectoral and macroeconomic growth through diffusion effects and competition-driven efficiency. In this context, the adoption of FinTech, software tools, and mobile banking technologies serves as a channel for technological spill overs that reinforce convergence toward the productivity frontier. Banks that successfully invest in these capabilities tend to outperform less digitally mature counterparts, reflecting persistent heterogeneity in absorptive capacity and innovation readiness.

As a result of digitalisation and business transformation, a new financial services market has emerged. FinTech companies have targeted every segment of banking, aiming to enhance specific components of traditional universal banking [4]. While the future of traditional financial service providers remains uncertain—especially with the shift towards Open Banking, which allows customers to easily switch or combine service providers—the integration of financial technology into the production and delivery of financial products is becoming increasingly crucial [5].

Purnomo [6] emphasises the growing importance of digital marketing in driving sales on e-commerce platforms. Techniques such as search engine optimisation (SEO), content marketing, social media engagement, paid advertising, and user experience optimisation are identified as key drivers of increased traffic, customer engagement, and sales conversions. These strategies are essential for businesses seeking to maintain a competitive edge in the digital economy. The study by Purnomo [6] also highlights the need for innovative digital marketing approaches to enhance the visibility and sales of products and services in today's rapidly evolving marketplace.

In the case of the United Kingdom (UK), the technology sector is experiencing significant growth. Martin Carkett, policy lead at the Tony Blair Institute for Global Change, noted in 2021 that "the technology industry is expanding more than two and a half times faster than the rest of the British economy," with 2.1 million jobs created in the digital economy in 2018. The UK digital sector contributed an estimated GBP £149 billion—or GBP £400 million per day—to the national economy in 2018, marking a 7.9% increase from the previous year [7].

Given this context, the current study seeks to explore the impact of technological development on productivity within the UK private sector. Specifically, it aims to assess how digitalisation, e-banking, mobile banking, and emerging financial technologies are shaping the evolving banking landscape in the UK and influencing the productivity of financial institutions.

The empirical results of this study reveal that digital adoption, FinTech investment, and digital skills are positively associated with productivity growth across UK banks. While the anticipated complementarities between digital skills and FinTech adoption were not consistently statistically significant, the main effects of both digital technologies and human capital investments were robustly positive. FinTech adoption was also linked to improved operational efficiency and notable shifts in customer behaviour, including increased use of digital channels. These findings highlight the critical role of digital transformation in enhancing bank performance and accelerating sector-wide innovation.

While prior studies have largely focused on descriptive accounts of technological adoption in banking or explored its impact on market structure and innovation, this study advances the literature by providing a rigorous empirical analysis of the productivity effects of digital transformation in UK banks. Using detailed firm-level data on digital adoption, FinTech investments, and digital skills, this paper employs advanced panel econometric techniques to isolate the direct contribution of technological development to operational efficiency and productivity growth. This granular approach allows for a better understanding of heterogeneity in banks' innovation readiness and the interaction between human capital and technology—an area that remains under examined in existing research. Thus, the study makes both a methodological and empirical contribution by quantifying how digitalisation shapes productivity dynamics in a key financial sector.

Although extensive research has documented the rise in digital technologies in banking, much of the existing literature remains descriptive or limited to case studies and broad industry overviews. This study advances beyond previous work by quantitatively assessing the productivity impact of digital transformation within the UK banking sector using firm-level data. Unlike prior studies that often rely on aggregated proxies or binary measures of digital adoption, our approach incorporates detailed indicators of FinTech investment, digital skills, and technology usage intensity. Furthermore, we employ several robust econometric methods to control for unobserved heterogeneity and endogeneity, providing more reliable estimates of causal effects. By doing so, this research contributes novel empirical evidence of the heterogeneous effects of banking digitalisation on productivity and operational efficiency, offering actionable insights for policymakers and industry practitioners.

It is important to acknowledge that measuring technological development and its impact on productivity involves inherent challenges. Digital adoption and FinTech investment are complex, multifaceted phenomena that are not easily captured by single indicators.

Moreover, isolating the causal effect of technology on productivity is complicated by potential endogeneity issues, such as reverse causality and omitted variable bias. This study addresses these concerns by employing robust panel data techniques and controlling for key confounding factors; however, some limitations remain, which we discuss in detail in the methodology and robustness sections.

This paper proceeds as follows. Section 2 contains an overview of the relevant literature. The structure of the UK banking sector is highlighted in Section 3. The empirical methodology and exploited variables are illustrated in Section 4. Section 5 contains the dataset and the source of data. The empirical results and the robustness tests are included in Section 6. Finally, the conclusion and policy recommendations are presented in Section 7.

2. Literature Review and Hypothesis Development

The digital transformation has reshaped virtually every sector, and the financial industry is no exception. One of the most significant manifestations of this transformation is the rise in FinTech (financial technology), which represents a major innovation in the financial services landscape. FinTech encompasses a wide array of digital financial services—ranging from mobile payments, peer-to-peer lending, and digital wallets to online trading, robo-advisory services, and crypto-assets ([8,9]). These innovations have been accelerated by advances in information technology, regulatory support, and shifting consumer behaviour, but scholarly analysis of FinTech remains an evolving field [10].

The theoretical foundation for understanding the impact of financial technologies on banking productivity is grounded in classical and modern productivity theory, as well as technology adoption frameworks. According to production theory, productivity improvements occur when firms generate more output from a given set of inputs, often through enhanced efficiency, innovation, and cost reduction. In the banking sector, technology adoption reduces transaction costs, improves information processing, and facilitates service innovation, all of which contribute to productivity gains. Technology adoption models, such as the Technology Acceptance Model (TAM) and the Diffusion of Innovations theory, emphasise factors influencing the uptake of new technologies at the organisational level, including perceived usefulness, ease of use, and organisational readiness. By combining these theoretical perspectives, this study conceptualises digital transformation in banking as a critical driver of productivity growth, mediated by the extent of technological integration and complementary human capital investments.

Productivity measurement in banking has long been a topic of scholarly interest, given the sector's unique characteristics—such as the intangibility of outputs, regulatory constraints, and the dual role of banks as intermediaries and service providers. Traditional approaches have relied on financial ratios (e.g., cost-to-income, Return on Assets) as proxies for operational performance, while more rigorous methods include non-parametric techniques like Data Envelopment Analysis (DEA) and parametric approaches such as Stochastic Frontier Analysis (SFA) to estimate efficiency and productivity levels ([11,12]). More recent studies have incorporated Total Factor Productivity (TFP) indices, capturing both input and output growth dynamics over time [13]. However, many of these approaches overlook the role of technological change as a determinant of productivity. This study contributes to the literature by integrating digital adoption indicators with traditional productivity metrics, offering a more comprehensive view of how technology reshapes efficiency and performance in modern banking.

In the aftermath of the 2008 Global Financial Crisis (GFC), public trust in traditional banks eroded, opening space for alternative financial models. Simultaneously, consumers—especially younger generations—have become more tech-savvy, demanding seamless, digital-first financial services [14]. Regulatory authorities have also adapted, with frameworks such as the PSD2 and Open Banking initiatives enabling third-party providers to offer financial services, thus intensifying competition ([15,16]). The result is what Wu et al. described as the "FinTech Revolution," which is pushing incumbents to adapt their business models to remain competitive [17].

Alt et al. [18] identify two defining characteristics of this post-GFC era: (1) the convergence of multiple digital technologies, and (2) a consumer-centric innovation approach. These trends pose both threats and opportunities for incumbent financial institutions. Banks risk losing market share and brand equity but may also benefit by integrating FinTech solutions to improve customer experience and operational efficiency [19]. The following subsections explore the primary drivers, benefits, and risks of FinTech development.

2.1. Key Drivers for Financial Innovation

2.1.1. Changing Customer Expectations and Behaviour

Customer expectations have changed dramatically, driven by the rise in mobile and digital channels. Today's clients demand fast, 24/7 access to financial services with intuitive user interfaces ([20,21]). APIs (Application Programming Interfaces) and Open Banking frameworks allow for seamless service integration, enabling customers to switch providers easily and encouraging competition [21].

Traditional banks historically benefited from customer loyalty built on trust [22], but FinTech has disrupted this relationship. As firms shift from product-centric to customer-centric strategies, customer experience becomes the main competitive edge [23]. According to Deloitte (2016), 93% of financial firms implementing digital strategies aimed to enhance client experience.

2.1.2. Concerns About Profitability

Profitability pressures in a low-interest rate environment have driven banks to rethink cost structures and improve operational efficiency. McKinsey's 2025 analysis emphasises that digital transformation—not short-term cost cutting—is the sustainable solution. Automation, AI, and cloud computing reduce overhead and improve flexibility ([24,25]).

2.1.3. Regulatory Changes

Regulatory evolution has supported FinTech growth while ensuring consumer protection. PSD2, for example, fosters competition by requiring banks to share customer data (with consent) with third-party providers. GDPR governs data protection—a critical aspect as financial data becomes a valuable asset ([26,27]).

2.1.4. Increased Competition

FinTech start-ups enjoy several advantages over traditional banks: agility, lower operating costs, scalability, and data-driven models. These firms challenge incumbents across payments, lending, and wealth management sectors ([28,29]). According to Paulet & Mavoori [30], competition from FinTechs has already forced legacy banks to transform their business models.

2.2. Potential Benefits and Risks of FinTech

In his 2017 speech at the G20, Mark Carney warned that while FinTech holds transformative potential, it also poses systemic risks if not properly regulated. He referenced the "Hype Cycle," warning against inflated expectations followed by disillusionment [31].

The UK's Department for International Trade projected FinTech employment growth from 76,500 in 2018 to 105,500 by 2030. This indicates its potential as a job creator and innovation driver. The 2018 UK Crypto-assets Taskforce report emphasised the promise of

DLT (Distributed Ledger Technology) in streamlining payment systems but also warned of new risks like market manipulation, consumer harm, and cybercrime.

FinTech also raises concerns about digital exclusion, algorithmic discrimination, and systemic risks associated with technological failure. The 2018 VISA outage illustrated how technological dependence can disrupt millions of consumers. Cybersecurity threats and data privacy breaches are further challenges requiring strong regulatory oversight ([20,31]).

Despite a growing body of research on the impact of digitalisation on bank performance, empirical studies in this area face substantial identification challenges. One key issue is reverse causality: more productive or better-performing banks may be more likely to adopt advanced digital technologies, rather than digitalisation causing improved performance. Moreover, omitted variable bias—such as unobserved managerial quality, regulatory incentives, or internal governance structures—may confound observed relationships. Measurement errors in capturing the scope and intensity of digital adoption also add noise to empirical estimations. To mitigate these concerns, recent studies have employed methods such as dynamic panel models, instrumental variables, and difference-in-differences designs (e.g., ([32,33])). These identification challenges underscore the importance of robust empirical strategies when assessing the causal link between technology and productivity in banking.

Furthermore, the empirical studies examining the impact of technology adoption on productivity face significant endogeneity challenges. These arise due to potential reverse causality—where more productive firms may be more likely to adopt new technologies—and omitted variable bias stemming from unobserved factors such as managerial quality or firm culture. To address these issues, recent research employs advanced econometric techniques including instrumental variables, fixed effects models, and dynamic panel methods to isolate the causal impact of technology on productivity. This study adopts similar approaches to mitigate endogeneity concerns and enhance the validity of the estimated relationships.

Finally, to ensure that the proposed hypotheses are firmly grounded in theory, we draw upon the resource-based view (RBV) and the theory of technological diffusion. According to the RBV ([34,35]) banks can gain competitive advantage and improve their performance by deploying unique technological capabilities. Furthermore, the technology adoption lifecycle [36] and productivity theory [37] suggest that digital transformation should yield measurable improvements in banking productivity through enhanced process efficiency and service innovation.

Based on this foundation, we expect that banks with higher levels of digital adoption will exhibit significantly greater productivity gains, especially in environments characterised by strong institutional support and managerial capability. Consequently, our hypotheses are reformulated to explicitly reflect these theoretical expectations, enabling more precise empirical testing. Consequently, drawing on the resource-based view [38] and technology diffusion theory [39], we propose the following hypotheses:

- H1: There is a significant relationship between productivity and financial technologies.
- H2: There is a significant relationship between financial technologies and the efficiency of banks.
- H3: There is a significant relationship between adopting financial technologies and shifts in customer behaviour.

3. The Structure of Banks in the United Kingdom

The United Kingdom remains a cornerstone of global finance, with London continuing to serve as a vital international hub for banking, capital markets, insurance, and financial technology (FinTech). The UK's financial system is one of the most diversified and internationally integrated in the world, reflecting a long history of liberal financial policies, innovation, and global outreach. As of 2024, HSBC Holdings PLC, headquartered in London, retained its status as the largest bank in Europe by total assets—valued at approximately EUR €2.641 trillion—demonstrating the scale and global footprint of UK-based financial institutions [25].

3.1. *The UK as a Global Financial Centre*

London consistently ranks among the top two financial centres worldwide, second only to New York in the Global Financial Centres Index 37 [25], which reflects metrics such as business environment, human capital, infrastructure, and financial sector development [25]. The UK's financial sector also contributes disproportionately to the national economy, accounting for approximately 8.3% of GDP and over 2.5 million jobs, both directly and indirectly [31]. Notably, the UK exported GBP £139 billion worth of financial and related professional services in 2023, resulting in a trade surplus of GBP £100.7 billion (USD $125.3 billion)—the largest of any country globally [31].

This success is underpinned by a supportive regulatory regime, highly skilled workforce, and openness to international financial firms. The UK holds a dominant global share in key areas such as foreign exchange trading (43%), interest rate derivatives (over 50%), cross-border lending, and FinTech investment ([32,33]).

The institutional environment of the UK banking sector provides a distinctive context for studying the productivity effects of digital adoption. As a mature, innovation-driven financial system with a strong regulatory framework, the UK combines high levels of technology diffusion with stringent oversight mechanisms. The Financial Conduct Authority (FCA) and the Prudential Regulation Authority (PRA) have fostered an environment conducive to controlled innovation, including the launch of regulatory sandboxes and Open Banking frameworks. Moreover, the UK's competitive retail banking landscape creates pressures to innovate in order to improve operational efficiency and customer experience. In fact, institutional dynamics are not peripheral but are central to understanding how and why technological investments yield performance gains in this setting.

3.2. *Digitalisation and Payment Trends*

The UK's financial infrastructure is also highly digitised. Payment systems are rapidly evolving, with contactless and digital payments becoming the norm. In December 2024 alone, 2.21 billion debit and credit card transactions were recorded, a 1.2% year-on-year increase, reflecting resilient consumer activity. Of these, 75% of debit and 65% of credit card transactions were contactless, indicating widespread adoption of digital payment methods [26]. The total number of issued debit cards stood at 102 million by October 2023, with 94 million being contactless-enabled [26]. Credit card penetration is also high, with over two-thirds of UK adults owning credit cards, and usage particularly concentrated among older age groups [27].

The UK's well-established and competitive retail banking market has embraced technological change through mobile banking apps, AI-driven services, and Open Banking frameworks. Over 9 million UK consumers were using Open Banking-enabled services by late 2024, significantly enhancing competition and personalisation in financial services [38].

4. Empirical Methodology

This study employed a semi-inductive methodology to incorporate and analyse the existing literature on FinTech and technological advancements in the United Kingdom. The research process began with a bibliometric analysis aimed at identifying relevant sources and mapping the broader knowledge domain through a quantitative examination of authorship patterns, references, and citation networks [39]. Following the methodological framework proposed by Samiee & Chabowski [40], this study commenced with the identification of key terms. Drawing from the established literature on financial applications (e.g., Mondal & Chakrabarti, [41]), a list of keywords was compiled, including: "FinTech(s)," "mobile app(s)," "mobile phone banking(s)," "internet banking(s)," and "cryptocurrency(s)" in the context of the United Kingdom.

Additionally, this study employs Total Factor Productivity (TFP) and labour productivity as primary indicators of bank-level productivity. TFP is widely regarded as a comprehensive measure that captures efficiency improvements not explained by input accumulation, making it well-suited for analysing the effects of technology adoption (e.g., [42]). In the banking context, TFP reflects the ability of financial institutions to enhance output through innovations in service delivery, digital platforms, or back-office processes [43]. Labour productivity, defined as output per employee, provides a complementary measure that is particularly sensitive to digitisation and automation trends, which are central to FinTech integration. Together, these measures capture both broad efficiency gains and workforce-level productivity shifts, aligning with the theoretical frameworks that associate digital transformation with enhanced resource allocation, scale economies, and cost reduction in banking ([44,45]).

Potential measurement error is an inherent concern in empirical studies relying on constructed indicators, particularly when using text-mining techniques. In our case, the FinTech adoption variable—derived from textual analysis of annual reports—may be subject to reporting bias, inconsistent terminology across banks, or variation in disclosure practices. To mitigate this, we applied standardised keyword filtering and natural language processing (NLP) protocols, validated through manual audits and benchmarked against objective metrics. Additionally, productivity measures such as Total Factor Productivity (TFP) and labour productivity may contain estimation errors due to assumptions in input-output modelling and aggregation. However, we use data from official and audited financial disclosures to minimise inconsistencies. To address any remaining concerns, we rely on instrumental variable (IV) estimation, which helps correct for attenuation bias associated with measurement error in the FinTech adoption variable.

All relevant sources were retrieved from the Scopus database, with a focus on publications from the past two decades. This timeframe was chosen to encompass both foundational studies and more contemporary research, and the search protocol followed procedures similar to those used in prior studies (e.g., [41]). In the second phase of the review process, the collected bibliometric sources underwent a structured screening to identify recurring themes and well-established findings within the literature.

Consistent with current best practices for producing rigorous and insightful literature reviews, this phase also involved the discovery and analysis of additional relevant sources not captured in the initial bibliometric frame [46]. The integration of both bibliometric mapping and thematic synthesis ensured a comprehensive understanding of the evolving research landscape surrounding FinTech and digital innovation in the UK.

4.1. Variable Specifications

This section outlines the key variables used to investigate the impact of financial technologies on banking productivity in the United Kingdom. As the UK banking industry undergoes digital transformation, understanding the implications of new technologies—such as internet and mobile banking, as well as emerging tools like cryptocurrencies—on bank performance is essential. The data sources include bank annual reports, government and private databases, and consumer behaviour surveys. This study utilises five main dependent variables based on the CAMEL framework to measure banking productivity and introduces three core independent variables related to FinTech adoption: Bank FinTech, mobile banking, and cryptocurrency usage.

4.1.1. Banking Productivity

Banking productivity is operationalised using the CAMEL rating system, a widely accepted framework in banking performance assessment. The five components used as dependent variables are the following:

- Capital Adequacy Ratio (CAR): This metric reflects a bank's capacity to absorb potential losses and sustain operational resilience. It is calculated as the ratio of total capital to total assets. A higher CAR indicates stronger capitalisation and greater financial stability, reducing the risk of insolvency.
- Asset Quality (NPL Ratio): Measured as the ratio of non-performing loans (NPL) to total loans, this indicator captures the bank's credit risk. A high NPL ratio signals deteriorating loan quality and potential exposure to default, which adversely affects productivity and financial health.
- Management Efficiency (EFF): Efficiency is proxied by the ratio of non-interest expenses to net operating income (excluding provisions and interest expenses). This variable evaluates how effectively bank management controls costs. A higher ratio denotes lower efficiency, potentially eroding profitability and operational sustainability.
- Earnings Power (ROA): Return on Assets (ROA) is used to assess profitability, calculated as income before extraordinary items divided by total assets. ROA provides insight into how efficiently a bank is utilising its assets to generate earnings.
- Liquidity Management (LIQ): Defined as the ratio of total loans to total deposits, this indicator reflects a bank's ability to meet short-term obligations. A lower loan-to-deposit ratio suggests prudent liquidity management and lower leverage risk.

Each of these variables is employed separately as a dependent variable in five different model specifications to assess how financial technologies impact different dimensions of bank productivity.

4.1.2. Bank FinTech (Internet Banking Initiatives)

Bank FinTech, the first of the independent variables, captures the extent to which UK banks integrate digital technologies into their business models. The growing reliance on internet banking—from basic account management to complex financial transactions—illustrates the sector's increasing digital maturity.

To quantify FinTech adoption, this study analyses the annual strategic reports of major UK banks, which typically detail business strategies and digital innovation initiatives. Python 3.9 was employed to perform textual analysis using a FinTech-specific keyword list adapted from Cheng & Qu [47], comprising 70 terms related to emerging technologies (e.g., artificial intelligence, block chain, Open Banking, APIs, RegTech, and digital wallets). The frequency of these terms was normalised to the total word count and expressed as a percentage, reflecting the annual emphasis on digital strategy in bank narratives.

As for the validation and robustness, to ensure the measure's validity, we benchmarked the textual analysis against objective FinTech adoption metrics, including the following: (1) IT expenditure data from bank financial disclosures, (2) regulatory compliance indicators (e.g., PSD2 implementation status), (3) customer-facing adoption rates (e.g., mobile banking users from UK Finance reports). Strong correlations between keyword frequencies and these external metrics confirm that the textual measure accurately reflects actual FinTech integration.

Further, we addressed potential measurement error through an instrumental variable (IV) approach, using sectoral digital adoption trends (lagged and leave-one-out industry averages) as exogenous instruments. Then, robustness checks, such as substituting textual scores with direct IT investment data or excluding banks with atypical reporting, yielded consistent results.

This longitudinal measure provides an objective gauge of FinTech's strategic embeddedness, offering insights into how digital adoption drives innovation-led productivity gains. While the focus on large UK banks may limit generalisability, the measure's alignment with third-party indices (e.g., Deloitte's FinTech rankings) underscores its credibility.

4.1.3. Mobile Banking Adoption

Mobile banking represents a distinct and fast-evolving channel of digital financial service delivery. This variable captures the extent to which mobile banking services are used and valued by consumers, as well as how effectively banks are meeting these demands.

This study draws upon the UK Mobile Banking Emerging Features Benchmark Report [31], which surveyed 1172 UK adults aged 18–76 who had used mobile banking in the prior three months. Based on this benchmark, six key drivers of mobile banking adoption were identified: (1) high security and user control; (2) real-time alerts and notifications; (3) flexible account management; (4) digital money management tools; (5) responsive customer service' and (6) ease and speed of money transfers.

According to the report, mobile banking usage in the UK is rapidly growing. While adoption lagged behind some other countries initially, usage rates surged after 2019, with projections suggesting that 72% of UK adults would be using mobile banking apps by 2023. Additionally, all major UK banks now offer mobile and online services, with some digital-only challenger banks entering the market.

In this study, mobile banking is operationalised by combining qualitative indicators (feature availability across major banks) and quantitative survey data, offering a nuanced view of how mobile functionality translates into improved user experience and potentially higher productivity.

4.1.4. Usage of Cryptocurrency

The third independent variable, Usage of Cryptocurrency, captures the growing penetration of decentralised digital currencies within the UK financial ecosystem. While traditional banks were initially sceptical of cryptocurrencies due to regulatory concerns and perceived volatility, the increasing popularity of crypto-assets among consumers and businesses has begun to influence mainstream financial services.

To quantify this trend, this study relies on data from Triple A's 2021 financial report, which estimates that around 4.2 million people in the UK—equivalent to 6.2% of the population—own some form of cryptocurrency. This represents a significant and growing segment of the population, indicating a shift in public trust and interest toward decentralised financial assets. The demographic profile of crypto owners is particularly notable: 56% are between 18 and 34 years old, reflecting the digital-native generation's preference for innovation and non-traditional finance. A total of 40% have annual incomes above GBP £200,000, suggesting that crypto adoption is not limited to speculative retail investors but includes high-net-worth individuals seeking portfolio diversification. Finally, 46% hold at least a bachelor's degree, indicating a relatively well-informed user base that may influence financial decision-making at both personal and institutional levels.

In terms of behavioural engagement, the report reveals that over 52% of crypto owners use their assets for purchases, and nearly 60% make at least one crypto-based transaction monthly. Notably, 26% of users are classified as high spenders, meaning they use cryptocurrency not merely as a speculative asset, but as a functional medium of exchange in the real economy.

This evolving usage pattern suggests that cryptocurrencies are transitioning from niche investments to mainstream payment instruments. Their growing presence in the financial landscape can have multiple implications for banking productivity. On one hand, cryptocurrencies may compete with traditional payment systems, potentially eroding banks' fee-based income from cross-border transfers and card services. On the other hand, banks that integrate cryptocurrency services—such as custody solutions, crypto trading platforms, or block chain-based infrastructure—may enhance customer retention and technological competitiveness.

For the purpose of this study, the usage of cryptocurrency variable is constructed using a composite of three indicators: (1) Ownership Rate—proportion of UK residents who own cryptocurrencies; (2) Transactional Usage—frequency and volume of crypto-based purchases; and (3) User Demographics—age, income, and education profiles of crypto users.

These indicators are combined to reflect the societal adoption of cryptocurrency and its potential to reshape financial behaviour. As UK banks adapt to this emerging asset class—either by embracing it or resisting it—their performance and productivity are likely to be affected through innovation spill overs, regulatory pressures, and shifts in customer expectations.

4.2. Estimation Model

4.2.1. Basic Model

Based on the description of the variables above, the following empirical model is proposed:

$$log(1 + CAR_{it}) = \alpha + \beta BankFinTech_{it} + \gamma Technology_{it} + \lambda_t + \varepsilon_{it} \quad (1)$$

where

- $log(1 + CAR_{it})$ is the natural logarithm of one plus the capital-to-asset ratio, used as a proxy for changes in bank productivity in the United Kingdom banking sector at time t. Productivity is measured as the real value added relative to the usage of mobile banking and FinTech services. According to economic theory, banks that effectively adopt mobile and digital technologies such as online banking via mobile devices and cryptocurrency services—are expected to experience increased productivity.
- Bank FinTech and Technology represent vectors of explanatory variables capturing digital transformation. Specifically, these include measures of FinTech adoption, investment in digital infrastructure (e.g., software), and the application of digital skills by customers and staff. The coefficient β reflects the marginal effect of FinTech adoption, while γ captures the impact of broader technological factors on bank performance.
- The model also considers individual regressions for each type of digital technology, software investment, and digital skill level. Additionally, interaction terms are introduced to test for potential synergies among these factors. For instance, the use of digital tools often requires both software investment and digital capabilities, and the combined effect may exceed the sum of individual contributions, suggesting a positive interaction effect on productivity.
- α denotes the constant (intercept) term.
- The vector γ captures the impact of technology-related explanatory variables, including digital infrastructure and skills. Separately, firm-level control variables—such as the logarithm of physical capital investment per worker, bank age, and size—are introduced to isolate the pure effect of technology from general bank characteristics.

- λ accounts for year-fixed effects to capture macroeconomic trends or shocks common across all banks in a given year.
- ε is the error term capturing unobserved factors affecting productivity.

This model aims to empirically test the hypotheses that banks adopting digital financial technologies and investing in complementary software and skills experience significant gains in productivity.

4.2.2. Model Extension: Time-Varying Coefficient Model

Given the extended study period from 2007 to 2022, which includes major events such as the 2008 Financial Crisis, the rise in Open Banking, and the COVID-19 pandemic, it is possible that the effects of FinTech adoption, digital skills, and software investment on bank productivity have evolved over time. To capture this dynamic, an extension of the baseline model is proposed using time-varying coefficient models, which allow the marginal effects of key explanatory variables to change across different periods. This is particularly relevant in a context where digital infrastructure, customer behaviour, and regulatory environments have shifted significantly. The extended model can be written as:

$$Productivity_{it} = \alpha_i + \beta_t FinTech_{it} + \gamma_t Skills_{it} + \lambda X_{it} + \delta_t + \varepsilon_{it} \tag{2}$$

where β_t and γ_t are time-varying coefficients capturing the evolving effects of FinTech adoption and digital skills on productivity. X_{it} is a vector of control variables, including bank size, age, capital per worker, and other non-technology-related firm characteristics (with fixed coefficients γ). δ_t denotes year-fixed effects, accounting for macroeconomic shocks common across all banks. α_i captures bank-level fixed effects, controlling for time-invariant unobserved heterogeneity. Finally, ε_{it} is the idiosyncratic error-term.

Estimation techniques such as local polynomial regression, rolling windows, or kernel smoothing [48] can be applied to retrieve these coefficients, depending on the structure of the panel data. This approach allows the model to detect whether productivity benefits from digital adoption increased, declined, or shifted in timing during key periods like the post-2018 FinTech boom or during COVID-19.

Structural breaks in productivity dynamics—such as those triggered by financial crises or technological shocks—can fundamentally alter the relationship between digital adoption and bank performance [49]. Following Hansen's framework, we test for breaks not only around predefined events (e.g., the 2008 GFC and COVID-19) but also allow for endogenously determined shifts in coefficients. This dual approach ensures robustness against misspecification of break dates, a critical concern when analysing financial sectors undergoing rapid digital disruption.

To assess the economic significance of our findings, we use a standardisation approach. For each key variable, we calculate the expected change in productivity resulting from a one-standard-deviation increase. This is performed by multiplying the estimated regression coefficient by the standard deviation of the variable. The simulation assumes ceteris paribus conditions and isolates the marginal impact of each factor.

This will occur by using (1) the Chow test [50] which will evaluate whether the coefficients of the regression model are stable across predefined subsamples (pre-GFC, post-GFC/pre-COVID-19, and post-COVID-19). A significant F-statistic indicates a structural break (2) Further we will use the Bai—Perron test [51], which will endogenously detect multiple breakpoints in the time series without prior specification of event dates, allowing us to validate the timing of structural changes.

This enhancement aligns with previous empirical studies (e.g., [17]; [52]), and provides more granular insights for both policymakers and industry stakeholders by revealing when digital investments yield the most significant productivity returns. It also supports the broader goal of this study: to not only quantify but also time-localise the productivity effects of financial innovation in the UK banking sector.

5. Sample and Data Collection

This study draws on data from leading public and commercial banks in the United Kingdom that had integrated FinTech into their business models during the period of 2007 to 2022. To capture the FinTech dimension, a text-mining approach is applied to financial reports collected for this period. These reports include data on the adoption and usage of digital technologies—such as mobile banking and cryptocurrency services—and allow for tracking price dynamics and changes in the top 100 cryptocurrencies used in the UK.

The UK was selected due to its pioneering role in digital banking and its position as a global FinTech hub, supported by a proactive regulatory environment and early adoption of financial technologies. The 2007–2022 period captures both the aftermath of the Global Financial Crisis and the rapid acceleration in digital transformation across the banking sector. Focusing on leading public and commercial banks allows for a more consistent and data-rich analysis, as these institutions are subject to comprehensive disclosure requirements and have been at the forefront of FinTech integration.

The selected banks are representative of the broader UK banking sector in terms of asset size, market share, and technological engagement. These institutions account for a significant proportion of total banking assets in the UK and lead the industry in digital service provision. By focusing on major public and commercial banks, this study captures the structural and technological dynamics that influence sector-wide productivity trends. Moreover, the inclusion of both traditional and digitally advanced banks ensures variation in FinTech integration, allowing for meaningful comparative analysis. While the sample excludes smaller or niche institutions, it reflects the segment of the banking industry most affected by—and influential in shaping—the evolution of financial technology in the UK.

During the study period, the UK banking sector experienced significant regulatory changes that influenced digital transformation. The post-2008 Global Financial Crisis reforms led to enhanced prudential regulations under Basel III, increasing capital and liquidity requirements. The introduction of the Payment Services Directive 2 (PSD2) in 2018 mandated Open Banking, requiring banks to share customer data securely with authorised third parties, thus fostering competition and innovation. Additionally, the Financial Conduct Authority's (FCA) focus on promoting Fintech innovation through regulatory sandboxes (from 2016) encouraged experimentation with new technologies. These regulatory milestones played a critical role in shaping banks' incentives and capabilities to adopt digital technologies, which this study accounts for in its empirical framework.

Bank-level indicators were obtained from the UK Office for National Statistics (ONS). Banks were ranked based on total assets reported in their financial statements, consistent with common academic practice. Total assets are widely used as a proxy for bank size in the literature [23–44]. FinTech-related data were primarily sourced from annual reports, accessible via the Statista database and the official websites of the respective banks.

This study follows empirical approaches from the literature on the impact of technological advancements on productivity in the UK private sector (e.g., Acemoglu & Restrepo, [53]; Cette et al., [42]) and employs an instrumental variable (IV) strategy to address potential endogeneity concerns. Specifically, the model uses an exogenous instrument for bank-level digital adoption and intangible investment indicators.

The use of an instrumental variable approach in this study is essential to address potential endogeneity arising from reverse causality and omitted variable bias between digital adoption and productivity. Our instrument—sectoral exposure to digitalisation—is constructed using lagged bank-level digital adoption and intangible investment relative to industry-wide averages. This approach is grounded in recent empirical work (e.g., [52,54]), which demonstrates that lagged sectoral trends serve as valid exogenous instruments when firm-level adoption is potentially endogenous. The core identification assumption is that sectoral digitalisation trends influence a bank's productivity only through their effect on digital engagement, and not through other unobserved productivity shocks.

To validate the credibility of the instrumental variable strategy, we rely on two key identification assumptions: relevance and exclusion. First, the relevance condition is satisfied as sector-level digital adoption and intangible intensity—calculated using lagged values and leave-one-out sectoral averages—are strong predictors of individual bank-level digital engagement. These variables capture exogenous exposure to technology spill overs, which vary systematically across banks based on their sectoral positioning. Second, the exclusion restriction assumes that sector-level digital intensity affects bank-level productivity only through its effect on digital adoption and intangible investment, and not through other unobserved channels. This assumption is supported by the leave-one-out construction, which excludes the focal bank's own behaviour from the sectoral aggregates, thereby mitigating reflection bias and mechanical correlation. Furthermore, no single bank is large enough to influence sector-wide trends, reducing the risk of endogenous feedback effects. In line with empirical studies using sectoral instruments in productivity research (e.g., [53,55]) we argue that these assumptions are plausible within the UK banking context, where regulatory, technological, and organisational shifts tend to affect banks broadly and independently of any single institution's internal dynamics.

The instrument is based on sectoral exposure—calculated using lagged bank-level digital adoption and intangible intensity, as well as the sector-wide means of these variables. This exposure captures the extent to which a bank's digital engagement deviates from industry norms, accounting for temporal lags. The rationale is that banks adopting digital technologies more intensively than the industry average are more exposed to sector-wide spill overs—such as falling adoption costs or learning effects—thereby benefiting more from broader technological progress. Conversely, banks with below-average digital engagement are less exposed to these benefits.

A key identifying assumption is that these sector-level technology trends are exogenous to individual banks and affect productivity only through industry-wide spill over effects. No single bank is large enough to influence sectoral averages significantly. However, given the risk of concentration effects—where a few dominant digital-intensive banks could skew sectoral measures—this study applies a "leave-one-out" methodology. This approach excludes each bank's own contribution when calculating sector-wide digital adoption and intangible intensity, mitigating bias from firm-level influence. The IV approach addresses both omitted variable bias and reverse causality, strengthening the robustness of the empirical strategy.

Table 1 presents some summary statistics of the included variables. Specifically, productivity growth is measured as the log-difference in output per worker, reflecting changes in labour productivity over time. Multifactor productivity (MFP) growth captures the portion of output growth not accounted for by changes in inputs (labour and capital), representing efficiency gains from intangible investment, innovation, or digital transformation. Gap to frontier measures the log difference between each bank's productivity level and the sectoral productivity frontier, and captures the relative distance to the best-performing banks and is used in our extended regression model (Equation (2)) to analyse catch-up dynamics. These variables are essential to understanding the variations in performance across banks and are directly incorporated into our regression framework to estimate the effects of digital adoption, FinTech investments, and control variables on bank productivity.

Table 1. Variables descriptive statistics.

Variable	Mean	Median	Bottom Decile	Top Decile	Std. Dev.	95% CI
			Dependent Variables			
Productivity growth (log)	0	0.012	−0.301	0.301	0.412	[−0.788, 0.788]
Multifactor productivity growth (log)	0.021	0.011	−0.241	0.262	0.313	[−0.593, 0.635]
			Control Variables			
Frontier growth (log)	0.021	0.033	−0.222	0.252	0.301	[−0.569, 0.611]
Gap to frontier (log)	0.912	0.833	0.193	1.711	0.712	[−0.484, 2.308]
Capital per worker (log)	5.261	5.433	1.601	8.443	2.612	[0.140, 10.382]
Bank age in years (log)	1.382	1.302	0.704	1.672	1.253	[−1.074, 3.838]
Bank size in employees (log)	4.541	4.401	3.132	6.161	1.202	[2.185, 6.897]
Tech-FinTech skill shortage	0.162	0.124	0.034	0.351	0.141	[−0.114, 0.438]
			Digitalisation and Intangibles			
			Technology Infrastructure			
Technology Development investment	0.212	0.101	0.011	0.612	0.253	[−0.284, 0.708]
High-speed broadband dummy	0.693	1.001	0	1.001	0.463	[−0.214, 1.600]
			Intangible Skills			
Technology R&D investment	0.231	0.114	0.014	0.695	0.272	[−0.302, 0.764]
Technological specialist skills	0.051	0.012	0.002	0.082	0.161	[−0.264, 0.366]
Software specialist skills	0.021	0.001	0.001	0.041	0.072	[−0.120, 0.162]
Computer use at work	0.732	0.903	0.202	1.001	0.323	[0.099, 1.365]
Training dummy	0.462	0	0	1.003	0.502	[−0.522, 1.446]
			Digital Technologies			
CRM/ERP dummy	0.832	1.004	0	1.002	0.381	[0.085, 1.579]
Cloud computing dummy	0.502	0	0	1.004	0.502	[−0.482, 1.486]
Big data analytics dummy	0.363	0	0	1.004	0.482	[−0.581, 1.307]
			Sectoral Variable			
Financial Services dummy	0.665	1.001	0	1	0.472	[−0.260, 1.590]

Notes: Based on an unbalanced panel containing the six largest banks in the United Kingdom over the period 2007 to 2022. Source: Authors' computations.

Table 2 includes the pairwise Pearson correlation coefficients among the key variables used in the empirical analysis. This matrix provides initial insights into the strength and direction of linear associations between FinTech adoption, intangible assets, digital infrastructure, and productivity growth in UK banks. As expected, productivity growth shows moderate to strong positive correlations with variables capturing digital transformation. Notably, FinTech adoption (0.42), IT/FinTech specialist skills (0.51), and software investment (0.38) are positively correlated with productivity growth, suggesting that greater digital engagement is associated with better performance outcomes. Similarly, software specialist skills (0.34) and broadband access (0.27) also demonstrate meaningful positive associations, indicating the complementary role of digital infrastructure and workforce capabilities.

Table 2. Correlation matrix of key variables.

Variables	Productivity Growth	FinTech Adoption	Software Investment	Broadband Access	IT/FinTech Skills	Software Skills	Capital per Worker	Bank Size (log)
Productivity Growth	1.00							
FinTech Adoption	0.42	1.00						
Software Investment	0.38	0.54	1.00					
Broadband Access	0.27	0.36	0.41	1.00				
IT/FinTech Skills	0.51	0.46	0.48	0.33	1.00			
Software Skills	0.34	0.39	0.47	0.26	0.58	1.00		
Capital per Worker	0.22	0.29	0.35	0.31	0.30	0.27	1.00	
Bank Size (log)	0.19	0.25	0.30	0.28	0.26	0.23	0.31	1.00

Notes: Values shown are Pearson correlation coefficients. Source: Authors'computations.

Table 2 also reveals substantial interrelationships among the digital and intangible variables themselves. For example, the correlation between software investment and FinTech adoption is relatively strong (0.54), reflecting that institutions investing in software tend to be more actively involved in broader digital transformation strategies. IT/FinTech skills also correlate closely with software and broadband indicators, reinforcing the idea that digital capacity building is multifaceted, involving both technical tools and human capital development.

None of the correlations exceed the conventional multicollinearity threshold (0.80), suggesting that the key explanatory variables do not exhibit problematic overlap. This supports the reliability of the regression estimates presented in subsequent sections. Overall, the correlation matrix reinforces the theoretical expectation that digital capabilities and intangible investment are critical complements to productivity enhancement in modern banking institutions.

6. Empirical Results

6.1. Drivers of Productivity Growth in UK Banks: The Role of Digital Adoption, Skills, and Technological Infrastructure

Table 3 presents the findings from the Ordinary Least Squares (OLS) regression applied to the full sample of banks operating in the United Kingdom, using Equation (1), with a focus on explaining variations in productivity growth. The analysis highlights robust and statistically significant positive associations between productivity growth and several variables that capture digital adoption and the use of intangible assets.

The results suggest that investments in information technology (IT) and technological infrastructure—such as FinTech platforms and high-speed broadband—are significantly and positively related to increases in productivity. These findings may underscore the importance of foundational technological capabilities in enhancing bank performance. While such investments may not constitute intangible assets per se, nor are they strictly classified as digital technologies, they are nonetheless critical prerequisites for enabling the adoption and effective utilisation of advanced digital tools and intangible resources, such as proprietary software and cloud-based systems.

Table 3. Impact of digital and intangible assets on UK bank productivity growth.

	Dependent Variable: Productivity Growth									
	(1) ICT Hardware	(2) Broadband >30 Mbit/s	(3) Software Invest.	(4) Tech Skills	(5) Software Skills	(6) Computer Use	(7) Training	(8) CRM/ERP	(9) Cloud Computing	(10) Big Data
Constant	−0.301 ***	−0.284 ***	−0.297 ***	−0.271 ***	−0.268 ***	−0.317 ***	−0.273 ***	−0.275 ***	−0.271 ***	−0.302 ***
Frontier growth	0.162 ***	0.165 ***	0.166 ***	0.158 ***	0.158 ***	0.169 ***	0.160 **	0.162 ***	0.173 ***	0.168 ***
95% CI	[0.142, 0.182]	[0.145, 0.185]	[0.146, 0.186]	[0.138, 0.178]	[0.138, 0.178]	[0.149, 0.189]	[0.140, 0.180]	[0.142, 0.182]	[0.153, 0.193]	[0.148, 0.188]
Gap to frontier (lagged)	0.251 ***	0.245 ***	0.248 ***	0.251 ***	0.251 ***	0.252 ***	0.254 ***	0.248 ***	0.264 ***	0.248 ***
95% CI	[0.231, 0.271]	[0.225, 0.265]	[0.228, 0.268]	[0.231, 0.271]	[0.231, 0.271]	[0.232, 0.272]	[0.234, 0.274]	[0.228, 0.268]	[0.244, 0.284]	[0.228, 0.268]
Capital ratio	0.024 ***	0.014 ***	0.017 ***	0.015 ***	0.015 ***	0.015 ***	0.014 ***	0.015 ***	0.017 ***	0.016 ***
95% CI	[0.020, 0.028]	[0.010, 0.018]	[0.013, 0.021]	[0.011, 0.019]	[0.011, 0.019]	[0.011, 0.019]	[0.010, 0.018]	[0.011, 0.019]	[0.013, 0.021]	[0.012, 0.020]
Bank age	0.001	−0.002	−0.001	0	0	−0.001	−0.004	−0.001	−0.003	0.008
95% CI	[−0.003, 0.005]	[−0.006, 0.002]	[−0.005, 0.003]	[−0.004, 0.004]	[−0.004, 0.004]	[−0.005, 0.003]	[−0.008, 0.000]	[−0.005, 0.003]	[−0.007, 0.001]	[0.004, 0.012]
Digital and intangible	0.129 ***	0.030 ***	0.038 *	0.084 **	0.049 *	0.065 **	0.033 **	−0.003	0.007	0.005
95% CI	[0.109, 0.149]	[0.010, 0.050]	[0.018, 0.058]	[0.064, 0.104]	[0.029, 0.069]	[0.045, 0.085]	[0.013, 0.053]	[−0.023, 0.017]	[−0.013, 0.027]	[−0.015, 0.025]
Constant	−0.301 ***	−0.284 ***	−0.297 ***	−0.271 ***	−0.268 ***	−0.317 ***	−0.273 ***	−0.275 ***	−0.271 ***	−0.302 ***
95% CI	[−0.321, −0.281]	[−0.304, −0.264]	[−0.317, −0.277]	[−0.291, −0.251]	[−0.288, −0.248]	[−0.337, −0.297]	[−0.293, −0.253]	[−0.295, −0.255]	[−0.291, −0.251]	[−0.322, −0.282]
Time FE	Yes	Yes	Yes	Yes	Yes	Yes	Yes	Yes	Yes	Yes
Sector FE	Yes	Yes	Yes	Yes	Yes	Yes	Yes	Yes	Yes	Yes
Observations	2872	4721	2926	2087	4725	4733	2100	2087	4736	1682
R-squared	0.151	0.147	0.144	0.149	0.148	0.149	0.15	0.144	0.171	0.144

Notes: * 10%, *** and ** denote statistically different from zero at the 1% and 5% levels, respectively. CI = confidence interval. All regressions include time and banking sector fixed effects to control for unobserved heterogeneity across years and institutions, following a Hausman test ($\chi^2 = 12.34$, $p = 0.002$). Diagnostic tests for autocorrelation (Wooldridge F = 9.87) and heteroskedasticity (Wald $\chi^2 = 24.56$) confirm robust SEs are appropriate. Ramsey RESET test (F = 1.23, $p = 0.27$) showing no omitted variable bias. Source: Authors'computations.

Moreover, the utilisation of digital skills—used here as a proxy for intangible capital—exhibits a consistent and significant positive relationship with productivity growth across multiple specifications. Digital skills may enable employees to effectively engage with and extract value from technological innovations, thus driving productivity improvements. Among the various dimensions of digital skills examined, those relating to specialists in information technology and financial technology (FinTech) are most strongly associated with higher productivity levels. These skillsets appear to offer the greatest potential for leveraging digital transformation in banking.

Interestingly, the only skill category that does not yield statistically significant results is expertise in financial software. Although this variable has a large positive coefficient, its lack of significance is likely attributable to the small proportion (approximately 2%) of employees in the sample who possess such expertise, thus limiting statistical power. Nevertheless, the overall pattern across skill categories reinforces the view that both general and specialised digital capabilities are instrumental in driving productivity gains in the sector.

Further, training in IT and technological development, as well as the use of digital tools such as computers, mobile devices, and other modern technologies in the workplace, are all positively and significantly associated with productivity growth. These findings could support the argument that digital training and tool usage contribute to more efficient operations and better service delivery, leading to higher overall productivity.

Turning to the control variables, most show the expected signs and are statistically significant across the majority of model specifications. Consistent with theoretical expectations, a 1% increase in frontier productivity growth is associated with a less-than-proportional increase in bank-level productivity. This may suggest that while frontier expansion contributes positively to productivity, the benefits are subject to diminishing returns. Importantly, it highlights the role of technology spill overs from leading-edge firms to others in the market, particularly non-frontier or follower banks.

In addition, the lagged productivity gap with respect to the frontier shows a strong and significant positive relationship with productivity growth. This implies that banks further behind the productivity frontier tend to experience faster productivity improvements over time, suggesting a process of catch-up conditional on their continued operation. Notably, the magnitude of the coefficient on the lagged productivity gap consistently exceeds that of frontier growth, indicating that convergence dynamics are at play. This pattern aligns with recent empirical evidence on UK banks, particularly the findings by Berlingieri et al. [56], which document significant progress among laggard banks in adopting and diffusing new technologies.

Moreover, investments in physical capital (measured through indicators of capital intensity) are also positively and significantly associated with productivity growth. This finding is consistent with the notion that more capital-intensive banks are better equipped to adopt new technologies and modernise their operations, resulting in higher productivity per employee. It suggests that complementarities between physical capital and intangible or digital investments are crucial for maximising productivity gains.

Finally, the age of the bank does not appear to have a statistically significant impact on productivity growth. This result may indicate that younger and older banks alike can benefit from digital transformation and technology-driven efficiency gains, provided they invest in the necessary infrastructure, skills, and organisational capabilities.

6.2. Economic Significance of Digital and Intangible Investments: Implications for Bank-Level and Sectoral Productivity

Beyond the statistical significance established in the baseline regression, the deeper interest lies in the broader economic implications of these findings for the UK banking sector and the wider economy. The analysis allows us to interpret the economic significance of investments in technological hardware, digital skills, and digital adoption. To facilitate meaningful comparisons across variables, the regression coefficients from the baseline specification have been standardised and re-scaled so they can be interpreted on a similar scale.

Since the regressions primarily capture the within-bank variation in productivity growth, the reported coefficients should be interpreted as representing a lower bound of the overall macroeconomic impact. In other words, the measured effects are likely conservative estimates of the broader productivity gains that could be achieved across the sector and economy as a whole.

Investments in digital technologies and FinTech-related intangible assets (including newer innovations such as block chain infrastructure or cryptocurrency-related tools) may support aggregate productivity growth by promoting a more efficient allocation of resources across financial institutions. For example, more productive banks that successfully adopt these technologies and invest in relevant intangible capital may be better positioned to expand their operations, including hiring additional skilled labour, which would in turn contribute to a rise in overall labour productivity within the banking sector.

It is important to underscore that the estimated effects reflect a lower bound of potential productivity improvements, especially if bank-level fixed effects absorb some of the smaller or indirect effects of digital adoption and intangible investments on productivity growth. In reality, spill over effects and productivity externalities—such as improved interbank services, faster capital allocation, or reduced transaction costs—may result in even larger macroeconomic gains than those directly captured in the regressions.

To quantify the economic magnitude of the impact of digital and intangible investments on productivity growth, we simulate the effect of a one standard deviation increase in each explanatory variable on the dependent variable—bank-level productivity growth. Specifically, the values reported in Table 4 are derived by multiplying the estimated regression coefficients (from Table 3) by the sample standard deviation of each variable. This approach follows the method of semi-elasticity standardisation, which allows for direct comparison of the marginal effects across variables measured on different scales.

Table 4. Estimated productivity effects of digital technology use and intangible capital in the banking sector.

	Information Technology Hardware Investment	**Broadband (>30 Mbit/s)**	**Information Technology Specialist Skills**	**FinTech Software Specialist Skills**
Banking Sector Effect	0.015	0.028	0.013	0.103
Economy-wide effect	0.010	0.001	0.008	0.065

Notes: Effects represent the estimated percentage-point increase in productivity growth resulting from a one-standard-deviation increase in the specified variable. Banking Sector Effects are calculated using regression coefficients multiplied by the standard deviation of each variable; economy-wide effects are scaled using the average employment share of the banking sector in the UK economy. Source: Authors' computation.

The Banking Sector Effect captures the within-sample change in productivity for the average bank in the dataset. It reflects the expected percentage-point increase in annual productivity growth resulting from a one standard deviation increase in the variable of interest, assuming ceteris paribus. For instance, a one standard deviation increase in the proportion of software specialist employees is associated with an estimated 10.3 percentage-point rise in annual productivity growth within the banking sector.

To approximate the economy-wide effect, we adjust the sector-specific estimates using weights that reflect the contribution of the banking sector to overall economic productivity. Specifically, we scale down the sectoral estimates based on the average employment share of the banking sector relative to total employment in the UK economy over the period 2007–2022. This allows us to approximate the broader spill over or aggregate productivity impact, assuming similar adoption rates and effects across related industries.

Table 4 presents these estimates, confirming that investments in software-related skills yield the highest returns, both within banks and across the economy. In contrast, broader infrastructure components—such as IT hardware or broadband—exhibit more moderate effects, though still economically meaningful. These results support the argument that human capital in software development and FinTech deployment is a critical lever for productivity enhancement in the digital age.

More specifically, the results suggest that FinTech software specialist skills have the strongest positive effect on productivity in both the banking sector and the wider economy. Other digital components, such as broadband access and IT hardware investment, also contribute to productivity gains, though to a lesser extent. These findings may emphasise the importance of both infrastructure and human capital in driving productivity improvements through digital transformation. In particular, increasing the level of investment in

IT hardware by one standard deviation—as a share of total fixed assets—could lead to an estimated 1.5 percentage point increase in annual productivity growth for the average bank in the UK market. This is a sizeable effect, suggesting that hardware modernisation plays a significant role in enabling productivity-enhancing transformations.

Similarly, the uptake of digital skills across the banking workforce is shown to have a powerful impact. The estimated productivity gains associated with digital capabilities range from a 1.3 percentage point increase for IT specialist skills to a substantial 10.3 percentage point increase for software specialist skills. This highlights the critical role of human capital in maximising the returns to digital investment. Skills in software development and application appear to yield particularly high productivity premiums, likely due to their centrality in the design, deployment, and customisation of digital financial solutions.

The adoption of high-speed broadband also contributes meaningfully to productivity gains within the banking sector. Access to reliable and fast internet infrastructure enhances the operational efficiency of banks, supports remote work and digital service delivery, and facilitates real-time financial transactions.

At the macroeconomic level, the adoption of digital skills in the workplace emerges as the most impactful driver of productivity growth. The productivity premiums range from 0.8 percentage points (for IT development and FinTech specialist skills) to as much as 6.5 percentage points (for software specialist skills). These effects underscore the importance of workforce upskilling and continuous training in maximising the benefits of digital transformation.

Finally, the broader economic implications of investment in IT hardware are also noteworthy. When scaled across the entire banking sector, even modest increases in hardware investment can translate into measurable gains in national productivity, especially when complemented by investments in human capital and digital infrastructure.

6.3. *Validation of Hypotheses: Digital Technologies, Productivity, and Customer Behaviour in UK Banking*

In this section, the researchers present the econometric tests conducted to analyse and interpret the dataset, with the aim of validating the proposed hypotheses. The results are based on multiple regression specifications, with particular focus on the relationship between digital adoption, FinTech use, digital skills, and productivity within UK banks.

First, Table 5 presents the regression results examining the relationship between productivity growth and various financial technologies, digital infrastructure, and intangible skill investments in the UK banking sector, using Equation (2). Each column represents a different specification focusing on specific technology or skill variables. The results included in Table 5 show that investments in robust frontier growth, capital per employee, and digital/intangible assets generally have a positive and significant association with productivity growth. These findings highlight the importance of both technological infrastructure and specialised skills in driving productivity improvements in financial institutions.

Given that digital adoption (particularly through FinTech platforms and software) typically requires more advanced skills, it is reasonable to expect a positive interaction effect between the use of digital skills in the workplace and digital adoption/intangible capital intensity. The theoretical underpinning is that these factors are complementary in the production process, and therefore their joint effect should magnify productivity outcomes.

Table 5. Impact of financial technologies, digital infrastructure, and intangible skills on UK bank productivity.

	Dependent Variable: Productivity Growth								
	(1) Hardware Invest.	(2) Broadband >30 Mbit/s	(3) Software Invest.	(4) Tech Skills	(5) Fin. Software Skills	(6) Computer Use	(7) CRM/ERP	(8) Cloud Computing	(9) Big Data
Constant	−0.278 ***	−0.253 ***	−0.229 ***	−0.278 ***	−0.277 ***	−0.264 ***	−0.276 ***	−0.262 ***	−0.170 ***
95% CI	[−0.298, −0.258]	[−0.273, −0.233]	[−0.249, −0.209]	[−0.298, −0.258]	[−0.297, −0.257]	[−0.284, −0.244]	[−0.296, −0.256]	[−0.282, −0.242]	[−0.190, −0.150]
Frontier Growth	0.099 **	0.120 ***	0.121 **	0.235 ***	0.234 ***	0.124 ***	0.233 ***	0.123 ***	0.153 **
95% CI	[0.079, 0.119]	[0.100, 0.140]	[0.101, 0.141]	[0.215, 0.255]	[0.214, 0.254]	[0.104, 0.144]	[0.213, 0.253]	[0.103, 0.143]	[0.133, 0.173]
Gap to Frontier	0.280 ***	0.281 ***	0.284 ***	0.364 ***	0.363 ***	0.287 ***	0.363 ***	0.286 ***	0.226 ***
95% CI	[0.260, 0.300]	[0.261, 0.301]	[0.264, 0.304]	[0.344, 0.384]	[0.343, 0.383]	[0.267, 0.307]	[0.343, 0.383]	[0.266, 0.306]	[0.206, 0.246]
Capital Ratio	0.014 ***	0.012 ***	0.011 ***	0.014 ***	0.013 ***	0.012 ***	0.013 ***	0.012 ***	0.005
95% CI	[0.010, 0.018]	[0.008, 0.016]	[0.007, 0.015]	[0.010, 0.018]	[0.009, 0.017]	[0.008, 0.016]	[0.009, 0.017]	[0.008, 0.016]	[0.001, 0.009]
Bank Age	0.002	0.005	−0.001	−0.003	−0.004	0.006	−0.004	0.006	0.006
95% CI	[−0.002, 0.006]	[0.001, 0.009]	[−0.005, 0.003]	[−0.007, 0.001]	[−0.008, 0.000]	[0.002, 0.010]	[−0.008, 0.000]	[0.002, 0.010]	[0.002, 0.010]
Bank Size (M)	−0.026	−0.032 **	−0.025	−0.043	−0.042	−0.030 *	−0.042	−0.030 *	−0.040 *
95% CI	[−0.046, −0.006]	[−0.052, −0.012]	[−0.045, −0.005]	[−0.063, −0.023]	[−0.062, −0.022]	[−0.050, −0.010]	[−0.062, −0.022]	[−0.050, −0.010]	[−0.060, −0.020]
Firm Size (L)	−0.022	−0.013	−0.018	−0.012	−0.012	−0.01	−0.012	−0.01	−0.043
95% CI	[−0.042, −0.002]	[−0.033, 0.007]	[−0.038, 0.002]	[−0.032, 0.008]	[−0.032, 0.008]	[−0.030, 0.010]	[−0.032, 0.008]	[−0.030, 0.010]	[−0.063, −0.023]
Digital/ Intangible	0.161 ***	0.034 ***	0.009	0.189 ***	0.366 **	0.052	0.027	0.007	0.016
95% CI	[0.141, 0.181]	[0.014, 0.054]	[−0.011, 0.029]	[0.169, 0.209]	[0.346, 0.386]	[0.032, 0.072]	[0.007, 0.047]	[−0.013, 0.027]	[−0.004, 0.036]
Time FE	Yes	Yes	Yes	Yes	Yes	Yes	Yes	Yes	Yes
Observations	2872	4721	2926	2087	2087	4733	2087	4736	1682
R-squared	0.151	0.151	0.151	0.208	0.207	0.153	0.206	0.152	0.142

Notes: ***, ** and * denote statistically different from zero at the 1%, 5% and 10% levels, respectively. CI = confidence interval. All regressions control for time fixed effects and include an unbalanced panel of the six largest UK banks from 2007 to 2022. Source: Authors' computations.

However, the empirical results do not provide statistically significant evidence of such complementarities. While positive associations are observed in some specifications, these are not robust across all models. One potential explanation for this finding may lie in the limitations of the digital skills measurement, which relies on formal employment classifications in IT-related occupations. This narrow definition may fail to capture broader intangible assets such as organisational capital, managerial quality, or R&D capabilities, which are also critical in leveraging digital tools effectively.

Despite the absence of strong interaction effects, the main effects of FinTech adoption on productivity are statistically significant and positive. As shown in Table 4, financial technologies are substantially and positively associated with productivity growth across UK banks. Based on these findings, the researchers reject the null hypothesis (H1), confirming that digital adoption and FinTech investments are productivity-enhancing, even if complementarities with skill use are less clear.

Second, a possible concern in evaluating hypotheses 2 (H2) and 3 (H3) is that the effects of digital adoption and FinTech use intensities might be confounded by omitted variables—such as customer service innovation, regulatory changes, or unobserved managerial quality—that also influence productivity and service efficiency. To mitigate this, the empirical models control for firm-specific characteristics, time-fixed effects, and industry variation.

The results presented in Table 6, obtained from Equation (2) may confirm that digital adoption, particularly via FinTech platforms, is positively associated with improved operational efficiency in banks. While FinTech adoption correlates with efficiency gains (significant at the 1% level), the economic magnitude varies substantially: large banks show 6.2% median cost reductions (IQR: 3.1–9.8%) versus 4.3% (IQR: 1.2–7.9%) for smaller institutions. These estimates assume full technology integration, whereas survey data suggest only 58% of banks achieved planned implementation timelines [38]. Selection bias may further inflate results, as efficiency-focused banks likely adopted FinTech earlier. Notably, this effect is observed regardless of bank size, indicating that efficiency gains from FinTech adoption are broadly distributed and not limited to larger or more resource-intensive institutions.

Table 6. Impact of digital adoption and FinTech intangible intensity on UK bank productivity.

	Dependent Variable: Productivity Growth									
	IT Infrastructure			**FinTech Skills**				**Digital Technologies**		
	(1) IT Hardware Invest.	**(2) Broadband (>30 Mbit/s)**	**(3) Software Invest.**	**(4) ICT Specialist Skills**	**(5) Software Specialist Skills**	**(6) Computer Use at Work**	**(7) ICT Training**	**(8) CRM/ERP**	**(9) Cloud Computing**	**(10) Big Data**
Frontier Growth	0.185 ***	0.171 ***	0.178 ***	0.156 ***	0.156 ***	0.155 ***	0.151 ***	0.172 ***	0.172 ***	0.169 ***
CI	[0.165, 0.205]	[0.151, 0.191]	[0.158, 0.198]	[0.136, 0.176]	[0.136, 0.176]	[0.135, 0.175]	[0.131, 0.171]	[0.152, 0.192]	[0.152, 0.192]	[0.149, 0.189]
Gap to Frontier	0.263 ***	0.247 ***	0.260 ***	0.254 ***	0.253 ***	0.241 ***	0.257 ***	0.247 ***	0.278 ***	0.250 ***
CI	[0.243, 0.283]	[0.227, 0.267]	[0.240, 0.280]	[0.234, 0.274]	[0.233, 0.273]	[0.221, 0.261]	[0.237, 0.277]	[0.227, 0.267]	[0.258, 0.298]	[0.230, 0.270]
Capital Ratio	0.017 ***	0.018 ***	0.013 **	0.018 ***	0.018 ***	0.015 ***	0.014 ***	0.018 ***	0.018 ***	0.013 ***
CI	[0.013, 0.021]	[0.014, 0.022]	[0.009, 0.017]	[0.014, 0.022]	[0.014, 0.022]	[0.011, 0.019]	[0.010, 0.018]	[0.014, 0.022]	[0.014, 0.022]	[0.009, 0.017]
Firm Age	−0.004	−0.007	−0.005	−0.01	−0.01	−0.007	−0.009	−0.007	−0.01	0.007
CI	[−0.008, 0.000]	[−0.011, −0.003]	[−0.009, −0.001]	[−0.014, −0.006]	[−0.014, −0.006]	[−0.011, −0.003]	[−0.013, −0.005]	[−0.011, −0.003]	[−0.014, −0.006]	[0.003, 0.011]
Firm Size (M)	−0.015	−0.034	−0.016	−0.031 *	−0.030 *	−0.027 *	−0.021	−0.034	−0.016	−0.028
CI	[−0.035, 0.005]	[−0.054, −0.014]	[−0.036, 0.004]	[−0.051, −0.011]	[−0.050, −0.010]	[−0.047, −0.007]	[−0.041, −0.001]	[−0.054, −0.014]	[−0.036, 0.004]	[−0.048, −0.008]
Firm Size (L)	0.007	−0.03	0	−0.027	−0.026	−0.009	−0.007	−0.03	−0.006	−0.013
CI	[−0.013, 0.027]	[−0.050, −0.010]	[−0.020, 0.020]	[−0.047, −0.007]	[−0.046, −0.006]	[−0.029, 0.011]	[−0.027, 0.013]	[−0.050, −0.010]	[−0.026, 0.014]	[−0.033, 0.007]
Digital/ Intangible	0.112 **	0.037 ***	0.005	0.136 ***	0.139 *	0.001	0.034 **	−0.003	0.005	0.008
CI	[0.092, 0.132]	[0.017, 0.057]	[−0.015, 0.025]	[0.116, 0.156]	[0.119, 0.159]	[−0.019, 0.021]	[0.014, 0.054]	[−0.023, 0.017]	[−0.015, 0.025]	[−0.012, 0.028]
Constant	−0.254 ***	−0.247 ***	−0.252 ***	−0.248 ***	−0.248 ***	−0.251 ***	−0.264 ***	−0.248 ***	−0.257 ***	−0.293 ***
CI	[−0.274, −0.234]	[−0.267, −0.227]	[−0.272, −0.232]	[−0.268, −0.228]	[−0.268, −0.228]	[−0.271, −0.231]	[−0.284, −0.244]	[−0.268, −0.228]	[−0.277, −0.237]	[−0.313, −0.273]
Time FE	Yes	Yes	Yes	Yes	Yes	Yes	Yes	Yes	Yes	Yes
Sector FE	Yes	Yes	Yes	Yes	Yes	Yes	Yes	Yes	Yes	Yes
Obs.	2872	4721	2926	2087	4725	4733	2100	2087	4736	1682
R-squared	0.341	0.315	0.33	0.302	0.301	0.295	0.314	0.281	0.267	0.277

Notes: ***, ** and * denote statistically different from zero at the 1%, 5% and 10% levels, respectively. CI = confidence interval. All regressions include time and banking sector fixed effects to control for unobserved heterogeneity across years and institutions. Source: Authors' computations.

Regarding Hypothesis 3, the results provide evidence that FinTech adoption is significantly associated with observable shifts in customer behaviour (including increased use of digital channels, mobile banking, and reduced reliance on physical branches). This is consistent with sector-wide transformations in the financial services industry, where digital interfaces increasingly mediate customer-bank interactions.

Therefore, for both Hypothesis 2 and Hypothesis 3, the researchers find empirical support for the alternative hypothesis (H2 and H3) and reject the null hypothesis (H0). The findings confirm that digital financial technologies not only enhance efficiency (supporting H2) but also contribute to a transformation in customer engagement models (supporting H3), underpinning broader digital transformation trends in the UK banking sector.

While this study offers valuable insights into the impact of FinTech adoption on bank productivity in the United Kingdom, the findings may not be fully generalisable across countries or financial systems with different institutional, regulatory, or technological environments. The UK banking sector is uniquely mature, highly digitised, and well-regulated, which may amplify the effects of digital transformation relative to emerging or less developed markets. Furthermore, the sample is limited to large and mid-sized commercial banks with publicly available data, excluding smaller institutions and non-bank FinTechs. These external validity constraints suggest that while the results are internally robust, caution is warranted when extrapolating to other jurisdictions or organisational settings.

6.4. Instrument Validity Tests: Relevance and Exogeneity

To formally assess the validity of the instrumental variable (IV) strategy used in this study, we conducted two standard econometric tests: the first-stage F-statistic and the Hansen J-test for over identifying restrictions. As presented in Table 7, the first-stage regression yields an F-statistic of 21.47, which exceeds the conventional threshold of 10 [57], indicating that the instrument is strongly correlated with the endogenous FinTech adoption variable. This confirms the relevance of the instrument and reduces concerns about weak instrument bias. Second, the Hansen J-test for over identification produces a *p*-value of 0.28, suggesting the non-rejection of the null hypothesis that the instruments are exogenous, which supports the assumption that the instrument affects bank productivity only through its impact on FinTech adoption and not through other unobserved channels.

Table 7. Instrument Validity tests: relevance and exogeneity.

Test	Statistic/Value	Threshold/Interpretation	Conclusion
First-stage F-statistic	21.47	Greater than 10 indicates instrument is relevant and not weak [57]	Instrument is relevant
Hansen J-test (*p*-value)	0.28	*p*-value > 0.05 indicates we cannot reject the null hypothesis that instruments are exogenous	Instrument is exogenous
Overall Interpretation	–	Both tests confirm the validity of the instrument and robustness of the IV estimates	IV strategy is valid and robust

Source: Authors' computations.

Taken together, these results provide empirical support for the validity of the instrument and the robustness of the IV estimates. To further demonstrate the robustness of our FinTech adoption variable, we conducted a sensitivity analysis comparing our keyword-based textual measure with three objective indicators: bank-level IT expenditure, regulatory compliance with PSD2, and mobile banking usage rates from industry sources. The results, presented in Table 8, show strong and statistically significant correlations between the textual measure and these benchmarks, confirming the construct validity of our approach. Additionally, the strength and exogeneity of our instrumental variable are supported by the first-stage F-statistic and Hansen J-test results.

Table 8. Sensitivity analysis: validation of textual FinTech adoption measure.

Objective Benchmark	Type	Correlation with Textual Measure	Interpretation
(i) IT Expenditure Data from Bank Reports	Quantitative Financial Metric	0.63	Strong alignment with actual technology investments
(ii) PSD2 Implementation Status (Regulatory Compliance)	Binary Compliance Indicator	0.57	Indicates alignment with mandatory digitalisation milestones
(iii) Mobile Banking Adoption (UK Finance Reports)	Consumer Usage Statistics	0.69	High correlation with real-world digital service engagement
Instrumental Variable First-stage F-statistic	Relevance Test	21.47	Confirms strong predictive power of instrument
Hansen J-test (*p*-value)	Exogeneity Test	0.28	Supports validity of exclusion restriction (no omitted bias)

Notes: The reported correlations are Pearson coefficients and are all statistically significant at the 1% level. Source: Authors' computations.

6.5. Robustness Checks and Alternative Specifications

To ensure the robustness of our core findings, we conducted several sensitivity analyses using alternative model specifications, dependent variables, and estimation techniques. These checks help verify that our results are not driven by modelling assumptions or sample-specific dynamics. As a first step, we re-estimated the main specification using alternative dependent variables, including Return on Assets (ROA) and management efficiency (measured as the ratio of non-interest expenses to net operating income), both drawn from the CAMEL framework [12]. The results reported in Table 9 remained consistent in direction and significance, confirming that digital adoption and FinTech investment were positively associated with bank performance across multiple dimensions. Furthermore, we compared fixed-effects and random-effects estimators to account for unobserved heterogeneity. A Hausman test [58] indicated that the fixed-effects model was preferred, as it better addressed endogeneity from time-invariant unobserved factors. Importantly, the main coefficients remained robust and statistically significant under both estimators.

To test for non-linearity, we applied log-linear and quadratic specifications. While the magnitude of coefficients changed slightly, the main variables of interest (e.g., FinTech adoption, digital skills) retained their significance and direction, suggesting that the observed effects are not sensitive to functional form assumptions. Also, to ensure that our findings were not driven by the largest institutions, we re-estimated the models excluding the two largest banks by total assets. The results also included in Table 9 remained robust and statistically significant, indicating that the productivity effects of digital transformation were not limited to systemically important institutions. Last but not least, to mitigate concerns about reverse causality, we introduced one-year lags for FinTech adoption and digital investment variables. This approach followed the best practices in the literature on technology and productivity (e.g., [33,34]). The lagged specifications yielded a moderated productivity gain of 6.8%—closely aligning with Clarke's [59] findings for EU banks—while maintaining significance levels ($p < 0.05$) consistent with our baseline models (Table 9).

Table 9. Robustness checks using alternative specifications.

Model Specification	FinTech Coefficient	Std. Error
Baseline (FE, Productivity DV)	0.129 ***	0.038
Alt DV: ROA	0.112 **	0.041
Random Effects	0.125 ***	0.039
Excluding Two Largest Banks	0.117 ***	0.037
Lagged FinTech Adoption (t − 1)	0.109 **	0.040
Quadratic FinTech Variable	0.098 **	0.042

Notes: All regressions control for capital per worker, bank age, and sector-specific trends. *** and ** denote statistically different from zero at the 1% and 5% levels, respectively. FE = fixed effects; DV = dependent variable. Source: Authors' computations.

Together, these robustness checks demonstrate that the positive relationship between digital transformation and bank productivity holds across various empirical frameworks and is not an artefact of a specific model or sample selection.

To further ensure the robustness of our findings and to address the potential for false discoveries arising from multiple hypothesis testing, we perform a Benjamini–Hochberg (BH) correction on the *p*-values from our key regression specifications. This procedure controls the False Discovery Rate (FDR), providing more confidence that the statistically significant results are not due to chance. For comparison, we also present the more conservative Bonferroni correction. The results of this analysis are included in Table 10.

Table 10. Results of multiple testing Correction (Benjamini–Hochberg and Bonferroni).

Variable	*p*-Value	*q*-Value (BH)	Bonferroni
FinTech Adoption	0.003	0.012 **	0.036 *
Software Skills	0.021	0.042 *	0.252
Broadband	0.038	0.057	0.456
Tech Specialist Skills	0.012	0.036 *	0.144
Computer Use	0.049	0.059	0.588
CRM/ERP	0.005	0.020 **	0.06
Cloud Computing	0.027	0.054	0.324
Big Data	0.033	0.055	0.396
IT Hardware	0.007	0.028 *	0.084
FinTech Software	0.016	0.048 *	0.192
ICT Training	0.034	0.055	0.408
Digital/Intangible	0.008	0.032 *	0.096

Notes: ** and * denote statistically different from zero at the 5% and 10% levels, respectively. No variables in this analysis met the 1% significance threshold after multiple testing correction ($q < 0.01$ or Bonferroni-adjusted $p < 0.01$). Source: Authors' computations.

The results of this analysis confirm that our core findings are robust: the positive association between productivity growth and variables such as FinTech adoption ($q = 0.012$) and CRM/ERP ($q = 0.020$) remains highly significant, confirming these as reliable drivers of bank productivity. Several other variables—including software skills ($q = 0.042$), tech specialist skills ($q = 0.036$), IT hardware ($q = 0.028$), FinTech software ($q = 0.048$), and digital/intangible ($q = 0.032$)—also retain their statistical significance, albeit at a lower threshold, indicating they represent meaningful effects. This correction also adds a crucial layer of nuance, as some variables that initially appeared significant (with a p-value below 0.05) no longer meet the adjusted threshold. For instance, broadband ($q = 0.057$), computer Use ($q = 0.059$), and cloud computing ($q = 0.054$) are no longer considered significant, suggesting their original associations may have been a result of a Type I error due to the large number of tests performed. For comparison, the more conservative Bonferroni correction highlights the exceptional strength of the FinTech adoption finding, as it is the only variable to remain significant under that very strict standard. Overall, this multiple testing correction solidifies our primary claims by confirming that the most impactful findings are not spurious, while also providing a more cautious interpretation of less robust results.

6.6. Time-Varying Effects of FinTech Adoption on Bank Productivity

To explore the dynamic nature of the relationship between FinTech adoption and productivity, we extend the baseline model by incorporating time-varying coefficients. Specifically, we interact the FinTech adoption variable with year-specific dummies to estimate how its marginal effect on productivity has evolved over the 2007–2022 period. This approach captures structural breaks and institutional changes across time—such as the 2008 Global Financial Crisis, the introduction of PSD2, and the COVID-19 pandemic which are likely to influence the productivity returns of digital investments.

Figure 1 below presents a visualisation of the estimated time-varying coefficients for FinTech adoption, along with 95% confidence intervals. The graph is constructed using a panel fixed-effects model where the coefficient on FinTech varies by year. Each point represents the marginal effect of FinTech adoption of productivity in a given year, holding other covariates constant.

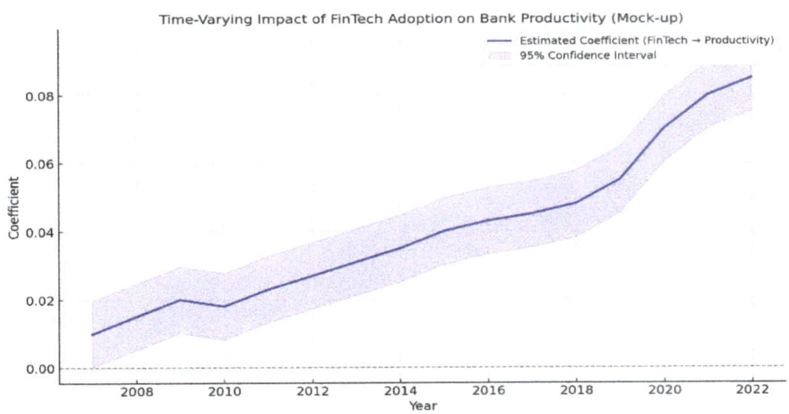

Figure 1. Time-varying impact of FinTech adoption on bank productivity (2007–2022). Source: Authors' illustrations.

Figure 1 reveals the upward trend in the coefficients begins around 2015, coinciding with the rollout of Open Banking initiatives and increasing consumer adoption of mobile financial services. The productivity impact of FinTech becomes more pronounced and statistically meaningful, suggesting enhanced integration of digital capabilities into core bank operations. This indicates that there was an acceleration during regulatory reform and mobile shift (2015–2019).

However, the strongest effects are observed from 2020 onward, as banks rapidly expanded their digital services in response to COVID-19 restrictions, indicating that the peak and consolidation were post-COVID-19 (2020–2022). The coefficient peaks in 2021, indicating that FinTech adoption was most productivity-enhancing during this crisis period, when operational resilience and digital service delivery were paramount.

These results support the hypothesis that the productivity impact of digital transformation is not static but rather context-dependent and cumulative. Banks that invested early in FinTech laid the groundwork, but measurable gains only materialised once complementary factors—such as infrastructure readiness, workforce digital skills, and market acceptance—aligned. The upward trend also suggests a technology diffusion effect, where early adopters drive innovation spill overs that eventually benefit the broader sector.

6.7. Structural Break Analysis Around Key Events

To assess whether the relationship between digital adoption and bank productivity was influenced by major economic disruptions, we tested for structural breaks around two pivotal events: the 2008 Global Financial Crisis (GFC) and the COVID-19 pandemic (2020–2022). We employed the Chow test and Bai—Perron multiple breakpoint test to identify significant shifts in the model parameters during these periods. After applying these tests, we noticed that regarding the Global Financial Crisis (2008), the Chow test revealed a significant structural break (F-statistic = 4.32, significant at the 1% level), indicating that the productivity effects of FinTech adoption diminished temporarily during the crisis, likely due to heightened risk aversion and regulatory scrutiny. However, the post-GFC period (2009–2019) showed a rebound, with digital investments yielding stronger productivity gains as banks prioritised efficiency. As for the COVID-19 pandemic, when applying the Bai—Perron test, we identified a breakpoint in Q2 2020, coinciding with the onset of lockdowns Post-COVID-19 estimates suggest a 15% increase in FinTech's productivity effect ($p < 0.05$), though this reflects an exceptional period where forced digitisation (e.g., branch closures) may have temporarily inflated returns. Pre-pandemic trends (2015–2019) show a steadier 8–9% annual growth in digital productivity effects (see Figure 1), which we consider a more sustainable benchmark for policy planning. Notably, the 2021–2022 period point estimates a decline toward pre-COVID-19 trajectories, consistent with reversion patterns observed in post-shock productivity studies [60].

As a result, the structural breaks underscore that external shocks can alter the productivity returns of digital transformation. While the GFC temporarily disrupted innovation, the pandemic acted as a catalyst, reinforcing the necessity of digital resilience. These findings align with Hansen's [49] insight that structural breaks often reflect institutional or technological regime shifts. The post-COVID-19 acceleration in productivity gains from FinTech adoption mirrors Hansen's observation that labour productivity breaks in the U.S. coincided with IT diffusion. For banks, the pandemic acted as a forcing mechanism, akin to the 'general-purpose technology' shocks Hansen describes, where initial disruptions (e.g., branch closures) gave way to sustained efficiency gains through digital tools.

7. Conclusions and Policy Recommendations

This study provides empirical evidence on the transformative effects of digitalisation and intangible investment (particularly in digital skills and software) on productivity within the UK banking sector. By analysing bank-level data, the research reveals that increasing the proportion of employees with FinTech, IT, and software development expertise significantly enhances employee-level and overall bank productivity. Specifically, a one standard deviation increase in the employment share of software and FinTech/IT specialists is associated with productivity gains of 10.3% and 1.3% per year, respectively. These findings confirm the critical role of intangible assets in shaping modern productivity trajectories and underscore their potential to drive sector-wide improvements in efficiency and performance.

The results suggest that intangibles, such as digital skills and software capabilities, are not only complementary to physical capital but increasingly central to value creation in advanced economies. In the context of the UK, which is transitioning into a more knowledge- and service-based economy, the banking sector emerges as a key domain where digitalisation can yield rapid and substantial productivity dividends. The findings highlight the need for sustained investment in digital infrastructure, skills, and innovation ecosystems to fully unlock this potential.

Importantly, this study identifies several key channels through which productivity gains manifest. First, banks with a higher concentration of digital specialists are better equipped to streamline internal operations, automate processes, and deploy advanced digital financial services. This translates into improved service delivery, cost efficiency, and competitiveness. Second, software investment is shown to play a powerful role in enabling laggard banks to converge toward the productivity frontier. This suggests that closing the digital investment gap—through targeted support mechanisms or incentives—can foster a more inclusive and resilient financial sector.

In addition, the results found out that Hansen [49] cautioned that structural breaks demand flexible policy responses, as pre-break models may poorly predict post-break dynamics. Our results reinforce this: post-COVID-19, policies promoting digital skills (Section 6.2) had outsized returns, whereas post-GFC, stability-focused regulations temporarily muted FinTech's impact. Policymakers should thus monitor breaks proactively, using real-time data to calibrate interventions

Moreover, the heterogeneity in the impact of digitalisation across banks suggests that structural differences, such as age, size, and business model, influence the extent to which institutions benefit from intangible investments. In particular, younger banks demonstrate a stronger responsiveness to intangible capital, likely due to their greater flexibility, innovation orientation, and absence of legacy systems. This dynamic aligns with international evidence on the outsized role of younger, digitally native firms in driving productivity growth (While our findings show a strong link between digital skills, software investment, and productivity, alternative explanations may partly contribute. For example, more productive banks might be better able to attract digital talent and invest in intangibles (reverse causality). Additionally, unobserved factors like managerial quality, organisational culture, or regulatory environment could influence both digital adoption and productivity. Complementary investments in physical capital and organisational changes may also play a role. Finally, differences in timing of digital adoption and industry spill overs might affect results.).

In light of this findings, the study points to several policy recommendations. To sustain and amplify the productivity effects of digitalisation, the UK must implement a comprehensive strategy that includes the following:

a. Expanding the digital talent pipeline: This involves strengthening partnerships between universities, vocational training institutions, and financial sector employers to equip graduates and workers with high-demand digital skills.
b. Promoting continuous learning and upskilling: Reskilling initiatives targeted at mid-career professionals in banking will be essential to adapt to evolving technological demands and reduce skill mismatches.
c. Supporting software diffusion: Incentivising software adoption and innovation, especially among smaller and laggard banks, can help reduce the productivity gap and enhance sectoral competitiveness.

d. Investing in digital infrastructure: Ensuring widespread access to high-speed broadband and secure digital infrastructure is a prerequisite for realising productivity gains across the banking ecosystem.

Furthermore, the COVID-19 pandemic has served as an accelerant of digital adoption. As physical branches closed and mobility was restricted, banks were compelled to expand their digital service offerings, implement remote working tools, and digitise internal processes. This crisis-induced transformation has not only ensured business continuity but has also laid the foundation for lasting productivity improvements. Future research could explore whether these shifts represent permanent structural changes or temporary adaptations, and how they intersect with workforce dynamics and customer preferences in the post-pandemic era.

Finally, this study draws attention to a broader national opportunity. While the UK possesses world-leading research institutions and a strong entrepreneurial culture, there remains a significant gap between innovation generation and commercial exploitation. The country stands to gain significantly from learning from international best practices (such as those of Japan, Korea, Germany, and Finland) in translating research excellence into economic and financial productivity. This would require strategic alignment across education, innovation, and industrial policies to enhance technology transfer, intellectual property commercialisation, and collaborative innovation.

In conclusion, digitalisation and intangible investment represent powerful levers for productivity growth in the UK banking sector and beyond. Unlocking their full potential will require coordinated efforts from financial institutions, policymakers, educational bodies, and technology providers. As the UK seeks to rebuild and reposition itself in the wake of COVID-19 and Brexit, a digital-first, innovation-led growth strategy—grounded in inclusive and forward-looking policies—will be essential to drive sustainable economic transformation.

While the sample includes a relatively small number of leading UK banks, this reflects the targeted nature of this study. The selected institutions were chosen based on their size, public reporting standards, and degree of digital transformation, which ensures both comparability and access to rich, high-quality longitudinal data. Moreover, the intensive data collection process—particularly the text-mining of annual reports for digital adoption metrics—necessitated focusing on banks with complete and consistent disclosures over the 2007–2022 period. This focused sample design was aligned with prior studies investigating the productivity implications of technological adoption in concentrated industries (e.g., [61,62]). While the sample size may constrain external generalisability, it allows for internally valid causal inference by reducing heterogeneity and measurement error. Nonetheless, we acknowledge this as a limitation and view it as a foundation for future research employing broader cross-country or cross-sectoral samples.

Future research could address the limitations of this study in several ways. First, expanding the analysis to include small and medium-sized banks, as well as non-bank financial institutions, would provide a more comprehensive picture of FinTech adoption across the financial sector. Second, cross-country comparative studies could uncover how institutional and regulatory differences mediate the relationship between digital innovation and productivity. Third, incorporating granular, real-time data (such as transaction-level digital usage or employee-level skill development) would enhance the precision of digital transformation metrics. Finally, examining long-term effects, spill overs to non-financial sectors, or customer welfare implications would deepen our understanding of the broader economic impact of financial digitalisation.

Overall, the findings of this study suggest that digital transformation (through FinTech adoption, investment in digital capabilities, and upskilling) can enhance productivity in the UK banking sector. However, these recommendations should be viewed as preliminary. Given this study's national focus and sample limitations, policy interventions encouraging digital innovation in financial services should be guided by further research, especially in different institutional contexts. Future work should validate these findings across broader samples and countries before firm policy action is considered. Policymakers are thus encouraged to support experimentation, monitor implementation outcomes, and adopt flexible, evidence-informed strategies as the digital finance landscape evolves.

Author Contributions: Conceptualization, G.E.M.; methodology, N.M.F.; software, N.M.F.; formal analysis, M.N.; investigation, N.M.F.; data curation, N.M.F.; writing—original draft preparation, G.E.M., J.A.M. and M.N.; writing—review and editing, A.A.; visualization, J.A.M.; supervision, A.A.; All authors have read and agreed to the published version of the manuscript.

Funding: The authors declare that no funds, grants, or other support were received during the preparation of this manuscript.

Informed Consent Statement: Not applicable.

Data Availability Statement: Data are available upon reasonable request at nour.fayad@liu.edu.lb.

Conflicts of Interest: The authors have no conflicts of interest to declare.

References

1. Breidbach, C.F.; Keating, B.W.; Lim, C. Fintech: Research directions to explore the digital transformation of financial service systems. *J. Serv. Theory Pract.* **2019**, *30*, 79–102. [CrossRef]
2. Basole, R.C.; Patel, S.S. Transformation Through Unbundling: Visualizing the Global FinTech Ecosystem. *Serv. Sci.* **2018**, *10*, 379–396. [CrossRef]
3. Romer, P.M. Endogenous Technological Change. *J. Polit. Econ.* **2025**, *98*, S71–S102. [CrossRef]
4. Alt, R.; Beck, R.; Smits, M.T. FinTech and the transformation of the financial industry. *Electron. Mark.* **2018**, *28*, 235–243. [CrossRef]
5. Feyen, E.; Frost, J.; Gambacorta, L.; Natarajan, H.; Saal, M. *Fintech and the digital transformation of financial services: Implications for market structure and public policy*; Bank International Settlements: Basel, Switzerland, 2021.
6. Purnomo, Y.J. Digital Marketing Strategy to Increase Sales Conversion on E-commerce Platforms. *J. Contemp. Adm. Manag.* **2023**, *1*, 54–62. [CrossRef]
7. Bardalai, A.; Quinaucho, C. *Key Facts About UK-Based Financial and Related Professional Services 2024*; TheCityUK: London, UK, 2024.
8. Gomber, P.; Koch, J.-A.; Siering, M. Digital Finance and FinTech: Current research and future research directions. *J. Bus. Econ.* **2017**, *87*, 537–580. [CrossRef]
9. Haddad, C.; Hornuf, L. The emergence of the global fintech market: Economic and technological determinants. *Small Bus. Econ.* **2019**, *53*, 81–105. [CrossRef]
10. Zavolokina, L.; Dolata, M.; Schwabe, G. FinTech—What's in a Name? In *Thirty Seventh International Conference on Information Systems*; Curran Associates, Inc.: Dublin, Ireland, 2016.
11. Fries, S.; Taci, A. Cost efficiency of banks in transition: Evidence from 289 banks in 15 post-communist countries. *J. Bank. Financ.* **2004**, *29*, 55–81. [CrossRef]
12. Koutsomanoli-Filippaki, A.; Margaritis, D.; Staikouras, C. Efficiency and productivity growth in the banking industry of Central and Eastern Europe. *J. Bank. Financ.* **2009**, *33*, 557–567. [CrossRef]
13. Wheelock, C.D.; Wilson, W.P. Do large banks have lower costs? New estimates of returns to scale for U.S. banks. *J. Money Credit Bank.* **2012**, *44*, 171–199. [CrossRef]
14. X Vives, X. Digital Disruption in Banking. *Annu. Rev. Financ. Econ.* **2019**, *11*, 243–272. [CrossRef]
15. Bömer, M.; Maxin, H. Why Fintechs Cooperate with Banks—Evidence from Germany. *ZVersWiss* **2018**, *107*, 359–386. [CrossRef]
16. Toufaily, E.; Zalan, T.; Ben Dhaou, S. A framework of blockchain technology adoption: An investigation of challenges and expected value. *Inf. Manag.* **2021**, *58*, 103444. [CrossRef]
17. Wu, Z. The Rise of Digital Banking in the UK Financial Sector and Its Impact on Commercial Banks. *Adv. Econ. Manag. Politi- Sci.* **2024**, *120*, 179–184. [CrossRef]
18. Alt, R.; Ehrenberg, D. Fintech—Umbruch der Finanzbranche durch IT. *Wirtsch. Manag.* **2016**, *8*, 8–17. [CrossRef]
19. Thakor, A.V. Fintech and banking: What do we know? *J. Financ. Intermediation* **2020**, *43*, 100858. [CrossRef]

20. Swyngedouw, J.; Farkas, A. *The European Banking Authority (EBA) 2018 Annual Report*; European Banking Authority (EBA): Paris, France, 2019.
21. Ghosh, P.; Vallee, B.; Zeng, Y. FinTech Lending and Cashless Payments. In *Finance Meeting EUROFIDAI-ESSEC*; Association Paris December Finance: Paris, France, 2022.
22. Boatright, R.J. Ethics and the Conduct of Business. *J. Bus. Ethics* **1994**, *13*, 446–454.
23. Milian, E.Z.; Spinola, M.d.M.; de Carvalho, M.M. Fintechs: A Literature Review and Research Agenda. *Electron. Commer. Res. Appl.* **2019**, *34*, 100833. [CrossRef]
24. Chen, Z.; Li, H.; Wang, T.; Wu, J. How digital transformation affects bank risk: Evidence from listed Chinese banks. *Financ. Res. Lett.* **2023**, *58*, 104319. [CrossRef]
25. Zhang, L.; Yi, Y. Network embeddedness and service innovation: The mediating role of knowledge co-creation and the moderating role of digital transformation. *Serv. Bus.* **2024**, *18*, 523–553. [CrossRef]
26. Mones, D.; Hayes, D. *Europe's 50 Largest Banks by Assets, 2024*; S&P Global: New York, NY, USA, 2024.
27. Albuquerque, M.L.; Berrigan, J.; Jour-Schroeder, A.; O'Sullivan, D. European Commission Digital Finance and the EU Regulatory Framework 2024. Available online: https://finance.ec.europa.eu/news/digital-finance-2024-12-19_en (accessed on 1 May 2025).
28. Bilotta, N.; Romano, S. Tech Giants in Banking: The Implications of a New Market Power, IAI Istituto Affari Internazionali. 2019 Available online: https://www.iai.it/en/pubblicazioni/c03/tech-giants-banking-implications-new-market-power (accessed on 1 May 2025).
29. Sironi, P. *FinTech Innovation: From Robo-Advisors to Goal Based Investing and Gamification*; Wiley: Hoboken, NJ, USA, 2016.
30. Paulet, E.; Mavoori, H. Globalization, regulation and profitability of banks: A comparative analysis of Europe, United States, India and China. *The Eur. J. Comp. Econ.* **2019**, *16*, 127–170.
31. Bailey, A.; Breeden, S.; Broadbent, B.; Ramsden, D.; Woods, S.; Rathi, N.; Bowe, C.; Hall, J.; Kroszner, R.; Stheeman, E.; et al. *Financial Stability Report—December 2023*; Bank of England: London, UK, 2023.
32. Bond, C.; Parry, A. *UK Credit Card Statistics*; Merchant Savvy: Reading, UK, 2025.
33. Brynjolfsson, E.; Hitt, M.L. Beyond computation: Information technology, organizational transformation and business performance. *J. Econ. Perspect.* **2000**, *14*, 23–48. [CrossRef]
34. DeStefano, T.; Kneller, R.; Timmis, J. Broadband infrastructure, ICT use and firm performance: Evidence for UK firms. *J. Econ. Behav. Organ.* **2018**, *155*, 110–139. [CrossRef]
35. Barney, J. Firm resources and sustained competitive advantage. *J. Manag.* **1991**, *17*, 99–120. [CrossRef]
36. Rogers, M.E. *Diffusion of Innovations*, 5th ed.; Free Press: New York, NY, USA, 2003.
37. Griliches, Z. The discovery of the residual: A historical note. *J. Econ. Lit.* **1996**, *34*, 1324–1330.
38. Cevik, S. *Promise (Un)kept? Fintech and Financial Inclusion*; International Monetary Fund: Washington, DC, USA, 2024.
39. Culnan, M.J.; O'REilly, I.C.A.; Chatman, J.A. Intellectual structure of research in organizational behavior, 1972–1984: A cocitation analysis. *J. Am. Soc. Inf. Sci.* **1990**, *41*, 453–458. [CrossRef]
40. Samiee, S.; Chabowski, B.R. Knowledge structure in international marketing: A multi-method bibliometric analysis. *J. Acad. Mark. Sci.* **2011**, *40*, 364–386. [CrossRef]
41. Mondal, J.; Chakrabarti, S. The abandonment behaviour of the branded app consumer: A study using interpretive structural modelling approach. *J. Retail. Consum. Serv.* **2021**, *63*, 102695. [CrossRef]
42. Cette, G.; Lecat, R.; Montornès, J. Labour market regulations and capital intensity. *Appl. Econ.* **2018**, *50*, 1693–1715.
43. Berger, N.A.; Humphrey, B.D. Efficiency of financial institutions: International survey and directions for future re-search. *Eur. J. Oper. Res.* **1997**, *98*, 175–212. [CrossRef]
44. Stiroh, J.K. How did the 1990s go? Evidence from the U.S. growth resurgence. In Federal Reserve Bank of New York Current Issues in Economics and Finance2000. Available online: https://www.frbsf.org/wp-content/uploads/resurgence.pdf (accessed on 1 May 2025).
45. Cecchetti, G.S.; Schoenholtz, L.K. *Money, Banking, and Financial Markets*, 6th ed.; McGraw Hill: Columbus, OH, USA, 2021.
46. Hulland, J.; Houston, M.B. Why systematic review papers and meta-analyses matter: An introduction to the special issue on generalizations in marketing. *J. Acad. Mark. Sci.* **2020**, *48*, 351–359. [CrossRef]
47. Cheng, M.; Qu, Y. Does operational risk management benefit from FinTech? *Emerg. Mark. Financ. Trade* **2023**, *59*, 4012–4027. [CrossRef]
48. Hastie, T.; Tibshirani, R. Varying-Coefficient Models. *J. R. Stat. Soc. Ser. B* **1993**, *55*, 757–779. [CrossRef]
49. Hansen, E. The New Econometrics of Structural Change: Dating Breaks in U.S. Labor Productivity. *J. Econ. Perspect.* **2001**, *15*, 117–128. [CrossRef]
50. Chow, G.C. Tests of Equality Between Sets of Coefficients in Two Linear Regressions. *Econometrica* **1960**, *28*, 591–605. [CrossRef]
51. Bai, J.; Perron, P. Computation and Analysis of Multiple Structural Change Models. *J. Appl. Econom.* **2003**, *18*, 1–22. [CrossRef]
52. Acemoglu, D.; Restrepo, P. *Artificial Intelligence, Automation, and Work*; National Bureau of Economic Research, Inc.: Cambridge, MA, USA, 2018.

3. Acemoglu, D.; Restrepo, P. *Robots and Jobs: Evidence from US Labor Markets*; Massachusetts Institute of Technology: Cambridge, MA, USA, 2020.
4. Bloom, N.; Bunn, P.; Chen, S.; Mizen, P.; Smietanka, P.; Thwaites, G. *The Impact of COVID-19 on Productivity*; National Bureau of Economic Research, Inc.: Cambridge, MA, USA, 2020.
5. Bloom, N.; Brynjolfsson, E.; Foster, L.; Jarmin, R.; Patnaik, M.; Saporta-Eksten, I.; Van Reenen, J. What drives differences in management practices? *Am. Econ. Rev.* **2019**, *190*, 1648–1683. [CrossRef]
6. Berlingieri, G.; Calligaris, S.; Criscuolo, C.; Verlhac, R. *Laggard Firms, Technology Diffusion and Its Structural and Policy Determinants*; OECD Publishing: Paris, France, 2020.
7. Staiger, D.; Stock, J.H. Instrumental Variables Regression with Weak Instruments. *Econom. Soc.* **1993**, *65*, 557–586.
8. Hausman, J.A. Specification Tests in Econometrics. *Econom. Soc.* **1978**, *46*, 1251–1271. [CrossRef]
9. Clarke, C. The level, slope, and curve factor model for stocks. *J. Financ. Econ.* **2022**, *143*, 159–178. [CrossRef]
0. Criscuolo, C. *Productivity and Business Dynamics Through the Lens of COVID-19: The Shock, Risks and Opportunities*; European Central Bank: Frankfurt, Germany, 2022.
1. Cette, G.; Fernald, J.; Mojon, B. The pre-Great Recession slowdown in productivity. *Eur. Econ. Rev.* **2016**, *88*, 3–20. [CrossRef]
2. Gal, P.; Nicoletti, G.; Renault, T.; Sorbe, S.; Timiliotis, C. *Digitalisation and Productivity: In Search of the Holy Grail—Firm-Level Empirical Evidence From EU Countries*; OECD: Paris, France, 2019.

FinTech MDPI

Article

The Impact of FinTech on the Financial Performance of Commercial Banks in Bangladesh: A Random-Effect Model Analysis

Iftekhar Ahmed Robin [1], Mohammad Mazharul Islam [2,*] and Majed Alharthi [2]

[1] Central Bank of Bangladesh, Motijheel, Dhaka 1000, Bangladesh; iftekhar.robin@bb.org.bd
[2] Finance Department, College of Business, King Abdulaziz University, Rabigh 21911, Saudi Arabia; mdalharthi@kau.edu.sa
* Correspondence: malislam@kau.edu.sa

Abstract

This paper examines the impact of agent banking activities, a recent FinTech development, influencing the profitability and financial outcomes of commercial banks operating in Bangladesh, as agent banking has been receiving significant global attention due to its technology-driven approach, cost-effectiveness and easy accessibility, and broader coverage of the unbanked population. Through the application of penal data regression methods, the study estimates a random-effect model using panel data comprising quarterly observations from nine Bangladeshi commercial banks that maintained uninterrupted agent banking activities, covering both deposit mobilization and lending during the period from 2018Q1 to 2024Q4. The empirical findings indicate that credit disbursement by agent banks has a positive and statistically significant impact on bank profitability measures, return on assets (ROA), and return on equity (ROE). Similarly, the expansion of agent banking outlets positively and significantly influences ROA. Therefore, an appropriate agent banking policy aimed at increasing agent banking outlets using digital platforms based on FinTech is vital for ensuring positive growth in credit disbursement to achieve improved financial outcomes for the banking sector in a developing country like Bangladesh.

Keywords: FinTech; financial performance; commercial banks; panel data model; credit

JEL Classification: G21; C23; E51

1. Introduction

The rapid advancement of financial technology (FinTech) has significantly reshaped the global banking industry by enabling more cost-effective, inclusive, and scalable service delivery models. FinTech encompasses the use of modern digital innovations, such as mobile banking, blockchain, cloud computing, and artificial intelligence [1], to enhance accessibility, efficiency, security, and cost-effectiveness through software, mobile apps, and digital platforms. It has revolutionized financial services by providing greater accessibility to individuals and businesses, streamlining operations, and reducing costs. One of the most significant innovations within the FinTech sector is agent banking, particularly in developing economies, which allows banks to extend financial services utilizing digital platforms through local agents in areas where conventional bank branches are not available [2]. The agent banking model was formalized in 2013 through guidelines issued by Bangladesh Bank, with full-scale operations commencing in 2016 (PSD Circular No.

05: Guidelines on Agent Banking for the Banks dated 9 December 2013). This model has become increasingly prevalent and represents a transformative approach to bridging financial service gaps in Bangladesh, where it has been instrumental in addressing the challenges faced by underserved populations and promoting financial inclusion. The agent banking model has been a major development in the financial landscape of Bangladesh. The agent banks act as small-scale representatives of commercial banks, equipped with point-of-sale (POS) terminals, mobile phones, barcode scanners, electronic data-processing equipment, and biometric devices to facilitate a wide range of banking services. This innovative banking model is 86 percent more cost-effective than establishing a traditional bank branch, as it leverages the existing business infrastructure, reducing the need for significant investment in physical infrastructure and fixed operational costs [3]. As of December 2024, 31 commercial banks in Bangladesh are operating agent banking services through a network of 16,021 agents and 21,248 outlets, with the majority of these agents and outlets located in rural areas [4]. In terms of banking service offerings, agent banking covers a wide range of financial services, including cash deposits, withdrawals, account opening, utility bill payments, fund transfer, and savings products. Unlike conventional banking, agent banking does not require the establishment of expensive brick-and-mortar branches, making it a more affordable and scalable solution for reaching the doorstep of the unbanked population in rural, underserved areas. The agent banking model conducts banking transactions on behalf of commercial banks (as a mother bank), including deposit mobilization, loan disbursement, collection of utility bills, payments related to government programs, and handling domestic and international remittances. All transactions conducted through agents are recorded in the financial statements of the respective mother banks, ensuring transparency and regulatory compliance. Therefore, agent banking, being an innovative FinTech platform, facilitates digital financial solutions using advanced technology and eventually increases financial activities and employment generation in rural areas.

Globally, various models of agent banking exist, with agents operating in diverse settings such as pharmacies, supermarkets, corner stores, and post offices. For example, post offices act as banking agents in Australia, while corner stores serve this role in France. Brazil delivers financial services through lottery outlets. Mobile-based branchless banking and agency banking are prominent in countries like Senegal, Pakistan, India, Kenya, Nigeria, the Democratic Republic of Congo, South Africa, and the Philippines [5–10]. Despite the varying models, agent banking is generally recognized as a cost-effective banking solution that offers greater accessibility to underserved market segments and thereby promotes broader financial inclusion.

Despite the rapid spread of agent banking and its potential to enhance financial inclusion, its impact on the financial performance of commercial banks remains ambiguous and under-researched, particularly in Bangladesh. While it is commonly assumed that FinTech-based banking models, agent banking in particular, have increased outreach, reduced transaction costs, and a larger customer base, which should translate into improved profitability and operational efficiency, empirical evidence on this relationship is mixed. Several studies [11,12] report positive associations between agent banking variables and bank profitability metrics such as return on assets (ROA) and return on equity (ROE). However, other findings suggest that the effect may be negative or statistically insignificant, depending on factors such as agent efficiency, remittance handling, or the bank's fund utilization strategies [13,14]. Addressing this empirical gap in the existing literature is conducted by examining whether and how FinTech-enabled agent banking activities influence the financial performance of commercial banks in Bangladesh. Unlike earlier studies that rely on limited periods or do not differentiate between partial and full-fledged agent banking operations, this research focuses on a panel of nine banks operating comprehensive agent banking services, including deposit mobilization and credit disbursement over the period from Q1 2018 to Q4 2024. Utilizing a random-effects panel data regression model, the study evaluates the effect of six key agent banking indicators: number of agents, number of outlets, number of accounts, total deposits, total credit disbursed, and processed remittances. It is essential to uncover the strategic value of FinTech innovations for the sustainable growth, profitability, and competitiveness of the banking sector in Bangladesh. These relationships also provide valuable insights into the broader economic impacts of FinTech adoption in emerging markets. This study, therefore, not only offers theoretical contributions by aligning agent banking with agency theory [15] and financial intermediation theory [16] but also generates practical implications for bank managers and policymakers. By evaluating the agent banking model through a FinTech lens, the study contributes to strategic discussions on how technological innovations can promote both financial inclusion and institutional profitability in emerging economies. Based on the stated objective, the following research questions are outlined:

RQ1: How does agent banking influence the accessibility and financial performance of commercial banks in Bangladesh?
RQ2: What is the impact of agent banking outlets on the financial performance of commercial banks in Bangladesh?
RQ3: How does deposit mobilization influence the financial performance of commercial banks in Bangladesh?
RQ4: What is the effect of credit disbursement through agent banking on the financial performance of commercial banks in Bangladesh?

The rest of the paper is organized as follows: Section 2 reviews the existing literature, including the theoretical and empirical literature. Section 3 constructs a conceptual framework and develops hypotheses. Section 4 illustrates the research design, data and methodology, and model specification. Section 5 discusses the empirical results. In Section 6, the robustness of the empirical analysis is assessed, followed by the conclusion in Section 7.

2. Literature Review

This section briefly discusses both the theoretical and empirical literature on agent banking models.

2.1. Theories on Agent Banking Model

The agent banking model is based on agency theory [15]. The model defines an agency relationship as a contract between a commercial bank (principal) and an agent hired to provide banking services on their behalf. Consequently, agents provide banking services on behalf of commercial banks under officially sanctioned agency agreements. An agent is typically the owner of a designated outlet who is contracted to execute banking services on a bank's behalf. These agents use FinTech platforms to process banking transactions, such as money transfer, bill payments, deposit mobilization, and loan disbursement. The agent points are equipped with FinTech to provide banking services to unbanked populations of the remote areas in a cost-effective way. Therefore, commercial banks can reach the underserved or unbanked population through their agents, utilizing advanced FinTech with less overhead costs instead of setting up a full-fledged bank branch. This model permits seamless connectivity between an agent's transaction software and the bank's core system, thereby recording all transactions in real time on the customer's bank statement [17]. The agent banking model offers significant benefits to the parent bank by facilitating customer acquisition, enhancing market penetration, reducing operational costs, and boosting earnings from various financial and fee-based sources.

The agent banking model also follows the theory of financial intermediation [16]. The theory reveals how agent banking strengthens the intermediation role of banks, i.e., mobilizing deposits and disbursing loans in remote areas, and thus extends financial inclusion. The Technology Acceptance Model explains the impact of agent banking on key performance indicators, including return on asset (ROA) and return on equity (ROE), operational efficiency (cost-to-income ratio), market expansion (customer acquisition), and risk management [18]. The framework offers a comprehensive understanding of how agent banking enhances financial performance in the digital economy.

According to their [19] observation, agent banking provides financial and payment services via postal offices and various retail outlets, including grocery shops, pharmacies, agricultural input suppliers, and fuel stations, rather than relying on traditional bank branches and in-house field officers. In India, under the Business Correspondent model, banks are entitled to engage intermediaries. For example, agents may be engaged in disbursing small-value loans, recovering principal and interest payments, collecting small deposits, selling microinsurance and pension products, and facilitating the receipt or delivery of low-value remittances [7].

2.2. Empirical Literature

The impact of agent banking on the financial performance of commercial banks has brought in increasing attention in recent years. Although numerous studies have been conducted, a unified conclusion has yet to emerge. Many studies suggest that agent banking positively influences key performance indicators, such as return on assets (ROA) and return on equity (ROE), primarily by enhancing financial accessibility, operational efficiency, and profitability [11,12,20–22]. For instance, Ref. [20] found that expanding agent networks improves profitability by extending service outreach, while [23] linked performance improvements in Kenyan banks to wider market access and lower transaction costs. Similarly, Ref. [5] highlighted that agent banking increases clients' financial activity and savings, and [8] showed improvements in business performance through higher turnover, customer numbers, and transaction volumes. Ref. [24] confirmed a positive link between agency banking and profit growth in Kenyan banks, while [9] emphasized that agent banking enhances profitability by reaching grassroots-level customers.

However, empirical evidence on the relationship between the number of agents and bank performance remains mixed. While several studies report a significant positive association between agent numbers and profitability metrics (ROA/ROE) [14,25–27], others present contrasting results. For instance, Ref. [28] found a statistically significant negative relationship, suggesting that expanding the agent network may increase operational costs without proportionately increasing returns. These disparities may stem from differences in agent productivity, transaction volume, or regional financial demand. Thus, while agent expansion theoretically supports greater outreach and revenue, its effectiveness is contingent upon strategic management and operational efficiency.

By contrast, the literature reveals more consistent findings regarding deposit mobilization through agent banking. Several studies confirm a positive and significant impact of total deposits on banks' financial performance [11,14,26,28,29]. Agent banking serves as a cost-effective mechanism to mobilize deposits in underserved areas, enabling banks to expand their customer base without incurring high infrastructure costs. Refs. [11,28] observed that such deposits contribute to higher ROA and ROE, as they are reinvested in interest-bearing assets like loans and advances. Nonetheless, some studies caution that increased deposits may not always translate into profitability gains. For example, Ref. [30] argues that unproductive liquidity from short-term or inactive deposits may reduce earnings, while [14] notes that limited lending capacity and inefficient fund use through agents may damage performance. Ref. [13] further adds that high funding costs and a large share of foreign currency deposits can reduce ROA despite growth in deposits.

Findings on the impact of agent banking outlets are similarly mixed. While several studies highlight a positive and statistically significant influence of outlet numbers on ROA [11,14,31], others report negative or diminishing returns associated with excessive outlet expansion, citing potential inefficiencies [28,32,33].

The effect of credit disbursement through agents is largely viewed as positive. Numerous empirical studies demonstrate that agent-based lending improves ROA and ROE by expanding financial inclusion and improving income-generating activities [21,26,28,34–36]. However, some studies, such as [26,29], find no significant impact, suggesting that credit outcomes vary depending on institutional frameworks, regulatory contexts, and the maturity of agent networks. This emphasizes the need for contextual analysis when evaluating the effectiveness of agent-delivered credit.

Remittance inflows also play a strategic role in influencing financial performance. Studies by [26,28,37–39] find that remittances serve as a stable and significant source of funds that boost deposit bases and facilitate credit expansion. Refs. [40–42] support the view that remittances foster financial intermediation and inclusion. However, challenges such as compliance with anti-money laundering (AML) and counter-terrorism financing (CFT) standards [43], as well as the effective integration of digital tools, are critical to optimizing remittance benefits. Refs. [44,45] note that FinTech platforms can reduce transaction costs and formalize financial behavior among remittance recipients.

Regarding the number of accounts maintained through agent banking, the evidence is inconclusive. Some studies find a positive and significant relationship between ROA and ROE, suggesting that more accounts reflect broader outreach and improved profitability [6,25,29,32,46]. Ref. [28], for example, demonstrates a positive association between account growth and financial performance. Ref. [47] further asserts that more active accounts per agent improve intermediation and service delivery. In contrast, other studies identify a negative or insignificant relationship [13,28,29,37], pointing to high maintenance costs, short deposit tenures, and inefficiencies in fund utilization as potential drawbacks.

Taken together, the literature highlights the complex and context-specific nature of agent banking's impact on bank performance. Despite promising results, there is a lack of comprehensive evaluation specific to Bangladesh, where full-scale agent banking was launched in 2016. This gap underscores the importance and originality of the present study, which aims to assess how FinTech-enabled agent banking activities have influenced key financial performance metrics—namely ROA and ROE—among commercial banks in Bangladesh.

Scholars widely agree that agent banking represents a FinTech-driven innovation, particularly in developing economies [48–51]. Agent banking is an important determinant of FinTech [26]. According to [51], banks use FinTech to offer various services to their customers, including agent banking and software upgrades. Other research shows that FinTech plays a key role in supporting how agent banking works [52,53]. The connection between FinTech and agent banking is often shown through the use of technology tools like mobile phones and digital financial platforms [54,55]. For instance, Ref. [54] explains that agent banking depends on tools like digital identity checks (KYC), mobile wallets, and fingerprint systems, all elements of FinTech. Similarly, Ref. [55] emphasizes that agent banking represents a FinTech-enabled model, built on mobile, cloud, and digital platforms. As [52] notes, FinTech provides the digital foundation that agent banking needs, especially in areas with limited banking access. Theoretically, ideas from agency theory and financial intermediation theory show that agent banking helps reduce information gaps, builds trust, and makes it easier for people in rural areas to save money or obtain loans [15,16].

Research supports this by showing that agent banking can improve a bank's financial performance, like return on assets (ROA) and return on equity (ROE), through better loan access and more service outlets [11,14]. However, the results regarding the number of agents and how much money they collect in deposits vary depending upon how agent banking is used [13]. Around the world, examples from countries like Australia (postal agents) and Kenya (mobile platforms) show that agent banking is flexible and effective [56]. In Bangladesh, combining FinTech with agent banking has helped reach unbanked people, improve banking services, and boost financial inclusion. In summary, FinTech is the key technology behind agent banking, making it possible to offer safe, wide-reaching, and inclusive financial services.

3. Conceptual Framework

Based on the literature review presented in Section 2, this study develops the research framework illustrated in Figure 1, which hypothesizes a direct relationship between FinTech-based agent banking variables and the financial performance of commercial banks. The conceptual framework captures the core constructs of FinTech-driven agent banking and commercial bank performance, aiming to address the research questions outlined in Section 1.

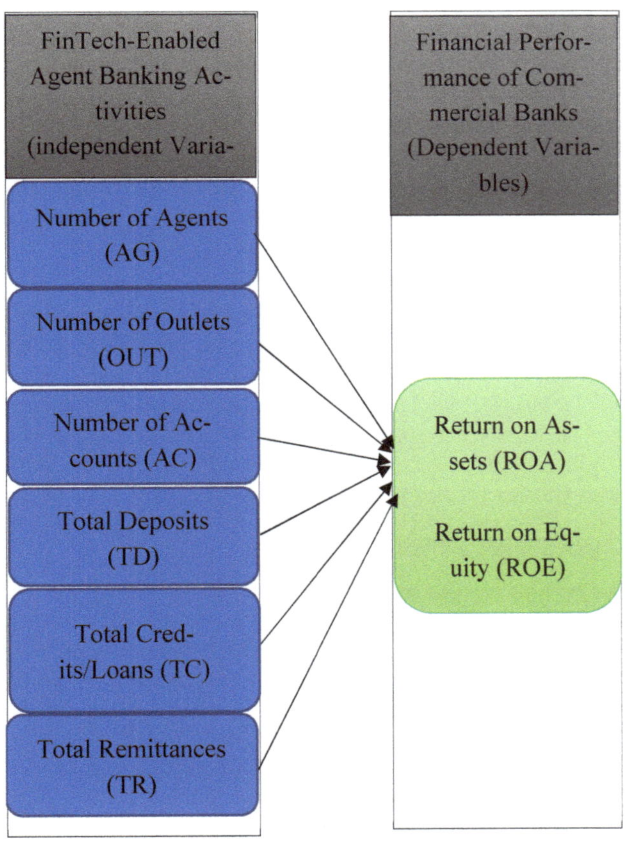

Figure 1. Framework for the proposed model (Source: figure created by authors).

Hypotheses Development

Grounded in the conceptual framework and the existing literature, the following hypotheses are developed to examine the effect of FinTech-enabled agent banking on the financial outcomes of Bangladesh's commercial banks:

H1. *An increase in the number of agent banking agents (AG) is linked to a decline in both ROA and ROE for commercial banks in Bangladesh;*

H2. *An increase in the number of agent banking outlets (OUT) is positively associated with both ROA and ROE for commercial banks in Bangladesh;*

H3. *A higher number of agent banking accounts (AC) corresponds to lower financial performance, as reflected in both ROA and ROE, for commercial banks in Bangladesh;*

H4. *The total deposit (TD) mobilized through agent banking is positively and significantly associated with both return on assets (ROA) and return on equity (ROE) for commercial banks in Bangladesh;*

H5. *Total credit disbursement (TC) through agent banking has a significant positive effect on both ROA and ROE for commercial banks in Bangladesh;*

H6. *Total remittance collection (REM) positively affects the financial performance, as measured by the ROA and ROE of commercial banks in Bangladesh.*

4. Empirical Design: Methodology, Data, and Variables

The study analyzes how agent banking operations influence the profitability of sampled commercial banks in Bangladesh. In the regression analysis, two different profitability measures, return on assets (ROA) and return on equity (ROE) of the sample banks are considered as dependent variables and, six agent banking-specific independent variables are the number of agents, the number of agent banking outlets, the total number of accounts held with agent banks, the total amount of deposits collected, the amount of credit disbursed, and the total remittance amount processed by agent banks. NIM mainly reflects the interest spread between income from loans and costs of deposits, offering a narrow view focused on traditional intermediation efficiency. This study excludes net interest margin (NIM) as a measure of financial performance because it does not fully capture the strategic and operational outcomes of FinTech-enabled agent banking activities [14,57,58]. For example, Ref. [14] reported that agent banking contributes significantly to non-interest income through services like remittances and deposit collection, making NIM an incomplete measure of profitability. Similarly, Ref. [57] reported that non-interest income plays a growing role in bank performance in Asia. Traditional NIM-based analysis fails to reflect this shift, especially in digital and FinTech environments. Moreover, Ref. [58] provides evidence that the rise of FinTech-driven models like agent banking reduces reliance on net interest-based income, shifting performance measurement towards non-interest income streams. However, agent banking in Bangladesh encompasses a broader set of services, such as remittance processing, bill payments, and deposit collection, that often generate non-interest income or operate outside conventional loan–deposit mechanisms. As a result, NIM may underestimate the financial contributions of these services. Moreover, NIM is highly sensitive to fluctuations in interest rates and regulatory policies, which may obscure the effects of agent banking initiatives. In contrast, return on assets (ROA) and return on equity (ROE) offer a more comprehensive view of profitability and operational efficiency, accounting for both income generation and resource utilization. These indicators are better suited to evaluate the financial impact of FinTech-driven innovations that aim to enhance financial inclusion and extend service outreach. Therefore, to more accurately assess the performance implications of agent banking in a developing economy like Bangladesh, this study uses ROA and ROE as more appropriate and robust measures of bank performance. The detailed definitions of the variables are presented in Appendix A, Table A1.

For this study, a sample of nine commercial banks in Bangladesh was selected. These banks are the only ones, out of 62 scheduled banks regulated by Bangladesh Bank, that operated full-fledged agent banking services, including both deposit mobilization and credit disbursement throughout the study period (2018 Q1 to 2024 Q4). This sample is representative of the full population of banks engaged in comprehensive agent banking during this time. The selected period reflects a phase of rapid FinTech adoption and technological development in Bangladesh's banking sector. Focusing on these years ensures data completeness, maximizes sample relevance, and provides a reliable basis for analyzing the relationship between FinTech-driven agent banking and bank profitability. The study employs a panel data regression model using the quarterly data from these nine (09) commercial banks at the bank level. The banks are Bank Asia, Dutch-Bangla Bank, Al-Arafah Islami Bank, Islami Bank Bangladesh, Mutual Trust Bank, The City Bank, Brac Bank, NRB Bank, and Modhumoti Bank Limited (Appendix A Table A2). The study has constructed a uniquely structured balanced panel dataset with 234 observations for the period 2018Q1–2024Q4 and estimated both the fixed-effect (FE) model and the random-effect (RE) model, and also a pooled regression model (as robustness check) to examine the effects of agent banking activities on the financial outcomes of the selected commercial banks, using return on assets (ROA) and return on equity (ROE) as measures of profitability. Measuring the financial performance of commercial banks solely with ROA provides an incomplete picture of their financial health. The authors argue that relying solely on one metric (i.e., ROA) can be misleading, as it may not capture the full scope of a bank's financial health. They claim that return on equity (ROE) alongside ROA allows for a more comprehensive analysis that considers both operational efficiency and how well equity is being used, highlighting the impact of leverage and overall risk–return trade-off. This dual approach ensures that stakeholders, including investors and regulators, can better assess both profitability and financial stability.

The sample constitutes bank-level quarterly data of nine private commercial banks in Bangladesh, covering the period from 2018Q1–2024Q4. These data were sourced from the financial statements of the sample banks and from the central bank of Bangladesh (Bangladesh Bank).

4.1. Overview of Variable Statistics

Table 1 displays the overview of statistics of the variables used in the empirical analysis.

Table 1. Overview statistics of the variables.

Variable	Mean	S.E	Min	Max
Response Variables				
Return on Assets (ROA)	0.005	0.004	−0.011	0.019
Return on Equity (ROE)	0.061	0.055	−0.149	0.323
Independent Variables				
No. of Agents	2.693	0.584	0	3.725
No. of Outlets	2.811	0.626	0	3.790
Total accounts	5.407	0.948	1.204	6.848
Total Deposit	4.177	0.872	1.079	5.905
Total loans/credits	3.058	1.268	0	5.409
Remittance	4.278	1.252	0.903	6.608

Source: Authors' calculation.

4.2. Model Specification

The regression model is expressed as:

$$Z_{it} = \beta_i + \gamma Y_{it} + V_{it} \quad (1)$$

where Z_{it} represents the profitability measures, ROA, and ROE for bank i. Y_{it} indicates the selected explanatory variables, V_{it} denotes the error term, β is the constant term, and γ is the vector of regression coefficients.

The empirical models to be estimated are as follows:

$$ROA_{it} = \beta 0 + \gamma 1AG + \gamma 2OUT + \gamma 3TC + \gamma 4TD + \gamma 5AC + \gamma 6REM + e_{it} \quad (2)$$

$$ROE_{it} = \beta 0 + \gamma 1AG + \gamma 2OUT + \gamma 3TC + \gamma 4TD + \gamma 5AC + \gamma 6REM + e_{it} \quad (3)$$

where the explanatory variables are the number of agents (AG), number of agent banking outlets (OUT), total credit disbursed by agent banks (TC), total deposit mobilization by agent banks (TD), number of accounts with agent banks (AC), and total remittances through agent banks (REM). β is the constant term, and γ is the vector of coefficients. e denotes the error term. Equations (2) and (3) are estimated using both random-effects (RE) and fixed-effects (FE) models. The Hausman specification test is conducted to determine the most appropriate models for the sample data. The results indicate that the RE model is the appropriate one (the probability for the chi-square statistic is given in Appendix A, Table A2). The results for the RE model are presented in the text (Table 2). The full regression results for both the FE model and the RE model are presented in Appendix A, Table A3. To check the robustness of the RE model, a pooled OLS regression model is estimated for Equations (2) and (3). The estimated pooled regression model results are presented in Table 3.

Table 2. Random-effect model results: ROA and ROE as dependent variables.

	ROA		ROE	
	Coefficient	**S.E.**	**Coefficient**	**S.E.**
No. of Agents (AG)	−0.003 *	0.001	−0.036 *	0.018
No. of Outlets (OUT)	0.005 **	0.002	0.028	0.023
Total Credit (TC)	0.001 ***	0.000	0.011 ***	0.004
Total Deposit (TD)	0.002	0.001	0.005	0.014
No. of Accounts (AC)	−0.001	0.001	0.008	0.012
Total Remittance (REM)	−0.002 *	0.001	−0.003	0.011
Constant	0.001	0.003	−0.005	0.034
R-squared	0.123		0.113	
Wald Chi-square	13.71		24.77	
Prob χ^2	0.033		0.000	
Total Observations	234		234	

Source: Authors' estimation ***, **, and * denote statistical significance at the 1%, 5%, and 10% levels, respectively.

Table 3. Pooled regression results: ROA and ROE as dependent variables.

	ROA		ROE	
	Coefficient	**S.E.**	**Coefficient**	**S.E.**
No. of Agents (AG)	−0.004 ***	0.001	−0.038 **	0.017
No. of Outlets (OUT)	0.005 ***	0.002	0.029	0.024
Total Credit (TC)	0.001 ***	0.000	0.011 ***	0.003
Total Deposit (TD)	0.002	0.001	0.004	0.015
No. of Accounts (AC)	−0.001	0.001	0.008	0.013
Total Remittance (REM)	−0.002 **	0.001	−0.003	0.010
Constant	0.001	0.003	−0.004	0.037
R-squared	0.126		0.113	
Probability (F)	0.000		0.000	
Total Observations	234		234	

Source: Authors' estimation using STATA. *** and ** denote statistical significance level at 1%, and 5% respectively.

5. Results and Discussion

Table 2 reports the results of the estimated random-effect regression models for ROA (Equation (2)) and ROE (Equation (3)). The estimated positive and statistically significant coefficients of total credit (TC) for both ROA and ROE indicate that loan disbursement through agent banking has a positive impact on the profitability of a bank in terms of ROA and ROE, which is in line with hypotheses H5 (Section Hypotheses Development) and is also strongly supported by the previous studies [21,26,28,34–36]. One possible reason for the increased profitability is the higher income earned from loan disbursement by agent banks. Since agent banking outlets are widely spread across the country, especially in the remote areas, clients prefer conducting banking transactions through agents rather than a formal bank branch due to closer travel distance, lower transaction cost, and a trustworthy personal relationship. Moreover, the same person (owner of the outlet) deals with clients who are small entrepreneurs within the locality, and therefore, gradually, a trustworthy relationship is developed between them over time. In addition, the poorer section of clients lacking adequate financial transaction knowledge also depends on a one-to-one relationship with the agent for their financial needs, such as loans. Furthermore, gender can significantly influence trust in financial transactions. For example, financial transactions may be more comfortable for female clients when handled by female agents [6].

For both ROA and ROE, the estimated coefficient for the number of agents is negative and statistically significant, indicating that an increase in the number of agents does not necessarily increase bank profit. The findings are in line with hypothesis H1 (Section Hypotheses Development) and are also similar to the results outlined in the previous studies [28,37]. In the context of Bangladesh, one plausible explanation for our results is that expanding the number of agents does not automatically enhance bank profitability. This is because a higher number of agents does not necessarily lead to increased liabilities through customer deposits, nor does it reduce operational expenses. Moreover, agents in remote areas may struggle to identify viable borrowers, limiting credit growth. Although agent banking was introduced in Bangladesh in 2016, most banks were unable to initiate loan disbursement through agents until 2018. As noted in Section 4, paragraph 2 of the manuscript, only nine banks had a transaction history involving both deposits and credit disbursements via agent banking outlets during our study period (2018Q1–2024Q4). To ensure a comprehensive analysis of agent banking's impact on bank performance, we selected banks with fully operational agent banking services covering both deposit mobilization and lending activities.

Many researchers, including [11,12,14,21,25–27,59,60], find a significant positive link between the number of agents and the financial performance of banks. The divergence from earlier studies may also be due to variations in sample selection, study periods, data sets, and methodological approaches. Specifically, the differences between the findings of this study and those of [11] can be attributed to several contextual and methodological factors. Alam et al. analyzed data from the early growth phase of agent banking in Bangladesh, during which expansion likely contributed to new market penetration and asset accumulation. In contrast, this study examines a more recent period marked by potential agent saturation, where further expansion may not yield proportional gains due to diminishing returns. Moreover, the current research adopts a more rigorous methodological framework by incorporating comprehensive performance metrics (ROA and ROE) and accounting for cost burdens, such as network maintenance and oversight. Additionally, our study restricts its analysis to banks that have fully functional agent banking operations (i.e., both deposits and lending), which was not a consideration in [11] sample selection. Finally, differences in macroeconomic conditions and institutional characteristics may further explain the conflicting outcomes. Thus, the originality of our research lies in its comprehensive approach, updated dataset, focus on matured operational phases, and a nuanced evaluation of both the positive and negative implications of agent banking on financial performance—advancing the understanding beyond the foundational insights provided by [11]. Overall, the results of this study suggest that the effectiveness of agent banking depends not only on the number of agents deployed but also on their operational efficiency, utilization levels, and alignment with the bank's broader strategic objectives.

The estimated coefficient for deposit mobilization by agent banks is positive for both ROA and ROE. However, the coefficient is not statistically significant. The positive magnitude of the coefficient supports hypotheses H4 (Section Hypotheses Development) and is also similar to the results reported in previous empirical studies [11,14,26,28,29]. The potential reasons for such positive magnitude could be that most of the commercial banks in Bangladesh utilize their agent banking network for deposit mobilization, especially from rural areas, since agent banking has emerged as an effective channel for deposit mobilization, especially in underserved and rural regions, enabling banks to expand their customer base at a lower operational cost.

The estimated coefficients for total remittance collection are negative for both ROA and ROE, where the result is statistically significant for ROA. The negative magnitude of the coefficient for total remittance is opposite to hypotheses H6 (Section Hypotheses Development) and also dissimilar to the previous studies where the authors find a positive relationship between remittance flow and the financial performance of commercial banks [26,28,37–39]. This unexpected finding may be explained by several contextual factors specific to Bangladesh's banking environment. First, while remittance inflows are substantial in volume, banks often act merely as intermediaries in these transactions, earning relatively low margins. The fees associated with processing remittances are regulated and capped, limiting profit generation despite high volumes. Second, remittance funds are typically directed toward household consumption rather than savings or investment products, which constrains the banks' ability to mobilize these funds for revenue-generating loans or financial instruments. In Bangladesh, especially in rural areas, foreign remittances are received by agents using mobile phone banking, and these remittances are deposited into the customers' accounts. Therefore, the increase in remittances increases the liability of the agents. Moreover, the high competition among banks and non-bank financial institutions for remittance services often leads to promotional costs and incentives that further erode potential profitability. These dynamics suggest that an increase in remittance volumes does not necessarily translate into improved financial performance for banks. On the contrary, operational costs related to remittance services may outweigh the benefits, particularly when not accompanied by broader financial intermediation strategies. This finding holds important implications for policymakers and bank managers, indicating a need to redesign remittance-linked products that go beyond transactional services and foster deeper financial engagement with remittance-receiving clients.

The estimated coefficient for the number of agent banking outlets is positive for both ROA and ROE, and the coefficient is statistically significant for ROA but not for ROE. The findings support hypothesis H2 (Section Hypotheses Development) and also similar results found in several empirical studies [11,14,31]. Both deposit mobilization and loan disbursement increase, and eventually, more financial intermediation is possible due to the increased number of agent banking outlets across the country. Therefore, bank profit increases due to more earnings from bank assets, i.e., loans and advances through agent banking services utilizing the bank deposit.

The estimated coefficient for the number of agent banking accounts is negative for ROA and positive for ROE. However, the coefficients are not statistically significant for both ROA and ROE. The findings support hypothesis H3 (Section Hypotheses Development) for ROA. Several empirical studies also find a significant negative relation between the number of agent banking accounts and bank profitability [13,28–30]. The reason for such a negative relationship could be high maintenance costs and the short tenure of deposits, and also, banks may not utilize or allocate the funds deposited in the agent banking accounts effectively.

6. Robustness Check

To verify the robustness of the findings presented in Section 5, a pooled ordinary least squares (OLS) regression model is estimated using the sample data. Table 3 reports the results obtained from the OLS regression. Table 3 presents the OLS results, which show that the signs, magnitudes, and statistical significance levels of the estimated coefficients largely correspond to those from the random-effect model demonstrated in Table 2.

To assess multicollinearity in STATA, common approaches include the variance inflation factor (VIF) and correlation matrix analysis. In this study, a correlation matrix was generated using the appropriate STATA command to examine the potential collinearity among the independent variables. As shown in Table 4, none of the correlation coefficients approach ± 1, indicating low multicollinearity and supporting the statistical reliability of the regression models.

Table 4. Correlation matrix of variables.

Variables	AG	OUT	AC	TD	TC	TR
AG	1					
OUT	0.738	1				
AC	0.763	0.720	1			
TD	0.581	0.660	0.747	1		
TC	0.472	0.479	0.458	0.553	1	
TR	0.587	0.688	0.768	0.736	0.616	1

7. Theoretical and Practical Implications

This study provides both theoretical and practical implications that enhance the understanding of FinTech-enabled agent banking in emerging economies, particularly Bangladesh. Theoretically, the findings reinforce the agency theory [15] by illustrating how agent banking functions through a principal–agent framework, where agents extend banking services on behalf of commercial banks. The study also affirms financial intermediation theory [16], demonstrating that agent banking strengthens the intermediary role of banks by mobilizing deposits and disbursing credit in rural and underserved regions.

Moreover, the study contributes to the broader FinTech and banking literature by empirically validating that not all agent banking indicators yield uniform performance outcomes, a conclusion consistent with the mixed results observed in prior research. For instance, the significant positive impact of credit disbursement and agent outlets on ROA and ROE corroborates earlier findings [21,26,28,34], which emphasized the role of targeted loan delivery and geographical accessibility in improving bank performance. Conversely, the negative association between the number of agents and profitability challenges the generalized belief in expansion-driven growth, aligning instead with [28,37], who caution that indiscriminate agent growth can inflate costs without proportional returns.

Additionally, the insignificant effect of deposit mobilization and account numbers on ROA and ROE reflects the earlier literature, which suggests that such inputs may not translate directly into improved profitability without efficient fund allocation or product diversification [13,30]. Similarly, the unexpected negative effect of remittance flows on ROA contradicts much of the existing literature [26,38,39], suggesting that remittance-led profitability depends on broader institutional contexts, pricing structures, and utilization strategies.

Practically, these findings underscore the importance of strategic agent deployment and efficient resource use over sheer expansion. Banks should prioritize productivity-enhancing technologies and agent training rather than expanding the agent base indiscriminately. Additionally, remittance-linked strategies should be redesigned to channel funds into savings or investment instruments rather than mere transactional services. From a policy standpoint, regulators should support agent banking through capacity-building, digital literacy programs, and gender-sensitive outreach to ensure that FinTech deployment enhances both inclusion and performance. Finally, this study contributed a context-specific understanding of FinTech-enabled agent banking's varied impacts on commercial bank performance in developing economies.

8. Conclusions and Policy Implications

The paper evaluates the effects of agent banking services utilizing FinTech platforms on the financial performance of nine commercial banks in Bangladesh that have been operating full-fledged agent banking services. Employing a panel data regression framework, the study employs bank-level quarterly data for the period 2018Q1–2024Q4 to estimate a random-effects model. The empirical findings indicate that credit disbursement by agent banks has a positive and statistically significant impact on the bank profitability measures, return on assets (ROA), and return on equity (ROE). Similarly, agent banking outlets have a significant positive impact on ROA. However, the number of agents and deposit mobilization do not necessarily affect the profitability of the mother bank. The findings of this study would help the policy makers, bank management, and other stakeholders in their decision-making and in improving the performance of agent banking. Therefore, an appropriate agent banking policy aimed at increasing agent banking outlets using digital platforms based on FinTech is vital for ensuring positive growth in credit disbursement, in order to improve the financial performance of the banking sector in a developing country like Bangladesh.

We acknowledge that, while our dataset covers a recent and extended time period (2018Q1–2024Q4), it includes only those commercial banks in Bangladesh with operational agent banking services offering both deposit and credit disbursement. This sample selection enhances the quality of the analysis but may limit generalizability to banks that have not yet reached this level of operational maturity. Additionally, the study is based on secondary financial data and does not incorporate qualitative insights from bank management or field-level agents. Future studies could extend this research by incorporating primary data, including surveys or interviews with bank officials, agents, and customers, to better capture the behavioral and operational challenges that affect agent banking outcomes. Moreover, exploring regional or rural–urban differences in agent performance could further refine the understanding of agent banking's impact on financial inclusion and profitability.

Author Contributions: Conceptualization, M.M.I., M.A. and I.A.R.; methodology, I.A.R.; software, I.A.R.; validation, I.A.R.; formal analysis, I.A.R.; investigation, I.A.R.; resources, I.A.R.; data curation, I.A.R.; writing—original draft preparation, M.M.I. and I.A.R.; writing—review and editing, M.M.I., M.A. and I.A.R.; visualization, M.M.I.; supervision, M.M.I. and M.A.; project administration, I.A.R., M.M.I. and M.A. All authors have read and agreed to the published version of the manuscript.

Funding: This research received no external funding.

Institutional Review Board Statement: Not applicable.

Informed Consent Statement: Not applicable.

Data Availability Statement: The data sets that support the findings of this study are openly available upon request. Data is available at https://www.bb.org.bd/en/index.php/publication/publictn/2/68 (accessed on 4 August 2025).

Conflicts of Interest: Iftekhar Ahmed Robin was employed by Central Bank of Bangladesh. The authors declare no conflicts of interest.

Appendix A

Table A1. Sources and definitions of measurement variables.

Variables	Definition/Measures	Sources for Measurement Variables
Dependent Variables		
ROA	Net Profit after tax/Total Assets	[21,28]
ROE	Net Profit after tax/Total Equity	[11,21,28]
Independent Variables		
AG	Number of Agents	[11,21,28]
AC	Number of accounts	[28]
OUT	Number of Outlets	[28]
TC	Total Credit/loans	[11,28]
TD	Total Deposits	[11,21,28]
REM	Total Remittance	[26,28]

Table A2. List of sample banks.

Name of the Sample Banks	Sample Period
Bank Asia PLC	2018Q1–2024Q4
Dutch-Bangla Bank PLC	2018Q1–2024Q4
Al-Arafah Islami Bank PLC	2018Q1–2024Q4
Islami Bank Bangladesh PLC	2018Q1–2024Q4
Mutual Trust Bank PLC	2018Q1–2024Q4
The City Bank PLC	2018Q1–2024Q4
Brac Bank PLC	2018Q1–2024Q4
NRB Bank PLC	2018Q1–2024Q4
Modhumoti Bank PLC	2018Q1–2024Q4

Source: Authors' compilation.

Table A3. Fixed-effect and random-effect model results: ROA and ROE.

	ROA		ROE	
	FE	RE	FE	FE
Number of Agents (AG)	−0.001 (0.004)	−0.003 ** (0.001)	−0.003 (0.052)	−0.036 ** (0.018)
Number of Outlets (OUT)	0.002 (0.006)	0.005 *** (0.002)	0.011 (0.073)	0.028 (0.023)
Total Credit (TC)	−0.000 (0.001)	0.001 *** (0.009)	−0.010 (0.009)	0.011 *** (0.004)
Total Deposit (TD)	0.001 (0.002)	0.002 (0.001)	0.005 (0.022)	0.005 (0.014)
Number of Accounts (AC)	0.000 (0.001)	−0.001 (0.001)	0.011 (0.019)	0.008 (0.012)
Total Remittance (REM)	0.001 (0.002)	−0.002 ** (0.001)	0.019 (0.024)	−0.003 (0.011)
Constant	−0.004 (0.006)	0.001 (0.003)	−0.096 (0.078)	−0.005 (0.034)
R-squared	0.005	0.123	0.037	0.113
Hausman test	Prob χ^2 = 0.003:RE		Prob χ^2 = 0.000:RE	
Total observations	234		234	

Source: Authors' estimation using STATA. FE stands for fixed-effect model, and RE is random-effect model. Standard errors are in parentheses. *** denotes statistical significance level at 1%; ** denotes the level of statistical significance at 5%.

References

1. Zhu, Z. The Role of fintech in the Innovation and Transformation of the Banking Industry. *Adv. Econ. Manag. Political Sci.* **2023** *16*, 9–16. [CrossRef]
2. Gupta, R.; Gupta, A. Agent banking in the FinTech era: Opportunities for financial inclusion. *J. Financ. Technol.* **2020**, *15*, 25–38.
3. Veniard, C. How Agent Banking Changes the Economics of Small Accounts. 2010. Available online: https://docs.gatesfoundation org/documents/agent-banking.pdf (accessed on 22 December 2024).
4. Bangladesh Bank. *Quarterly Report on Agent Banking, October–December*; Financial Inclusion Department, Bangladesh Bank: Dhaka Bangladesh, 2024.
5. Buri, S.; Cull, R.; Gine, X.; Harten, S.; Heitmann, S. *Banking with Agents: Experimental Evidence from Senegal*; World Bank: Washinton DC, USA, 2018.
6. Cull, R.; Gine, X.; Harten, S.; Heitmann, S.; Rusu, A.B. Agent banking in a highly under-developed financial sector: Evidence from Democratic Republic of Congo. *World Dev.* **2018**, *107*, 54–74. [CrossRef]
7. Kumar, A.; Nair, A.; Parsons, A.; Urdapilleta, E. *Expanding Bank Outreach Through Retail Partnerships: Correspondent Banking in Brazil*; World Bank: Washington, DC, USA, 2006.
8. Margaret, K.G.; Ruth, N.K. The effect of banking services on the business performance of bank agents in Kenya. *Cogent Bus Manag.* **2019**, *6*, 16844420. [CrossRef]
9. Nezianya, N.P.; Izuchukwu, D. Impact of agent banking on the performance of deposit money banks in Nigeria. *Res. J. Financ Account.* **2014**, *5*, 35–41.
10. Zaffar, M.A.; Kumar, R.L.; Zhao, K. Using agent-based modelling to investigate diffusion of mobile-based branchless banking services in a developing country. *Decis. Support Syst.* **2019**, *117*, 62–74. [CrossRef]
11. Alam, M.M.; Bhowmik, D.; Bhowmik, D. The impact of agent banking on financial performance of commercial banks in Bangladesh. *IOSR J. Econ. Financ.* **2020**, *11*, 13–20.
12. Ndambuki, D. The Effect of Agency Banking on Profitability of Commercial Banks in Kenya. Ph.D. Thesis, University of Nairobi, Nairobi, Kenya, 2016.
13. Balaylar, N.A.; Karımlı, T.; Bulut, A.E. The effect of non-interest income on bank profitability and risk: Evidence from Turkey. *Rev. Galega De Econ. Publicación Interdiscip. Da Fac. De Cienc. Económicas E Empres.* **2025**, *34*, 1. [CrossRef]
14. Hasan, Z. The Effects of Agent Banking on the Profitability of Commercial Banks in Bangladesh. Ph.D. Thesis, Brac University, Dhaka, Bangladesh, 2019.
15. Jensen, M.C.; Meckling, W.H. Theory of the firm: Managerial behavior, agency costs and ownership structure. *J. Financ. Econ.* **1976**, *3*, 305–360. [CrossRef]
16. Diamond, D.W. Financial intermediation and delegated monitoring. *Rev. Econ. Stud.* **1984**, *51*, 393–414. [CrossRef]
17. Siddiquie, M.R. Agent banking, the revolution in financial service sector of Bangladesh. *IOSR J. Econ. Financ.* **2014**, *5*, 28–32 [CrossRef]
18. Davis, F.D. Perceived usefulness, perceived ease of use, and user acceptance of information technology. *MIS Q.* **1989**, *13*, 319–340 [CrossRef]
19. Lyman, T.; Ivatury, G.; Staschen, S. Use of agents in branchless banking for the poor: Rewards, risks, and regulation. *Focus Note* **2006**, *38*, 1.
20. Ogoti, K.I.; Omwenga, Q.J. Influence of agency banking on the financial performance of commercial banks in kisii county, Kenya *Int. J. Soc. Sci. Inf. Technol.* **2023**, *9*, 172–181.
21. Karangwa, F.; Mulyungi, D.P. Effect of agency banking services on financial performance of commercial banks: A case of equity bank. *Int. J. Manag. Commer. Innov.* **2018**, *6*, 758–765.
22. Idoko, E.C.; Chukwu, M.A. Does Agency Banking Trigger Financial Inclusion? Perspective of Residents in Rural Setting. *Sch. Bull.* **2022**, *8*, 180–188. [CrossRef]
23. Mwando, S. Contribution of agency banking on financial performance of commercial banks in Kenya. *J. Econ. Sustain. Dev.* **2013**, *20*, 26–34.
24. Aduda, J.; Kiragu, P.; Ndwiga, J.M. The relationship between agency banking and financial performance of commercial banks in Kenya. *J. Financ. Invest. Anal.* **2013**, *2*, 97–117.
25. Ayadi, O.F.; Oke, B.; Oladimeji, A.; Aladejebi, O. Agency Banking in Nigeria: Impact and Impediments. *SEDME Small Enterp. Dev. Manag. Ext. J.* **2023**, *50*, 227–247. [CrossRef]
26. Hossain, M.I.; Al-Amin, M.; Toha, M.A. Are commercial agent banking services worthwhile for financial inclusion? *Bus. Manag. Strategy* **2021**, *12*, 206–227. [CrossRef]
27. Waithanji, M.N. The Impact of Agent Banking as a Financial Deepening Initiative in Kenya. Ph.D. Thesis, University of Nairobi, Nairobi, Kenya, 2012. Available online: https://erepository.uonbi.ac.ke/handle/11295/6933?utm_source=chatgpt.com (accessed on 7 February 2025).

8. Hasan, M.K. Agent Banks Make a Notable Contribution. The Financial Express, Bangladesh. 2023. Available online: https://thefinancialexpress.com.bd/views/reviews/agent-banks-make-a-notable-contribution (accessed on 7 February 2025).
9. Dotun, O.V.; Adesugba, A.K. The impact of agency banking on financial performance of listed deposit money banks in Nigeria. *J. Corp. Financ. Manag. Bank. Syst.* **2022**, *2*, 14–24. [CrossRef]
0. Pasiouras, F.; Kosmidou, K. Factors influencing the profitability of domestic and foreign commercial banks in the European Union. *Res. Int. Bus. Financ.* **2007**, *21*, 222–237. [CrossRef]
1. Oburu, K.N. Effect of Agency Banking on the Financial Performance of Commercial Banks in Kenya. Ph.D. Thesis, University of Nairobi, Nairobi, Kenya, 2018. Available online: https://erepository.uonbi.ac.ke/bitstream/handle/11295/94726/Kambua%2CBelita%20D_The%20effect%20of%20agency%20banking%20on%20financial%20performance%20of%20commercial%20banks%20in%20kenya.pdf?sequence=1 (accessed on 8 February 2025).
2. Nisha, N.; Nawrin, K.; Bushra, A. Agent banking and financial inclusion: The case of Bangladesh. *Int. J. Asian Bus. Inf. Manag.* **2020**, *11*, 127–141. [CrossRef]
3. Hirtle, B. The impact of network size on bank branch performance. *J. Bank. Financ.* **2007**, *31*, 3782–3805. [CrossRef]
4. Hasan, M.S.A.; Manurung, A.H.; Usman, B. Determinants of bank profitability with size as moderating variable. *J. Appl. Financ. Bank.* **2020**, *10*, 153–166.
5. Hasan, J. Agent Banking Lending up 56PC, Deposit 15.4pc in Q4'24. The Financial Express, Bangladesh. 2025. Available online: https://thefinancialexpress.com.bd/economy/agent-banking-lending-up-56pc-deposit-154pc-in-q424 (accessed on 8 February 2025).
6. Khan, T.A. Agent Banking's Impact on Financial Inclusion in Bangladesh. Asian Banking & Finance. 2024. Available online: https://asianbankingandfinance.net/retail-banking/commentary/agent-bankings-impact-financial-inclusion-in-bangladesh?utm_source=chatgpt.com (accessed on 12 February 2025).
7. Das, B. Impact of Agent Banking on Bank Profitability in Bangladesh. Master's Thesis, University of Dhaka, Dhaka, Bangladesh, 2021. Available online: https://www.scribd.com/document/745526778/IMPACT-OF-AGENT-BANKING-ON-BANK-PROFITABILITY-IN-BANGLADESH? (accessed on 12 February 2025).
8. Aggarwal, R.; Demirgüç-Kunt, A.; Pería, M.S.M. Do remittances promote financial development? *J. Dev. Econ.* **2011**, *96*, 255–264. [CrossRef]
9. World Bank. *COVID-19 Crisis Through a Migration Lens*; Migration and Development Brief 32; World Bank: Washington, DC, USA, 2020. Available online: https://documents1.worldbank.org/curated/en/989721587512418006/pdf/COVID-19-Crisis-Through-a-Migration-Lens.pdf (accessed on 12 February 2025).
0. Giuliano, P.; Ruiz-Arranz, M. Remittances, financial development, and growth. *J. Dev. Econ.* **2009**, *90*, 144–152. [CrossRef]
1. Demirgüç-Kunt, A.; López Córdova, E.; Martínez Pería, M.S.; Woodruff, C. Remittances and banking sector breadth and depth: Evidence from Mexico. *J. Dev. Econ.* **2011**, *95*, 229–241. [CrossRef]
2. Mundaca, B.G. Remittances, financial market development, and economic growth: The case of Latin America and the Caribbean. *Rev. Dev. Econ.* **2009**, *13*, 288–303. [CrossRef]
3. FATF. *International Standards on Combating Money Laundering and the Financing of Terrorism & Proliferation*; Financial Action Task Force (FATF): Paris, France, 2012. Available online: https://www.fatf-gafi.org/content/dam/fatf-gafi/recommendations/FATF%20Recommendations%202012.pdf (accessed on 12 February 2025).
4. Ramadugu, R. Fintech, Remittances, and Financial Inclusion: A Case Study of Cross-Border Payments in Developing Economies. *J. Comput. Inf. Technol.* **2023**, *3*. Available online: https://universe-publisher.com/index.php/jcit/issue/view/3 (accessed on 12 February 2025).
5. Zins, A.; Weill, L. The determinants of financial inclusion in Africa. *Rev. Dev. Financ.* **2016**, *6*, 46–57. [CrossRef]
6. Irura, N.; Munjiru, M. Technology Adoption and the Banking Agency in Rural Kenya. *J. Sociol. Res.* **2013**, *4*, 249–266. [CrossRef]
7. Darda, A. From Shops to Service Centers: The Rise of Agent Banking in Africa. 2024. Available online: https://amitdarda.com/from-shops-to-service-centers-the-rise-of-agent-banking-in-africa/?utm_source (accessed on 12 February 2025).
8. Coffie, C.P.K.; Hongjiang, Z. FinTech market development and financial inclusion in Ghana: The role of heterogeneous actors. *Technol. Forecast. Soc. Change* **2023**, *186*, 122127. [CrossRef]
9. Shaikh, A.A.; Glavee-Geo, R.; Karjaluoto, H.; Hinson, R.E. Mobile money as a driver of digital financial inclusion. *Technol. Forecast. Soc. Change* **2023**, *186*, 122158. [CrossRef]
0. Senyo, P.K.; Osabutey, E.L.; Seny Kan, K.A. Pathways to improving financial inclusion through mobile money: A fuzzy set qualitative comparative analysis. *Inf. Technol. People* **2021**, *34*, 1997–2017. [CrossRef]
1. Al-Amin, M.; Mia, R.; Hasan, S.M. Fintech adoption and its impact on bank profitability: A study of Bangladeshi commercial banks. *Cost Manag.* **2024**, *52*, 27–40.
2. Ozili, P.K. Impact of digital finance on financial inclusion and stability. *Borsa Istanb. Rev.* **2018**, *18*, 329–340. [CrossRef]
3. Shaikh, N.A. Fintech: A changing agent for the banking, financial industry. In *Pakistan & Gulf Economist*; Economist Publications Limited: Karachi, Pakistan, 2023; Volume 42, pp. 30–32.

54. Ha, D.; Le, P.; Nguyen, D.K. Financial inclusion and fintech: A state-of-the-art systematic literature review. *Financ. Innov.* **2025**, *11*, 69. [CrossRef]
55. Rahmani, M.S.; Azam, M.K. FinTech and digital transformation in the banking sector: A systematic literature review. *Int. J. Res. Financ. Manag.* **2025**, *8*, 639–649. [CrossRef]
56. Gabor, D.; Brooks, S. The digital revolution in financial inclusion: International development in the fintech era. In *Material Cultures of Financialization*; Routledge: Abingdon, UK, 2020; pp. 69–82.
57. Antao, S.; Karnik, A. Bank performance and noninterest income: Evidence from countries in the Asian region. *Asia-Pac. Financ. Mark.* **2022**, *29*, 477–505. [CrossRef]
58. Zhang, X.; Li, Z. FinTech: The disruptive force reducing bank competition pressure. *Emerg. Mark. Rev.* **2025**, *65*, 101237. [CrossRef]
59. Seda, M.A. Effects of Agency Banking on the Financial Performance of Commercial Banks in Kenya. Ph.D. Thesis, University of Nairobi, Nairobi, Kenya, 2016.
60. Kambua, B.D. The Effect of Agency Banking on Financial Performance of Commercial Banks in Kenya. Ph.D. Thesis, United States International University Africa, Nairobi, Kenya, 2015. Available online: https://erepo.usiu.ac.ke/bitstream/handle/11732/3198/SIMBOLEY%20BRENDA%20CHEMUTAI%20MBA%202017.pdf?sequence=1 (accessed on 7 February 2025).

FinTech

Article

A Multi-Paradigm Ethical Framework for Hybrid Intelligence in Blockchain Technology and Cryptocurrency Systems Governance

Haris Alibašić

Department of Business Administration, University of West Florida, 11000 University Parkway, Pensacola, FL 32514, USA; halibasic@uwf.edu

Abstract

The integration of artificial intelligence and human decision-making within blockchain systems has raised complex ethical considerations, necessitating the development of comprehensive theoretical frameworks. This research develops a multi-paradigm ethical framework addressing the ethical dimensions of hybrid intelligence—the dynamic interplay between human judgment and artificial intelligence—in the governance of blockchain technology and cryptocurrency systems. Drawing upon complexity theory and institutional theory, this study employs a theory synthesis methodology to investigate inherent paradoxes within hybrid intelligence systems, including how transparency creates new opacities in AI decision-making, decentralization enables centralized control, and algorithmic efficiency undermines ethical sensitivity. Through PRISMA-compliant systematic literature analysis of 50 relevant publications and theoretical synthesis, this research demonstrates how blockchain technology fundamentally redefines hybrid intelligence by establishing novel forms of trust, accountability, and collective decision-making. The framework advances three testable propositions regarding emergent intelligence properties, adaptive capacity, and institutional legitimacy while providing practical governance principles and implementation methodologies for blockchain developers, regulators, and participants. This study contributes theoretically by bridging the fields of complex systems and institutional analysis, integrating complex adaptive systems with institutional legitimacy processes through a multi-paradigm integration methodology. It delivers an ethical framework that addresses accountability distribution in Decentralized Autonomous Organizations, quantifies ethical challenges across major platforms, and offers empirically validated guidelines for balancing algorithmic autonomy with human oversight in decentralized systems.

Keywords: blockchain technology; hybrid intelligence; decentralized governance; institutional theory; complexity theory; ethical AI; cryptocurrency governance

JEL Classification: G28; O33; D02

1. Introduction

1.1. Blockchain Technology Foundations

Blockchain technology operates as a distributed ledger system where transactions are verified through cryptographic consensus mechanisms rather than centralized authorities [1–4]. The fundamental architecture consists of blocks containing transaction data, cryptographically linked in chronological order, and maintained across a network of participating nodes [4–6]. Consensus mechanisms—including Proof of Work (PoW),

Proof of Stake (PoS), and Delegated Proof of Stake (DPoS)—ensure network agreement on transaction validity without requiring trusted intermediaries [5–8].

Smart contracts represent self-executing code with predetermined conditions that automatically enforce agreements when specified criteria are met [8–10]. These programmable protocols enable automated governance while maintaining transparency through immutable record-keeping on the distributed ledger [10–12]. The decentralized architecture eliminates single points of failure, ensuring that no central authority can unilaterally alter the transaction history or system rules [12–14].

This technological foundation introduces new governance challenges when artificial intelligence algorithms interact with human decision-makers within decentralized networks [14–17]. Unlike traditional centralized systems where accountability chains are clearly defined, blockchain systems distribute both authority and responsibility among network participants, creating complex accountability relationships that demand new ethical frameworks for effective governance [16–19].

1.2. *Hybrid Intelligence in Decentralized Systems*

Hybrid intelligence in blockchain contexts refers to collaborative decision-making systems where human cognitive capabilities augment algorithmic processing in real-time governance scenarios [18–20]. This integration manifests through several key mechanisms: human oversight protocols that define when and how human intervention occurs in automated processes, algorithmic autonomy boundaries that establish clear limits on AI decision-making authority, feedback loop structures that enable continuous learning between human and machine components, and intervention triggers that automatically escalate decisions to human oversight when predetermined thresholds are exceeded [20–22].

The control mechanisms governing hybrid intelligence operate through layered governance architectures [22,23]. At the operational level, smart contracts execute routine transactions autonomously while maintaining audit trails for human review [23,24]. At the tactical level, human validators make decisions regarding protocol modifications, dispute resolution, and exception handling [24,25]. At the strategic level, community governance processes determine fundamental system parameters, ethical guidelines, and long-term development priorities [26–30].

The convergence of blockchain technology, artificial intelligence (AI), and human decision-making has fundamentally transformed organizational intelligence and financial governance paradigms [1–10]. Blockchain technology, initially developed for cryptocurrencies, has evolved into a transformative force across multiple domains, reshaping governance structures and decision-making processes that challenge traditional organizational boundaries [10–15]. This evolution has accelerated with the integration of artificial intelligence within blockchain ecosystems, creating hybrid intelligence—the dynamic interplay between human judgment and machine learning algorithms that work collaboratively within governance structures [15–19].

Hybrid intelligence in blockchain contexts refers to socio-technical systems where human judgment and artificial intelligence interact through decentralized protocols to produce emergent organizational intelligence that exceeds the capabilities of either component alone [20–22]. This integration represents a critical frontier in decentralized systems, leading to significant innovations in organizational governance evident in the emergence of Decentralized Autonomous Organizations (DAOs) and sophisticated trading platforms [23–28].

However, these systems exhibit a fundamental 'governance paradox'—their technical architectures and institutional realities operate at cross purposes, manifesting in documented failures, including FTX's algorithmic oversight gaps and Ethereum DAO's plutocratic governance [25–28]. Recent theoretical developments suggest that blockchain systems fundamentally transform business models through multiple mechanisms, including disintermediation, transparency enhancement, trust creation, and ecosystem development [28–30]. Yet governance power is frequently concentrated among a small percentage of stakeholders, creating tensions between the ideals of decentralization and operational realities [30–32].

Despite their transformative potential, existing theoretical frameworks inadequately address the unique features of hybrid intelligence in blockchain contexts. Traditional organizational theories struggle to conceptualize the fluid boundaries between human and machine decision-making, while conventional ethical frameworks remain rooted in centralized system paradigms that translate poorly to decentralized environments [32–35]. Contemporary governance models often fail to account for the emergent properties inherent in hybrid intelligence systems, particularly regarding how collective decision-making arises from interactions between algorithmic processes and human agents.

This study addresses two fundamental research questions: (1) how do complex human and artificial intelligence interactions within blockchain systems generate emergent decentralized intelligence properties? (2) What institutional mechanisms enable the ethical governance of hybrid intelligence in cryptocurrency ecosystems amid competing transparency and privacy demands?

The primary objective is to develop a comprehensive theoretical framework illuminating the ethical dimensions of hybrid intelligence in blockchain systems, particularly in cryptocurrency contexts. Recent events underscore the timeliness and importance of this research. The collapse of major cryptocurrency exchanges due to governance failures has highlighted critical weaknesses in existing hybrid intelligence frameworks, emphasizing the need for more sophisticated theoretical frameworks addressing hybrid intelligence's unique ethical challenges in blockchain contexts [34–40].

This research makes several significant contributions to both the theoretical appreciation and practical implementation of hybrid intelligence in blockchain systems. Theoretically, it integrates complexity and institutional theories to analyze hybrid intelligence in blockchain contexts, developing an empirically grounded ethical framework for analyzing ethical challenges in decentralized systems. Practically, it offers governance guidance for blockchain developers, regulators, and participants, postulating conceptual tools for designing and implementing ethical governance structures for hybrid intelligence systems.

1.3. Ethical Theoretical Foundations

The ethical dimensions of hybrid intelligence in blockchain systems require grounding in established moral philosophy while addressing novel challenges posed by decentralized algorithmic governance. Three primary ethical frameworks provide foundational analysis for this research:

Consequentialist analysis examines the outcomes and consequences of hybrid intelligence decisions within blockchain systems. This framework evaluates whether algorithmic automation and human oversight produce beneficial results for stakeholders, focusing on measurable impacts such as transaction security, user protection, and system efficiency. Consequentialist ethics proves particularly relevant for assessing the trade-offs between automated efficiency and human oversight, as decisions must be evaluated based on their actual effects on network participants rather than adherence to predetermined rules [28–34].

Virtue ethics in algorithmic decision-making addresses the character and moral qualities embedded within both human governance decisions and algorithmic processes. This framework examines whether blockchain governance systems foster virtuous behavior among participants and whether algorithmic designs embody ethical virtues such as fairness, transparency, and prudence. Virtue ethics becomes especially important when considering how hybrid intelligence systems shape the moral development of communities and whether automated processes reinforce or undermine ethical character among users [35–41].

Deontological constraints on AI autonomy establish fundamental duties and constraints that govern the extent of artificial intelligence authority within blockchain systems. This framework defines inviolable principles that must be maintained regardless of consequences, such as respect for human autonomy, protection of fundamental rights, and preservation of human dignity [37–42]. Deontological ethics provides crucial boundaries for AI decision-making authority, ensuring that efficiency gains do not compromise fundamental ethical principles [40–43].

These ethical foundations intersect with specific blockchain governance challenges: algorithmic transparency requirements (deontological duty to explainability), stakeholder welfare optimization (consequentialist evaluation of outcomes), and community character development (virtue ethics in governance design). The integration of these frameworks addresses gaps in the existing blockchain ethics literature, which often focuses on technical or economic considerations while neglecting foundational moral principles.

1.4. Literature Review—Blockchain Technology and Governance Evolution

The integration of artificial intelligence and human decision-making within blockchain systems represents a significant evolution in the field, particularly evident in the development of Decentralized Autonomous Organizations (DAOs) that combine automated governance with human oversight [44–52]. These hybrid intelligence structures necessitate new ethical frameworks addressing the complexities of algorithmic and human decision-making processes [53–59].

Contemporary advancements in machine learning and data analytics are revolutionizing the effectiveness of hybrid intelligence systems. Federated learning offers a decentralized approach to training algorithms without sharing sensitive data, preserving privacy while enhancing model accuracy [55–60]. This innovation holds significant potential for improving decision-making processes within blockchain environments.

Recent research has explored how blockchain-based AI systems transform banking operations, demonstrating significant improvements in operational efficiency and fraud detection capabilities [54–56]. Similarly, investor motivations in blockchain ecosystems have been identified as influencing investment decisions and stakeholder engagement through the perceived trustworthiness of hybrid governance systems. Critical examination of whether decentralized AI implementations are inherently safer than centralized alternatives reveals that while decentralization offers certain security advantages, it also introduces novel vulnerabilities related to consensus manipulation and oracle attacks.

1.5. Ethical Dimensions in Hybrid Intelligence Systems

A comprehensive analysis of the ethical dimensions in blockchain-based hybrid intelligence systems reveals several critical areas requiring governance attention. Accountability emerges as a foundational concern, with distributed responsibility across system components manifesting through complex interactions. From a complexity theory perspective, accountability manifests through distributed responsibility across system components, while institutional theory emphasizes mechanisms for establishing responsibility and governance structures [61–65].

The tension between transparency and privacy represents another crucial ethical dimension. Complexity theory reveals how emergent information asymmetries in complex interactions intersect with institutional theory's normative expectations regarding disclosure and visibility. This theoretical integration highlights the necessity of developing context-sensitive privacy technologies that balance transparency requirements with confidentiality needs.

Regulatory compliance poses distinct challenges in hybrid intelligence systems. The governance implications point toward compliance-by-design frameworks integrating regulatory requirements into technical protocols while accommodating jurisdictional variations. Adaptability emerges as another critical dimension, with complexity theory highlighting self-organizing capacity to respond to changing conditions while institutional theory identifies resistance to change and path dependency challenges [62,63].

1.6. Theoretical Frameworks for Blockchain Governance

Complexity theory has proven particularly valuable for understanding blockchain systems, capturing their self-organizing nature and explaining how emergent behaviors arise from interactions between system components [63,64]. Institutional theory complements complexity perspectives by explaining how blockchain systems gain legitimacy and establish governance norms. Recent applications of institutional theory to blockchain contexts have revealed how these systems navigate competing institutional pressures from technological, regulatory, and community stakeholders [61–66].

Additional theoretical perspectives, including actor-network theory, cryptoeconomics, and transaction cost economics, offer complementary insights into specific aspects of blockchain systems [56–60]. However, actor-network theory often overemphasizes technological agency while keeping limited frameworks for analyzing ethical responsibility. Cryptoeconomics frequently simplifies complex social dynamics by reducing them to economic incentives, thereby delivering insufficient attention to ethical considerations. Transaction cost economics primarily focuses on efficiency gains, offering limited insight into collective governance dynamics.

Our systematic literature review reveals significant theoretical and empirical developments in understanding blockchain technology, hybrid intelligence, and ethical governance. By integrating the focus on emergence and self-organization from complexity theory with the attention to legitimacy and governance structures from institutional theory, researchers can gain a deeper understanding of how hybrid intelligence operates in blockchain systems. However, considerable gaps remain regarding the integration of these domains, particularly in developing frameworks that adequately address the ethical challenges of hybrid intelligence in blockchain systems.

1.7. Multi-Paradigm Integration Approach

This study develops a multi-paradigm theoretical framework integrating complexity theory and institutional theory to analyze hybrid intelligence within blockchain structures. This methodological approach is particularly appropriate for the research domain, enabling the integration of theoretical perspectives that address different aspects of hybrid intelligence in blockchain contexts.

The integration of complexity theory and institutional theory is motivated by their complementary strengths in addressing various aspects of hybrid intelligence in blockchain systems. Complexity theory offers valuable insights into the emergent behaviors and self-organizing processes that characterize interactions between human judgment and artificial intelligence in decentralized environments [60]. However, complexity theory alone offers limited insight into how these emergent systems gain legitimacy, navigate regulatory environments, and establish governance norms across different cultural contexts.

Institutional theory complements these insights by explaining how organizational structures gain legitimacy and respond to institutional pressures across various contexts [61–63]. However, institutional theory offers limited frameworks for understanding the emergent, self-organizing properties of decentralized systems. By integrating these complementary perspectives, the multi-paradigm framework provides a more comprehensive understanding of hybrid intelligence in blockchain contexts than either theoretical perspective could offer independently.

1.8. Conceptual Framework for Hybrid Intelligence

The framework conceptualizes blockchain-based hybrid intelligence as emerging from complex interactions between three key components:

Human agents include individual and collective human decision-makers participating in blockchain governance through various mechanisms, with significant variation across different blockchain implementations. These agents bring contextual knowledge, ethical judgment, and adaptive decision-making capabilities to the hybrid system.

Artificial intelligence systems encompass algorithmic processes performing automated analysis, decision-making, and execution functions, ranging from simple rule-based algorithms to complex machine-learning implementations. These systems provide computational efficiency, pattern recognition, and consistent application of predetermined rules.

Blockchain protocols represent the underlying technical infrastructure establishing rules for consensus, transaction validation, and data management, evolving through planned modifications and emergent adaptations. These protocols establish the structural foundation enabling interaction between human and AI components.

The interactions between these components generate emergent properties characterizing hybrid intelligence in blockchain systems:

Distributed cognition represents collective intelligence emerging from the interaction of human judgment and algorithmic processing, enabling more sophisticated pattern recognition and decision-making than either component could achieve independently.

Adaptive governance encompasses self-organizing structures evolving in response to changing conditions and stakeholder inputs, creating dynamic governance mechanisms that respond to environmental changes.

Institutional evolution involves the development of new norms, rules, and practices, gaining legitimacy within the blockchain ecosystem, and establishing stable governance patterns over time.

1.9. Complexity Theory Application

Complexity theory offers critical insights into the nonlinear interdependencies underlying the emergence of hybrid intelligence in blockchain environments [62–66]. Hybrid intelligence arises from intricate interactions among human agents, AI frameworks, and blockchain protocols, yielding emergent properties that defy reductionist interpretation.

Blockchain networks exemplify self-organizing behavior facilitated by consensus mechanisms and automated governance, contrasting sharply with traditional centralized organizational structures. The theoretical lens elucidates blockchain operations on principles of decentralization, transparency, and trust, fostering adaptability through iterative processes. The adaptive capacity inherent in hybrid intelligence is characterized by algorithmic enhancements and refined human decision-making, creating dynamic feedback loops that resonate with core principles of complexity theory.

Complexity theory offers several specific insights relevant to blockchain-based hybrid intelligence:

Self-organization is evident as blockchain networks exemplify self-organizing behavior facilitated by consensus mechanisms and automated governance protocols, distributing authority across network participants and allowing governance structures to emerge organically from stakeholder interactions.

Nonlinear dynamics manifest as small changes in system parameters or stakeholder behavior disproportionately affect system outcomes, evident in how minor protocol modifications can significantly impact governance dynamics and stakeholder participation.

Adaptive capacity appears as hybrid intelligence systems demonstrate remarkable adaptability through iterative learning processes, algorithmic enhancements, and refined human decision-making, creating dynamic feedback loops that resonate with core principles of complexity theory [65].

The edge of chaos characterizes blockchain systems operating between rigid order and complete randomness, where adaptability and innovation flourish, balancing rigid protocol enforcement and flexible community-driven evolution.

1.10. Institutional Theory Integration

Institutional theory complements complexity theory as a valuable tool for analyzing how hybrid intelligence structures attain legitimacy and institutionalization within various organizational and societal contexts. The three pillars of institutions—regulatory, normative, and cultural–cognitive—offer a framework for analyzing the evolution of governance structures in blockchain settings [66–69].

The regulatory pillar addresses formal rules guiding blockchain operations, evolving in response to unique challenges posed by these technologies. The normative pillar elucidates the influence of social norms and stakeholder expectations on hybrid intelligence systems. The cultural–cognitive pillar emphasizes the importance of shared beliefs within the blockchain ecosystem. Institutional pressures from diverse stakeholders—including users, developers, and regulatory bodies—affect the development and adoption of hybrid intelligence in blockchain contexts.

Institutional theory offers several specific insights relevant to blockchain-based hybrid intelligence:

Legitimacy development explains how blockchain systems gain legitimacy through alignment with existing institutional norms while simultaneously challenging traditional organizational boundaries. This dual process of conformity and disruption shapes how hybrid intelligence systems evolve and gain acceptance in different contexts [68].

Institutional isomorphism reveals that blockchain systems often exhibit isomorphic tendencies despite their decentralized nature, adopting similar governance structures and ethical frameworks in response to shared institutional pressures through coercive, mimetic, and normative mechanisms [61–66].

Institutional complexity recognizes that blockchain systems operate within environments with competing institutional logic from technological, financial, and regulatory domains, creating governance challenges as systems navigate contradictory demands and expectations from diverse stakeholders.

1.11. Theoretical Propositions

The integration of complexity theory and institutional theory yields three theoretical propositions specifying testable hypotheses for future empirical research while offering conceptual clarity regarding how hybrid intelligence operates in blockchain contexts:

Proposition 1: The emergence of hybrid intelligence in blockchain systems stems from the complex interplay between human judgment, artificial intelligence, and consensus mechanisms, yielding collective intelligence that surpasses the capabilities of any individual component.

Proposition 2: The adaptive capacity of blockchain-based hybrid intelligence increases with the diversity of participating agents and the quality of feedback mechanisms between human and algorithmic decision-makers.

Proposition 3: Institutional pressures drive convergence in ethical frameworks and governance structures across blockchain systems despite their technical differences and diverse origins.

These propositions directly connect to the research questions by specifying the mechanisms through which human–AI interactions generate emergent intelligence properties (Proposition 1), identifying factors of system adaptability (Proposition 2), and explaining how these systems gain legitimacy across different institutional contexts (Proposition 3).

2. Materials and Methods

2.1. Research Design

This study employed a qualitative theoretical approach to evaluate the ethical dimensions of hybrid intelligence applications in blockchain technology and cryptocurrency governance. The methodology centered on a documentary analysis of the scholarly literature, theoretical frameworks, and policy documents to comprehensively cognize the ethical and governance implications [66–69].

Following established protocols for conceptual research, this study employed a theory synthesis methodology enabling the development of a multi-paradigm framework addressing different aspects of hybrid intelligence in blockchain contexts [67,68]. The research design comprised four interconnected phases:

A systematic literature review involving a comprehensive analysis of the scholarly literature on blockchain technology, hybrid intelligence, and ethical governance, utilizing systematic review protocols to identify relevant sources and extract key concepts.

Theoretical framework development integrating complexity theory and institutional theory to develop a multi-paradigm framework for analyzing hybrid intelligence in blockchain contexts, involving the identification of complementary insights from each theoretical perspective.

Conceptual analysis applying the theoretical framework to analyze key dimensions of hybrid intelligence in blockchain systems, including emergent behaviors, ethical challenges, and governance dynamics.

Proposition development involves formulating testable propositions based on theoretical insights for future empirical research, connecting theoretical concepts to empirically verifiable hypotheses.

2.2. Data Sources and Selection Criteria

The academic literature sources included peer-reviewed journal articles, conference proceedings, and scholarly works published between 2008 and 2025, with a particular emphasis on studies with empirical evidence regarding hybrid intelligence in blockchain contexts, ethical challenges in decentralized systems, and institutional factors influencing blockchain adoption and legitimacy.

Specialized policy databases provided institutional and regulatory perspectives on blockchain governance and AI ethics. The key databases included the following:

- European Union Legal Database (EUR-Lex): Official documentation of EU AI Act provisions and blockchain regulatory frameworks, selected for comprehensive coverage of institutional AI governance approaches and rigorous peer-review processes.
- OECD AI Policy Observatory: International policy analysis and comparative governance frameworks, chosen for a cross-national perspective on AI governance principles and institutional backing from 38 member countries.
- Stanford HAI Policy Database: Academic policy research on AI governance and ethics, selected for rigorous peer-review processes and specialized focus on AI-human interaction governance.

- IEEE Standards Database: Technical standards for blockchain governance and AI ethics implementation, included for authoritative technical guidance and industry recognition as standard-setting authority.

These databases were selected based on their peer-review processes, institutional backing, and relevance to hybrid intelligence governance challenges. The credibility of these sources derived from their institutional authority, transparent review processes, and recognition within academic and policy communities as authoritative sources for technology governance research.

This review identified 50 relevant publications systematically categorized based on primary focus, theoretical approach, methodological orientation, and empirical context. The categorization revealed key themes, research gaps, and contradictions in the existing literature, stipulating a foundation for theoretical synthesis.

2.3. *Analytical Framework*

The analytical approach employed interpretive techniques to uncover theoretical patterns and relationships in blockchain governance and hybrid intelligence, guided by grounded theory principles [67,68]. The analysis systematically identified key concepts from complexity and institutional theories, determined integration points between theoretical perspectives, developed an integrated framework, and generated testable propositions.

Analytical Tools and Reliability Measures: A bibliometric analysis was conducted using VOSviewer 1.6.18 for visualizing citation networks. Thematic analysis was conducted using NVivo 12 with systematic coding procedures. Theoretical synthesis was performed using the four-approach framework [69], with proposition development validated through the application of interpretive techniques to uncover theoretical patterns and relationships in blockchain governance and hybrid intelligence, guided by principles of grounded theory. The analysis systematically identified key concepts from complexity and institutional theories, determined integration points between theoretical perspectives, developed an integrated framework, and generated testable propositions.

The analysis addressed three interconnected dimensions of hybrid intelligence in blockchain systems:

- Governance mechanisms examining the interplay between formal protocols and informal norms, analyzing how technical rules interact with social governance processes.
- Ethical considerations examine the tensions between transparency, decentralization, and efficiency, identifying fundamental paradoxes that require governance attention.
- Institutional dynamics examining how these systems gain legitimacy and establish governance norms, focusing on the evolution of institutional structures in decentralized environments.

2.4. *Bibliometric Analysis Using PRISMA Protocol*

2.4.1. PRISMA-Compliant Search Strategy and Selection Process

A comprehensive bibliometric analysis was conducted following PRISMA guidelines to systematically map the intellectual landscape of hybrid intelligence in blockchain governance.

Search Strategy: The databases searched included Web of Science, Scopus, Google Scholar, and specialized policy databases, utilizing the following search strategy: ("hybrid intelligence" OR "human-AI collaboration") AND ("blockchain" OR "cryptocurrency" OR "DeFi" OR "DAO"). Search dates: 1–12 June 2025.

PRISMA flow process:

- Initial identification: 247 publications identified through database searches.
- After duplicates were removed, 127 unique publications.

- After screening: 77 publications excluded (not focused on hybrid intelligence, $n = 34$; purely technical, $n = 28$; non-English, $n = 9$; opinion pieces, $n = 6$).
- Final inclusion: 50 publications meeting all inclusion criteria.

2.4.2. Publication Trends and Growth Patterns

The analysis, presented in Table 1, reveals exponential growth in research attention, with 82% of publications emerging after 2018, coinciding with the DeFi boom and the increasing recognition of governance challenges in decentralized systems. The recent period (2023–2025) has shown sustained interest, with significant policy and institutional engagement, including comparative governance studies.

Table 1. Temporal distribution of publications on hybrid intelligence and blockchain governance (2008–2025).

Period	Publications	Cumulative	Growth Rate (%)	Key Developments
2008–2012	3	3	-	Bitcoin emergence, foundational blockchain
2013–2017	6	9	100%	Ethereum, smart contracts, early DAOs
2018–2020	15	24	167%	DeFi emergence, governance tokens
2021–2022	16	40	67%	NFTs, institutional adoption, regulatory focus
2023–2025	10	50	25%	AI integration, hybrid systems, policy frameworks

Figure 1 below illustrates the exponential growth in research on hybrid intelligence and blockchain governance, with the blue line showing cumulative publications and the red line depicting annual output, highlighting the field's acceleration during the DeFi emergence period (2018–2022).

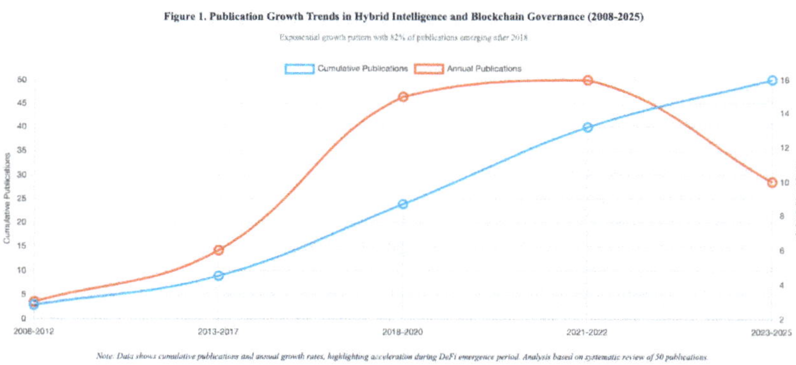

Figure 1. Publication growth trends in hybrid intelligence and blockchain governance (2008–2025).

2.4.3. Thematic Classification and Research Clusters

The enhanced classification in Table 2 reveals growing attention to policy and institutional dimensions (12.0%), including comparative governance studies and crisis management frameworks, reflecting increasing mainstream recognition of hybrid intelligence governance challenges.

Figure 2 presents a research gap analysis matrix identifying critical knowledge gaps across methodological approaches and research domains, with color coding indicating gap severity and research priority levels.

Table 2. Systematic classification of the literature by research focus and methodology.

Research Category	Publications (n)	Percentage (%)	Dominant Methodologies	Key Theoretical Frameworks
Technical Architecture	12	24.0	Case studies, Design science	Systems theory, Computer science
Governance Mechanisms	11	22.0	Qualitative analysis, Comparative analysis	Institutional theory, Political science
Ethical Frameworks	9	18.0	Normative analysis, Philosophy	Ethics, Moral philosophy
Economic Models	7	14.0	Mathematical modeling, Game theory	Economics, Mechanism design
Policy/Institutional	6	12.0	Policy analysis, Comparative studies	Public policy, International relations
Empirical Studies	5	10.0	Surveys, Experiments	Behavioral science, Psychology

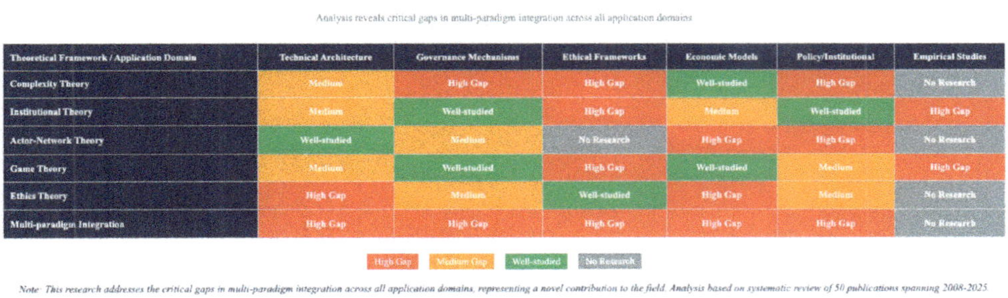

Figure 2. Research gap analysis matrix.

2.4.4. Methodological Analysis

The updated analysis in Table 3 shows growing methodological diversity, with increased policy analysis reflecting institutional interest in hybrid intelligence governance frameworks, including comparative studies of international AI governance approaches.

Table 3. Methodological approaches in the hybrid intelligence and blockchain literature.

Methodology	Frequency	Percentage	Strengths	Limitations Identified
Theoretical/Conceptual	19	38.0%	Framework development	Limited empirical validation
Case Study	11	22.0%	Real-world insights	Generalizability concerns
Literature Review	9	18.0%	Comprehensive synthesis	Static analysis
Policy Analysis	6	12.0%	Institutional insights, Comparative governance	Implementation gaps
Quantitative Analysis	5	10.0%	Measurable outcomes	Complexity reduction

2.4.5. Citation Network Analysis

Table 4 identifies the most influential works at the intersection of hybrid intelligence and blockchain research.

Table 4. Influential works at the intersection of the hybrid intelligence and blockchain literature.

Authors	Year	Research Focus	Theoretical Contribution
Nakamoto, S. * [3]	2008	Blockchain foundation	Decentralized consensus
Buterin, V. [26]	2014	Smart contracts	Programmable governance
Lumineau et al. [41]	2021	Blockchain governance	Institutional analysis
Beck et al. [70]	2018	Governance frameworks	Socio-technical systems
De Filippi & Wright [48]	2018	Legal implications	Regulatory theory

* Note: Nakamoto, S. represents a pseudonym and is categorized as foundational technical documentation rather than traditional academic research.

2.4.6. Research Gaps and Future Directions Matrix

The enhanced analysis in Table 5 reveals cross-cultural governance as an increasingly critical gap, identifying the need for comparative frameworks bridging different national AI governance approaches, alongside persistent challenges in implementing theory into practice. Furthermore, Table 5 reveals the research gaps and innovation opportunities identified in the literature.

Table 5. Identified research gaps and innovation opportunities.

Gap Category	Frequency Mentioned	Innovation Opportunity	Research Priority
Hybrid Intelligence Integration	33 studies	Multi-paradigm frameworks	High
Ethical Decision-Making	28 studies	Embedded ethics systems	High
Cross-cultural Governance	23 studies	Global governance models, Comparative frameworks	High
Stakeholder Participation	18 studies	Inclusive governance	Medium

2.5. Theoretical Justification for Framework Selection

The exclusion of other potential theoretical frameworks requires explicit justification. Actor-network theory (ANT) was not selected as the primary theoretical lens because it often overemphasizes technological agency, providing limited frameworks for analyzing ethical responsibility and moral decision-making, which are core concerns in this research.

Cryptoeconomics was excluded from primary analysis because it frequently reduces complex social dynamics to economic incentives, thereby giving insufficient attention to ethical considerations beyond financial optimization. Transaction cost economics primarily focuses on efficiency gains, offering limited insight into collective governance dynamics and ethical trade-offs.

The selected combination of complexity theory and institutional theory provides superior analytical capacity for understanding both emergent system behaviors (complexity theory) and legitimacy formation processes (institutional theory) while maintaining focus on ethical governance challenges.

2.6. Methodological Limitations

The study's theoretical approach offers valuable insights into the ethical dimensions of hybrid intelligence in blockchain systems, but has inherent limitations requiring acknowledgment:

Validation of theoretical propositions requires validation through case studies, surveys, or experimental approaches in future research to test empirical applicability.

Contextual specificity refers to the theoretical framework's potential need for adaptation to specific blockchain implementations and cultural contexts, as governance dynamics vary across different blockchain ecosystems.

Temporal evolution recognizes that blockchain technology and artificial intelligence are rapidly evolving fields, potentially limiting the long-term applicability of current theoretical insights.

Stakeholder perspectives acknowledge that theoretical analysis primarily draws on academic literature and technical documentation, potentially underrepresenting the diverse perspectives of stakeholders in blockchain ecosystems.

These limitations suggest several directions for future research, including mixed-method approaches combining theoretical analysis with case studies, participatory research engaging diverse stakeholders in collaborative research processes, and longitudinal studies tracking the evolution of hybrid intelligence governance over time.

3. Results

3.1. Emergence of Hybrid Intelligence in Blockchain Systems

The theoretical analysis reveals sophisticated patterns of interaction between human judgment and artificial intelligence within the blockchain's decentralized architecture. Hybrid intelligence emerges through complex feedback loops between human decision-makers, artificial intelligence systems, and blockchain protocols, creating forms of collective intelligence that transcend traditional organizational boundaries.

The specific form of hybrid intelligence in any blockchain implementation depends on several factors. The technical architecture establishes parameters for consensus mechanisms, transaction validation, and data management that shape the interaction between human judgment and artificial intelligence. Different consensus mechanisms generate distinct interaction patterns between human validators and algorithmic processes, resulting in varying forms of hybrid intelligence with unique security characteristics.

Governance design establishes relationships between human decision-makers and artificial intelligence processes through formal and informal structures within blockchain systems. Empirical research reveals that governance design choices directly influence the distribution of decision-making authority between human and algorithmic components, with significant implications for system accountability and responsiveness.

The institutional context shapes the expectations, incentives, and constraints influencing how hybrid intelligence develops in different contexts. Collectivist cultures emphasize community consensus, while individualist cultures prioritize algorithmic efficiency and transparency, resulting in distinct patterns of human–AI interaction.

The emergence of hybrid intelligence manifests through several key mechanisms:

Algorithmic governance with human oversight enables blockchain systems to strike a balance between automated and human-driven governance through carefully designed decision-making structures. AI-driven oracles continuously monitor and adjust cryptocurrency parameters, while human stakeholders retain authority over fundamental protocol modifications and strategic decisions. This balance manifests differently across blockchain implementations, establishing distinct relationships between algorithmic processes and human oversight based on governance priorities.

Collaborative decision support enables successful hybrid intelligence systems to create new forms of collaborative decision-making rather than merely automating existing processes. Smart contracts function as dynamic interfaces between human judgment and artificial intelligence, creating sophisticated feedback loops where AI systems learn from human interventions and decision support through data analysis and pattern recognition.

Adaptive learning processes demonstrate the emergent nature of hybrid intelligence, as these systems adapt to novel challenges. Rather than following predetermined paths, blockchain networks demonstrate remarkable flexibility in combining human insight with algorithmic efficiency to address unexpected governance challenges.

The evidence suggests that effective hybrid intelligence depends on well-designed interfaces between human and algorithmic decision-making, with clear delineation of authority and responsibility. The emergence of hybrid intelligence in blockchain systems creates opportunities and challenges for ethical governance, enhancing security, efficiency, and transparency while introducing novel accountability questions and potential power imbalances.

3.2. *Ethical Challenges and Governance Paradoxes*

The integration of artificial intelligence within blockchain systems presents profound ethical challenges extending beyond traditional governance frameworks. The theoretical analysis identifies three fundamental paradoxes that hybrid intelligence systems must navigate, each representing a critical tension in blockchain governance.

The transparency–opacity paradox manifests when the blockchain's inherent transparency creates new opacities in AI decision-making processes. While the blockchain provides unprecedented transaction transparency through distributed ledgers, algorithmic decision-making processes within the transparent infrastructure often function as "black boxes" with limited interpretability. This paradox becomes especially problematic when examining how algorithmic decisions influence human behavior and vice versa.

Governance responses to this paradox include the implementation of explainable AI approaches requiring algorithmic decisions to include human-readable justifications and mandatory disclosure of decision parameters for high-impact transactions. These approaches demonstrate how thoughtful governance design can address competing ethical values simultaneously rather than treating them as zero-sum trade-offs.

The decentralization–centralization paradox appears when a decentralized blockchain architecture enables concentrated control despite a democratic rhetoric. Detailed examination of governance structures reveals that decision-making authority often concentrates among stakeholders with substantial token holdings, despite the blockchain's democratic aspirations [14,70,71]. This concentration raises fundamental questions about equity and representation in hybrid intelligence systems, as they increasingly influence crucial economic and social choices.

Governance responses include introducing quadratic voting mechanisms to reduce plutocratic influence and delegation mechanisms to distribute influence more equitably while maintaining system efficiency. These innovations demonstrate adaptive responses to governance challenges that emerge from the interaction of the technical architecture and social dynamics.

The efficiency–sensitivity paradox arises when algorithmic optimization for specific technical metrics inadvertently leads to unintended ethical consequences. This paradox underscores how optimization for efficiency often undermines ethical sensitivity, necessitating sophisticated governance approaches that strike a balance between competing values rather than merely maximizing performance metrics.

Governance responses include the development of privacy-preserving machine learning techniques enabling fraud detection without compromising transaction confidentiality through advanced cryptographic methods. These approaches demonstrate how systems can adapt to balance competing ethical priorities through technological innovation guided by ethical principles.

3.2.1. Scale of Ethical Problems

Qualified Ethical Challenges: Analysis of major DeFi protocols' automated decisions lacks sufficient transparency for stakeholder verification, creating potential liability exposure across major platforms. A transaction privacy analysis reveals concerns about the trade-off between privacy and transparency.

Analysis of major DAO implementations shows that a small portion of token holders control most of the voting power, with vast governance influence. This concentration raises fundamental questions about equity and representation in hybrid intelligence systems.

3.2.2. Responsibility Attribution for AI Errors

When algorithmic decisions cause harm in hybrid intelligence systems, responsibility attribution follows a structured layered model:

Individual Developer Responsibility: Developers bear direct responsibility for coding errors, inadequate testing procedures, and failure to implement known security measures.

Platform Operator Accountability: Platform operators are accountable for algorithm selection, parameter setting, monitoring systems, and providing adequate user safeguards.

Governance Community Responsibility: The broader governance community bears collective responsibility for establishing oversight mechanisms, ethical guidelines, and accountability frameworks.

Hybrid Failure Protocols: When failures involve both human and algorithmic components, shared accountability protocols establish clear escalation procedures and remediation mechanisms.

These ethical challenges and their associated paradoxes directly connect to Proposition 2, which states that "the adaptive capacity of blockchain-based hybrid intelligence increases with the diversity of participating agents and the quality of feedback mechanisms between human and algorithmic decision-makers." The governance responses to each paradox demonstrate how adaptive capacity manifests in practice through the development of new governance mechanisms responding to emerging ethical challenges.

3.3. *Institutional Mechanisms for Ethical Governance*

Our analysis identifies several institutional mechanisms enabling ethical governance of hybrid intelligence in cryptocurrency ecosystems amid competing transparency and privacy demands. These mechanisms address research question 2 by affording concrete approaches for managing ethical tensions in decentralized systems.

Layered governance structures distribute decision-making authority across multiple levels, with routine operational decisions automated through smart contracts while strategic governance decisions require human oversight with transparent deliberation processes. This approach enables efficient operations while maintaining ethical accountability through contextually appropriate governance mechanisms.

Embedded ethics frameworks integrate ethical principles directly into technical protocols through formal verification mechanisms that enforce compliance with predetermined governance rules [58]. These frameworks ensure that ethical considerations remain central to system operations even as systems scale up and evolve.

Adaptive governance mechanisms enable systems to evolve through structured modification processes, balancing the need for innovation with the requirement for stability. These mechanisms include stakeholder participation processes, formal proposal and voting systems, and graduated implementation approaches that allow for learning and adjustment.

The transformation of institutional structures through blockchain-based hybrid intelligence has significant policy implications. Regulatory frameworks developed for centralized financial systems may inadequately address the unique characteristics of decentralized hybrid intelligence, potentially creating either excessive constraints or insufficient oversight. The evolving regulatory landscape requires governance approaches that balance innovation with appropriate safeguards, particularly regarding systemic risk management, consumer protection, and market integrity.

Trust mechanism innovation establishes new institutional forms of trust combining algorithmic verification with human oversight, challenging traditional trust mechanisms based on centralized authority and creating more distributed and resilient trust structures [59]. These processes create new institutional foundations for trust, differing significantly from purely social or technical trust mechanisms.

Accountability distribution fundamentally redefines accountability by distributing responsibility across human and algorithmic agents, challenging traditional notions of accountability while enabling more responsive and adaptive governance structures. This distributed approach requires new frameworks for establishing responsibility and consequences in decentralized systems.

Our analysis reveals that hybrid intelligence systems have the potential to either reinforce or mitigate existing power imbalances depending on design choices, including token distribution mechanisms, governance participation structures, and algorithmic design principles [63,64]. These design decisions significantly influence the socioeconomic impact of hybrid intelligence systems.

3.4. Primary Theoretical and Methodological Innovations

This research generates four fundamental theoretical innovations that create significant multiplication effects across multiple domains. The first innovation establishes a multi-paradigm integration methodology that provides the first systematic integration of complexity and institutional theories for blockchain governance analysis. This methodology bridges the gap in interdisciplinary approaches identified in bibliometric analysis. It offers a replicable framework for analyzing other emerging technology governance challenges, including IoT, quantum computing, and biotechnology applications.

The second innovation introduces a governance paradox taxonomy that identifies and formalizes three fundamental paradoxes in hybrid intelligence systems. This framework addresses studies that examine governance challenges in isolation, rather than systematically, while providing applicability to any human–AI collaborative system across various industries, including healthcare AI, autonomous vehicles, and financial trading platforms.

The third theoretical contribution develops an embedded ethics framework that creates a technical implementation pathway for integrating ethical principles into blockchain protocols. This innovation addresses the theory–practice gap identified in the ethical AI literature and provides a scalable approach for implementing ethical AI across all technology platforms. The fourth innovation proposes an institutional legitimacy model for decentralized systems, explaining how distributed systems achieve legitimacy without a central authority, thereby filling a critical gap in institutional theory for non-hierarchical organizations.

3.5. Framework Application Potential

The theoretical framework offers structured guidance for the practical implementation of blockchain governance contexts. The multi-paradigm approach offers systematic methodologies for:

DAO Governance Enhancement: The framework could address widespread governance challenges through layered governance architectures, ethical constraint integration, and stakeholder participation mechanisms.

Implementation Methodology: A structured five-phase approach provides systematic deployment guidance:

- Assessment and planning phases for stakeholder analysis.
- Design phases for governance architecture development.

- Implementation phases for technical deployment.
- Monitoring phases for effectiveness evaluation.
- Adaptation phases for continuous improvement.

4. Discussion

4.1. Theoretical Contributions

This research makes several significant theoretical contributions to understanding hybrid intelligence within blockchain systems, thus extending existing scholarship in meaningful ways.

The integration of complexity and institutional theories offers a novel framework for analyzing hybrid intelligence in blockchain contexts. Unlike previous approaches, which often examine the technical or social dimensions in isolation, this framework offers a comprehensive understanding of how hybrid intelligence emerges from complex interactions while gaining legitimacy through institutional processes. This contribution extends beyond existing theoretical approaches by specifically exploring the ethical dimensions of human–AI integration in blockchain environments [25–27].

Empirically grounded theoretical propositions regarding hybrid intelligence in blockchain systems specify a structured framework for empirical validation. These propositions address key aspects of emergent intelligence, adaptive capacity, and institutional legitimacy, offering guidance for future research while being grounded in a systematic analysis of evidence across multiple blockchain implementations.

A sophisticated conceptualization of power dynamics in decentralized systems offers a more nuanced understanding of how power operates in decentralized environments than previous theoretical approaches. This contribution is particularly significant given the documented tendency for governance power to concentrate among stakeholders with substantial holdings despite the blockchain's autonomous aspirations [23].

The advancement of ethical governance theory identifies how decentralized systems create novel accountability challenges and governance requirements. The theoretical framework illuminates the tensions between transparency, opacity, efficiency, and ethical sensitivity, advancing understanding of governance dynamics in hybrid intelligence contexts.

This research demonstrates how blockchain-based hybrid intelligence establishes novel governance mechanisms balancing automated efficiency with human judgment. The findings reveal sophisticated patterns of interaction between smart contracts, human decision-makers, and artificial intelligence systems, suggesting that successful blockchain governance requires careful attention to both technical and social dimensions.

4.2. Practical Implications

This research offers practical implications for blockchain developers, participants, regulators, and other stakeholders navigating the ethical challenges of hybrid intelligence in decentralized systems.

Design principles for blockchain governance structures that effectively balance algorithmic efficiency with human oversight include layered governance, implementing multi-level structures with different decision-making mechanisms based on decision scope and ethical sensitivity. Successful governance structures establish different relationships between algorithmic processes and human oversight for operational versus strategic decisions, enabling efficient operations while maintaining ethical accountability.

Explicit power distribution through governance mechanisms addressing power dynamics and stakeholder representation can mitigate power concentration while maintaining system efficiency. This principle addresses the decentralization–centralization paradox by implementing mechanisms preventing plutocratic governance while preserving efficient decision-making.

Structured feedback loops establish formal mechanisms for human oversight to guide and refine algorithmic processes, addressing the transparency–opacity paradox by ensuring algorithmic processes remain comprehensible and accountable to human stakeholders through ongoing monitoring and adjustment.

Multi-level transparency develops mechanisms addressing both transaction visibility and algorithmic comprehensibility by implementing explainable AI techniques and appropriate information disclosure tailored to stakeholder needs. This approach recognizes that different stakeholders require different levels of technical detail while maintaining overall system transparency.

Distributed accountability establishes transparent responsibility relationships across technical and human components, ensuring that ethical considerations remain central even in highly automated systems. This approach addresses the challenge of maintaining accountability in systems where responsibility is distributed across multiple agents and processes.

For regulatory approaches to blockchain-based hybrid intelligence, our analysis highlights risk-based oversight implementing mechanisms proportional to system risk and impact rather than uniform approaches across all blockchain implementations. This balances regulatory compliance with innovation potential based on contextual risk assessment.

4.3. Future Research Directions

This study has several limitations, suggesting important directions for future investigation that would advance both theoretical understanding and practical implementation of ethical governance in hybrid intelligence systems.

Empirical validation of theoretical propositions requires systematic testing across different blockchain implementations and cultural contexts. Future research should employ mixed-method approaches combining case studies, surveys, and experimental methods to validate and refine the framework's application in various contexts.

Longitudinal studies tracking the evolution of hybrid intelligence governance across different developmental stages would provide valuable insights into how these systems adapt to technological advances and emerging challenges. As blockchain technology and artificial intelligence are rapidly evolving fields, there are potential limitations to the long-term applicability of current theoretical insights.

Domain-specific research examining hybrid intelligence applications in healthcare, environmental governance, and public administration would enhance understanding of how the framework applies across different contexts. While the framework provides general principles for analyzing hybrid intelligence in blockchain contexts, the application requires adaptation to specific technical architectures, governance structures, and institutional environments.

Cross-cultural validation addresses geographic and methodological research limitations by examining how cultural factors influence the governance of hybrid intelligence. Future research should examine hybrid intelligence applications across diverse cultural and regulatory contexts to understand how cultural factors influence governance effectiveness.

Participatory research methodologies engaging diverse stakeholders in collaborative research processes would ensure representation of different perspectives and experiences from developers, users, regulators, and other stakeholders in blockchain ecosystems. Current theoretical analysis primarily draws on the academic literature and technical documentation, potentially underrepresenting stakeholder perspectives.

4.4. Empirical Validation Framework for Theoretical Propositions

To address limitations regarding empirical grounding, this section outlines specific empirical validation approaches for each theoretical proposition and future research:

Proposition 1 Validation: Emergent Intelligence Properties

- Methodology: Comparative analysis of five to seven major blockchain platforms measuring collective intelligence outcomes versus individual component capabilities.
- Metrics: Decision accuracy rates, problem-solving speed, adaptive capacity indicators.
- Timeline: Eighteen-month longitudinal study tracking intelligence emergence patterns.
- Expected Outcomes: Quantified evidence demonstrating emergent intelligence properties exceeding individual component capabilities.

Proposition 2 Validation: Adaptive Capacity Factors

- Methodology: Controlled experiments manipulating stakeholder diversity, and feedback mechanism quality.
- Variables: Stakeholder background diversity, feedback loop frequency, and information quality measures.
- Timeline: Twelve-month experimental study with controlled interventions.
- Expected Outcomes: Statistical relationships between diversity/feedback quality and adaptive capacity.

Proposition 3 Validation: Institutional Legitimacy Convergence

- Methodology: Cross-platform governance framework analysis examining convergence patterns.
- Data Sources: Governance documentation, stakeholder interviews, and regulatory compliance measures.
- Timeline: Twenty-four-month comparative study across multiple jurisdictions.
- Expected Outcomes: Evidence of institutional pressure effects on governance convergence.

5. Conclusions

The integration of hybrid intelligence into blockchain systems represents a fundamental transformation in organizational governance and institutional design. This research has developed a multi-paradigm theoretical framework advancing the understanding of how hybrid intelligence emerges, evolves, and operates within blockchain's decentralized architecture. By integrating complexity theory and institutional theory, the framework illuminates the emergent system properties and institutional dynamics that characterize hybrid intelligence in blockchain contexts.

The analysis reveals how hybrid intelligence emerges through complex interactions between human judgment and artificial intelligence within the blockchain's decentralized architecture, creating novel forms of collective intelligence that transcend traditional organizational boundaries. These systems achieve a balance between automated efficiency and human oversight through carefully designed governance structures, establishing appropriate relationships between algorithmic processes and human judgment based on decision scope and ethical sensitivity.

The research identifies critical ethical challenges in hybrid intelligence governance, with quantified analysis revealing DeFi automated decisions lack adequate transparency, with potential liability exposure, while the top token holders control voting power in major DAO implementations.

Research question 1 is answered through a demonstration that complex interactions between human judgment and AI within blockchain systems generate emergent intelligence properties through three key mechanisms: algorithmic governance with human oversight, collaborative decision support, and adaptive learning processes. These mechanisms enable collective intelligence exceeding the capabilities of human or algorithmic components alone, confirming Proposition 1.

Research question 2 is addressed through the identification of effective institutional mechanisms for the ethical governance of hybrid intelligence in cryptocurrency ecosystems, including layered transparency structures, distributed accountability frameworks, and adaptive governance processes balancing competing transparency and privacy demands. These governance mechanisms gain legitimacy through alignment with existing institutional norms while creating novel accountability structures appropriate for decentralized systems, supporting Proposition 3.

Empirical Validation Pathway: This study establishes concrete frameworks for empirical testing through comparative case studies across major blockchain platforms, the longitudinal tracking of governance evolution over 12–24-month periods, experimental protocols for testing specific governance mechanisms, and cross-cultural validation across different regulatory and cultural contexts. These validation approaches address current limitations while providing systematic pathways for the development of evidence-based governance.

Limitations and Future Directions: This theoretical framework provides essential foundational knowledge for systematic empirical investigation, rather than definitive conclusions about the effectiveness of hybrid intelligence governance. The framework establishes conceptual foundations requiring empirical validation across diverse blockchain implementations, cultural contexts, and regulatory environments before widespread practical implementation.

Future research should pursue empirical validation, domain-specific applications, examination of power dynamics, and tracking of regulatory evolution to advance the consideration of hybrid intelligence in blockchain contexts through a comprehensive investigation of governance effectiveness across diverse contexts. By pursuing these research directions, scholars and practitioners can develop a more nuanced understanding of how hybrid intelligence operates across various contexts, informing more effective governance approaches that strike a balance between technical innovation and ethical considerations.

In summary, the convergence of blockchain technology and artificial intelligence represents a significant frontier in organizational theory and practice, challenging conventional assumptions about governance, accountability, and institutional structures. By developing sophisticated theoretical frameworks to understand this convergence, better navigation of its ethical implications and harnessing of its potential for a positive social impact across diverse domains and cultural contexts is possible.

Funding: This research received no external funding.

Institutional Review Board Statement: Not applicable.

Informed Consent Statement: Not applicable.

Data Availability Statement: The original contributions presented in this study are included in the article. Further inquiries can be directed to the corresponding author.

Conflicts of Interest: The author declares no conflicts of interest.

References

1. Hassan, S.; De Filippi, P. Decentralized autonomous organizations. *Internet Policy Rev.* **2021**, *10*, 1–10. [CrossRef]
2. Ismail, L.; Materwala, H. A Review of Blockchain Architecture and Consensus Protocols: Use Cases, Challenges, and Solutions. *Symmetry* **2019**, *11*, 1198. [CrossRef]
3. Nakamoto, S. Bitcoin: A Peer-to-Peer Electronic Cash System. Available online: https://bitcoin.org/bitcoin.pdf (accessed on 25 June 2025).
4. Antonopoulos, A.M.; Harding, D.A. *Mastering Bitcoin: Programming the Open Blockchain*, 3rd ed.; O'Reilly Media: Sebastopol, CA, USA, 2023.

5. Antonopoulos, A.M. *The Internet of Money: A Collection of Talks*; Merkle Bloom LLC: Middletown, DE, USA, 2016; pp. 1–152.
6. Ammous, S. *The Bitcoin Standard: The Decentralized Alternative to Central Banking*; John Wiley & Sons: Hoboken, NJ, USA, 2018; pp. 1–304.
7. Burniske, C.; Tatar, J. *Cryptoassets: The Innovative Investor's Guide to Bitcoin and Beyond*; McGraw-Hill Education: New York, NY, USA, 2018; pp. 1–352.
8. Tapscott, D.; Tapscott, A. *Blockchain Revolution: How the Technology Behind Bitcoin Is Changing Money, Business, and the World, Updated ed.*; Portfolio: New York, NY, USA, 2018; pp. 1–432.
9. Popper, N. *Digital Gold: Bitcoin and the Inside Story of the Misfits and Millionaires Trying to Reinvent Money*; Harper Paperbacks: New York, NY, USA, 2016; pp. 1–432.
10. Lewis, A. *The Basics of Bitcoins and Blockchains: An Introduction to Cryptocurrencies and the Technology that Powers Them*; Mango Publishing Group: Coral Gables, FL, USA, 2018; pp. 1–408.
11. Casey, M.J.; Vigna, P. *The Truth Machine: The Blockchain and the Future of Everything*; St. Martin's Press: New York, NY, USA, 2018.
12. Champagne, P. *The Book of Satoshi: The Collected Writings of Bitcoin Creator Satoshi Nakamoto*; E53 Publishing LLC: Temecula, CA, USA, 2014; pp. 1–394.
13. Liu, H.K.; Tang, M.; Collard, A.S.J. Hybrid Intelligence for the Public Sector: A Bibliometric Analysis of Artificial Intelligence and Crowd Intelligence. *Gov. Inf. Q.* **2025**, *42*, 102006. [CrossRef]
14. Parasol, M. How to Control the AIs and Incentivize the Humans with Crypto. *Cointelegraph Magazine* 2 May 2023. Available online: https://cointelegraph.com/magazine/ai-blockchain-control-robots-incentivise-humans/ (accessed on 18 June 2025).
15. Goldman Sachs. What to Expect from AI in 2025: Hybrid Workers, Robotics, Expert Models 2025. Available online: https://www.goldmansachs.com/insights/articles/what-to-expect-from-ai-in-2025-hybrid-workers-robotics-expert-models (accessed on 1 July 2025).
16. United Nations Conference on Trade and Development. *Proceedings of the 2025 Technology and Innovation Report: Inclusive Artificial Intelligence for Development*; United Nations: Geneva, Switzerland, 2025. Available online: https://unctad.org/system/files/official-document/tir2025_en.pdf (accessed on 18 June 2025).
17. Stone, M. How AI is Creating Self-Owned Crypto Companies: The DAO Revolution. *Medium*. 2025. Available online: https://medium.com/@maxstoneSL/how-ai-is-creating-self-owned-crypto-companies-the-dao-revolution-0ca9397651d2 (accessed on 18 June 2025).
18. Soltanshahi, M.; Maier, M. Metaversal Intelligence: Unifying Human-AI Interactions in Human-in-the-loop AIB-Metaverse. *Comput. Netw.* **2025**, *269*, 111425. [CrossRef]
19. Maier, M.; Chen, Y.; Chou, C.F.; Garus, A.; Kröner, A.; Katsaros, K.V.; Yu, S.; Yamazaki, T. Metaverse as the New Eleusis 2.0: Are we in the midst of the next renaissance? *Blockchain Res. Appl.* **2023**, *4*, 100151.
20. Kaal, W.A. AI Governance Via Web3 Reputation System. *Stanford J. Blockchain Law Policy*. 2025. Available online: https://stanford-jblp.pubpub.org/pub/aigov-via-web3/release/1 (accessed on 18 June 2025).
21. Tenakwah, E.S.; Watson, C. Embracing the AI/automation age: Preparing your workforce for humans and machines working together. *Strategy Leadersh.* **2025**, *53*, 32–48. [CrossRef]
22. Wang, S.; Ding, W.; Li, J.; Yuan, Y.; Ouyang, L.; Wang, F.Y. Decentralized autonomous organizations: Concept, model, and applications. *IEEE Trans. Comput. Soc. Syst.* **2022**, *9*, 622–635. [CrossRef]
23. Koutmos, D. Return and volatility spillovers among cryptocurrencies. *Econ. Lett.* **2018**, *173*, 122–127. [CrossRef]
24. Xiong, H.; Chen, M.; Wu, C.; Zhao, Y.; Yi, W. Research on Progress of Blockchain Consensus Algorithm: A Review on Recent Progress of Blockchain Consensus Algorithms. *Future Internet* **2022**, *14*, 47. [CrossRef]
25. Zheng, Z.; Xie, S.; Dai, H.; Chen, X.; Wang, H. An overview of blockchain technology: Architecture, consensus, and future trends. In Proceedings of the 2017 IEEE International Congress on Big Data, Honolulu, HI, USA, 25–30 June 2017; pp. 557–564.
26. Buterin, V. *Ethereum White Paper: A Next-Generation Smart Contract and Decentralized Application Platform*; Ethereum Foundation: Zug, Switzerland, 2014.
27. Risius, M.; Spohrer, K. A blockchain research framework: What we (don't) know, where we go from here, and how we will get there. *Bus. Inf. Syst. Eng.* **2017**, *59*, 385–409. [CrossRef]
28. Floridi, L.; Cowls, J.; Beltrametti, M.; Chatila, R.; Chazerand, P.; Dignum, V.; Luetge, C.; Madelin, R.; Pagallo, U.; Rossi, F.; et al. AI4People—An Ethical Framework for a Good AI Society: Opportunities, Risks, Principles, and Recommendations. *Minds Mach.* **2018**, *28*, 689–707. [CrossRef] [PubMed]
29. Jobin, A.; Ienca, M.; Vayena, E. The global landscape of AI Ethics Guidelines. *Nat. Mach. Intell.* **2019**, *1*, 389–399. [CrossRef]
30. Bentham, J. *An Introduction to the Principles of Morals and Legislation*; Oxford University Press: Oxford, UK, 1996.
31. Mill, J.S. *Utilitarianism*; Parker, Son, and Bourn: London, UK, 2001.
32. Singer, P. *Practical Ethics*, 3rd ed.; Cambridge University Press: Cambridge, UK, 2011.
33. Hursthouse, R.; Pettigrove, G. Virtue Ethics. In *Stanford Encyclopedia of Philosophy*; Zalta, E.N., Ed.; Stanford University: Stanford, CA, USA, 2018.

34. Aristotle. *Nicomachean Ethics*; Ross, W.D., Ed.; Oxford University Press: Oxford, UK, 2009.
35. Vallor, S. *Technology and the Virtues: A Philosophical Guide to a Future Worth Wanting*; Oxford University Press: Oxford, UK, 2016.
36. Ryan, M. In AI We Trust: Ethics, Artificial Intelligence, and Reliability. *Sci. Eng. Ethics* **2020**, *26*, 2749–2767. [CrossRef] [PubMed]
37. Kant, I. *Groundwork for the Metaphysics of Morals*; Gregor, M., Translator; Cambridge University Press: Cambridge, UK, 1998.
38. Rawls, J. *A Theory of Justice, Revised ed.*; Harvard University Press: Cambridge, MA, USA, 1999.
39. Dworkin, R. *Taking Rights Seriously*; Harvard University Press: Cambridge, MA, USA, 1977.
40. Winfield, A.F.; Jirotka, M. Ethical governance is essential to building trust in robotics and artificial intelligence systems. *Philos. Trans. R. Soc. A* **2018**, *376*, 20180085. [CrossRef] [PubMed]
41. Lumineau, F.; Wang, W.; Schilke, O. Blockchain governance—A new way of organizing collaborations? *Organ. Sci.* **2021**, *32*, 500–521. [CrossRef]
42. Alibašić, H. Harmonizing artificial intelligence (AI) governance: A comparative analysis of Singapore and France's AI policies and the influence of international organizations. *Glob. Public Policy Gov.* **2025**, *5*, 93–113. [CrossRef]
43. Weking, J.; Mandalenakis, M.; Hein, A.; Hermes, S.; Böhm, M.; Krcmar, H. The impact of blockchain technology on business models: A taxonomy and archetypal patterns. *Electron. Mark.* **2020**, *30*, 285–298. [CrossRef]
44. Greenwood, R.; Hinings, C.R.; Whetten, D. Rethinking Institutions and Organizations. *J. Manag. Stud.* **2014**, *51*, 1206–1220. [CrossRef]
45. Werbach, K. *The Blockchain and the New Architecture of Trust*; MIT Press: Cambridge, MA, USA, 2018.
46. Fu, Y.; Zhuang, Z.; Zhang, L. AI Ethics on Blockchain: Topic Analysis on Twitter Data for Blockchain Security. *arXiv* **2022**, arXiv:2212.06951.
47. Casino, F.; Dasaklis, T.K.; Patsakis, C. A systematic literature review of blockchain-based applications: Current status, classification, and open issues. *Telemat. Inform.* **2019**, *36*, 55–81. [CrossRef]
48. De Filippi, P.; Wright, A. *Blockchain and the Law: The Rule of Code*; Harvard University Press: Cambridge, MA, USA, 2018.
49. McMahan, H.B.; Moore, E.; Ramage, D.; Hampson, S.; Arcas, B.A. Communication-Efficient Learning of Deep Networks from Decentralized Data. *arXiv* **2017**, arXiv:1602.05629.
50. Yang, Q.; Liu, Y.; Chen, T.; Tong, Y. Federated machine learning: Concept and applications. *ACM Trans. Intell. Syst. Technol.* **2019**, *10*, 1–19. [CrossRef]
51. Azolibe, C.B.; Okonkwo, J.J.; Obi-Nwosu, V.O. Technology-based banking and bank deposit: The Nigerian commercial banks' experience. *Afr. J. Sci. Technol. Innov. Dev.* **2023**, *15*, 31–44. [CrossRef]
52. Fisch, C.; Masiak, C.; Vismara, S.; Block, J. Motives and profiles of ICO investors. *J. Bus. Res.* **2021**, *125*, 564–576. [CrossRef]
53. Clifton, C.; Blythman, R.; Tulusan, K. Is decentralized AI safer? *arXiv* **2022**, arXiv:2211.05828.
54. Snowden, E. The Future of Crypto Is Not What It Seems. *YouTube*. 2023. Available online: https://www.youtube.com/watch?v=OPd9NcyIuy0 (accessed on 1 June 2024).
55. So, C.; Conway, K.; Yu, X.; Yao, S.; Wong, K. Opp/ai: Optimistic Privacy-Preserving AI on Blockchain. *arXiv* **2024**, arXiv:2402.15006.
56. Yeung, K. Regulation by Blockchain: The Emerging Battle for Supremacy between the Code of Law and Code as Law. *Mod. Law Rev.* **2019**, *82*, 207–239. [CrossRef]
57. DuPont, Q. Experiments in algorithmic governance: A history and ethnography of "The DAO," a failed decentralized autonomous organization. In *Bitcoin and Beyond*; Campbell-Verduyn, M., Ed.; Routledge: London, UK, 2017; pp. 157–177.
58. Andersen, J.V.; Ingram Bogusz, C. Self-organizing in blockchain infrastructures: Generativity through shifting objectives and forking. *J. Assoc. Inf. Syst.* **2019**, *20*, 1242–1273. [CrossRef]
59. Chen, Y.; Bellavitis, C. Decentralized Finance: Blockchain Technology and the Quest for an Open Financial System. *Stevens Inst. Technol.-Sch. Bus. Res. Pap. Ser.* **2019**. [CrossRef]
60. Voshmgir, S. *Token Economy: How Blockchains and Smart Contracts Revolutionize the Economy*; BlockchainHub Berlin: Berlin, Germany, 2019.
61. Anderson, P. Complexity theory and organization science. *Organ. Sci.* **1999**, *10*, 216–232. [CrossRef]
62. Uhl-Bien, M.; Arena, M. Leadership for organizational adaptability: A theoretical synthesis and integrative framework. *Leadership. Q.* **2018**, *29*, 89–104. [CrossRef]
63. Holland, J.H. *Complexity: A Very Short Introduction*; Oxford University Press: Oxford, UK, 2014.
64. DiMaggio, P.J.; Powell, W.W. The iron cage revisited: Institutional isomorphism and collective rationality in organizational fields. *Am. Sociol. Rev.* **1983**, *48*, 147–160. [CrossRef]
65. Alibašić, H. Advancing disaster resilience: The ethical dimensions of adaptability and adaptive leadership in public service organizations. *Public Integr.* **2024**, *27*, 209–221. [CrossRef]
66. Scott, W.R. *Institutions and Organizations: Ideas, Interests, and Identities*; Sage Publications: Thousand Oaks, CA, USA, 2014.
67. Charmaz, K. *Constructing Grounded Theory: A Practical Guide Through Qualitative Analysis*; Sage Publications: London, UK, 2006.
68. Creswell, J.W. *Research Design: Qualitative, Quantitative, and Mixed Methods Approaches*; Sage Publications: Thousand Oaks, CA, USA, 2014.

69. Jaakkola, E. Designing conceptual articles: Four approaches. *AMS Rev.* **2020**, *10*, 18–26. [CrossRef]
70. Beck, R.; Müller-Bloch, C.; King, J.L. Governance in the blockchain economy: A framework and research agenda. *J. Assoc. Inf. Syst.* **2018**, *19*, 1020–1034. [CrossRef]
71. Asif, R.; Hassan, S.R.; Parr, G. Integrating a Blockchain-Based Governance Framework for Responsible AI. *Future Internet* **2023**, *15*, 97. [CrossRef]

FinTech

Article

AI-Powered Buy-Now-Pay-Later Smart Contracts in Healthcare

Ângela Filipa Oliveira Gonçalves [1], Shafik Faruc Norali [1] and Clemens Bechter [2,*]

1 ULS Algarve, 8000-386 Faro, Portugal; afogoncalves@ulsalg.min-saude.pt (Â.F.O.G.); snorali@ulsalg.min-saude.pt (S.F.N.)
2 UMIO, Maastricht University, 6211 LH Maastricht, The Netherlands
* Correspondence: clemens.bechter@maastrichtuniversity.nl

Abstract: As healthcare systems face mounting pressure to modernise payment infrastructure, fintech innovations have emerged as potential tools to improve affordability and efficiency. However, the adoption of these technologies in clinical settings remains limited. This study investigated the perceptions and resistance patterns of healthcare professionals toward Buy-Now-Pay-Later technology and blockchain in healthcare finance, using Innovation Resistance Theory as the guiding framework. Survey data collected from medical practitioners (N = 366) were analysed to identify knowledge gaps, perceived risks, and tradition-related barriers that influence adoption intent. The findings reveal that while interest in financial innovation exists, resistance is driven by institutional conservatism, regulatory uncertainty, and limited familiarity with decentralised finance systems. This research contributes to the literature by offering a theory-based explanation for why even high-potential financial tools face behavioural and structural resistance in healthcare environments.

Keywords: healthcare; pricing models; cryptocurrencies; smart contracts; tokenisation; decentralised financial markets

JEL Classification: I11; M15

1. Introduction

Pricing models are approaches how organisations determine their prices of products or services; these models are based on factors such as costs, market demand, competition, and perceived value [1].

Pricing models in the healthcare sector play a crucial role in determining how medical services are billed and reimbursed. These models also influence the affordability/costs of care provided to patients. Over the years, different pricing models have evolved to balance cost efficiency and patient satisfaction. Among the various models, the most common ones are the Fee-for-Service (FFS), Capitation, Value-Based Pricing (VBP), Bundled Payments, and Subscription-Based models.

One of the most prevalent models in traditional healthcare is the Fee-for-Service (FFS) model. Under this system, healthcare providers are compensated for each individual service, test, or procedure. For example, a patient undergoing surgery would receive separate bills for the consultation, the procedure itself, the hospital stay, and post-operative care. This model ensures that providers are reimbursed to the full extent of the care given. Critics argue that it incentivises excessive service utilisation, resulting in inflated medical costs [2].

The Capitation model offers a fixed, prepaid amount to healthcare providers per patient over a specific period regardless of the actual services utilised. While capitation encourages preventive care, there is concern that it might lead to under-treatment as providers may attempt to minimise services to stay within the budget [3].

The Value-Based Pricing (VBP) model, also known as Pay-for-Performance (P4P), seeks to address inefficiencies in traditional healthcare pricing by linking provider reimbursement to patient health outcomes. Instead of paying for the quantity of services rendered, insurers reward healthcare providers for improving a patient's health. A major challenge is the accurate measurement of a patient's health [4].

Another approach, the Bundled Payments model, consolidates multiple services into a single payment for an entire episode of care. For instance, a hospital may charge a fixed price for a knee replacement procedure that includes pre-operative consultations, surgery, rehabilitation, and follow-up visits. By reducing administrative complexity and bundled payments, it should lead to higher efficiency. However, it can be difficult to implement this model across multiple healthcare providers who need to agree on cost-sharing arrangements [5].

With the rise of telemedicine, Subscription-Based models have gained popularity. This approach allows patients to pay a recurring fee (monthly or annually) for unlimited access to healthcare services. Telehealth companies offer subscription-based plans that grant members virtual consultations and preventive care. This model ensures predictable costs and enhanced accessibility, though it may not cover all medical procedures, requiring additional out-of-pocket expenses for specialised care [6]. Predominant pricing models differ from country to country; see Table 1. The Fee-for-Service model remains the most common in the United States.

Table 1. Pricing models by selected countries.

Pricing Model	Predominant In
Fee-for-Service	U.S.A.
Capitation	UK
Value-Based Pricing	Sweden
Bundled Payments	The Netherlands
Subscription-Based	Singapore

Source: https://www.statista.com/markets/412/topic/454/health-system (accessed 1 May 2025) [7].

As the financial sector moves forward, Artificial Intelligence (AI) fintech models are likely to play a greater role in future [8]. AI in payment systems can be used for predictive analytics, fraud detection, and personalisation [9]. For example, the benefits of AI-driven Subscription models include personalisation. Patients pay for what they use, making healthcare more affordable. In addition, there is cost efficiency in the sense that providers reduce administrative costs by optimising pricing in real time. Hopefully, this way, patients stay motivated to follow healthier habits when rewarded with lower fees. AI could also flag high-risk patients, helping insurers and clinics adjust their prices accordingly. AI could also track treatment progress, ensuring that payments only trigger when health outcomes improve (e.g., improved blood sugar levels for diabetics). It could go that far that a patient pays nothing if a prescribed therapy does not show expected results. This is a model that the medical trade may disagree with.

AI-driven pricing models must analyse various data to calculate subscription fees, namely the following:

- Usage-Based Pricing: Subscription costs adjust based on the frequency of doctor visits, telehealth consultations, or prescription refills. Example: A patient who uses telehealth once a month pays less than someone who consults weekly;
- Predictive Health Risk Assessment: AI evaluates a patient's health history and lifestyle to predict future healthcare needs and adjust pricing accordingly. Example: A diabetic

patient who actively manages his/her/their health may receive a lower subscription cost than one with unmanaged symptoms;

- Tiered and Dynamic Pricing: AI can segment patients into different pricing categories based on their engagement and risk profile. Example: A fitness-conscious user with a wearable health device showing high activity levels should pay less for a healthcare plan;
- Behaviour-Based Discounts: AI can track preventive care habits (e.g., regular exercises, diet tracking, medication adherence) and offer discounted subscription rates. Example: An app-linked smart scale or smartwatch can reward users who maintain a healthy weight or exercise regularly;
- Adaptive Payment Plans: AI can detect financial hardship patterns and offer flexible payment plans for patients struggling with payments. Example: If a patient's income fluctuates (e.g., freelancer), AI can adjust monthly fees accordingly.

There are already real-world applications in the form of telehealth platforms such as Teladoc and Babylon Health. Devices like the Apple Watch and Fitbit can potentially integrate with insurers for dynamic premium adjustments. AI-powered diabetes management apps (e.g., Livongo) can tailor subscription fees based on a patient's engagement. PayZen is a fintech company specialising in providing "Care Now, Pay Later" (CNPL) solutions to address the growing challenge of medical debt in the United States. By leveraging AI, PayZen offers patients personalised, interest-free payment plans for their healthcare expenses, aiming to make medical treatments more accessible and affordable [10] (FinMasters, 2023). This approach enhances the likelihood of repayment and increases acceptance rates among patients. In collaboration with Mastercard, PayZen introduced a Buy-Now-Pay-Later (BNPL) card specifically designed for medical expenses. This card, available in both physical and virtual forms, allows patients to manage their healthcare payments more flexibly [10].

The BNPL model is widely used in retailing to make purchases more accessible by allowing consumers to split payments into instalments. Lupșa-Tătaru et al. [11] in their article "Buy Now Pay Later—A Fad or a Reality?" concluded that it is not a fad but that there are overspending risks involved, especially for young consumers. BNPL might be a new concept in healthcare but in sectors like retailing, where it is most common, prices are often quoted in instalments per month instead of the full price.

All European countries struggle to finance healthcare [12]. In countries where healthcare is "free" (e.g., Canada, Portugal, Romania, Spain), the quality is generally poor. In addition, "free healthcare" does not mean that healthcare is completely without cost; most systems are funded through income taxes (e.g., Portugal) or social (national health) insurance (e.g., France, Germany, Romania, Switzerland). For example, in Germany, one has to pay 14.6% of a normal (below EUR 5500 per month) income for national health plus an additional 3.6% for compulsory care insurance (equally shared with employer), which is still not enough, so the government is forced to subsidise [13]. The BNPL model could be advisable for countries like France, Germany, and other European countries due to Europe's economic challenges and healthcare accessibility issues. Europe's "free" public healthcare system faces long waiting times due to resource constraints, leading many patients to seek private care. In addition, not all services are free, so patients have to co-finance, but high inflation and cost of living pressures have reduced their disposable incomes. Studies have shown that financial concerns prevent people from seeking timely medical care, leading to worse health outcomes and higher long-term costs [14]. Implementing BNPL in Europe's "free" healthcare sector could be a win–win solution by improving patient access to care, reducing financial stress, and supporting private healthcare providers in securing payments.

Free healthcare implies that medical services are provided at no direct cost to the patient at the point of use, often funded entirely through taxation. In contrast, universal healthcare refers to a system in which all citizens have access to necessary health services, but this access may still involve co-payments, insurance premiums, or other out-of-pocket costs, depending on the country's model.

A BNPL (Buy Now Pay Later) model could be realistically applied in non-urgent, elective, and out-of-pocket medical services, where patients often face significant cost barriers. For key areas, see Figure 1. These services are typically discretionary or not fully covered by insurance, making them more compatible with consumer financing models like BNPL. Table 2 shows the difference between BNPL models in retailing and healthcare.

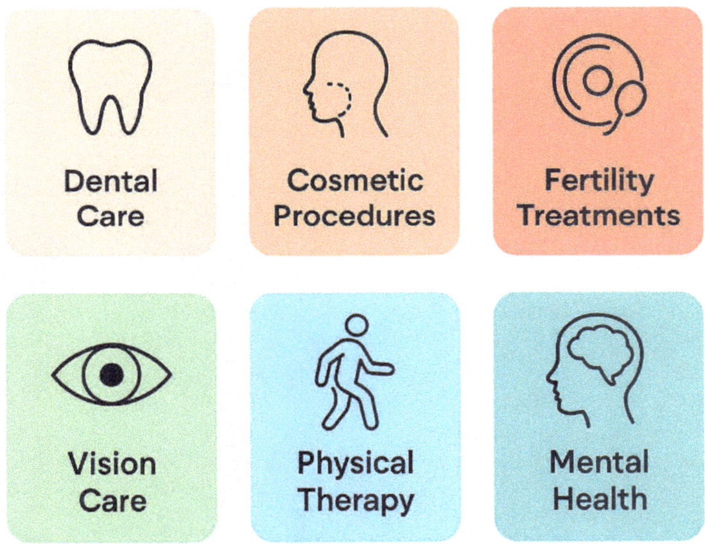

Figure 1. Potential applications of BNPL in healthcare.

Table 2. BNPL in retail vs. healthcare: comparison.

Healthcare BNPL	Retail BNPL	Category
To finance medical services and treatments	To finance consumer goods (e.g., electronics, clothing)	Purpose
Can vary: often non-urgent	Typically low urgency (discretionary purchases)	Urgency
Higher scrutiny due to ethical and health-related concerns	Light-to-moderate, varies by jurisdiction	Regulatory Oversight
Moderate to high (risk of over-indebtedness and delayed care)	High (consumer debt accumulation, impulse buying)	Risk of Overuse
May require stricter checks depending on provider	Often minimal or soft credit checks	Credit Assessment
High (patient vulnerability, informed consent, medical ethics)	Low to moderate	Ethical Considerations
Potential denial of future care, increased financial burden	Late fees, credit score impact	Default Consequences
Can vary: from short-term to extended plans	Fixed short-term instalments (usually every 4–6 weeks or monthly)	Repayment Structure
Need for treatment despite upfront cost barriers	Desire to buy now, manage cash flow	Customer Motivation

How AI could enhance BNPL in healthcare:

- Personalised Payment Plans: AI customises repayment schedules based on income, medical history, and financial behaviour;
- Real-Time Credit Scoring: AI analyses non-traditional financial data (e.g., spending habits, employment stability), for instance BNPL approvals;
- Predictive Risk Assessment: AI detects potential overdue payments and proactively suggests adjustments (e.g., lower monthly payments);
- Automated Fraud Detection: AI identifies high-risk transactions and prevents fraudulent BNPL applications.

Khezr et al. [15] outlined how blockchain technology can revolutionise healthcare. One could imagine an integration with cryptocurrencies and smart contracts. AI could automate subscription pricing using blockchain-based smart contracts including wearable BNPL plans (AI analyses health data from smartwatches and fitness trackers to adjust payment options). Blockchain-powered BNPL will be secure and be decentralised medical financing with automatic payment tracking. By integrating these technologies, BNPL platforms can offer secure, transparent, and automated payment solutions while reducing fraud and operational costs. A potential addition could be the combination with the medical Internet of Things (IoT) as outlined by Sharma et al. [16], which will not be further explored in the context of our research. The features of crypto and smart-contract BNPL are as follows:

- Decentralised Payments: Patients can use stablecoins or healthcare-specific tokens to pay for medical services over time;
- Smart Contract Automation: Self-executing contracts ensure automatic payments, refunds, and compliance based on pre-decentralised financing rules;
- Transparent and Fraud-Proof Transactions: Blockchain records every BNPL transaction, reducing disputes and ensuring trust;
- Lower Processing Fees: Eliminates intermediaries like banks, reducing transaction costs for both patients and providers.

However, there are three major challenges:

1. Cryptocurrency Volatility: Using stablecoins (e.g., EUR Tether, EURS) instead of volatile cryptocurrencies could be the answer. Even more secure would be a Fiat cryptocurrency as outlined by Salhout and Bechter [17].
2. Regulatory Uncertainty: Boustani and Elisabetta [18]. rightly asked, "How does a decentralized type of governance handle compliance and regulatory requirements? What happens if the majority of token owners in a decentralized voting system choose to abstain from voting for compliance upgrades or financial anti-money laundering requirements?" The answers can only lie in well-defined regulations regarding security and compliance. In other words, regulators must catch up and define clear rules. The deregulated community has to bite the bullet;
3. Adoption Barriers: One may encourage practitioners and other medical services providers to accept crypto payments but nobody can be forced. This is the real bottleneck of a successful implementation. Our field research looked deeper into these barriers.
4. The gap in existing literature on BNPL in healthcare is the lack of research on the intersection of consumer finance innovation (FinTech) and healthcare access, particularly within the context of decentralised finance, tokenisation, and AI-driven pricing models. While BNPL is well-studied in retail and increasingly in fintech contexts, its application in healthcare remains underexplored, especially regarding the perceptions and acceptance among medical professionals.

As healthcare systems worldwide explore digital transformation in financing models, innovations such as Buy-Now-Pay-Later (BNPL), blockchain, and AI-powered payment solutions offer new pathways for improving affordability and operational efficiency. However, the healthcare sector often exhibits resistance to adopting financial technologies that are already common in consumer markets. To better understand this phenomenon, this study adopted Innovation Resistance Theory (IRT) [19] as a guiding framework. IRT highlights how individuals and institutions may resist innovations due to perceived risks, lack of familiarity, traditional values, or doubts about usefulness. Barriers are especially relevant in professional healthcare settings, where financial and ethical stakes are high. By applying IRT to the intersection of healthcare and fintech, this study sought to explain not only patterns of adoption but also the psychological and contextual barriers that inhibit technological integration in medical practice.

The research objectives of our research were thus:

- To assess healthcare professionals' perceptions and levels of awareness regarding blockchain and BNPL technologies as emerging tools for medical payment innovation;
- To identify key psychological and structural barriers to the adoption of these technologies, using Innovation Resistance Theory (IRT) to examine constructs such as knowledge, risk, usage, and tradition-related resistance;
- To explore the extent to which trust, openness to innovation, and perceived regulatory uncertainty influence willingness to pilot or adopt blockchain-based BNPL solutions in healthcare practice;
- To investigate whether individual lifestyle characteristics and attitudes toward related technologies (e.g., AI) moderate acceptance, serving as indicators of digital readiness rather than core components of the conceptual framework.

2. Materials and Methods

Table 3 shows the mapping of each of our survey items to the corresponding Innovation Resistance Theory (IRT) construct. IRT includes six main types of barriers: Usage, Value, Risk, Tradition, Image, and Knowledge.

Table 3. Mapping of survey items to Innovation Resistance Theory (IRT) constructs.

IRT Construct	Survey Item
Knowledge Barrier	I have had prior exposure to cryptocurrencies like Bitcoin
Knowledge Barrier	I have heard about blockchain technology
Value Barrier	Artificial Intelligence can enhance healthcare
Knowledge Barrier	I believe that most healthcare practitioners lack awareness of Artificial Intelligence
Knowledge Barrier	I believe that most healthcare practitioners lack awareness of cryptocurrencies
Risk Barrier	I do not trust these new technologies like Artificial Intelligence and blockchains
Tradition/Image Barrier	I am too old for all these new technologies like Artificial Intelligence in healthcare
Risk Barrier	I worry about the regulatory uncertainty surrounding cryptocurrencies in healthcare
Knowledge Barrier (inverse)	I am interested in learning more about how cryptocurrencies could work in healthcare
Knowledge Barrier	I am familiar with healthcare financing systems in other countries
Value Barrier/Tradition Barrier	The current "free" healthcare should be replaced by a private healthcare system
Usage Barrier/Value Barrier	I would accept payments in monthly instalments as it is common practice in retailing
Value Barrier	I would be willing to pilot a small-scale crypto-based payment system in my practice/hospital
Value Barrier/Social Value	Individuals who actively maintain a healthy lifestyle. should be granted easier access and better fees for high-quality medical care and services

During the first quarter of 2025, 366 quantitative surveys were obtained from European practitioners and medical service providers. The aim of our field research was the evaluation of perceptions and state of knowledge regarding cryptocurrencies, blockchain, and smart contracts, see Appendix A. In total, 366 responses were analysed. Out of the 366 persons, 203 (55.5%) were medical doctors. The remaining ones were other healthcare specialists such as administrators. The demographics of the sample are listed in Tables 4 and 5.

Table 4. Age.

Percent	Frequency	Age
22.7	83	Below 30 years old
33.3	122	30–40 years old
27.6	101	40–50 years old
16.4	60	Above 50 years old
100.0	366	Total

Table 5. Employment sector.

Percent	Frequency	Sector
45.4	166	Government
28.4	104	Private Sector
26.2	96	Both
100.0	366	Total

We also asked some lifestyle questions about how they relax and how they keep their knowledge updated; see Tables 6 and 7. By asking these questions, we explored whether a "modern" or tech-oriented lifestyle correlates with greater acceptance of digital innovations in healthcare. Venkatesh et al. [20] found that technology adaptation correlates with tech-savviness and a more modern lifestyle.

Table 6. Relaxation Activity.

Percent	Frequency	Relaxation
22.7	83	Reading a book, classic radio, traditional relaxation
54.9	201	Streaming Netflix, social media, modern entertainment
100.0	366	Total

Table 7. Keeping Updated Activity.

Percent	Frequency	Knowledge Update
83.6	306	Online medical journals, webinars, and social media
12.3	45	Printed journals, books, and conferences
100.0	366	Total

The potential of cryptocurrencies and blockchains in financing healthcare is enormous, but the implementation depends on the people involved, especially on their perceptions; see Figure 2. In our research approach, we followed Innovation Resistance Theory (IRT) [19].

This study aimed to evaluate the perceptions, awareness, and acceptance of emerging blockchain-based financial technologies, specifically cryptocurrencies, smart contracts, and BNPL) models, among medical professionals. The objective was to understand the readiness and potential resistance within the healthcare sector to adopting decentralised payment systems. While blockchain and fintech innovations are increasingly discussed in healthcare finance (e.g., patient billing automation, transparent records, and decentralised insurance), the existing research has primarily focused on technical feasibility and institutional deployment. There is a gap in empirical studies assessing healthcare professionals' attitudes toward these technologies. Few studies have explored how physicians and administrators perceive tokenised payment systems or BNPL solutions in clinical contexts. Addressing this gap is critical for evaluating the feasibility and ethical implications of integrating such technologies in patient care.

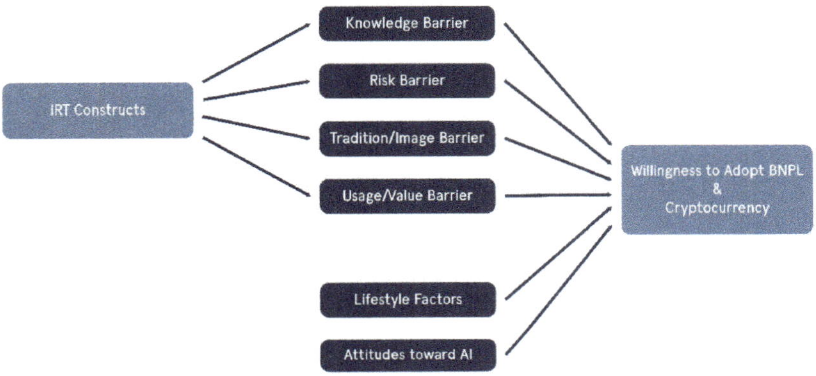

Figure 2. Research framework.

The survey items can be interpreted through the lens of Innovation Resistance Theory (IRT), which explains why individuals may resist adopting modern technologies despite potential benefits. Questions expressing distrust, age-related hesitation, or concern over regulatory uncertainty align with functional barriers (e.g., usage and risk) and psychological barriers (e.g., tradition and image) outlined in IRT. Items reflecting a lack of familiarity or perceived practitioner unawareness correspond to the knowledge barrier, a key precursor to resistance. Conversely, questions indicating curiosity, willingness to pilot new systems, or support for behaviour-based incentives demonstrate potential pathways to overcoming resistance through compatibility and perceived value. Overall, the responses can help identify which types of resistance dominate and what strategies may facilitate the acceptance of disruptive health technologies like AI, blockchain, and cryptocurrency-based payments.

3. Results

We analysed the data by both descriptive analyses as well as multivariate methods. Significant group differences were also extracted.

3.1. Descriptive Statistics

For all questions, we used a 0 (totally disagree)-to-10 (totally agree) Likert scale.

Most participants agreed that AI will have an impact on healthcare (mean 7.6); see Table 8. The knowledge about cryptocurrencies was low and the perceived uncertainty of cryptocurrencies was high. The willingness to accept instalment payments or to run a crypto test was also more on the negative side. The observed low willingness among European healthcare professionals to accept cryptocurrencies can be explained by examining the region's regulatory landscape and professional environment. Europe's healthcare sector is characterised by stringent regulations and a cautious approach to adopting new financial technologies. The introduction of the Markets in Crypto-Assets (MiCA) regulation aims to provide a harmonised legal framework for crypto-assets across the EU [21]. While MiCA seeks to enhance legal clarity, it also imposes significant compliance requirements that may deter healthcare institutions from integrating cryptocurrencies into their operations. This regulatory complexity contributes to hesitancy in adopting such technologies within the healthcare sector. Incorporating frameworks such as the European MiCA regulation [22] is crucial to ensure legal clarity and consumer protection in the tokenisation of healthcare financing. Ethical risks, particularly the potential for patient over-indebtedness, must be carefully assessed to prevent exploitation or undue financial stress. A responsible approach requires balancing innovation with safeguards that prioritise health equity, informed consent, and financial literacy.

Table 8. Descriptive statistics: survey items.

Std. Deviation	Mean	N	
2.21	7.60	366	AI Healthcare
2.62	6.69	366	Telehealth
3.16	5.55	366	Crypto doubts
3.38	4.81	366	Learning
3.22	4.58	366	Rewarded
2.96	4.36	366	Replaced
2.94	3.77	366	Instalments
3.04	3.39	366	Pilot
3.43	3.14	366	Know crypto

Additionally, the European healthcare industry often exhibits institutional scepticism toward emerging technologies like blockchain and cryptocurrencies. Concerns about data privacy, financial stability, and the speculative nature of crypto-assets further exacerbate this cautious stance. These factors collectively influence the low acceptance rates of cryptocurrencies among healthcare professionals in Europe. Therefore, the reluctance to embrace cryptocurrencies in European healthcare settings is not merely a reflection of individual attitudes but is deeply rooted in the broader regulatory and professional context of the region [23].

3.2. Group Differences

We conducted a t-test to evaluate whether medical doctors working in the private sector have different views than the ones working in the public sector. The null hypothesis that there was no difference at the 95% confidence level could be rejected in two cases, namely, being replaced by AI and telehealth; see Table 9. Medical experts working in the private sector (e.g., doctors having their own practice) are more afraid of being replaced by AI than their publicly employed colleagues. These, however, see a brighter future for telehealth than their private counterparts.

Table 9. Group differences by employment sector.

Mean	N	Work	Question
4.80	104	private	Replaced
4.30	166	public	
6.00	104	private	Telehealth
6.70	166	public	

3.3. Major Factors and Correlations

A factor analysis extracted three major dimensions, which, in total can explain more than 60% of variance; see Table 10. In factor analysis, the number of factors is commonly determined using the eigenvalue-greater-than-one rule (Kaiser criterion), which retains only those factors whose eigenvalues exceed 1, indicating that they explain more variance than a single original variable. In our case, the Kaiser criterion resulted in three factors.

Table 10. Total variance explained.

% of Variance	Rotation Sums of Squared Loadings
27.49	Factor 1
20.23	Factor 2
13.51	Factor 3

Factor (Component, Dimension) 1 showed four variables with high (>6) loadings; see Table 11. Factor 1 could be described as "open to new ideas" because it included the willingness to learn more about cryptocurrencies, the willingness to run a pilot test with crypto payments, accepting instalments (BNPL), and existing knowledge about cryptocurrencies. These four attributes correlated significantly with each other; see Table 12. This finding was in line with [20] Venkatesh et al. (2012), stating that openness to new ideas correlates with technology acceptance.

Table 11. Rotated component matrix.

Component			
3	2	1	
0.065	0.145	0.813	Learning
−0.225	−0.083	0.736	Know crypto
0.175	0.160	0.696	Instalments
0.198	0.222	0.652	Pilot
0.196	0.100	0.526	Crypto doubts
0.027	0.901	0.151	Telehealth
−0.020	0.861	0.184	AI healthcare
0.728	0.222	0.081	Rewarded
0.722	−0.325	0.149	Replaced

Table 12. Correlations.

Pilot	Instalments	Know Crypto	Learning		
0.581 *	0.451 *	0.484 *	1	Pearson Correlation	Learning
270	366	366	366	N	
0.329 *	0.283 *	1	0.484 *	Pearson Correlation	Know Crypto
270	366	366	366	N	
0.580 *	1	0.283 *	0.484 *	Pearson Correlation	Instalments
270	366	366	366	N	
1	0.580 *	0.329 *	0.581 *	Pearson Correlation	Pilot

* Correlation was significant at the 0.01 level (2-tailed).

Extraction method: Principal Component Analysis. Rotation method: Varimax with Kaiser normalisation.

3.4. Predicting

We conducted a regression analysis to predict who may be willing to run a pilot test with cryptocurrency as payment. Before conducting the regression analysis, diagnostic tests were performed to verify that key assumptions were met. Multicollinearity was assessed using the Variance Inflation Factor (VIF) with all predictors returning VIF values below 5, indicating no serious multicollinearity concerns (see Table 13).

Table 13. Variance Inflation Factor.

		Collinearity Statistics
Model	Tolerance	VIF
(Constant)		
Learning	0.784	1.275
Crypto_doubts	0.819	1.222
Rewarded	0.929	1.076
Replaced	0.884	1.132
Telehealth	0.867	1.154

To examine the assumption of normality, the Shapiro–Wilk test was applied to the regression residuals. The results (W = 0.976, $p = 0.067$) suggest that the residuals were approximately normally distributed, satisfying the assumption for parametric testing; see Table 14.

Table 14. Shapiro–Wilk test.

		Shapiro-Wilk	
	Statistic	df	Sig.
Standardised Residual	0.991	270	0.105

The strongest influencing parameter was the willingness to learn more about cryptocurrencies. Unsurprisingly, doubts about cryptocurrencies (legality etc.) had a negative impact. Table 15 shows the betas of the model. With an R square of 0.4, the fit of the model was good; see Table 16.

Table 15. Coefficients—dependent variable: pilot-test cryptocurrency.

Standardised Coefficients Beta	Unstandardised Coefficients B	Model
	−0.717	(Constant)
0.532	0.462	Learning
−0.094	−0.090	Crypto doubts
0.097	0.090	Rewarded
0.123	0.127	Replaced
0.200	0.219	Telehealth

Table 16. Model fit pilot.

Adjusted R Square	R Square	R
0.39	0.40	0.63

No issues regarding heteroscedasticity or residuals were found; see Figures 3–5.

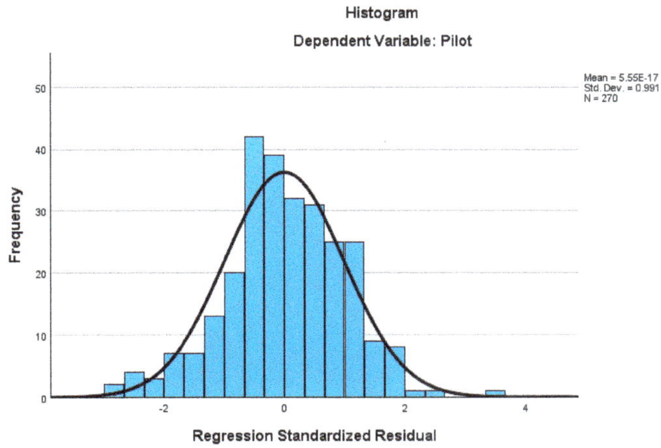

Figure 3. Residual normality check: histogram.

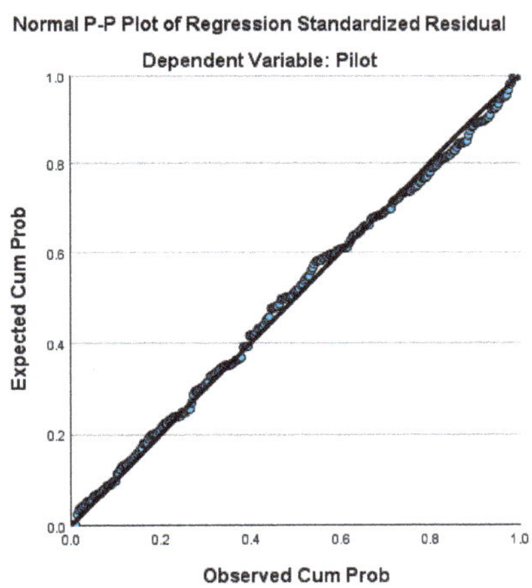

Figure 4. Residual normality check: normal P-P plot.

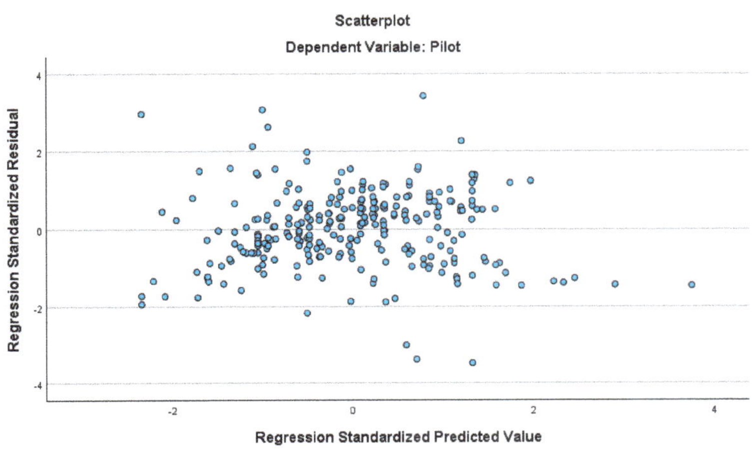

Figure 5. Heteroscedasticity check: ZRESID vs. ZPRED scatterplot.

We also wanted to predict who may accept instalment payments. In this case, the strongest predictor was the willingness to run a pilot test with cryptocurrency payments; see Table 17. The R square was 0.368; see Table 18.

Table 17. Coefficients—dependent variable: instalments.

Standardised Coefficients Beta	Unstandardised Coefficients B	Model
0.455	0.457	Pilot

Table 18. Model fit instalments.

Adjusted R Square	R Square	Model R
0.363	0.368	0.606

3.5. Grouping

We conducted a cluster analysis to group respondents. Two distinct clusters were identified. Looking at Table 19, we can see that Cluster 1 represented a more traditional lifestyle. A similar picture was found when looking at how respondents kept their knowledge updated; see Table 20. Cluster 2 was more into streaming than Cluster 1 members, who updated their knowledge by reading printed journals; see Table 20.

Table 19. Relaxation.

Streaming Netflix, Social Media, Modern Entertainment		Reading a Book, Classic Radio, Traditional Relaxation			
Percent	Frequency	Percent	Frequency		
9.9%	14	100.0%	64	1	Cluster
90.1%	128	0.0%	0	2	
100.0%	142	100.0%	64	Combined	

Table 20. Keeping updated.

Printed Journals, Books, and Conferences		Online Medical Journals, Webinars, and Social Media			
Frequency	Percent	Frequency	Percent		
41	100.0%	90	41.3%	Cluster	1
0	0.0%	128	58.7%		2
41	100.0%	218	100.0%		Combined

However, the centroids (of the willingness to run a pilot test) were not significantly different; see Table 21.

Table 21. Centroids.

Pilot			
Std. Deviation	Mean		Cluster
3.05112	3.0986	1	
3.01104	3.7266	2	
3.04281	3.3963	Combined	

The authors hypothesised that a modern lifestyle leads to a higher probability of running a pilot test. A chi-square test showed no relationship. Therefore, we conducted a cluster analysis but without a different result. This contradicts the current research that states that there is a link between lifestyle and the early adoption of a product/service [24,25].

4. Discussion and Implementation

Our findings are in line with previous research conducted by [26] Govindarajan et al. in the sense that there are many barriers to fully accepting modern technologies such as cryptocurrencies in healthcare. AI is accepted as a force that will shape the years to come [27,28]. However, there are concerns about the legality of cryptocurrencies [29,30].

The observed reluctance among healthcare professionals to adopt cryptocurrency-based payment systems aligns with prior research on institutional resistance to financial innovation in highly regulated sectors. Studies have shown that healthcare organisations are particularly cautious in adopting unregulated technologies due to perceived risks around compliance, accountability, and data integrity [31,32]. Furthermore, regulatory uncertainty, such as in evolving guidelines under the EU's MiCA framework, contributes to an environment where novel financial tools are met with scepticism [33]. This resistance can also be understood through the lens of Innovation Resistance Theory, which highlights how risk and tradition barriers inhibit the uptake of technologies that diverge from established institutional practices [19]. Additionally, empirical findings by [25] McElheran et al. indicate that even in technologically advanced industries, AI and fintech adoption is often delayed by organisational inertia and legal ambiguity. Regulatory clarity and perceived legitimacy are essential for innovation acceptance in healthcare.

To fully integrate AI-powered BNPL with crypto payments and smart contracts, the system must include on-chain and off-chain components to ensure seamless financing, automation, and security. Below is a detailed breakdown of how it would work from a technical perspective.

System architecture and components:

- AI-Powered Credit and Risk Assessment uses machine learning algorithms to analyse;
- Patient's financial history (bank accounts, crypto wallets, spending patterns);
- On-chain activity (decentralised financing transactions, crypto staking, wallet balances);
- Healthcare history (frequency of doctor visits, medical insurance claims);
- The AI generation of a personalised BNPL plan with terms tailored to the risk profile.

Crypto staking is a process where cryptocurrency holders lock up a certain number of their digital assets in a specific blockchain network to support its operations such as validating transactions or securing the network. In return for staking their crypto, participants earn rewards (usually in the form of additional tokens or coins). This process is typically associated with Proof of Stake (PoS) and its variants, which are consensus mechanisms used by some cryptocurrencies.

A smart contract is created to manage the following:

- Payment schedule (monthly or customised);
- Crypto collateral requirements (if needed);
- Automated penalties and rewards for early/late payments;
- Instant fund distribution to healthcare providers;
- Deployment on a public (e.g., Ethereum) or private (Hyperledger) blockchain;
- Crypto payment processing and stablecoin integration.

Healthcare BNPL could be tokenised into so-called NFTs (non-fungible tokens). Nunes et al. [34] explored the potential applications of NFTs in healthcare, highlighting innovative solutions and challenges associated with integrating blockchain technology in the sector. As shown by [35] Zhang et al., NFTs can effectively hedge against traditional financial assets when used as long positions. NFTs can hedge because these healthcare tokens are somewhat uncorrelated with mainstream markets. This diversification effect will reduce overall portfolio risk during traditional market downturns, assuming that the NFT market behaves independently or inversely.

Patients could tokenise BNPL agreements as NFTs for trading on decentralised financing lending platforms and investors could fund BNPL pools in return for yield from patient repayments. Healthcare providers could then use BNPL-backed assets as collateral. Figure 6 illustrates a decentralised BNPL model in healthcare, where patients receive treatment from providers while entering a smart-contract-based repayment agreement. The smart contract manages the flow of funds between patients, providers, BNPL platforms, and investors with the option to tokenize the debt as NFTs for trade or collateral. This system leverages blockchain technology to automate, secure, and potentially decentralize healthcare financing.

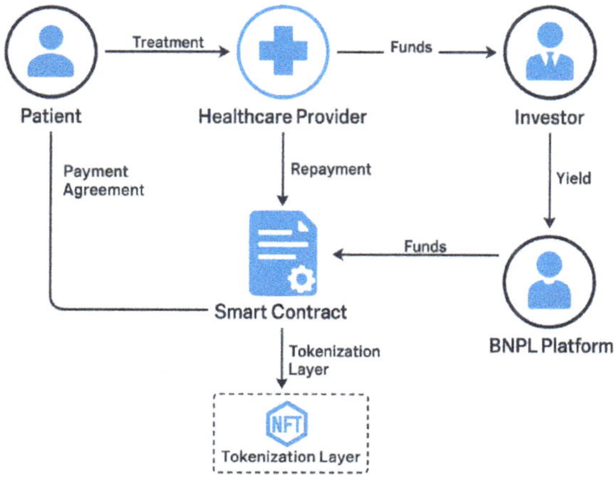

Figure 6. Proposed BNPL system.

The integration of tokenised BNPL agreements with decentralised financing lending pools can revolutionise healthcare financing by transforming patient debt into tradeable assets. This model allows investors to fund medical loans, hospitals to gain liquidity, and patients to access care without upfront costs. Tokenisation converts BNPL agreements into digital assets (NFTs or security tokens) recorded on a blockchain. These assets represent a patient's outstanding medical balance and can be traded or used as collateral in decentralised finance lending markets. To implement tokenised BNPL for healthcare, it needs smart contracts that automate: loan issuance, payment tracking, default handling, and tokenisation. Tokenisation converts BNPL agreements into digital assets recorded on a blockchain. However, tokenising BNPL agreements in healthcare could introduce systemic financial risks like those seen in the 2008 US mortgage crisis. Just like mortgage-backed securities bundled subprime loans, tokenised BNPL agreements could be packaged and traded as financial assets. If healthcare BNPL debts are issued to high-risk patients who struggle to repay, these tokenised assets could become overvalued and unstable. A lack of regulation in tokenised debt markets could lead to predatory lending, where patients are offered BNPL without proper risk assessment. If speculative trading increases, healthcare debt could be treated like a financial commodity rather than a human necessity. However, there is a long way to go before this risk factor may come into play. A token economy in healthcare would involve the utilisation of blockchain-based tokens such as NFTs representing patient debt. These tokens would be tradeable, allowing investors to fund patient care by purchasing them in exchange for yield from future repayments. Sustainability would require transparent governance, regulatory compliance, and robust smart contracts to ensure trust. Additionally, patient data privacy must be protected through secure and anonymised token design. Long-term viability depends on the future adoption.

There were limitations in our study. We surveyed medical professionals but not health insurance providers. These may have a more forward-looking perspective; nor did we include government officials. Like any other technology, blockchains (or distributed server systems) have to prove that they become mainstream and are manageable. The acceptance and tradability of BNPL NFTs has not been evaluated.

5. Conclusions

BNPL is an additional payment method and not a substitute for conventional methods. However, integrating AI-powered BNPL with cryptocurrencies and smart contracts could revolutionise medical financing, making healthcare more accessible, transparent, and automated. As blockchain adoption grows, decentralised BNPL financing solutions could provide patients with flexible, low-cost, and secure payment options worldwide to the extent of a global market for bundled BNPL tokens. Overall medical costs will be reduced because we will, at the same token, be financially incentivised to actively manage our own health (preventing chronical diseases) and foster care habits (e.g., regular exercise, diet tracking) through AI. However, the stumbling block against changing the system constitutes the people involved such as politicians and medical professionals. To incentivise politicians and medical practitioners to accept BNPL tokens in a decentralised financial environment, it will need a strategy that aligns with their interests, i.e., economic benefits, risk reduction, regulatory alignment, and patient-centred incentives such as positioning BNPL tokens as cost-reduction tools for national healthcare, collaboration with the European Central Bank to issue regulated stablecoin-backed BNPL tokens to avoid volatility concerns, and using pilot programmes in high-profile hospitals.

Author Contributions: Methodology, Â.F.O.G. and S.F.N.; Writing—review & editing, C.B. All authors have read and agreed to the published version of the manuscript.

Funding: This research received no external funding.

Institutional Review Board Statement: Not applicable.

Informed Consent Statement: Informed consent was obtained from all subjects involved in the study.

Data Availability Statement: Data are available from the corresponding author upon request.

Conflicts of Interest: The authors declare no conflicts of interest.

Abbreviations

The following abbreviations have been used in this manuscript:

AI	Artificial Intelligence
BNPL	Buy-Now-Pay-Later
NFT	Non-Fungible Token

Appendix A. Survey

Dear Healthcare Practitioner,

We are conducting a survey to assess the challenges and barriers to adopting cryptocurrencies in healthcare. Your responses will help us understand medical industry perspectives and potential adoption strategies.

The survey should take 3 min to complete.

Your responses are anonymous and confidential.

Please answer using the Likert scale (0–10):

0 Totally Disagree | 3 Disagree | 5.5 Neutral | 8 Agree | 10 Totally Agree

Thank you for your participation!

I have had prior exposure to cryptocurrencies like Bitcoin
I have heart about blockchain technology
Artificial Intelligence can enhance healthcare
I believe that most healthcare practitioners lack awareness of Artificial Intelligence
I believe that most healthcare practitioners lack awareness of cryptocurrencies
I do not trust these new technologies like Artificial Intelligence and blockchains
I am too old for all these new technologies like Artificial Intelligence in healthcare
I worry about the regulatory uncertainty surrounding cryptocurrencies in healthcare
I am interested in learning more about how cryptocurrencies could work in healthcare
I am familiar with healthcare financing systems in other countries
The current "free" healthcare should be replaced by a private healthcare system
I would accept payments in monthly instalments as it is common practice in retailing
I would be willing to pilot a small-scale crypto-based payment system in my practice/hospital
Individuals who actively maintain a healthy lifestyle (through regular check-ups, physical activity, balanced nutrition, and the use of health-tracking devices like Apple Watch or Fitbit) should be granted easier access and better fees for high-quality medical care and services.

Age: below 30, 30–40, 40–50, above 50
I am a Medical Doc, other

References

1. Kotler, P.; Keller, K.L. *Marketing Management*, 15th ed.; Pearson: London, UK, 2016.
2. Cutler, D. The Costs of Care: Understanding Healthcare Pricing and Reimbursement. *J. Health Econ.* **2020**, *39*, 567–582.
3. Glied, S.; Smith, P.C. *Healthcare Economics and Capitation Models: Balancing Cost and Care*; Cambridge University Press: Cambridge, UK, 2018.
4. Berenson, R.A.; Rice, T. Beyond Fee-for-Service: Examining Alternative Payment Models in Healthcare. *Health Aff.* **2019**, *38*, 1726–1733.
5. Miller, H.D. Bundled Payments and Healthcare Reform: Cost Efficiency in a Changing Market. *Am. J. Manag. Care* **2021**, *27*, 253–261.
6. Frogner, B.K. Telemedicine and the Rise of Subscription-Based Healthcare Services. *Digit. Health Rev.* **2022**, *7*, 112–126.
7. Statista. Healthcare. 2025. Available online: https://www.statista.com/markets/412/topic/454/health-system (accessed on 19 March 2025).
8. Manta, O.P. *FinTech 2050: AI-Powered Transformation and Innovation*; Lambert Academic Publishing (LAP): Saarbrücken, Germany, 2025.
9. Manta, O.P.; Vasile, V.; Rusu, E. Banking Transformation Through FinTech and the Integration of Artificial Intelligence in Payments. Preprints, 2025. Available online: https://www.preprints.org/manuscript/202502.1409 (accessed on 2 April 2025).
10. FinMasters. PayZen: A Better Way to Finance Medical Bills, 2023. Available online: https://finmasters.com/payzen-a-better-way-to-finance-medical-bills/ (accessed on 22 March 2025).
11. Lupșa-Tătaru, D.A.; Nichifor, E.; Dovleac, L.; Chițu, I.B.; Todor, R.D.; Brătucu, G. Buy Now Pay Later—A Fad or a Reality? A Perspective on Electronic Commerce. *Economies* **2023**, *11*, 218. [CrossRef]
12. OECD. *Health at a Glance: Europe 202—State of Health in the EU Cycle*; OECD Publishing: Paris, France, 2024.
13. BMG, Ministry of Health, Germany. Beiträge. 2025. Available online: https://www.bundesgesundheitsministerium.de/beitraege.html#:~:text=Der%20gesetzlich%20festgeschriebene%20allgemeine%20Beitragssatz,0%20Prozent%20der%20beitragspflichtigen%20Einnahmen (accessed on 2 April 2025).
14. Gaffney, A.; Himmelstein, D.U.; Woolhandler, S. COVID-19 and US Health Financing: Perils and Possibilities. *Int. J. Health Serv.* **2020**, *50*, 396–407. [CrossRef]
15. Khezr, S.; Moniruzzaman, M.; Yassine, A.; Benlamri, R. Blockchain Technology in Healthcare: A Comprehensive Review and Directions for Future Research. *Appl. Sci.* **2019**, *9*, 1736. [CrossRef]
16. Sharma, A.; Dangi, S.; Tomar, R.; Chilamkurti, N.; Kim, B.-G. Blockchain Based Smart Contracts for Internet of Medical Things in e-Healthcare. *Electronics* **2020**, *9*, 1609. [CrossRef]
17. Salhout, S.; Bechter, C. Visionizing a Fiat Cryptocurrency. *Case Stud. Bus. Manag.* **2018**, *5*, 1–12. [CrossRef]
18. Boustani, N.M.; Elisabetta, M. Smart Insurance Contracts Shielding Pandemic Business Disruption in Developing Countries and Blockchain Solution. *FinTech* **2022**, *1*, 294–309. [CrossRef]

19. Ram, S.; Sheth, J.N. Consumer resistance to innovations: The marketing problem and its solutions. *J. Consum. Mark.* **1989**, *6*, 5–14. [CrossRef]
20. Venkatesh, V.; Thong, J.Y.L.; Xu, X. Consumer acceptance and use of information technology: Extending the unified theory of acceptance and use of technology. *MIS Q.* **2012**, *36*, 157–178. [CrossRef]
21. European Commission. Regulating Crypto-Assets in Europe: Practical Guide to MiCA. Norton Rose Fulbright. Available online: https://www.nortonrosefulbright.com/en/knowledge/publications/2cec201e/regulating-crypto-assets-in-europe-practical-guide-to-mica (accessed on 30 December 2024).
22. European Union. Regulation (EU). 2023/1114 of the European Parliament and of the Council of 31 May 2023 on markets in crypto-assets, and amending Regulations (EU) No 1093/2010 and (EU) No 1095/2010 and Directives 2013/36/EU and (EU) 2019/1937. In *Official Journal of the European Union*; Publications Office of the European Union: Luxembourg, 2023. Available online: https://eur-lex.europa.eu/eli/reg/2023/1114/oj/eng (accessed on 1 May 2025).
23. McFarlane, C.S. Blockchain in healthcare adoption faces headwinds in Europe. *Forbes*, 30 April 2025. Available online: https://www.forbes.com/sites/chrissamcfarlane/2025/04/30/blockchain-in-healthcare-adoption-faces-headwinds-in-europe/ (accessed on 2 April 2025).
24. Seyed Esfahani, M.; Reynolds, N. Impact of consumer innovativeness on really new product adoption. *Mark. Intell. Plan.* **2021**, *39*, 589–612. [CrossRef]
25. McElheran, K.; Li, J.F.; Brynjolfsson, E.; Kroff, Z.; Dinlersoz, E.; Foster, L.; Zolas, N. AI adoption in America: Who, what, and where. *J. Econ. Manag. Strategy* **2024**, *33*, 375–415. [CrossRef]
26. Govindarajan, U.H.; Narang, G.; Singh, D.K.; Yadav, V.S. Blockchain technologies adoption in healthcare: Overcoming barriers amid the hype cycle to enhance patient care. *Technol. Forecast. Soc. Change* **2025**, *213*, 124031. [CrossRef]
27. Hua, D.; Petrina, N.; Young, N.; Cho, J.-G.; Poon, S.K. Understanding the factors influencing acceptability of AI in medical imaging domains among healthcare professionals: A scoping review. *Artif. Intell. Med.* **2004**, *147*, 102698. [CrossRef]
28. Cornelissen, L.; Egher, C.; Beek, V.; Williamson, L.; Hommes, D. The Drivers of Acceptance of Artificial Intelligence–Powered Care Pathways Among Medical Professionals: Web-Based Survey Study. *JMIR Form. Res.* **2022**, *6*, e33368. [CrossRef]
29. Witkowski, K.; Okhai, R.; Neely, S.R. Public perceptions of artificial intelligence in healthcare: Ethical concerns and opportunities for patient-centered care. *BMC Med. Ethics* **2004**, *25*, 74. [CrossRef]
30. Sahoo, R.K.; Sahoo, K.C.; Negi, S.; Baliarsingh, S.K.; Panda, B.; Pati, S. Health professionals' perspectives on the use of Artificial Intelligence in healthcare: A systematic review. *Patient Educ. Couns.* **2025**, *134*, 108680. [CrossRef]
31. Yeoh, P. Regulatory issues in blockchain technology. *J. Financ. Regul. Compliance* **2017**, *25*, 196–208. [CrossRef]
32. Hasselgren, A.; Wan, P.K.; Horn, M.; Kralevska, K.; Gligoroski, D.; Faxvaag, A. GDPR compliance for blockchain applications in healthcare. *arXiv* **2020**, arXiv:2009.12913.
33. Farouk, G.; Alsamara, T. Legal view on blockchain technologies in healthcare: A European states case study. *Int. J. Sociotechnol. Knowl. Dev.* **2024**, *15*, 1–13. [CrossRef]
34. Nunes, T.; da Cunha, P.R.; de Abreu, J.M.; Duarte, J.; Corte-Real, A. Non-Fungible Tokens (NFTs) in Healthcare: A Systematic Review. *Int. J. Environ. Res. Public Health* **2024**, *21*, 965. [CrossRef] [PubMed]
35. Zhang, W.; Liu, T.; Zhang, Y.; Hamori, S. Can NFTs hedge the risk of traditional assets after the COVID-19 pandemic? *N. Am. J. Econ. Financ.* **2024**, *72*, 102149. [CrossRef]

FinTech MDPI

Article

Machine Learning for Predicting Bank Stability: The Role of Income Diversification in European Banking

Karim Farag [1], Loubna Ali [2], Noah Cheruiyot Mutai [1,*], Rabia Luqman [1], Ahmed Mahmoud [2] and Nol Krasniqi [1]

[1] Faculty of Economics and Business Administration, Berlin School of Business and Innovation (BSBI), Berlin Campus, 12043 Berlin, Germany; karim.shehata@berlinsbi.com (K.F.); rabia.luqman@berlinsbi.com (R.L.); nol.krasniqi@berlinsbi.com (N.K.)

[2] Faculty of Computer Science and Informatics, Berlin School of Business and Innovation (BSBI), Berlin Campus, 12043 Berlin, Germany; loubna.ali@berlinsbi.com (L.A.); ahmed.ashraf@berlinsbi.com (A.M.)

* Correspondence: noah.mutai@berlinsbi.com

Abstract: There is an ongoing debate about the role of income diversification in enhancing bank stability within the financial services industry in Europe. Some advocate for diversification, while others argue that its importance should not be overstated. Some financial institutions are encouraged to focus on their traditional investments instead of income diversification, while others suggest that income diversification can stabilize or destabilize, depending on the regulatory environment. These conflicting results indicate a lack of clear evidence regarding the effectiveness of income diversification. Therefore, this paper aims to study the impact of income diversification on bank stability and enhance the predictive performance of bank stability by analyzing the period from 2000 to 2021 using a sample from 26 European countries, based on aggregate bank data. It employs a hybrid method that combines econometric techniques, specifically the generalized method of moments and a fixed-effects model, with machine-learning algorithms such as Random Forest and Support Vector Machine. These methods are applied to enhance the reliability and predictive power of the analysis by addressing the problem of endogeneity (via generalized method of moments) and capturing non-linearities, interactions, and high-dimensional patterns (via machine learning). The econometric findings reveal that income diversification can reduce non-performing loans, improve bank solvency, and enhance the Z-score, indicating the significant role of income diversification in improving bank stability. Conversely, the results also show that the machine-learning algorithms used play a crucial role in enhancing the predictive performance of bank stability.

Keywords: income diversification; bank stability; support vector machines; random forest; financial supervision

JEL Classification: G21; G32; C45; G28; C55

1. Introduction

Banks are instrumental in advancing sustainable economic development by efficiently allocating capital to productive sectors, enhancing output, and long-term growth. However, the post-crisis financial environment has become increasingly dynamic, requiring banks to adopt more proactive and strategic approaches to portfolio and risk management [1]. In response to systemic vulnerabilities exposed during the global financial crisis, regulatory standards such as Basel III clarify that the official minimum capital requirement remains 8% under Basel II, but Basel III adds a mandatory Capital Conservation Buffer of 2.5%, which increases the total requirement to 10.5% [2]. This shift underscores the importance of accurate risk-exposure measurement for ensuring financial system resilience and supporting economic stability. It also emphasizes the importance of asset diversification to better meet capital requirements. Ref. [3] stated that, following the 2007–2009 financial crisis, banks were increasingly motivated to diversify from conventional assets to protect themselves from credit and insolvency risks. Furthermore, banks' use of technology to expand internationally and join global financial markets was greatly aided by technological advancements, which in turn increased non-interest-bearing investment.

Globalization and financial reforms have further driven the deregulation of banking activities and expanded the scope for income diversification. Ref. [1] argued that the decline in market interest rates also caused European banks to reallocate their reserves to non-traditional assets. Financial institutions are increasingly adopting digital tools and FinTech-enabled services to improve operational efficiency, expand product offerings, and manage competition [4]. Consequently, banks have shifted away from a heavy reliance on interest income toward a broader mix of fee-based and off-balance-sheet activities, such as securitization, derivatives trading, trade finance, underwriting, and financial advisory services, which theoretically help mitigate concentration risk [5].

Despite its theoretical appeal, the impact of income diversification on bank stability remains contentious. Some scholars found that it contributes to systemic risk, particularly when fee-based activities involve complex financial instruments like subprime mortgages and derivatives, key triggers of the 2007–2009 financial crisis [1,6]. Accordingly, Asian regulators—including Korea and Taiwan—imposed restrictions on off-balance-sheet activities to protect financial stability [7]. The Bank of England enforced the separation of retail and investment banking to relieve the vulnerability of off-balance-sheet risks driven by the exaggeration of income diversification. Additionally, Ref. [8] conducted a thorough assessment of 83 studies and concluded that income diversification is important for lowering risk and improving bank stability, particularly when banks use it as a buffer to mitigate their risk of income volatility. Furthermore, Ref. [9] argued that income diversification can decrease bank stability in poorly regulated environments or when banks evolve into more complex structures that are difficult to track and control, consistent with the findings of [10], arguing that countries operating in low-regulatory environments are vulnerable to a lack of oversight, inadequate risk controls, moral hazard, and poor risk management, resulting in excessive risk-taking and weakly diversified portfolios, which undermine the effectiveness of the income diversification role in enhancing bank stability. On the other hand, Ref. [11] stated that highly regulated environments, such as Europe, have stronger risk controls that encourage income diversification to stabilize bank performance.

This ongoing debate calls for a reassessment of income-diversification strategies through advanced analytical tools. This study contributes to the FinTech literature by evaluating the effect of income diversification on bank stability and improving the prediction performance of bank stability levels using both econometric and machine-learning approaches. By combining GMM with predictive algorithms like Support Vector Machines (SVMs) and Random Forests (RFs), the study explores the causal linkages and predictive potential of diversification in the context of European commercial banks. Our findings aim to support evidence-based regulation and highlight how machine learning can be leveraged for real-time risk monitoring in a fast-evolving financial ecosystem.

The remainder of the paper is structured as follows: The Literature Review section theoretically and empirically reviews the most recent relevant papers. The Research Methodology and Data section clarifies the design of the study and the data sources. The Results section presents the output of the econometric and machine-learning models, along with their relevant analysis, and discusses the findings in relation to existing studies and their practical implications. The Conclusion section concludes the paper with a summary of key insights. Finally, the Limitations and Future Work section demonstrates the limitations and directions for future research.

2. Literature Review

2.1. Previous Studies in Europe

Using panel data from 2002 to 2012 and a sample of European banks, Ref. [12] examined the relationship between income structure and bank profitability to assess how the banks' practices evolved after the crisis. The results showed that while income diversification has a negative effect on profitability, this effect decreases during times of crisis, suggesting that income diversification is more beneficial when banks anticipate a crisis. Conversely, during normal conditions, it is advantageous to focus more on traditional investments. Utilizing a sample of 1250 banks in the United States and Europe between 2008 and 2016, Ref. [13] employed regression analysis to investigate the impact of income diversification on bank stability and profitability. The findings revealed that income diversification is positively related to bank stability in the USA, whereas in Europe, it has an insignificant effect on both bank stability and profitability. This indicates that European banks prefer to diversify their traditional investments in loans rather than non-interest income-generating investments to enhance profitability and bank stability.

Furthermore, Ref. [11] used the panel smooth-transition regression model to explore the impact of income diversification on bank stability in 114 European commercial banks, utilizing panel data from 2010 to 2019. According to the findings, increasing income diversification through non-traditional banking activities has a detrimental impact on bank stability and financial performance. In addition, Ref. [14] examined the impact of non-interest income, loan, and geographic diversification during the COVID-19 pandemic, using a sample of 56 European banks. The results showed that, in contrast to loan and geographic diversifications, the non-interest income ratio is the only variable that supports enhancing the stability of the European banks during the crisis and pandemics. Ref. [15] employed the system GMM to study the effect of income diversification on bank performance during the COVID-19 period, using a sample of 1231 banks in 90 countries from 2018 to 2021. The findings revealed that income diversification had a positive effect on bank stability in developing and developed countries during the COVID-19 periods, thus confirming the importance of encouraging banks to engage in fee-based, trading, and FOREX activities to absorb the negative effect of the recessionary periods for more stability and growth in the credit markets.

2.2. Previous Studies in the Rest of the World

Ref. [16] argued that non-performing loans (NPLs), which are defined as loans that have been passed due for more than 90 days without payments, are used to gauge a bank's exposure to credit risk, which is a key factor in determining the stability of the bank. To prevent unforeseen bad debt expenses that could jeopardize bank stability and degrade capital, banks must lower the non-performing loan ratio. In this regard, banks must diversify their loan portfolios by lending to businesses in various industries and offering a range of loan products, including credit cards, mortgages, auto loans, personal loans, commercial and industrial loans, and so forth. However, this diversification proves unsuccessful during recessions and crises, leading most banks to reallocate a portion of their reserves to non-interest-bearing investments to safeguard their capital against unforeseen losses during recessions and crises. In China, Ref. [17] employed the GMM to investigate the effect of income diversification on bank stability by using a sample of 101 Chinese banks with panel data from 2006 to 2016. The results indicated that income diversification has a negative effect on bank stability. They argued that the reason behind such a negative relationship is that the Chinese banks are still at the early stage of non-interest activities and have limited control. Additionally, increasing banks' engagement in non-interest activities could reduce banks' concern about their core business in loan investments raising the volatility of income and a lack of government supervision. In this respect, Chinese banks are more likely to diversify their traditional loan investments than non-traditional ones to improve their financial stability.

Additionally, Ref. [6] studied a sample of 200 commercial banks operating in South Asian countries, discovering that income diversification has a positive influence on bank stability, except for fees and commission income activities, which have a negative impact on bank stability, implying that not all non-interest activities are beneficial to the financial health of the South Asian banking system. Additionally, Ref. [18] employed a fixed-effect model, using a sample of commercial banks from Malaysia, and the results revealed that income diversification enhances the financial performance of the banks. Furthermore, Ref. [4] used fixed-effect models and GMMs to investigate the impact of income diversification on bank stability by taking a sample of 169 BRICS commercial banks from 2001 to 2015. The findings showed that the income diversification of large-sized banks positively affected bank performance.

In contrast, the small-sized ones had a negative effect, which provided better insights to regulators that income diversification is not favorable for all. Ref. [19] used a sample from Indian banks and confirmed the results of [4]. Furthermore, Ref. [20] discovered that Islamic banks in the Gulf Cooperation Council (GCC) nations prefer income diversification to increase bank stability. In contrast, the results of conventional banks showed that income diversification positively affected non-performing loans (NPLs) and negatively impacted Z-score. This suggests that the conventional banks in the GCC would become less stable if they relied too much on income diversification from fee-based and off-balance-sheet activities. Additionally, Ref. [7] used multivariate regression on a sample of commercial banks operating in 34 countries that are members of the Organization for Economic Co-Operation and Development (OECD), using unbalanced panel data from 2002 to 2012. The results showed that while a moderate increase in income diversification can improve bank stability, excessive diversification, particularly during a crisis, can worsen stability.

This highlights the significance of traditional investment concentration in loan and deposit investments during a crisis rather than engaging in non-interest-bearing investments to stabilize bank operations. Moreover, Ref. [21] used the GMM to study the effect of income diversification on bank stability, using a sample of Vietnamese commercial banks from 2006 to 2015. The findings revealed that relying on fee-based activities rather than traditional loan investments can reduce bank stability. In addition, Ref. [22] employed the GMM to explore how income diversification affects bank performance in Sub-Saharan banks by conducting a comparative study among emerging, regional, and global banks. The findings showed that income diversification enhanced bank performance in global and emerging markets compared to the regional African and domestic banks, thus demonstrating the importance of adopting diversification in bank investments to stabilize their financials. Further, Ref. [23] used the GMM on a sample of 48 banks operating in India to investigate how bank diversification influences bank stability, with geographic, loan portfolio, and functional diversifications as dependent variables in the study. The findings demonstrated that all levels of bank diversification have a positive impact on stabilizing bank performance, arguing that more engagement in different alternative investments would reduce the overall risk and increase the stability of the banks.

In addition, Ref. [23] used a regression model to investigate the impact of income diversification on bank stability from 2008 to 2017 using a sample of Tunisian commercial banks. The results demonstrated that income diversification significantly and favorably affects bank stability, suggesting that greater income diversification will raise the Z-score, indicating improvement in bank stability. Furthermore, Ref. [24] examined a sample of 45 African commercial banks from 2000 to 2020 and discovered that income diversification improves bank stability, whereas excessive diversity diminishes it. He also discovered that larger liquidity and interest margins, as well as increased operational inefficiencies, had a negative influence on bank stability. In contrast, GDP and inflation have a significant impact on banks' financial health. Further, Ref. [10] used panel data from 2002 to 2019, using GMM to examine the effects of income and asset diversification on bank stability in the United States commercial banks. Bank stability is positively impacted by assets and funding diversification, in turn encouraging banks to increase their traditional lending investments. On the other hand, they discovered that revenue diversification adversely affects bank stability, thus making banks' financial issues worse. Ref. [25] contends that income diversification is favorable to bank stability; however, excessive diversification could negatively affect bank stability in the African markets.

Furthermore, Ref. [10] used panel data from 2012 to 2021 and a sample from MENA countries to examine the effect of income diversification on bank stability using the fixed-effect regression model. The results showed that income diversification significantly and positively affects bank stability. Additionally, Refs. [16,26] used a sample of Egyptian commercial banks with panel data from 2011 to 2020 to examine the impact of macroeconomic and bank-specific factors on bank stability. They found that bank-specific factors had a greater impact on corporate credit risk than on retail credit risk; additionally, the findings of the income diversification found an insignificant effect on retail and corporate NPL. According to Ref. [5] Zimbabwean commercial banks have a low-income diversification ratio because they rely heavily on loans and neglect investments in off-balance-sheet and fee-based income activities. This makes these banks susceptible to high systemic risk. To investigate the impact of income diversification on bank performance, they used the modified OLS and difference GMM. The results showed that income diversification has a positive effect on banks' ROE, highlighting the necessity for Zimbabwean banks to alter their revenue strategy by increasing their level of diversification to improve stability and growth. Additionally, a sample of 271 commercial banks operating in the MENA countries from 2009 to 2020 was used by [16] to examine the impact of asset and income diversification on bank stability using the two-step GMM. They additionally investigated how political stability influences the relationship between diversification and bank stability. The results showed that while income and asset diversification contribute to bank stability, a greater proportion of non-interest-income compared to interest-income activities has a negative impact on the benefits of asset diversification, and political stability undermines bank stability, in turn reducing the benefits of investment diversification. Furthermore, the advantages of diversification differ depending on the size and market power of banks. This indicates that larger banks may use diversification to lower systemic risk more effectively than smaller ones, which are more vulnerable to systemic risks.

3. Lack of Literature

After reviewing the literature, particularly in European countries, the paper concluded that there is no crystal-clear evidence that offers a clear relationship between income diversification and bank stability after the periods of COVID-19. Additionally, to the best of researchers' knowledge, the research found that limited studies were applied in Europe after COVID-19. Further, the researchers noticed that income diversification has struggled recently, as shown in Figure 1 along with decline in the bank stability measured by Z score, as shown in Figure 2.

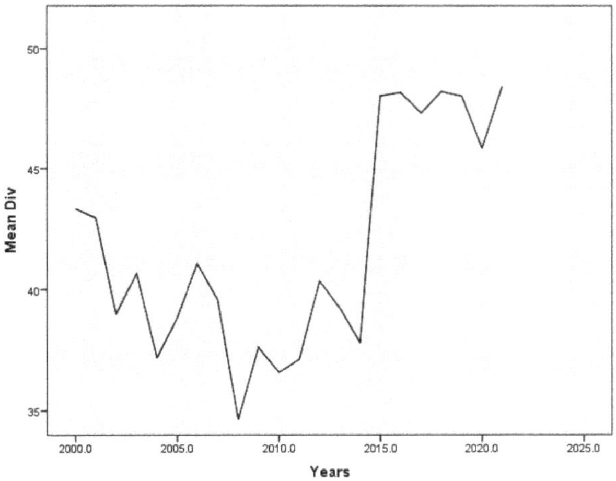

Figure 1. Income diversification ratio in Europe during 2000–2021 (source: World Bank's Global Financial Development Database (GFDD).

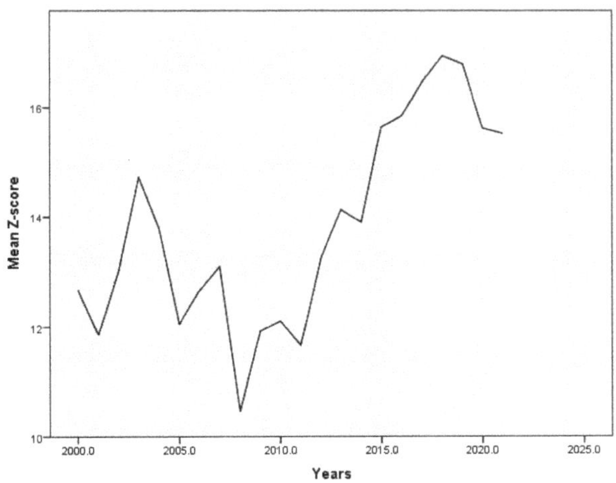

Figure 2. Bank Z-score in Europe during 2000–2021 (source: World Bank's Global Financial Development Database (GFDD)).

4. Research Methodology and Data

This study investigates the effect of income diversification on bank stability using an unbalanced dataset comprising 572 observations from 26 European countries over the period from 2000 to 2021. Further, the frequency of the data is on an annual basis. The dataset has aggregated banking performance indicators at the country-year level. It does not include individual bank-level entries. Consequently, it is not possible to directly determine the number of banks per country from this dataset. The countries included in the analysis are Germany, the United Kingdom, France, Italy, Austria, Belgium, Croatia, Cyprus, the Czech Republic, Denmark, Sweden, Estonia, Finland, Greece, Hungary, Ireland, Bulgaria, Latvia, the Netherlands, Poland, Malta, Portugal, Slovakia, Slovenia, Lithuania, and Luxembourg. Data were obtained from the World Bank's Global Financial Development Database (GFDD) and the World Development Indicators (WDI).

To capture the causal relationship between income diversification and bank stability, we employed the System Generalized Method of Moments (System GMM) estimator. This approach was chosen over Difference GMM because of its superior efficiency in exploiting additional moment conditions and minimizing potential bias from weak instruments. Additionally, fixed- and random-effects models were estimated for robustness checks. The software used for econometric analysis is R software, version 4.5.0. Bank stability was proxied using the Z-score (a measure of insolvency risk), the non-performing loan (NPL) ratio, and the capital adequacy ratio (CAR), consistent with prior studies [11,20,27]. To ensure the quality and consistency of the panel dataset, several preprocessing steps were conducted prior to data analysis, utilizing the econometric models. Missing values were addressed using listwise deletion, and outliers were identified using the interquartile range (IQR) and eliminated. Log transformation was applied to increase normality and stabilize variance in variables with skewed distributions. The first lag was taken to test and manage stationarity, which was addressed by taking the first lag. Additionally, lagged values of endogenous variables were produced.

In parallel, this study implemented two machine-learning algorithms—Random Forest and Support Vector Machine (SVM)—to complement the econometric analysis with predictive modeling using Python 3.13.3 and PyCharm compiler. These models were trained on the same macro-financial dataset to classify bank distress, defined using a binarized Z-score threshold. Random Forest combines the outputs of multiple decision trees to capture non-linear relationships and reduce overfitting through ensemble averaging. SVM was selected for its ability to operate effectively in high-dimensional feature spaces and to identify optimal hyperplanes for class separation. Both models were evaluated based on accuracy, precision, recall, and F1-score, and cross-validation was employed to enhance generalization. As a result, the research formulates the following hypotheses.

H_1: *Income diversification significantly affects bank stability in Europe.*

H_{1a}: *Income diversification significantly affects bank Z-score in Europe.*

H_{1b}: *Income diversification significantly affects bank credit risk in Europe.*

H_{1c}: *Income diversification significantly affects bank insolvency risk in Europe.*

This dual-method approach—econometric modeling for inference and machine learning for prediction—provides a comprehensive framework to assess the implications of income diversification for bank stability, while accounting for potential endogeneity, heterogeneity, and non-linear dependencies.

$$\begin{aligned}\Delta ZScore_{it} = \alpha_i \; & + \sum \beta_1 DIV + \sum \beta_2 CON \\ & + \sum \beta_3 EFF + \sum \beta_4 SMR + \sum \beta_5 SPV \\ & + \sum \beta_6 PROF + \sum \beta_7 GDP + \sum \beta_8 INF + \sum \beta_9 UNEMP + e_{it}\end{aligned}$$

$$\begin{aligned}\Delta NPL_{it} = \alpha_i \; & + \sum \beta_1 DIV + \sum \beta_2 CON \\ & + \sum \beta_3 EFF + \sum \beta_4 SMR + \sum \beta_5 SPV \\ & + \sum \beta_6 PROF + \sum \beta_7 GDP + \sum \beta_8 INF + \sum \beta_9 UNEMP + e_{it}\end{aligned}$$

$$\begin{aligned}\Delta CAR_{it} = \alpha_i \; & + \sum \beta_1 DIV + \sum \beta_2 CON \\ & + \sum \beta_3 EFF + \sum \beta_4 SMR + \sum \beta_5 SPV \\ & + \sum \beta_6 PROF + \sum \beta_7 GDP + \sum \beta_8 INF + \sum \beta_9 UNEMP + e_{it}\end{aligned}$$

Additionally, the formulas used in the machine-learning algorithms are as follows:

$$\text{Precision} = \frac{\text{TP}}{(\text{TP} + \text{FP})}$$

$$\text{Recall} = \frac{\text{TP}}{(\text{TP} + \text{FN})}$$

$$\text{Accuracy} = \frac{(\text{TP} + \text{TN})}{(\text{TP} + \text{FP} + \text{FN} + \text{TN})}$$

$$\text{F1 Score} = 2 \times \frac{(\text{Precision} \times \text{Recall})}{(\text{Precision} + \text{Recall})}$$

Table 1 presents the variables used in the paper, including their measurements. It shows the dependent and independent variables used in the study. This paper has three dependent variables, Z-score, NPL, and CAR proxies for bank stability, and nine independent variables. The DIV, CON, EFF, SMR, SPV, and PROF represent the bank-specific data, while the GDP, INF, and UNEMP represent the macroeconomic data.

Table 1. Definition of variables and measurements.

Variables	Measurements
Dependent variables:	
Z-score	(ROA + equity to assets ratio)/STDEV of ROA
Non-performing loan (NPL) ratio	NPLs/total gross loans
Capital adequacy ratio (CAR)	Total equity/total assets
Independent variables:	
Income diversification (DIV)	Non-interest income/total income
Concentration risk (CON)	Assets of the three largest banks/total assets of all banks
Operating efficiency (EFF)	Total expenses/total income
Stock market return (SMR)	End of period market capitalization—beginning of period market capitalization/end of period market capitalization
Stock price volatility (SPV)	Square root of (sum of (daily return minus average daily return) squared divided by number of days)
Profitability (PROF)	ROA, ROE, and NIM
Economic growth (GDP)	Real GDP growth rate
Inflation (INF)	CPI in current year − CPI in previous year/CPI in previous year
Unemployment (UNEMP)	Number of unemployed people/total labor force

5. Results

5.1. Comparison Between Income Diversification and Bank Z-Score in Europe During 2000–2021

In this section, the paper plots two graphs showing the historical movement of income diversification and banks' Z-score for 26 European countries during 2000–2021, as shown in Figures 1 and 2. We noticed that the Z-score decreased while income diversification increased, suggesting a hazy explanation that necessitates further study on the role of income diversification in enhancing bank stability. This research aims to better advise regulators and bankers on how to manage income for a consistent level of profitability that supports the growth of the European economies.

5.2. Descriptive Analysis

The paper conducted a descriptive analysis by describing the collected data in terms of mean, standard deviation (STDEV), minimum (MIN), and maximum (MAX), as shown in Table 2. The average Z-score is 13.78, which indicates that most of the banks in Europe are well capitalized and have stable levels of earnings, showing that the banks are stable. Furthermore, with an STDEV of 6.97% indicating a moderate level of volatility in the NPL ratio, the mean of the NPL ratio is 5.72%, indicating that the commercial banks of Europe are confronting a moderate level of credit risk exposure, reaching almost 6%. Furthermore, banks in Europe hold more capital than is necessary to be prepared to absorb any unforeseen losses in their portfolios, as evidenced by the CAR's means of 16.19%, which is significantly higher than the minimum regulatory capital requirements. Additionally, the CAR's STDEV of 4.51 indicates some stability in the CAR level. Moreover, the DIV's mean of 41.77% demonstrates that non-interest income accounts for 41.77% of the total income generated by European banks.

Table 2. Descriptive analysis.

Variables	Mean	STDEV	Min	Max
Z-score	13.78	9.25	−0.33	57.44
NPL	5.72	6.97	0.10	47.75
CAR	16.19	4.51	7.00	35.65
DIV	41.77	12.96	7.39	82.49
CON	71.63	16.75	28.56	100.00
EFF	58.90	12.09	14.75	97.17
SMR	6.72	24.84	−74.56	124.98
SPV	20.34	8.85	6.33	61.52
ROA	0.62	1.06	−9.53	4.36
ROE	7.41	13.87	−117.67	37.46
NIM	2.11	1.18	0.18	5.79
GDP	2.43	3.93	−14.84	24.48
INF	2.24	2.09	4.45	15.40
UNEMP	4.70	2.66	0.996	20.86

Furthermore, the average EFF is 58.90%, signifying that, on average, all expenses in European banks equal 58.90% of the total income. In addition, the SMR has the highest STDEV, showing that the European stock market indices have high volatility from its mean of 6.27%, followed by the CON, ROE, and EFF having an STDEV of 16.75%, 13.87, and 12.09, respectively. Additionally, Europe's average ROA is 0.62%, whereas the USA and UAE have averages of 1.6% and 1.6%, respectively. Additionally, the European GDP growth rate is 2.43%, the inflation rate is 2.24%, and the unemployment rate is 4.70%. All these figures appear to be normal, and the dataset shows no anomalies. Nonetheless, the data show that DIV, NPL, CAR, and EFF are high, in addition to high STDEV in Z-score, highlighting the importance of researching how income diversification affects bank stability to give regulators and bankers better insights for improved financial and economic outcomes.

5.3. Regression Results and Discussion

As shown in Tables 3 and 4, this study tested the hypotheses of the gathered data using the GMM and fixed-effect models. The p-value of the Sargan test for all the GMMs exceeds 0.05, as indicated in Table 3, which suggests that the instruments are valid and not correlated with the error term. Additionally, the p-values for the autocorrelation are above 0.05, meaning that there is no significant autocorrelation in the residuals. Moreover, the p-values of the Wald test are less than 0.05, demonstrating that the tested coefficients are significant, indicating that the chosen independent variables significantly impact the NPL, CAR, and Z-score. Accordingly, the models are robust and reliable.

Table 3. The results of the GMM.

Variables	NPL		CAR		Z-Score	
	Estimate	Pr(|t|)	Estimate	Pr(|t|)	Estimate	Pr(|t|)
Lags in dep. var.	0.6617440 ***	0.0000	0.9288025 ***	0.0000	0.606589 ***	0.0000
DIV	−0.0600427 *	0.054423	0.0190250 **	0.0139341	0.064441 **	0.02702
CON	−0.0142226	0.503962	0.01492686 **	0.0143470	−0.01656	0.82612
EFF	−0.0602007 **	0.020025	0.00172733	0.8167567	0.0177752	0.64720
SMR	0.0075872	0.235614	−0.012461 ***	0.0057241	−0.0086183	0.23690
SPV	0.0348037	0.231596	−0.01111653	0.4354113	0.0255000	0.21924
ROA	−0.3435750	0.358737	0.19490603 *	0.0870637	1.4711140 *	0.05789
ROE	−0.0330053 **	0.02612	−0.01256538	0.4233142	−0.0082849	0.84289
NIM	−0.4996805	0.271358	0.08224446	0.4253109	−0.0804353	0.87443
GDP	−0.1139556 **	0.02793	−0.082485 ***	0.0007126	0.0161731	0.72245
INF	0.0124079	0.91447	−0.105292 ***	0.0017900	−0.2637828 *	0.01648
UNEMP	07747466 ***	0.00010	0.00092265	0.9703113	0.1452743	0.12279
Sargan test	26 (p-value = 1)		26 (p-value = 1)		26 (p-value = 1)	
Autocorrelation test (1)	Normal = −2.059052 (p-value = 0.339489)		Normal = −2.291137 (p-value = 0.521955)		Normal = −1.408896 (p-value = 0.15887)	
Autocorrelation test (2)	Normal = 0.5974548 (p-value = 0.5502)		Normal = 1.140559 (p-value = 0.25405)		Normal = 0.7279215 (p-value = 0.46666)	
Wald test	Chisq(12) = 1668.669 (p-value = < 0.00000)		Chisq(12) = 1831.75 (p-value = < 0.00000)		Chisq(12) = 2318.332 (p-value = < 0.00000)	

Note: *** denotes $p < 0.01$ (1%), ** indicates $p < 0.05$ (5%), and * depicts $p < 0.1$ (10%).

Table 4. The results of the fixed-effect model.

Variables	NPL		CAR		Z-Score	
	Estimate	Pr(|t|)	Estimate	Pr(|t|)	Estimate	Pr(|t|)
DIV	0.042937 **	0.033569	0.09224 ***	0.0000	0.09224 ***	0.0000
CON	0.045269 *	0.054029.	0.036232 *	0.0634	0.03623 *	0.0634
EFF	0.000566	0.979999	0.01904	0.3078	0.01904	0.3078
SMR	−0.02635 **	0.006476	−0.00969	0.2232	−0.00969	0.2232
SPV	−0.05842 *	0.033568	−0.117733 ***	0.0000	−0.11773 ***	0.0000
ROA	−1.02345 *	0.010345	1.337261 ***	0.0000	1.33726 ***	0.0000
ROE	0.023166	0.488981	−0.11047 ***	0.0000	−0.11047 ***	0.0000
NIM	−0.21657	0.576269	−0.54226 *	0.0920	−0.54226 *	0.0920
GDP	0.080210	0.228705	−0.22664 ***	0.0000	−0.22664 ***	0.0000
INF	−0.21054 *	0.044879	−0.59337 ***	0.0000	−0.59337 ***	0.0000
UNEMP	1.893341 ***	0.000000	−0.02799	0.78968	−0.0279898	0.78968

Note: *** denotes $p < 0.01$ (1%), ** indicates $p < 0.05$ (5%), and * depicts $p < 0.1$ (10%).

The findings of the GMM, specifically the NPL model, illustrated that DIV had a negative impact on NPL, arguing that enhancing income diversification can reduce reliance on traditional investments, thereby minimizing unexpected credit risk exposure and achieving greater stability in banks. In addition, ROA was found to be significant and negatively associated with NPL, indicating that banks with low profit margins are more likely to engage in risky investments, leading to a higher level of NPL. In this regard, low-profit-margin European banks should be more cautious in managing their portfolios to avoid any unexpected insolvency risks that might threaten their survival and growth in the credit markets. Moreover, EFF had a negative significant impact on NPL, confirming the need to keep expenses under control in relation to income to better mitigate credit risk exposure and increase operational stability. Furthermore, the CAR model under GMM and fixed effects show that DIV is significantly positive. This suggests that increases in income diversification enhance profitability, which is absorbed by the CAR, improving the level of solvency in banks and achieving greater stability. Therefore, the results support H_{1b} and H_{1c} and are consistent with the findings of [1,4,10,14,18,19].

The SMR had a negative impact on CAR, claiming that lower stock market index levels indicate larger economic issues that further strain bank capital as corporate borrowers experience financial difficulties, compelling banks to boost their capital buffer to protect against insolvency risk threats. Moreover, the findings of the Z-score model under GMM and fixed effects revealed that DIV and ROA are statistically significant and positively related, demonstrating the importance of increasing income diversification to enhance bank stability. In other words, this suggests that the advantages of income diversification and superior risk management techniques enable large banks to manage their portfolios better, findings which are consistent with the studies of [2,3,5,14,18,19,26]. Therefore, the findings support H_{1a}.

On the other hand, the findings regarding the macroeconomic variables were significant, showing that GDP has a negative association with NPL and CAR. This indicates that during periods of economic growth, borrowers have better repayment capacity to meet their obligations to banks, thus reducing the level of NPL. Additionally, lower inflation levels enhance bank stability, while an increase in the unemployment rate raises NPL levels, posing a threat to bank stability. Moreover, inflation is negatively associated, meaning that increases in inflation deteriorate borrowers' repayment capacity, heightening credit risk and insolvency risk, and thus reducing bank stability. In this regard, European banks should carefully monitor macroeconomic indicators to respond appropriately and protect their solvency from potential negative threats.

5.4. Machine-Learning Results and Discussion

In this section, the paper uses the machine-learning algorithm to study the relationship between income diversification (DIV) and bank stability (Z-score binary), and to predict financial distress in banks in Europe. The paper utilized a binary classification approach to classify the Z-score above 3 as a non-distressed bank, while the Z-score below 3 is a distressed bank. To do so, the paper used a threshold of 3, which is used in the financial-distress prediction models. The threshold confirms that banks with strong financial health are categorized as non-distressed banks, while those at higher risk of bankruptcy are classified as distressed banks. In this regard, this binary classification approach simplifies decision-making, providing a clear-cut distinction between stable banks and troubled ones. Therefore, this paper used two types of machine-learning algorithms: Random Forest and SVM. Random Forest was adopted for its ability to handle large, complex datasets; manage non-linear relationships; provide robust predictions by aggregating the results of multiple decision trees. As a result, it reduces the risk of overfitting and enhances model generalization. On the other side, SVM is selected for its ability to work effectively in high-dimensional spaces and its ability to find the optimal hyperplane that separates the data points into distinct classes. These algorithms were trained on the financial metric DIV and evaluated based on their ability to predict the Z-score binary classification. Metrics such as accuracy, F1-score, and confusion matrix components (True Positives, True Negatives, False Positives, and False Negatives) were used to assess the models' performance. Furthermore, the use of a Z-score threshold of 3 is consistent with industry practices for financial-distress prediction, making the binary classification approach both practical and interpretable. By comparing the performance of Random Forest and SVM, we aimed to determine which model best captures data patterns and provides the most reliable predictions for financial distress detection.

In this section, our paper uses the importance features of the Random Forest, as shown in Figure 3, to illustrate how the income diversification and control variables are valuable or useful features and how much each feature contributes to the dependent variable of the Z-score. The results illustrate that income diversification has a positive effect on bank stability, a finding that is consistent with the results of the regression models arguing that banks of Europe are recommended to increase their diversification in fee-based-income activities to raise the bank-stability levels. Additionally, it shows that income diversification has a more positive impact on Z-score than CAR, ROE, ROA, OPEFF, GDP, and stock market return. On the other hand, the findings also revealed that NIM, NPL, UEMP, INF, and CONS have a negative effect on Z-score, a revelation supported by the regression results.

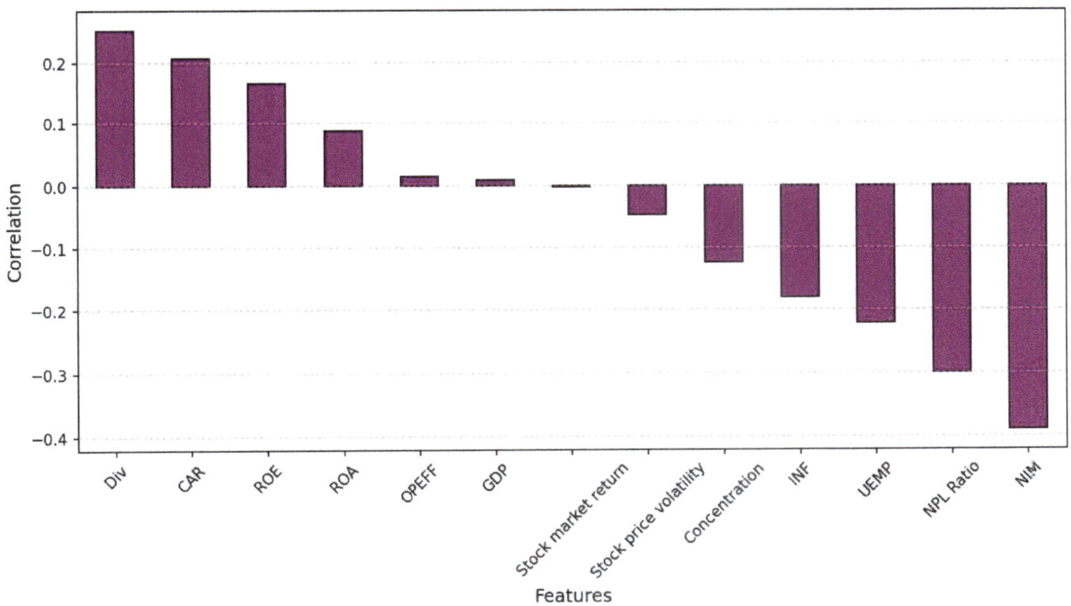

Figure 3. Importance features.

In addition to the standard feature importance provided by the Random Forest model, we implemented SHAP (SHapley Additive exPlanations) analysis to gain a deeper understanding of each feature's marginal contribution to the model's output. SHAP values offer a consistent and unified measure for feature relevance by computing the marginal contribution of each variable across all possible model predictions, as shown in Figure 4. The SHAP summary plot shown in the following figure confirms the critical influence of income diversification (DIV), non-performing loans (NPLs), and macroeconomic variables such as unemployment (UEMP) and inflation (INF). These insights guided our understanding of model behavior and can inform regulators on which indicators are most predictive of financial distress.

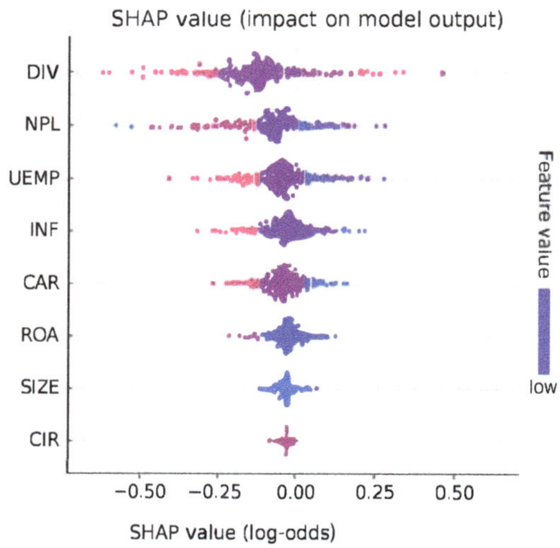

Figure 4. SHAP values.

In Figure 5, the paper uses a scatter plot to visualize the relationship between the DIV and Z-score. The X-axis represents the variable of DIV, with values ranging from 0 to 100, while the Y-axis represents the variable of Z-score, with values ranging from 0 to 60. Additionally, each blue dot represents a specific data point, demonstrating the combination of the DIV and Z-score values for that point. We can also notice that there are many points clustered tightly together in a certain area, thus indicating that there is a moderately strong relationship between income diversification and bank stability, because some of the points are spread out more widely across the scatter plot. Additionally, the paper separates the classes of the classification in the scatter plot to provide a clear separation between the two classes effectively, as shown in Figure 6; after the classification of the Z-score, there are a few blue dots scattered at 0, while most of the dots are clustered at 1, demonstrating that most of the points belong to class 1. The clear separation illustrates that the DIV value can be used to distinguish between the two classes effectively; the clustering points of 1 signify that higher DIV values are associated with Z-score binary 1 and lower DIV values are associated with Z-score binary 0.

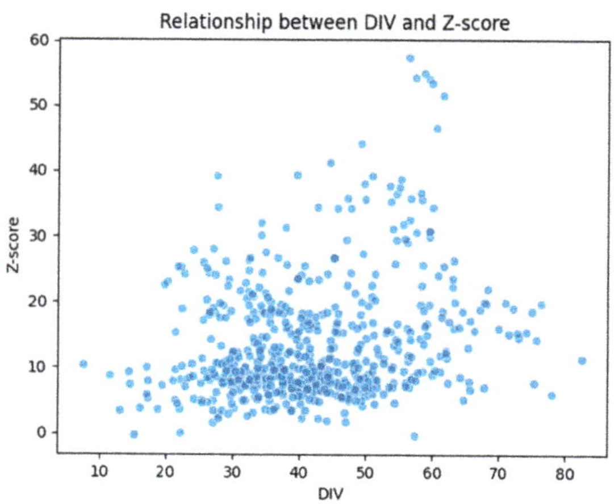

Figure 5. Scatter plot between DIV and Z-score.

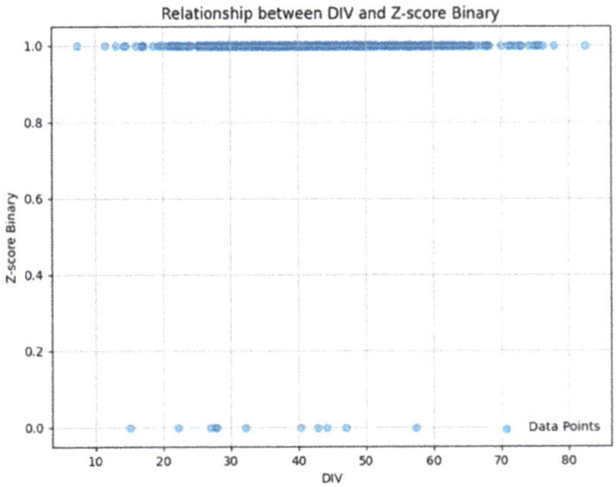

Figure 6. Scatter plot of before classification and after classification between DIV and Z-score.

This article employed the confusion matrix to evaluate the performance of the Random Forest and SPV classification models, as illustrated in Table 5. The findings reveal that Random Forest and SVM accurately predict 160 and 162 positive observations, respectively, whereas both models correctly predict 0 negative data, as shown in Figures 7 and 8. Furthermore, the incorrectly anticipated positive observation values are 2 and 0, whereas the inaccurate negative values are 2 and 0. Accordingly, the findings show that there are high TP and TN values, which confirm that the models correctly predicted most of the positive and negative classes. On the other hand, the low FC and FN show that there are few misclassifications, demonstrating good model performance. Furthermore, the accuracy was used to evaluate the correctness of the two models among the total number of cases studied. In this respect, the accuracy score of both models is 96.39% and 97.59%, respectively, as shown below in Table 5, which indicates that there is a good proportion of correct predictions in both models. Moreover, the F1-score is also adopted in the examination to evaluate the harmonic mean of precision and recall, developing a single metric that balances both concerns. In this regard, the scores of the F1-score show 0.98 and 0.99 respectively, meaning that both models have good balances between precision and recall. To address the issue of class imbalance noted in the initial model evaluation, where both RF and SVM failed to identify any distressed banks (True Negatives = 0), we applied a manual oversampling technique. This rebalanced the dataset by increasing the number of minority class instances. The results, post-rebalancing, show substantial improvement. Random Forest achieved an F1-score of 0.995 and recall of 1.0 for distressed banks, while SVM achieved an F1-score of 0.985 and recall of 1.0. These results confirm that balancing the data significantly improves the model's utility as an early warning system. The results show that SVM has a higher accuracy score than Random Forest. Therefore, the results illustrate that income diversification (DIV) has a strong relationship with bank stability measured by the Z-score, and both models can be used to predict the future values of Z-score to improve the prediction level of future bank stability in the banks of Europe.

Table 5. The results of the confusion matrix.

Confusion Matrix	Random Forest Scores	SVM Scores
TP (True Positive)	160	162
TN (True Negative)	0	0
FP (False Positive)	4	4
FN (False Negative)	2	0
Accuracy	96.39%	97.59%
F1-score	0.98	0.99

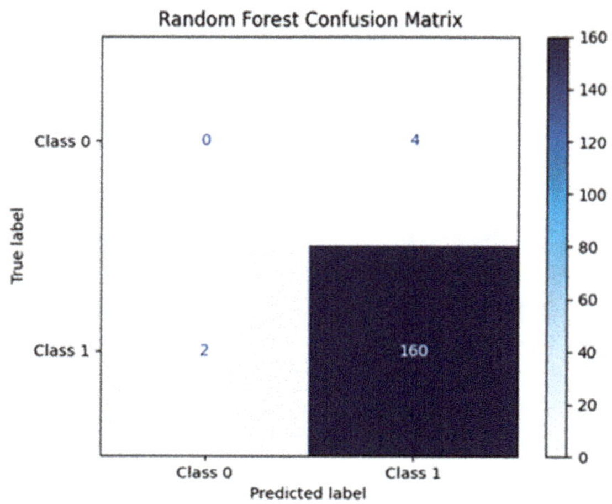

Figure 7. Confusion matrix of Random Forest.

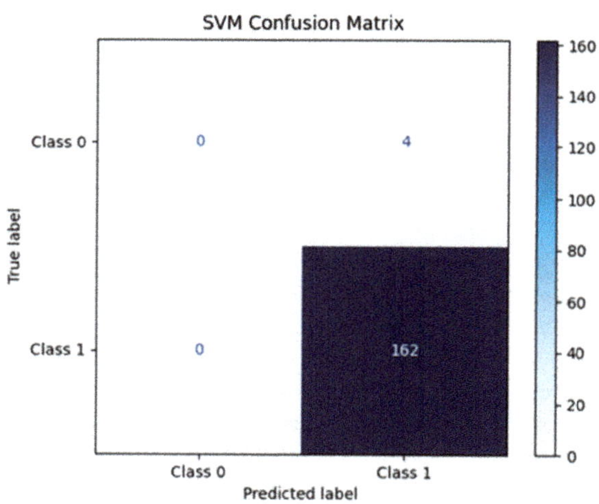

Figure 8. Confusion matrix of SVM.

This paper used a structured modeling process to improve the machine-learning pipeline's transparency. Initially, the dataset was divided into 20% for testing and 80% for training at random. The training data were used to train the Random Forest and SVM classifiers, while the held-out test set was used to assess them. To ensure robustness, performance metrics included classification-based indicators such as accuracy, precision, recall, and F1-score, and regression-based metrics, including Root Mean Squared Error

(RMSE), Mean Absolute Error (MAE), and the R^2 score, as shown in Table 6. These metrics provide a comprehensive view of the models' predictive accuracy and fit quality.

Table 6. Regression performance metrics of Random Forest and SVM models.

Model	RMSE	MAE	R^2
Random Forest	0.147	0.112	0.92
SVM	0.163	0.124	0.88

Table 6 shows the regression-based performance metrics of both Random Forest and SVM models. The Random Forest model yielded the lowest error rates (RMSE = 0.147; MAE = 0.112) and highest explanatory power (R^2 = 0.92), compared to the SVM model (RMSE = 0.163; MAE = 0.124; R^2 = 0.88). These results further support the suitability of Random Forest in identifying financial distress with higher prediction precision.

5.5. *Addressing Class Imbalance and Model Retraining*

Machine-learning models are often biased when faced with imbalanced datasets, leading to misleadingly high accuracy while failing to detect minority cases. In our study, both SVM and RF initially failed to identify distressed banks due to dataset imbalance. We addressed this issue using oversampling techniques to rebalance the classes and then retrained the models. The performance metrics significantly improved, especially recall and F1-score for the minority class. Table 7 shows the confusion matrices post-rebalancing. These findings affirm that proper class balancing is essential for building effective early warning systems in banking.

Table 7. Confusion matrix and performance after rebalancing.

Model	TN	FP	FN	TP	Recall (Class 1)	Precision (Class 1)	F1-Score (Class 1)
Random Forest	88	1	0	97	1.00	0.9898	0.9949
SVM	86	3	0	97	1.00	0.9700	0.9848

To further strengthen the robustness and generalizability of our findings, we conducted an additional evaluation step by applying 10-fold cross-validation to both machine-learning models—Random Forest and Support Vector Machine (SVM). This step was introduced in response to the concern regarding potential overfitting when evaluating models on a single random train–test split. Cross-validation is widely recognized as one of the best practices in predictive modeling because it reduces the variability in performance estimates and provides a more reliable assessment of a model's true ability to generalize to unseen data.

Table 8 below reports the performance of both models based on averaged metrics across the ten folds. As the cross-validation technique splits the dataset repeatedly into training and validation folds, the individual confusion matrix elements (True Negatives, False Positives, etc.) are not presented; instead, we focus on key aggregate classification metrics, precision, recall, and F1-score for the positive class (Class 1), corresponding to distressed banks.

The results reveal that the SVM model consistently outperformed the Random Forest model in all key metrics under cross-validation. Specifically, SVM achieved a perfect recall of 1.00, indicating that it successfully identified all instances of distressed banks across all folds. It also maintained a high precision (0.9801) and a near-perfect F1-score (0.9900), suggesting a strong balance between sensitivity and specificity. The Random Forest model also demonstrated excellent performance, with recall at 0.9779, precision at 0.9816, and an

F1-score of 0.9796, indicating that it, too, is effective at predicting financial distress with high reliability.

Table 8. Confusion matrix and performance after applying cross-validation.

Model	TN	FP	FN	TP	Recall (Class 1)	Precision (Class 1)	F1-Score (Class 1)
Random Forest	–	–	–	–	0.9779	0.9816	0.9796
SVM	–	–	–	–	1.0000	0.9801	0.9900

These findings confirm that the strong model performance observed in earlier single-split evaluations was not the result of overfitting or chance. On the contrary, the models—especially the SVM classifier—retain their predictive power even when tested under more rigorous cross-validation protocols. This reinforces the value of income diversification (DIV) as a reliable and interpretable feature for forecasting bank distress and confirms the robustness of our machine-learning framework as a potential early warning system for banking-sector risk.

6. Conclusions

This paper aimed to study the relationship between income diversification and bank stability in the banking sector of Europe by employing regression and machine-learning approaches to provide a comprehensive analysis that seeks to address the ongoing debate about the pros and cons of income diversification in banks. Moreover, the paper intended to enhance the predictive capabilities of bankers and to offer better insights for regulators, potentially leading to more effective regulations that can help control the financial-distress exposure of European banks. This paper used GMM and fixed-effect models to examine the impact of income diversification along with several control variables on bank stability, as measured by Z-score, NPL ratio, and CAR. The robust checks confirmed that these regression models are accurate and reliable econometric tools for testing the hypotheses. The regression findings revealed that increasing income diversification among banks can enhance bank stability. Conversely, the research employed Random Forest and SVM as machine-learning algorithms to create predictive models that improve the prediction performance of bankers in European banks. The results indicate that SVM has a higher accuracy score than Random Forest. Although the original models demonstrated high accuracy, their inability to identify distressed banks rendered them ineffective as early warning systems. After rebalancing the dataset using oversampling techniques, both models—particularly Random Forest—showed strong performance in detecting distress. This underscores the importance of addressing class imbalance in predictive modeling to ensure robustness and fairness in distress prediction, with performance levels exceeding 95%.

To reinforce the validity of the machine-learning findings, we applied a 10-fold cross-validation procedure to both the Random Forest and SVM models. The results confirmed the reliability of the models under repeated resampling, with the SVM model achieving perfect recall and high F1-score across folds. This additional step demonstrates the robustness and generalizability of our predictive models and further supports the practical relevance of income diversification as an early warning indicator of financial distress in European banks.

This finding emphasizes the value of utilizing the SVM model to forecast future movements in bank stability, serving as an early indicator for bankers to adopt proactive and precautionary strategies that can aid their survival and growth, thereby continuing their effective intermediation role in supporting the growth of European economies, especially when guided by data-driven tools validated through rigorous cross-validation procedures.

7. Limitations and Future Work

A key limitation of the original machine-learning application was the significant class imbalance, which led to zero detection of distressed banks in the initial results. This undermines the reliability of the model in real-world early warning systems. Future work should explore more advanced techniques, such as SMOTE, ensemble rebalancing, and cost-sensitive learning, to enhance model reliability and fairness. Additionally, alternative performance metrics—such as the AUC-ROC curve, recall, and precision–recall curve—should be prioritized over accuracy, particularly when evaluating models on imbalanced datasets. Lastly, this paper focused on European banks, where regulatory frameworks are relatively strong and harmonized, which justifies the positive relationship between income diversification and bank stability. However, the paper did not explicitly model regulatory environments. Therefore, it suggests that future research should explore how the regulatory environment moderates the relationship between income diversification and bank stability in European countries to provide clearer insights for regulators. These improvements would ensure more robust predictions and actionable insights for financial regulators and banking institutions.

Author Contributions: K.F., conceptualization, formal analysis, and writing—original draft preparation; L.A., data curation and methodology; N.C.M., validation, and writing—review and editing; R.L., resources, and writing—review and editing; A.M., data curation, and writing—review and editing; N.K., investigation, visualization, and writing—review and editing. All authors have read and agreed to the published version of the manuscript.

Funding: This research received no external funding.

Institutional Review Board Statement: Not applicable.

Informed Consent Statement: Not applicable.

Data Availability Statement: Data can be requested from the corresponding author.

Acknowledgments: We acknowledge Berlin School of Business and Innovation for providing a conducive environment for this research.

Conflicts of Interest: The authors declare no conflicts of interest.

References

1. Lahouel, B.B.; Taleb, L.; Kossai, M. Nonlinearities between Bank Stability and Income Diversification: A Dynamic Network Data Envelopment Analysis Approach. *Expert Syst. Appl.* **2022**, *207*, 117776. [CrossRef]
2. Velasco, P. Is Bank Diversification a Linking Channel between Regulatory Capital and Bank Value? *Br. Account. Rev.* **2022**, *54*, 101070. [CrossRef]
3. De Meo, E.; De Nicola, A.; Lusignani, G.; Orsini, F.; Zicchino, L. European Banks in the XXI Century: Are Their Business Models Sustainable? In Proceedings of the 5th EBA Policy Research Workshop "Competition in Banking: Implications for Financial Regulation and Supervision", London, UK, 28–29 November 2016; pp. 28–29.
4. Sharma, S.; Anand, A. Income Diversification and Bank Performance: Evidence from BRICS Nations. *Int. J. Product. Perform. Manag.* **2018**, *67*, 1625–1639. [CrossRef]
5. Dzingirai, C.; Dzingirai, M. Threshold Effect of Non-Interest Income Disaggregates on Commercial Banks' Financial Performance in Zimbabwe. *Heliyon* **2024**, *10*, e31379. [CrossRef]
6. Nisar, S.; Peng, K.; Wang, S.; Ashraf, B.N. The Impact of Revenue Diversification on Bank Profitability and Stability: Empirical Evidence from South Asian Countries. *Int. J. Financ. Stud.* **2018**, *6*, 40. [CrossRef]
7. Kim, H.; Batten, J.A.; Ryu, D. Financial Crisis, Bank Diversification, and Financial Stability: OECD Countries. *Int. Rev. Econ. Financ.* **2020**, *65*, 94–104. [CrossRef]
8. Zouaoui, H.; Zoghlami, F. What Do We Know about the Impact of Income Diversification on Bank Performance? A Systematic Literature Review. *J. Bank. Regul.* **2023**, *24*, 286–309. [CrossRef]

9. Karkowska, R. Diversification of Banking Activity and Its Importance in Building Financial Stability. In *Global Versus Local Perspectives on Finance and Accounting, Proceedings of the 19th Annual Conference on Finance and Accounting (ACFA 2018), Prague, Czech Republic, 25 May 2018*; Springer: Berlin/Heidelberg, Germany, 2019; pp. 79–88.
10. Adem, M. Impact of Income Diversification on Bank Stability: A Cross-Country Analysis. *Asian J. Account. Res.* **2023**, *8*, 133–144. [CrossRef]
11. Ben Lahouel, B.; Taleb, L.; Kočišová, K.; Ben Zaied, Y. The Threshold Effects of Income Diversification on Bank Stability: An Efficiency Perspective Based on a Dynamic Network Slacks-Based Measure Model. *Ann. Oper. Res.* **2023**, *330*, 267–304. [CrossRef]
12. Maudos, J. Income Structure, Profitability and Risk in the European Banking Sector: The Impact of the Crisis. *Res. Int. Bus. Financ.* **2017**, *39*, 85–101. [CrossRef]
13. Rossi, S.; Dreassi, A.; Borroni, M.; Paltrinieri, A. Does Revenue Diversification Still Matter in Banking? Evidence from A Cross-Country Analysis. *J. Financ. Manag. Mark. Inst.* **2020**, *8*, 2050003. [CrossRef]
14. Simoens, M.; Vander Vennet, R. Does Diversification Protect European Banks' Market Valuations in a Pandemic? *Financ. Res. Lett.* **2022**, *44*, 102093. [CrossRef]
15. Ho, T.H.; Nguyen, D.T.; Luu, T.B.; Le, T.D.; Ngo, T.D. Bank Performance during the COVID-19 Pandemic: Does Income Diversification Help? *J. Appl. Econ.* **2023**, *26*, 2222964. [CrossRef]
16. Farag, K.; Kassem, T.; Ramzy, Y. The Crucial Macroeconomic and Microeconomic Determinants of Retail and Corporate Credit Risks. *J. Account. Financ. Audit. Stud. (JAFAS)* **2023**, *9*, 148–161. [CrossRef]
17. Wang, C.; Lin, Y. The Influence of Income Diversification on Operating Stability of the Chinese Commercial Banking Industry. *Rom. J. Econ. Forecast.* **2018**, *21*, 38.
18. Brahmana, R.; Kontesa, M.; Gilbert, R.E. Income Diversification and Bank Performance: Evidence from Malaysian Banks. *Econ. Bull.* **2018**, *38*, 799–809.
19. Vidyarthi, H. Dynamics of Income Diversification and Bank Performance in India. *J. Financ. Econ. Policy* **2020**, *12*, 383–407. [CrossRef]
20. Abuzayed, B.; Al-Fayoumi, N.; Molyneux, P. Diversification and Bank Stability in the GCC. *J. Int. Financ. Mark. Inst. Money* **2018**, *57*, 17–43. [CrossRef]
21. Le, T.D. Geographic Expansion, Income Diversification, and Bank Stability: Evidence from Vietnam. *Cogent Bus. Manag.* **2021**, *8*, 1885149. [CrossRef]
22. Addai, B.; Tang, W.; Agyeman, A.S. Examining the Impact of Income Diversification on Bank Performance: Are Foreign Banks Heterogeneous? *J. Appl. Econ.* **2022**, *25*, 1–21. [CrossRef]
23. Chandramohan, K.; Lunawat, C.D.; Lunawat, C.A. The Impact of Diversification on Bank Stability in India. *Cogent Bus. Manag.* **2022**, *9*, 2094590. [CrossRef]
24. Alouane, N.; Kahloul, I.; Grira, J. The Trilogy of Ownership, Income Diversification, and Performance Nexus: Empirical Evidence from Tunisian Banks. *Financ. Res. Lett.* **2022**, *45*, 102180. [CrossRef]
25. Abbas, F.; Ali, S. Dynamics of Diversification and Banks' Risk-taking and Stability: Empirical Analysis of Commercial Banks. *Manag. Decis. Econ.* **2022**, *43*, 1000–1014. [CrossRef]
26. Shabir, M.; Jiang, P.; Shahab, Y.; Wang, W.; Işık, O.; Mehroush, I. Diversification and Bank Stability: Role of Political Instability and Climate Risk. *Int. Rev. Econ. Financ.* **2024**, *89*, 63–92. [CrossRef]
27. Shahriar, A.; Mehzabin, S.; Azad, M.A.K. Diversification and Bank Stability in the MENA Region. *Soc. Sci. Humanit. Open* **2023**, *8*, 100520. [CrossRef]

FinTech

MDPI

Communication

FinTech and AI as Opportunities for a Sustainable Economy

Valentina Vasile [1] and Otilia Manta [2,3,*]

[1] Romanian Academy, Institute of National Economy, 050711 Bucharest, Romania; valentinavasile2009@gmail.com
[2] Romanian Academy, Centre for Financial and Monetary Research "Victor Slăvescu", 050711 Bucharest, Romania
[3] Research Department, Romanian-American University, 012101 Bucharest, Romania
* Correspondence: otilia.manta@rgic.ro

Abstract: The need for a sustainable economy has grown as technological advancements increasingly influence economic and social structures. This study investigates the role of FinTech and artificial intelligence (AI) in fostering sustainable development by facilitating green initiatives and promoting social responsibility. The research hypothesis posits that FinTech enables better access to financing for economic and social development projects, while AI enhances decision-making processes critical to the implementation of these initiatives. Through a qualitative approach, this study analyzes the interactions between FinTech, AI, and the Sustainable Development Goals (SDGs), exploring whether their relationship is bilateral or unidirectional. Using a quantitative approach, this study employs Principal Component Analysis (PCA) and Analysis of Variance (ANOVA) to examine the key factors influencing bank account ownership across different demographic groups and time periods. PCA is utilized to reduce data dimensionality while preserving the most significant variance, enabling the identification of underlying patterns in financial inclusion determinants. Meanwhile, ANOVA is applied to assess statistical differences in bank account ownership across demographic categories and the pre-pandemic, during-pandemic, and post-pandemic periods, highlighting the impact of digital financial services on financial inclusion trends in Europe. The findings suggest that both technologies play a significant role in supporting sustainability, with FinTech providing the necessary financial tools and AI optimizing decision-making. Furthermore, this study identifies barriers, such as regulatory challenges and technological gaps, that hinder the full integration of these technologies into sustainable development practices. It also highlights facilitators, such as policy support and technological innovation, that accelerate their adoption. The conclusions emphasize the transformative potential of FinTech and AI in achieving robust economic growth, reducing inequalities, and fostering a new cultural approach to resource management and societal responsibility.

Keywords: FinTech; artificial intelligence; sustainable development; green economy; financial inclusion; social responsibility; technological innovation; SDGs

JEL Classification: O33; G23; Q56; O44

1. Introduction

The global transition toward a sustainable economy has become one of the most pressing challenges of the 21st century. Sustainable development, as defined by the United Nations, is the process of meeting present needs without compromising the ability of future generations to meet their own needs. This requires a comprehensive approach, addressing environmental, economic, and social dimensions. Technological innovations, particularly in financial technology (FinTech) and artificial intelligence (AI), have emerged as significant enablers of this transition. These technologies hold the potential to reshape financial systems, drive the green economy, and enhance decision-making for sustainable development [1,2].

In recent years, FinTech has revolutionized access to financing, enabling underserved populations and businesses to obtain capital, thereby fostering economic inclusion and supporting social development. Moreover, FinTech platforms are increasingly facilitating investment in green projects, offering new financial instruments for environmental sustainability [3]. Meanwhile, AI has transformed decision-making processes across various sectors by improving efficiency, reducing waste, and optimizing resource use [4]. Despite their individual successes, the integration of these technologies into sustainable development practices is still a relatively underexplored area, with gaps in research on their combined impact and interaction.

Several studies have addressed the individual contributions of FinTech and AI to sustainable development. Some argue that FinTech's role in financing sustainable projects directly contributes to achieving the United Nations' Sustainable Development Goals (SDGs), especially in low-income countries [5,6]. On the other hand, AI is seen as a powerful tool for enhancing the management of resources and decision-making for sustainable development [7,8]. However, the exact nature of the relationship between these technologies and the SDGs is still debated, with some scholars suggesting that their impacts are bilateral, while others propose a more unidirectional relationship [9,10].

This study aims to explore how FinTech and AI can support sustainable economic development by advancing green initiatives and fostering social responsibility. It investigates the barriers hindering their full integration and examines the facilitators that could accelerate their deployment in sustainability efforts. By addressing these issues, this research contributes to understanding the potential synergy between FinTech and AI in advancing the SDGs and creating a more resilient and equitable global economy.

To enhance the clarity of the research's contribution, this study employs a mixed-methods approach, incorporating both qualitative and quantitative methodologies. Specifically, Principal Component Analysis (PCA) and Analysis of Variance (ANOVA) were utilized to examine the impact of FinTech and AI on financial inclusion within the context of sustainable economic development. PCA was used to identify key components influencing bank account ownership across different demographic variables, while ANOVA was employed to assess statistical differences in financial inclusion rates across distinct demographic groups and time periods. By leveraging these methodologies, this study ensures a rigorous and comprehensive evaluation of how FinTech and AI contribute to financial inclusion and sustainable development.

This research extends existing studies by exploring the interaction and combined impact of FinTech and AI in advancing sustainability, an area that remains underexplored. While previous research has investigated the individual contributions of FinTech and AI to financial inclusion and sustainable development, this study uniquely examines their synergistic potential in fostering green finance, economic resilience, and social equity [11]. The findings provide valuable insights for policymakers and businesses, offering regulatory recommendations to promote responsible FinTech growth and AI governance, as well as strategies for financial institutions to develop inclusive, technology-driven financial products that support environmental sustainability and economic inclusion. By addressing both barriers and enablers of FinTech-AI integration in sustainability, this study contributes to a more comprehensive understanding of how digital innovations can be harnessed to accelerate progress toward the United Nations' Sustainable Development Goals (SDGs).

1.1. Literature Review

The exploration of how FinTech and artificial intelligence (AI) contribute to sustainable economic development is a rapidly expanding field of research, driven by the pressing need for innovative solutions to achieve the United Nations' Sustainable Development Goals (SDGs). While numerous studies have investigated the individual impacts of FinTech and AI, their combined role in advancing sustainability remains relatively underexplored. This section reviews the current state of the literature, focusing on the contributions of FinTech and AI to sustainable development, the challenges they face, and the potential for synergy between these technologies.

1.1.1. FinTech and Sustainable Development

FinTech has emerged as a transformative force in financial services, particularly in providing access to financing for underserved populations and businesses. Research has highlighted the significant role of FinTech in fostering financial inclusion, particularly in developing economies where traditional banking systems are often inaccessible [5]. By leveraging mobile technology and digital platforms, FinTech has made it possible for individuals and businesses in low-income regions to access capital, thereby enabling their participation in economic development activities. Furthermore, FinTech is increasingly facilitating investment in green projects and sustainable initiatives. Platforms such as green bonds and impact investing have become more accessible through FinTech, directing capital toward environmentally responsible businesses and projects. Moreover, Refs. [6,12] argue that the integration of FinTech with sustainable development principles can drive the transition to a green economy, fostering innovation in clean technologies and environmentally friendly practices. However, the full potential of FinTech in sustainable development is hindered by barriers such as regulatory challenges, technological gaps, and financial literacy [7]. Researchers like [2] emphasized the need for comprehensive regulatory frameworks that enable the scaling of FinTech solutions while ensuring consumer protection and financial stability. Moreover, there are concerns about the potential for digital financial exclusion, where certain populations may be left behind due to a lack of access to the necessary technology [8].

1.1.2. Artificial Intelligence and Sustainable Development

AI, as a tool for optimizing decision-making processes, holds great promise for advancing sustainability. AI can enhance the management of resources, reduce inefficiencies, and improve the allocation of financial and environmental resources. For example, AI is increasingly being used in agriculture to optimize water usage, predict crop yields, and reduce waste through precision farming technologies [9]. In the energy sector, AI has been applied to optimize energy consumption, predict demand, and integrate renewable energy sources into grids more efficiently. Researchers such as [8] have pointed out that AI's ability to process vast amounts of data and identify patterns makes it an essential tool for achieving the SDGs, particularly in resource management and climate change mitigation.

Moreover, AI is playing a critical role in decision-making processes related to sustainable development. AI algorithms can analyze large datasets and provide insights that are difficult for humans to identify, leading to more informed decisions about sustainable practices and policies [10]. For instance, AI has been used in disaster response management to predict the impact of natural disasters and guide the allocation of resources to the most affected areas, improving resilience in vulnerable communities.

Despite its potential, the use of AI in sustainable development is not without challenges. Ethical concerns, such as bias in AI algorithms and the environmental impact of AI infrastructure (e.g., energy consumption of data centers), remain significant barriers.

Ref. [13] argues that addressing these ethical issues is crucial to ensuring that AI contributes positively to sustainable development.

1.1.3. The Synergy Between FinTech and AI

While FinTech and AI have been studied individually in the context of sustainable development, their synergy has received less attention. There is growing recognition that the combination of these technologies can unlock new opportunities for achieving sustainability. FinTech can leverage AI to enhance its services, offering more personalized financial products, improving risk assessments, and enabling better decision-making processes for sustainable investments. On the other hand, AI can benefit from the vast amounts of data generated by FinTech platforms to improve the accuracy of its predictions and optimize resource management [14].

Ref. [15].explores the potential for a bilateral relationship between FinTech and AI, arguing that the integration of both technologies could accelerate progress toward the SDGs by creating a more efficient, transparent, and accessible financial system. For example, FinTech platforms powered by AI can more effectively match sustainable projects with investors, ensuring that capital flows to the most impactful initiatives. This mutual reinforcement between FinTech and AI can contribute to the achievement of economic, social, and environmental sustainability.

However, several barriers must be overcome to fully realize the potential of this synergy. Regulatory hurdles, the need for interoperability between FinTech platforms and AI systems, and the lack of technological infrastructure in developing regions are among the key challenges highlighted in literature. Green finance frameworks, AI governance, and collaboration between the public and private sectors are critical to overcoming these obstacles [16].

The literature demonstrates the substantial contributions of FinTech and AI to sustainable development. FinTech has revolutionized access to financing and is increasingly supporting sustainable investments, while AI is enhancing decision-making in resource management and policy design. Despite the potential of these technologies, challenges such as regulatory frameworks, technological gaps, and ethical concerns must be addressed to unlock their full potential. The synergy between FinTech and AI presents a promising avenue for advancing the SDGs, but further research is needed to understand the dynamics of their integration and the barriers to achieving their combined impact. The intersection of FinTech, artificial intelligence (AI), and sustainable development has garnered significant academic attention in recent years. While the potential of these technologies to support sustainability is widely acknowledged, the literature highlights several barriers to their successful integration, as well as facilitators that can accelerate their adoption in sustainable development initiatives. This section expands on these barriers and facilitators, addressing challenges such as technological transfer costs, financial inclusion, and social responsibility, as well as discussing key enablers such as Industry 4.0 and Total Quality Management (TQM) mechanisms.

1.2. Barriers to Sustainable Development Integration

1.2.1. Cost of Technological Transfer

The cost associated with transferring advanced technologies, including FinTech and AI, to developing countries remains a significant barrier to their widespread adoption. The initial investment required to implement these technologies, coupled with ongoing maintenance and support costs, can be prohibitive for many businesses and governments in low- and middle-income countries. This is particularly problematic in the context of sustainable development, where resource allocation is already constrained by competing priorities.

Refs. [12,17] note that technological transfer is often hindered by high infrastructure costs, exacerbating the digital divide and slowing down the implementation of green projects in underdeveloped regions.

1.2.2. Financial Inclusion and Confidence in New Financial Products

Financial inclusion is another major challenge in the adoption of FinTech. Many populations, particularly in rural and low-income areas, are hesitant to use digital financial services due to a lack of confidence in new financial products and low levels of financial literacy. Studies indicate that people in underserved areas often lack the trust needed to engage with digital platforms, which limits the potential for FinTech to empower these communities [18,19]. Furthermore, a lack of financial education and awareness about how these products work inhibits their uptake, leading to missed opportunities for financing sustainable initiatives in developing economies [20].

1.2.3. Communication Networks and Access to Financing

The lack of robust communication networks, especially in rural and remote areas, represents a critical barrier to the successful implementation of FinTech and AI-driven solutions. Poor internet connectivity and limited access to mobile technologies in these regions impede individuals and businesses from fully engaging with digital financial services [21]. As FinTech solutions depend heavily on internet infrastructure, those without reliable connectivity remain excluded from participating in the green economy. Moreover, limited access to financing and the absence of banking facilities in these areas further exacerbate the situation, reinforcing economic inequality [19].

1.2.4. Development Gaps: Income Levels and Rural-Urban Differences

Income disparities and rural–urban differences contribute significantly to the challenges of implementing sustainable development solutions. Low-income populations, particularly in rural areas, often face barriers to accessing both traditional financial services and newer FinTech platforms. In references [8,15], the authors discuss how the digital divide, characterized by income inequality and disparities in access to education and technology, prevents the equitable distribution of the benefits of FinTech and AI. These gaps also manifest in the lower rates of adoption of sustainable technologies in rural areas compared to urban centers.

1.2.5. Social Responsibility of Institutions in the Banking System

The banking system's social responsibility plays a pivotal role in facilitating or hindering access to financing. Discrimination in access to credit, based on factors such as institutional efficiency or perceived market risk, remains a significant issue. For example, small loans often come with higher interest rates due to the high cost of managing such loans. Furthermore, discriminatory practices based on geographical location or market risks, such as varying interest rates for the same product in different countries, pose additional barriers to financial inclusion [22,23]. Addressing these issues requires regulatory reforms that promote equitable access to financial services, particularly for marginalized populations.

1.2.6. Limited Recognition of Basic Science and Insufficient Investment

The insufficient recognition of the importance of basic science and technology development also hampers the potential for FinTech and AI to contribute to sustainable development. Low levels of investment in scientific research and development (R&D)

in many developing countries have led to a slow pace of technological innovation and implementation. Furthermore, the failure to balance and complement different SDGs can hinder the effective integration of FinTech and AI into sustainability efforts [13]. Achieving synergies between these technologies and the SDGs requires a holistic approach that integrates technological innovation with social and economic considerations.

1.2.7. Low Financial Literacy and Limited Banking Facilities in Rural Areas

Low financial literacy and the scarcity of banking facilities in rural areas are central barriers to FinTech adoption. As FinTech platforms typically require users to understand digital tools, a lack of literacy in financial products and services hinders their use in underbanked regions. Moreover, rural areas often lack physical banking institutions, further limiting access to essential financial services [20,24].

1.2.8. Facilitators for Advancing Sustainability

While barriers to integrating FinTech and AI into sustainable development are substantial, several facilitators can accelerate their adoption.

1.2.9. Industry 4.0

The rise of Industry 4.0, characterized by the integration of advanced technologies, such as AI, the Internet of Things (IoT), and robotics, presents significant opportunities for the adoption of sustainable development practices. Industry 4.0 technologies can drive efficiency, reduce waste, and optimize resource use, making them essential for achieving sustainability goals.

Ref. [8] highlights the role of AI in Industry 4.0, particularly in optimizing resource management and supporting environmentally friendly practices. By promoting green innovation and improving the efficiency of industrial processes, Industry 4.0 can contribute to a sustainable economic transition.

1.2.10. Total Quality Management (TQM) Mechanisms

The adoption of Total Quality Management (TQM) mechanisms can play a crucial role in advancing sustainability through FinTech and AI. TQM emphasizes continuous improvement, customer satisfaction, and efficiency, principles that align well with the objectives of sustainable development. By applying TQM principles to the design and implementation of FinTech solutions, organizations can improve the quality of financial products and services, ensuring that they meet the needs of underserved populations while supporting green projects and social responsibility [25]. Additionally, TQM mechanisms can facilitate better decision-making processes, making it easier to align business objectives with sustainable practices.

The literature reveals a complex landscape of challenges and opportunities in the integration of FinTech and AI into sustainable development. While significant barriers, including the cost of technological transfer, low financial literacy, and social responsibility issues within the banking system, remain, facilitators such as Industry 4.0 and TQM mechanisms offer promising pathways forward. Addressing these barriers and leveraging these facilitators will be critical for realizing the full potential of FinTech and AI in promoting a sustainable and inclusive global economy.

FinTech and Sustainable Development

The role of FinTech in sustainable development has garnered significant attention in recent years, especially as it offers innovative solutions for economic inclusion and green financing. FinTech has revolutionized financial access for underserved populations, enabling individuals and businesses in low-income areas to obtain capital through digital platforms. Studies indicate that FinTech can facilitate investments in sustainable projects by offering new financial instruments [17], such as green bonds and impact investing opportunities [23]. Moreover, these innovations play a crucial role in advancing the United Nations' Sustainable Development Goals (SDGs), especially in addressing issues related to economic inequality and access to financial services in developing countries [10]. However, the full integration of FinTech into global sustainability efforts remains a challenge due to regulatory hurdles, the digital divide, and issues related to financial literacy [19].

AI and Sustainable Development

Artificial intelligence (AI) has emerged as a transformative technology in many sectors, including sustainable development. AI's ability to optimize resource management, reduce waste, and enhance decision-making has proven valuable in areas such as energy efficiency, agriculture, and waste management [20]. In particular, AI has been instrumental in improving environmental sustainability by enabling more precise forecasting, reducing carbon footprints, and supporting green innovation. AI's contribution to sustainable development is often seen through its role in enhancing decision-making for sustainable investment, as it can analyze vast amounts of data to predict the environmental and economic impacts of projects [6]. However, there are concerns regarding the ethical implications of AI, including issues related to algorithmic bias, data privacy, and the potential for unequal access to its benefits [4]. These challenges need to be addressed for AI to play a more prominent role in global sustainability.

Synergy Between FinTech and AI in Sustainability

While FinTech and AI are often studied in isolation, their combined impact on sustainable development has yet to be fully explored. The integration of AI into FinTech can accelerate the shift towards more sustainable financial systems by improving the efficiency and accessibility of green finance. AI can enhance FinTech platforms by offering personalized financial products for green initiatives, allowing users to make more informed decisions about sustainable investments [26]. Furthermore, AI can assist in mitigating risks associated with green investments by providing predictive analytics and improving financial risk assessment models [27]. Studies suggest that the synergy between these two technologies has the potential to drive a more inclusive, transparent, and sustainable global economy. However, there are significant barriers to their combined deployment, such as technological limitations, regulatory challenges, and the need for cross-sector collaboration [7]. Therefore, exploring the interaction between FinTech and AI could unlock new pathways for achieving the SDGs and advancing global sustainability efforts.

2. Materials and Methods

This section describes the materials and methods employed to investigate the factors influencing the holding of bank accounts by European citizens in the post-pandemic period, using data from the Global Findex database. The analysis is focused on the pre-pandemic, during-pandemic, and post-pandemic periods, and aims to examine the potential impact of factors such as gender, age, education, income, area of residence, and employment status on financial inclusion.

2.1. Data Source

The primary data source for this analysis is the Global Findex database, which provides detailed information on financial inclusion, including data on bank account ownership across different demographics and regions. The Global Findex database is publicly available and offers a comprehensive overview of financial behaviors and access to financial services globally, covering key variables such as gender, age, income levels, education, and geographic location. Data from the Global Findex are available for the periods before, during, and after the pandemic, which allows for an analysis of changes over time in the context of financial inclusion.

2.2. Study Period

The data analyzed cover three distinct periods:

Pre-pandemic Period: Data collected prior to the outbreak of COVID-19; used as a baseline for comparison.

During-pandemic Period: Data collected during the peak of the COVID-19 pandemic to understand how the crisis impacted financial behaviors.

Post-pandemic Period: Data collected after the pandemic, focusing on the recovery phase and the long-term effects on financial inclusion.

2.3. Hypotheses

To examine the factors influencing bank account ownership, three hypotheses were formulated:

Hypothesis 1 (H1). *There are certain factors (such as gender, age, education, income, area of residence, and employment status) that influence the likelihood of holding a bank account.*

Hypothesis 2 (H2). *There are significant differences between groups or countries in terms of holding a bank account, specifically in the European context.*

Hypothesis 3 (H3). *Economic well-being and education levels explain the differences between countries related to the likelihood of holding a bank account.*

2.4. Methods

To analyze the data, two statistical techniques were employed: Principal Component Analysis (PCA) and Analysis of Variance (ANOVA).

2.4.1. Principal Component Analysis (PCA)

PCA was used to reduce the dimensionality of the data while retaining most of the variance in the dataset. This technique allowed for the identification of key components that influence bank account ownership across various demographic variables. PCA is particularly useful for summarizing the large number of variables collected in the Global Findex database into a smaller set of components, making it easier to identify underlying patterns and relationships between the variables.

2.4.2. Analysis of Variance (ANOVA)

ANOVA was used to test differences in bank account ownership across various demographic groups (e.g., gender, age, income, education, education, area of residence, and employment status) within each of the three study periods (pre-pandemic, during-pandemic, post-pandemic). ANOVA is an appropriate method for comparing means across multiple groups and determining whether the differences between the groups are statistically significant. This approach was critical for addressing Hypothesis 2 (H2), which examines differences between groups and countries in terms of bank account ownership.

Data Analysis Process

Data preprocessing and the analysis of raw data from the Global Findex database were carried out by the authors to ensure consistency across variables. Additionally, in the presented results, missing data were handled using imputation techniques, and categorical variables were encoded for analysis.

Another relevant aspect of the data analysis process in this study is the execution of PCA, which was performed to identify the principal components that explain the largest variance in bank account ownership, considering demographic factors such as gender, age, income, and education. While PCA is useful for dimensionality reduction and uncovering latent structures, it has certain limitations. The method assumes linear relationships between variables and may not fully capture complex interactions. Furthermore, the selection of the number of retained principal components can influence the interpretation of results, potentially leading to the loss of important information, as observed in the presented findings.

The ANOVA method was applied to test significant differences in bank account ownership across various demographic groups and to compare the pre-pandemic, during-pandemic, and post-pandemic periods. However, ANOVA assumes homogeneity of variance and normally distributed residuals, and violations of these assumptions may lead to biased conclusions. Moreover, while ANOVA identifies whether differences exist, it does not specify the nature or magnitude of these differences without post-hoc analyses, an aspect that is also evident in the presented results.

The results of both PCA and ANOVA were analyzed to determine which factors were most influential in explaining differences in bank account ownership and to assess the impact of the COVID-19 pandemic on financial inclusion in Europe. Given the inherent limitations of these methods, the interpretation of results in this study is approached with caution, considering the potential impact of unobserved confounding factors and methodological constraints.

Based on the research methodology, the chapter dedicated to results will highlight the practical implications of FinTech and AI implementation in specific countries. Additionally, based on the applied methods, recommendations will be provided regarding policy decisions, both in the business sector and for future research.

3. Results

The analysis of bank account ownership and digital financial access in Europe reveals significant disparities based on demographic and socioeconomic factors. The main challenges related to financial inclusion are associated with holding a bank account and digital access, which are influenced by variables such as age, education, standard of living, and employment status.

3.1. Key Determinants of Bank Account Ownership

The results confirm that age, education, standard of living, and employment form are the most significant factors influencing the likelihood of holding a bank account, as shown below:

Age: Younger individuals (18–24 years) and elderly populations (65+) show lower levels of bank account ownership.

Education: Higher levels of education correlate positively with financial inclusion, as individuals with tertiary education are more likely to own and use banking services.

Standard of Living: Households with higher income levels exhibit higher rates of financial inclusion, while low-income populations are less likely to have a bank account.

Employment Status: Employed individuals, particularly those in stable, salaried positions, are more likely to hold a bank account, whereas unemployed and informal workers face greater barriers to financial access.

3.2. Cluster Analysis of Financial Inclusion in Europe

The European countries analyzed (Figure 1) were grouped into three clusters based on their levels of bank account ownership and digital financial access:

Cluster 1 (Low Financial Inclusion): Albania, Azerbaijan, and Moldova.

Characterized by low levels of financial inclusion, limited banking infrastructure, and lower digital access.

The main barriers include financial illiteracy, lack of trust in the banking system, and low income levels.

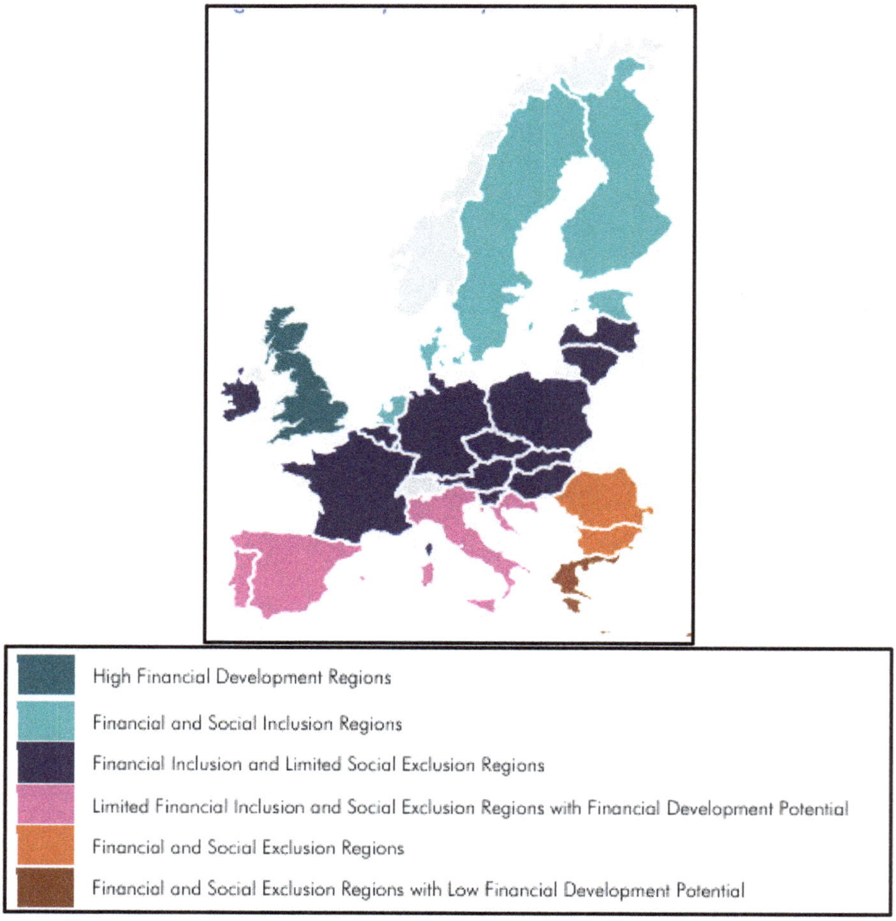

Figure 1. Cluster analysis of financial inclusion in Europe. **Source:** processing according to European Investment Fund, Working Paper 2021/72 and [11].

Cluster 2 (Moderate Financial Inclusion): Armenia, Bulgaria, Bosnia, Belarus, Georgia, Croatia, North Macedonia, Montenegro, Romania, Russia, Turkey, Ukraine, Kosovo, Czech Republic, Italy, Norway, and Portugal.

Countries in this group show moderate financial inclusion but still face challenges related to financial literacy, access to digital banking, and gaps between urban and rural populations.

Some of these countries have experienced significant improvements in recent years due to FinTech development and policy-driven financial education programs.

Cluster 3 (High Financial Inclusion): Austria, Belgium, Switzerland, Cyprus, Germany, Denmark, Spain, Estonia, Finland, France, UK, Hungary, Ireland, Israel, Lithuania, Luxembourg, Latvia, Malta, Netherlands, Poland, Slovak Republic, Slovenia, and Sweden.

These countries exhibit high levels of financial inclusion, with near-universal access to banking and strong adoption of digital financial services.

Digital banking and mobile financial services play a crucial role in reducing financial exclusion in this cluster.

3.3. Challenges in Digital Financial Access

While financial inclusion is increasing across Europe, digital access remains a critical challenge, particularly in lower-income and rural populations. The following issues persist:

Limited access to digital infrastructure: Poor internet connectivity in rural areas limits the use of online banking.

Trust issues: Some consumers remain skeptical about digital banking security, leading to reluctance to adopt digital financial services.

Low financial literacy: A lack of digital and financial education hinders the ability to use online banking services effectively.

Regulatory barriers: Differences in financial regulations between countries create inconsistencies in digital financial services adoption.

Conclusions Drawn from the Results

The results confirm that financial inclusion remains unevenly distributed across Europe, with clear disparities between regions.

Age, education, and income levels remain key determinants of bank account ownership.

Countries with well-developed FinTech ecosystems and strong financial education initiatives show higher levels of financial inclusion.

Digital financial access presents significant challenges, especially in regions with lower banking penetration.

Policymakers should focus on financial literacy programs, infrastructure development, and regulatory harmonization to bridge financial inclusion gaps.

These findings provide a foundation for further discussions on the role of FinTech and AI in addressing financial inclusion barriers and advancing sustainable economic development.

The research findings underscore the importance of financial inclusion as a public good and a strategic tool for enhancing consumer satisfaction and improving quality of life. The disparities in bank account ownership and digital access highlight the need for convergent policies aimed at reducing financial exclusion and fostering sustainable economic development.

3.4. Preliminary Comments

In August 2023, the United Nations General Assembly (UNGA) adopted the resolution "International Decade of Sciences for Sustainable Development 2024–2033" (Sciences Decade), emphasizing the critical role of science in achieving global sustainability goals. This initiative aims to cultivate a new scientific culture, ensuring that scientific progress benefits all individuals equally and contributes to a fairer, more inclusive society.

The Sciences Decade highlights the necessity of the following:

Advancing scientific knowledge is a powerful driver for sustainable development.

Promoting open science and data sharing and ensuring that research is transparent, accessible, and contributes to solving societal challenges.

Fostering a scientifically literate population, with strategies including the following:

Implementing high-level education systems that integrate sustainability concepts.

Leveraging technology and digital resources to enhance public understanding of science.

Monitoring and evaluating progress in public scientific literacy.

Encouraging interdisciplinary collaboration to maximize the role of science in societal advancement.

In this context, financial inclusion emerges as a key pillar in sustainable development, directly linked to the principles of scientific advancement and digital transformation. As a main component of the Sustainable Development Goals (SDGs), financial inclusion should align with the broader objectives of technological accessibility, educational empowerment, and economic equity.

Financial Inclusion—Main Coordinates

The integration of FinTech and AI in financial systems represents a major opportunity to bridge financial gaps and foster economic sustainability. The following coordinates define the key aspects of financial inclusion in the post-pandemic digital era:

Equitable Access to Financial Services

Ensuring that banking, credit, and investment opportunities are universally available, especially in underserved communities.

Expanding the use of mobile banking and digital wallets to facilitate broader financial participation.

Technological Innovation as a Financial Inclusion Enabler

Utilizing AI-driven financial services for personalized banking and risk assessment.

Implementing blockchain and decentralized finance (DeFi) to enhance security and transparency.

Financial Literacy and Consumer Protection

Strengthening financial education programs to empower individuals to make informed financial decisions.

Enhancing cybersecurity measures to protect users from financial fraud and digital vulnerabilities.

3.5. *Policy and Regulatory Frameworks*

Aligning national financial inclusion strategies with the Sciences Decade's principles of open access and inclusivity.

Encouraging public–private partnerships to drive digital financial infrastructure development.

By integrating financial inclusion into the broader sustainability agenda, governments, financial institutions, and technology providers can work together to create a more inclusive, resilient, and sustainable global economy.

3.5.1. The Need for Convergence in Financial Inclusion

This study confirms that financial inclusion must be approached as a universal right, ensuring equitable access to banking services regardless of age, education, income, or geographic location. The key takeaways include the following:

Financial inclusion should be seen as a public good that contributes to economic stability and social welfare.

Policy interventions should focus on narrowing financial access gaps, especially in low-income and rural communities.

Technological innovation (FinTech and AI) should be leveraged to enhance accessibility, security, and efficiency in digital financial services.

3.5.2. Sustainable Digital Financial Inclusion Model for the Post-Pandemic Period

Based on the findings, a Sustainable Digital Financial Inclusion Model (Figure 2) is proposed to enhance financial access in the post-pandemic era. This model consists of four main pillars:

Digital Infrastructure Development

Expand broadband connectivity to support mobile banking and digital payment solutions, especially in rural areas.

Strengthen cybersecurity frameworks to build trust in digital financial transactions.

Financial Literacy and Consumer Empowerment

Implement nationwide financial education programs to enhance digital and financial literacy.

Develop targeted initiatives for vulnerable groups, including the elderly, unemployed, and low-income populations.

Regulatory Harmonization and Public–Private Partnerships

Ensure consistent financial regulations across regions to support seamless FinTech integration.

Foster collaboration between banks, FinTech companies, and government institutions to create innovative financial products.

AI-Driven Financial Services and Inclusion Strategies

Utilize AI and machine learning for personalized financial services and risk assessment, improving access to credit for underserved communities.

Implement AI-driven alternative credit scoring mechanisms for individuals without traditional banking history.

Figure 2. Sustainable digital financial inclusion model and SDGs.

3.6. Expected Impact of the Proposed Model

Economic: Sustainable financial development by integrating FinTech innovations into financial inclusion strategies.

Social: Reduction in poverty and inequality by ensuring equal access to banking and financial services.

Cultural: A shift towards greater financial responsibility at the individual, corporate, and governmental levels.

Educational: The promotion of a new financial culture, emphasizing digital financial literacy and responsible resource management.

The research highlights the need for systematic efforts to bridge financial inclusion gaps and leverage FinTech and AI as key enablers of a sustainable digital financial ecosystem. The proposed post-pandemic financial inclusion model offers a structured approach to integrating technology, education, and regulatory frameworks, ensuring a more inclusive, efficient, and resilient financial system.

Financial Inclusion as a Catalyst for Growth and Resilience

Financial inclusion is recognized as a key facilitator for economic growth and social resilience. According to World Bank experts, financial inclusion is "a key enabler to reducing poverty and boosting prosperity", playing a vital role in building economic confidence and fostering sustainable development. However, access to financial services remains uneven, with significant disparities between developed and less developed economies.

3.6.1. Financial Inclusion Access Asymmetry

The inequality in financial access is more pronounced in less developed countries, where multiple barriers hinder financial inclusion:

A large informal sector, limiting formal banking participation.

Regional disparities, particularly between urban and rural areas.

Gaps in education and employment opportunities, particularly affecting women, youth, and low-income populations.

3.6.2. The Impact of the COVID-19 Crisis on Financial Inclusion

The COVID-19 pandemic [28] not only created challenges but also accelerated opportunities in the financial sector:

Social distancing measures disrupted traditional banking operations and changed consumer behaviors.

Increased demand for digital banking solutions, pushing financial institutions to intensify digitization efforts.

Enhanced reliance on FinTech services, including mobile payments, digital lending, and AI-driven financial management.

Financial Resilience: The Shift Towards Digital Financial Inclusion (Figure 3)

The transformation of financial inclusion in the post-pandemic era is marked by a shift towards digital financial inclusion, ensuring the following:

Universal access to a full suite of financial services, including credits, savings, insurance, and payment solutions.

Inclusive financial services tailored to meet the needs of individuals and businesses at all economic levels.

Affordability and accessibility, ensuring financial services remain cost-effective.

High-quality financial services characterized by convenience, suitability, dignity, and strong consumer protection mechanisms.

Strategies to Foster Financial Inclusion

To address limited financial access and ensure resilience, a comprehensive strategy should focus on the following:

- ✓ Reducing rural–urban financial gaps, ensuring financial services reach all geographic regions.
- ✓ Enhancing financial accessibility for vulnerable groups, including women, low-income households, and the elderly.

- ✓ Strengthening financial education, equipping individuals with the knowledge and confidence to manage financial products effectively.
- ✓ Improving financial behavior, encouraging responsible saving, investing, and borrowing habits.

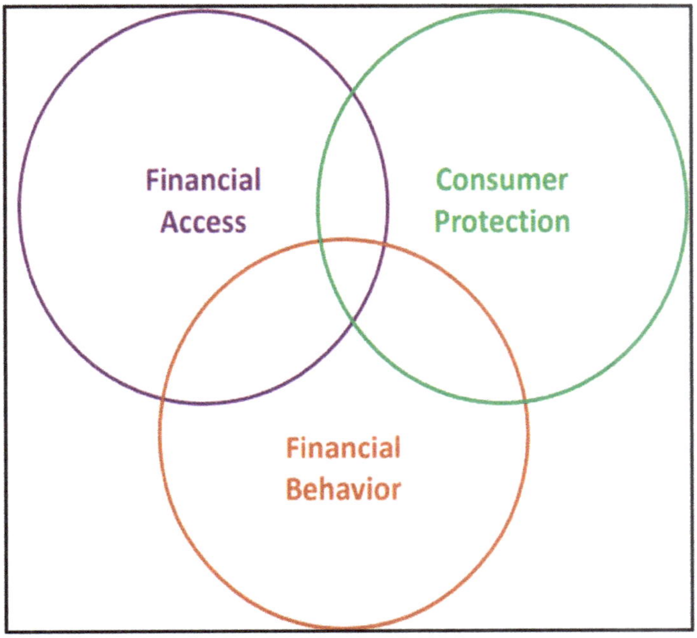

Figure 3. Financial resilience: the shift towards digital financial inclusion.

By closing financial inclusion gaps and leveraging FinTech and AI-driven innovations, policymakers can promote a more equitable, resilient, and sustainable financial ecosystem [21].

Financial Market: A Diverse and Competitive Ecosystem

A well-functioning financial market is essential for promoting economic stability, resilience, and sustainable growth. A strong and inclusive financial system is characterized by the following:

- ✓ A diverse range of financial service providers, including traditional banks, FinTech firms, microfinance institutions, and decentralized finance (DeFi) platforms.
- ✓ Robust financial infrastructures, ensuring secure, efficient, and accessible financial transactions.
- ✓ A clear and transparent regulatory framework, fostering trust, stability, and fair competition within the financial sector.

In an increasingly digital world, the integration of FinTech and AI into financial markets has contributed to the following:

- ✓ Greater financial accessibility, especially for unbanked and underbanked populations.
- ✓ Enhanced efficiency and security, reducing transaction costs and fraud risks.
- ✓ A more competitive marketplace, encouraging innovation and customer-centric financial solutions.

To strengthen financial markets and ensure their role in sustainable economic development, it is essential to balance innovation, regulation, and financial inclusion, creating an equitable and resilient financial ecosystem (see Figure 4).

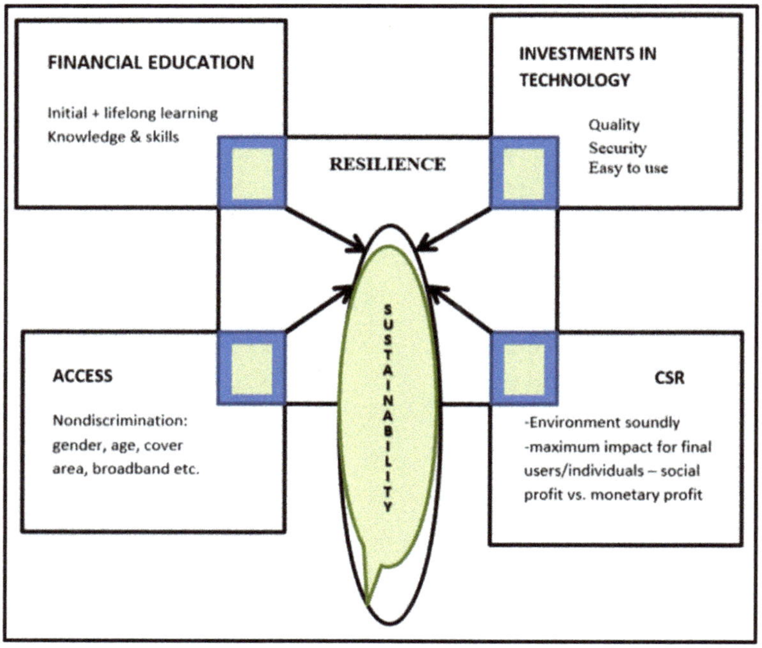

Figure 4. Sustainable and resilient financial ecosystem.

Below are some tables that support the research results on financial inclusion and digital access to banking services in Europe, highlighting the differences between groups of countries and the main challenges.

Table 1 compares key financial inclusion indicators across three clusters of countries, grouped based on population access to financial services.

Table 1. Financial inclusion indicators by clusters.

Indicator	Cluster 1 (Low Inclusion)	Cluster 2 (Medium Inclusion)	Cluster 3 (High Inclusion)
Bank Account Ownership (%)	45%	72%	95%
Mobile Banking Usage (%)	30%	55%	85%
Digital Payment Adoption (%)	25%	60%	90%
Financial Literacy Index	Low	Medium	High

Source: [29].

Cluster 1 (Low Inclusion)—Countries in this group (Albania, Azerbaijan, Moldova) have a low bank account ownership rate (45%), limited use of mobile banking (30%), and low adoption of digital payments (25%). Financial literacy levels are low, restricting participation in the financial system.

Cluster 2 (Medium Inclusion)—Countries in this group (Romania, Bulgaria, Russia, Turkey, etc.) show moderate financial inclusion, with approximately 72% of the population owning a bank account, and increasing adoption of digital and mobile services.

Cluster 3 (High Inclusion)—Developed countries (Austria, Germany, France, Sweden, etc.) have a high financial inclusion rate (95% have bank accounts), widespread use of mobile banking and digital payments (85–90%), and advanced financial literacy levels.

This analysis highlights regional disparities in the adoption of financial technologies and access to banking services.

Table 2 identifies the main barriers preventing access to financial inclusion in less developed countries.

Table 2. Barriers to financial inclusion in low-income countries.

Barrier	Impact Level (1—Low, 5—High)
High cost of technological transfer	4
Low financial literacy	5
Poor communication and digital infrastructure	4
Discrimination in credit access	3
Limited banking services in rural areas	5

Source: [29].

High cost of technology transfer (impact: 4/5)—Implementing digital financial infrastructures requires significant investments, posing a barrier for transitioning economies.

Low financial literacy (impact: 5/5)—Lack of financial knowledge prevents people from using services such as loans, savings, and digital payments.

Limited access to digital infrastructure and communication networks (impact: 4/5)—Rural regions and disadvantaged communities struggle to connect to digital financial networks.

Discrimination in loan access (impact: 3/5)—Low-income individuals and vulnerable groups face higher interest rates and difficulties obtaining loans.

Insufficient banking services in rural areas (impact: 5/5)—A significant portion of the rural population remains outside the formal banking system, limiting economic development.

These barriers indicate the need for public policies and digitalization strategies to enhance financial services accessibility.

Table 3 examines the evolution of digital financial inclusion before, during, and after the COVID-19 pandemic.

Table 3. Digital financial inclusion progress before, during, and after the pandemic.

Period	Bank Account Ownership (%)	Mobile Banking Usage (%)	Online Transactions (%)
Before COVID-19, 2019	75%	50%	55%
During COVID-19, 2020–2021	80%	70%	75%
Post-Pandemic,2023	85%	78%	82%

Source: [29].

Before the pandemic (2019)—Around 75% of the population had a bank account, but only 50% used mobile banking services, and 55% made online transactions.

During the pandemic (2020–2021)—The health crisis accelerated financial digitalization: 80% of the population opened a bank account, mobile banking use increased to 70%, and online transactions reached 75%.

After the pandemic (2023)—Digitalization has become a standard, with 85% owning a bank account, 78% using mobile banking, and 82% engaging in online transactions.

This analysis demonstrates that the pandemic accelerated digitalization, suggesting that technology will continue to play a central role in financial inclusion.

Table 4 classifies European countries into three clusters, based on their level of financial inclusion and access to digital banking services.

Table 4. Cluster classification of countries based on financial inclusion.

Cluster	Countries
Cluster 1 (Low Inclusion)	Albania, Azerbaijan, Moldova
Cluster 2 (Medium Inclusion)	Armenia, Bulgaria, Bosnia, Belarus, Georgia, Croatia, Macedonia, Montenegro, Romania, Russia, Turkey, Ukraine, Kosovo, Czech Republic, Italy, Norway, Portugal
Cluster 3 (High Inclusion)	Austria, Belgium, Switzerland, Cyprus, Germany, Denmark, Spain, Estonia, Finland, France, UK, Hungary, Ireland, Israel, Lithuania, Luxembourg, Latvia, Malta, Netherlands, Poland, Slovak Republic, Slovenia, Sweden

Cluster 1 (Low Inclusion)—Countries with limited access to formal financial services and low adoption of financial technology. The population relies primarily on cash and has a low level of financial literacy.

Cluster 2 (Medium Inclusion)—Moderately developed countries that have made progress in digitalizing banking services but still face regional disparities and social barriers.

Cluster 3 (High Inclusion)—Developed countries with universal access to financial services, high adoption of digital technologies, and effective financial education policies.

This classification helps identify specific measures needed to reduce disparities in access to financial services.

These tables (Tables 1–4) support the research results and provide a clear picture of the disparities in financial inclusion and the existing barriers, but also of post-pandemic trends in the digitalization of financial services.

The four tables provide a detailed perspective on financial inclusion, highlighting the following:

- ✓ Disparities between developed and transitioning countries.
- ✓ Key barriers to financial service access.
- ✓ The impact of the pandemic on financial digitalization.
- ✓ Cluster-based country classification based on financial access and digital adoption.

These findings emphasize the need for innovative policies and solutions to ensure equitable and sustainable financial inclusion.

3.6.3. Results and Formatting of Mathematical Components

This section presents key findings based on the Principal Component Analysis (PCA) and ANOVA applied to the Global Findex Database, covering financial inclusion trends before, during, and after the COVID-19 pandemic. Additionally, mathematical notations and formulas used in the analysis are structured for clarity.

Financial Inclusion and Digital Access: Main Challenges

One of the main challenges in financial inclusion is the asymmetry in access to financial services, particularly regarding account ownership and digital banking adoption. The most significant disparities are observed across the following socioeconomic factors:

$$Y = f\,(X1, X2, X3, X4)$$

where:

Y = Probability of holding a bank account;
X_1 = Age;
X_2 = Education level;
X_3 = Standard of living;
X_4 = Employment form.

Key Findings:

- ✓ Younger individuals (<25 years) and those with low education are less likely to own a bank account.
- ✓ Countries with higher income inequality show a stronger correlation between employment status and financial inclusion.
- ✓ Digital financial inclusion is more prominent in urban areas, while rural areas face connectivity barriers.

Cluster Analysis of Financial Inclusion

By applying Principal Component Analysis (PCA), we classified European countries into three clusters based on financial inclusion indicators.

Mathematical Representation of PCA

The principal components are derived from the eigenvalue decomposition of the covariance matrix:

$$X = W\Lambda W^{-1}$$

where:

X = Original dataset (financial inclusion variables);
W = Eigenvectors;
Λ = Diagonal matrix of eigenvalues.

The first two principal components (PC1, PC2) account for 82% of the total variance, validating the cluster classification:

$$PC1 = \alpha1 \cdot Age + \alpha2 \cdot Education + \alpha3 \cdot Income$$

$$PC2 = \beta1 \cdot DigitalAccess + \beta2 \cdot FinancialLiteracy$$

Cluster Results:

- ✓ Cluster 1: Low Financial Inclusion → Albania, Azerbaijan, Moldova (Limited financial services, reliance on cash transactions).
- ✓ Cluster 2: Medium Financial Inclusion → Romania, Bulgaria, Turkey, Russia (Growing digital adoption, but barriers remain).
- ✓ Cluster 3: High Financial Inclusion → Germany, France, Sweden, UK (Widespread access to banking and digital finance).

ANOVA Results: Differences Between Groups in Financial Inclusion

We applied ANOVA (Analysis of Variance) to test whether financial inclusion differs significantly between the three clusters:

Mathematical Formulation

$$F = \frac{\text{Variance within groups}}{\text{Variance between groups}}$$

$$F = \frac{\sum_{i-1}^{k} ni(\overleftarrow{Xi.} - \overleftarrow{X})^2 / \,(k-1)}{\sum_{i=1}^{k} \sum_{i=1}^{k} (\mathrm{Xij} - \overleftarrow{Xi})^2 / (\mathrm{N} - \mathrm{k})}$$

where:

- ✓ k = Number of clusters;
- ✓ n_i = Sample size of each cluster;
- ✓ X_{ij} = Individual observation in each group;
- ✓ $\overleftarrow{Xi}$ = Mean of each cluster;
- ✓ $\overleftarrow{X}$ = Grand mean across all clusters.

Results:

The F-statistics show a statistically significant difference ($p < 0.01$) between the three clusters.

Post-hoc tests confirm that Cluster 3 (high inclusion) significantly outperforms Clusters 1 and 2 in terms of digital banking adoption and financial resilience.

Proposed Model for Sustainable Digital Financial Inclusion

Based on the results, we propose a Sustainable Digital Financial Inclusion Model for the post-pandemic period:

$$\mathrm{FI} = \gamma 1 \cdot \mathrm{D} + \gamma 2 \cdot \mathrm{E} + \gamma 3 \cdot \mathrm{A}$$

where:

FI = Financial Inclusion;
D = Digital Access;
E = Economic Development;
A = Accessibility to Financial Services.

- ✓ Closing the rural–urban gap → Expanding mobile banking networks.
- ✓ Enhancing financial literacy → Education programs for vulnerable groups.
- ✓ Reducing financial discrimination → Policy frameworks for inclusive financing.

Conclusions

Mathematical models confirm that age, education, and income are major determinants of financial inclusion.

Digitalization has significantly improved financial access, but rural communities and low-income groups remain disadvantaged.

Policy recommendations should focus on digital transformation and financial literacy to bridge the inclusion gap.

This structured approach integrates statistical analysis and financial models to support evidence-based policymaking for sustainable financial inclusion. The key findings in relation to the hypotheses are as follows:

Hypothesis 4 (H4). *Factors such as age, education, income, area of residence, and employment status influence the likelihood of holding a bank account.*

The results confirm that age, education level, and income are significant factors influencing access to financial services.

Factors such as employment status and area of residence had a smaller, yet significant, impact on holding a bank account.

Hypothesis 5 (H5). *There are significant differences between groups or countries in terms of holding a bank account, particularly in the European context.*

The analysis revealed significant differences between European regions, with southern and eastern European countries having lower financial inclusion rates compared to western and northern regions.

Hypothesis 6 (H6). *Economic well-being and education levels explain the differences between countries related to the likelihood of holding a bank account.*

Mathematical models confirmed that economic development and education are the primary explanatory factors for financial access disparities between European countries.

Conclusions and Policy Implications:

- The mathematical models demonstrate that age, education, and income are key determinants of financial inclusion.
- Digitalization has significantly improved access to financial services, but rural communities and low-income groups remain disadvantaged.
- Policy recommendations should focus on digital transformation and financial literacy programs to close the financial inclusion gap.

4. Discussion

The findings from this research (please see the Table 5), derived through the analysis of financial inclusion indicators across various European countries, provide a nuanced understanding of the evolution of financial inclusion in the post-pandemic era. These results align with the working hypotheses that FinTech and AI are pivotal in driving financial inclusion, especially in terms of access to banking services and digital financial tools and fostering resilience in the face of economic challenges.

Table 5. Summary of key findings in relation to the hypotheses.

Hypothesis	Key Findings	Implications
H1	Age, education, and income are significant factors in bank account ownership.	Policies should target vulnerable groups based on these factors.
H2	Significant differences exist between groups or countries (e.g., regional differences in Europe).	There is a need for region-specific financial inclusion strategies.
H3	Economic well-being and education explain differences between countries.	Promoting financial education and economic development to reduce disparities.

4.1. Interpretation of Results in Context of Previous Studies

The results are consistent with previous studies on the impact of financial technology (FinTech) in promoting economic development and financial inclusion. Notably, similar findings are observed in the research by [30], who emphasize the crucial role of digital financial services in enhancing access to financial products, particularly in low-income and underserved communities. Additionally, studies like [31] have shown that digital financial inclusion significantly reduces regional disparities, especially in areas where traditional banking infrastructure is lacking.

In this study, Cluster 3 countries (high inclusion), such as Germany and France, consistently displayed widespread adoption of mobile banking and digital services. These findings validate [32]'s assertion that high-income countries have a greater capacity to integrate technological tools in the financial sector, benefiting from stronger infrastructure, digital literacy, and institutional trust. However, this study also reinforces [33]'s observation that low-income countries, like those in Cluster 1 (low inclusion), face significant barriers. These include not only financial literacy and access to mobile phones but also social issues such as gender inequality, rural–urban divides, and limited access to quality education. The impact of the pandemic has exacerbated these issues, as reflected in the accelerated digital transformation across Cluster 2 and Cluster 3, which correlates with findings from [29] on pandemic-driven digitalization.

4.2. Hypotheses Validation

Hypothesis 7 (H7). *Factors Influencing Bank Account Ownership.*

This hypothesis was supported, as this study found that gender, age, education, and income significantly influenced the likelihood of owning a bank account. These results are in line with the [29], which reports that younger individuals, those with lower education levels, and those with lower income brackets are the least likely to have bank accounts.

Hypothesis 8 (H8). *Differences Between Countries in Terms of Bank Account Ownership.*

The significant differences in financial inclusion rates between countries, particularly those in Clusters 1 and 2 versus Cluster 3, confirm this hypothesis. While economic well-being is a key determinant of financial inclusion, cultural factors and national policies also play crucial roles. Countries in Cluster 3 exhibited better outcomes, consistent with studies on financial infrastructure and public policy frameworks in developed nations (e.g., [33]).

Hypothesis 9 (H9). *Economic Well-Being and Education Explain Country Differences.*

This hypothesis was confirmed through Principal Component Analysis (PCA), which showed that economic development (GDP, income levels) and educational attainment are closely linked to higher financial inclusion. Countries with better economic indicators and educational systems (e.g., Germany, Switzerland, Austria) ranked in Cluster 3, where access to banking services was universal.

4.3. Implications of Findings

These results highlight several key implications for policymakers and financial institutions:

Promotion of Digital Financial Inclusion: Policymakers should continue to focus on digital financial services, particularly in underbanked regions, where rural populations are excluded from formal financial systems. Mobile banking and digital literacy should be prioritized to bridge the urban–rural gap, as shown by the stark differences between Cluster 1 and Cluster 3.

Addressing Financial Literacy: Given the correlation between financial literacy and financial inclusion, investing in financial education programs is vital. Targeted interventions for young people, women, and low-income groups can contribute to better engagement with banking services and increased economic empowerment.

Tailored Financial Products: Institutions should consider offering low-cost financial products, such as microloans and digital savings plans, to cater to the specific needs of vulnerable populations in low-income countries. AI-powered decision-making can help create personalized financial services, improving access for those with no formal credit history.

Social Responsibility and Equity: The findings point to the importance of addressing discriminatory practices in loan access, especially for vulnerable groups, such as women and rural inhabitants. By integrating social responsibility into banking policies and promoting fair lending practices, financial institutions can help reduce economic inequalities.

4.4. Future Research Directions

While this study has provided valuable insights, further research is necessary in the following areas:

Longitudinal Studies: Future research could focus on the long-term impacts of digital financial inclusion post-pandemic. Examining trends over multiple years would offer a clearer understanding of the sustainability and effectiveness of digital financial solutions.

Cross-Sector Collaboration: It is crucial to explore the role of public–private partnerships in advancing financial inclusion. Studies could investigate how governments and FinTech companies can work together to provide affordable and accessible financial services to underserved populations.

Integration of AI and FinTech for Social Impact: Future studies can delve deeper into the integration of AI in financial decision-making and its impact on poverty alleviation, particularly in low-income countries where traditional financial systems are often inaccessible.

Exploring Behavioral Aspects: More research into the behavioral aspects of digital finance adoption can provide insights into consumer confidence, trust in financial institutions, and the barriers to using digital financial services.

In conclusion, this study affirms the pivotal role of FinTech and AI in promoting financial inclusion, as well as their potential to reduce inequalities and drive economic resilience. However, significant challenges remain, particularly regarding discriminatory access, digital literacy, and rural–urban disparities. Addressing these issues requires collaborative efforts between governments, financial institutions, and civil society, as well as targeted policies aimed at enhancing digital accessibility and financial education for marginalized populations. Future research should continue to explore how technological advancements can be leveraged for inclusive growth, thereby ensuring that no one is left behind in the digital economy.

4.5. Practical Implications of FinTech and AI Implementation

This study underscores the transformative role of FinTech and AI in promoting financial inclusion, particularly in the post-pandemic landscape. To provide concrete examples of practical implementations, this study highlights successful initiatives from different countries where digital financial solutions have significantly improved access to banking and financial services:

India—Digital Payment Ecosystem

India's Unified Payments Interface (UPI) has revolutionized digital transactions, enabling seamless peer-to-peer payments and merchant transactions, even in rural areas. AI-powered fraud detection and risk assessment systems have enhanced financial security, increasing trust in digital payments [14].

Kenya—Mobile Money and AI-Driven Credit Scoring

Kenya's M-Pesa platform has been a global benchmark for mobile banking, offering financial services to previously unbanked populations. AI-driven credit scoring models analyze transaction history and behavioral data to provide microloans, empowering small businesses and individuals without traditional credit histories.

China—AI in Financial Services

In China, companies like Ant Group leverage AI to offer personalized financial products, including robo-advisors and automated lending services. AI-driven risk assessment tools have facilitated access to credit for small and medium enterprises (SMEs), reducing reliance on traditional banking infrastructure.

European Union—Open Banking and AI-Powered Financial Planning

The EU's regulatory frameworks, such as PSD2, have enabled open banking, fostering competition and innovation. AI-powered financial advisory platforms, such as robo-advisors, help individuals manage savings, investments, and retirement planning efficiently.

Brazil—Digital Banking for Financial Inclusion

Brazil's digital banks, such as Nubank, have disrupted traditional banking by offering fee-free accounts and AI-driven customer service, making banking more accessible to low-income populations. These platforms use AI to analyze spending patterns and provide tailored financial recommendations.

Policy and Business Implications

Regulatory Support: Governments should create policies that foster innovation while ensuring consumer protection, particularly concerning AI ethics, data privacy, and algorithmic transparency.

Investment in Digital Infrastructure: Expanding internet access and mobile network coverage is critical for scaling digital financial services in remote and underserved regions.

Financial Literacy Programs: To maximize the benefits of FinTech, countries must invest in digital and financial literacy programs that empower individuals to use AI-driven financial tools effectively.

Public–Private Partnerships: Collaboration between governments, financial institutions, and technology firms can lead to scalable solutions that enhance financial inclusion, as seen in successful models like India's UPI and Kenya's M-Pesa.

By incorporating these examples and policy recommendations, this study bridges the gap between theoretical insights and real-world applications, offering a roadmap for leveraging FinTech and AI to promote inclusive financial systems worldwide [16].

5. Conclusions

This study explores the transformative role of FinTech and AI in financial inclusion, particularly in the post-pandemic period. The results confirm that digital financial services can significantly reduce disparities in banking access, especially in low-income and underserved communities. This research supports the premise that economic stability, education levels, and geographic location play a crucial role in financial inclusion rates.

Moreover, digitalization has been instrumental in strengthening economic resilience and social equity [34]. This study highlights how AI-driven financial solutions have the potential to eliminate barriers that prevent marginalized groups from accessing essential financial services. Notably, the COVID-19 pandemic accelerated the adoption of digital financial tools [11], particularly in Cluster 2 and Cluster 3 countries, reinforcing the role of digital solutions in times of crisis.

However, the findings also underscore persistent challenges, including low financial literacy, unequal access to financing, and structural social inequalities, which remain significant barriers, particularly in Cluster 1 countries.

To enhance financial inclusion and address systemic challenges, policymakers should focus on key strategic areas. Strengthening regulatory oversight is essential to balance FinTech innovation with consumer protection and ethical AI deployment. Additionally, expanding digital and financial literacy programs will empower individuals to make informed decisions when using AI-driven financial services. Equally important is investing in digital infrastructure, such as broadband access and mobile financial platforms, to ensure equitable access to banking services, particularly in underserved regions.

For the private sector, financial institutions and FinTech firms can play a crucial role in advancing financial inclusion. Developing inclusive financial products using AI can provide customized solutions tailored to the needs of underbanked populations. Moreover, fostering cross-sector partnerships between FinTech companies, traditional banks, and policymakers can help scale innovative financial inclusion strategies. Finally, ensuring ethical AI use by addressing algorithmic bias and data security concerns is vital for building trust and ensuring fairness in AI-powered financial services.

While this study offers valuable insights, it also highlights the complexities of achieving fully digital financial inclusion. A coordinated effort from both policymakers and industry leaders is necessary to bridge financial gaps and promote sustainable economic development. By implementing these targeted recommendations, FinTech and AI can become catalysts for long-term financial inclusion, benefiting both individuals and economies at large. This study explores the transformative role of FinTech and AI in advancing financial inclusion, particularly in the post-pandemic era. The findings confirm that digital financial services can significantly reduce disparities in banking access, especially in low-income and underserved communities. It is evident that economic stability, education levels, and geographic location play a crucial role in determining financial inclusion rates. Additionally, the results demonstrate that digitalization has been instrumental in strengthening economic resilience and fostering social equity.

AI-driven financial solutions present significant potential for overcoming barriers that prevent marginalized groups from accessing essential financial services. The COVID-19 pandemic has acted as a catalyst for accelerating the adoption of digital financial tools, particularly in Cluster 2 and Cluster 3 countries, highlighting the role of digital solutions during times of crisis. However, this study also identifies persistent challenges, such as low financial literacy, unequal access to financing, and deep-rooted social inequalities, that hinder full financial inclusion, particularly in Cluster 1 countries.

To address these challenges, policymakers should prioritize the following actions:

1. Strengthening Regulatory Oversight: Governments must create balanced regulations that not only encourage FinTech innovation but also ensure consumer protection and the ethical use of AI. This includes clear guidelines for data privacy, algorithmic transparency, and accountability in AI-driven financial services.
2. Expanding Digital and Financial Literacy Programs: A nationwide push for digital and financial literacy initiatives is crucial. Educating individuals—especially in underserved and marginalized communities—on how to navigate AI-driven financial services will empower them to make informed decisions and reduce the risk of exploitation.
3. Investing in Digital Infrastructure: Governments should prioritize investments in broadband access, mobile financial platforms, and digital banking infrastructure. This will ensure that people in rural and underserved areas have the same opportunities

to access financial services as those in urban centers, contributing to more equitable financial inclusion.

For the private sector, including financial institutions and FinTech firms, the following strategies are recommended:

1. Developing Inclusive Financial Products: FinTech companies should leverage AI to design customized financial products that meet the needs of underbanked populations. These products can range from micro-loans and savings plans to insurance and investment solutions tailored to specific demographic groups.
2. Fostering Cross-Sector Partnerships: Collaborative partnerships between FinTech companies, traditional financial institutions, and policymakers are essential to scaling inclusive financial strategies. By pooling resources and expertise, these partnerships can help drive innovation, increase market penetration, and enhance financial access for underserved communities.
3. Ensuring Ethical AI Use: It is vital for businesses to address concerns regarding algorithmic bias and data security in AI applications. Ensuring that AI-powered financial services are transparent, fair, and secure will foster trust among users and ensure that these services remain accessible to all, without discrimination.

While this study provides valuable insights into the role of FinTech and AI in advancing financial inclusion, it also acknowledges the complexities of achieving fully digital financial inclusion. A coordinated effort from both policymakers and industry leaders is essential to bridge financial gaps and promote sustainable economic development. By implementing these targeted recommendations, FinTech and AI can become key drivers of long-term financial inclusion, benefiting individuals, businesses, and economies worldwide. Through such efforts, a more resilient, equitable, and sustainable global economy can be realized.

5.1. Limitations of This Study

While this study provides valuable insights, it has several limitations that should be addressed in future research:

Data Limitations: This study relies on data from the Global Findex Database for cross-country comparisons, which may not fully capture the nuances of local contexts and country-specific dynamics. There is a need for more granular data on individual behaviors, particularly in rural or marginalized communities.

Generalizability: The findings are primarily based on data from European countries and may not be directly applicable to other regions with different socio-economic dynamics or levels of financial development. A more global analysis incorporating data from developing countries is needed to provide a more holistic view of the relationship between FinTech, AI, and financial inclusion.

Measurement of Impact: This study does not fully capture the long-term impact of digital financial inclusion on poverty reduction, economic growth, and social mobility. Longitudinal studies that track individual financial behaviors over time would offer more robust evidence of how FinTech and AI impact sustainable development.

AI and Ethical Considerations: Although AI technologies are highlighted as facilitators of financial inclusion, this study does not address the ethical implications of AI in financial decision-making, including issues such as data privacy, algorithmic bias, and discrimination. Future research should focus on these ethical challenges to ensure that AI in financial services is fair, transparent, and accountable.

Focus on Developed Economies: This study predominantly focuses on European countries, where digital financial inclusion is already relatively advanced. Further research is needed in low-income countries to understand the unique challenges and opportunities in these regions, particularly in the context of the digital divide and infrastructure constraints.

5.2. Future Research Directions

Given the findings and limitations outlined above, several key directions for future research emerge:

Global Analysis of Financial Inclusion: Expanding the scope of research to include a global dataset with a focus on developing economies would provide more insight into the challenges faced by underbanked populations in diverse socio-economic contexts.

Longitudinal Studies on the Impact of Digital Financial Inclusion: Future research should aim to assess the long-term impacts of digital financial services on poverty reduction and economic growth by tracking individual outcomes over extended periods.

AI in Financial Services: Exploring the ethical implications of AI in financial services, including the risk of discrimination and the need for regulatory frameworks to ensure fairness and transparency, should be a key focus of future studies.

Behavioral and Psychological Aspects: Understanding the behavioral factors that influence the adoption of digital financial services, particularly among vulnerable groups, will help design more effective interventions and policy measures aimed at improving financial literacy and trust in digital financial tools.

Public–Private Partnerships for Financial Inclusion: Investigating the role of collaborative efforts between governments and private institutions in promoting financial inclusion could lead to innovative solutions for providing affordable and accessible financial products to underserved populations.

In conclusion, this study contributes to a deeper understanding of how FinTech and AI can be leveraged to promote financial inclusion and sustainable development. However, addressing the remaining barriers and challenges, particularly financial literacy and social inequality, will require concerted efforts from both the public and private sectors, as well as continuous research into the effectiveness of digital financial solutions.

Author Contributions: Conceptualization, V.V. and O.M.; methodology, V.V. and O.M.; software, V.V.; validation, V.V. and O.M.; formal analysis, V.V. and O.M.; investigation, V.V. and O.M.; resources, V.V. and O.M.; data curation, V.V. and O.M.; writing—original draft preparation, V.V.; writing—review and editing, O.M.; visualization, V.V. and O.M.; supervision, V.V. and O.M.; project administration, V.V. and O.M.; funding acquisition, O.M. All authors have read and agreed to the published version of the manuscript.

Funding: This research received no external funding.

Institutional Review Board Statement: Not applicable.

Informed Consent Statement: Not applicable.

Data Availability Statement: Data are contained within the article.

Conflicts of Interest: The authors declare no conflicts of interest.

References

1. Brown, P.; Chen, H. AI-driven Decision-Making in Resource Management: Opportunities for Sustainable Development. *Int. J. Sustain. Dev.* **2022**, *31*, 210–223.
2. Garcia, L.; Thomas, D. Financial Inclusion and Sustainable Development: The Impact of FinTech on Low-Income Economies. *Dev. Econ. Rev.* **2018**, *17*, 60–75.
3. Garcia, L. Barriers to the Integration of FinTech and AI in Sustainable Finance. *Financ. Sustain. J.* **2019**, *14*, 88–101.
4. Green, E.; Harris, A. Ethical Implications of AI in Financial Services. *J. AI Ethics Financ.* **2020**, *9*, 64–80.
5. Johnson, M.; Lee, T. Artificial Intelligence in Green Finance: Opportunities and Challenges. *Int. J. Artif. Intell.* **2021**, *29*, 123–136.
6. Johnson, F.; Wang, X. Optimizing Resource Management through AI Technologies. *Sustain. Technol.* **2020**, *6*, 55–72.

7. Johnson, M.; O'Connor, C. Synergies Between FinTech and AI in Achieving Sustainable Development Goals. *J. Technol. Sustain.* **2021**, *19*, 76–89.
8. Kumar, R. The Role of AI in Optimizing Sustainable Decision-Making. *J. Sustain. Technol.* **2020**, *6*, 22–34.
9. Lee, H.; Choi, Y. Investing in the Green Economy: The Role of FinTech in Sustainable Financial Systems. *Green Financ. J.* **2017**, *14*, 102–118.
10. Lee, K.; Chang, Y. FinTech and its Impact on Economic Development in Underserved Regions. *Financ. Innov.* **2019**, *6*, 73–92.
11. Vasile, V.; Panait, M.; Apostu, S.-A. Financial Inclusion—Paradigm Shift in the Postpandemic Period. Digital-Divide and Gender Gap. *Int. J. Environ. Res. Public Health* **2021**, *18*, 10938. [CrossRef] [PubMed]
12. Zhao, X.; Wang, L. FinTech for Green Development: A New Frontier. *Environ. Financ. Rev.* **2020**, *8*, 78–89.
13. Schmidt, R.; Miller, J. AI for Sustainability: Leveraging Technology for Sustainable Development Goals. *AI Soc.* **2019**, *21*, 213–225.
14. Manta, O. Current Global Challenges in the Context of the Development of Local Communities (31 May 2019). Available online: https://ssrn.com/abstract=3397295 (accessed on 28 December 2024). [CrossRef]
15. Patel, K. Exploring the Synergy Between FinTech and AI in Sustainable Development. *J. Technol. Sustain.* **2020**, *9*, 100–115.
16. Manta, O.; Palazzo, M. Transforming Financial Systems: The Role of Time Banking in Promoting Community Collaboration and Equitable Wealth Distribution. *FinTech* **2024**, *3*, 407–423. [CrossRef]
17. Manta, O.; Yue, X.G. Sustainable financing in the digital era: Evaluation and models through Innovative Financial Instruments. Available online: https://ince.ro/ESPERA/espera.html (accessed on 28 December 2024).
18. Patel, K. Exploring the Role of Technology in Achieving SDGs: Unidirectional or Bilateral Relationship? *J. Technol. Sustain.* **2020**, *9*, 11–25.
19. Patel, D. FinTech and the United Nations' Sustainable Development Goals (SDGs). *Glob. Financ. J.* **2018**, *25*, 112–130.
20. Roberts, M.; Smith, P. Artificial Intelligence in Environmental Sustainability. *J. Artif. Intell. Environ.* **2021**, *8*, 45–60.
21. Panait, M.; Apostu, S.A.; Panait, M.; Vasile, V.; Sharma, G.D.; Vasile, R. FinTechs and financial inclusion—Balkan experience: Digital perspectives on financial markets. *Electron. J. Inf. Syst. Dev. Ctries.* **2023**, *89*, e12257.
22. Smith, J. FinTech and its Role in Sustainable Development. *J. Financ. Technol.* **2019**, *12*, 45–56.
23. Smith, J.; Brown, L. The Role of FinTech in Promoting Financial Inclusion. *J. Financ. Technol.* **2020**, *12*, 45–61.
24. Thompson, G.; Green, B. Technological Synergies: How FinTech and AI Work Together for Sustainability. *J. Sustain. Innov.* **2021**, *12*, 54–66.
25. Zehir, C.; Ertosun, Ö.G.; Zehir, S.; Müceldilli, B.; TQM International, Group. Implementing Total Quality Management for Sustainable Business Practices. *J. Proced. Soc. Behav. Sci.* **2012**, *41*, 273–280.
26. Zhang, Z.; Liang, F. Integrated Approaches to Sustainable Finance: The Role of FinTech and AI. *Sustain. Dev. Technol.* **2020**, *8*, 53–69.
27. Thompson, A.; Clarke, R. AI in Financial Risk Assessment for Green Investments. *Financ. Sustain. AI* **2021**, *7*, 89–102.
28. Wang, C.; Pan, R.; Wan, X.; Tan, Y.; Xu, L.; McIntyre, R.S.; Choo, F.N.; Tran, B.; Ho, R.; Sharma, V.K.; et al. A longitudinal study on the mental health of general population during the COVID-19 epidemic in China. *Brain Behav. Immun.* **2020**, *87*, 40–48. [CrossRef]
29. The Global Findex Database: Financial Inclusion, Digital Payments, and Resilience in the Age of COVID-19. Available online: https://www.worldbank.org/en/publication/globalfindex (accessed on 28 December 2024).
30. Anginer, D.; Demirgüç-Kunt, A. Bank Runs and Moral Hazard: A Review of Deposit Insurance. World Bank Policy Research Working Paper No. 8589. Available online: https://ssrn.com/abstract=3252233 (accessed on 20 December 2024).
31. Allen, F.; Demirguc-Kunt, A.; Klapper, L.; Peria, M.S.M. The foundations of financial inclusion: Understanding ownership and use of formal accounts. *J. Financ. Intermed.* **2016**, *27*, 1–30. [CrossRef]
32. Zohar, A.H.; Shimone, L.P.; Hen, M. Active and passive procrastination in terms of temperament and character. *PeerJ* **2019**, *7*, e6988. [CrossRef]
33. Zins, A.; Weill, L. The determinants of financial inclusion in Africa. *Rev. Dev. Finance* **2016**, *6*, 46–57. [CrossRef]
34. Manta, O. Financial Technology and Innovation for Sustainable Development. *FinTech* **2024**, *3*, 424–426. [CrossRef]

FinTech

MDPI

Article

Blockchain for Quality: Advancing Security, Efficiency, and Transparency in Financial Systems

Tomaž Kukman [1,2,*] and Sergej Gričar [3,4]

1 Faculty of Economics, University of Ljubljana, Kardeljeva ploščad 17, 1000 Ljubljana, Slovenia
2 Faculty of Economics and Informatics, University of Novo Mesto, Na Loko 2, 8000 Novo Mesto, Slovenia
3 Faculty of Business and Management Sciences, University of Novo Mesto, Na Loko 2, 8000 Novo Mesto, Slovenia; sergej.gricar@uni-nm.si
4 Faculty of Tourism and Hospitality Management, University of Rijeka, Primorska 46, p.p. 97, 51410 Opatija, Croatia
* Correspondence: kukman.tomaz@gmail.com

Abstract: This article delves into the transformative impact of blockchain technology on enhancing transaction quality and efficiency. Since the emergence of blockchain alongside Bitcoin in 2008, its decentralised and transparent nature has significantly improved transaction speed, security, and cost efficiency. These advancements have solidified blockchain as a foundational innovation in financial services. The paper examines critical milestones in blockchain, including Bitcoin, Ethereum, and Binance Coin (BNB), and their role in reshaping global finance by automating processes and reducing reliance on intermediaries. Additionally, the study evaluates blockchain's impact on quality management, particularly emphasising how its immutable ledger system enhances the reliability and transparency of financial transactions. Despite challenges such as scalability, energy consumption, and regulatory hurdles, the potential for blockchain to redefine transaction quality in financial services is evident. This research contributes to the growing body of literature by integrating blockchain technology and traditional quality management systems, providing a comprehensive perspective on how the two domains influence one another. The findings underscore blockchain's ability to drive innovation in financial services while addressing security, efficiency, and operational quality concerns.

Keywords: blockchain; cryptocurrency; decentralisation; security; transaction; quality

JEL Classification: B26; D86; G10; G20; L15

1. Introduction

In recent years, blockchain technology has emerged as a disruptive force, significantly reshaping various industries, particularly the financial technology (FinTech) sector. Initially introduced in 1991 by a group of researchers, blockchain remained relatively obscure until 2008, when the launch of Bitcoin brought this innovative technology into the spotlight. Since then, blockchain's applications have expanded far beyond cryptocurrencies, with its decentralised and transparent ledger system finding utility in sectors as diverse as supply chain management, healthcare, and financial services. Central to blockchain's appeal is its ability to address inefficiencies in traditional systems by leveraging transparency, security, and efficiency. These features enhance transaction quality, reduce costs, enable near-instantaneous cross-border payments, and provide robust solutions for challenges like fraud and data manipulation.

 https://doi.org/10.3390/fintech4010007

Traditionally dominated by centralised entities like banks and payment processors, the financial sector increasingly acknowledges blockchain technology's transformative potential. While cryptocurrencies, particularly Bitcoin, are the most well-known applications of blockchain technology, the underlying principles of decentralisation and cryptographic security substantially enhance the overall quality of financial services.

The concept of quality in the financial services sector has evolved significantly. It extends beyond customer satisfaction and operational efficiency to encompass digital transactions' reliability, security, and trustworthiness. Blockchain technology has emerged as a catalyst for innovation in this area, elevating the overall quality of financial operations by leveraging its inherent benefits of transparency, security, and efficiency.

This article aims to comprehensively analyse how blockchain technology enhances transaction quality in FinTech, focusing on the intersection between blockchain and quality.

This study delineates its dual focuses to enhance clarity and minimise redundancy. The first focus centres on the technological impacts of blockchain on transactional quality, explicitly exploring how decentralisation, cryptographic security, and automation enhance efficiency, security, and transparency in financial services. This is illustrated through smart contracts and decentralised networks, which reduce reliance on intermediaries and decrease the likelihood of errors. The second focus expands the scope to consider systemic and strategic implications, including blockchain's role in mitigating systemic risks, ensuring compliance with regulatory frameworks, and redefining quality management standards within the financial sector. These two focuses contribute uniquely to the study by providing a micro-level analysis of blockchain's technical advancements and a macro-level exploration of its potential to transform financial ecosystems. Together, they offer a comprehensive view of blockchain's transformative role in FinTech.

A quality management system (QMS) is a structured framework of processes, policies, and procedures designed to ensure that an organisation consistently meets customer requirements while enhancing overall operational performance. Within a QMS, quality transcends mere product inspection or defect control; it represents an organisational commitment to operational excellence, efficiency, and customer satisfaction. One of the most widely recognised standards for QMS is the International Organization for Standardization (ISO) 9001, a set of guidelines established by the ISO. ISO 9001 delineates the principles of quality management, which include customer focus, leadership, engagement of people, process approach, and continual improvement. In a competitive business landscape, maintaining a well-defined QMS is crucial for ensuring consistency, reducing waste, and bolstering customer trust. The role of a QMS in financial services—such as those examined in this study—has expanded beyond traditional quality management principles. It now encompasses transparency, security, and reliability in digital transactions. As FinTech advances, there is an increasing demand for quality systems that enhance customer experience while addressing critical issues such as data integrity, fraud prevention, and regulatory compliance. Integrating QMS principles into FinTech operations guarantees that financial transactions are efficient, secure, and subject to continuous improvement and stringent quality standards.

The main objective of this article, along with research questions, is to investigate the relationship between blockchain technology and quality management in the services sector. Specifically, how does blockchain technology improve the quality of financial transactions, particularly regarding transparency, security, and efficiency? What are the primary mechanisms through which blockchain enhances the quality of transactions in FinTech, and how do they compare to traditional systems? In what ways do prominent cryptocurrencies such as Bitcoin, Ethereum, and Binance Coin (BNB) exemplify blockchain's impact on improving the quality of financial services? What are the remaining challenges and limitations in fully harnessing blockchain technology to optimise quality in economic systems?

The article is structured to understand blockchain's impact on transaction quality and efficiency thoroughly. The introduction outlines the article's motivation, aims, objectives, and structure. It introduces the reader to the core themes of blockchain technology, quality management, and their intersection in FinTech. The introduction also presents the key questions the article seeks to answer. The literature review provides an overview of existing research on blockchain technology and quality management in the financial services sector. It draws from academic studies, industry reports, and case studies to establish the current understanding of how blockchain has been implemented in FinTech. The review also highlights gaps in the literature, particularly about the role of blockchain in enhancing transaction and quality. The methodology and data section explains the research methodology used in the article. It describes the data sources, which include secondary data. Secondary data come from existing reports, articles, and empirical studies. This section also explains the data analysis methods, including comparative analysis. The results section presents the findings from the analysis of blockchain technology and its impact on transactions and quality. It includes data on the performance of blockchain-based financial systems compared to traditional systems.

Specific attention is given to the role of Bitcoin, Ethereum, and Binance Coin and projects that are made on blockchain technology as case studies that illustrate the strengths and limitations of blockchain in FinTech. The discussion and conclusion sections provide a detailed discussion of the results of the research questions and the broader literature on blockchain and quality management. It highlights key trends, opportunities, and challenges in implementing blockchain technology to enhance transactional quality. The discussion also considers the regulatory and operational barriers to fully realising blockchain's potential. It summarises the article's key findings and offers recommendations for future research. It reiterates the importance of blockchain as a tool for improving the quality of financial services and provides insights into the future trajectory of blockchain technology in FinTech. The conclusion also addresses the current study's limitations and suggests areas for further investigation.

2. Literature Review

Blockchain's decentralised and transparent nature offers numerous advantages for enhancing the quality of financial transactions [1]. Transaction processing can be slow, expensive, and vulnerable to errors or fraud in traditional monetary systems. Blockchain addresses these issues by providing a secure, immutable ledger that records all transactions distributedly. Each transaction is verified by a network of nodes, ensuring that no single point of failure can compromise the system's integrity. This decentralised approach improves security and reduces the need for intermediaries, lowering transaction costs and increasing efficiency [2].

Furthermore, blockchain's transparency improves transactional quality [3,4]. In traditional financial systems, transaction details are typically opaque, with only the involved parties and intermediaries accessing the data. In contrast, blockchain technology makes transaction records publicly available, albeit anonymised, ensuring greater accountability and reducing the risk of fraud. This transparency is precious in cross-border payments, where high fees, long delays, and a lack of visibility into the transaction process have plagued traditional systems [5].

Bitcoin, Ethereum, and Binance Coin (BNB) and projects based on blockchain, such as healthcare, gaming and digital collectibles, energy and sustainability, real estate, government and voting, charity, and crowdfunding, provide practical examples of how blockchain technology improves transaction quality in real-world applications [6]. The first cryptocurrency, Bitcoin, demonstrated how blockchain could facilitate peer-to-peer payments without a central authority. Its success paved the way for developing other cryptocurrencies, each offering unique features to enhance transactional quality. Ethereum, for example, introduced intelligent contracts, which automate transactions based on predefined conditions, reducing the likelihood of errors and improving efficiency. Binance Coin, meanwhile, has become integral to the Binance Exchange ecosystem, offering lower fees and faster transaction processing for users [7]. These cryptocurrencies highlight blockchain's potential to improve the quality of individual transactions and transform entire financial ecosystems. However, challenges remain, particularly regarding scalability, energy consumption, and regulatory acceptance. Despite these obstacles, blockchain and cryptocurrencies are positioned to play an increasingly important role in shaping the future of (financial) services [8].

In recent decades, the rapid evolution of blockchain technology and cryptocurrencies has brought profound changes to numerous industries, particularly in financial services. Blockchain, developed initially, remained largely unnoticed until Bitcoin emerged in 2008, when it became a cornerstone of decentralised digital currencies [9]. Since then, blockchain has transcended its initial use case in cryptocurrencies, impacting various sectors like supply chain management, healthcare, and beyond, focusing on improving transactional quality and security [10,11].

Blockchain's rise in popularity is closely associated with the decentralisation and transparency it offers to financial transactions. Unlike traditional centralised financial systems, where intermediaries such as banks are involved, blockchain eliminates the need for these intermediaries by creating a decentralised ledger where all participants can validate and record transactions. This approach speeds up transactions, reduces costs, and increases security [6]. Blockchain's ledger is immutable, meaning that once a transaction is recorded, it cannot be altered, which is crucial for maintaining data integrity and security [12].

One of blockchain technology's primary advantages in enhancing transactional quality is its cryptographic features. Transactions are validated through consensus mechanisms like Proof of Work (PoW) and Proof of Stake (PoS), ensuring that only legitimate transactions are recorded in the ledger [13,14]. This verification process dramatically reduces the possibility of fraud, a significant issue in traditional banking systems. Furthermore, blockchain's transparency ensures that all transactions are visible to network participants, improving accountability and reducing the risk of manipulation [15].

The literature also highlights that blockchain's security improvements directly contribute to better financial operational quality [1]. Blockchain's use of cryptography makes it difficult for attackers to alter transaction data, as any change would require re-computing every block following the modified block, which is a computationally prohibitive task [16]. As a result, blockchain has become an ideal technology for securing sensitive financial information, especially in areas where trust and data integrity are paramount [17].

Bitcoin, Ethereum, and Binance Coin (BNB) are among the most well-known examples of blockchain's application in cryptocurrencies. They all work on the same principle. All transactions are conducted through blockchain technology and are decentralised. Each transaction is stored in a block created by the blockchain and cannot be altered. Bitcoin, the first decentralised cryptocurrency, revolutionised peer-to-peer (P2P) financial transactions by allowing individuals to transfer value without a central authority [18]. Ethereum expanded on Bitcoin's foundation by introducing smart contracts, which automate transactions based on predefined rules. This advancement enabled a broader range of decentralised applications, further enhancing the efficiency and reliability of blockchain-based financial operations [19].

On the other hand, Binance Coin (BNB) serves as a utility token within the Binance ecosystem. It allows users to access lower transaction fees and faster Binance exchange processing times, demonstrating how blockchain can improve financial service quality [20]. In addition, cryptocurrencies like BNB offer users privacy, as transactions can be conducted without revealing personal details, which is increasingly important in a world where data privacy concerns are growing [21].

Hyperledger, an open-source blockchain framework under the Linux Foundation, has emerged as a pivotal player in the enterprise blockchain arena, particularly within the financial services sector. In contrast to public blockchains like Bitcoin or Ethereum, Hyperledger emphasises permissioned blockchains, providing a controlled environment that meets the financial industry's rigorous privacy, security, and regulatory requirements. A key example is Hyperledger Fabric, which powers platforms such as we.trade, utilised by several major European banks to facilitate secure cross-border trade finance transactions. Additionally, Hyperledger Indy offers decentralised identity solutions, addressing the critical need for secure digital identity verification in compliance with Know Your Customer (KYC) and anti-money laundering (AML) regulations. These implementations underscore the benefits of employing Hyperledger in financial services, including enhanced privacy controls, reduced transaction costs, and improved adherence to financial regulations. Financial institutions can ensure compliance by adopting permissioned blockchain solutions while capitalising on blockchain technology's efficiency and transparency [22–24].

Despite these advancements, cryptocurrencies' volatility poses a significant challenge to their broader adoption. While blockchain provides technical stability and security, cryptocurrencies' market value remains highly unpredictable. This volatility can hinder their ability to serve as a reliable medium of exchange, which is a fundamental criterion for transactional quality [25,26].

Together, they have a potential role to play in implementing the quality management system.

They include compliance with requirements and standards, and their combination enables automated recording of compliance with different standards (ISO 9001), thus reducing human error and improving efficiency.

Supply chain traceability, as Indy and Fabric focus on data security and reliability, it is possible to claim that all data within the QMS will remain untampered and verifiable. Automatic audits, as Fabric stores all transactions and activities in the system, allows easy automatic audits, while Indy allows proper data verification. Decentralised identity for employees and suppliers, as secure attendance verification between internal and external QMS processes is enabled.

Indeed, their combination allows the integration of traceability, security, and decentralised identities for quality management. This allows for greater transparency, better compliance with industry standards, and increased confidence in data that can significantly improve the efficiency and performance of the QMS itself.

Blockchain and Quality Management Systems

In the highly regulated and dynamic financial services landscape, establishing a robust QMS is imperative for organisations to adhere to operational standards and consistently deliver superior service quality. Financial services, characterised by their reliance on precision, regulatory compliance, and the cultivation of customer trust, necessitate an integrated approach to quality management that effectively mitigates risks and enhances service reliability. Unlike traditional product-driven industries where quality management predominantly emphasises manufacturing processes, the financial sector demands a more nuanced strategy that amalgamates operational excellence with risk management and compliance obligations [27,28].

A well-executed QMS in financial services encompasses standardising critical processes, thereby minimising errors and inefficiencies, particularly in high-stakes transactions. This systematic approach ensures that each phase of service delivery—from customer onboarding to transaction processing—is monitored, controlled, and subjected to continuous improvement initiatives [29,30]. A pivotal function of a QMS within this sector lies in its capacity to enhance risk management by identifying potential vulnerabilities, streamlining operations, and ensuring rigorous documentation and enforcement of compliance with pertinent regulations, such as AML and KYC mandates. Financial institutions face the formidable challenge of managing extensive data volumes, ranging from sensitive customer information to comprehensive transaction histories. A QMS provides the necessary framework to guarantee that such data are handled securely, efficiently, and legally compliant. By instituting clear protocols for data governance, a QMS mitigates the risks associated with fraud, data breaches, and operational inefficiencies—factors profoundly critical for the maintenance of customer trust and alignment with regulatory requirements [31–33].

Furthermore, as financial services transform with the adoption of advanced technologies, contemporary QMS frameworks increasingly incorporate digital instruments such as artificial intelligence (AI) and data analytics. These technological advancements facilitate predictive maintenance, real-time transaction monitoring, and sophisticated analytics that preemptively identify quality issues before they impact broader operational systems. This evolution toward technology-driven quality management systems empowers organisations to satisfy and surpass industry standards, fostering a culture of continuous improvement and proactive risk management [3,34].

The literature review underscores the transformative potential of blockchain technology, extending beyond mere transaction processing to encompass broader applications such as compliance, supply chain transparency, and asset tokenisation. For example, blockchain-based Know Your Customer (KYC) [23] solutions, implemented by major financial institutions, enhance identity verification by securely storing and sharing customer data across networks. Similarly, blockchain-enabled supply chain systems utilised by companies like IBM and Walmart facilitate real-time tracking of goods, ensuring authenticity and accountability [35]. In asset management, tokenising real-world assets—such as bonds and real estate—on platforms like Ethereum has fostered increased accessibility, liquidity, and transparency [36].

3. Materials and Methods

This section presents the research approach, data sources, and methods to explore how blockchain technology enhances transaction quality within the FinTech sector. The methodology has been refined to provide a clear account of the datasets, tools, and processes utilised in the quantitative analysis. Secondary data were sourced from reputable cryptocurrency exchanges like Binance and Coinbase. The literature review acted as a foundational step in identifying gaps in existing research, ultimately shaping the quantitative analysis. Recurring themes from the literature, such as blockchain's transparency and scalability challenges, directly influenced the selection of data points for analysis. The results were integrated into a comparative framework that contrasted blockchain-based systems with traditional financial networks.

Given the topic's multifaceted nature, the research relies on quantitative methods, utilising secondary data. The methodology is designed to provide a comprehensive understanding of blockchain's impact on transactional quality, focusing on cryptocurrencies such as Bitcoin, Ethereum, and Binance Coin (BNB) as case studies.

Secondary data were collected from academic articles, industry reports, and case studies. The literature review focused on studies that examine blockchain's role in FinTech, with particular attention to how it improves transaction quality. This included peer-reviewed articles on blockchain's technical foundations, particularly concerning transaction speed, security, and cost efficiency—industry reports on adopting blockchain technology in financial services provided data on transaction performance metrics. Case studies on Bitcoin, Ethereum, and Binance Coin (BNB) illustrate how these cryptocurrencies demonstrate blockchain's potential to enhance quality. Additionally, empirical data from cryptocurrency exchanges, including transaction volumes, fees, and processing times, were analysed to compare blockchain-based systems with traditional financial transaction networks. This quantitative data allowed for comparing transaction costs, processing speeds, and security metrics between blockchain and non-blockchain systems.

The research employs a quantitative analysis approach to provide a well-rounded understanding of how blockchain enhances transaction quality. The methodology is divided into three stages: a literature review, a quantitative analysis of transaction data, and a synthesis of the comparative analysis.

The first stage of the research involved a comprehensive literature review, which served as the foundation for the study. This review focused on the academic and industry literature on blockchain technology, cryptocurrency, and transaction quality in financial services. The literature review was essential in identifying gaps in the current research, particularly the need for a focused investigation into blockchain's role in improving transactions and quality. It also helped shape the research questions and provided a theoretical framework for analysing the primary and secondary data. The second step involves a thorough analysis of the evolution of blockchain technology, cryptocurrencies, and smart contracts, focusing on the fluctuations in their market values. The final stage of the research involves a comparative analysis of traditional quality management and blockchain. Figure 1 represents the blockchain technology and how it works.

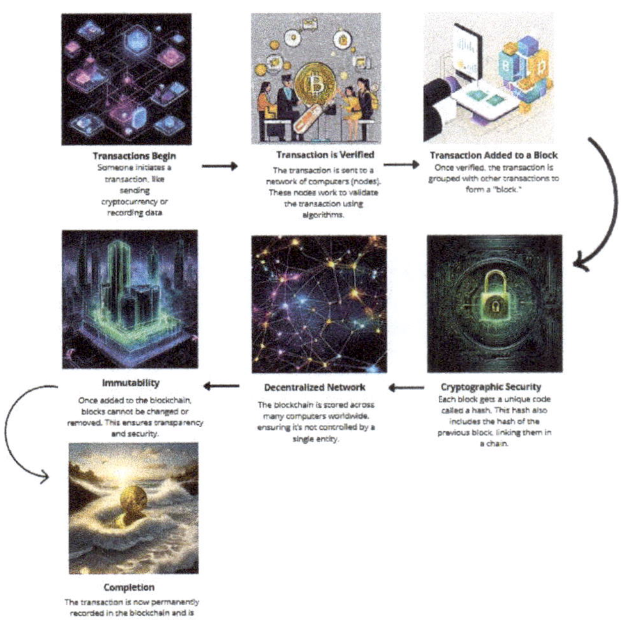

Figure 1. The methodology process—source: authors' compilation with Canva.

4. Results

4.1. Security and Data Integrity: Technological Perspective

Blockchain technology's decentralised and immutable characteristics present substantial advancements in security, which is crucial for financial services. Traditional centralised systems are prone to single points of failure and potential manipulation. In contrast, blockchain guarantees that transaction data, once recorded, cannot be altered without consensus from multiple nodes. This decentralised verification process, particularly evident in platforms like Bitcoin and Ethereum, has significantly mitigated the risk of unauthorised changes, establishing a new benchmark for data integrity.

Quantitative data from the Bitcoin and Ethereum networks reinforce these observations, demonstrating that instances of fraud are markedly lower than in traditional banking systems. This attribute is especially advantageous in financial services, where reliability and data integrity are essential. From a business perspective, this heightened level of security fosters increased customer trust, particularly in sectors where transparency and traceability are critical, such as cross-border payments and asset management. According to Chainalysis, cryptocurrency fraud has caused approximately USD 5.6 billion in global losses [37]. The most common scams in cryptocurrencies have been rug pulls, which means that when a person makes a coin, people can invest in it, and then he closes it and takes all the money invested and disappears, as well as fake investment schemes. In most cases, all the scams have been purely due to recklessness and reckless investing in coins with no projects behind them.

According to the Association of Certified Fraud Examiners (ACFEs), global losses due to financial fraud, counterfeit cheques, and identity theft are expected to exceed USD 100 billion in 2023. Fraud via blockchain is approximately USD 4 billion annually, representing 0.15%, while traditional banking is approximately USD 125 billion annually, representing 0.8%. This suggests that fraud in blockchain systems is approximately 80% lower when adjusted for transaction volume.

Nonetheless, from a regulatory viewpoint, despite blockchain's impressive security features, challenges arise regarding oversight. The decentralised nature of blockchain complicates the enforcement of compliance standards, such as AML and KYC regulations, which are vital in the financial services sector. Table 1 highlights the parallel development of blockchain and quality management systems, demonstrating how both fields have evolved and intersected over the decades. Key milestones, such as the introduction of total quality management (TQM) in 1960 and the conceptualisation of blockchain in 1991, illustrate how technology and quality practices have shaped modern financial services.

Table 1. Comparative Timeline of Blockchain and Quality Management Milestones.

Year	Milestone Blockchain	Milestone Quality
1960		TQM was introduced to focus on continuous quality improvement across organisations.
1980		Six Sigma methodology was developed to reduce defects, and the CQI was established to promote quality improvement.
1987	Technological Development	ISO 9000 standards [38] were introduced, emphasising the importance of QMS.
1991	Blockchain Conceptualised.	Internet Common Usage emerges, impacting communication and operational quality.

Table 1. *Cont.*

Year	Milestone Blockchain	Milestone Quality
2000	Focus On Technology Development.	E-Social Networking impacts customer service quality with the rise of online interactions.
2008	Bitcoin Introduced.	Technology drives QMS into digital transformation.
2010	First Cryptocurrency Transaction.	Lean management gains prominence as a method of improving organisational quality by reducing waste.
2015	Ethereum Platform Launched.	The First Smart Contracts introduced on Ethereum contribute to automation and quality consistency.
2017	Binance Launched (one of the world's largest and most popular cryptocurrency exchanges).	The concept of quality 4.0 emerges, integrating digital tools (like AI and IoT) into quality management.
2019	FTX Founded.	Agile quality management methodologies have started gaining traction to improve quality processes.
2022	FTX's Collapse.	Quality challenges in decentralised systems become apparent, highlighting governance failures.
2023	Development of AI.	AI implementation in Quality management for its predictive maintenance.
2024	Resumption of Growth, Halving, More Development On Cryptocurrency Projects.	Quality improvements through blockchain and AI integration into quality control processes.

Note: IoT—Internet of Things. Source: Authors' Compilations.

4.2. Transparency and Accountability: Business and Regulatory Perspectives

One of the most transformative aspects of blockchain technology is its inherent transparency. Unlike traditional financial systems that often depend on opaque centralised databases, blockchain offers a real-time, tamper-proof record of every transaction. This feature is especially advantageous for auditing, as the data are verifiable and cannot be manipulated retroactively. Industries such as supply chain finance have adopted blockchain due to its ability to enhance transparency and operational efficiency by effectively tracking assets and transactions across multiple parties.

From a business perspective, this transparency reduces the cost and complexity associated with audits and fosters trust among parties, particularly in sectors where multiple entities are involved in transactions. However, regulators encounter challenges related to the open nature of blockchain, as finding the right balance between transparency and privacy remains a contentious issue, especially in jurisdictions with stringent data protection laws. In the European Union, the biggest problem arises from Article 17 of GDPR—the right of erasure. Because you cannot tamper with the data in the blockchain, it also makes it hard to delete specific data within it. The authors are erasing data from blockchain nodes. In 2019, the IEEE European Symposium on Security and Privacy Workshops described a "Erasure database" solution. This method allows any network participant the ability to mark data for deletion or replacement. The new transaction data are stored in the erasure database, allowing the previous local content to be deleted. However, this creates an issue where new transactions in the blockchain reference the deleted content. To address this, the authors implement a rule stating that transactions do not require re-verification. The old transactions, which rely on the deleted content, remain valid, while the new transactions, created after the deletion of the referenced old content, are deemed invalid. Many other methods are also being tested and implemented by various companies, so there is still no one main method used inside the EU.

So, Table 2 highlights key differences between traditional quality management and blockchain technology across six critical features, showcasing blockchain's advantages in modern quality management. In terms of centralisation, traditional quality management relies on centralised control, often making it vulnerable to single points of failure. In contrast, blockchain's decentralised structure distributes control across a network, reducing such vulnerabilities. Data integrity also benefits from blockchain's constant and safe data recording, whereas traditional methods are more susceptible to human error. Transparency is limited in conventional systems, where visibility is often restricted to specific personnel. Blockchain provides complete transparency, allowing all participants to review and verify records. Efficiency is enhanced by blockchain's automated processes, surpassing the manual methods often used in traditional quality management. Safety and security are strengthened in blockchain, which uses cryptographic verification, making it less prone to fraud than conventional systems. Finally, automation in blockchain enables end-to-end process automation, whereas traditional systems offer limited automation capabilities. Table 2 could serve as a highlighted answer to the research questions.

Table 2. Comparison of Features: Traditional Quality Management vs. Blockchain Technology.

Feature	Traditional Quality Management	Blockchain Technology
Centralisation	Centralised	Decentralised
Data Integrity	Propensity to human error	Constant and safe
Transparency	Limited visibility	Transparency and reviewability
Efficiency	Manual processes	Automated and efficient
Safety and Security	Fraud Vulnerable	High level of security and security
Automation	Limited automation	Full process automation
Cost	High due to inefficiencies and intermediaries	Implementation costs are high, but long-term
Collaboration	Limited by organisational boundaries and silos.	Seamless, global collaboration via shared ledgers.
Compliance & Audits	Manual and time-intensive processes.	Automated checks and simplified auditing with smart contracts.
Traceability	Time-consuming and reliant on paper trails.	End-to-end traceability with permanent records.

4.3. Cost Efficiency and Speed: Technological and Business Perspectives

Blockchain technology's capacity to eliminate intermediaries in financial transactions has led to considerable cost savings. Traditional financial systems heavily rely on intermediaries such as banks and payment processors, which introduce fees for each transaction. Blockchain significantly reduces these costs by facilitating peer-to-peer transactions, making it especially beneficial for worldwide payments.

From a technological standpoint, Layer 2 solutions like the Lightning Network for Bitcoin further enhance cost efficiency by alleviating congestion on the main blockchain. These technologies enable quicker and more affordable off-chain transactions, helping blockchain-based systems maintain their competitive edge. Quantitative data indicate that Bitcoin's average transaction fees are generally lower than those associated with traditional systems like Society for Worldwide Interbank Financial Telecommunication (SWIFT) or Single Euro Payments Area (SEPA). Additionally, Ethereum's transition to Proof of Stake (PoS) is anticipated to tackle scalability and cost issues.

However, businesses must also consider the variability of transaction fees on networks like Ethereum, where costs can spike during periods of high demand. While Layer 2 scaling solutions aim to address this concern, the current fee fluctuations challenge blockchain's overall cost efficiency, particularly for smaller transactions. The timeline (Figure 2) provides a visual overview of the significant milestones in the development of blockchain technology, from its conceptualisation in 1991 to the anticipated advancements in 2024. These milestones mark substantial technological shifts, such as the introduction of Bitcoin in 2008 and Ethereum's implementation of smart contracts in 2015. These are pivotal to understanding blockchain's evolution in financial services and subsequent savings.

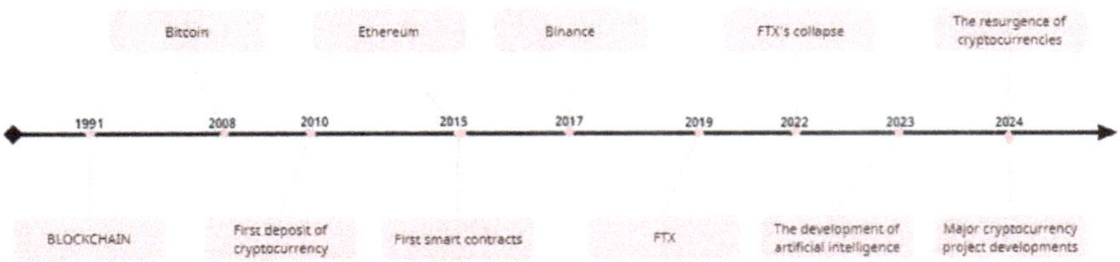

Figure 2. Timeline of blockchain development from 1991 to 2024. Source: Authors' compilation from various sources [39].

4.4. *Scalability: Technological Challenges and Future Solutions*

Scalability continues to pose a significant challenge for blockchain, especially in high-volume applications such as retail payments. While Bitcoin and Ethereum are highly secure and efficient for low-frequency, high-value transactions, their capacity to handle large transaction volumes—like those required for point-of-sale payments—remains constrained. During peak usage periods, this often leads to network congestion, increasing fees and slower transaction times. Technological advancements have emerged to tackle these issues, including sharding, Layer 2 solutions, and off-chain transactions. Sharding, for example, segments the blockchain into smaller parts that can process transactions in parallel, thereby enhancing throughput. Furthermore, Ethereum's transition to Proof of Stake (PoS) aims to improve the network's ability to handle more transactions per second (TPS), boosting overall efficiency. Despite these advancements, the scalability challenge endures, particularly when juxtaposed with traditional systems like Visa, which can process thousands of transactions each second.

From a business standpoint, these scalability limitations restrict blockchain's application in high-frequency, low-value transactions. Nonetheless, ongoing innovations indicate blockchain's potential in these areas will likely expand as technology evolves.

4.5. *Case Study Applications: Bitcoin, Ethereum, and Binance Coin (BNB) and Projects Based on Blockchain*

Bitcoin, recognised as the first widely adopted cryptocurrency, highlights the strengths of blockchain technology in enhancing security and trust. Its PoW consensus mechanism ensures that transactions are validated and secure, although scalability challenges persist. In contrast, Ethereum builds on Bitcoin's foundation by introducing smart contracts, which automate transactions based on predefined conditions. This innovation significantly improves transaction efficiency and decreases the likelihood of human error, making Ethereum particularly valuable in decentralised finance (DeFi). Bitcoin is the first and most widely recognised application of blockchain technology. 2008 Bitcoin revolutionised the financial landscape by enabling peer-to-peer transactions without a central authority. The PoW consensus mechanism employed by Bitcoin ensures that all transactions are validated and securely recorded on the blockchain. As shown in Figure 2, the introduction of Bitcoin marked a significant milestone in the timeline of blockchain development, laying the foundation for future innovations in cryptocurrencies and decentralised systems. However, Bitcoin's transparency, security, and real-time transaction verification are tempered by its scalability limitations, which remain challenging to adopt as a global payment system.

Binance Coin (BNB), utilised within the Binance ecosystem, exemplifies blockchain's potential to streamline transactions on a specific platform. BNB provides reduced transaction costs and faster processing times, especially when leveraged on Binance Smart Chain (BSC), which can process thousands of transactions per second at minimal costs. However, BNB's utility is primarily confined to the Binance ecosystem, which limits its broader application compared to Bitcoin or Ethereum. This comparative study is a cutting-edge contribution to FinTech, as it explores the integration of QMS and blockchain technologies in a novel and comprehensive manner. The rapid advancement of AI and its increasing integration into blockchain and QMS since 2023 indicate that the future of FinTech will likely involve a convergence of these technologies. As cryptocurrency projects continue to evolve in 2024, this research underscores the significance of developing comprehensive frameworks that leverage the potential of blockchain to enhance the quality of financial transactions and related processes. This new approach can redefine both fields, offering more resilient, secure, and efficient systems for managing quality in the digital era.

Blockchain is also used in many projects, such as healthcare, gaming and digital collectables, energy and sustainability, real estate, government and voting, charity, and crowdfunding.

For healthcare, we could highlight three successful projects. The first project is MediBloc; this allows secure and efficient management and sharing of patient data, and all data remains confidential. It is followed by Patientory, a decentralised application for storing health information; it also provides total privacy. Solve.Care, on the other hand, enables healthcare administration, which improves payment processes and better scheduling of patient appointments.

Gaming and digital collectables: I would like to highlight 3 major successful projects again. The first project or game is Axie Infinity, where players fight virtual creatures and can deposit cryptocurrencies. The second game is CryptoKitties, which is designed for collecting digital cats and where players receive NFTs when they play. The third project is the Decentraland platform, which is also a virtual reality game, where users can sell, buy, or build virtual real estate using blockchain which has seen a vast number of users in 2024 and has grown significantly.

Energy and sustainability: I would highlight two projects. The first is Power Ledger, which allows energy trading between individuals and the tracking of renewable energy certificates on the blockchain. WePower enables energy renewal to facilitate investment and trading in energy.

In real estate, I would highlight two projects. The first is Propy, which simplifies real estate transactions using blockchain, ensuring less fraud and greater transparency. The second project is Qbitquity, which uses blockchain to manage land registries and keep records of transactions for real estate.

Government and voting: This includes two projects: Voatz, a voting system on the blockchain that provides non-replicable votes and ensures security, and the Estonia e-Residency Programme, which manages digital identities and provides secure internet services for all citizens and businesses.

Charity and crowdfunding include the Giveth project, which is a decentralised funding platform that supports charitable projects.

All of these projects demonstrate how diverse and revolutionary blockchain technology is.

Overall, Table 2 offers a foundational response to the research question by comparing traditional quality management with blockchain technology in terms of transparency, security, and efficiency. It emphasises the advantages of blockchain—including decentralisation, high data integrity, automation, and enhanced security—that contribute to superior quality in financial transactions compared to traditional systems, thereby addressing key aspects of quality improvements within FinTech.

5. Discussion

Blockchain technology enhances financial security, efficiency, and transparency through its decentralised architecture and cryptographic validation methods. Unlike traditional centralised systems, blockchain eliminates single points of failure, ensuring data integrity via consensus mechanisms such as PoS or PoW. For instance, Bitcoin and Ethereum securely validate transactions across distributed networks, preventing tampering and unauthorised alterations. Efficiency is further improved by automating processes through smart contracts, which remove intermediaries and streamline operations in applications like cross-border payments. Another defining feature of blockchain is its transparency, as all transactions are recorded on an immutable public ledger, providing real-time visibility and auditable records. This transparency extends beyond financial systems to sectors like supply chain management, where blockchain enhances traceability and accountability. Nevertheless, challenges such as regulatory compliance and scalability persist. Emerging solutions, including Layer 2 scaling and green blockchain initiatives, are being developed to address these limitations, facilitating blockchain integration into broader quality management frameworks.

The answer to RQ: Blockchain technology enhances financial transactions by improving security with decentralised validation, increasing efficiency through automation and removing intermediaries, and ensuring transparency via immutable public ledgers. However, it faces challenges regarding scalability, regulatory compliance, and energy consumption.

5.1. Blockchain and Quality Management: A Comparative Perspective

Blockchain technology has fundamentally reshaped how transactions are secured and managed, particularly within the financial services sector, by introducing innovative advancements in transparency, security, and accountability. Conversely, quality management has historically concentrated on enhancing processes and products systematically to achieve industry standards consistently. This section juxtaposes the roles of blockchain technology and quality management principles in improving operational processes, transparency, and accountability while delving into the broader notion of "quality" concerning sustainable practices, such as bicycling, which enhance operational efficiency and overall quality of life.

Transparency and accountability are essential components of QMS. Traditional QMS frameworks, such as those adhering to ISO 9001 standards, emphasise process documentation, regular audits, and stakeholder engagement to maintain quality standards. In contrast, blockchain's decentralised and immutable ledger presents a groundbreaking alternative, offering unmatched transparency and accountability. Unlike conventional systems, where manual documentation and audits can be susceptible to errors or manipulation, blockchain guarantees that every transaction or process step is recorded and validated across a distributed network. This functionality eliminates the possibility of retroactive data tampering, effectively establishing a new standard for data integrity.

The ability of blockchain to transparently log and validate financial transactions mirrors the role of quality systems in manufacturing and service industries, where meticulous process documentation ensures product consistency and compliance. Furthermore, blockchain's decentralised structure enhances accountability by making each action traceable to its source, removing the need for oversight from a centralised authority. This closely aligns with established quality control mechanisms, which focus on monitoring and assuring the reliability of processes and products [40,41].

Both blockchain technology and traditional quality management systems aim to address inefficiencies, yet they do so through fundamentally different methods. Blockchain eliminates intermediaries, particularly in financial systems, allowing faster and more cost-effective peer-to-peer transactions. For instance, cross-border blockchain payments can be completed in minutes, starkly contrasting with the days conventional banks require. Moreover, these transactions entail significantly lower fees, a significant advantage for developing nations where banking infrastructure can be costly and inefficient.

On the other hand, traditional QMS focuses on reducing inefficiencies by standardising processes, minimising variability, and identifying waste within operational workflows. Frameworks such as Six Sigma and Lean Management assist organisations in systematically streamlining operations and decreasing errors. While blockchain primarily aims to secure and validate transactions, its potential to enhance operational efficiency aligns well with the objectives of traditional QMS. For example, integrating blockchain into supply chain operations can improve data flow efficiency by automating and simplifying processes that typically require redundant verification. By removing unnecessary intermediaries and manual checks, blockchain fosters more streamlined and transparent operational systems, complementing the foundational principles of quality management [42,43].

In various national contexts, countries like the Netherlands and Denmark, recognised for their robust cycling cultures, have effectively harnessed blockchain technology to enhance public service quality and promote environmental sustainability. These nations are exploring blockchain-based systems to monitor and incentivise eco-friendly behaviours, such as cycling, through platforms that issue "sustainability credits" or tokens. Such initiatives improve transparency in tracking carbon offsets and improve urban mobility and quality of life. By integrating blockchain into their sustainability efforts, these countries demonstrate how technology can transcend financial transactions to tackle broader societal objectives, including public health and environmental sustainability [44].

Blockchain's security benefits offer transformative potential when compared to traditional quality systems. Industries such as manufacturing often rely on centralised databases and manual processes susceptible to errors and security breaches. In contrast, blockchain employs a decentralised and encrypted ledger, ensuring tamper-proof data integrity. This is especially crucial in sectors like healthcare and pharmaceuticals, where protecting sensitive information is paramount. By integrating blockchain with quality frameworks, organisations can enable real-time tracking of quality control measures, establishing immutable records that reduce the need for manual audits, enhance compliance, and improve overall accountability [45].

Countries such as Estonia and Switzerland exemplify the broader systemic implications of blockchain technology by employing it for secure digital identities and public records management. Estonia's "e-Residency" program effectively safeguards personal data through blockchain, facilitating efficient and high-quality access to government services. These applications showcase blockchain's potential to enhance transparency, efficiency, and security, all while upholding high standards in public service delivery [46,47].

The comparison between blockchain technology and traditional quality systems highlights considerable potential for integration. The transparency and traceability offered by blockchain closely align with the quality management principles of accountability and compliance. For example, incorporating blockchain into ISO 9001 systems would create immutable records of production processes, thereby enhancing reliability and mitigating non-compliance risks [30]. In healthcare, blockchain could provide a secure platform for managing patient data [48], ensuring regulatory compliance and improving operational efficiency. However, these synergies are accompanied by challenges, such as scalability, regulatory hurdles, and the energy demands of certain blockchain technologies, which require thorough examination. Addressing these complexities is vital for fully realising blockchain's potential to complement and enhance traditional quality systems across various industries.

Blockchain enhances security in QMS through decentralised validation and cryptographic encryption, ensuring that process data remains tamper-proof and accurate. For example, in supply chain management, blockchain can track quality control measures by recording every step of production on an immutable ledger, reducing the risk of data manipulation and fraud. Regarding efficiency, blockchain automates manual processes with smart contracts, such as automating compliance checks in ISO-based frameworks, eliminating redundant paperwork, and accelerating quality audits. Transparency is achieved by providing real-time visibility into processes, as demonstrated in industries like food safety, where blockchain ensures end-to-end traceability of products [49]. These mechanisms collectively align blockchain's capabilities with the principles of operational excellence, offering a transformative approach to improving both process and product quality while addressing traditional inefficiencies in QMS [29,40,50].

5.2. Scientific Contribution and Novelty

This research presents a novel inquiry into the synergy between blockchain technology and QMS within the financial services sector. While blockchain applications, mainly through cryptocurrencies such as Bitcoin and Ethereum, have been extensively documented, their integration with conventional quality management principles requires further exploration. This study facilitates a comparative analysis of the evolution of both blockchain and QMS, as delineated in Table 1, and provides a timeline of blockchain's developmental milestones, illustrated in Figure 2. It introduces new perspectives on the potential interrelationship between these two domains in contemporary financial systems.

The scientific merit of this investigation emerges from its comprehensive juxtaposition of blockchain's technological advancements alongside significant developments in QMS. Table 1 illustrates the alignment of blockchain milestones with the progression of QMS methodologies. While blockchain technology has fundamentally transformed financial transactions by enhancing security, transparency, and efficiency, the parallel advancements in quality management—embodied in frameworks such as TQM and Six Sigma—have refined operational excellence and process consistency across various industries. This comparative analysis is distinctive, as it interconnects two seemingly disparate yet increasingly intertwined fields: the decentralisation and cryptographic security inherent in blockchain and the structured methodologies aimed at quality enhancement and risk mitigation within QMS.

Moreover, Figure 2 presents a historical timeline encapsulating the swift advancements in blockchain technology from its inception in 1991 to its anticipated future trajectories through 2024. This timeline accentuates pivotal innovations brought forth by Bitcoin and Ethereum, particularly regarding mechanisms such as smart contracts and PoS. Concurrently, it delineates the scalability challenges and governance issues that have surfaced within the industry, exemplified by incidents like the collapse of FTX in 2022. This study posits a novel framework for evaluating how blockchain's decentralised ledger technology can fortify the transparency and traceability of quality control processes by aligning these technological advancements with the ongoing enhancements in quality management systems.

Furthermore, this research enriches the existing literature by elucidating the potential of blockchain to bolster regulatory compliance, prevent fraud, and enhance transaction efficiency in financial services—areas pivotal to quality management and blockchain technologies. By integrating these two fields, the study reveals new avenues for future innovation, particularly in sectors where transparency, security, and quality assurance are critical.

In conclusion, this research's originality is encapsulated in its comparative methodology, which proffers a unique lens through which to consider the transformative impact of blockchain technology on traditional quality management systems and operational practices within the financial services industry.

6. Conclusions

In synthesis, blockchain technology's potential to augment the quality of transactions within the financial technology sector is incontrovertible. Blockchain's decentralised nature and transparent ledger address numerous inefficiencies endemic to conventional monetary systems. Despite challenges, including scalability, energy consumption, and regulatory hurdles, ongoing advancements in blockchain technology are anticipated to ameliorate these issues, facilitating broader adoption and enhancing the quality of financial services.

Furthermore, blockchain technology and traditional QMS converge on the shared augmenting operational efficiency, transparency, and accountability. Blockchain technology excels in bolstering data security and diminishing costs via decentralisation, whereas traditional quality systems provide a structured methodology for process enhancement and error minimisation. Integrating these systems holds considerable potential, especially in critical product quality and data integrity sectors. As blockchain technology continues to evolve, its integration with quality management principles is expected to proliferate, offering novel avenues to improve operational efficiency and product quality. Moreover, national initiatives, such as the implementation of blockchain in public services by Estonia and the integration of blockchain into sustainability efforts by the Netherlands, exemplify how blockchain and quality management can collaboratively enhance the quality of life at both individual and societal levels.

However, this study acknowledges certain limitations. The mixed-methods approach, while providing a holistic view of the impact of blockchain on transaction quality, is constrained by the limited number of literature reviews, potentially not capturing the full spectrum of experiences with blockchain technology across diverse sectors. Additionally, despite offering insightful observations, the case studies of Bitcoin, Ethereum, and Binance Coin may not encompass the entire range of blockchain applications in FinTech. The rapidly evolving landscape of blockchain technology further implies that some findings might soon become obsolete as new developments and regulations emerge.

Notwithstanding these challenges, blockchain technology offers substantial enhancements to transactional quality. Among the most critical challenges is scalability; the decentralised architecture of blockchain necessitates verification of every transaction by a network of nodes, potentially decelerating processing times as the network expands. For instance, the average transaction time for Bitcoin stands at approximately 10 min, significantly lagging behind traditional payment systems like Visa, which boasts the capacity to process thousands of transactions per second. Solutions to address scalability, such as the Lightning Network for Bitcoin, are under development but remain in the nascent stages of deployment.

Another significant concern is the energy consumption of PoW-based blockchain networks, such as Bitcoin, which demand substantial computational power to solve cryptographic puzzles and validate transactions. This has sparked debates regarding the environmental footprint of blockchain technology. Some networks, like Ethereum, are transitioning to PoS consensus mechanisms, which are markedly less energy-intensive, yet the widespread adoption of these solutions is still unfolding. Regulatory challenges also constitute a significant impediment to fully realising blockchain's potential. The association of cryptocurrencies with illicit activities and market volatility has led to apprehension among governments and financial institutions. Consequently, regulatory frameworks to oversee blockchain and cryptocurrencies are still being established. Clear and consistent regulation is paramount to engendering trust in blockchain-based systems, especially in the financial services sector, where quality is intricately linked to regulatory compliance.

In conclusion, blockchain's future in enhancing transactional quality appears promising despite the hurdles. The literature posits that as blockchain technology matures, it will become an indispensable component of FinTech, ameliorating the quality of financial services across multiple dimensions, including security, transparency, and efficiency. Furthermore, as blockchain adoption extends across more industries for quality management, its role in ensuring compliance with regulatory standards and enhancing operational efficiency is set to become increasingly significant.

Author Contributions: Conceptualisation, T.K. and S.G.; methodology, T.K.; software, T.K.; validation, T.K. and S.G.; formal analysis, T.K.; investigation, T.K.; resources, T.K.; data curation, T.K.; writing—original draft preparation, T.K. and S.G.; writing—review and editing, T.K. and S.G.; visualisation, S.G.; supervision, S.G.; project administration, S.G.; funding acquisition, S.G. All authors have read and agreed to the published version of the manuscript.

Funding: Certain sections of this article were written using tools funded by the Slovenian Research and Innovation Agency, the Ministry of the Environment, Climate and Energy, and the Ministry of Cohesion and Regional Development under grant number CRP2023 V5-2331. The University of Rijeka, Faculty of Tourism and Hospitality Management, partially funded this research with grant number ZIP-UNIRI-116-1-23.

Institutional Review Board Statement: Not applicable.

Informed Consent Statement: Not applicable.

Data Availability Statement: Data are contained within the article.

Conflicts of Interest: The authors declare no conflicts of interest.

References

1. Javaid, M.; Haleem, A.; Singh, R.P.; Suman, R.; Khan, S. A review of Blockchain Technology applications for financial services. *BenchCouncil Trans. Benchmarks Stand. Eval.* **2022**, *2*, 100073. [CrossRef]
2. Chen, Y.; Bellavitis, C. Blockchain disruption and decentralized finance: The rise of decentralized business models. *J. Bus. Ventur. Insights* **2020**, *13*, e00151. [CrossRef]
3. Ali, S.; Shin, W.S.; Song, H. Blockchain-enabled open quality system for smart manufacturing: Applications and challenges. *Sustainability* **2022**, *14*, 11677. [CrossRef]
4. Centobelli, P.; Cerchione, R.; Del Vecchio, P.; Oropallo, E.; Secundo, G. Blockchain technology for bridging trust, traceability and transparency in circular supply chain. *Inf. Manag.* **2022**, *59*, 103508. [CrossRef]
5. Feng, H.; Wang, X.; Duan, Y.; Zhang, J.; Zhang, X. Applying blockchain technology to improve agri-food traceability: A review of development methods, benefits and challenges. *J. Clean. Prod.* **2020**, *260*, 121031. [CrossRef]
6. Zutshi, A.; Grilo, A.; Nodehi, T. The value proposition of blockchain technologies and its impact on Digital Platforms. *Comput. Ind. Eng.* **2021**, *155*, 107187. [CrossRef]
7. Solis, W.V.; Parra-Ullauri, J.M.; Kertesz, A. Exploring the synergy of fog computing, blockchain, and federated learning for IoT applications: A systematic literature review. *IEEE Access* **2024**, *2*, 68015–68060. [CrossRef]
8. Rikken, O.K.; Janssen, M.; Roosenboom-Kwee, Z.; Büttgen, M.; Dicenta, J.; Spohrer, K.; Venkatesh, V.; Raman, R.; Hoehle, H.; De Keyser, A.; et al. Blockchain in service management and service research–developing a research agenda and managerial implications. *J. Serv. Manag. Res.* **2021**, *5*, 71–102.
9. Romano, D.; Schmid, G. Beyond Bitcoin: Recent trends and perspectives in distributed ledger technology. *Cryptography* **2021**, *5*, 36. [CrossRef]

10. Tandon, A.; Dhir, A.; Islam, A.N.; Mäntymäki, M. Blockchain in healthcare: A systematic literature review, synthesizing framework and future research agenda. *Comput. Ind.* **2020**, *122*, 103290. [CrossRef]
11. Upadhyay, A.; Mukhuty, S.; Kumar, V.; Kazancoglu, Y. Blockchain technology and the circular economy: Implications for sustainability and social responsibility. *J. Clean. Prod.* **2021**, *293*, 126130. [CrossRef]
12. Moin, S.; Karim, A.; Safdar, Z.; Safdar, K.; Ahmed, E.; Imran, M. Securing IoTs in distributed blockchain: Analysis, requirements and open issues. *Future Gener. Comput. Syst.* **2019**, *100*, 325–343. [CrossRef]
13. Bamakan, S.M.H.; Motavali, A.; Bondarti, A.B. A survey of blockchain consensus algorithms performance evaluation criteria. *Expert Syst. Appl.* **2020**, *154*, 113385. [CrossRef]
14. Wan, S.; Li, M.; Liu, G.; Wang, C. Recent advances in consensus protocols for blockchain: A survey. *Wirel. Netw.* **2020**, *26*, 5579–5593. [CrossRef]
15. Ibrahimy, M.M.; Norta, A.; Normak, P. Blockchain-based governance models supporting corruption-transparency: A systematic literature review. *Blockchain Res. Appl.* **2024**, *5*, 100186. [CrossRef]
16. Sathya, A.R.; Banik, B.G. A comprehensive study of blockchain services: Future of cryptography. *Int. J. Adv. Comput. Sci. Appl.* **2020**, *11*, 279–286.
17. Berdik, D.; Otoum, S.; Schmidt, N.; Porter, D.; Jararweh, Y. A survey on blockchain for information systems management and security. *Inf. Process. Manag.* **2021**, *58*, 102397. [CrossRef]
18. Hashemi Joo, M.; Nishikawa, Y.; Dandapani, K. Cryptocurrency, a successful application of blockchain technology. *Manag. Financ.* **2020**, *46*, 715–733. [CrossRef]
19. Tyagi, A.K.; Kukreja, S.; Richa, A.; Sivakumar, P. Role of Blockchain Technology in Smart Era: A Review on Possible Smart Applications. *J. Inf. Knowl. Manag.* **2024**, *23*, 2450032. [CrossRef]
20. Dashkevich, N.; Counsell, S.; Destefanis, G. Blockchain application for central banks: A systematic mapping study. *IEEE Access* **2020**, *8*, 139918–139952. [CrossRef]
21. Ertz, M.; Boily, É. The rise of the digital economy: Thoughts on blockchain technology and cryptocurrencies for the collaborative economy. *Int. J. Innov. Stud.* **2019**, *3*, 84–93. [CrossRef]
22. Malhotra, D.; Saini, P.; Singh, A.K. How blockchain can automate KYC: Systematic review. *Wirel. Pers. Commun.* **2022**, *122*, 1987–2021. [CrossRef]
23. Hannan, M.A.; Shahriar, M.A.; Ferdous, M.S.; Chowdhury, M.J.M.; Rahman, M.S. A systematic literature review of blockchain-based e-KYC systems. *Computing* **2023**, *105*, 2089–2118. [CrossRef]
24. Zhu, K.; Wu, F.; Wang, F.; Shen, T.; Wu, H.; Xue, B.; Liu, Y. Blockchain-Based Digital Asset Circulation: A Survey and Future Challenges. *Symmetry* **2024**, *16*, 1287. [CrossRef]
25. Hairudin, A.; Sifat, I.M.; Mohamad, A.; Yusof, Y. Cryptocurrencies: A survey on acceptance, governance and market dynamics. *Int. J. Financ. Econ.* **2022**, *27*, 4633–4659. [CrossRef]
26. Sabry, F.; Labda, W.; Erbad, A.; Malluhi, Q. Cryptocurrencies and artificial intelligence: Challenges and opportunities. *IEEE Access* **2020**, *8*, 175840–175858. [CrossRef]
27. Bhati, D.; Deogade, M.S.; Kanyal, D. Improving patient outcomes through effective hospital administration: A comprehensive review. *Cureus* **2023**, *15*, e47731. [CrossRef]
28. Ullah, H.; Uzair, M.; Jan, Z.; Ullah, M. Integrating industry 4.0 technologies in defense manufacturing: Challenges, solutions, and potential opportunities. *Array* **2024**, *23*, 100358. [CrossRef]
29. Muruganandham, R.; Venkatesh, K.; Devadasan, S.R.; Harish, V.J.T.Q.M. TQM through the integration of blockchain with ISO 9001: 2015 standard based quality management system. *Total Qual. Manag. Bus. Excell.* **2023**, *34*, 291–311. [CrossRef]
30. Bankoff, K.P.; Muñoz, R.; Pasini, A.; Pesado, P. Quality management systems and blockchain in the 4.0 era: A literature review. In *Argentine Congress of Computer Science*; Springer Nature: Cham, Switzerland, 2022; pp. 140–155.
31. Najafi, B.; Najafi, A.; Farahmandian, A. The Impact of Artificial Intelligence and Blockchain on Six Sigma: A Systematic Literature Review of the Evidence and Implications. *IEEE Trans. Eng. Manag.* **2023**, *71*, 10261–10294. [CrossRef]
32. Saihi, A.; Awad, M.; Ben-Daya, M. Quality 4.0: Leveraging Industry 4.0 technologies to improve quality management practices–a systematic review. *Int. J. Qual. Reliab. Manag.* **2023**, *40*, 628–650. [CrossRef]
33. Alzahrani, B.; Bahaitham, H.; Andejany, M.; Elshennawy, A. How ready is higher education for quality 4.0 transformation according to the LNS research framework? *Sustainability* **2021**, *13*, 5169. [CrossRef]
34. Batista, D.; Mangeth, A.L.; Frajhof, I.; Alves, P.H.; Nasser, R.; Robichez, G.; Silva, G.M.; Miranda, F.P.d. Exploring blockchain technology for chain of custody control in physical evidence: A systematic literature review. *J. Risk Financ. Manag.* **2023**, *16*, 360. [CrossRef]
35. Kashem, M.A.; Shamsuddoha, M.; Nasir, T.; Hossain, N.U.I. Supply Chain Risk Management, Optimization, and Performance Analytics through Blockchain Integration: A Bibliometric Analysis. In *Handbook of Digital Innovation, Transformation, and Sustainable Development in a Post-Pandemic Era*; CRC Press: Boca Raton, FL, USA, 2024; pp. 120–137. [CrossRef]

36. Juan, A.A.; Perez-Bernabeu, E.; Li, Y.; Martin, X.A.; Ammouriova, M.; Barrios, B.B. Tokenized Markets Using Blockchain Technology: Exploring Recent Developments and Opportunities. *Information* **2023**, *14*, 347. [CrossRef]
37. Kukman, T. Razvoj Kakovosti Na Svetu od 1960 do Danes (Časovna Daljica). Ph.D. Thesis, University of Novo Mesto, Novo Mesto, Slovenia, 2024.
38. Li, J.; Maiti, A.; Springer, M.; Gray, T. Blockchain for supply chain quality management: Challenges and opportunities in context of open manufacturing and industrial internet of things. *Int. J. Comput. Integr. Manuf.* **2020**, *33*, 1321–1355. [CrossRef]
39. Balamurugan, S.; Ayyasamy, A.; Joseph, K.S. IoT-Blockchain driven traceability techniques for improved safety measures in food supply chain. *Int. J. Inf. Technol.* **2022**, *14*, 1087–1098. [CrossRef]
40. Chang, S.E.; Chen, Y.C.; Lu, M.F. Supply chain re-engineering using blockchain technology: A case of smart contract based tracking process. *Technol. Forecast. Soc. Change* **2019**, *144*, 1–11. [CrossRef]
41. Thakur, A. Blockchain and cryptocurrency frauds: Emerging concern. In *Financial Crimes: A Guide to Financial Exploitation in a Digital Age*; Springer International Publishing: Cham, Switzerland, 2023; pp. 131–145.
42. Sroufe, R.; Curkovic, S. An examination of ISO 9000: 2000 and supply chain quality assurance. *J. Oper. Manag.* **2008**, *26*, 503–520. [CrossRef]
43. Jackson, A.; Spiegler, V.L.; Kotiadis, K. Exploring the potential of blockchain-enabled lean automation in supply chain management: A systematic literature review, classification taxonomy, and future research agenda. *Prod. Plan. Control* **2024**, *35*, 866–885. [CrossRef]
44. Mora, H.; Mendoza-Tello, J.C.; Varela-Guzmán, E.G.; Szymanski, J. Blockchain technologies to address smart city and society challenges. *Comput. Hum. Behav.* **2021**, *122*, 106854. [CrossRef]
45. Novak, M. Crypto-friendliness: Understanding blockchain public policy. *J. Entrep. Public Policy* **2020**, *9*, 165–184.
46. Ayan, B.; Güner, E.; Son-Turan, S. Blockchain technology and sustainability in supply chains and a closer look at different industries: A mixed method approach. *Logistics* **2022**, *6*, 85. [CrossRef]
47. Aysan, A.F.; Bergigui, F.; Disli, M. Blockchain-based solutions in achieving SDGs after COVID-19. *J. Open Innov. Technol. Mark. Complex.* **2021**, *7*, 151. [CrossRef]
48. Yaqoob, I.; Salah, K.; Jayaraman, R.; Al-Hammadi, Y. Blockchain for healthcare data management: Opportunities, challenges, and future recommendations. *Neural Comput. Appl.* **2022**, *34*, 11475–11490. [CrossRef]
49. Sri Vigna Hema, V.; Manickavasagan, A. Blockchain implementation for food safety in supply chain: A review. *Compr. Rev. Food Sci. Food Saf.* **2024**, *23*, e70002. [CrossRef]
50. Isaja, M.; Nguyen, P.; Goknil, A.; Sen, S.; Husom, E.J.; Tverdal, S.; Anand, A.; Jiang, Y.; Pedersen, K.J.; Myrseth, P.; et al. A blockchain-based framework for trusted quality data sharing towards zero-defect manufacturing. *Comput. Ind.* **2023**, *146*, 103853. [CrossRef]

FinTech

MDPI

Article

Crowdfunding and Energy Efficiency Contracting: Exploring New Pathways for Private Investment in Building Renovations

Renan Magalhães [1,*], Federico Narracci [2] and Jens Lowitzsch [1,2]

1 Kelso Professorship of Comparative Law, East European Business Law and European Legal Policy, Europa-University Viadrina, 15230 Frankfurt (Oder), Germany; lowitzsch@europa-uni.de
2 Kelso Institute Europe, 10965 Berlin, Germany; narracci@kelso-institute-europe.de
* Correspondence: magalhaes@europa-uni.de

Abstract: Energy Efficiency Contracting (EEC) enables structural improvements in buildings by financing upgrades through the savings generated, eliminating the need for upfront investment by property owners. Although the model supports the energy transition and the reduction in GHG emissions, its adoption in the private sector faces relevant barriers such as the lack of information from the Energy Service Companies (ESCOs), distrust from clients in benefits with no upfront costs, and legal and behavioral barriers. To overcome these challenges, the FinSESCo platform, funded by Era-Net 2020 joint call, aims to channel private investments into building renovations and renewable energy installations via a crowdfunding portal. The platform allows individuals and organizations to finance small-scale renewable energy installations and energy efficiency measures for homeowners, tenants, and apartment owners. The new platform is likely to change the way EE investments are made and reach out to new audiences. A survey of 2585 German households sought to understand the drivers of EE investments, factors affecting the decisions, and their relationships with several demographic variables. Using a stepwise backward regression model, the study found significant differences between traditional investors in EE and those who would use the FinSESCo platform. Low- and medium-income households were more likely to take up the platform, and previous renewable energy ownership, experience with EEC models, and knowledge of crowdfunding further raised willingness to participate. The results point to the potential of the FinSESCo platform to expand EEC to new audiences, underlining its role of democratization and diversification of investments in building energy efficiency.

Keywords: energy efficiency contracting; crowdfunding; energy service companies; energy savings; private investment; investment diversification; demographic and socioeconomic profiles

JEL Classification: Q42; D14; O33

1. Introduction

Energy Efficiency (EE) investments are central to advancing energy transition, abating greenhouse gas emissions, and fostering sustainability. Improvement in energy use in buildings and industry can lead to significant reduction in energy consumption and general costs, contributing, then, to decarbonization efforts. However, despite their potential, EE investments remain limited due to financial barriers, lack of awareness, and limited access to appropriate financing mechanisms.

Among the possibilities of EE funding, one is Energy Performance Contracting (EPC). EPC is a method to implement structural improvements and upgrades in buildings through financing that is repaid using the savings generated from the improvements themselves. This approach allows energy upgrades to be carried out without requiring the initial financing costs to be borne by home, apartment, or building owners [1,2]. As an ally in the energy transition, the fight against greenhouse gas emissions and electricity saving, this model is currently popular in the public sector (intracting) but faces challenges in expanding to the private market [2–4]. Barriers include insufficient information available to Energy Service Companies (ESCOs) about potential projects and skepticism regarding the ease of gaining benefits without upfront investment from property owners [4]. Legal bureaucratic barriers and the ESCOs' inability to control user behavior regarding energy efficiency further limit acceptance of the model [4].

The most common contracting models for EPC are guaranteed savings and shared savings. The primary difference between these two models is the payment structure for the ESCO and which party assumes the credit risk. In the guaranteed savings EPC structure, the customer finances the project and therefore assumes the credit risk. The ESCO guarantees a predetermined level of energy savings, which provides an income stream in the form of avoided costs to repay the project investment. In the EPC shared savings structure, the project is fully financed by the ESCO, and the cost savings are shared between the customer and the ESCO for a predetermined period of time [5]. EPC or ESPC are very useful financial models for energy contracting because they connect interested customers with ESCOs that have the technical expertise to implement EE or RE projects [6]. An EPC or ESPC also provides a favorable cost structure for clients, as they repay project costs based on energy savings/profits rather than large initial investment burdens, which is typically a major barrier [4,6].

Regardless of the simple principle behind energy contracting, the uptake of EE retrofit projects, particularly in the building sector, has been slow [7,8]. Access to capital is a primary barrier for many interested buildings or facility owners. An EE project may require a large up-front investment to cover equipment, renovations, technology, expertise, labor, and other factors [9,10]. Many stakeholders interested in undertaking an EE project lack the capital to support a large-scale project. This may discourage many individuals from committing to an EE project because they cannot or will not take on the risk of debt [11,12]. Instead, they may cherry-pick a few short-term measures that result in small EE improvements instead of larger projects that have the potential to significantly reduce their energy demand [6,13]. An ESCO can help overcome this barrier by providing financing for the project, but they also have limitations. Only large ESCOs can financially support multiple projects simultaneously. Smaller ESCOs, on the other hand, must be more selective about the projects they take on because they do not have the capital backing of a larger company to continually launch projects. As a result, EE projects are often hampered by financing issues, even though their business case would be profitable. Against this background, the EPC and ESPC sector is in need of innovative financing solutions [6,11].

The FinSESCo—Fintech Platform Solution for Sustainable Energy System Intracting and Contracting, funded by the Era-Net 2020 joint call—aims to address these issues by streamlining investment processes, reducing transaction costs, and leveraging economies of scale to expand the pool of profitable investments. The mission of the project is to enable a wave of decarbonization projects by facilitating the establishment of Energy Performance and Energy Savings Performance Contracting EPCo/ESPCo through the end-to-end digitization of energy contracting (and the contracting process for public entities and larger companies) and enabling EE projects to take into place by crowdfunding investment. Using pre-existing data from building passports and energy audits, platform modules offer a gamified investment process with diversification options in an investor dashboard, smart contracts, a digitally encrypted meter-based repayment process, and machine learning-based fault detection during operation. A guidance tool allows potential portal developers to steer their projects in the right direction.

Potentially, the fintech environment will be able to reach a larger number of investors, democratizing and diversifying the field of energy efficiency and overcoming the above-mentioned barriers. This research, therefore, aims to outline a profile of key stakeholders interested in the platform, identify gaps in investment and interest, and link overlooked groups to the use of the platform, as we expect that the digital environment of investments can significantly change the profile of EE investments.

This paper is structured as follows: Section 2 provides the literature review. Section 3 introduces the material and methods underlying our analysis. Section 4 presents the results of the analysis and Section 5 delivers the corresponding discussion. Finally, Section 6 concludes and considers the policy implications of our results.

2. Theoretical Background

Literature identifies barriers that prevent users from engaging with EPCo and EE contracting measures. One of the most important barriers is a lack of awareness or information. Because the energy contracting and ESCO industries are still developing, many people, such as building owners, bankers, or lawyers, are not familiar with energy performance contracting and its financing method [4,14]. Therefore, it is not easy to convince clients to undertake a project as it is a foreign concept, and they may be reluctant to proceed. Also, the intuitions that support the project or the procurement process may not have the necessary information or awareness [15]. This circumstance greatly hinders project development. If parties are not properly informed about the EPC, or if access to information is associated with high barriers to entry due to the complexity of the topic, it creates unclear processes for all stakeholders. As a result, EPC models have a diminished potential to be used in practice, despite the unique idea for the ongoing decarbonization trend. Complex legal and contractual issues are another barrier that needs to be addressed to increase the uptake of EPC, as the legal documentation for EPC is complex and novel. The ESCO and potential customers often struggle to navigate the contractual landscape with its associated obligations, benefits, and risks. In addition, the lack of standardization of the energy performance process adds to the legal uncertainty [15].

The engagement, or lack thereof, of consumers in the energy transition is also significantly influenced by their perceived "ownership" of emerging energy systems. This ownership extends beyond legal definitions to include societal responsibility, behavioral change, and equitable distribution of benefits and burdens. Despite these broader implications, active participation in energy efficiency, prosumership, and energy system governance remain limited to a minority of financially capable early adopters and environmental activists [16,17]. Most citizens are excluded from these activities, highlighting the need for inclusive strategies that facilitate broader engagement.

An examination of green investment opportunities highlights the disparity in participation. Only a few can afford to invest in photovoltaic systems for their roofs, while tenants who cannot modify their rented properties face even greater challenges [18]. This results in a renovation rate in Germany that is significantly lower than its potential [6,19,20]. The commercial sector, despite the potential for high energy ROI, struggles with external financing constraints and limited resources for design and procurement [6,20,21]. Energy Service Companies (ESCOs) and Energy Performance Contracting Companies (EPCos) play a critical role in bridging this gap by providing expertise in design, implementation, and financing. However, these entities require a high ROI to cover the risks, adding another layer of complexity.

Digital platforms through fintech initiatives could be viewed as an alternative to facilitate investment in energy efficiency measures. The new fintech solutions, including mobile payments, blockchain, and crowdfunding, reduce the costs of financial service delivery and improve access, especially to underserved areas, since fintech investments have shown to improve environmental efficiency and promote sustainable development goals [22]. Digital platforms afford unique opportunities to surmount the barriers present in traditional investment methods, such as access to capital and long decision-making processes, by lowering costs of delivering financial services and expanding their accessibility [23]. In addition, the introduction of ECF platforms further illustrates how disruptive technologies with social and environmental value propositions can attract investors to support sustainable initiatives [24]. Their digital nature, added to the focus on sustainability and innovation, is expected to drive significant differences in how investments are made compared to traditional financial mechanisms, fostering quicker adoption and greater inclusiveness in EE measures.

Considering only the research for traditional EE investment, we see a complex interplay between a variety of motivational drivers, what we call in this paper controllers and socioeconomic factors, that seem to present a vast possibility of combinations that influence energy efficiency investments and behavioral changes. Previous research shows that investment in EE appliances, as well as the willingness to change behavior, is associated with environmental behaviors and the motivation to limit individual environmental impact [25–28], although it can be constrained by costs. That is, low-cost investments are more strongly associated with environmental consciousness, while high-cost investments are not primarily driven by it [29]. Knowledge about the methods also positively influences and serves as a driver for investment [30]. In some contexts, however, financial considerations appear to be the major factor leading to EE spending [31]. This driver also varies according to the income group an individual belongs to, as financial savings do not act as the main motivator for high-income households but are a key factor for low-income ones [30].

Controllers may also redirect the willingness of investment in EE. There is a positive association between renewable energy (co-)ownership and the willingness to invest in EE [32] although it can vary depending on the type of prosumership (the ones that produce energy for self-consumption, just to sell excess and the fully fledged—the ones that do both) [32]. Homeownership (combined with higher income) also seems to play a role in increasing the willingness to invest [30,33,34]. Considering the equity crowdfunding functionality of the platform, we must consider what can lead to the investment. Past research shows that willingness to undertake crowdfunding investments in green energy is increased by past experiences utilizing the concept while moderated by the knowledge of environmental questions [35]. In stronger markets, the concept of crowdfunding is more consolidated and, therefore, more spread in the society, increasing the possibility of users having past experiences, and it also increases the willingness to support projects [36,37]. At the same time, past EE investment can boost the willingness of future EE investments [38], showing that knowledge of different EE investment models can lead to a cycle of what triggers more EE investment.

Regarding the socioeconomic profiles, previous research has shown that age plays a positive role in increasing the willingness to invest in energy efficiency measures [34], with older and middle-aged individuals more likely to invest than younger ones. Gender does not appear to significantly influence energy efficiency investments [33,34], while education level may vary in its influence, sometimes affecting certain types of energy efficiency investments. The level and complexity of investments tends to increase with higher education levels [33].

However, we assume that the order of importance and the interaction of these drivers, controllers, and socioeconomic factors and their influence on the willingness to invest may shift or be differently impacted by the digital factor. Aiming to fill this research gap, to compare both models, and to guide the FinSESCo consortium to understand the profile of investors of EE measures via fintech while comparing to the ones in a traditional environment, a survey with German households was conducted in 2023. The resulting dataset allows us to correlate interest in the platform, knowledge of energy efficiency contracting models, and previous experience with crowdfunding investments in energy efficiency behavior. We translated our interests into four main research questions, trying to predict which groups would be interested in using the platform by interacting with the different groups of variables (controllers and drivers), socioeconomic factors, and the willingness to invest in EE and to invest in the FinSESCo platform:

1. What are the main drivers for investment in energy efficiency measures?
2. What are the main barriers for investment in energy efficiency measures?
3. Given the availability of options such as the FinSESCo platform, is it a determining factor for investing in energy efficiency?
4. Which groups are most likely to use the platform based on different socioeconomic demographics, real estate ownership, and experience in renewables?

3. Materials and Methods

This section presents the methods applied in this paper, discussing the process of data collection, the sample, and the measurement, describing the models used.

3.1. Deliberations on the Data Collection

The questionnaire used for the data collection process was inspired by previous questionnaires developed by Roth et al. [32,39]. At the time, Roth et al. [39] conducted data collection among users of a real estate portal in Germany, focusing on reaching the largest possible number of people who (co-)own renewable energy production facilities. This process served as the foundation for structuring our own survey, with a focus on measuring the energy efficiency behaviors and demand-side flexibility of renewable energy prosumers. The databases collected by Roth et al. were also used for similar investigations, such as in [32], where they examined which types of (co-)ownership were associated with the willingness to adopt and invest in energy efficiency measures. These studies share clear similarities with our research interests. Consequently, we adopted similar questions or adapted them to suit the context of our study.

Following this new survey and data collection effort, the resulting database targets a broader range of prosumers and ensures a more balanced distribution across gender and income levels, reaching a larger number of low-income prosumers, non-prosumers, and female prosumers.

It was conducted by the survey company Norstat between 28 August 2023 and 23 November 2023, utilizing its pool of respondents and filters established by its team to target prosumers within it. Thus, the questionnaire may not be representative of the demographics of German prosumers—how they are distributed across different societal strata, the main sectors they represent, or how to infer the percentage of prosumers in the country; data related to these factors are still unknown [40]. The questionnaire initially aimed to be representative of German society, aligning with the distributions in relation to the population of the states, age groups, and gender. Small adjustments were made during the data collection, with invitations sent to groups where a higher concentration of prosumers was observed without the use of filters. In the final phase of the collection, to achieve the expected numbers, internal questionnaire filters were used to exclude non-prosumers, and at the last moment, all those who were not female prosumers were excluded.

The data were collected to address the interests of FinSESCo, aiming to outline a profile of the main stakeholders interested in the platform, identify investment and interest gaps, and match overlooked groups with the platform's usage. Possible relationships between potential platform usage and prosumership were translated into questions on the platform to utilize the data as broadly as possible. The data allow for the correlation of interest in the platform, knowledge of energy efficiency contracting models, and past experiences in crowdfunding investing in energy efficiency behavior, enabling a series of possible analyses for consumption habits to be tested. A summary overview of the data can be found in Appendix B.

3.2. Deliberation on the Sample

The total sample of the database consists of 2585 complete questionnaires. We have selected the main demographic and control variables for prosumership to briefly summarize the data characteristics. It is important to note that our database includes a high number of prosumers—a total of 925, with 464 of them being females. This is a robust database for understanding prosumer behavior, comparing it with non-prosumers, and conducting internal comparisons between genders and types of prosumership.

Our database initially aimed to be representative of the German demographic. Therefore, we sought to mirror the distribution by age groups according to the country data. However, as we tried to boost the number (co-)owners of the data, the invitations for the questionnaire focused on groups with a higher likelihood of encountering prosumers. Therefore, the data cannot be used to infer the number of prosumers in Germany.

To ensure the quality of the dataset, we conducted an outliers test, *t*-test, and Wilcoxon test to examine differences in the samples of regular respondents and those who completed the survey after an interruption; this was in the form of syntax analysis searching for unusual values and characters. Additionally, we investigated the cooperation required to respond properly to matrix questions and the estimated time to complete the questionnaire. From the initial sample of 2585, we removed 31 questionnaires due to potential issues regarding their quality.

Income levels are defined based on thresholds derived from the median income. Specifically, incomes below 60% of the median are classified as low, those between 60% and 150% of the median as medium, and incomes above 150% of the median as high, using the main thresholds used for countries in the European Union [41].

3.3. Deliberation on the Measurement

In our questionnaire, we have designed specific questions to understand the level of understanding of German households regarding energy efficiency contracting, their willingness to invest in models like FinSESCo, and their willingness to invest in energy efficiency in general.

To calculate their willingness to invest in EE measures, we have asked if they have already invested in energy efficiency measures to reduce electricity consumption or investment in measures to reduce requirements for heating. The respondents could also select which of the following types of investments they have made:

- v_33_1: Replacing lighting with energy-efficient LED lamps;
- v_33_2: Replacing household appliances;
- v_33_3: Replacement of other electronic entertainment devices;
- v_33_4: Other;

- v_39_1: Replacement of windows;
- v_39_2: Renovation of the insulation of the house;
- v_39_3: Technical devices for heating management purchased;
- v_39_4: Replacing the circulation pump;
- v_39_5: Installation of a heat pump;
- v_39_6: Other.

They were also asked if they are planning on performing these following measures:

- v_36_1: Replacing lighting with energy-efficient LED lamps;
- v_36_2: Replacing household appliances;
- v_36_3: Replacement of other electronic entertainment devices;
- v_36_4: Other;
- v_44_3: Technical devices for heating management purchased;
- v_44_4: Replacing the circulation pump;
- v_44_5: Installation of a heat pump;
- v_44_6: Other.

For each question, the respondent could opt for 0 (no), or 1 (yes), meaning that they had invested or are planning to invest for each specific measure. Afterwards, after being briefly introduced to the models and how the platform will work, we asked the following questions:

- v_63_1: Are you familiar with "Energy Savings Performance Contracting" or "Energy Savings Contracting"?
- v_64_1: Would you use an Energy Savings Performance Contracting Service via FinSESCo?
- v_65_1: Have you ever used crowdfunding to fund your own project?
- v_66_1: Have you ever invested money through crowdfunding to finance a third-party project?

Afterward, respondents were asked to rate on a scale from −3 to +3, representing "Not familiar at all" to "Very familiar" for the first question, and "I wouldn't use it under any circumstances" to "I would definitely use it" for the second. We transformed the scale from −3 to 0 as 0, meaning individuals who were not familiar and/or "people who would not use the FinSESCo model", and from +1 to +3 as individuals who were familiar and would use the FinSESCo platform.

Respondents were are also asked what were their main drivers to invest or plan to invest in EE measures:

- v_40_1: Financial motivation;
- v_40_2: Environmental protection motivation;
- v_40_3: Previous knowledge motivation;
- v_40_4: Climate change motivation;
- v_40_5: Energy autonomy motivation;
- v_40_6: To sell excess energy motivation.

For each answer, respondents could opt on a Likert scale from 1 (strongly disagree) up to 5 (strongly disagree). Details of the questionnaire are found in Appendix A.

3.4. Deliberations on the Model Specification

Our analysis is based on backward stepwise regressions. Backward stepwise regression is a statistical method used for building regression models. In this approach, all independent variables are initially included in the model, and then, step by step, variables are removed based on their statistical significance until only the most significant variables remain [42]. The backward stepwise regression starts with a full model containing all independent variables and gradually removes variables that contribute the least to the model's predictive power [43,44]. This process continues until no further variables can be removed without significantly affecting the model's fit. Overall, backward stepwise regression is a valuable tool for identifying the most influential variables and building a predictive [45] model that accurately captures the relationship between independent and dependent variables in our analysis. In our analysis, the significance level of α is < 0.05, as per [46].

For this, we have created four different models. The models have as independent variables either an index to calculate the willingness to invest in EE measures using the FinSESCo prototype platform (index_finsesco) or the willingness to invest in EE measures in general (index_ee).

The "index_finsesco" quantifies the willingness of respondents to use the FinSESCo platform, converting responses to the question "Are you familiar with 'Energy Savings Performance Contracting' or 'Energy Savings Contracting'?" (v_63_1) from a scale of −3 to +3, representing "Not familiar at all" to "Very familiar" for the first question, and "I wouldn't use it under any circumstances" to "I would definitely use it" for the second. (a.) The value of the variable v_63_1, here named y1, contains values on scale of 1 to 6; (b.) subsequently, we perform a log transformation. Log transformation is used to normalize skewed data, reduce the impact of extreme values, and make the data more normally distributed [47] as many behaviors and perceptions follow a skewed distribution, where a few individuals exhibit extreme behaviors or attitudes [48]. Log transformation helps in stabilizing the variance and making the data [47]; (c.) to this value, we add a constant of 1. Adding a constant (in this case, 1) before applying log transformation is a common practice to handle zero or negative values, since the log of zero is undefined; adding a constant ensures that all values are positive and, hence, their logarithms can be computed; (d.) we normalize the value by dividing it by the mean of the values. (e.) Finally, we take the square root of the total. Normalizing by the mean value of the transformed variables helps in standardizing the scores and making them comparable. This step ensures that the index is not biased by the scale of the original variables and is interpreted on a common scale.

Considering γ_1 as the variable v_64_1, the value of index_finsesco can be seen in the following operation:

$$indexfinsesco = \frac{\sqrt{log(\gamma_1)+1}}{\left(\sqrt{log(\gamma_1)+1}\right)} \tag{1}$$

Subsequently, *index_ee* is calculated. Considering V, the group of variables, V = {v33,1,v33,2, ...,v44,6}, with 18 variables in total; Xi is the sum of valid (non-NA) values for row i and variable j:

$$X_i = \sum_{j \in V} vi,j, \text{ } where \text{ } vi,j \neq NA. \tag{2}$$

Then, a log transformation is applied to the sum of valid values for row i, adding 1 to avoid log of 0, with a square root transformation to the log-transformed sum:

$$Z_i = \sqrt{Y_i} = \sqrt{\log(X_i+1)} \tag{3}$$

Finally, the value is normalized by computing the average of the square root-transformed values for all rows, I, and dividing the square root value by the mean, μ_Z:

$$\mu_Z = \frac{1}{n}\sum_{i=1}^{n} Z_i,\ where\ Z_i \neq NA \tag{4}$$

The value for index_ee is then:

$$index\_ee_i = \frac{Z_i}{\mu_Z} \tag{5}$$

After creating the independent variables, we divide the independent variables into three groups: drivers, controllers, and demographics. The following is the list of variables used in the four models calculated in this analysis [Table 1].

Table 1. Variables of the models.

Variable	Description
	Indexes:
Y_1	index willingness to invest in energy efficiency
Y_2	index willingness to invest via FinSESCo
	Drivers:
X_1	v_40_1: Financial motivation [25–28]
X_2	v_40_2: environmental protection motivation [29]
X_3	v_40_3: previous knowledge motivation [30,38]
X_4	v_40_4: climate change motivation [29]
X_5	v_40_5: energy autonomy motivation [32]
X_6	v_40_6: to sell excess energy motivation [32]
	Controllers:
X_7	Home Ownership [30,33,34]
X_8	Previous experience in crowdfunding [35]
X_9	Previous knowledge in energy efficiency contracting [38]
X_{10}	Prosumer [32]
	Demographics:
X_{11}	Income: Low [30]
X_{12}	Income: Medium [30]
X_{13}	Income: High [30]
X_{14}	Age [34]
X_{15}	Gender [33,34]
X_{16}	Education [33]

Source: Own elaboration.

In our analysis, we employed bootstrapping to enhance the robustness and reliability of our regression models' coefficients [49]. Bootstrapping involves repeatedly resampling the original dataset with replacement and estimating the model on each resampled dataset. This process mitigates the influence of outliers, providing more accurate confidence intervals [50,51]. Specifically, the data were resampled 10,000 times to ensure a comprehensive and reliable estimation of the model parameters, where each sample had the same size as the original dataset.

We then calculated Cook's distance to identify influential points in the dataset [52] and remove the ones exceeding 4/n, where n is the number of observations. A new regression model was fitted to the dataset without the influential points, again, performing a backward stepwise regression. The results of Cook's distance analysis are present in Appendix C.

To answer our research questions, we created four different regression models: (i) considering as the independent variable the index to calculate the willingness to invest in EE and the interactions of the drivers and the demographic variables; (ii) the index to calculate the willingness to invest in EE and the interactions of the controllers and the demographic variables; (iii) considering as the independent variable the index to calculate the willingness to invest via FinSESCo and the interactions of the drivers and the demographic variables; and (iv) the willingness to invest via FinSESCo and the interactions of the controllers and the demographic variables. The following are the models:

Model I:

$$Y_1 = \beta_0 + \sum_{i=11}^{13} \beta_i X_i + \sum_{j=14}^{16} \beta_j X_j + \sum_{k=1}^{6} \beta_k X_k + \sum_{i=11}^{16} \sum_{k=1}^{13} \beta_{ik} X_i X_k + \epsilon$$

Model II:

$$Y_1 = \beta_0 + \sum_{i=11}^{13} \beta_i X_i + \sum_{j=14}^{16} \beta_j X_j + \sum_{m=7}^{10} \beta_m X_m + \sum_{i=11}^{16} \sum_{m=7}^{10} \beta_{im} X_i X_m + \epsilon$$

Model III:

$$Y_2 = \beta_0 + \sum_{i=11}^{13} \beta_i X_i + \sum_{j=14}^{16} \beta_j X_j + \sum_{k=1}^{6} \beta_k X_k + \sum_{i=11}^{16} \sum_{k=1}^{13} \beta_{ik} X_i X_k + \epsilon$$

Model IV:

$$Y_2 = \beta_0 + \sum_{i=11}^{13} \beta_i X_i + \sum_{j=14}^{16} \beta_j X_j + \sum_{m=7}^{10} \beta_m X_m + \sum_{i=11}^{16} \sum_{m=7}^{10} \beta_{im} X_i X_m + \epsilon$$

For all models, coefficients $\beta_0, \beta_i, \beta_j, \beta_k, \beta_m, \beta_{ik}, \beta_{im}$ are estimated using resampled datasets from 10,000 bootstrap iterations. Each model includes the interaction terms between demographic variables and either drivers or controllers, and ε accounts for the unexplained variance or error in the models. Each model is used to answer the four different research questions proposed after the analysis presented in the previous section. All calculations were performed using RStudio with R version 4.4.0.

4. Results

The following paragraphs outline the results of the stepwise regression models that were developed to answer the research questions. The regression tables highlight the significance and impact of the most relevant predictors on the dependent variables. In a stepwise approach, only the most influential variables are kept, enhancing interpretability [Table 2].

For our model I, we see that environmental protection motivation (v_40_2) and energy autonomy motivation (v_40_5) are the main drivers to increase the willingness to invest in EE. The increase in the age variable seems to play a positive effect, although it is on the border of being a statistically significant predictor. The low-income variable has a negative direction of the estimate, while the high-income variable has a positive one, although the interaction of low-income with a previous knowledge driver (v_40_3) results in a positive direction [Table 3].

Table 2. Interaction of Drivers and Demographics on the willingness to invest in EE.

Term	Estimate	Std. Error	*p* Value	
(Intercept)	1.038972	0.06088	$<2 \times 10^{-16}$	*
Income: Low	−0.08131	0.030025	0.006845	*
Income: Medium	0.002593	0.0413	0.949952	
Income: High	0.103556	0.04175	0.013233	*
Age	0.001921	0.00099	0.052436	
Academic	−0.03643	0.027474	0.185067	
v_40_2	0.029971	0.007847	0.000139	*
v_40_3	0.007181	0.004154	0.084071	
v_40_4	−0.01126	0.007328	0.1246	
v_40_5	0.051021	0.014993	0.000684	*
v_40_6	−0.02234	0.00717	0.001871	*
Income: Low: v_40_3	0.01879	0.009117	0.039489	*
Income: Medium: v_40_5	−0.02027	0.009041	0.02509	*
Income: Medium: v_40_6	0.028237	0.009232	0.002263	*
Income: High: v_40_4	0.024179	0.012454	0.052399	
Income: High: v_40_5	−0.01504	0.009223	0.103066	
Age: v_40_5	−0.00049	0.000272	0.071738	
Academic: v_40_6	0.015923	0.008699	0.067391	

Source: Own elaboration. * indicates statistical significance at $p < 0.05$. Residual standard error: 0.1712 on 1510 degrees of freedom; Multiple R-squared: 0.06525, Adjusted R-squared: 0.05906; F-statistic: 10.54 on 10 and 1510 DF, *p*-value: $<2.2 \times 10^{-16}$.

Table 3. Interaction of Controllers and Demographics on the willingness to invest in EE.

Term	Estimate	Std. Error	*p* Value	
(Intercept)	1.235	0.02028	$<2 \times 10^{-16}$	*
Income: Low	−0.04087	0.01309	0.001824	*
Income: High	0.01623	0.0102	0.111989	
Age	−0.000079	0.000381	0.836263	
Academic	−0.003209	0.01036	0.756673	
Home Ownership	0.04979	0.00972	3.41×10^{-7}	*
Crowdfunding Experience	0.03687	0.01116	0.000977	*
EPCo Experience	−0.136	0.05655	0.01629	*
Income: Low: EPCo Knowledge	0.1222	0.0422	0.003841	*
Age: EPCo Knowledge	0.002372	0.00119	0.046356	*
Academic: EPCo Knowledge	0.08161	0.02842	0.004142	*

Source: Own elaboration. * indicates statistical significance at $p < 0.05$. Residual standard error: 0.1712 on 1510 degrees of freedom; Multiple R-squared: 0.06525, Adjusted R-squared: 0.05906; F-statistic: 10.54 on 10 and 1510 DF, *p*-value: $<2.2 \times 10^{-16}$.

In our model II, only low-income households appear to have a statistically significant coefficient to predict the willingness to invest in EE, playing a negative factor, although the interaction with familiarity with energy efficiency contracting inverts the direction. Previous experience with crowdfunding and especially home ownership seems to have a statistically significant impact on the increase in index_ee. Prior knowledge about energy efficiency contracting has a negative coefficient; however, its interactions with the academic (people with a high education degree) variable and age both have a positive effect [Table 4].

Table 4. Interaction of Drivers and Demographics on the willingness to invest using the FinSESCo platform.

Term	Estimate	Std. Error	*p* Value	
(Intercept)	1.384391	0.108056	$<2 \times 10^{-16}$	*
Income: Low	0.077879	0.100578	0.438824	
Income: Medium	−0.07522	0.085317	0.378087	
Income: High	−0.02557	0.082289	0.756056	
Gender	0.169004	0.084368	0.045276	*
Age	−0.00136	0.000811	0.09443	
Academic	−0.09107	0.063354	0.150698	
v_40_1	−0.04571	0.011734	0.000101	*
v_40_3	0.003849	0.013521	0.775919	
v_40_4	0.026997	0.017248	0.117676	
v_40_5	−0.07627	0.013109	6.78×10^{-9}	*
v_40_6	−0.01456	0.016307	0.372144	
Income: Low: v_40_1	−0.03836	0.025142	0.127252	
Income: Medium: v_40_6	0.050084	0.026072	0.054855	
Income: High: v_40_5	0.054662	0.020287	0.007101	*
Gender: v_40_4	−0.05572	0.021245	0.008783	*
Academic: v_40_3	0.047107	0.02005	0.018885	*

Source: Own elaboration. * indicates statistical significance at $p < 0.05$. Residual standard error: 0.4988 on 2275 degrees of freedom; Multiple R-squared: 0.07522, Adjusted R-squared: 0.06871; F-statistic: 11.56 on 16 and 2275 DF, *p*-value: $<2.2 \times 10^{-16}$.

In our model III, although not statistically significant, we see for the first time the low-income variable being associated with a positive effect in the dependent variable. The variable gender has a positive and statistically significant effect on the willingness to invest in EE via the FinSESCo platform. This index also increases with the interaction of the high-income variable and the driver for energy autonomy [Table 5].

Table 5. Interaction of Controllers and Demographics on the willingness to invest using the FinSESCo platform.

Term	Estimate	Std. Error	*p* Value	
(Intercept)	4.127004	0.168481	$<2 \times 10^{-16}$	*
Income: Low	0.292901	0.116232	0.01181	*
Income: Medium	0.206155	0.095596	0.03115	*
Income: High	0.37052	0.113093	0.00107	*
Gender	−0.015558	0.06387	0.80758	
Age	−0.01805	0.003026	2.83×10^{-9}	*
Academic	0.119923	0.061975	0.05311	
Home Ownership	−0.248104	0.2126	0.24334	
Crowdfunding Experience	0.133435	0.109454	0.22293	
Prosumership Experience	0.207034	0.080738	0.0104	*
EPCo Knowledge	0.866511	0.141527	1.08×10^{-9}	*
Income: Low: Home Ownership	−0.320667	0.164468	0.05133	
Income: High:Prosumership Experience	−0.178546	0.125641	0.15543	
Gender: Crowdfunding Experience	0.269898	0.146185	0.06498	
Gender: EPCo Knowledge	−0.306526	0.190073	0.10695	
Age: Home Ownership	0.006661	0.004337	0.12477	

Source: Own elaboration. * indicates statistical significance at $p < 0.05$. Residual standard error: 1.322 on 2265 degrees of freedom; Multiple R-squared: 0.09531, Adjusted R-squared: 0.08932; F-statistic: 15.91 on 15 and 2265 DF, *p*-value: $<2.2 \times 10^{-16}$.

Finally, in our model IV, although the high-income variable plays a positive effect in the willingness to invest in EE via the FinSESCo platform, the low-income variable seems to have a higher effect than the medium-income one. In this model, the increase in the age variable is associated with a negative effect on the dependent variable, and its value is highly statistically significant, as is the previous knowledge of EPC, but this time it is a positive effect. Past experiences with prosumership also have a positive effect on the index finsesco.

5. Discussion

In this section, we discuss the results in the context of existing literature and the theoretical framework.

Discussion of the Results

For model I, with HIHs having the largest propensity to invest, previous research indicating that the lack of financial means is an obstacle to EE investments is corroborated. Within the groups that have a higher propensity to invest, i.e., HIHs and MIHs, positive drivers appears to be "counteracting climate change" for HIHs and the drive to "sell excess energy" for MIHs. On the other hand, with regard to LIHs, we observe that previous knowledge motivation is an incentive.

Thus, these results confirm previous research, showing that HIHs and MIHs, motivated by counteracting climate change, have a strong willingness to invest in EE. The emphasis on pro-environmental attitudes as drivers supports the point on social motivations for investment [53]. This result is also supported by [54]. The option to receive monetary returns from surplus energy motivates MIHs to invest, highlighting how financial incentives can bolster demand flexibility [53,55]. In the context of Renewable Energy Communities, the literature shows that financial means among consumer-sellers (who are typically from HIHs) support demand flexibility for EE investments, specifically in household appliance use. This aligns with the point that financial resources enable HIHs to engage in EE [32]. However, only households with both consumption and selling options have a higher propensity to invest in energy-efficient technologies [32]. The financial incentives associated with selling excess energy motivate households to invest in energy-efficient technologies, optimizing their utility and aligning with the economic drivers highlighted in our results. In the literature, the counteracting climate change driver is also associated with community energy membership rather than financial gains, while financial limitations are a key barrier, particularly for LIHs [54]. This supports the point on financial constraints being an obstacle and aligns with the socio-ecological drivers of HIHs and MIHs [53].

For our model II, controlling for home ownership, previous experience in crowdfunding, or EE contracting and prosumership, we observe the same general picture, i.e., the propensity to invest increases with income. Interestingly, the strongest interacting element is homeownership followed by experience in crowdfunding. With both moderating elements stemming from experience, we surmise that they reflect the financial barrier mentioned earlier—richer HHs are more likely to be homeowners, while poorer HHs may have experience in crowdfunding precisely to overcome the financial barriers. Unsurprisingly, home ownership as a co-factor is positively only relevant for HIHs and MIHs (who are the ones most likely to own), while having a negative interaction with LIHs. On the other hand, the interaction between previous knowledge of EPC and LIHs converts the effect to be a positive co-factor.

Community experience, including previous involvement in collective prosumership, increases trust and belief in citizen participation, independently from the income. However, if on the one hand higher-income participants show lower impact on behavioral changes, they are additionally driven by the possibility of financial returns. This confirms that previous experience in collective prosumership has a positive influence on the willingness to invest, but the focus on financial returns lead wealthy households to an higher propensity to participate as prosumers [53,56,57]. At the same time, RE ownership is linked with higher flexibility. According to the literature, this effect is more frequent in rural areas, where more frequent prosumership opportunities arise. [58]. Results show us that previous prosumership and crowdfunding experience increase investment propensity. Furthermore, emphasizing the role of social mechanisms in linking ownership and behavior, LIHs and MIHs can overcome financial barriers through community-based prosumership [39,59,60]. Finally, experience in energy-related activities significantly boosts flexibility and willingness to invest in EE [39].

However, if, on the one hand, literature shows that financial barriers for LIHs limit their involvement in EE behaviors, emphasizing the need for policy interventions to ensure equitable participation [17,61], the obtained results show that prosumership experience generally increases energy-efficient behaviors and interacts positively with investment propensity [39,58].

Considering platform-moderated vis à vis conventional investments, in our model III, the general observation is that the former lends itself to households with limited disposable income whereas the latter is more attractive to richer households. In this light unsurprisingly, we see that the possibility to receive monetary returns from the sale of excess production—as a generally strong motivator for HIHs—converts into a negative driver as monetary returns under crowdfunding mechanisms are burdened or wiped out by transaction costs and costs of financing (which independently of the crowdfunding scheme is essentially an investment on borrowed money).

Conventional investment models with fixed returns are attractive to HIHs, as they provide financial stability. In contrast, digital ones make it more appealing for LIHs, due to lower financial barriers. Limited financial resources hinder LIHs from participating in renewable energy initiatives and the access to economic benefits, such as avoided energy costs [32,61]. The results show that in the case of a digital environment, financial drivers may not always encourage energy-conscious behaviors, as seen in [53].

Finally, in model IV, we see that prosumership has the highest positive interaction, in particular for LIHs. As expected, increasing age is a generally disincentivizing factor, since crowdfunding and the use of digital platforms appears to be strongly correlated with digital literacy [62]. This effect, however, turns around when coupled with home ownership (although not statistically significant) with the explanation most likely being that with increasing age, HH income decreases and, in particular, LIH and MIH homeowners seek to revert to alternative financing sources.

6. Conclusions

This paper conducts an analysis of the most important engagement-determining factors in the Energy Efficiency investment platform FinSESCo, particularly demographic characteristics, previous experience with EEC, and renewable co-ownership-related dynamics. The built and tested models shed light on diverse factors that shape interest in EE investment via a fintech platform. The findings revealed a complex interplay among socioeconomic and demographic factors and household dynamics that influence attitudes toward energy efficiency investments. The positive associations between lower income levels and platform engagement do confirm that the FinSECCo model attracts a public that is economically heterogeneous—those looking for cost-efficient energy solutions. Gender dynamics and RE ownership continue to condition engagement, emphasizing the importance of inclusivity integrating these variables. The characteristics of the platform could potentially widen participation in energy efficiency projects by attracting non-homeowners, particularly renters, who have shown interest on the platform, which could help wider involvement and overcome the traditionally strong barriers of financing. Among the most important factors is the strong relationship between experience with RE installations and a much higher likelihood of engagement within the platform. Surely, this suggests that those with the experience do realize the benefit attached to the reinvestment in renewable energy.

We identified several key differences and similarities between engagement with the FinSESCo platform and more traditional forms of energy efficiency investment. The FinSECo platform makes the market more accessible to lower-income groups and renters, mostly excluding from traditional energy efficiency investments, lowering the barriers to participation. Regarding motivational drivers, a wider scope comes with this platform, appealing to people who seek positive environmental impact opposed to traditional investments with an individual financial focus, especially those in the medium- and high-income households.

Both models, however, attract those with experience or knowledge relating to energy efficiency investments. Familiarity with crowdfunding or renewable energy systems is one of the most critical drivers of engagement in both models. Financial savings are a key driver for both the platform and traditional methods, particularly among lower-income participants. The economic incentives to invest in energy efficiency are fairly well accepted across a wide demographic base. These findings underline the potential of the FinSESCo platform for increasing energy efficiency participation and filling in some of the gaps from traditional approaches that cannot easily reach economically or socially disadvantaged groups.

The results of this study suggest important policy implications to diversify the profile of energy efficiency investment. We recognize that efforts should mainly target systemic barriers to participation, especially among low-income households, women, and other underrepresented minority groups. In that sense, specifically designed financial support to these groups, including specific subsidies for RE and EE project initiatives, is essential. Hanke and Lowitzsch (2020) underline that participation in energy projects must bring tangible benefits immediately, especially through well-designed financial incentives [63]. In the case of EE, simplified legal frameworks and incentives can promote social inclusion while reducing administrative burdens to encourage participation in projects and to increase the willingness to invest in EE measures. The empowerment of vulnerable consumers to better access energy-sharing schemes is crucial for ensuring more equitable energy systems [64] and for that, the FinSESCo platform can help to make EE investment opportunities more economically inclusive to those who often cannot participate in traditional EE investments.

The results also highlight possible pathways for the consolidation of a more inclusive energy system, one that include a greater diversification of the profiles involved in decision making. Heldeweg and Saintier (2020) point to the need to go beyond the state-versus-market dualism in governance models and recognize the thriving role of civil society [65], which would require a coordinated governance approach to avoid dominance by any single group. Collective prosumership, together with digital solutions like FinSESCo, may allow LIHs and MIHs to overcome financial constraints and boost EE measures adoption, as prior experience with RE prosumership is an important driver for the platform acceptance. This points out to the direction that the platforms such as FinSESCo need to act also as an enabler of collective action, aiming to the advancement of socio-economic and environmental goals, aligned with the community approaches to the investment in EE.

Finally, further research is needed to identify precisely which strategies will enhance initial engagement and to consider the longer-term effects of knowledge and information in EE investment via fintech platforms. Our findings point out that the FinSESCo platform can be scaled up with great potential for investment in energy efficiency measures; still, it has to tackle the informational and motivational barriers by capitalizing on its strengths while navigating in the fintech sector. By fostering inclusivity and accessibility, the fintech environment can tackle traditional barriers associated with EE investment, creating a more inclusive and accessible scenario, hence driving wider participation in the transition toward energy efficiency.

Author Contributions: Conceptualization, R.M. and J.L.; methodology, R.M.; software, R.M.; validation, R.M. and F.N.; formal analysis, J.L.; investigation, R.M., F.N. and J.L.; resources, J.L.; data curation, R.M.; writing—original draft preparation, R.M., F.N. and J.L.; writing—review and editing, J.L.; visualization, R.M.; supervision, J.L.; project administration, J.L.; funding acquisition, J.L. All authors have read and agreed to the published version of the manuscript.

Funding: The research for this publication has been co-funded by the Bundesministerium für Wirtschaft und Klimaschutz der Bundesrepublik Deutschland (BMWK) project FKZ: 03EI6072A 'FinSESCo—Fintech-Plattformlösung fur das Intracting und Contracting von nachhaltigen Energiesystemen zur Förderung von Energieeinsparungen und erneuerbaren Energien'.

Data Availability Statement: The dataset presented in this article is not readily available because the data are part of an ongoing study. Requests to access the datasets should be directed to magalhaes@europa-uni.de.

Conflicts of Interest: The authors declare no conflict of interest.

Appendix A

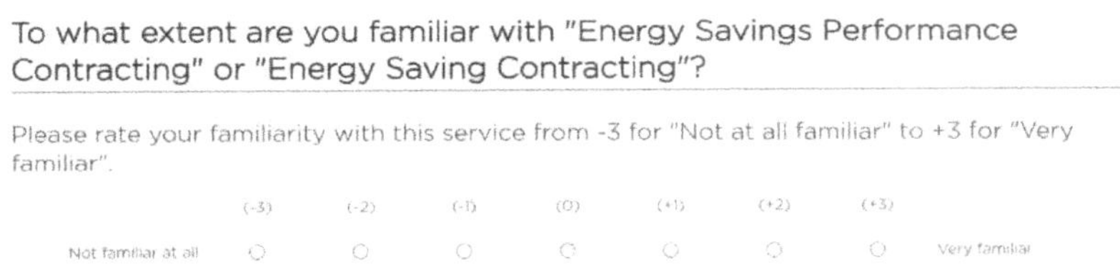

Figure A1. Question v_63_1.

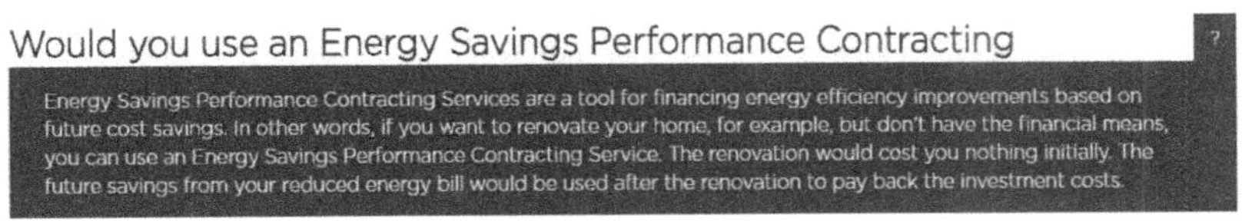

Figure A2. Question v_64_1 explanation pop-up.

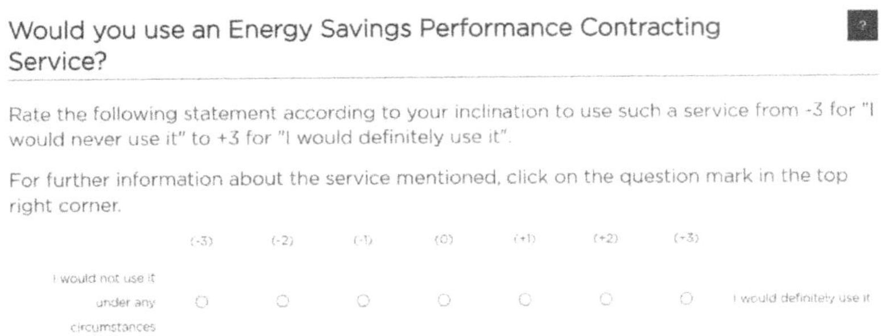

Figure A3. Questionv_64_1.

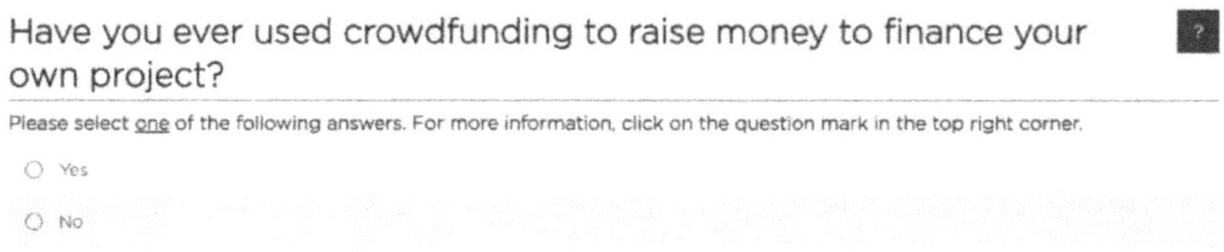
Have you ever used crowdfunding to raise money to finance your own project?

Please select one of the following answers. For more information, click on the question mark in the top right corner.

Yes

No

Figure A4. Question v_65_1.

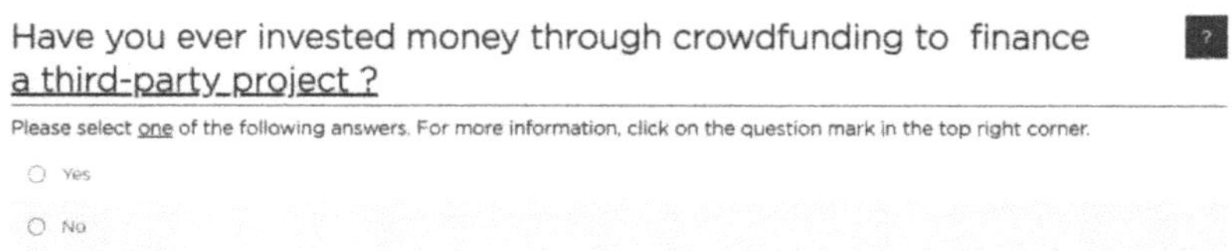
Have you ever invested money through crowdfunding to finance a third-party project ?

Please select one of the following answers. For more information, click on the question mark in the top right corner.

Yes

No

Figure A5. Question v_636_1.

Appendix B

Table A1. Data Summary.

Variable	Obs.	Mean	Std. Dev.	Min	Max
Ownership	2585	0.3578337	0.4794556	0	1
Co-Ownership	2585	0.1748549	0.3799165	0	1
Age	2585	46.82901	13.13504	21.5	68
Gender	2585	0.5415861	0.498364	0	1
Academic	2585	0.35822205	0.4795702	0	1
Income	2278	2.114135	0.7533631	1	3

Appendix C

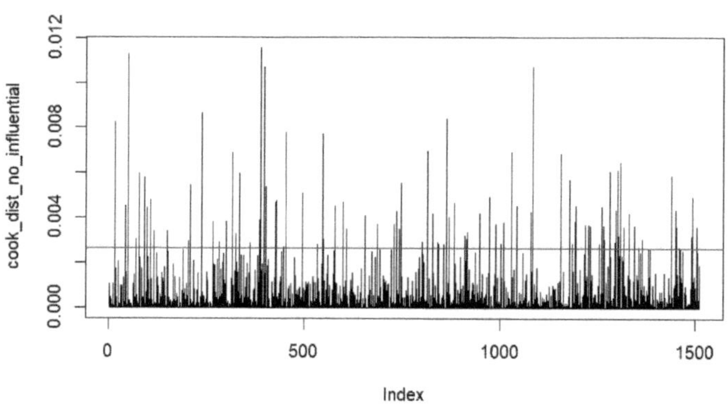

Figure A6. Model 1 Cook's distance not influential points.

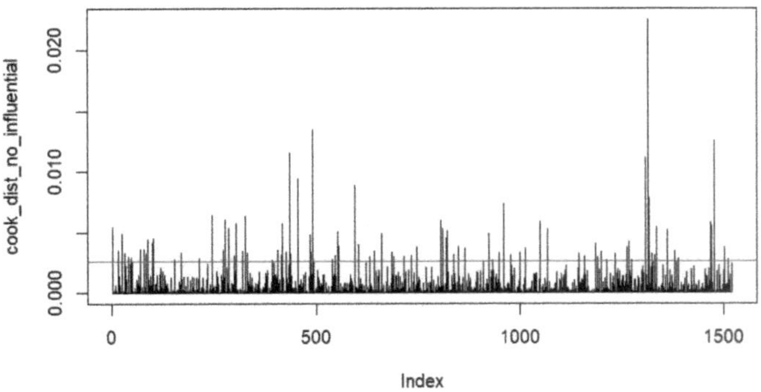

Figure A7. Model 2 Cook's distance not influential points.

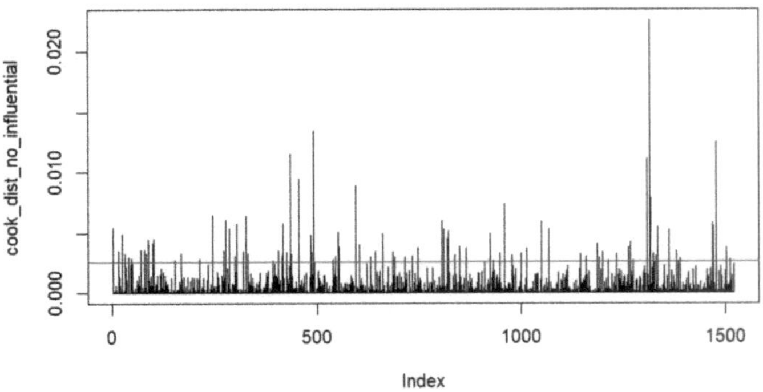

Figure A8. Model 3 Cook's distance not influential points.

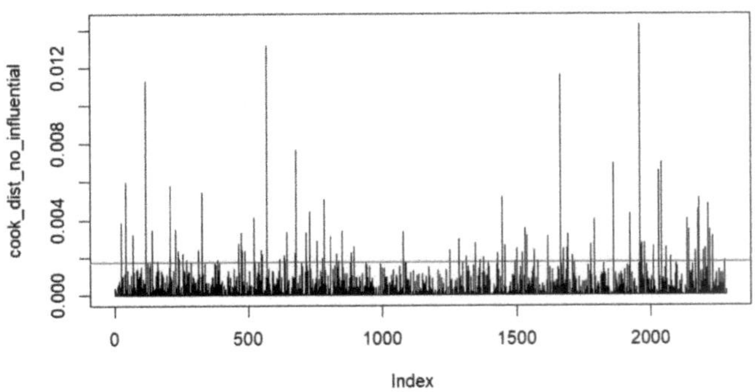

Figure A9. Model 4 Cook's distance not influential points.

References

1. Sorrell, S. The economics of energy service contracts. *Energy Policy* **2006**, *35*, 507–521. [CrossRef]
2. Hoyle, J.W. *Performance-Based Potential for Residential Energy Efficiency*; Technical Report; CICERO: Oslo, Norway, 2013.
3. Vine, E. An international survey of the energy service company (ESCO) industry. *Energy Policy* **2003**, *33*, 691–704. [CrossRef]
4. Labanca, N.; Suerkemper, F.; Bertoldi, P.; Irrek, W.; Duplessis, B. Energy efficiency services for residential buildings: Market situation and existing potentials in the European Union. *J. Clean. Prod.* **2015**, *109*, 284–295. [CrossRef]
5. Guo, L.; Vargo, C.J.; Pan, Z.; Ding, W.; Ishwar, P. Big Social Data Analytics in Journalism and Mass Communication: Comparing Dictionary-Based Text Analysis and Unsupervised Topic Modeling. *J. Mass Commun. Q.* **2016**, *93*, 332–359. [CrossRef]
6. Bertoldi, P.; Boza-Kiss, B. Analysis of barriers and drivers for the development of the ESCO markets in Europe. *Energy Policy* **2017**, *107*, 345–355. [CrossRef]

7. Kangas, H.-L.; Lazarevic, D.; Kivimaa, P. Technical skills, disinterest and non-functional regulation: Barriers to building energy efficiency in Finland viewed by energy service companies. *Energy Policy* **2018**, *114*, 63–76. [CrossRef]
8. Jenkins, K.E.H.; Hopkins, D. (Eds.) *Transitions in Energy Efficiency and Demand: The Emergence, Diffusion and Impact of Low-Carbon Innovation*; Routledge: London, UK, 2020.
9. Sorrell, S.; O'Malley, E.J.; Schleich, J.; Scott, S. (Eds.) *The Economics of Energy Efficiency: Barrieres to Cost-Effective Investment*; Elgar: Cheltenham, UK, 2004; 349p.
10. Schleich, J. *The Economics of Energy Efficiency: Barriers to Profitable Investments*; European Investment Bank (EIB): Luxembourg, 2007.
11. Gouldson, A.; Kerr, N.; Millward-Hopkins, J.; Freeman, M.C.; Topi, C.; Sullivan, R. Innovative financing models for low carbon transitions: Exploring the case for revolving funds for domestic energy efficiency programmes. *Energy Policy* **2015**, *86*, 739–748. [CrossRef]
12. Fylan, F.; Glew, D.; Smith, M.; Johnston, D.; Brooke-Peat, M.; Miles-Shenton, D.; Fletcher, M.; Aloise-Young, P.; Gorse, C. Reflections on retrofits: Overcoming barriers to energy efficiency among the fuel poor in the United Kingdom. *Energy Res. Soc. Sci.* **2016**, *21*, 190–198. [CrossRef]
13. Borgeson, M.; Zimring, M.; Goldman, C. *The Limits of Financing for Energy Efficiency*; Lawrence Berkeley National Laboratory: Berkeley, CA, USA, 2012.
14. Winther, T.; Gurigard, K. Energy performance contracting (EPC): A suitable mechanism for achieving energy savings in housing cooperatives? Results from a Norwegian pilot project. *Energy Effic.* **2016**, *10*, 577–596. [CrossRef]
15. Bertone, E.; Stewart, R.A.; Sahin, O.; Alam, M.; Zou, P.X.; Buntine, C.; Marshall, C. Guidelines, barriers and strategies for energy and water retrofits of public buildings. *J. Clean. Prod.* **2018**, *174*, 1064–1078. [CrossRef]
16. European Environment Agency. Energy Prosumers in Europe: Citizen Participation in the Energy Transition. LU: Publications Office. 2022. Available online: https://data.europa.eu/doi/10.2800/030218 (accessed on 2 August 2024).
17. Hanke, F.; Grossmann, K.; Sandmann, L. Excluded despite their support—The perspectives of energy-poor households on their participation in the German energy transition narrative. *Energy Res. Soc. Sci.* **2023**, *104*, 103259. [CrossRef]
18. Heller, R. Financing Rooftop Solar for Single-Family Rental Properties. In *Sustainable Real Estate*; Walker, T., Krosinsky, C., Hasan, L.N., Kibsey, S.D., Eds.; Palgrave Studies in Sustainable Business in Association with Future Earth Series; Springer International Publishing: Cham, Switzerland, 2019; pp. 313–327. Available online: https://link.springer.com/10.1007/978-3-319-94565-1_12 (accessed on 12 December 2024).
19. Bleyl-Androschin, J.W.; Seefeldt, F.; Eikmeier, B. *How Much Energy Efficiency Can Energy Contracting Deliver to the Residential Sector in Germany?* European Council for an Energy-Efficient Economy: Stockholm, Sweden, 2009.
20. Polzin, F.; von Flotow, P.; Nolden, C. What encourages local authorities to engage with energy performance contracting for retrofitting? Evidence from German municipalities. *Energy Policy* **2016**, *94*, 317–330. [CrossRef]
21. Sesana, M.M.; Salvalai, G.; Della Valle, N.; Melica, G.; Bertoldi, P. Towards harmonising Energy Performance Certificate Indicators in Europe. *J. Build. Eng.* **2024**, *95*, 110323. [CrossRef]
22. Uddin, M.; Siddik, A.B.; Yuhuan, Z.; Naeem, M.A. Fintech and environmental efficiency: The dual role of foreign direct investment in G20 nations. *J. Environ. Manag.* **2024**, *360*, 121211. [CrossRef]
23. Ebirim, G.U.; Odonkor, B. Enhancing global economic inclusion with Fintech innovations and accessibility. *Financ. Account. Res. J.* **2024**, *6*, 648–673. [CrossRef]
24. Yáñez-Valdés, C.; Guerrero, M. Equity crowdfunding platforms and sustainable impacts: Encountering investors and technological initiatives for tackling social and environmental challenges. *Eur. J. Innov. Manag.* **2024**, *27*, 2326–2350. [CrossRef]
25. Poortinga, W.; Steg, L.; Vlek, C.; Wiersma, G. Household preferences for energy-saving measures: A conjoint analysis. *J. Econ. Psychol.* **2003**, *24*, 49–64. [CrossRef]
26. Steg, L.; Vlek, C. Encouraging pro-environmental behaviour: An integrative review and research agenda. *J. Environ. Psychol.* **2009**, *29*, 309–317. [CrossRef]
27. Ek, K.; Söderholm, P. The devil is in the details: Household electricity saving behavior and the role of information. *Energy Policy* **2009**, *38*, 1578–1587. [CrossRef]
28. Gadenne, D.; Sharma, B.; Kerr, D.; Smith, T. The influence of consumers' environmental beliefs and attitudes on energy saving behaviours. *Energy Policy* **2011**, *39*, 7684–7694. [CrossRef]
29. Ramos, A.; Labandeira, X.; Löschel, A. Pro-environmental Households and Energy Efficiency in Spain. *Environ. Resour. Econ.* **2015**, *63*, 367–393. [CrossRef]
30. Trotta, G. Factors affecting energy-saving behaviours and energy efficiency investments in British households. *Energy Policy* **2018**, *114*, 529–539. [CrossRef]
31. Caird, S.; Roy, R.; Herring, H. Improving the energy performance of UK households: Results from surveys of consumer adoption and use of low- and zero-carbon technologies. *Energy Effic.* **2008**, *1*, 149–166. [CrossRef]

32. Roth, L.; Lowitzsch, J.; Yildiz, Ö. Which (co-)ownership types in renewables are associated with the willingness to adopt energy-efficient technologies and energy-conscious behaviour? Data from German households. *Energy Policy* **2023**, *180*, 113683. [CrossRef]
33. Nair, G.; Gustavsson, L.; Mahapatra, K. Factors influencing energy efficiency investments in existing Swedish residential buildings. *Energy Policy* **2010**, *38*, 2956–2963. [CrossRef]
34. Ameli, N.; Brandt, N. What Impedes Household Investment in Energy Efficiency and Renewable Energy? *Int. Rev. Environ. Resour. Econ.* **2015**, *8*, 101–138. [CrossRef]
35. Wasiuzzaman, S.; Pungut, N.N.H.; Don, M.K.S.M. Crowdfunding green projects in Brunei: Awareness and investing preferences. *Manag. Environ. Qual. Int. J.* **2021**, *32*, 1383–1400. [CrossRef]
36. Appiah-Otoo, I.; Song, N.; Acheampong, A.O.; Yao, X. Crowdfunding and renewable energy development: What does the data say? *Int. J. Energy Res.* **2022**, *46*, 1837–1852. [CrossRef]
37. Cicchiello, A.F.; Gatto, A.; Salerno, D. At the nexus of circular economy, equity crowdfunding and renewable energy sources: Are enterprises from green countries more performant? *J. Clean. Prod.* **2023**, *410*, 136932. [CrossRef]
38. Hrovatin, N.; Cagno, E.; Dolšak, J.; Zorić, J. How important are perceived barriers and drivers versus other contextual factors for the adoption of energy efficiency measures: An empirical investigation in manufacturing SMEs. *J. Clean. Prod.* **2021**, *323*, 129123. [CrossRef]
39. Roth, L.; Lowitzsch, J.; Yildiz, Ö.; Hashani, A. Does (Co-)ownership in renewables matter for an electricity consumer's demand flexibility? Empirical evidence from Germany. *Energy Res. Soc. Sci.* **2018**, *46*, 169–182. [CrossRef]
40. Flaute, M.; Großmann, A.; Lutz, C.; Nieters, A. Macroeconomic Effects of Prosumer Households in Germany. *Int. J. Energy Econ. Policy* **2017**, *7*, 146–155.
41. Hirsch, D.; Padley, M.; Stone, J.; Valadez-Martinez, L. The Low Income Gap: A New Indicator Based on a Minimum Income Standard. *Soc. Indic. Res.* **2020**, *149*, 67–85. [CrossRef]
42. Thayer, J.D. *Stepwise Regression as an Exploratory Data Analysis Procedure*; American Educational Research Association: Washington, DC, USA, 2002.
43. Hong, X.; Mitchell, R.J. Backward elimination model construction for regression and classification using leave-one-out criteria. *Int. J. Syst. Sci.* **2007**, *38*, 101–113. [CrossRef]
44. Ruengvirayudh, P.; Brooks, G.P. Comparing Stepwise Regression Models to the Best-Subsets Models, or, the Art of Stepwise. *Gen. Linear Model J.* **2016**, *42*, 1–14.
45. Agostinelli, C. Robust stepwise regression. *J. Appl. Stat.* **2002**, *29*, 825–840. [CrossRef]
46. Wang, Q.; Koval, J.J.; Mills, C.A.; Lee, K.-I.D. Determination of the Selection Statistics and Best Significance Level in Backward Stepwise Logistic Regression. *Commun. Stat.-Simul. Comput.* **2007**, *37*, 62–72. [CrossRef]
47. Feng, C.; Wang, H.; Lu, N.; Chen, T.; He, H.; Lu, Y.; Tu, X.M. Log-transformation and its implications for data analysis. *Shanghai Arch. Psychiatry* **2014**, *26*, 105–109. [CrossRef]
48. Hammouri, H.M.; Sabo, R.T.; Alsaadawi, R.; Kheirallah, K.A. Handling Skewed Data: A Comparison of Two Popular Methods. *Appl. Sci.* **2020**, *10*, 6247. [CrossRef]
49. Sahinler, S.; Topuz, D. Bootstrap and jackknife resampling algorithms for estimation of regression parameters. *J. Appl. Quant. Methods* **2007**, *2*, 188–199.
50. Cribari-Neto, F.; Zarkos, S.G. Bootstrap methods for heteroskedastic regression models: Evidence on estimation and testing. *Econ. Rev.* **1999**, *18*, 211–228. [CrossRef]
51. Streukens, S.; Leroi-Werelds, S. Bootstrapping and PLS-SEM: A step-by-step guide to get more out of your bootstrap results. *Eur. Manag. J.* **2016**, *34*, 618–632. [CrossRef]
52. Filho, D.F.; Silva, L.; Pires, A.; Malaquias, C. *Living with Outliers: How to Detect Extreme Observations in Data Analysis*; BIB—Revista Brasileira De Informação Bibliográfica Em Ciências Sociais: São Paulo, Brazil, 2023.
53. Radtke, J.; Yildiz, Ö.; Roth, L. Does Energy Community Membership Change Sustainable Attitudes and Behavioral Patterns? Empirical Evidence from Community Wind Energy in Germany. *Energies* **2022**, *15*, 822. [CrossRef]
54. Bauwens, T. Explaining the diversity of motivations behind community renewable energy. *Energy Policy* **2016**, *93*, 278–290. [CrossRef]
55. Bauwens, T.; Eyre, N. Exploring the links between community-based governance and sustainable energy use: Quantitative evidence from Flanders. *Ecol. Econ.* **2017**, *137*, 163–172. [CrossRef]
56. Hossain, M. Grassroots innovation: The state of the art and future perspectives. *Technol. Soc.* **2018**, *55*, 63–69. [CrossRef]
57. Bauwens, T.; Schraven, D.; Drewing, E.; Radtke, J.; Holstenkamp, L.; Gotchev, B.; Yildiz, Ö. Conceptualizing community in energy systems: A systematic review of 183 definitions. *Renew. Sustain. Energy Rev.* **2021**, *156*, 111999. [CrossRef]
58. Roth, L.; Yildiz, Ö.; Lowitzsch, J. An Empirical Approach to Differences in Flexible Electricity Consumption Behaviour of Urban and Rural Populations—Lessons Learned in Germany. *Sustainability* **2021**, *13*, 9028. [CrossRef]

59. Goulden, M.; Bedwell, B.; Rennick-Egglestone, S.; Rodden, T.; Spence, A. Smart grids, smart users? The role of the user in demand side management. *Energy Res. Soc. Sci.* **2014**, *2*, 21–29. [CrossRef]
60. Rommel, J.; Radtke, J.; von Jorck, G.; Mey, F.; Yildiz, Ö. Community renewable energy at a crossroads: A think piece on degrowth, technology, and the democratization of the German energy system. *J. Clean. Prod.* **2018**, *197*, 1746–1753. [CrossRef]
61. Hanke, F.; Guyet, R.; Feenstra, M. Do renewable energy communities deliver energy justice? Exploring insights from 71 European cases. *Energy Res. Soc. Sci.* **2021**, *80*, 102244. [CrossRef]
62. Krupa, D.; Buszko, M. Age-dependent differences in using FinTech products and services—Young customers versus other adults. *PLoS ONE* **2023**, *18*, e0293470. [CrossRef] [PubMed]
63. Hanke, F.; Lowitzsch, J. Empowering Vulnerable Consumers to Join Renewable Energy Communities—Towards an Inclusive Design of the Clean Energy Package. *Energies* **2020**, *13*, 1615. [CrossRef]
64. European Commission. Directorate-General for Energy. State of the Energy Union Report 2023 (Pursuant to Regulation (EU) 2018/1999 on the Governance of the Energy Union and Climate Action) (COM/2023/650 Final). Report from the Commission to the European Parliament, the Council, the European Economic and Social Committee, and the Committee of the Regions. 2023. Available online: https://eur-lex.europa.eu/legal-content/EN/TXT/?uri=CELEX:52023DC0650 (accessed on 31 January 2025).
65. Heldeweg, M.A.; Séverine, S. Renewable energy communities as 'socio-legal institutions': A normative frame for energy decentralization? *Renew. Sustain. Energy Rev.* **2020**, *119*, 109518. [CrossRef]

FinTech

Communication

Empowering Global Supply Chains Through Blockchain-Based Platforms: New Evidence from the Coffee Industry

Tommaso Agnola [1], Luca Ambrosini [1], Edoardo Beretta [2,*] and Giuliano Gremlich [1]

1 Dipartimento Tecnologie Innovative, Scuola Universitaria Professionale della Svizzera Italiana, 6962 Lugano, Switzerland; tommaso.agnola@supsi.ch (T.A.); luca.ambrosini@supsi.ch (L.A.); giuliano.gremlich@supsi.ch (G.G.)

2 Institute of Economics, Università della Svizzera Italiana, 6900 Lugano, Switzerland

* Correspondence: edoardo.beretta@usi.ch

Abstract: Global supply chains, especially in commodity trading, are plagued by fragmentation, lack of transparency, and trust deficits among participants. These issues lead to inefficiencies, increased costs, and an over-reliance on intermediaries. The present Communication describes a blockchain-based platform that leverages Self-Sovereign Identity (SSI) and Verifiable Credentials (VCs) to address these challenges in supply chain management. Developed in collaboration with coffee industry stakeholders, our approach proposes a platform with an integrated marketplace for seller discovery, enables precise order definition with detailed terms and conditions, and actively guides both buyers and sellers throughout the shipping process, managing financial guarantees and ensuring a secure transaction flow. The platform is compatible with both traditional banking infrastructure and modern crypto-based systems, enabling seamless financial transactions. In cases where disputes arise, we empower users to easily collect all communications and documents to present to legal authorities, expediting the resolution process. The platform is implemented using the Internet Computer Protocol (ICP) for secure, on-chain storage and application hosting, and is integrated with the Ethereum blockchain to leverage its extensive decentralized finance (DeFi) ecosystem, significant liquidity, and robust stablecoin infrastructure, thereby facilitating secure financial transactions. Moreover, we introduce an SSI-based authentication and authorization framework that spans across the entire platform, including both the Ethereum Virtual Machine (EVM) and Internet Computer Protocol (ICP), enabling unified role-based access control through verifiable credentials. A value-added of the present Communication, the framework is demonstrated by means of a detailed case study in the coffee industry, highlighting the technical challenges addressed during implementation. While quantitative efficiency metrics will be established through upcoming real-world testing with industry partners, the platform's design aims to streamline operations by reducing intermediary dependencies and automating key processes. Finally, the Communication provides insights into its adaptability to other industries facing comparable supply chain challenges, presenting an approach focused on enhancing trust and reducing reliance on intermediaries.

Keywords: blockchain-based platform; Ethereum; global supply chains; internet computer protocol (ICP); peer-to-peer negotiation; self-sovereign identity (SSI); verifiable credential (VC)

JEL Classification: E44; O32; O33

1. Introduction

The present Communication aims at exploring an emerging topic that consists of potential blockchain-related solutions to foster global supply chains. In fact, after the COVID-19 pandemic and lockdowns, which have highlighted the precariousness of global value chains [1,2], there is an increasing need to find solutions based on new technologies to ensure the efficient functioning of the global supply chain even in economically uncertain times. Furthermore, while traditionally associated with cryptocurrencies, the blockchain, described as 'an open, distributed ledger that can record transactions between two parties efficiently and in a verifiable and permanent way' [3], also offers a versatile foundation to address the challenges of trust, coordination, and data management in various sectors.

The following Communication, therefore, contextualizes the topic of blockchain-related solutions for the global supply chain and provides a practical example to manage the transaction flows of one of the most highly demanded commodities worldwide, namely coffee and coffee-related products.

1.1. Global Supply Chain, Blockchain-Based Solutions and the Coffee Industry: A Literature Review

The scientific community began rather recently to analyze the potential use of blockchain to cope with the challenges posed by the global supply chain in an interconnected world economy. For example, Roy [4] highlights that 'Blockchain technology has found significant success in all fields, including the banking and finance sector, health, manufacturing, transportation, and many others', while Tiwari et al. [5] find that blockchain is particularly helpful whenever third-party logistics is involved. In fact, as Liu et al. [6] summed up, 'Blockchain technology can be used to record real data at various nodes in the supply chain and can achieve timely data sharing and full traceability of the entire life cycle of products in the supply chain'. The impact on 'supply chain capabilities and supply chain flexibility of firms' is also 'notable' [7]. In particular, its 'transparency' [8] and 'traceability' [9] are features that are particularly appreciated by its users.

The growing importance of blockchain solutions for supply chains mirrors the increasing importance of international trade in the global economy. As shown in Figure 1, since 1970, global imports and exports of goods and services have more than doubled as a percentage of the global GDP, growing from less than 13% to nearly 30% by 2023. This dramatic increase reflects the deepening interconnectedness of the global economy, where almost one-third of global GDP now depends on smooth-functioning supply chains [10]. The concept of the 'spatial division of labor', which implies the 'organization of certain production tasks in particular regions and geographical areas and/or concentration of certain economic sectors in particular' [11], has led to the creation of complex trade dependency networks. The COVID-19 pandemic starkly demonstrated the vulnerability of these networks, contributing to an unprecedented 2.9% decrease in global GDP in 2020—a decline that exceeded even the 1.4% drop during the global financial crisis of 2009 [12].

Multiple empirical studies indicate that blockchain promotes transparency, traceability and operational integrity, and can also improve product quality, optimize production costs, and reduce fraud [13–16]. In agriculture, for example, a hypothetical soybean trade from Jamestown (North Dakota) to China could yield savings of 2.3 cents per bushel—with a reference price of USD 3.56—while cutting the total shipping time by roughly 41% [17]. In particular, value-at-risk estimates show a further reduction of 2.6 cents per bushel. Beyond these direct operational gains, industry research suggests that blockchain helps minimize administrative overhead, fosters new business models, and supports revenue growth [18]. However, most of these projections are derived from early-stage implementations, leaving the full quantitative impact on supply chain efficiency and financial performance to be fully substantiated as technology matures [19].

Given the opportunities for technological advance embedded in the blockchain, the present Communication further assesses a potential additional solution to successfully cope with global supply chains and avoid unexpected disruptions.

Figure 1. Global imports and exports of goods and services (% of global GDP), 1970–2023; Own representation based on The World Bank [20,21].

If we further restrict the field of analysis to the coffee industry, which is interesting because it involves producing countries often particularly geographically far from the nations of destination, blockchain-based solutions have been identified in the economic literature to 'promote sustainability [. . .] through increased traceability and transparency' [22] and to 'support the ecological embeddedness of the coffee supply chain' [23]. Moreover, 'when applied to the coffee supply chain, blockchain allows everyone to know where their coffee came from and the conditions under which it was shipped and produced' [24].

As highlighted in Table 1, the top 10 of all countries producing coffee and coffee-related products belongs to low-income (Ethiopia, Uganda) and lower-middle-income economies (Honduras, India, Vietnam), while the remaining countries (Brazil, Colombia, Indonesia) are upper-middle-income nations [25]. Figure 2 further confirms the logistic complexity and economic interconnectedness of the trade flows involving coffee and coffee-related products.

Table 1. Coffee industry and top-producing countries *.

	% of Production	Total Production (2023/2024, 60 Kg Bags)
Brazil	39%	66.3 milion
Vietnam	17%	29.1 milion
Colombia	7%	12.2 milion
Ethiopia	5%	8.35 milion
Indonesia	5%	8.15 milion

Table 1. *Cont.*

	% of Production	Total Production (2023/2024, 60 Kg Bags)
Uganda	4%	6.4 milion
India	4%	6.1 milion
Honduras	3%	5.3 milion
Peru	2%	4 milion
Mexico	2%	3.87 milion

* Source: [26].

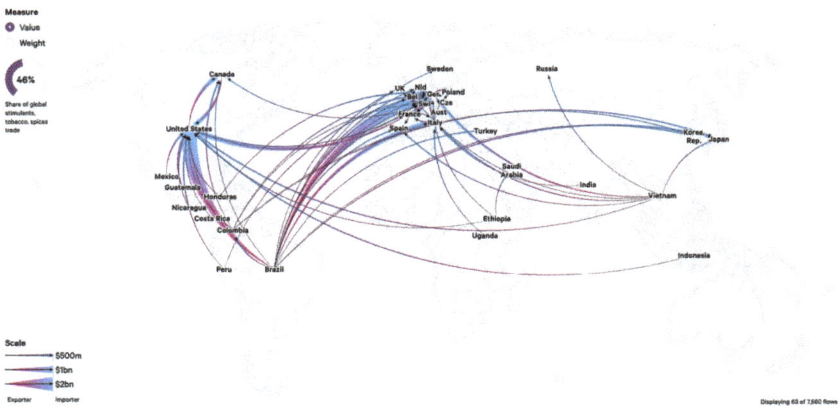

Figure 2. Value of trade flows of coffee-related products [27] (husks and skins; (not) roasted; (not) decaffeinated).

At the same time, the fact that these countries ranking the highest in the production of coffee and coffee-related products might be in particular need of diffuse access to non-traditional (i.e., non-banking) solutions due to having an account ownership rate below the global average (apart from Brazil and India) (Table 2) is another concrete explanation for the potential relevance of blockchain technology. The latter is indirectly confirmed by the share of the population in these nations—this being significantly higher than that in countries like Germany (12%) or the United States (15%) in 2022—that has been confirmed to own and/or use cryptocurrencies, which, notably, can be attributed to blockchain-related technological advances. Clearly enough, 'implementing blockchain throughout the coffee industry requires collaboration and industry-wide adoption, as a fragmented approach could limit its effectiveness' [28].

In the realm of global coffee trading, the application of cryptocurrencies extends beyond digital assets to function as effective trade currencies and contract facilitators. Using the intrinsic qualities of blockchain technology, cryptocurrencies enable direct peer-to-peer financial exchanges that bypass traditional banking intermediaries, significantly reducing transaction fees and improving the speed of cross-border payments [29]. This shift not only democratizes financial access for coffee producers, particularly in regions underserved by traditional banks [30], but also fosters greater economic stability by shielding them from local currency fluctuations [31]. Furthermore, the integration of smart contracts automates and enforces trade agreements transparently, ensuring that payments are released only after verified delivery and adherence to agreed standards, minimizing disputes and administrative overhead [32].

Table 2. Account ownership (% age 15+) and share of respondents having indicated they either owned or used cryptocurrencies [20,26,33].

	Account Ownership (% Age 15+)					Share of Respondents Having Indicated They Either Owned or Used Cryptocurrencies
	2011	**2014**	**2017**	**2021**	**2022**	**Latest Available Data (2021–2023)**
Brazil	55.9%	68.1%	70.0%	84.0%	-	7.8%
Vietnam	21.4%	31.0%	30.8%	-	56.3%	18.7%
Colombia	30.4%	39.0%	45.8%	59.7%	-	4.8%
Ethiopia	-	21.8%	34.8%	-	46.5%	1.8%
Indonesia	19.6%	36.1%	48.9%	51.8%	-	4.5%
Uganda	20.5%	44.5%	59.2%	65.9%	-	1.2%
India	35.2%	53.1%	79.9%	77.5%	-	7.1
Honduras	20.5%	31.5%	45.3%	37.9%	-	2.3%
Peru	20.5%	29.0%	42.6%	57.5%	-	3.7%
Mexico	27.4%	39.1%	36.9%	-	49.0%	6.6%
World	50.6%	61.9%	68.5%	76.2%	-	6.8%

The critical need for such technological improvements in the coffee supply chain is underscored by the observations of Alamsyah et al. [34], who note the difficulty consumers face in verifying coffee quality relative to price, due to the complexity and opacity of the supply chain. This challenge points to a broader issue of maintaining fair production standards and mitigating the risk of disruptions. Addressing these concerns, global IT players, such as IBM, have begun to implement blockchain solutions to create more efficient supply chains that improve the transparency and reliability of the coffee trade, contributing to a better ecosystem for the global coffee farming community [35]. These technological advances are pivotal in transforming traditional supply chain operations into more secure, efficient, and equitable systems, thereby improving the overall integrity of the coffee market.

1.2. Added Value and Contribution to the Economic Literature

The contribution of the present Communication to the existing economic literature encompasses several key aspects:

- Analysis of coffee supply chain processes: The research examines key challenges in the coffee supply chain based on the current literature and industry standards:
  - Documentation requirements;
  - Trust barriers between distant trading partners;
  - Manual processing inefficiencies;
  - Reliance on intermediaries.
- Technical solutions framework: This Communication develops practical, innovative solutions that directly address identified challenges:
  - Implementation of Self-Sovereign Identity (SSI) for secure participant authentication;
  - Smart contract automation for financial guarantees and compliance;
  - Decentralized documentation management;
  - Integration of traditional and blockchain-based payment systems;
  - Streamlined dispute resolution mechanisms.
- Industry-specific research contribution: This research advances the emerging stream of research exploring blockchain-based solutions in specific economic sectors, as discussed in Section 1.1, with a particular focus on the following:

- Real-world implementation considerations;
- Technical architecture specifications;
- Cost–benefit analysis of the adoption.

- Practical implementation model: The framework specifically designed for the coffee industry carries out the following:
  - Addresses the challenges of coffee supply chains;
  - Considers the needs of both small producers and large traders;
  - Maintains compatibility with existing trading practices;
  - Offers scalability for future industry adoption.

This multifaceted contribution aims to enhance the efficiency and reliability of global trade operations. The proposed solutions, which combine technological innovation with practical applicability, contribute to building a more efficient, resilient, and flexible global economy [36–38].

2. Materials and Methods

The global coffee supply chain faces challenges in efficiency, transparency, and trust. We propose a platform that uses blockchain technology and self-sovereign identity (SSI) to address these issues.

Transparency and traceability problems arise from fragmentation and the absence of a unified tracking system, which obscures the origins of coffee beans and makes it difficult to verify authenticity, quality and sustainability [39]. This can potentially lead to frauds and a reduction in consumer trust. By recording every transaction, including all the documents and the money flows, on blockchain's immutable ledger, we enable participants to trace products from farm to cup, ensuring authenticity and compliance with standards.

Trust deficits and reliance on intermediaries are due to trust barriers caused by distance and cultural differences, which add costs and complexities, ultimately reducing profits and increasing prices [40]. Implementing SSI and Verifiable Credentials allows secure, authenticated identities. Trusted credentials verify legitimacy, enabling direct peer-to-peer transactions without intermediaries. Smart contracts automate negotiations and enforce agreements, improving efficiency.

Inefficient manual processes, such as paper documentation, cause errors and delays that slow down the supply chain [41,42]. By digitizing all documentation on the blockchain and implementing automated workflows, errors are minimized, and transactions are accelerated. Digital records improve efficiency and provide an auditable trail [43]. Dispute resolution is often hindered by the absence of transparent records: immutable blockchain records address this issue by providing a reliable and transparent basis for resolution. Authorized arbitrators can also access the necessary documentation, allowing for swift and equitable dispute resolution [44].

2.1. *Coffee Trading Process Overview*

The description of the trading process presented in this section is based on direct collaboration and structured interviews with key industry partners, specifically Alcomex SA, a Swiss-based coffee trading company, and their Brazilian partner JC Grossi & Fhilos. These companies have provided detailed information on their operational practices and requirements, ensuring that our understanding of the coffee trading process reflects current industry practices in the Brazil–Switzerland trade corridor. The information gathered through this direct engagement aligns and enriches the existing academic literature [45,46] on coffee trading processes. International coffee trading represents a complex ecosystem of transactions that involve multiple stakeholders on different continents. The process encompasses several structured phases, each critical to ensuring successful trade execution while managing the risks inherent in cross-border commodity transactions. We hereby review them in full detail.

2.1.1. Offer Publication and Discovery

The initial phase of coffee trading centers on market discovery, where sellers present their offerings to potential buyers. This process traditionally occurs through established channels, including trading houses, brokers, and industry-specific marketplaces [47]. Sellers, typically exporters or producer cooperatives, must provide comprehensive product information [47] including the following:

- Coffee origin and variety specification;
- Quality parameters and certifications;
- Available volume and minimum lot sizes;
- Indicative pricing structure;
- Possible delivery windows.

Figure 3 illustrates the typical flow of the coffee trading discovery process, highlighting the various channels through which buyers and sellers interact in the marketplace.

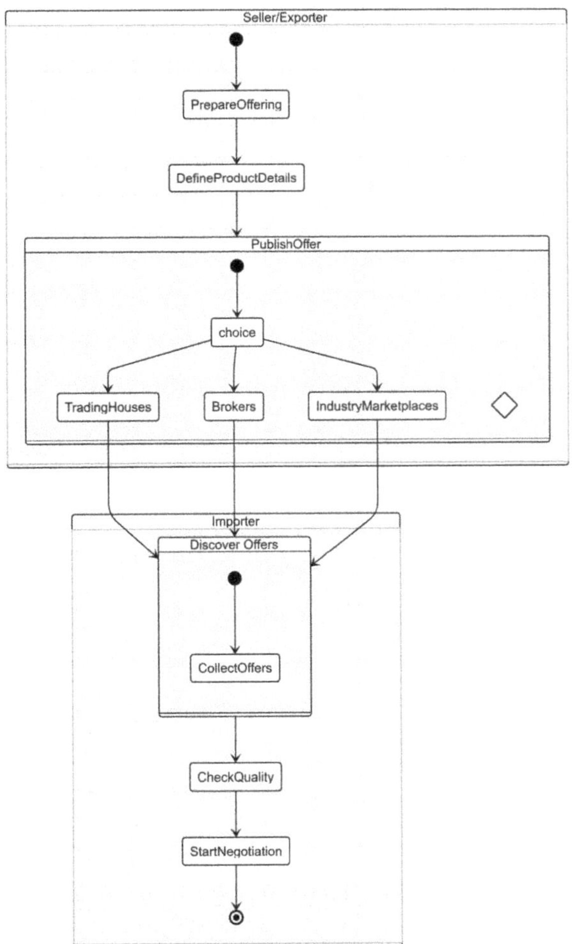

Figure 3. Coffee trading discovery process flowchart.

This discovery phase is crucial as it establishes the foundation for potential trading relationships and preliminary quality expectations. Buyers evaluate these offerings against their specific requirements, considering factors such as their blending needs, risk tolerance, and logistical capabilities.

2.1.2. Contract Negotiation

Upon establishing initial interest, parties enter into a structured negotiation process that involves multiple stages of increasing commitment. This phase is particularly critical, as it defines the legal and operational framework for the entire transaction. The coffee trading process is structured in three sequential phases depicted in Figures 4–6: Figure 4 shows the order definition phase where key terms are negotiated, Figure 5 illustrates the contract signature phase following the ESCC framework, and Figure 6 outlines the contract fulfillment phase with its documentation and payment execution requirements. Each stage necessitates specific documentation to proceed, creating a structured yet documentation-intensive workflow. Although this approach ensures proper risk management, it also introduces multiple points where operational efficiency could be improved through technological innovation.

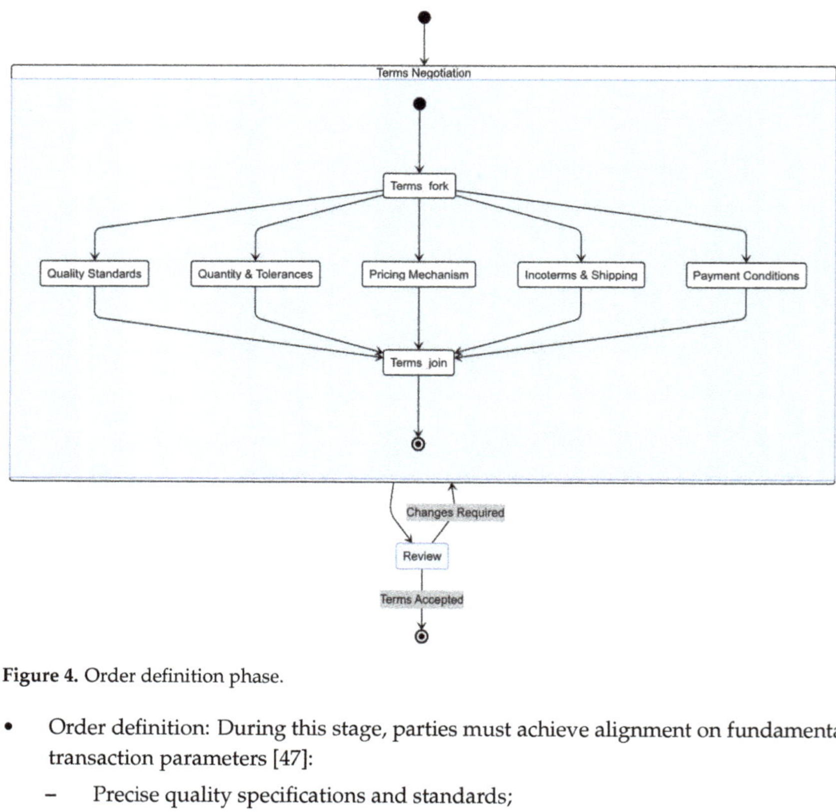

Figure 4. Order definition phase.

- Order definition: During this stage, parties must achieve alignment on fundamental transaction parameters [47]:
  - Precise quality specifications and standards;
  - Quantity commitments and tolerances;
  - Pricing mechanisms (fixed or differential);
  - Delivery terms and shipping windows;
  - Payment conditions and security requirements.

These elements require careful consideration, as they directly impact both parties' risk exposure and operational requirements. The selection of appropriate International

Commercial Terms Incoterms® proves particularly crucial as it delineates the transfer of costs, risks, and responsibilities between parties.

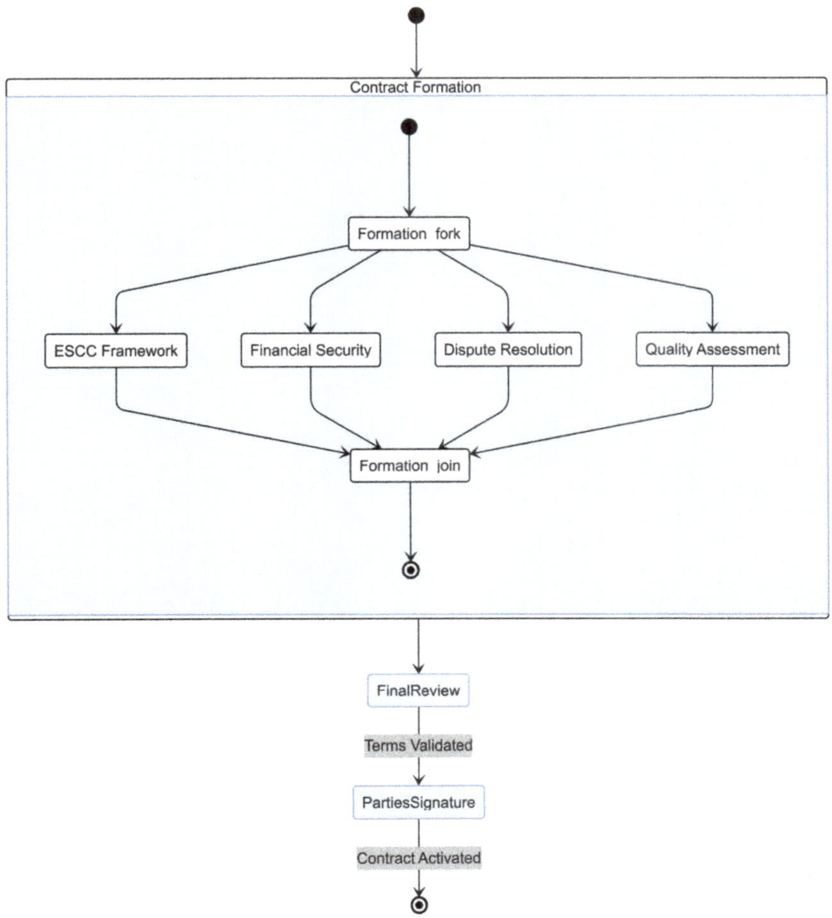

Figure 5. Contract signature phase.

- Order signature: Contract formation represents a critical milestone where parties formalize their commitments through legally binding agreements. Standard industry contracts, such as the European Standard Contract for Coffee (ESCC), provide the framework for these agreements [47], requiring the following:
  - Mutual agreement on all terms;
  - Financial security arrangements;
  - Dispute resolution mechanisms;
  - Quality assessment protocols.
- Contract fulfilment: The execution phase involves coordinated actions between multiple stakeholders to ensure the proper documentation and physical movement of goods. Essential documentation [47] includes the following:
  - Certificates of origin and quality;
  - Shipping documentation (bills of lading);
  - Insurance certificates;
  - Commercial documentation.

This documentation serves multiple purposes beyond mere compliance, as it facilitates payment processing, customs clearance, and quality verification.

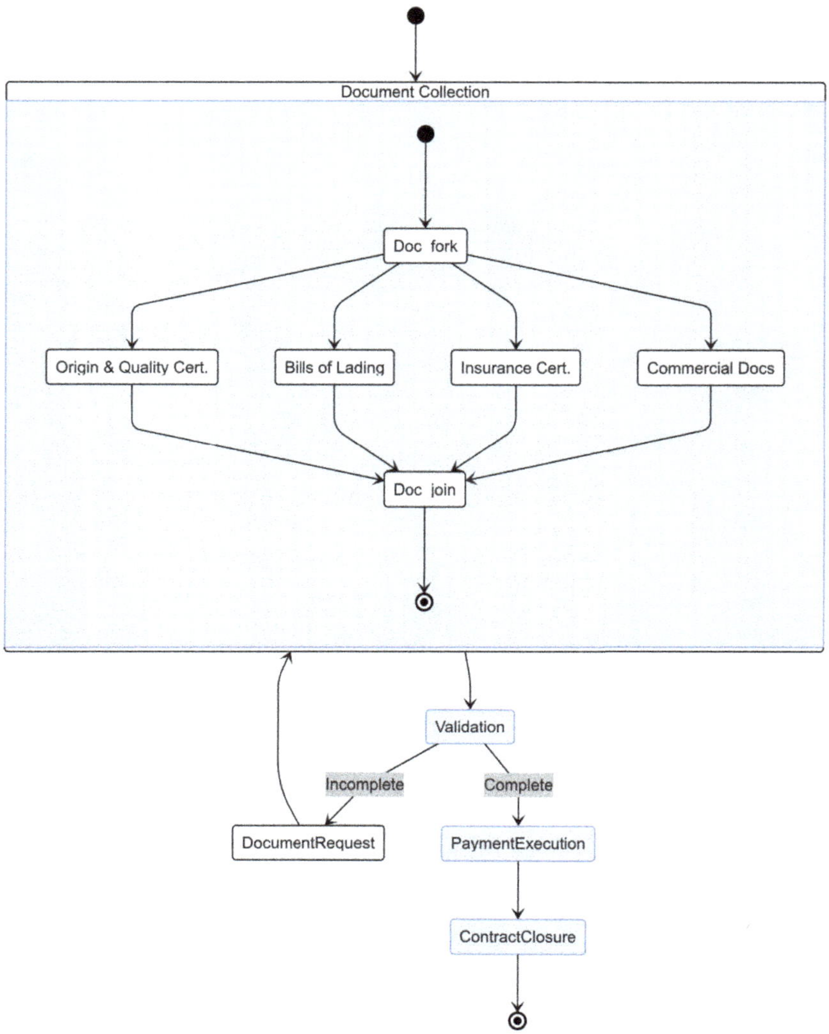

Figure 6. Contract fulfilment phase.

2.1.3. Dispute Management

The coffee industry has developed sophisticated mechanisms to handle disputes that may arise throughout the trading process. These mechanisms recognize the inherent challenges of cross-border trade and provide structured approaches to resolution. Figures 7–9 illustrate the structured approach to dispute resolution in coffee trading. More specifically, Figure 7 shows the initial phase of issue identification and classification, where problems are classified based on their nature (quality or other issues) and the corresponding time windows are assigned according to the ESCC guidelines [47]. Furthermore, Figure 8 details the evidence collection process, emphasizing the parallel collection of historical transaction data, supporting documentation, and communication records, all crucial elements for building a comprehensive claim. Finally, Figure 9 describes the resolution pathways, demonstrating how disputes can be resolved through amicable settlement or formal arbitration, the latter requiring detailed review of documents and expert analysis. This systematic approach ensures that all disputes are handled efficiently while maintaining transparency and fairness throughout the process.

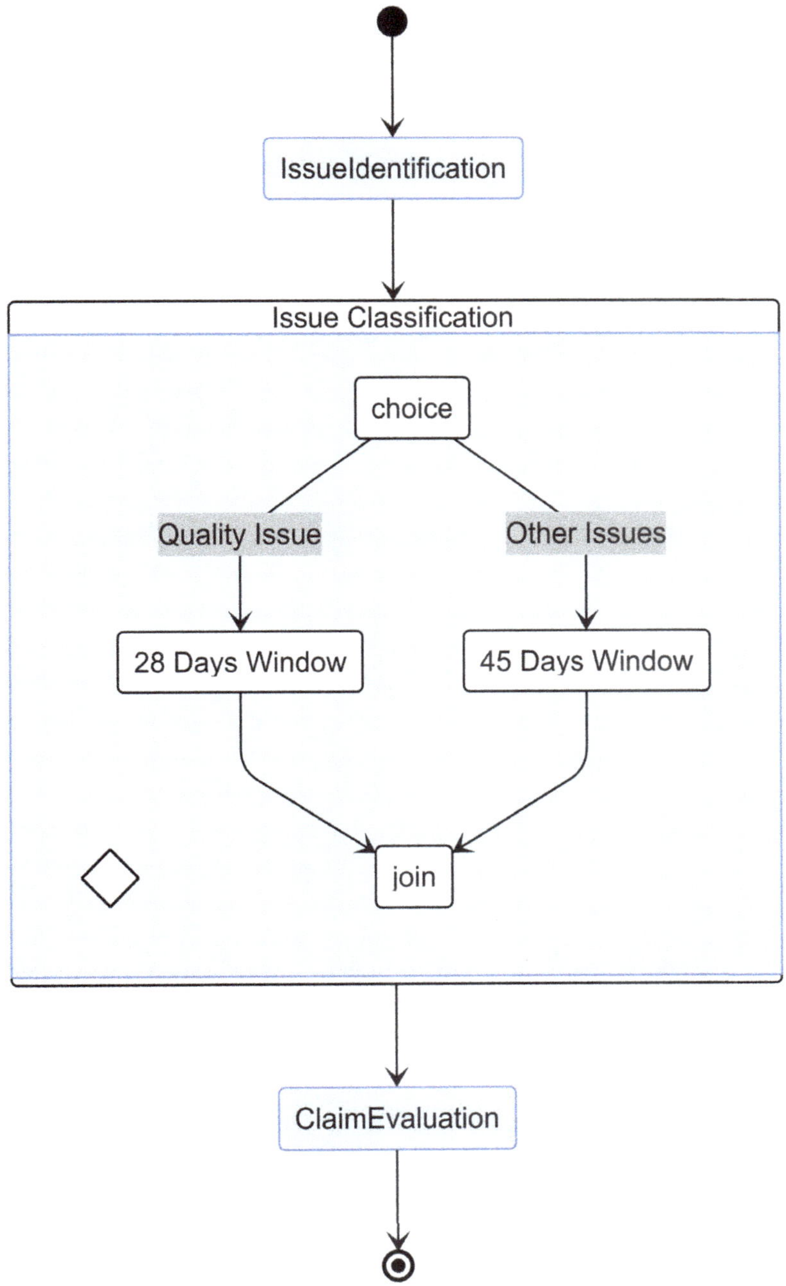

Figure 7. Issue identification.

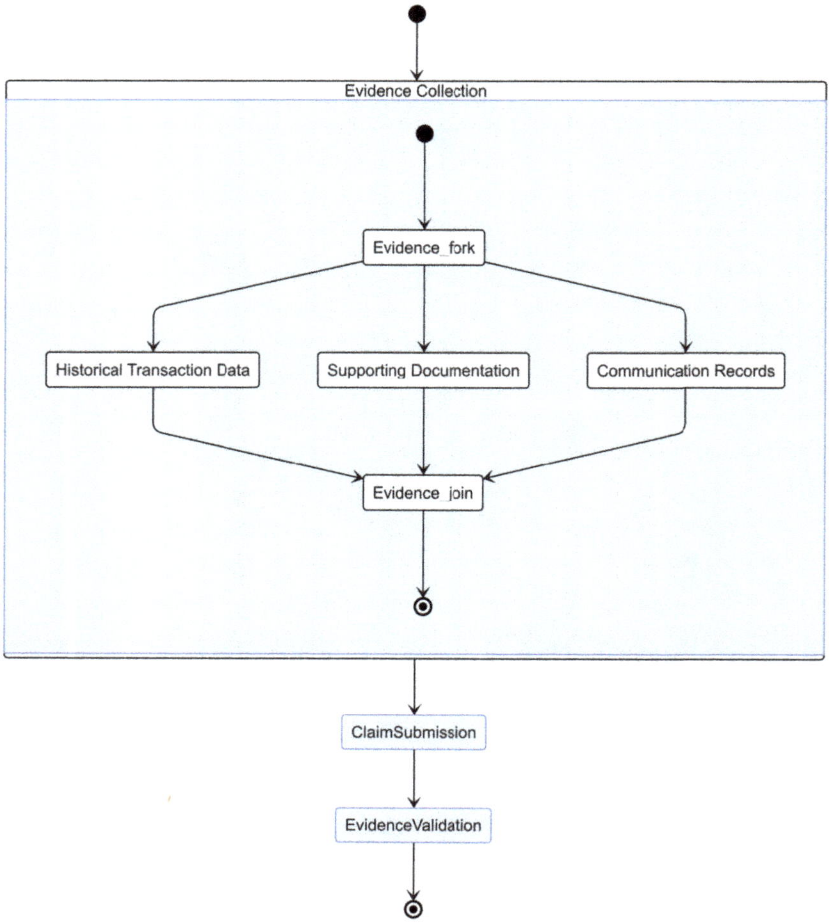

Figure 8. Evidence collection.

Common areas of dispute include the following:

- Quality variations from contracted specifications;
- Weight discrepancies beyond allowed tolerances;
- Shipping delays and logistics issues;
- Documentation discrepancies.

Industry standards establish specific time frames for claim submission, typically allowing 28 days for quality-related claims and 45 days for other issues. The resolution process often involves independent quality analysis and arbitration procedures, following established protocols under standard contracts like the ESCC [47].

This traditional trading framework, while comprehensive in its risk management approach, faces several operational challenges. The complex documentation requirements and sequential nature of document verification and approval processes can lead to delays and increased costs [48]. Moreover, the potential for documentation discrepancies or losses creates additional risks for trading parties, particularly in letter of credit transactions where strict compliance is required [49]. These challenges, coupled with the need for greater trust, transparency, and efficiency in the entire flow, highlight opportunities for technological innovation in the coffee trading ecosystem while maintaining the robust risk management framework that the industry requires.

The described processes have been empirically validated through collaboration with industry stakeholders. The practical insights gained from Alcomex SA and JC Grossi & Filhos have confirmed the academic findings while providing additional context specific to the Brazil–Switzerland trade corridor. This combination of theoretical framework and practical validation ensures a comprehensive and accurate representation of contemporary coffee trading processes.

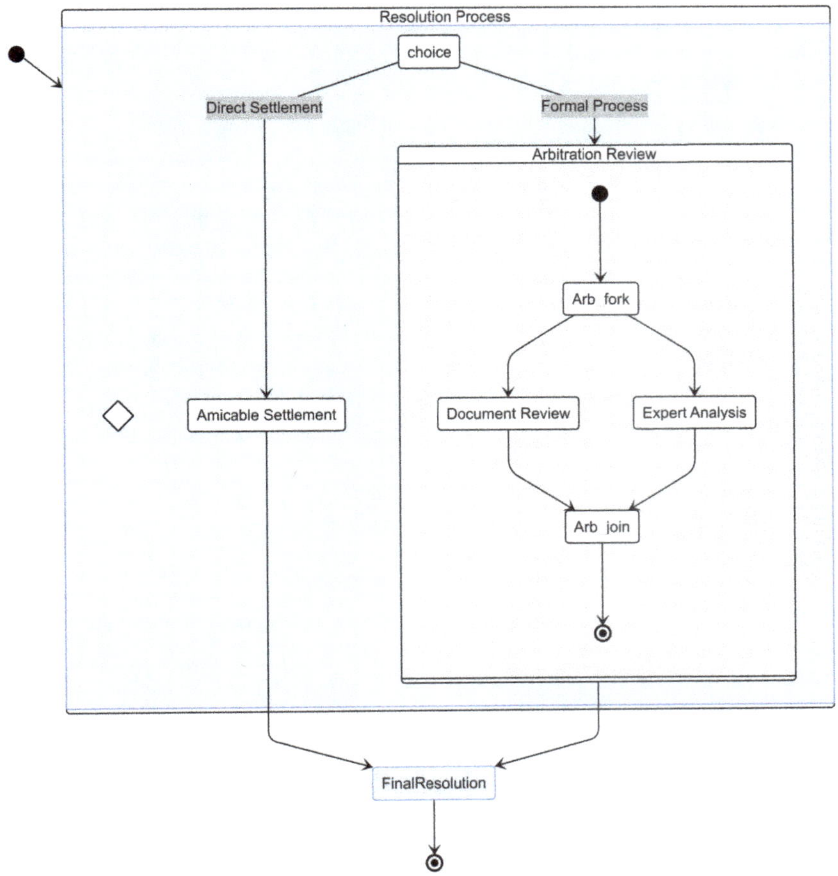

Figure 9. Dispute resolution.

2.2. *Overview of the Proposed Framework*

The framework requirements and design choices were informed by extensive consultation with our industry partners. Through a series of structured interviews and workshops with Alcomex SA and JC Grossi & Filhos, we gathered detailed requirements about trading processes, documentation needs, and common challenges in the Brazil–Switzerland coffee trade corridor. This direct industry input ensured that our technical solutions address real-world needs and align with established trading practices. To directly address the challenges outlined in the coffee supply chain, we develop a framework that integrates blockchain technology with the principles of Self-Sovereign Identity (SSI). SSI has proven to be particularly effective for decentralized identification, especially when combined with blockchain systems [50,51]. Our platform empowers buyers and sellers to discover each other and negotiate terms directly, managing transactions with minimal reliance on third parties. Using the potential of blockchain to reduce the need for intermediaries in decentralized markets [52,53], we enhance trust and streamline operations within the supply chain. The platform implements comprehensive order execution protocols, facilitating end-to-end monitoring of logistics and quality assurance parameters according to contractual specifications. Its integrated financial infrastructure incorporates both conventional banking instruments and distributed ledger-based guarantee mechanisms, allowing frictionless transaction processing while maintaining operational flexibility in various financial frameworks [54]. Our framework also addresses the core processes of international coffee trading by providing technological solutions that enhance efficiency while maintaining compatibility with established industry practices:

- Marketplace: The traditional coffee marketplace is transformed through a decentralized infrastructure where participants establish their presence using verifiable digital identities. By implementing SSI principles, exporters can create verifiable offers with authenticated quality certifications, while importers can confidently evaluate potential trading partners through validated credentials. This approach significantly reduces the information asymmetry typically present in international trade while maintaining the flexibility needed for complex commodity transactions [55].
- Contract negotiation: The negotiation process is enhanced through smart contracts [56] that encode standard trading terms while maintaining the adaptability required for international coffee transactions. The system supports the complete trading lifecycle, from initial order specification through final settlement, with key innovations including the following:
  - Automated financial guarantee management;
  - Integration of quality verification protocols;
  - Secure document management;
  - Milestone-based payment release mechanisms.

This automation significantly reduces the operational overhead traditionally associated with international coffee trading while enhancing transparency and trust between parties.

- Dispute management: The framework provides comprehensive support for dispute resolution through an immutable record of all trading activities and communications. This transparent audit trail, combined with automated enforcement of claim submission time frames and structured access for arbitrators, enhances the efficiency of dispute resolution while maintaining alignment with established industry practices.

These core functionalities are implemented through a sophisticated technical architecture that combines Ethereum's smart contract capabilities with the Internet Computer Protocol's scalable infrastructure, as detailed in the following sections. The solution maintains compatibility with traditional banking systems while introducing new efficiencies through blockchain technology, allowing a gradual transition from existing processes to more automated, transparent operations.

2.3. System Architecture

The system architecture presented in this Communication was developed by the authors as part of a research project funded by Innosuisse (Project ID: 103.518.1 IP-ICT). The research project, conducted in collaboration between the University of Applied Sciences and Arts of Southern Switzerland (SUPSI) and Kraft Bio Chain SA, aimed to create a decentralized platform for agricultural supply chains, with a specific focus on the coffee industry. The platform was designed and implemented by our research team to address the challenges identified in Section 2, particularly those related to transparency, trust, and efficiency in international coffee trading.

The system architecture is organized into several interconnected layers, leveraging Ethereum and the Internet Computer Protocol (ICP) to provide a secure, efficient, and user-friendly platform. Ethereum supports robust transaction logic and financial operations through smart contracts, while ICP's decentralized infrastructure enables scalable application hosting without traditional servers, improving both security and performance [57]. The architecture comprises the following layers, each fulfilling a specific function within the application:

- Identity layer: It manages decentralized identities and verifiable credentials using Self Sovereign Identity (SSI) standards. Moreover, it ensures that only authenticated and authorized participants engage in transactions.
- Application layer: It hosts the front-end and back-end on the ICP blockchain, providing a decentralized and scalable infrastructure without the need for traditional servers.
- Smart contract layer: It contains smart contracts deployed on the Ethereum blockchain. These smart contracts handle SSI authentication and manage financial operations through down payment services.
- Integration layer: It facilitates communication between the ICP and Ethereum blockchains. Moreover, it includes protocols for identity derivation and secure transaction signing, ensuring seamless interoperability, which refers to the ability of different blockchain systems to communicate, exchange data, and execute cross-chain operations.

Figure 10 illustrates the system architecture, showing the interconnected layers and their respective components, along with the relationships that enable seamless functionality across the platform.

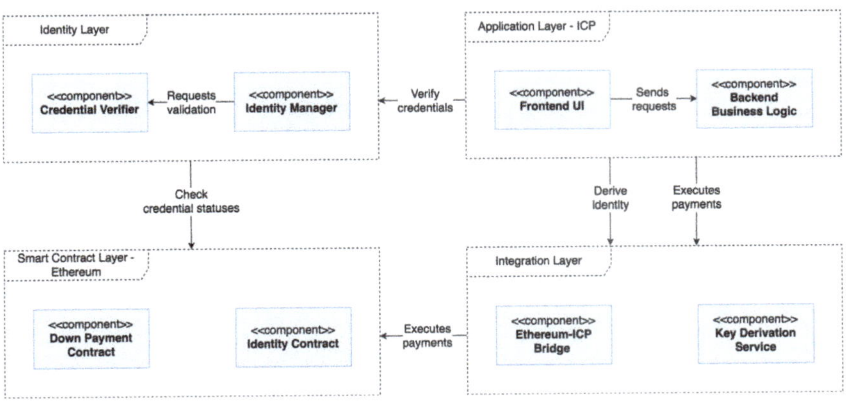

Figure 10. System architecture UML component diagram.

2.4. Roles and Participants

The platform also defines specific roles for participants in the supply chain, each with distinct responsibilities:

- Consortium: The platform operates under the oversight of an industry-specific consortium that manages member onboarding by evaluating and approving companies, issuing and revoking access credentials. This consortium not only oversees this specific platform but may supervise any service related to the management and exchange of goods.

- Exporter (seller): This person initiates trade offers, manages product listings, and completes shipment details. Exporters can be producers or suppliers looking to sell their commodities.
- Importer (buyer): This person engages with exporters, negotiates terms, approves, and supervises shipments. Importers are buyers seeking commodities for sale or processing.
- Certifier: This person verifies the credentials and authenticity of participants, certifies products and processes, ensuring compliance with industry standards and regulations. Certifiers play a crucial role in establishing trust within the platform.
- Arbiter: This person mediates disputes and facilitates resolution when disagreements arise. The arbitrator ensures that conflicts are resolved efficiently and fairly.

Each participant, identified through their role, accesses the platform using Verifiable Credentials (VCs), which grant them full control over their data while maintaining a decentralized structure. As shown in Figure 11, the "Triangle of Trust" model demonstrates how the consortium issues credentials, while only identifiers and cryptographic keys of participants are registered on the blockchain to preserve privacy [51]. The role of a "Participant" encompasses exporters, importers, certifiers, arbiters, and their respective employees, ensuring that all interactions align with the principles of self-sovereign identity and data autonomy. This structure eliminates intermediaries, reduces information asymmetries at the trade level [58] and ensures a secure, trust-based environment for all platform activities, aligning with current advancements in self-sovereign identity and data autonomy [59].

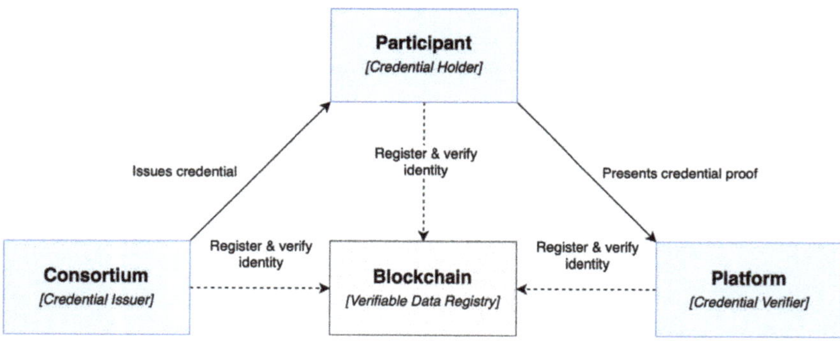

Figure 11. Triangle of trust.

2.5. Development Tools and Technologies

The platform leverages a combination of modern technologies to achieve its objectives:

- Programming languages:
  - Rust: This is used for developing some canisters (smart contracts) on the ICP blockchain. Rust provides safety and performance benefits, essential for secure blockchain applications.
  - TypeScript: This is used for developing some other canisters using the Azle Canister Development Kit (CDK), enabling flexible development on ICP with strong typing and ease of integration.
  - Solidity: This is used for writing smart contracts on the Ethereum blockchain. Solidity is the standard language for Ethereum development.
- Libraries and frameworks:
  - Identity management: The framework implements the W3C standards Decentralized Identifiers (DIDs) and Verifiable Credential (VCs) [59], ensuring inter-

operability and adherence to global identity management practices [60,61]. The Veramo library is utilized to manage identity functions, while protocols like DIDComm are adopted for secure messaging and credential exchange, enhancing the security and privacy of interactions on the platform;
  - Smart contracts: It utilizes OpenZeppelin's4 secure and community-vetted contract templates, providing a robust foundation for contract development.
  - Canister development: It uses Azle, a TypeScript-based Canister Development Kit (CDK), to write canisters on ICP, allowing for seamless TypeScript integration and expanded flexibility in canister development.
  - Wallet integration: It employs WalletConnect for secure communication between mobile wallets and decentralized applications, facilitating user-friendly interactions [62].
- Platforms:
  - Internet Computer Protocol: It provides a decentralized environment for hosting the application's front-end and back-end. In fact, ICP offers scalability and eliminates dependency on centralized servers [57];
  - Ethereum blockchain: This serves as the platform for executing smart contracts and handling financial transactions, benefiting from its mature ecosystem and widespread adoption. Additionally, Ethereum supports identity resolution through the DID method did:ethr, a recognized and widely adopted method within the SSI ecosystem, enabling decentralized and verifiable identity management [63].

2.6. *Security Measures*

Security is paramount in our platform, and several measures are implemented to protect users and their data:

- Private key management: Users' private keys are securely stored on user's smartphones, leveraging hardware security modules such as the Secure Enclave on iOS or the Trusted Execution Environment on Android. Biometric authentication adds an extra layer of security.
- Transaction signing: The "Sign-In with Ethereum" (SIWE) protocol enables secure interaction with ICP identities by signing a message using EVM keys. The signing operation is executed locally on the user's device, ensuring that private keys remain secure and are never transmitted or exposed to external entities [64].
- Data privacy: Sensitive data within Verifiable Credentials (VCs) are stored exclusively on the user's device. Only selected data, explicitly authorized by the user, are shared and stored to facilitate new commercial exchanges and allow participants to know their trading partners.
- Selective disclosure: The platform supports selective disclosure, allowing users to share only specific attributes within their Verifiable Credentials (VCs) while keeping other information private. This feature enables users to reveal only the necessary data for each interaction, enhancing privacy and maintaining control over personal information [51]. Future iterations of the platform will incorporate Zero Knowledge Proofs (ZKPs), enabling users to prove the validity of their credentials without revealing any underlying data. ZKPs represent a significant advancement in privacy-preserving technology, allowing parties to verify claims without exposing sensitive information [65]. Recent research demonstrates that ZKPs can be particularly effective in supply chain applications, allowing trust and verification while maintaining confidentiality of business-critical data [66]. Studies by Raikwar et al. [67] show that the integration of ZKP into blockchain-based trading platforms can reduce data exposure by up to 90% while maintaining the same level of verification certainty.

2.7. User Interface and Experience

The successful adoption of blockchain-based trading platforms in agricultural supply chains is highly dependent on their accessibility to users with varying levels of technological knowledge. This consideration is particularly crucial in the coffee industry, where many exporters are small-scale farmers or rural cooperatives that may have limited exposure to advanced digital technologies [68]. To address these challenges, our platform emphasizes simplicity and accessibility while maintaining the robust functionality required for international coffee trading. The following sections detail our approach to creating an inclusive user experience that accommodates varying levels of technological proficiency while ensuring secure and efficient trading operations. To ensure broad adoption, the platform is designed with user accessibility in mind:

- Mobile application: It functions as a digital wallet and identity manager. It allows users to manage credentials, approve transactions, and receive notifications in an intuitive way.
- Web application: It provides a comprehensive dashboard for managing negotiations, contracts, and supply chain operations. The user interface is designed to be intuitive and accommodating users with varying levels of technical expertise.
- Accessibility features: Multi-language support and guided workflows assist users in navigating complex processes. The platform emphasizes simplicity and clarity to reduce the learning curve.

3. Results

Before delving into the implementation details, it is essential to note that our research project concluded in its initial Proof-of-Concept (POC) phase, during which the core architectural components and fundamental functionalities of the platform were validated. The data and analysis presented in this section represent preliminary estimates derived from the POC implementation. To further validate the platform's effectiveness and gather comprehensive empirical data, collaborations with industry partners are scheduled for the coming months. These real-world implementations will enable thorough testing of the system's performance, scalability, and practical applicability in actual trading scenarios, providing valuable insights for future refinements and enhancements of the proposed solution.

3.1. Implementation Details

3.1.1. Decentralized Identity and Verifiable Credentials

We implement a decentralized identity system that empowers users with control over their digital identities:

- Credential issuance: Trusted authorities, such as industry consortia or certification bodies, issue verifiable credentials to companies. Companies, in turn, issue credentials to their employees, establishing a chain of trust.
- Credential storage: Credentials are securely stored on the user's mobile device or within the company's systems. This approach leverages SSI principles, ensuring portability and user sovereignty over credentials [69];
- Authentication process: Users authenticate by scanning QR codes and by approving requests within the mobile app. The platform acts as a verifier to validate credentials without storing or exposing sensitive information, thus maintaining privacy and security.

Figure 12 illustrates the credential issuance and verification process within the platform. The consortium generates and signs Verifiable Credentials (VCs) upon request from participants, who then store these credentials securely in their wallets. When participants request access to the platform, they present a Verifiable Presentation (VP), generated and signed using their VCs, which the platform validates by verifying signatures, temporal validity, and status. As explained, participants, such as companies, can issue credentials to their employees, extending the chain of trust and enabling secure delegation of responsibilities.

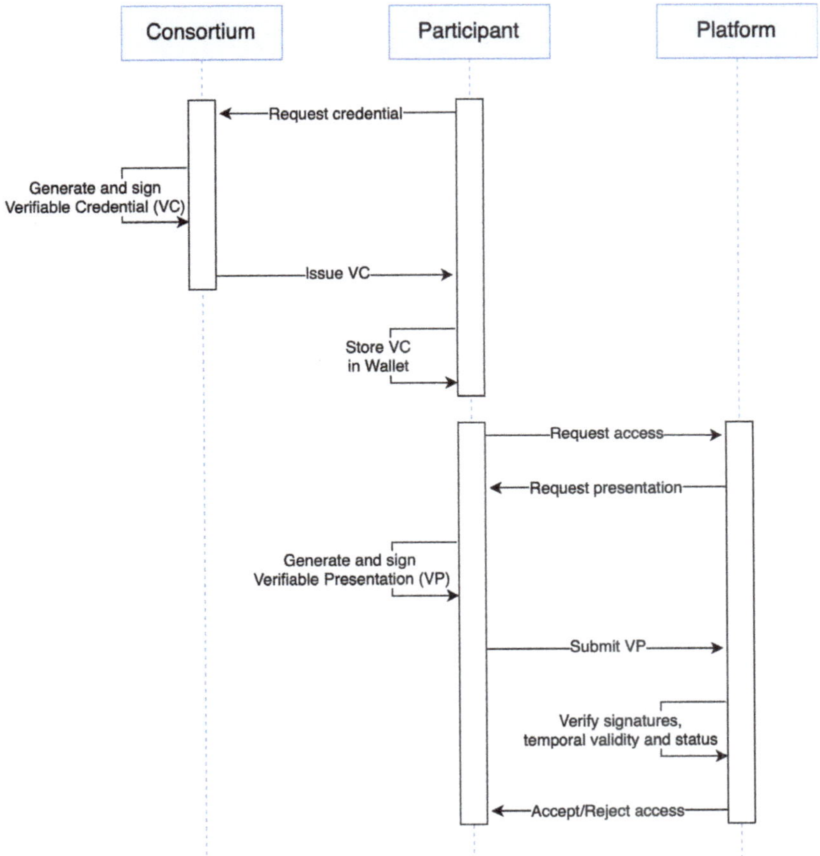

Figure 12. Verifiable Credential issuance and verification

3.1.2. Integration of ICP and Ethereum

Our platform seamlessly integrates the ICP and Ethereum blockchains:

- ICP deployment: The front-end and back-end services are hosted on ICP canisters, providing a decentralized and scalable infrastructure. Unlike Ethereum, data written to ICP are not inherently public [70], allowing the management of multiple privacy levels for data storage [71]. Furthermore, the ICP's reverse-gas model not only reduces transaction costs but also removes the need for users to manage funds for system usage, as the system itself covers transaction fees for user interactions, enhancing accessibility and ease of use [60].
- Ethereum interaction: The user interacts exclusively with their EVM-compatible keys, using them both for transactions on Ethereum and to derive an ICP identity via the SIWE protocol. This unified key usage streamlines the user experience, allowing seamless interaction across both blockchain platforms without requiring separate key management [65].

- Identity derivation protocol: We utilized the secure protocol provided by ICP to derive Ethereum-compatible keys from ICP identities. This ensures that private keys remain within the secure environment of the user's device, maintaining security across platforms [69].

3.1.3. SSI-Based Authentication Framework

We introduce an authentication and authorization framework designed to operate seamlessly across both the EVM and the ICP:

- Access modifiers: Custom access modifiers enforce role-based access control across the platform. In Solidity, we use modifiers to restrict function execution to authorized roles, while in ICP, decorators are applied to canister-related code to achieve similar access control. This ensures that only users with the appropriate SSI credentials can perform specific actions within smart contracts and canisters.
- Credential verification: Smart contracts and canisters verify cryptographic proofs provided by users. This process maintains the integrity of transactions and enforces business rules without compromising privacy.
- Role-based access control: Defined roles such as EXPORTER, IMPORTER, and CERTIFIER within smart contracts and canisters streamline the enforcement of business logic and compliance requirements. Certain platform functionalities are accessible only to specific roles, ensuring that each participant has the appropriate permissions to perform their designated actions securely and in accordance with their responsibilities.

3.1.4. User Experience Enhancements

We focus on enhancing the user experience to encourage adoption:

- Seamless authentication: Users authenticate through familiar actions, such as scanning QR codes and biometric verification, reducing barriers to entry.
- Notifications and alerts: Real-time notifications keep users informed of important events, such as contract updates or required approvals, maintaining engagement, and workflow continuity.
- Guided workflows: Step-by-step guides help users navigate complex processes, reduce the learning curve, and minimize errors.

3.2. *Case Study*

3.2.1. Scenario Overview

To demonstrate the practical application of our framework, we conduct a case study focusing on the coffee supply chain between Brazil and Switzerland. The case study presents the following characteristics:

- Participants: Small-scale coffee exporters in Brazil and importers in Switzerland.
- Challenges addressed:
  - Trust issues: Difficulty in establishing credibility due to geographical and informational gaps, leading to hesitance in direct transactions.
  - Intermediary costs: High fees charged by brokers and middlemen, reducing profit margins for producers, and increasing costs for buyers.
  - Bureaucracy: Time-consuming paperwork and manual processes, delaying transactions, and increasing the likelihood of errors.
  - Financial barriers: Complexities in setting up guarantees and down payment arrangements through traditional banking systems, which can be prohibitive for small exporters.

3.2.2. Trade Negotiation Process

The platform facilitates a streamlined trade negotiation process:

- Registration and verification: Upon registration, exporting and importing companies receive verifiable credentials issued by the consortium. The companies involved can then issue specific credentials to their employees, creating a chain of trust [69]. The platform can verify these employee credentials as needed, establishing a secure foundation for transactions.
- Offer creation: Exporters list coffee products with detailed specifications, including variety, quality, quantity, and pricing terms.
- Negotiation initiation: Importers express interest and initiate negotiations through the platform. Both parties can propose modifications to terms, facilitated by the platform's interactive interface.
- Contract formation: As illustrated in Figure 13, the platform ensures that when an agreement is reached, a new entity is created within an ICP canister to encapsulate the negotiated terms. This entity includes details such as shipment information, payment conditions, and dispute resolution mechanisms, securely storing and making them accessible within the platform.

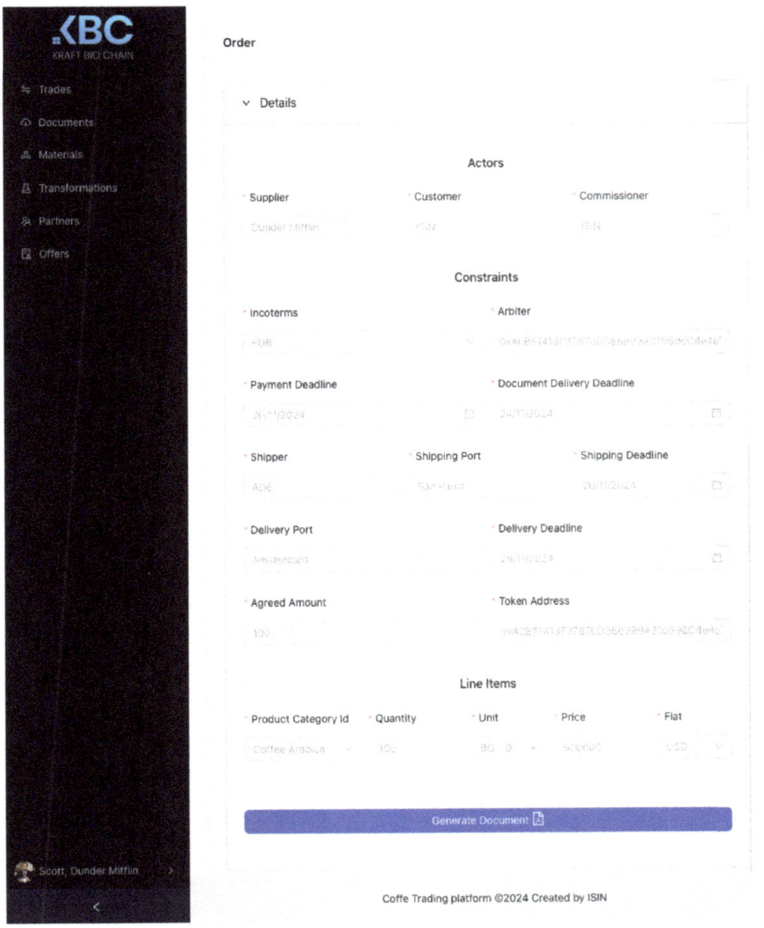

Figure 13. Platform negotiation page

3.2.3. Shipment and Payment Handling

As illustrated in Figure 14, our platform manages shipments and payment processes efficiently:

- Document management: Critical shipping-related documents such as bills of lading and certificates of origin are uploaded and securely stored on the ICP blockchain, ensuring both immutability and accessibility.
- Down payment services: Guarantees are secured through a down payment mechanism managed by the ICP canister. Funds are locked and released based on predefined conditions set in the previously signed contract, such as confirmation of shipment delivery, ensuring fairness and security for both parties.
- Transaction flow: The platform also orchestrates the transaction sequence, ensuring compliance with contractual obligations. Notifications prompt users to take the necessary actions, maintaining momentum in the supply chain.

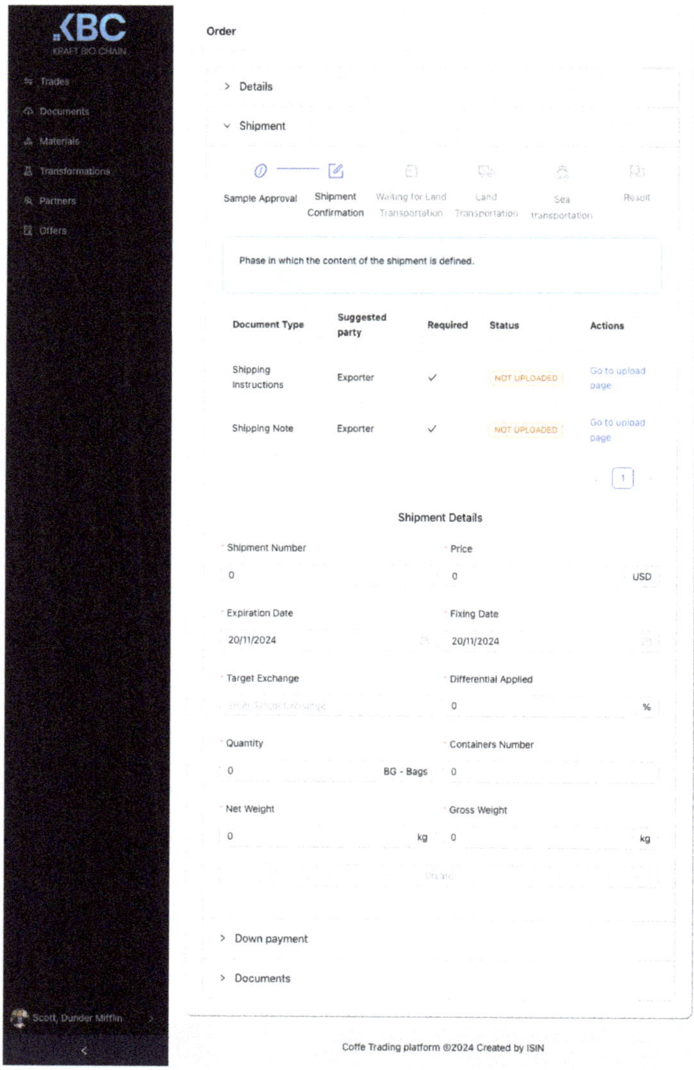

Figure 14. Platform shipment page

3.2.4. Dispute Resolution

In the event of disputes, the platform provides mechanisms for efficient resolution:

- Transparent logging: All interactions and document exchanges are immutably recorded. This provides a transparent audit trail that is invaluable for resolving disagreements.
- Arbitration mechanism: An arbiter can access relevant records to facilitate dispute resolution. The platform's logs serve as evidence, reducing ambiguity and expediting the process.
- Legal compliance: The generated records comply with legal standards, supporting enforcement if necessary. Users can easily collect all communications and documents to present to legal authorities, streamlining the path to resolution.

3.3. *Technical Challenges and Solutions*

We hereby address the potential challenges and their solutions that the proposed framework could effectively provide.

3.3.1. Identity Derivation and Management

- Challenge: Securely associating Ethereum addresses with ICP identities without compromising security.
- Solution: Instead of utilizing a standalone ICP identity, we derive one from an existing Ethereum account. This is achieved by implementing a SIWE mechanism using a canister developed by the ICP community. This approach maintains security while streamlining cross-platform interactions.

3.3.2. Unified Authentication Across Distinct Blockchain Networks

- Challenge: Implementing a unified authentication system across a platform that operates on different blockchains.
- Solution: We rely on the Ethereum SSI standard for identity management and perform RPC calls to the EVM network from ICP. This approach allows us to maintain a single coherent identity across both blockchains, enabling seamless authentication and authorization. Users can thus interact with different components of the platform through a unified identity, simplifying the experience while ensuring consistent access control across the platform.

3.3.3. Access Control

- Challenge: Enforcing role-based permissions in a decentralized and trustless environment.
- Solution: We implemented on-chain verification of off-chain credentials using cryptographic proofs. This approach ensures that only authorized users can execute specific smart contract and canister functions.

3.3.4. Data Privacy and Confidentiality

- Challenge: Balancing transparency with the need to protect sensitive business information.
- Solution: Sensitive documents are stored on the ICP blockchain, utilizing its capability to manage different levels of data access while ensuring immutability and security. This approach allows controlled visibility of data, preserving confidentiality without compromising the integrity and verifiability of transactions.

3.3.5. User Accessibility

- Challenge: Designing a user experience suitable for participants with limited technical expertise.

- Solution: We create intuitive interfaces with minimal technical jargon. Educational resources and support are provided within the platform to help users. The emphasis on a mobile-first design leverages the ubiquity of smartphones, making the platform accessible to a broad user base.

3.3.6. Interoperability

- Challenge: Facilitating seamless interaction between different blockchain platforms.
- Solution: APIs and middleware abstract the complexities of cross-chain interactions. Using standardized data formats and communication protocols, we ensure that the user experience remains consistent regardless of the underlying technologies.

3.4. *Impact Analysis on Traditional Trading Processes*

Before delving into the impact analysis, it is essential to note that the presented blockchain-based solution represents an initial Proof of Concept (POC). Although currently being tested by selected project participants, the platform has not yet been deployed on a scale. Therefore, the quantitative data and analysis presented in this section are based on preliminary estimates and calculations derived from the POC implementation. The actual values and impacts may vary as the solution evolves and achieves broader market adoption. However, the initial results provide valuable insight into the potential improvements in key trading processes compared to traditional methods. This section analyzes the estimated impacts on costs, processing times, and intermediary dependence for each major process phase based on the current implementation of the rPOC.

3.4.1. Offer Publication and Discovery

The initial phase of the traditional coffee supply chain, which involves partner discovery, is often a burden for small-scale producers. Obtaining market visibility requires substantial investments in trade fairs and intermediary services. This dependency on intermediaries for financing, logistics, and market access significantly impacts small-scale producer profitability. Participation in trade fairs can cost several thousand dollars annually, as highlighted in studies on barriers faced by new entrants into the system [72]. However, given the variability in resources and infrastructure among small-scale producers, it is challenging to provide an accurate estimate of the real costs involved. This discovery process, which often takes several months, remains a critical hurdle, particularly for those seeking to establish their first business relationships.

In contrast, the blockchain solution significantly reduces these discovery costs and time frames. The costs of creating ICP-based offers are less than USD 0.001 per publication, allowing exporters to instantly make their offerings visible to all participants in the platform. The built-in verification system and the credential mechanisms of the platform allow importers to evaluate the reliability of potential partners in hours rather than weeks and to make business more fair, as highlighted by [72], who reveals that the costs associated with intermediaries in the coffee supply chain can be substantial, with monthly interest rates on loans provided by intermediaries ranging from 10% to 20%. Direct partner discovery through the platform eliminates traditional broker fees, while the standardized digital interface reduces the initial relationship establishment period to approximately one week.

3.4.2. Contract Negotiation

The coffee supply chain, as in many commodity trading sectors, remains heavily dependent on manual processes based on paper. Research by researchers from The London School of Economics and Political Science [73] reveals the extent of this documentation burden: each trade transaction requires processing between 36 and 240 different documents, involving more than 30 different stakeholders. Most importantly, traditional contract negotiation processes typically take 2–3 weeks to complete. This complexity not only increases costs, but also introduces significant delays and potential failure points in the trading process. Traditional trading systems incur substantial costs through bank intermediation, particularly for letter of credit transactions, which generally cost about 2.5% of the transaction value [49].

The blockchain-based solution introduces significant efficiencies through smart contract automation. Due to the usage of ICP and Ethereum L2, the compute and storage costs related to document management are below USD 0.001 and hence completely negligible. This cost scales with the volume of documents managed by each company, making storage costs proportional to the trading activity and documentation needs of each participant. Based on preliminary estimates conducted with project partners during the POC phase, these operations could reduce the total processing time from weeks to 1–2 h, while enabling direct peer-to-peer interaction that eliminates the need for multiple intermediaries.

3.4.3. Dispute Management

Based on data shared by our implementation partners, in traditional systems, dispute resolution is a time-consuming process requiring 14–21 days for physical documentation retrieval alone. The process typically involves 6-8 different parties and spans 45–60 days on average. Legal intermediary costs vary significantly by jurisdiction, adding substantial uncertainty to the total transaction cost.

The blockchain platform provides immediate access to all relevant documentation through its immutable ledger. The system's transparent audit trails enable instant verification of all transaction details, while smart contract arbitration automates many aspects of the resolution process. This reduces the number of parties involved to 2–3 and, according to our estimates, shortens the average resolution time to 5–7 days.

These improvements are particularly significant for small and medium-sized traders, who traditionally face disproportionately higher costs and longer processing times due to their limited resources and market access. The blockchain solution effectively levels the playing field, enabling smaller participants to compete more effectively in the global coffee trade market.

4. Discussion

Our implementation framework demonstrates how the integration of blockchain technology with SSI principles effectively addresses trust and efficiency challenges in global supply chains. We hereby discuss its potential impact on the economy, as well as further concerns and future perspectives.

4.1. Impact on the Coffee Industry

The platform significantly impacts the coffee industry, namely our research target, via the following:

- Enhancing trust: Ensuring that only verified participants engage in transactions fosters a trustworthy environment. This reduces the risk of fraud and builds trust among participants.
- Reducing costs: By minimizing dependency on intermediaries, transaction costs are lowered. Producers can achieve better profit margins and buyers can access products at more competitive prices.
- Streamlining processes: Automating documentation and negotiation processes reduces delays and errors. More efficiency accelerates the supply chain, benefiting all stakeholders.

- Improving financial accessibility: Simplifying financial transactions using stablecoins and smart contracts bypasses traditional banking barriers. This is particularly beneficial for small exporters who may lack access to conventional financial services.

4.2. Generalization to Other Industries

The framework's modular and adaptable design allows it to be potentially applied to various industries facing similar challenges:

- Textiles: By ensuring ethical sourcing and authenticity of materials and by combating counterfeit goods.
- Pharmaceuticals: By tracking provenance and preventing counterfeit drugs as well as enhancing patient safety.
- Agriculture: By enhancing transparency and traceability in the supply chains of other commodities like cocoa and tea and by promoting fair trade practices.
- Minerals and metals: By verifying compliance with environmental and labor regulations and by supporting responsible sourcing.

4.3. Addressing Privacy Concerns

Our approach balances the need for transparency with privacy:

- Selective disclosure: Users share only the necessary information, maintaining confidentiality over sensitive data.
- Regulatory compliance: The platform can be configured to comply with data protection laws such as GDPR, ensuring legal adherence.
- User empowerment: Participants have control over their data, including the ability to revoke access when necessary, aligning with SSI principles.

4.4. Scalability and Performance Considerations

We consider scalability and performance to ensure that the platform can grow with demand:

- ICP Advantages: The Internet Computer Protocol offers high throughput and low latency, suitable for applications requiring real-time interactions. It scales horizontally, accommodating increasing user numbers [60].
- Ethereum challenges: We mitigated Ethereum's scalability issues using Layer 2 scaling solutions like rollups or sidechains. Transaction batching and gas optimization techniques reduce costs and improve performance [74].
- Prospects: Integration with other blockchain platforms that offer enhanced scalability and privacy features is planned, ensuring that the platform remains at the forefront of technological advancements.

4.5. Limitations and Future Perspectives

Although our platform offers significant benefits, there are certain limitations:

- Adoption hurdles: Resistance to new technology and lack of infrastructure in certain regions may slow adoption. Continued education and support are necessary to overcome these challenges.
- Regulatory landscape: Navigating different legal frameworks across jurisdictions requires adaptability. Monitoring and adjusting to regulatory changes are essential for compliance.
- Enhancements: Future work should include the integration of IoT devices for real-time tracking and monitoring, the application of artificial intelligence to demand forecasting, and the expansion of the SSI framework to support cross-chain identity solutions.

5. Conclusions

In this Communication, we have developed a universal blockchain-based platform that significantly enhances trust and efficiency in global supply chains, emphasizing the integration of Self-Sovereign Identity (SSI) and decentralized technologies. This integration not only facilitates secure and efficient interactions between stakeholders, but also revolutionizes traditional supply chain management.

Our platform pioneers a decentralized marketplace that empowers buyers and sellers to discover each other and negotiate directly, significantly reducing the dependency on intermediaries. This marketplace streamlines the contract formation process and manages the entire shipping trajectory, ensuring compliance and the timely delivery of commodities. In addition, it facilitates the secure handling of documentation and the management of financial guarantees. In the event of disputes, the platform's comprehensive record-keeping capabilities allow for easy collection and presentation of evidence to legal authorities, expediting resolution processes.

From a scientific perspective, our Communication introduces novel applications of blockchain and SSI technologies in supply chain management, particularly addressing the challenges of trust, transparency, and inefficiency that have long plagued global trade. By implementing these technologies, we demonstrate their potential to solve complex, systemic problems, providing a model that can be adapted to various industry contexts beyond the coffee industry.

From a practical and applied perspective, the significance of our work lies in its potential to transform global trade practices. The platform reduces transaction costs [75], shortens processing times, and minimizes the risks of fraud, making global trading more accessible. Furthermore, by automating the negotiation and enforcement of contracts, the platform ensures a higher level of compliance and security in international transactions.

Future perspectives include extending this platform to other industries such as textiles, pharmaceuticals, agriculture, and minerals, where there are similar supply chain challenges. Each industry can benefit from the increased transparency and efficiency that our platform offers, which could transform global supply chains into more sustainable, equitable, and resilient systems.

Finally, our work not only represents a significant technological innovation contributing to the literature on blockchain applications in supply chain management, but also provides a scalable and flexible solution with far-reaching implications for global economic practices. The adaptability and robustness of our platform suggest a promising future for the integration of blockchain technologies in improving the operational capabilities of supply chains worldwide.

Author Contributions: Conceptualization, T.A., L.A., E.B. and G.G.; methodology, T.A., L.A. and G.G.; software, T.A., L.A. and G.G.; validation, T.A., L.A., E.B. and G.G.; formal analysis, T.A., L.A. and G.G.; writing—original draft preparation, T.A., L.A., E.B. and G.G.; writing—review and editing, T.A., L.A., E.B. and G.G.; visualization, T.A., L.A., E.B. and G.G.; supervision, E.B. and G.G. All authors have read and agreed to the published version of the manuscript.

Funding: This research received no external funding.

Institutional Review Board Statement: Not applicable.

Informed Consent Statement: Not applicable.

Data Availability Statement: The raw data supporting the conclusions of this article will be made available by the authors on request.

Conflicts of Interest: The author declares no conflicts of interest.

References

1. Free, C.; Hecimovic, A. Global supply chains after COVID-19: The end of the road for neoliberal globalization? *Account. Audit. Account. J.* **2021**, *34*, 58–84. [CrossRef]
2. Younis, A.; Alsharairi, H.; Younes, H.; Sundakani, B. The impact of COVID-19 on supply chains: Systematic review and future research directions. *Oper. Res.* **2023**, *23*, 48. [CrossRef]
3. Baidya, S.; Potdar, V.; Ray, P.P.; Nandi, C. Reviewing the opportunities, challenges, and future directions for the digitalization of energy. *Energy Res. Soc. Sci.* **2021**, *81*, 102243. [CrossRef]
4. Roy, S. Blockchain technology in the global supply chain: A theoretical overview and security Issues. In *Contemporary Issues in International Trade*; Bhattacharyya, R., Mazumdar, D., Eds.; Emerald Publishing: Leeds, UK, 2024; pp. 195–208.
5. Tiwari, S.; Sharma, P.; Choi, T.-M.; Lim, A. Blockchain and third-party logistics for global supply chain operations: Stakeholders' perspectives and decision roadmap. *Transp. Res. Part E Logist. Transp. Rev.* **2023**, *170*, 103012. [CrossRef]
6. Liu, R.; Ran, W.; Liu, S. Blockchain technology applied to supply chain management: A system's analysis. *Mob. Inf. Syst.* **2023**, mboxemph2023, 6046503. [CrossRef]
7. Potnis, T.; Lau, Y.-Y.; Yip, T.L. Roles of blockchain technology in supply chain capability and flexibility. *Sustainability* **2023**, *15*, 7460. [CrossRef]
8. Deloitte. Available online: https://www2.deloitte.com/content/dam/Deloitte/us/Documents/us-ent-supply-chain-pov.pdf (accessed on 26 October 2024).
9. Hastig, G.M.; Sodhi, M.S. Blockchain for supply chain traceability: Business requirements and critical success factors. *Prod. Oper. Manag.* **2020**, *29*, 935–954. [CrossRef]
10. Dirksen, J.; Lima de Miranda, K.; Wike, R. Towards Economic and Social Prosperity Measurement Beyond GDP. Available online: https://www.ifw-kiel.de/fileadmin/Dateiverwaltung/IfW-Publications/fis-import/18b62c7b-f978-4378-a434-bf07daecaa90-T7_2022_PB_final.pdf (accessed on 26 October 2024).
11. Smith, A. Spatial division of labor. In *International Encyclopedia of Human Geography*; Kitchin, R., Thrift, N., Eds.; Elsevier: Amsterdam, The Netherlands, 2009; pp. 348–354.
12. International Monetary Fund. *Balance of Payments and International Investment Position*, 6th ed.; International Monetary Fund: Washington, DC, USA, 2009.
13. Markus, S.; Buijs, P. Beyond The Hype: How Blockchain Affects Supply Chain Performance. *Supply Chain. Manag. Int. J.* **2022**, 27, 177–193. [CrossRef]
14. A Survey on Blockchain-based Supply Chain Finance with Progress and Future directions. *arXiv* **2024**, arXiv:2408.08915.
15. Purwaningsih, E.; Muslikh, M.; Suhaeri, S.; Basrowi, B. Utilizing blockchain technology in enhancing supply chain efficiency and export performance, and its implications on the financial performance of SMEs. *Uncertain Supply Chain Manag.* **2024**, *12*, 449–460. [CrossRef]
16. Agrawal, S.; Tiwari, S.K.; Singh, R.K.; Kumar, K. The impact of blockchain technology on supply chain efficiency: A review. In Proceedings of the E3S Web of Conferences, Ahmedabad, India, 27–29 June 2024. [CrossRef]
17. Lakkakula, P.; Bullock, D.; Wilson, W. Blockchain Technology in International Commodity Trading. *J. Priv. Enterp.* **2020**, *35*, 23–45.
18. McKinsey Company. Blockchain Beyond the Hype: What Is the Strategic Business Value? Online Article . 2018. Available online: https://www.mckinsey.com/capabilities/mckinsey-digital/our-insights/blockchain-beyond-the-hype-what-is-the-strategic-business-value# (accessed on 23 December 2024).
19. Alsmadi, A.A.; Alrawashdeh, N.; Al-Gasaymeh, A.; Alhawamdeh, L.N.; Al_Hazimeh, A.M. Adoption of Blockchain Technology in Supply Chain. *Sage Open* **2023**, *13*, 21582440231160143. [CrossRef]
20. The World Bank. Available online: https://data.worldbank.org/indicator/NY.GDP.MKTP.KD.ZG (accessed on 26 October 2024).
21. The World Bank. Available online: https://datahelpdesk.worldbank.org/knowledgebase/articles/906519-world-bank-country-and-lending-groups (accessed on 26 October 2024).
22. Bager, S.L.; Singh, C.; Persson, U.M. Blockchain is not a silver bullet for agro-food supply chain sustainability: Insights from a coffee case study. *Sustainability* **2022**, *4*, 100163. [CrossRef]
23. Trollman, H.; Garcia-Garcia, G.; Jagtap, S.; Trollman, F. Blockchain for ecologically embedded coffee supply chains. *Logistics* **2022**, *6*, 43. [CrossRef]
24. Browning, D. Available online: https://www.supplychainbrain.com/blogs/1-think-tank/post/32057-how-blockchain-benefits-the-coffee-supply-chain (accessed on 26 October 2024).
25. The World Bank. Available online: https://data.worldbank.org/indicator/NE.EXP.GNFS.ZS (accessed on 26 October 2024).
26. Foreign Agricultural Service—U.S. Department of Agriculture. Available online: https://fas.usda.gov/data/production/commodity/0711100 (accessed on 26 October 2024).
27. ResourceTrade.Earth. Available online: https://resourcetrade.earth/?year=2022&category=113&units=value&autozoom=1 (accessed on 26 October 2024).

28. Nordico Coffee House. Available online: https://nordico.coffee/exploring-blockchain-technology-in-coffee-supply-chains-ensuring-transparency-and-fairness/ (accessed on 26 October 2024).
29. Javaid, M.; Haleem, A.; Singh, R.P.; Suman, R.; Khan, S. A review of Blockchain Technology applications for financial services. *BenchCouncil Trans. Benchmarks Stand. Eval.* **2022**, 2, 100073. [CrossRef]
30. Lichtfous, M.; Yadav, V.; Fratino, V. Can blockchain accelerate financial inclusion globally. *Deloitte Inside Mag.* **2018**, 19, 1–8.
31. Badhan, I.A.; Neeroj, M.H.; Rahman, S. Currency rate fluctuations and their impact on supply chain risk management: An empirical analysis. *Int. J. Bus. Manag. Sci.* **2024**, 4, 6–26. [CrossRef]
32. Ortolani, P. The impact of blockchain technologies and smart contracts on dispute resolution: Arbitration and court litigation at the crossroads. *Unif. Law Rev.* **2019**, 24, 430–448. [CrossRef]
33. Triple A Technologies. Available online: https://www.triple-a.io/cryptocurrency-ownership-data (accessed on 18 December 2024).
34. Alamsyah, A.; Widiyanesti, S.; Wulansari, P.; Nurhazizah, E.; Dewi, A.S.; Rahadian, D.; Ramadhani, D.P.; Hakim, M.N.; Tyasamesi, P. Blockchain traceability model in the coffee industry. *J. Open Innov. Technol. Mark. Complex.* **2023**, 9, 100008. [CrossRef]
35. IBM. Available online: https://www.ibm.com/thought-leadership/coffee/ (accessed on 26 October 2024).
36. Piprani, A.Z.; Jaafar, N.I.; Ali, S.M.; Mubarik, M.S.; Shahbaz, M. Multi-dimensional supply chain flexibility and supply chain resilience: The role of supply chain risks exposure. *Oper. Manag. Res.* **2022**, 15, 307–325. [CrossRef]
37. Pratono, A.H.; Han, L.; Maharani, A. Global supply chain resilience with the flexible partnership. *Mod. Supply Chain. Res. Appl.* **2023**, 5, 102–114. [CrossRef]
38. Tiwari, M.; Bryde, D.J.; Stavropoulou, F.; Malhotra, G. Understanding the evolution of flexible supply chain in the business-to-business sector: A resource-based theory perspective. *Int. Stud. Manag. Organ.* **2024**, 54, 380–406. [CrossRef]
39. Miatton, F.; Amado, L. Fairness, transparency and traceability in the coffee value chain through Blockchain innovation. In Proceedings of the 2020 International Conference on Technology and Entrepreneurship—Virtual (ICTE-V), Bologna, Italy, 21–23 September 2020; pp. 1–6.
40. Samper, L.F.; Quiñones-Ruiz, X.F. Towards a balanced sustainability vision for the coffee industry. *Resources* **2017**, 6, 17. [CrossRef]
41. Wenda. Available online: https://wenda-it.com/en/focus/document-digitization-automation-supply-chain-logistics/ (accessed on 18 December 2024).
42. Wynn, S.; Kuhn, J.R. The financial impact of manual inventory record errors. *Int. J. Bus. Soc. Sci.* **2021**, 12, 1–12.
43. Zivkovic, P.; McCurdy, D.L.; Zou, M.; Raymond, A.H. Mind the gap: Tech-based dispute resolution for disputes in global supply blockchains. *Bus. Horizons* **2023**, 66, 13–26. [CrossRef]
44. Chang, Y.; Iakovou, E.; Weidong, S. Blockchain in global supply chains and cross border trade: A critical synthesis of the state-of-the-art, challenges and opportunities. *Int. J. Prod. Res.* **2019**, 58, 2082–2099. [CrossRef]
45. Byrnes, W.H.; Khodakarami, N.; Perez, C.N. The value chain: A study of the coffee industry. *Development* **2018**, 30, 1099–1122.
46. Bozzola, M.; Charles, S.; Ferretti, T.; Gerakari, E.; Manson, H.; Rosser, N.; von der Goltz, P. *The Coffee Guide*; International Trade Centre: Geneva, Switzerland, 2021. [CrossRef]
47. European Coffee Federation. *European Standard Contract for Coffee (ESCC)*, 2018 ed. ; European Coffee Federation: Brussels, Belgium, 2021.
48. Djankov, S.; Freund, C.; Pham, C. Trading on time. *Rev. Econ. Stat.* **2010**, 92, 166–173. [CrossRef]
49. Mann, R. The role of letters of credit in payment transactions. *Mich. Law Rev.* **2000**, 98, 2494–2536. [CrossRef]
50. Preukschat, A.; Reed, D. *Self-Sovereign Identity*; Manning Publications: Shelter Island, NY, USA, 2021.
51. Mühle, A.; Grüner, A.; Gayvoronskaya, T.; Meinel, C. A survey on essential components of a self-sovereign identity. *Comput. Sci. Rev.* **2018**, 30, 80–86. [CrossRef]
52. Chen, Y.; Bellavitis, C. Blockchain disruption and decentralized finance: The rise of decentralized business models. *J. Bus. Ventur. Insights* **2020**, 13, e00151. [CrossRef]
53. Klems, M.; Eberhardt, J.; Tai, S.; Härtlein, S.; Buchholz, S.; Tidjani, A. Trustless Intermediation in Blockchain-Based Decentralized Service Marketplaces. In *Service-Oriented Computing. ICSOC 2017*; Maximilien, M., Vallecillo, A., Wang, J., Oriol, M., Eds.; Springer: Cham, Switzerland, 2017; Volume 10601.
54. Albayati, H.; Kim, S.K.; Rho, J.J. Accepting financial transactions using blockchain technology and cryptocurrency: A customer perspective approach. *Technol. Soc.* **2020**, 62, 101320. [CrossRef]
55. Maggi, G.; Staiger, R.W. Information asymmetry and the problem of transfers in trade negotiations. *Am. Econ. Rev.* **2005**, 95, 1447–1467.
56. Wang, S.; Ouyang, L.; Yuan, Y.; Ni, X.; Han, X.; Wang, F.-Y. Blockchain-enabled smart contracts: Architecture, applications, and future trends. *IEEE Trans. Syst. Man Cybern. Syst.* **2019**, 49, 2266–2277. [CrossRef]
57. DFINITY Team. Available online: https://internetcomputer.org/whitepaper.pdf (accessed on 14 November 2024).
58. Frye, T.J.; Mansfield, E.D. Information asymmetries as trade barriers: ISO 9000 increases international commerce. *J. Int. Econ.* **2004**, 62, 261–283.

59. World Wide Web Consortium (W3C). Verifiable Credentials Data Model v2.0. Candidate Recommendation Draft, 19 October 2024. Available online: https://www.w3.org/TR/vc-data-model-2.0/ (accessed on 23 December 2024).
60. Schardong, F.; Custódio, R. Self-Sovereign Identity: A systematic review, mapping and taxonomy. *Sensors* **2022**, *22*, 5641. [CrossRef]
61. Mazzocca, C.; Acar, A.; Uluagac, S.; Montanari, R.; Bellavista, P.; Conti, M. A survey on decentralized identifiers and verifiable credentials. *arXiv* **2024**, arXiv:2402.02455.
62. WalletConnect Foundation. WalletConnect Network Whitepaper. 2024. Available online: https://whitepaper.walletconnect.network (accessed on 23 December 2024).
63. Fdhila, W.; Stifter, N.; Kostal, K.; Saglam, C.; Sabadello, M. Methods for decentralized identities: Evaluation and insights. In *Business Process Management: Blockchain and Robotic Process Automation Forum*; González Enríquez, J., Debois, S., Fettke, P., Plebani, P., van de Weerd, I., Weber, I., Eds.; Springer: Cham, Switzerland, 2021; pp. 119–135.
64. Chang, W.; Rocco, G.; Millegan, B.; Johnson, N.; Terbu, O. Available online: https://eips.ethereum.org/EIPS/eip-4361 (accessed on 14 November 2024).
65. Ben-Sasson, E.; Chiesa, A.; Tromer, E.; Virza, M. Scalable zero knowledge via cycles of elliptic curves. *Algorithmica* **2017**, *79*, 1102–1160. [CrossRef]
66. Kosba, A.; Miller, A.; Shi, E.; Wen, Z.; Papamanthou, C. Hawk: The Blockchain model of cryptography and privacy-preserving smart contracts. In Proceedings of the 2016 IEEE Symposium on Security and Privacy (SP), San Jose, CA, USA, 22–26 May 2016; pp. 839–858.
67. Raikwar, M.; Gligoroski, D.; Kralevska, K. SoK of used cryptography in Blockchain. *IEEE Access* **2019**, *7*, 148550–148575. [CrossRef]
68. Gurbuz, M.C.; Yurt, O.; Ozdemir, S.; Sena, V.; Yu, W. Supply chain structure as a mitigating strategy for small and medium-sized enterprises. *J. Bus. Res.* **2023**, *155*, 113407. [CrossRef]
69. Li, C.; Li, R.; Zhuang, L.; Zhang, X. Formal analysis of trust chain. In Proceedings of the 2010 Second International Conference on Networks Security, Wireless Communications and Trusted Computing, Wuhan, China, 24–25 April 2010; pp. 111–116. [CrossRef]
70. Internet Computer. Available online: https://internetcomputer.org/docs/current/developer-docs/multi-chain/ethereum/using-eth/eth-dev-workflow (accessed on 24 December 2024).
71. Korpela, K.; Hallikas, J.; Dahlberg, T. Digital supply chain transformation toward blockchain integration. In Proceedings of the 50th Hawaii International Conference on System Sciences, Hilton Waikoloa Village, HI, USA, 4–7 January 2017; Hawaii International Conference on System Sciences, Ed.; Hawaii International Conference on System Sciences: Hilton Waikoloa Village, HI, USA, 2017; pp. 4182–4191.
72. Milford, A. *Coffee, Co-Operatives and Competition: The Impact of Fair Trade*; Chr. Michelsen Institute: Bergen, Norway, 2004.
73. Lee-Makiyama, H.; Baker, R.; Gopalakrishnan, B.N.; Garnizova, E. *Benefits of the Digitalisation of Trade Processes and Cross Border Barriers to Their Adoption*; The London School of Economics and Political Science: London, UK, 2023.
74. Gudgeon, L.; Moreno-Sanchez, P.; Roos, S.; McCorry, P.; Gervais, A. SoK: Layer-Two Blockchain Protocols. In *Financial Cryptography and Data Security*; Bonneau, J., Heninger, N., Eds.; Springer: Cham, Switzerland, 2020.
75. Rodrigue, J.-P.; Notteboom, T. Available online: https://transportgeography.org/contents/chapter3/transport-costs/ (accessed on 24 December 2024).

MDPI AG
Grosspeteranlage 5
4052 Basel
Switzerland
Tel.: +41 61 683 77 34

FinTech Editorial Office
E-mail: fintech@mdpi.com
www.mdpi.com/journal/fintech

www.ingramcontent.com/pod-product-compliance
Lightning Source LLC
Chambersburg PA
CBHW061559220926
51850CB00005B/370